D0179149

STREET ATLAS
Somerset

First published 2002 by

Philip's, a division of
Octopus Publishing Group Ltd
2–4 Heron Quays, London E14 4JP

First edition 2002
First impression 2002

ISBN 0-540-08221-X (pocket)

© Philip's 2002

Ordnance Survey®

This product includes mapping data licensed
from Ordnance Survey® with the permission
of the Controller of Her Majesty's Stationery
Office. © Crown copyright 2002. All rights
reserved. Licence number 100011710

Printed and bound in Spain
by Cayfosa-Quebecor

Contents

III **Key to map symbols**

IV **Key to map pages**

VI **Route planning**

X **Administrative and Postcode boundaries**

1 **Street maps** at 2½ inches to 1 mile

122 **Street maps** at 1¼ inches to 1 mile

200 **Street maps** at 2½ inches to 1 mile

226 **Street map of Bristol and Bath city centres** at 5 inches to 1 mile

229 **Index** of towns and villages

231 **Index** of streets, hospitals, industrial estates, railway stations, schools, shopping centres, universities and places of interest

Digital Data

The exceptionally high-quality mapping found in this atlas is available as digital data in TIFF format, which is easily convertible to other bit mapped (raster) image formats.

The index is also available in digital form as a standard database table. It contains all the details found in the printed index together with the National Grid reference for the map square in which each entry is named.

For further information and to discuss your requirements, please contact Philip's on 020 7531 8439 or ruth.king@philips-maps.co.uk

(228)	**Motorway** with junction number
	Primary route – dual/single carriageway
	A road – dual/single carriageway
	B road – dual/single carriageway
	Minor road – dual/single carriageway
	Other minor road – dual/single carriageway
	Road under construction
	Rural track, private road or narrow road in urban area
	Gate or obstruction to traffic (restrictions may not apply at all times or to all vehicles)
	Path, bridleway, byway open to all traffic, road used as a public path
	Pedestrianised area
DY7	**Postcode boundaries**
	County and unitary authority boundaries
	Railway, railway under construction
	Tramway, tramway under construction
	Miniature railway
Walsall	**Railway station**
	Private railway station
South Shields	**Metro station**
	Tram stop, tram stop under construction
	Bus, coach station

◆	**Ambulance station**
◆	**Coastguard station**
◆	**Fire station**
◆	**Police station**
✚	**Accident and Emergency entrance to hospital**
H	**Hospital**
✚	**Place of worship**
i	**Information Centre** (open all year)
P	**Parking**
P&R	**Park and Ride**
PO	**Post Office**
⚕	**Camping site**
⚐	**Caravan site**
⚑	**Golf course**
⚔	**Picnic site**
Prim Sch	**Important buildings, schools, colleges, universities and hospitals**
River Medway	**Water name**
	River, stream
	Lock, weir
	Water
	Tidal water
	Woods
	Built up area
Church	**Non-Roman antiquity**
ROMAN FORT	**Roman antiquity**
87	**Adjoining page indicators and overlap bands** The colour of the arrow and the band indicates the scale of the adjoining or overlapping page (see scales below)
228	

Acad	Academy	Inst	Institute	Recn Gd	Recreation Ground
Allot Gdns	Allotments	Ct	Law Court		
Cemy	Cemetery	L Ctr	Leisure Centre	Resr	Reservoir
C Ctr	Civic Centre	LC	Level Crossing	Ret Pk	Retail Park
CH	Club House	Liby	Library	Sch	School
Coll	College	Mkt	Market	Sh Ctr	Shopping Centre
Crem	Crematorium	Meml	Memorial	TH	Town Hall/House
Ent	Enterprise	Mon	Monument	Trad Est	Trading Estate
Ex H	Exhibition Hall	Mus	Museum	Univ	University
Ind Est	Industrial Estate	Obsy	Observatory	Wks	Works
IRB Sta	Inshore Rescue Boat Station	Pal	Royal Palace	YH	Youth Hostel
		PH	Public House		

■ The small numbers around the edges of the maps identify the 1 kilometre National Grid lines ■ The dark grey border on the inside edge of some pages indicates that the mapping does not continue onto the adjacent page

The scale of the maps on the pages numbered in blue is 3.92 cm to 1 km • 2½ inches to 1 mile • 1: 25344	0 ... ¼ ... ½ ... ¾ ... 1 mile
	0 ... 250m ... 500m ... 750m ... 1 kilometre
The scale of the maps on pages numbered in green is 1.96 cm to 1 km • 1¼ inches to 1 mile • 1: 50688	0 ... ¼ ... ½ ... ¾ ... 1 mile
	0 ... 250m 500m 750m 1kilometre
The scale of the maps on pages numbered in red is 7.84 cm to 1 km • 5 inches to 1 mile • 1: 12672	0 ... 220 yards ... 440 yards ... 660 yards ... ½ mile
	0 ... 125m ... 250m ... 375m ... ½ kilometre

IV

Key to map pages

227	Map pages at 5 inches to 1 mile
113	Map pages at 2½ inches to 1 mile
141	Map pages at 1¼ inches to 1 mile

Scale

0	5	10	15	20 km
0	5		10 miles	

Cardiff, Swansea and the Valleys STREET ATLAS

Caerphilly

Pyle

Bridgend

Pencoed

Llantrisant

Cowbridge

Llantwit Major

Rhoose

Cardiff

Penarth

Barry

47

Brean 65

84

103

Lynton

Brendon **122**

123 Porlock Weir

124 Porlock

125

Minehead

Luccombe

200 201

Watchet **202**

Kilve

Stogursey **134**

Stretcholt **135**

126

127

Simonsbath

128 Exford

129 Wheddon Cross

Timberscombe

130

Washford

131

Williton

132

Holford

133

Nether Stowey

Cannington

Spaxton **152**

208 Bridgwater

153 North Petherton

Emmett's Grange

145

Withypool

146

Winsford **147** Exton

Hawkridge

Kingsbridge

148 Brompton Regis

149 Clatworthy

Stogumber

150

Crowcombe

151

Brompton Ralph

Lydeard St Lawrence

Broomfield

West Anstey **162**

Dulverton

163 Brushford

Knowstone

164

Chipstable

165 Shillingford

Bampton

Bishop's Lydeard

Wiveliscombe **210** Milverton

166

167

Langford Budville

Bradford on Tone

A358

168

169

212 213 Taunton

Creech St Micha

South Molton

Holcombe Rogus **178** Sampford Peverell

179 Westleigh

Wellington **222**

180

181

Rosemary Lane

Staplehay

Staple Fitzpaine **182**

Tiverton

Cullompton

Bolham Water **191** Rawridge

Churchinford

192 Yarcombe

193

Crediton

Honiton

Axminster

Exeter

Ottery St Mary

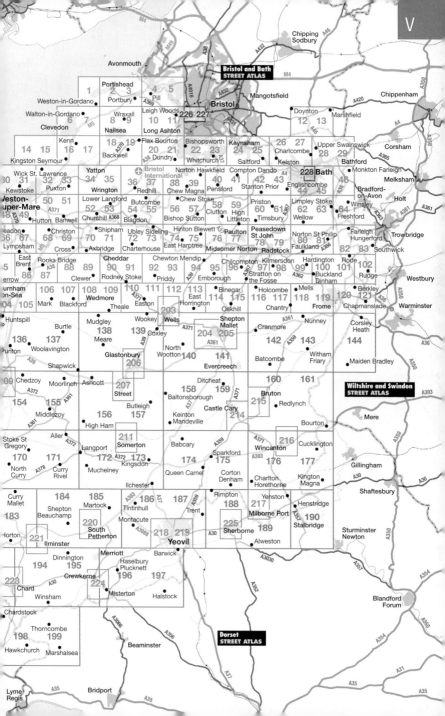

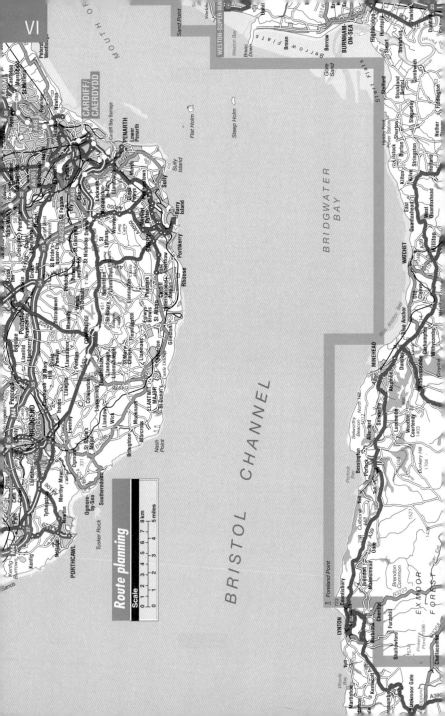

Route planning

Scale

0 1 2 3 4 5 6 7 8 km
0 1 2 3 4 5 miles

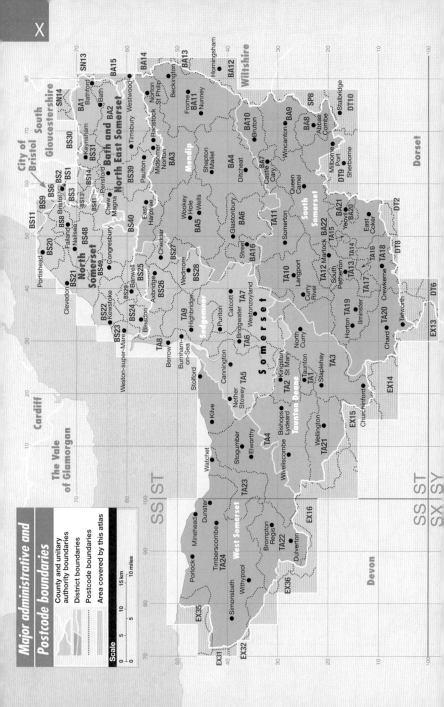

A B C D E F

8

Battery Point
Portishead Point
WOODLANDS RD
East Wood
PH
Pier

7

Portishead Point
Woodhill Bay
Woodhill
Kilkenny Bay
Marina Lake
PIER RD
ROYAL TERR
Old Pier

77

Lake Grounds
BEACH RD W
Portishead Dock

6

Sugar Loaf Beach
IRB Sta
Slipway
Mariners Path
PH
NORE RD
St Joseph's RC Prim Sch
Dry Hill
BLOCKHOUSE MEWS
COMBE AVE
Parish Liby
Portishead Wharf Est
STATION RD A369
L Ctr
Harbour Road Trad Est
Portbury Wharf

5

West Hill
CABOT RISE
FROBISHER AVE
DRAKES WAY
ADMIRAL'S WLK
St Barnabas CE Prim Sch
Portishead Prim Sch
COMBE FIELDS
STOKE RD
Portishead Bsns Pk
THE PRECINCT
Portishead Bsns Pk
WYNDHAM WAY
(dis)
PEARTREE

76

DENNY VIEW
MINDOP CL
MANOR CL
CHARLTON VIEW
LOWER DOWN RD
ROATH RD
NEWLANDS
CHURCH RD
VICTORIA CT
St Peters CE Prim Sch
BLACKTHORN DR
LADYMEAD CONFERENCE CL
Moor Farm
THE PARK

4

High Down Jun & Inf Schs
THE DOWNS
THE ROWANS
ELM WLK
CEDAR WAY
NEWLANDS HILL
CHURCH RD
DANDY'S MDW
1 BLADEN CL
2 TUDOR RD
3 COTSWOLD CL
RD DENSTON CL
AELFRIC MDW
JACOBS MDW
CONFERENCE CL
SHEEPWAY

PORTISHEAD
ST MARY'S
SPRINGFIELD RD
THE SPINNEY
B3124
BRISTOL RD
STAFFORD
THATCHER
GLEBE AVE
PORT CL
PORTBURY COMM
4 BRAMPTON WAY
5 CADBURY HO
6 GLEBE HO
Middle Bridge
THE PORTBURY HUNDRED A

3

Portishead Down
West Wood
Gordano Sec Sch
LIPGATE
CLEVEDON RD
Cemy
BS20

75

Allot Gdns
Weston Big Wood
North Weston
Oakfield Place

2

Woodside Grange
How Ham Farm

B3124

1

ROCK VILLAS
B3124
Sperrings Farm
Cherry Orchard Farm
Clapton Farm
Brook Farm
Clapton Dro
Clapton in Gordano
Stratton
NAISH HILL

74

45 A B 46 C D 47 E F

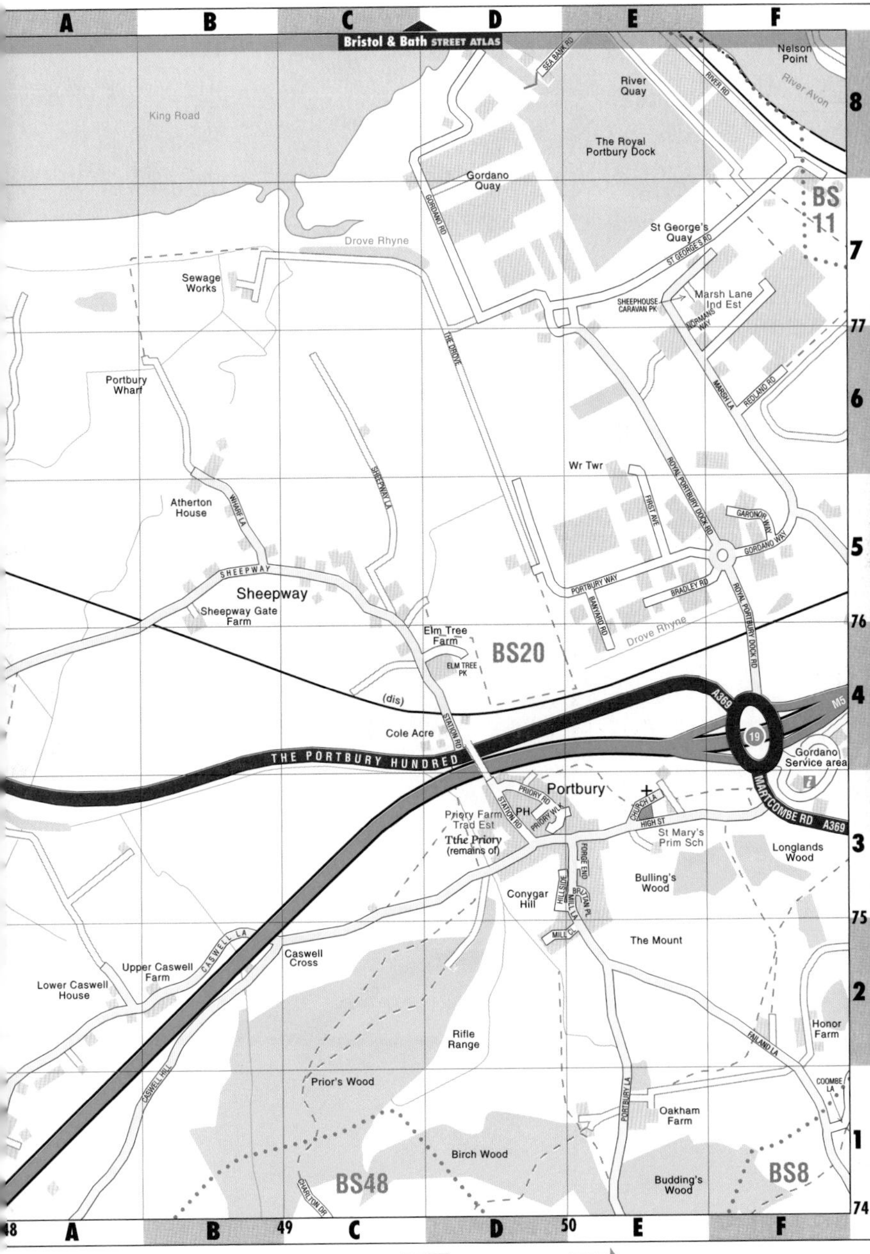

Bristol & Bath STREET ATLAS
King Road
Nelson Point
River Avon
River Quay
SEA BANK RD
RIVER RD
The Royal Portbury Dock
Gordano Quay
GORDANO RD
BS 11
St George's Quay
ST GEORGE'S RD
Drove Rhyne
Sewage Works
SHEEPHOUSE CARAVAN PK
Marsh Lane Ind Est
NORMANS WAY
THE DROVE
Portbury Wharf
MARSH LA
REDLAND RD
SHEEPWAY LA
Wr Twr
FIRST AVE
ROYAL PORTBURY DOCK RD
Atherton House
WHARF LA
GARONOR WAY
GORDANO WAY
SHEEPWAY
Sheepway
PORTBURY WAY
BRADLEY RD
BANYARD RD
Sheepway Gate Farm
Drove Rhyne
Elm Tree Farm
ELM TREE PK
BS20
(dis)
A369
M5
Cole Acre
STATION RD
19
THE PORTBURY HUNDRED
Gordano Service area
Portbury
PRIORY RD
PH
PRIORY WLK
CHURCH LA
HIGH ST
MARTCOMBE RD
A369
Priory Farm Trad Est
The Priory (remains of)
St Mary's Prim Sch
Longlands Wood
FORGE END
Bulling's Wood
Conygar Hill
HILLSIDE
BRITTAN PL
MILL LA
MILL CL
The Mount
CASWELL LA
Caswell Cross
Upper Caswell Farm
Lower Caswell House
Rifle Range
Honor Farm
FAILAND LA
CASWELL HILL
Prior's Wood
COOMBE LA
PORTBURY LA
Oakham Farm
Birch Wood
BS48
CHARLTON DR
Budding's Wood
BS8
A
B
C
D
E
F
8
7
77
6
5
76
4
3
75
2
1
74
48
49
50

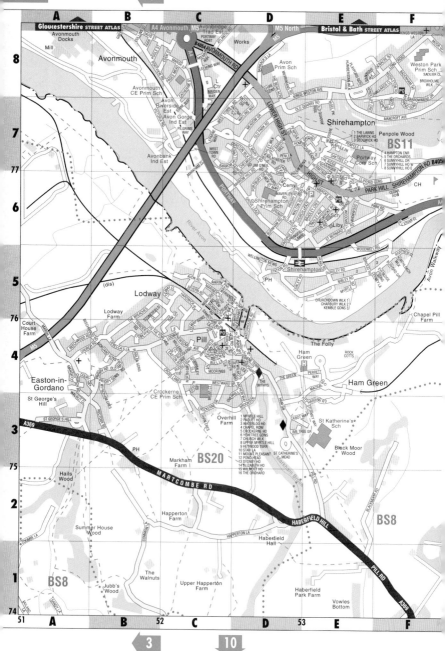

Gloucestershire STREET ATLAS   A4 Avonmouth, M5   M5 North   **Bristol & Bath** STREET ATLAS

Avonmouth
Docks

Mill

Avonmouth

Avonmouth
CE Prim Sch

Avon
Riverside
Est
Avon Gorge
Ind Est

Avonbank
Ind Est

Works

Avon
Prim Sch

Shirehampton

BS11

1 THE LAWNS
2 BARWICK HO
3 SEDGWICK HO
4 HAMPTON CNR
5 THE ORCHARDS
6 SUNNYHILL DR
7 SUNNYHILL HO W
8 SUNNYHILL HO

Penpole Wood

Portway
Com Sch

PARK HILL   SHIREHAMPTON RD B4054

Shirehampton
Prim Sch

Sch

Liby

River Avon

(dis)

Lodway

Lodway
Farm

Pill

PO

Shirehampton

PH

CHURCHDOWN WLK 1
CHARBURY WLK 2
KEMBLE GDNS 3

Chapel Pill
Farm

Court
House
Farm

The Folly

Ham
Green

Ham Green

Easton-in-
Gordano

St George's
Hill

Crockerne
CE Prim Sch

The
Withies

ROCK
COTTS

PERRETT
WAY

St Katherine's
Sch

ST GEORGE'S HILL

Overhill
Farm

1 MYRTLE HILL
2 PAQUET HO
3 WATERLOO HO
4 CHAPEL ROW
5 CROCKERNE HO
6 YEW TREE GDNS
7 CHURCH WLK
8 UPPER MYRTLE HILL
9 HEYWOOD TERR
10 STAR LA
11 MOUNT PLEASANT
12 POND HEAD
13 SYDNEY HO
14 ELIZABETH HO
15 WILMOTT HO
16 THE ORCHARD

St Catherine's
Mead

Black Moor
Wood

A369

PH

Markham
Farm

BS20

MARTCOMBE RD

Hails
Wood

Happerton
Farm

HABERFIELD HILL

Haberfield
Hall

BS8

Summer House
Wood

Happerton La

PILL RD

Jubb's
Wood

The
Walnuts

Upper Happerton
Farm

Haberfield
Park Farm

Vowles
Bottom

A369

BS8

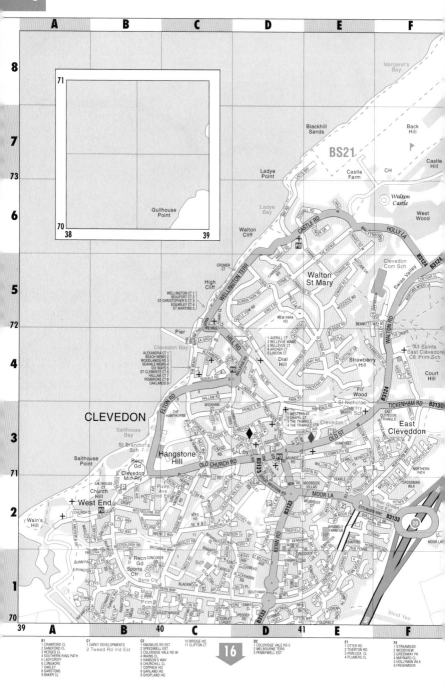

CLEVEDON

BS21

A
B1
1 CRAWFORD CL
2 SANDFORD CL
3 HEDGES CL
4 SOUTHERN RING PATH
5 LADYCROFT
6 LONGACRE
7 OAKLEY
8 GARSTONS
9 BAKER CL

C1
1 CAREY DEVELOPMENTS
2 Tweed Rd Ind Est

C2
1 KNOWLES RD EST
2 SPEEDWELL EST
3 COLERIDGE VALE RD W
4 WAINS CL
5 HARBON'S WAY
6 CHURCHILL CL
7 COPPACK HO
8 GARLAND HO
9 SHOPLAND HO

10 BRIDGE HO
11 CLIFTON CT

D2
1 COLERIDGE VALE RD E
2 MELBOURNE TERR
3 PENNYWELL EST

E1
1 OTTER RD
2 TIVERTON RD
3 PORLOCK CL
4 PLUMERS CL

F3
1 STREAMSIDE
2 WOODVIEW
3 GREENWAY PK
4 MAYNARD CL
5 HOLLYMAN WLK
6 FRESHMOOR

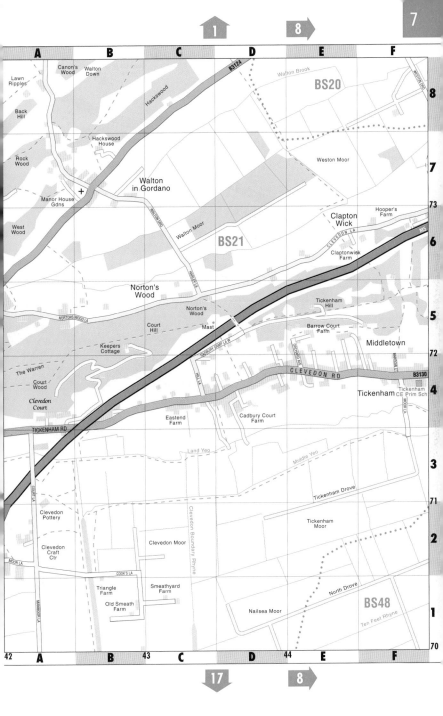

A   B   C   D   E   F

Lawn Ripples

Canon's Wood

Walton Down

Hackswood

BS20

Walton Brook

Back Hill

8

Rock Wood

Hackswood House

Weston Moor

7

West Wood

Manor House Gdns

Walton in Gordano

Walton Moor

BS21

Clapton Wick

Hooper's Farm

73

Claptonwick Farm

6

Norton's Wood

Norton's Wood

Tickenham Hill

M5

NORTONS WOOD LA

Court Hill

Mast

Barrow Court Farm

Middletown

5

Keepers Cottage

CADBURY CAMP LA W

The Warren

Court Wood

HILL LA

CLEVEDON RD

B3130

72

Clevedon Court

Tickenham

Tickenham CE Prim Sch

4

TICKENHAM RD

Eastend Farm

Cadbury Court Farm

Land Yeo

Middle Yeo

Tickenham Drove

3

COURT LA

Clevedon Pottery

71

Tickenham Moor

Clevedon Craft Ctr

Clevedon Moor

Clevedon Boundary Rhyne

2

MOOR LA

COOK'S LA

MANMOOR LA

Triangle Farm

Old Smeath Farm

Smeathyard Farm

Nailsea Moor

North Drove

BS48

Ten Feet Rhyne

1

42   A   B   43   C   D   44   E   F   70

D1	E1	E2
1 MIZZYMEAD CL	1 FARMHOUSE CT	1 CHRISTCHURCH CL
2 BEAUFORT GDNS	2 BERENDON GDNS	2 CLEVEDON WLK
3 AMBERLEY GDNS	3 MENDIP CL	3 SOMERSET SQ
4 CLAREMONT GDNS	4 SELWORTHY GDNS	4 COLLIERS WLK
5 DOWNLAND CL	5 DUNSTER GDNS	5 CROWN GLASS PL
6 DORCHESTER CL	6 BIDDISHAM CL	6 VALLEY CL
		7 FARMHOUSE CL

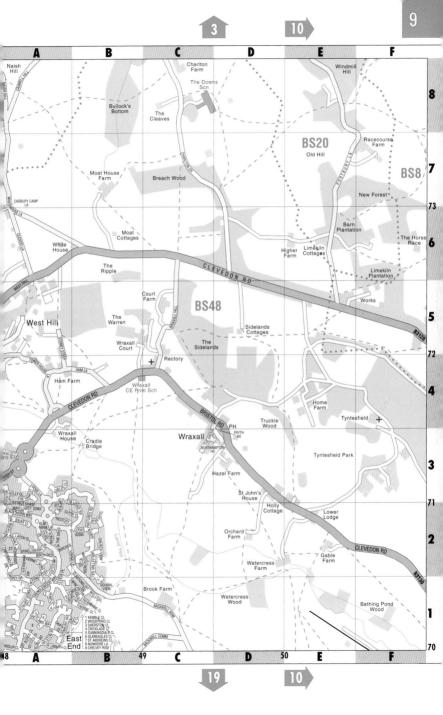

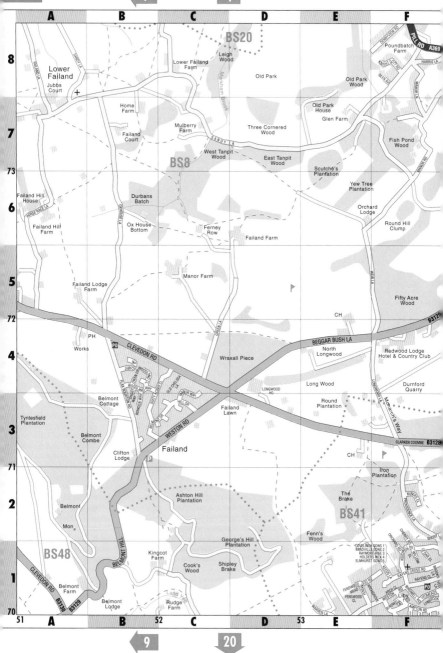

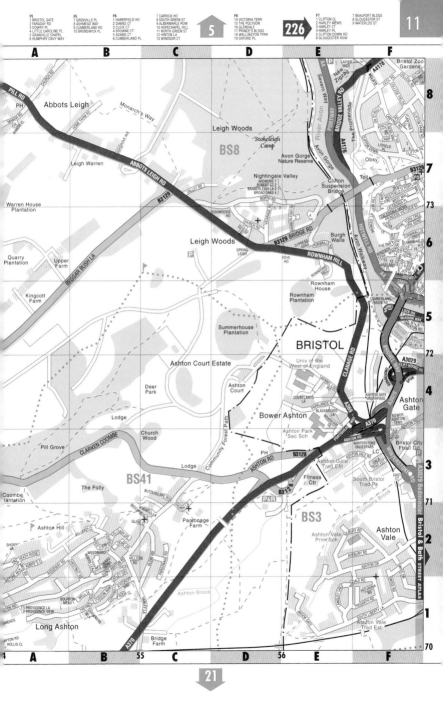

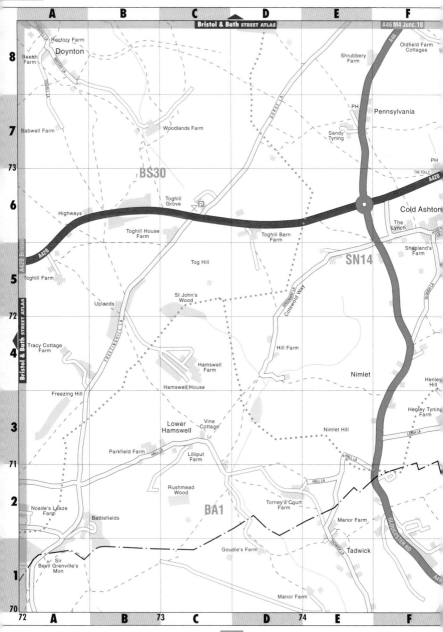

A46 M4 Junc. 18

Oldfield Farm Cottages

Shrubbery Farm

Rectory Farm

Doynton

Beebh Farm

8

Babwell Farm

7

Woodlands Farm

Pennsylvania

PH

Sandy Tyning

73

BS30

PH

THE FOLLY

A420

6

Highways

Toghill Grove

P

Cold Ashton

The Lynch

Toghill House Farm

Toghill Barn Farm

Shapland's Farm

A420 Bristol

A420

Tog Hill

SN14

Toghill Farm

5

Bristol & Bath STREET ATLAS

St John's Wood

72

Uplands

Colswold Way

Tracy Cottage Farm

4

Hill Farm

Nimlet

Henley Hill

Hamswell Farm

Hegley Tyning Farm

Freezing Hill

Hamswell House

LEIGH LA

Lower Hamswell

Vine Cottage

Nimlet Hill

3

Parkfield Farm

HALL LA

Lilliput Farm

HALL LA

71

Rushmead Wood

HALL LA

2

Noade's Leaze Farm

Battlefields

BA1

Torney's Court Farm

Manor Farm

GLOUCESTER RD

Tadwick

Sir Bevil Grenville's Mon

Goudie's Farm

1

A4

Manor Farm

70

A B C D E F

A420

Oldfield Farm

Almshouses

Hillcrest Bellum Marshfield

SN14

Folly Farm

Fuddlebrook Hill

Cotswold Way

Little Moody's Wood

73

Great Moody's Wood

Holly Barn

Fuddlebrook Rudgway

Manor House

BEEK LA

Halldoor La

Poulson's Farm

Coombes Wood

Halldoor Wood

72

Trull's Wood

AYFORD LA

Henley Hill

Tipper's Wood

Fry's Farm

LEIGH LA

Beek's Farm

Beek's Cottages

Nailey Farm

Monkswood Resr

Beek's Mill

St Catherine's Brook

Limestone Link

Ayford Bridge

Ayford Farm

71

Monk Woods

St Catherine's End House

Cripp's Farm

The Hermitage

Hunterwick Wood

BA1

Summerhill Wood

Coombe Wood

Court Farm

Hartley Wood

Hartley Farm

Stillcombe Wood

St Catherine

GLOUCESTER RD A46

Charmy Down

Airfield (dis)

St Catherine's Court

Cowleaze Wood

70

A B 76 C D 77 E F

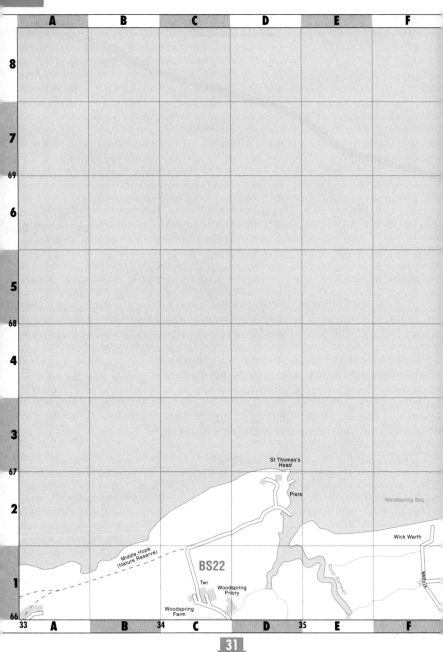

St Thomas's
Head

Piers

Woodspring Bay

Wick Warth

Middle Hope
(Nature Reserve)

BS22

River Banwell

Twr

Woodspring
Priory

Woodspring
Farm

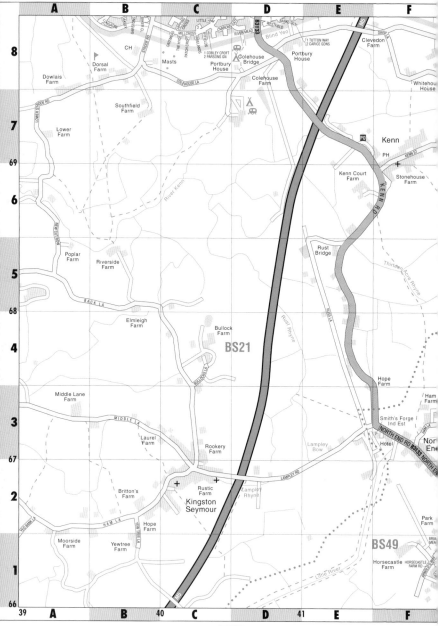

A B C D E F

8

CH
Dorsal
Farm
Masts
LITTLE HAM
GREENLANDS
MILLCROSS
THE HYERCROFT
STROUDE RD
RIVER MEAD
B3133
Blind Yeo
WESTFIELD
BRAND DK
DAVIS
1 TUTTON WAY
2 CARICE GDNS
Clevedon
Farm
Whitehouse
House
Dowlais
Farm
Southfield
Farm
1 COBLEY CROFT
2 PARSONS GN
Colehouse
Bridge
Portbury
House
Portbury
House
Colehouse
Farm
COLEHOUSE LA

7

Lower
Farm
LOWER EXE ROCK RD
Kenn
PO
Kenn
KENN ST
PH

69
River Kenn
Kenn Court
Farm
Stonehouse
Farm
KENN RD

6

5
Poplar
Farm
NEW CUT RD/CLAY
Riverside
Farm
Rust
Bridge
Thirteen Acre Rhyne

68
BACK LA
Elmleigh
Farm
Bullock
Farm
BS21
RUST LA
Rust Rhyne

4
BULLOCK LA
Hope
Farm
Ham
Farm

3
Middle Lane
Farm
MIDDLE LA
Laurel
Farm
Rookery
Farm
Lampley
Bow
Smith's Forge
Ind Est
NORTH END RD B3133 NORTH END
Nor
En

67
Britton's
Farm
Rustic
Farm
Kingston
Seymour
Lampley
Rhyne
LAMPLEY RD
Hotel

2
YEO BANK LA
Hope
Farm
HAM LA
YEW TREE LA
Park
Farm
BS49
BRIA
MEA

1
Moorside
Farm
Yewtree
Farm
Horsecastle
Farm
Horsecastle
FARM RD
HORSECASTLE LANE

66
M5
Little River

39 A 40 B C 41 D E F

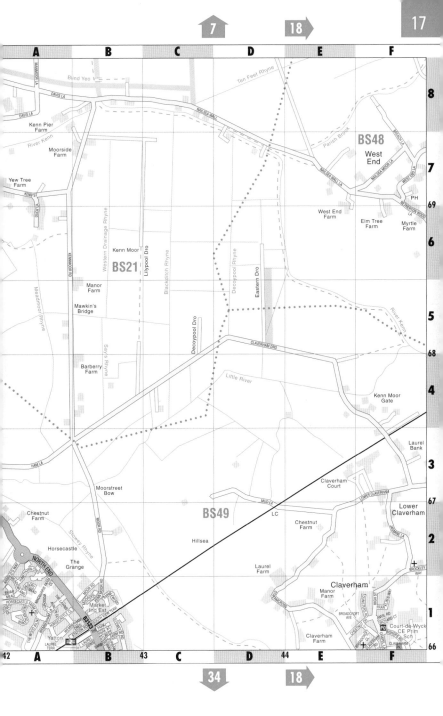

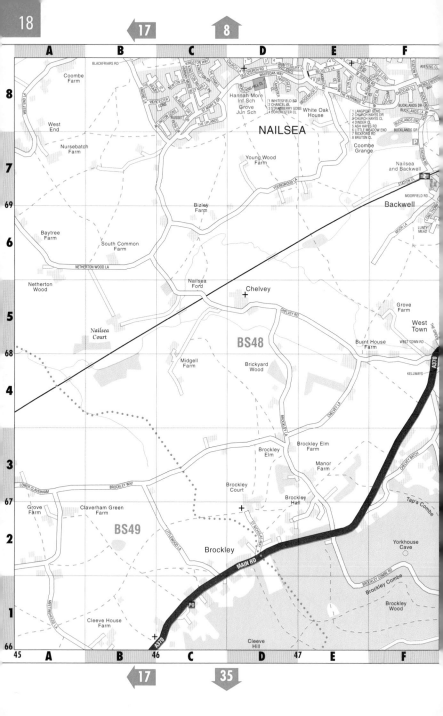

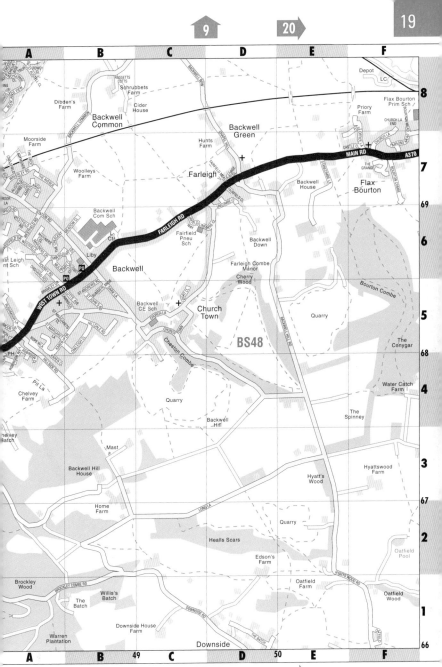

19
10

A   B   C   D   E   F

B3130
CLEVEDON RD
Kingcott Mill
Farm
Cambridge
Batch
Gatcombe
Court
Ashton
Watering
Long Ashton
Research Station

8

Ct
STATION RD
ORCHARD CL
HEAD

OLD WESTON RD
REDWOOD LA
WESTON RD

BS41

BRADVILLE GDNS 1
RAYMORE RISE 2
HOLDERS WLK 3
ELMHURST GDNS 4

Monarch Way

PH
Eastfield

A370   MAIN RD

7

A3

69

Breach Hill
Wood

Redwood
Farm

The
Fillies

Barrow

REDWOOD LA

WILDCOUNTRY LA

6

Crossgrove
Wood

VICARAGE LA
Hillside
Barrow
Mill

Barrow
Wood

The
Vicarage

School
Farm

Church
Wood

5

The
Triangle

Farleigh
Hill

BARROW COURT LA

Barrow
Court

BS48   BARROW ST

Barrow
Gurney

Home
Farm

SCHOOL LA

HERM LA

Water
Works

68

Park
Cottages

Slade
Wood

Dead Hill
Wood

SLADE CL

Steps Farm

B3130

A38

4

SLADE LA

Batches
Wood

HOBBS LA

Barrow
Hill

Stevens'
Farm

Hill
Farm

Stevens'
Wood

Resrs

3

• Mon

67

Freeman's
Farm

NAISH LA

B3130

FREEMANS LA

Dial
Farm

PH

Glenville House
Farm

2

BRIDGWATER RD

BARROW LA

Einell Brook

Yewtree
Farm

ROCKS LA

DIAL LA

BENDLLS LA

Hartcliff
Rocks

ELRELL LA

B3130

1

PH
Potters
Hill

A38

CURRELLS LA

BS40

66

51   A   B   52   C   D   53   E   F

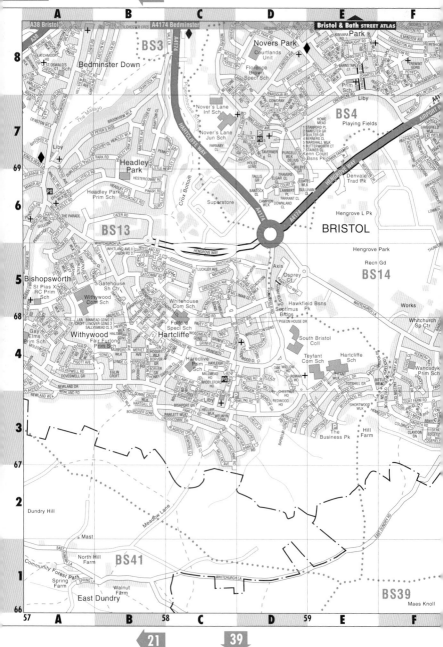

BS4

BS4

Flowers Hill Trad Est

P&R

8

Brislington Sch

Scotland Farm

Sports Gd

Sports Gd

WEST TOWN LA

B3119

Flowers Hill

The Coots

7

Ilsyngrove

SWALLOW

69

Petherton Road Inf Sch

Central Pk

1 FIRST AVE
2 SIXTH AVE
3 SEVENTH AVE
4 EIGHTH AVE
5 THIRD AVE
6 SECOND AVE
7 FOURTH AVE
8 FIFTH AVE

Tyning Hengrove Jun Sch

Hengrove Sch

Hengrove

New Fosseway Sch

David's Rd

Hollyridge

6

St Bernadette RC Prim Sch

St Bernadette RC Sch

Dutton Wlk

Stockwood

Burgis Rd

Cornish

ANDEREACH CL 1
ALLANMEAD RD 2
EDGEWOOD CL 3

Griggfield

1 CHARTER WLK
2 PYRACANTHA WLK
3 KING EDWARD CL

Perry Court Jun & Inf Schs

Knightstone Rd

Burnbush Prim Sch

Liby

Waycroft Prim Sch

5

Whitchurch District Ctr

The Drive

ROBIN

Hooper

LANGDOWN CT

WATERMAN

GOSLET RD

68

COPELAND DR 1
WEDGWOOD CL 2
EXTON CL 3
CURLAND GR 4
BLACKDOWN CT 5
WANSDYKE CT 6
SHIPHAM CL 7

Craydon Rd

Craydon Gr

Binley Gr

Stockwood Green Prim Sch

BS14

Whitchurch

Maggs La

Whitchurch Prim Sch

4

Whitchurch

OLD VICARAGE

Manor Farm

Church Mdws

Newlands

3

Dundry Hill

BLACKROCK LA

67

BRISTOL RD

Queen Charlton La

Cemy

BS31

2

Nursery

Whitewood Farm

The Cot

BS39

1

MAGOTSFIELD LA

GIBBET LA

GIBBET LA

BLACKROCK LA

HURSLEY LA

66

Bristol & Bath STREET ATLAS

A4 Bristol
A4174 Bristol Northern Ring Road

BS4

BS15

BS30

8

Hicks
Gate

BS8

Scotland Bottom

Keysham Hams

Factory

Somerdale

River Avon

7

Oaklease
Farm

Durleypark

DURLEY HILL

Cemy

Recn Gd

CH

Wood
Covert

Stockwood
Vale

Broadlands
Sch

Keysham

BRISTOL RD

STATION RD

KEYNSHAM RD A4175

69

6

BS14

Charlton Bottom

Broadlands
House

St Francis Rd

Temple
Jun Sch

THE
HYDE

THE
REGENTS

B3116 HIGH ST

BATH RD

5

Heathfield Cl

Westfield Cl

Keynsham
Prim Sch

St John's
Prim Sch

Handel Ave

Sherwood
Rd

Temple
Inf Sch

BATH RD B3116

68

4

Lays
Bsns Ctr

Lays
Farm

Box Wlk

Walnut Wlk

Warwick Rd

Coronation Ave

Castle
Prim Sch

Chelmer Gr

Chandag Rd

3

Queen Charlton

Parkhouse
Farm

Parkhouse Lane

KEYNSHAM

BS31

Community Forest Path

67

Manor
Farm

Queen Charlton
La

Wellfield
House

Manor
Farm

Chewton
Place

Courtenay Rd

2

Highwall La

Newlynch La

Poplars
Cottage

Chew
Keynsham

1

Charlton Field

Harvey's
Ditch

Warners
Farm

66

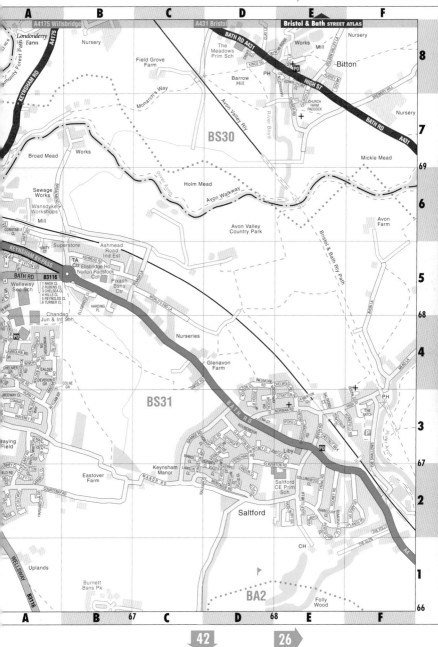

26

A · **B** · **C** · **D** · **E** · **F**

A4175 Willsbridge

A431 Bristol

BATH RD A431

Bristol & Bath STREET ATLAS

Londonderry Farm

Nursery

Field Grove Farm

The Meadows Prim Sch

Works

Mill

Nursery

8

Community Forest Path

KEYNSHAM RD · A4175

Monarch's Way

Barrow Hill

Bitton

PH

PO

HIGH ST

Avon Valley Rly

River Boyd

CHURCH FARM PADDOCK

BATH RD

A431

Nursery

7

BS30

Broad Mead

Works

River Avon

Holm Mead

Mickle Mead

69

Sewage Works

Avon Walkway

Avon Farm

6

Wansdyke Workshops

Mill

Avon Valley Country Park

Bristol & Bath Rly Path

CONSTABLE CL

Superstore

Ashmead Road Ind Est

5

KEYNSHAM BY-PASS

UNITY CT

TA Ctr

Elisbridge Ho

Norton Radstock Coll

Pixash Bsns Ctr

BATH RD · B3116

Wellsway Sec Sch

1 NASH CL
2 RUBENS CL
3 CHELSEA CL
4 HILLS CL
5 REYNOLDS CL
6 TURNER CL

WORLD'S END LA

HARDING PL

68

Chandag Jun & Inf Sch

Nurseries

4

PO

LAMBOURN RD

Glenavon Farm

BS31

BATH RD

INEDMORE RD

CHELWO

STRATTON

CAMERTON

THE BATCH

PH

P

River Avon

3

NORMAN RD

Liby

PO

67

Playing Field

Eastover Farm

Keynsham Manor

MANOR RD

WITNEY CL

CLAVERTON RD

GLAVERTON RD

Collingwood

Saltford CE Prim Sch

2

WELLSWAY · B3116

Uplands

Saltford

CH

THE GLEN

THE TOLL

A4

1

Burnett Bsns Pk

BA2

Folly Wood

66

A · **B** · 67 · **C** · **D** · 68 · **E** · **F**

42

26

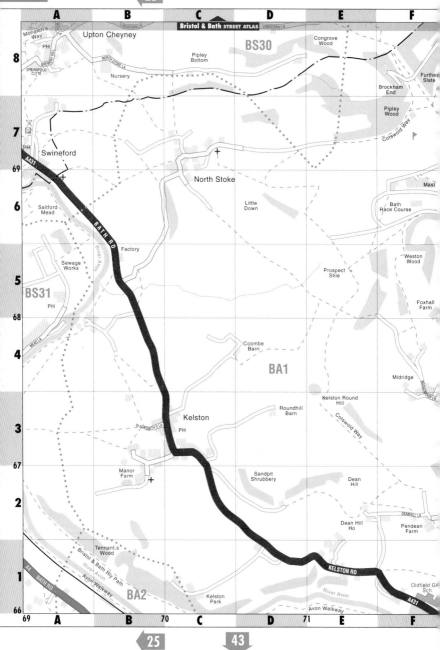

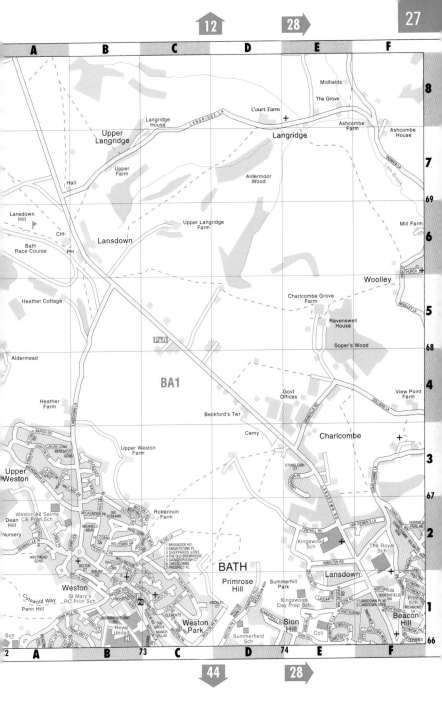

A B C D E F

8
7
69
6
5
68
4
67
3
2
1
66

Midfields
The Grove
Court Farm
Langridge House
LANGRIDGE LA
Langridge
Ashcombe Farm
Ashcombe House
Upper Langridge
Upper Farm
Hall
Aldermoor Wood
FADDICK LA
Lam Brook
Lansdown Hill
CH
PH
Lansdown
Upper Langridge Farm
Mill Farm
Bath Race Course
HIGH CHURCH
Woolley
WOOLLEY LA
Heather Cottage
Charlcombe Grove Farm
Ravenswell House
P&R
Soper's Wood
Aldermead
BA1
Govt Offices
View Point Farm
Heather Farm
LANSDOWN LA
Beckford's Twr
GRANVILLE RD
COLLIERS LA
Charlcombe
Cemy
Upper Weston Farm
CHARLCOMBE LA
Napier Rd
LEVEL
DUNCAN GDNS
BERESFORD GDNS
STONELEIGH CT
Upper Weston
Rohannon Farm
LANSDOWN
FAIRFIELD PARK RD
Weston All Saints CE Prim Sch
Dean Hill
SIX STREAMS
Nursery
BROADMOOR PK
MICHAELS MEAD
HOLCOMBE GN
HOLCOMBE GR
WEAL FARM
BURL LA
Kingswood Sch
VAN DIEMEN'S LA
The Royal Sch
WESTMEAD GDNS
BELTON CT
BIBURY HO
HARCOURT GDNS
1 BROOKSIDE HO
2 KNIGHTSTONE PL
3 SHEPPARDS GDNS
4 THE OLD BREWHOUSE
5 GAINSBOROUGH CT
6 CHELSOMEL
7 PROSPECT PL
FONTHILL RD
HAMILTON RD
Lansdown
NORTHFIELDS
Weston
St Mary's RC Prim Sch
Cotswold Way
Penn Hill
BATH
Primrose Hill
Summerhill Park
Kingswood Day Prep Sch
LANSDOWN PL
1 LANSDOWN PL
2 LANSDOWN CRES
Prim Sch
RICHMOND
Beacon Hill
BERNARD WEARD HO
Royal United
H
THE GROVE MANOR VILLAS
Weston Park
HOOLEY CT
Sion Hill
Coll
SOMERSET
LANSDOWN RD
RICHARDSON
STEPHEN'S
Summerfield Sch
Sch
2 73 C 74 E F

27 13

8
7
69
6
68
5
4
3
67
2
1
66

A B C D E F

GLOUCESTER RD
A46

Charmy Down
Airfield (dis)
Down Farm
Wingfield Farm
Mast
Holts Down
Lyegrove Wood
Stoney La

Cherrywell Wood
Bailey's Wood

Short Wood
Charmydown Farm
Ramscombe Bottom
RAMSCOMBE LA
The Hill Farm

Crossleaze Farm
Manor Farm
Kent La
BLACKSMITH'S LA
Upper Swainswick
Swainswick Prim Sch
Chilcombe Bottom
Northend
EAGLE LA

Lam Brook
Little Solsbury Hill
BA1
Church Farm
Batheaston
CATHERINE WAY
CHURCH LA
Batheaston CE Prim Sch
PH

Twinfield Farm
SWAINSWICK LA
SOLSBURY LA
SOLSBURY CT
SOLSBURY LINK
LONDON RD

Meadow Farm
Lower Swainswick
Bailbrook
BAILBROOK LA
GEORGES BLDGS
KYRLE GDNS
Hotel Bathampton Bridge (Toll)
Limestone Link

BATH
RAGLAN TERR 1
FAIRFIELD VIEW 2
MELROSE TERR 3
FAIRFIELD TERR 4
Larkhall
VALLEY VIEW
FERNDALE
GARFIELD TERR 1
BROUGHAM PL 2
COTTAGE PL 3
EDEN TERR
PITMAN
St Mark's CE Sch
Bailbrook Coll
BA2
LONDON RD W
A4
River Avon
Bathampton Prim Sch

Fairfield Park
Lambridge
UPPER LAMBRIDGE ST
P
Bathampton
CANAL TERR
PO
St Nicholas
PH

Grosvenor
Grosvenor High Sch
LONDON RD
A4
Avon Walkway
Kennet & Avon Canal
DEVONSHIRE RD

27 45

A1
1 MOUNT BEACON ROW
2 BELGRAVE TERR
3 MALVERN VILLAS
4 MALVERN TERR
5 SEYMOUR RD
6 DOVER PL
7 CATHCART HO
8 HIGHBURY COTTS
9 HIGHBURY VILLAS
10 HIGHBURY TR
11 COBURG VILLAS
12 STANLEY VILLAS
13 GILLINGHAM TERR
14 EVELYN TERR
15 TYNNING TERR
16 KINGSDOWN VIEW
17 SOLSBURY VIEW
18 COLLEGE VIEW

B1
1 BRUNSWICK ST
2 HANOVER ST
3 WALMSLEY TERR
4 WALMSLEY TERR
5 HANOVER TERR
6 FRANKLEY TERR
7 CHILTON CT
8 BEAUFORT VILLAS
9 GROSVENOR VILLAS
10 ST SAVIOUR'S TERR
11 BEAUFORT W
12 ALEXANDER BLDGS
13 PERCY PL

C1
1 LAMBRIDGE BLDGS
2 VICTORIA PL
3 BEAUFORT MEWS
4 ST SAVIOURS WAY
5 LAMBRIDGE MEWS
6 LAMBRIDGE
7 LAMONT HO
8 MONTAGUE HO
9 EASTON HO
10 HAMPTON HO
11 BRIDGE HO

SN14

Colerne

The Oaks Farm

ROAD HILL

Upper Northend Farm

DARTFORD LA

oney La

Rodney Farm

8

Alcombe Manor

Grubbins Wood

7

Mast

69

St Catherine's Brook

Limestone Link

Oldhouse Farm

Lower Shockerwick Farm

6

Banner Down

Shockerwick House

STELWAY LA

Starfall Farm

Sheep Sleight

Shockerwick Farm

Shockerwick

A4 Chippenham

BA1

The Mount

BANNERDOWN RD

BATH RD

5

A4

Wiltshire STREET ATLAS

68

ELMHURST EST

Sheylor's Farm

Box Bridge

4

Ashley House

SHOCKERWICK LA

Ashley Wood La

LONDON RD

Ashley House

SN13

3

PH

BOX RD

Mill

By Brook

ASHLEY RD

Kingsdown

Ashley Wood Farm

LOWER KINGSDOWN RD

KINGSDOWN DN

67

A363

Bathampton Farm

River Avon

LC

PH

BATHFORD HILL

PO

JOUBERT LA

MOUNTAIN WOOD

2

Ashley Wood

BA2

Limestone Link

BRADFORD RD

CHURCH ST

COURT LA

Bathford Prim Sch

Bathford

Kennet & Avon Canal

on Walkway

HOLCOMBE LA

Warleigh Lodge

WARLEIGH LA

A363

Brown's Folly

P

BA15

EMLEIGH RISE

FARLEIGH RISE

1

66

A   B   79   C   D   80   E   F

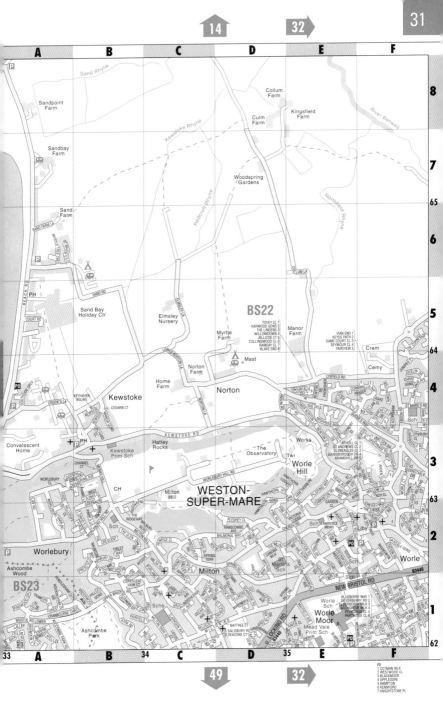

BS21

Tutshill
Ear

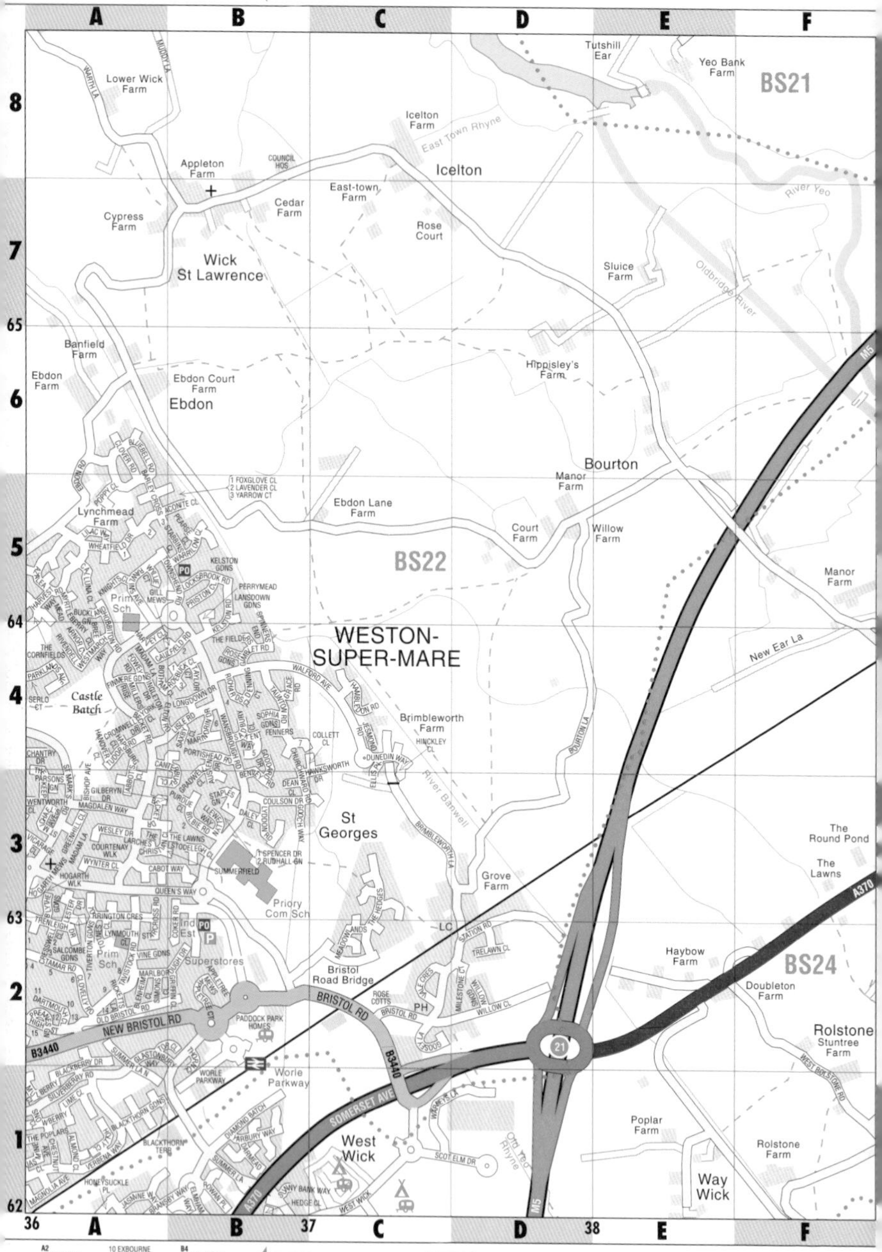

Yeo Bank
Farm

Lower Wick
Farm

Icelton
Farm

East Town Rhyne

Icelton

River Yeo

Appleton
Farm

COUNCIL
HOS

Cedar
Farm

East-town
Farm

Cypress
Farm

Rose
Court

Sluice
Farm

Oldbridge River

Wick
St Lawrence

Banfield
Farm

Hippisley's
Farm

Ebdon
Farm

Ebdon Court
Farm

Ebdon

Bourton

Manor
Farm

M5

Lynchmead
Farm

1 FOXGLOVE CL
2 LAVENDER CL
3 YARROW CT

Ebdon Lane
Farm

Court
Farm

Willow
Farm

Manor
Farm

BS22

**WESTON-
SUPER-MARE**

New Ear La

Castle
Batch

Brimbleworth
Farm

Hinckley

The
Round Pond

St
Georges

The
Lawns

A370

Grove
Farm

River Banwell

Priory
Com Sch

Haybow
Farm

BS24

Bristol
Road Bridge

NEW BRISTOL RD

BRISTOL RD

Doubleton
Farm

Rolstone
Stuntree
Farm

B3440

Paddock Park
Homes

Superstores

PH

21

Worle
Parkway

SOMERSET AVE

Poplar
Farm

Rolstone
Farm

West
Wick

Way
Wick

Boot Elm Dr

M5

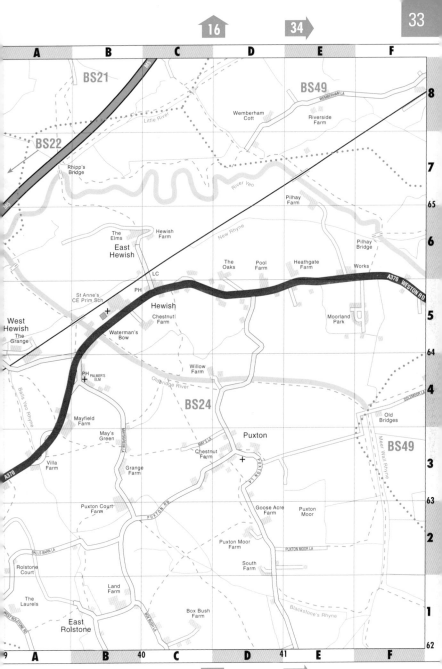

A B C D E F

8

BS21

BS22

BS49

Little River

Wemberham Cott

WEMBERHAM LA

Riverside Farm

Rhipp's Bridge

7

River Yeo

65

Pilhay Farm

The Elms

Hewish Farm

East Hewish

New Rhyne

6

Pilhay Bridge

LC

The Oaks

Pool Farm

Heathgate Farm

Works

A370 WESTON RD

St Anne's CE Prim Sch

PH

Hewish

5

Chestnut Farm

Moorland Park

West Hewish

The Grange

Waterman's Bow

64

PH PALMER'S ELM

Willow Farm

Oldbridge River

4

Old Bridges

VOLEMOOR LA

BS24

Mayfield Farm

May's Green

MAY'S LA

Puxton

MAYSFIELD LA

BS49

Meer Wall Rhyne

Villa Farm

Grange Farm

Chestnut Farm

3

PUXTON RD

Puxton Court Farm

Goose Acre Farm

Puxton Moor

63

BALLS BARN LA

Puxton Moor Farm

PUXTON MOOR LA

2

Rolstone Court

South Farm

The Laurels

Land Farm

Box Bush Farm

BOX BUSH LA

Blackstone's Rhyne

East Rolstone

1

62

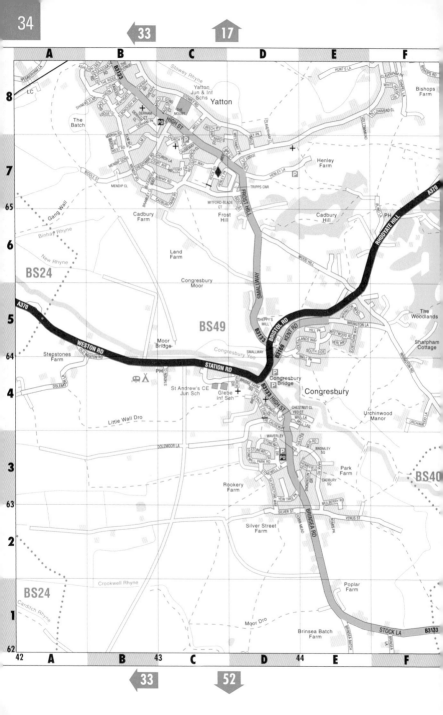

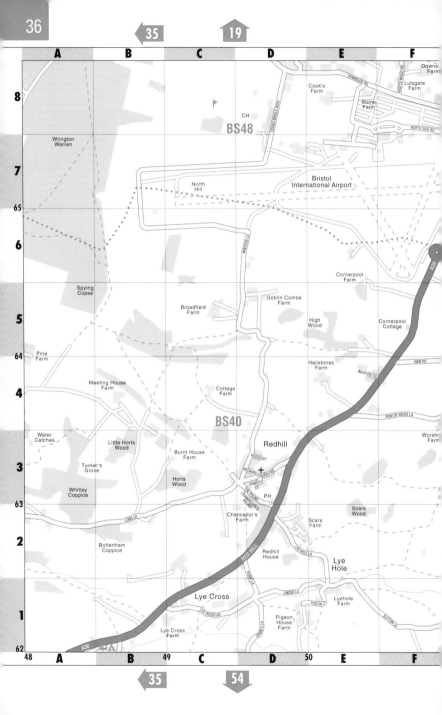

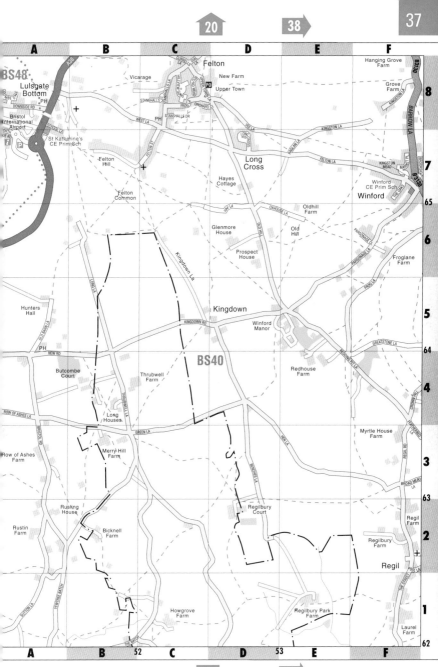

| A | B | C | D | E | F |

BS48

Lulsgate Bottom

DOWNSIDE RD
PH

Bristol International Airport

St Katherine's CE Prim Sch

Vicarage

STANSHALLS

WEST LA

PH

STANSHALLS DR

Felton Hill

+

Felton Common

Felton

New Farm

Upper Town

PO

ORCHARD CT

TEE LA

LONG CROSS

KINGSTON LA

Hanging Grove Farm

Grove Farm

8

DOWNSIDE RD

Hayes Cottage

Long Cross

FELTON LA

Winford CE Prim Sch

Winford

7

KINGSTON MEAD

MAY

B3130

BARROW LA

65

JAY LA

OXHOUSE LA

Oldhill Farm

Glenmore House

OLD HILL

Old Hill

Prospect House

Froglane Farm

6

Kingdown La

PARSONAGE CT

PARSONAGE LA

FROG LA

Hunters Hall

OLD DERN LA

Kingdown

KINGDOWN RD

Winford Manor

REDHILL FIVE LA

GREASTONE LA

5

PH

NEW RD

BS40

64

Butcombe Court

Thrubwell Farm

Redhouse Farm

Myrtle House Farm

4

ROW OF ASHES LA

THRUBWELL LA

Long Houses

GREEN LA

TEE LA

BROAD MEAD LA

3

Row of Ashes Farm

BRISTOL RD

Merry Hill Farm

BACK LA

63

Rusking House

Regilbury Court

Regil Farm

2

Rustin Farm

Bicknell Farm

Regilbury Farm

+

Regil

POST LA

REGIL RD

SUTTON LA

PENTHOUSE HATCH

Howgrove Farm

Regilbury Park Farm

1

Laurel Farm

BATCH

| A | B | C | D | E | F |

BS41

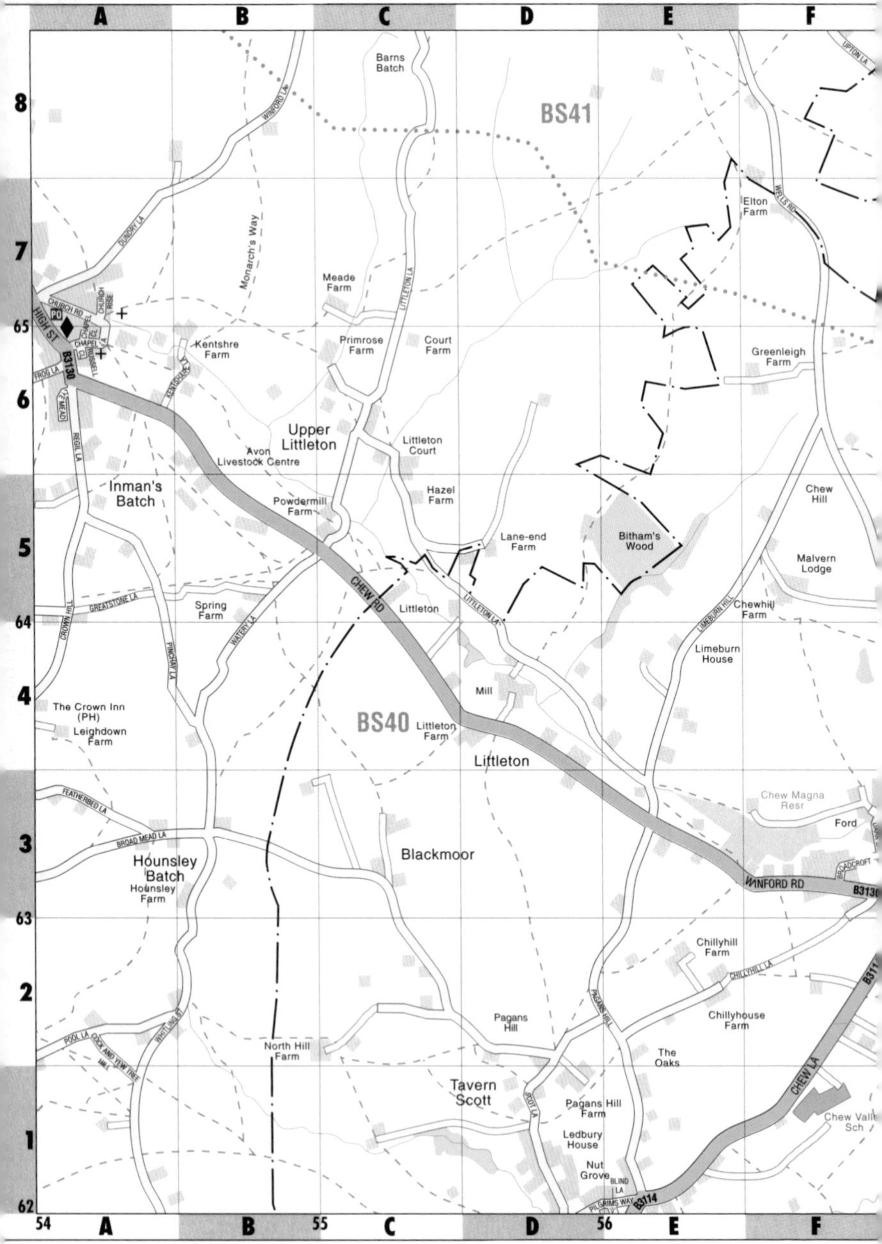

A B C D E F

8

7

65

6

5

64

4

63

3

2

1

62

54 55 56

Barns Batch

Windmill La

Dursley La

Monarch's Way

Meade Farm

Littleton La

Kentshre Farm

Primrose Farm

Court Farm

Chapel

High St

Greens La

Bristol Rd

Littleton Court

Upper Littleton

Avon Livestock Centre

Powdermill Farm

Hazel Farm

Lane-end Farm

Bitham's Wood

Chew Hill

Malvern Lodge

Chewhill Farm

Limeburn La

Inman's Batch

Chew Rd

Spring Farm

Greatstone La

Pinch La

Water La

Littleton

Littleton La

Limeburn House

The Crown Inn (PH)

Leighdown Farm

Church Town La

BS40

Mill

Littleton Farm

Littleton

Chew Magna Resr

Ford

Featherbed La

Broad Mead La

Hounsley Batch

Hounsley Farm

Blackmoor

Winford Rd

B3130

B3114

Chillyhill Farm

Chillyhill La

Chillyhouse Farm

Pool La

Gas And Tar Tar La

North Hill Farm

Ridge La

Pagans Hill

Pagan La

Pagans Hill

The Oaks

Chew La

Tavern Scott

Pagans Hill Farm

Ledbury House

Nut Grove

Blind La

Pilgrims Walk

B3114

Chew Valley Sch

Chew La

Elton Farm

Wells Rd

Lipson La

Greenleigh Farm

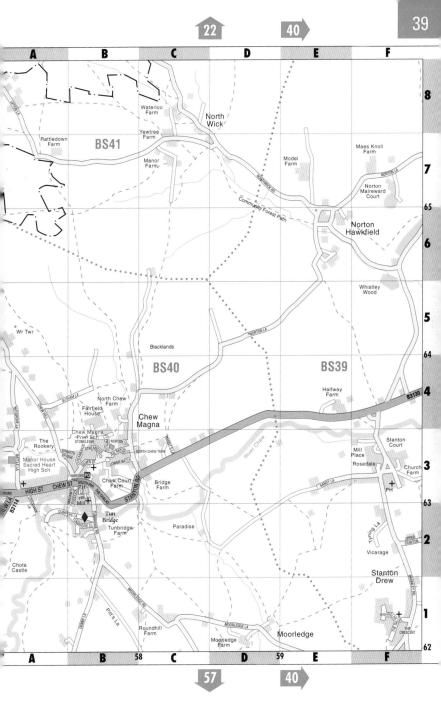

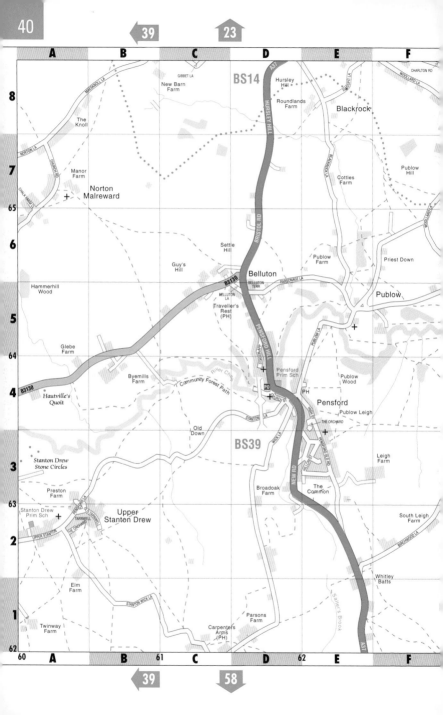

BS14

CHARLTON RD

GIBBET LA

New Barn Farm

Hursley Hill

Roundlands Farm

Blackrock

WOOLARD LA

MAESBURY LA

8

The Knoll

NORTON LA

CHURCH RD

7

Manor Farm

Norton Malreward

HURSLEY HILL

WORLE HILL

BLACKROCK LA

Publow Hill

Cottles Farm

CHALK WELL CS

65

BRISTOL RD

Settle Hill

6

Guy's Hill

B3130

Belluton

BELLUTON TERR

PARSONAGE LA

Publow Farm

Priest Down

Publow

WOOLARD LA

Hammerhill Wood

BELLUTON LA

Traveller's Rest (PH)

5

Glebe Farm

64

Byemills Farm

River Chew

Community Forest Path

PENSFORD HILL

PUBLOW LA

Pensford Prim Sch

Publow Wood

B3130

Hautville's Quoit

NEW SHOPS

Old Down

CHURCH ST

STANTON LA

PO

PH

PENSFORD RD

Pensford

Publow Leigh

THE ORCHARD

Leigh Farm

4

BS39

HILLCREST

BILBIE LA

Stanton Drew Stone Circles

3

Preston Farm

Broadoak Farm

NEW RD

The Common

South Leigh Farm

63

Stanton Drew Prim Sch

THE DIMROAD

TARNWELL

Upper Stanton Drew

UPPER STANTON

THE DIMROAD

2

Elm Farm

STANTON WICK LA

Parsons Farm

Whitley Batts

BIRCHWOOD LA

Twinway Farm

Carpenters Arms (PH)

Salter's Brook

A37

1

62

60

A

B

61

C

D

62

E

F

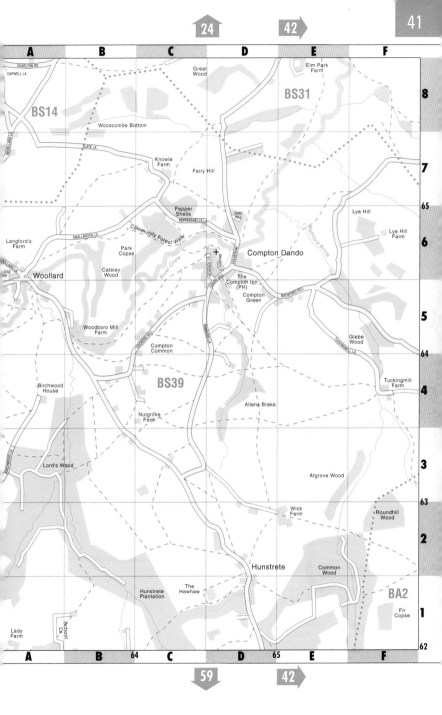

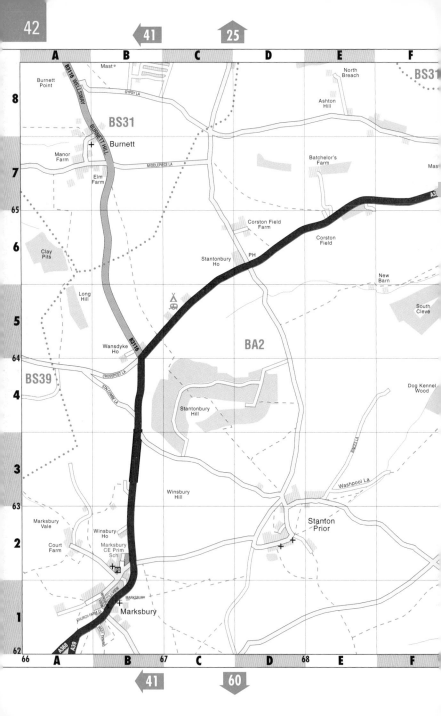

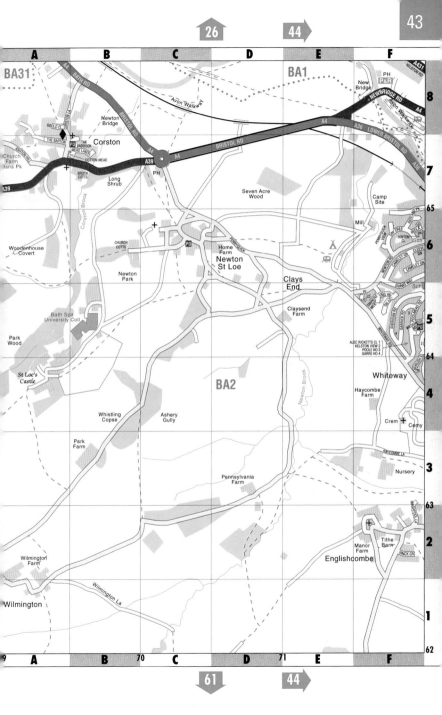

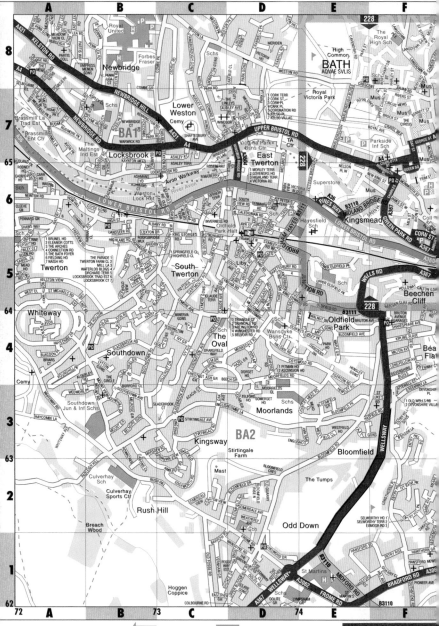

A B C D E F

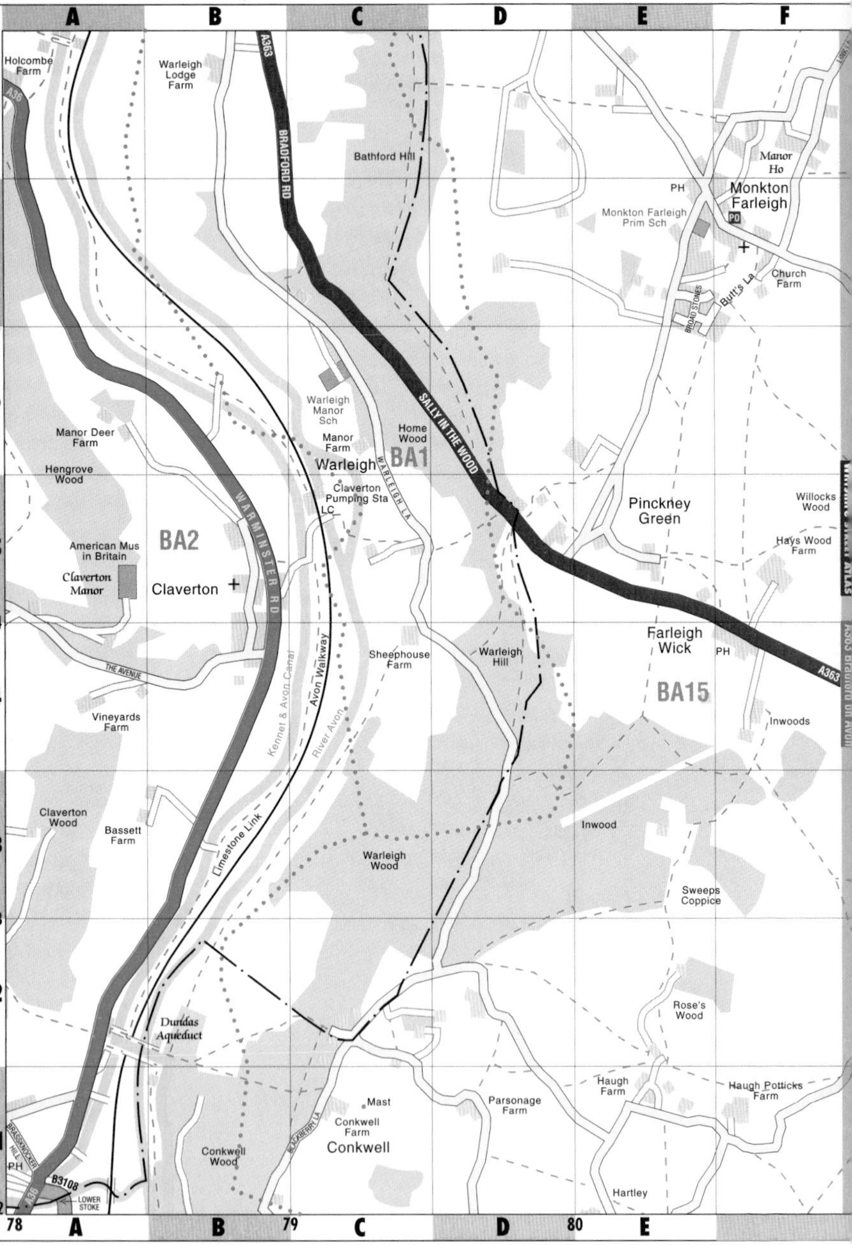

8

Holcombe
Farm

Warleigh Lodge
Farm

Manor
Ho

Bathford Hill

Monkton
Farleigh

PH

7

Monkton Farleigh
Prim Sch

Burt's La

Church
Farm

65

6

Warleigh
Manor
Sch

Home
Wood

BA1

SALLY IN THE WOOD

Manor
Farm

Warleigh

Manor Deer
Farm

Pinckney
Green

Willocks
Wood

Hengrove
Wood

Claverton
Pumping Sta
LC

Hays Wood
Farm

5

BA2

American Mus
in Britain

WARMINSTER RD

Farleigh
Wick

PH

Claverton
Manor

Claverton +

64

Sheephouse
Farm

Warleigh
Hill

BA15

A363

THE AVENUE

4

Vineyards
Farm

Kennet & Avon Canal

River Avon

Avon Walkway

Inwoods

3

Claverton
Wood

Bassett
Farm

Limestone Link

Warleigh
Wood

Inwood

Sweeps
Coppice

63

2

Dundas
Aqueduct

Rose's
Wood

1

PH

B3108

LOWER
STOKE

Conkwell
Wood

Mast

Conkwell
Farm

Conkwell

Parsonage
Farm

Haugh
Farm

Haugh Potticks
Farm

Hartley

62

78 A B 79 C D 80 E

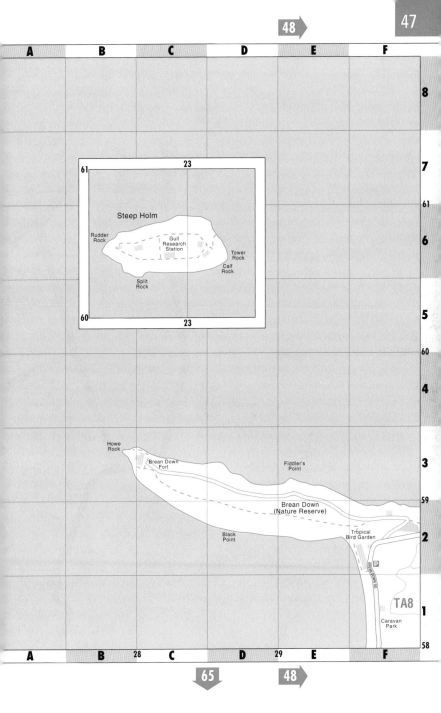

Steep Holm

Rudder
Rock

Gull
Research
Station

Tower
Rock

Calf
Rock

Split
Rock

Howe
Rock

Brean Down
Fort

Fiddler's
Point

Brean Down
(Nature Reserve)

Black
Point

Tropical
Bird Garden

TA8

Caravan
Park

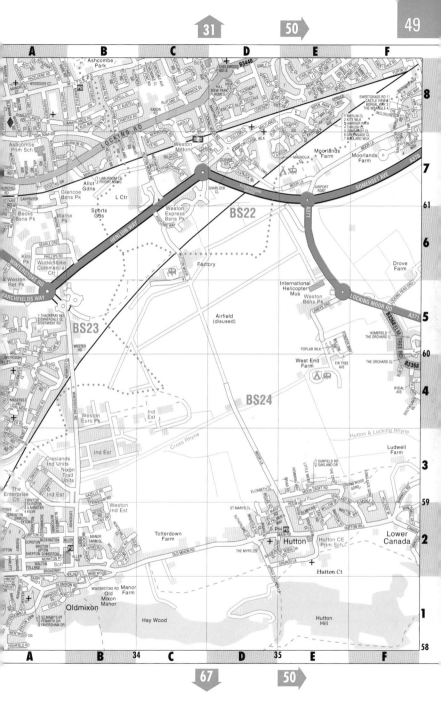

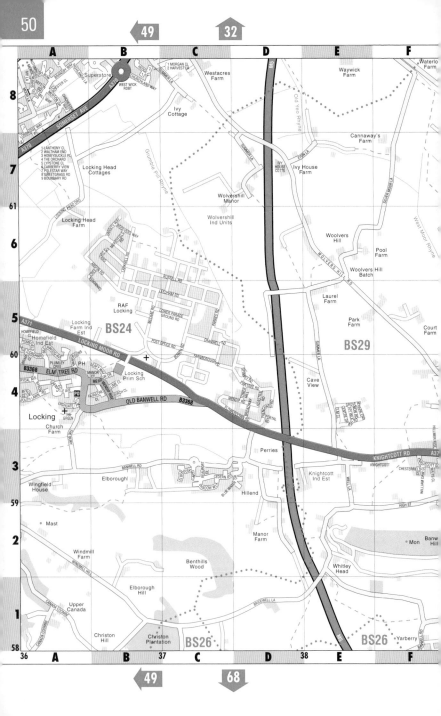

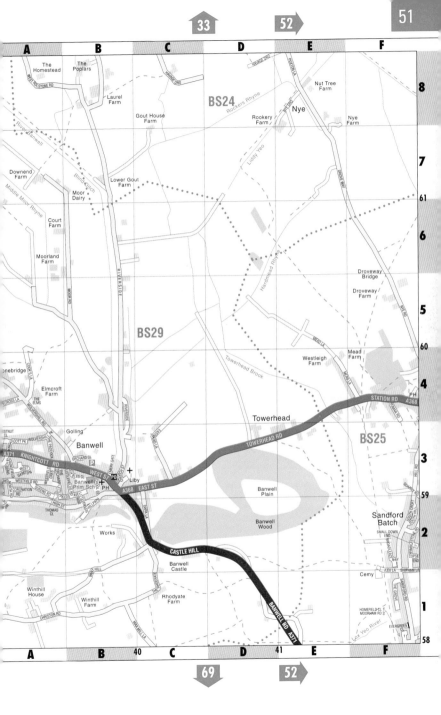

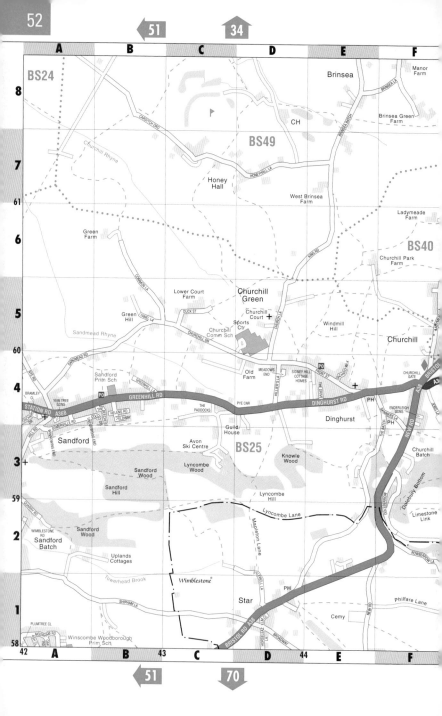

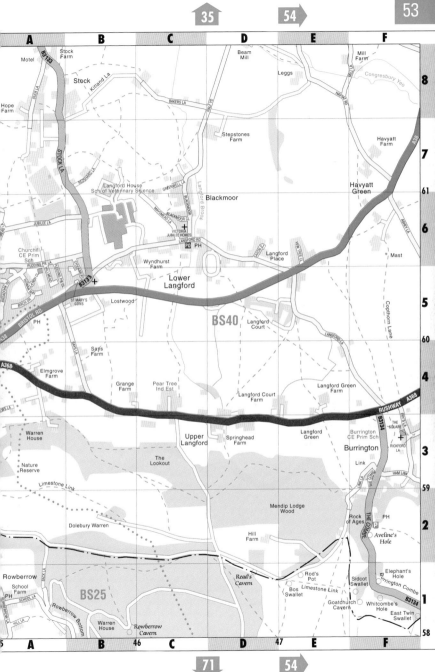

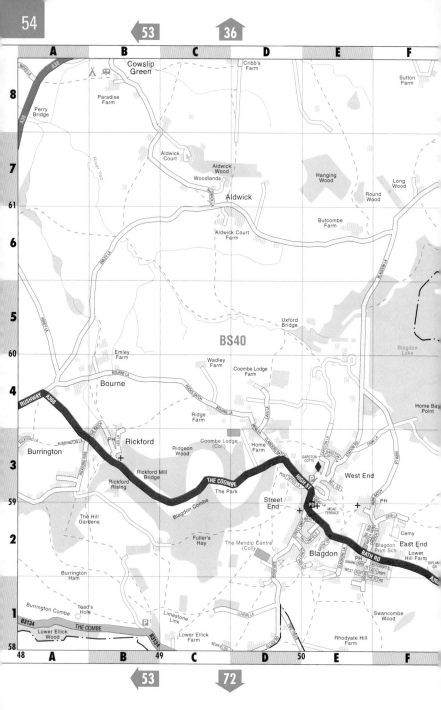

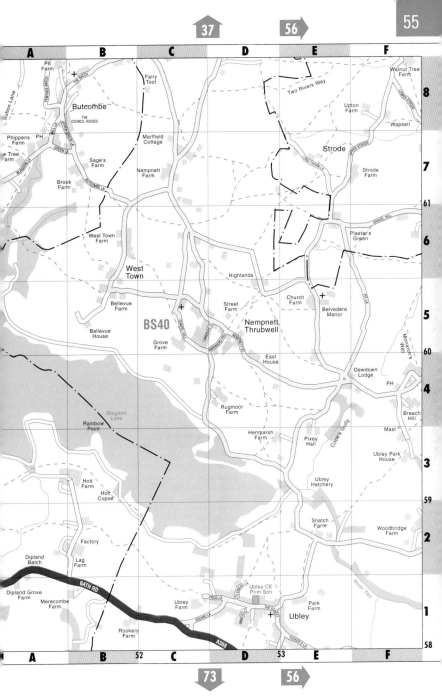

8
7
61
6
5
60
4
3
59
2
1
58

A · B · C · D · E · F

Pit Farm
THE BATCH
Fairy Toot
Two Rivers Way
Walnut Tree Farm
Upton Farm
Wapsell
Butcombe
THE COUNCIL HOUSES
Marlfield Cottage
Strode
UPPER STRODE
Phippens Farm
PH
Sage's Farm
Nempnett Farm
Strode Farm
w Tree arm
BLAGDON LA
GREEN LA
MILL LA
UPPER GREEN LA
Brook Farm
BUTCOMBE LA
NEW TOWN LA
Plaster's Green
GRAVEL HILL
West Town Farm
West Town
Highlands
Plaster's Green
Bellevue Farm
Street Farm
Church Farm
Belvedere Manor
PIT LA
BS40
GRAVEL HILL
Nempnett Thrubwell
Bellevue House
Grove Farm
LANSDOWN CL
MAYNARD'S RD
NEMPNETT ST
East House
Monarch's Way
Dewdown Lodge
PH
Blagdon Lake
Rugmoor Farm
Breach Hill
Rainbow Point
Henmarsh Farm
Pixey Hall
Cook's Gully
Mast
Ubley Park House
Holt Farm
Ubley Hatchery
Holt Copse
Snatch Farm
Woodbridge Farm
Factory
Dipland Batch
Lag Farm
Dipland Grove Farm
BATH RD
STEEL LA
Ubley CE Prim Sch
PROS LA
Park Farm
River Yeo
Merecombe Farm
Ubley Farm
SQUIRE LA
MINION'S LA
THE STREET
Ubley
Rookery Farm
A368
TUCKER'S LA

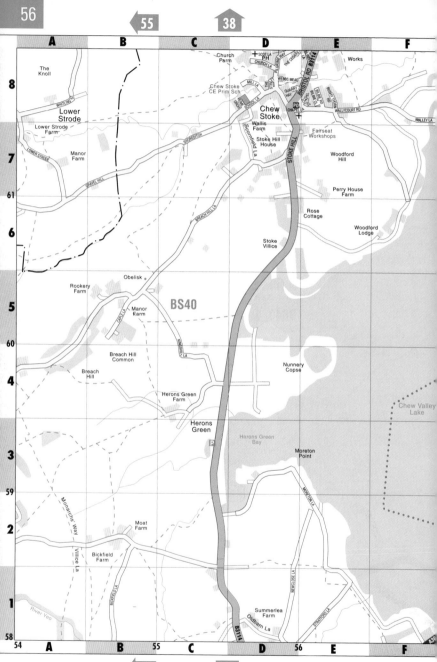

A   B   C   D   E   F

8

The
Knoll

Church
Farm

PH

THE CROSS

Works

Chew Stoke
CE Prim Sch

WEBBS MEAD

BRISTOL RD B3114

MILL LA

SCHOOL LA

Lower
Strode

Chew
Stoke

QUARRY
WAY

Lower Strode
Farm

Wallis
Farm

CHAPEL LA

WALLYCOURT RD

VALLEY LA

7

Manor
Farm

SCORFIELD LA

Stoke Hill
House

Fairseat
Workshops

Woodford
Hill

SHOREDITCH

STOKE HILL

Perry House
Farm

61

GRAVEL HILL

LOWER STRODE

Rose
Cottage

Woodford
Lodge

6

BREACH HILL LA

Stoke
Villice

Obelisk

Rookery
Farm

BS40

5

Manor
Farm

KINGSHILL LA

60

Breach Hill
Common

Nunnery
Copse

Breach
Hill

4

Herons Green
Farm

Chew Valley
Lake

Herons
Green

P

Herons Green
Bay

3

Moreton
Point

59

Monarch's Way

MORETON LA

2

Villice La

Moat
Farm

Bickfield
Farm

BICKFIELD LA

NEWBURLA

1

River Yeo

Summerlea
Farm

OLDBURN LA

B3114

Oldbarn La

STRODE LA

A37

58

54   A   B   55   C   D   56   E   F

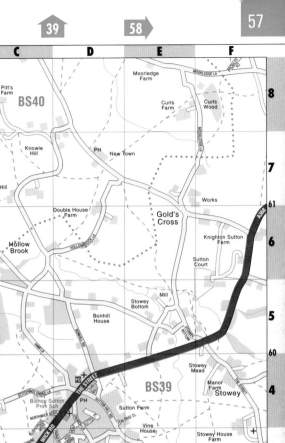

A   B   58   C   D   59   E   F

Woodbarn Farm
Pitt's La
Pitt's Farm
BS40
Moorledge Farm
MOORLEDGE LA
Curls Farm
Curls Wood
Nature Trails
Knowle Hill
PH
New Town
Knowle Hill Farm
Works
Double House Farm
HOLLOW BROOK LA
Gold's Cross
Knighton Sutton Farm
Hollow Brook
Sutton Court
Denny Island
Stowey Bottom
Mill
Bonhill House
STOWEY BOTTOM
Stowey Mead
THE STREET
Manor Farm
Stowey
BS39
PO
Bishop Sutton Prim Sch
PH
Sutton Farm
Vine House
Stowey House Farm
PH
WICK RD
BATTLE LANE RD
YEW TREE CL
Wick Farm
Castle Wood
Bishop Sutton
WOODCROFT
Broad Wood
Wick Green Copse
Hillside Farm
Barelegs Brake
Stowey Quarry
Sutton Wick
Weeks Green Farm
Burledge Hill
Hill View House
New Manor Farm
Hart's Farm Cottage
Burledge Common
White Cross
North Widcombe
Sparrow Grove
Curtis' Barn
BS40
Herriott's Bridge

River Chew

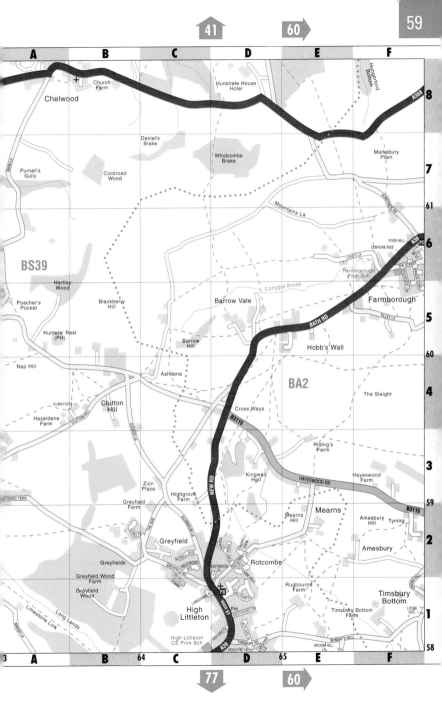

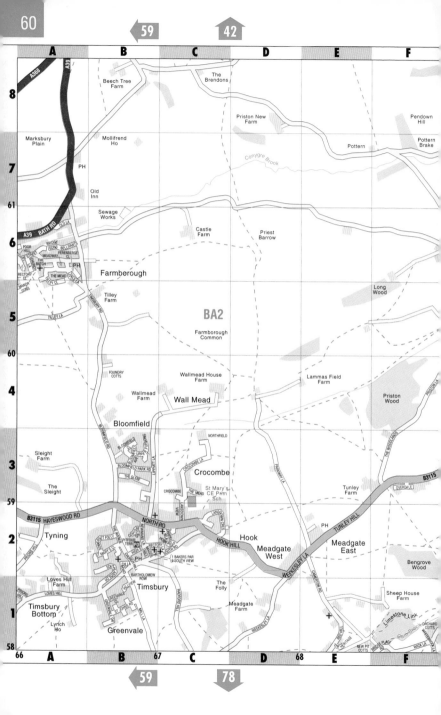

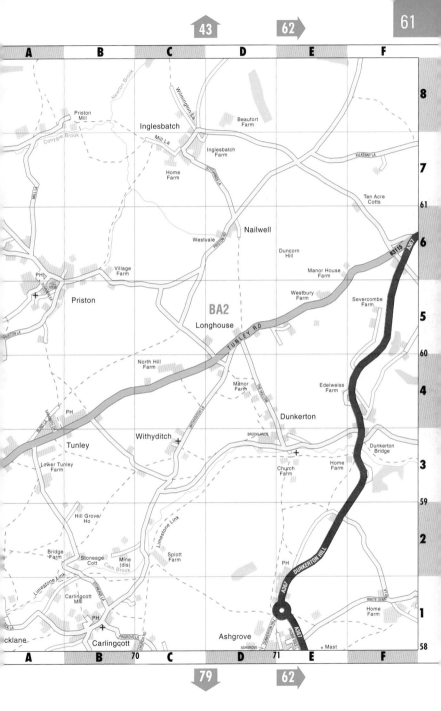

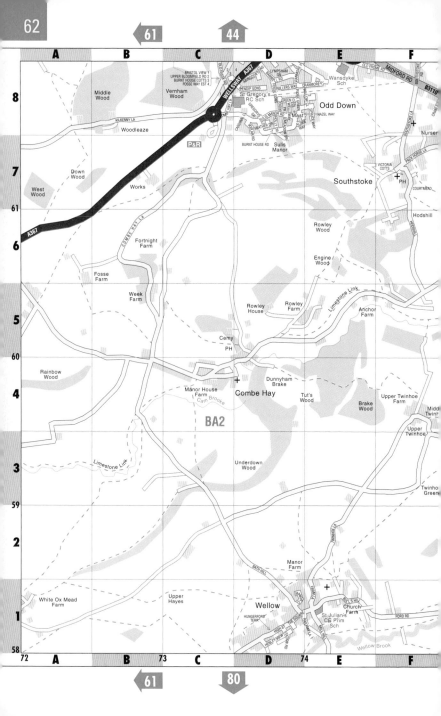

A   B   C   D   E   F

8

BRISTOL VIEW 1
UPPER BLOOMFIELD RD 2
BURNT HOUSE COTTS 3
FOSSE WAY EST 4

Middle
Wood

Vernham
Wood

A367

WELLSWAY

MENDIP GDNS

St Gregory's
RC Sch

FULLERS WAY

CRANMORE PL

Wansdyke
Sch

Old FROME RD

MIDFORD RD

B3110

Odd Down

Mast

HAZEL WAY

Kilkenny La

Woodleaze

CARMEL

BURNT HOUSE RD

Sulis
Manor

Nurser

VICTORIA
COTTS

BACK HORSE LA

7

Down
Wood

Works

P&R

Southstoke

PH

COURTMEAD

West
Wood

61

Rowley
Wood

Hodshill

A367

6

Fortnight
Farm

COMBE WAY LA

Engine
Wood

Fosse
Farm

Limestone Link

5

Week
Farm

Rowley
House

Rowley
Farm

Anchor
Farm

Cemy

PH

60

Rainbow
Wood

Manor House
Farm

Cam Brooke

Combe Hay

Dunnyham
Brake

Tut's
Wood

Upper Twinhoe
Farm

Middl
Twin

4

BA2

Brake
Wood

Upper
Twinhoe

Limestone Link

Underdown
Wood

3

59

Twinho
Green

2

BATH HILL

Manor
Farm

WYNSOE LA

White Ox Mead
Farm

Upper
Hayes

Wellow

Church
Farm

FORD RD

1

HUNGERFORD
TERR

HIGH ST

THE SQUARE

St Julian's
CE Prim
Sch

WELL'S HILL

HENLEY VIEW

Wellow Brook

58

72   A   B   73   C   D   74   E   F

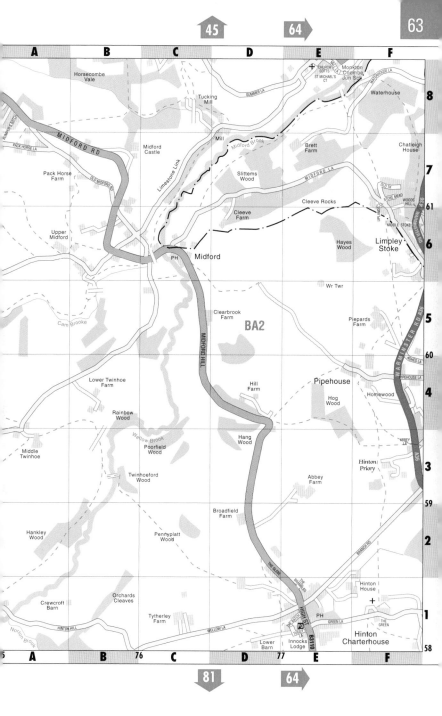

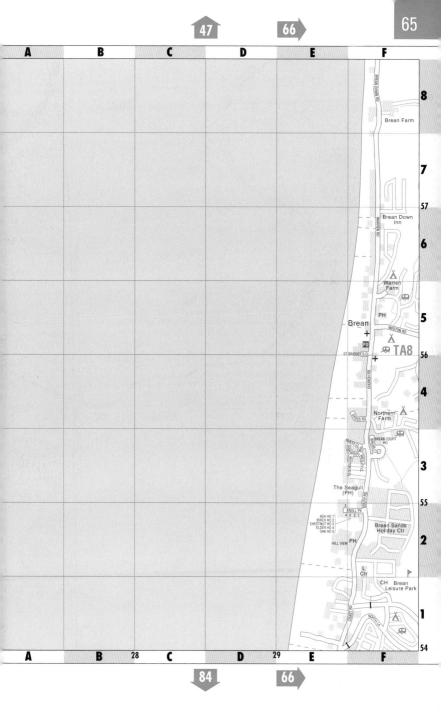

A   B   C   D   E   F

BREAN DOWN RD

Brean Farm

WARREN RD

Brean Down Inn

Warren Farm

PH

Brean

WESTON RD

PO

TA8

ST BRIDGES CL

CHURCH RD

Northern Farm

BREAN COURT HO

BIRCH RD

RUETT CL

FIRE STN

PIKE WOOD CL

VICTORIA CL

The Seagull (PH)

KNOLL PK
5 4 3 2 1

ASH HO 1
BIRCH HO 2
CHESTNUT HO 3
ELDER HO 4
OAK HO 5

HILL VIEW

PH

Brean Sands Holiday Ctr

L Ctr

CH Brean Leisure Park

COAST RD

NORTH RD

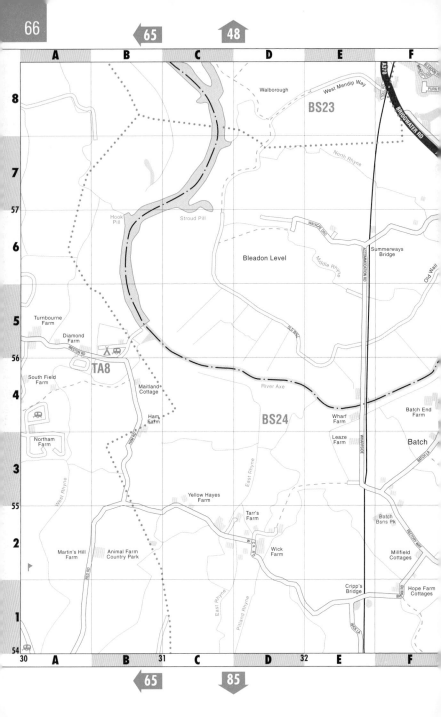

A B C D E F

8

Walborough

West Mendip Way

BS23

7

North Rhyne

57

Hook Pill

Stroud Pill

6

Bleadon Level

Middle Rhyne

Wavape Rd

Summerways Bridge

Accommodation Rd

Old Wall

5

Turnbourne Farm

Diamond Farm

Old Wall

56

Weston Rd

TA8

Maitland Cottage

River Axe

4

South Field Farm

Ham Farm

Wharf Farm

Batch End Farm

Leaze Farm

Batch

Northam Farm

BS24

Wharfside

Batch La

3

West Rhyne

East Rhyne

55

Yellow Hayes Farm

Tarr's Farm

Batch Bsns Pk

Red Rd

Beach Way

2

Martin's Hill Farm

Animal Farm Country Park

W C La Rd

Wick Farm

Millfield Cottages

East Rhyne

Pitland Rhyne

Cripp's Bridge

Hope Farm Cottages

Back La

1

54

30 A B 31 C D 32 E F

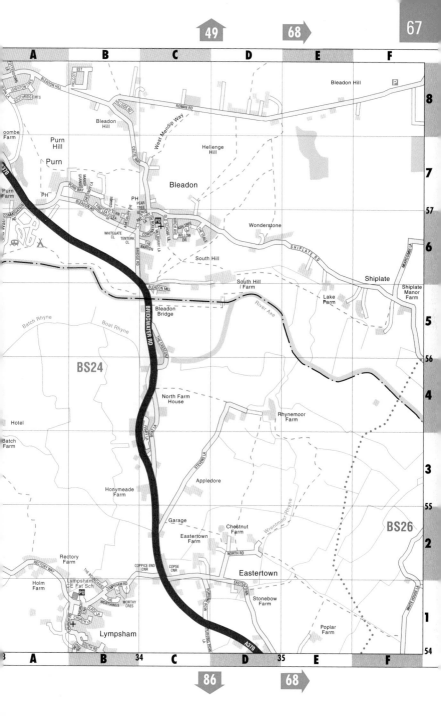

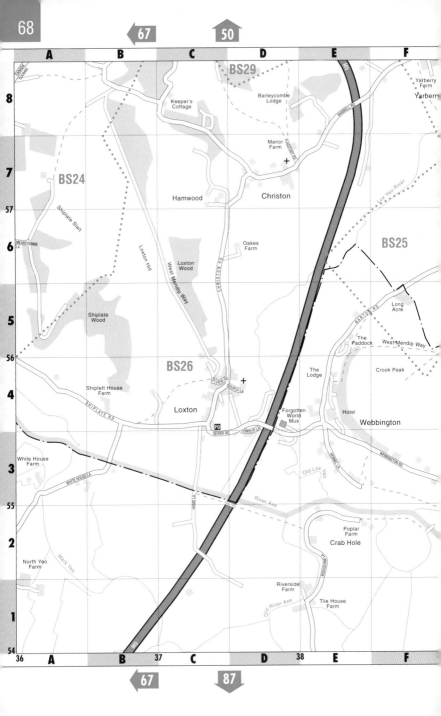

67
50

A B C D E F

8

BS29

Yarberry Farm

Keeper's Cottage

Barleycombe Lodge

Yarberry

7

BS24

Manor Farm

Shiplate Slait

Hamwood

Christon

Lox Yeo River

57

6

MEARCOMBE LA

Oakes Farm

BS25

Loxton Hill

Loxton Wood

Christon Rd

West Mendip Way

Long Acre

5

Shiplate Wood

The Paddock

West Mendip Way

Barton Rd

Crook Peak

56

BS26

The Lodge

Shiplett House Farm

Plum Rd

Church La

4

Shiplate Rd

Loxton

Forgotten World Mus

Hotel

Webbington

PO

Sevier Rd

Cowslip La

Webbington Rd

White House Farm

3

White House La

Old Lox Yeo

Kennel La

Hams La

River Axe

55

North Yeo Farm

Mark Yeo

Poplar Farm

Crab Hole

2

Riverside Farm

Old River Axe

Tile House Farm

1

M5

54

36 A B 37 C D 38 E F

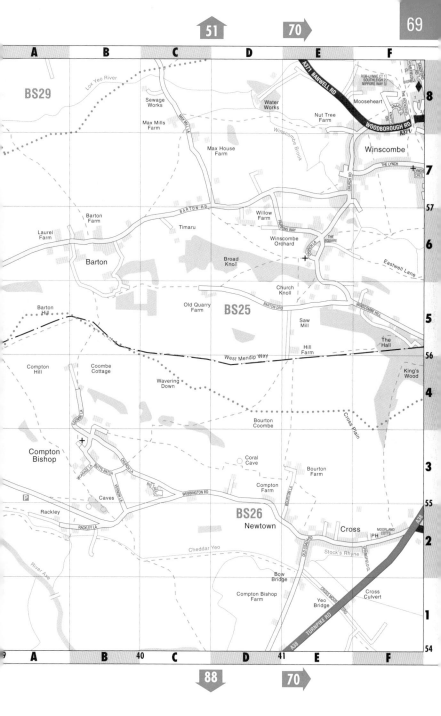

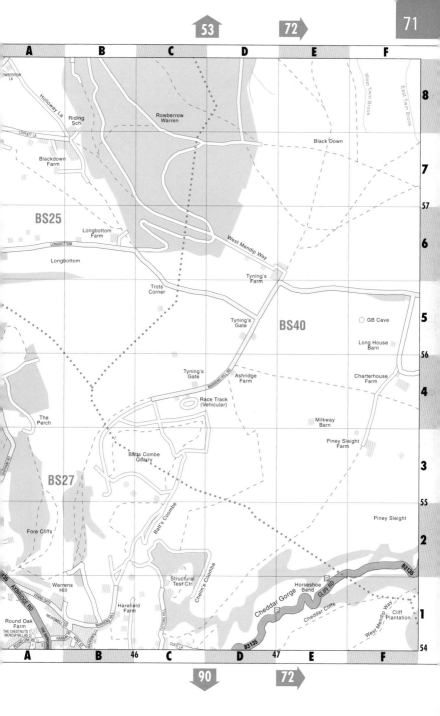

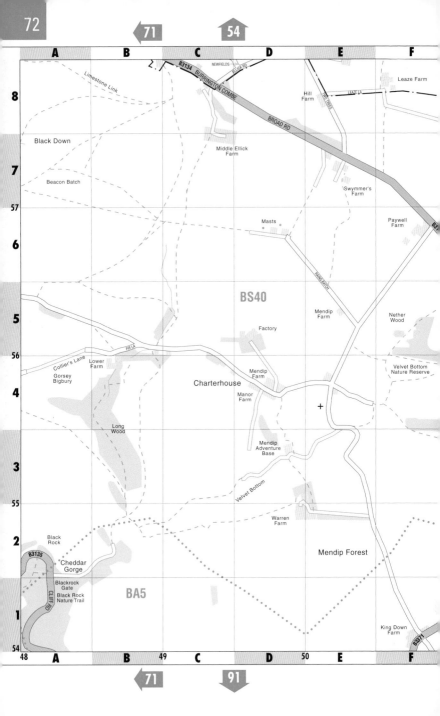

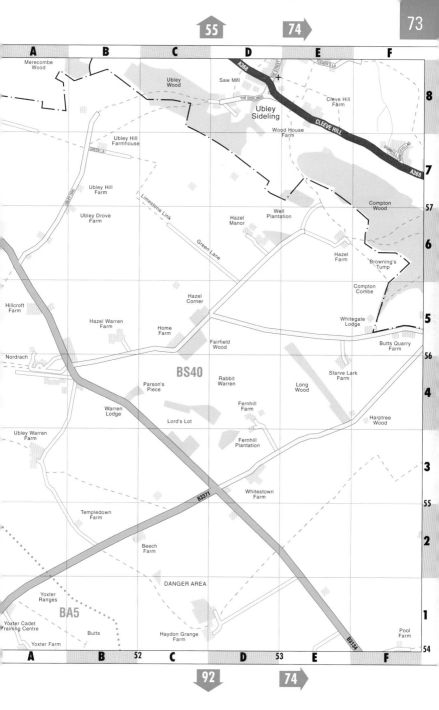

A   B   C   D   E   F

8

NEWCLOSE LA
B3114
STRATFORD LA
PH
Lower
Gurney Farm
A368

Bickfield House
Farm
Greenacres
Farm
White Cross
Farm

BOXWELL LA
TIMBER LA
River Yeo
VILLAGE LA

Compton
Martin

UNDERTOWN LA
THE BATCH
UNDERTOWN LA
HIGHROAD LA
THE COMBE
THE BUILDINGS

7

A368
Ring of
Bells
(PH)
THE STREET
PO

57

Fairash
Poultry Farm

Tilly Manor
Farm
PH
West
Harptree
B3114
NEWTON CL
PO
RISE & CMG
THE COURTYARD

WHISTLEY LA
Whistley
Farm

6

The
Wrangle

Limestone Link
COW LANE LA
RIDGEWAY LA

Bungalow
Farm
Cemy

WEST HARPTREE RD B 31

Beaconsfield
Farm

Molly Brook

East Harptree
Prim Sch
PO
THE
CROSS
Harptree
Court

5

HARPTREE HILL
BELLUXES LA
The
Wellsway
Inn
(PH)
Ridge
RIDGE LA

B 31
+

WHITECROSS RD

56

Harptree Hill
Farm

Monarch's Way

Shortcombe
Farm
BS40
Castle
East Harptree
PH
GREY
HOLLOW
COCKHILL LA
ORCHARD
END

4

WESTERN LA
Harptree
Combe
Wallace
COCKABLE LA
PROUD
CROSS
BARN
END
CAVER LA
WILLS LA
Newhou
HIGHFIELD LA

3

Gibbets
Brow
Lamb Leer
Cavern
Garrow Bottom
Garrow

55

OLD BRISTOL RD

Vale
Hollow
Farm
East Harptree
Woods
Chy
Smitham
Hill
The
Grove
Morgan's
Cottage

2

1

Lamb Bottom
The
Belt
Spring
Farm
P
X
Pitt
Farm
BA3

54

54   A   B   55   C   D   56   E   F

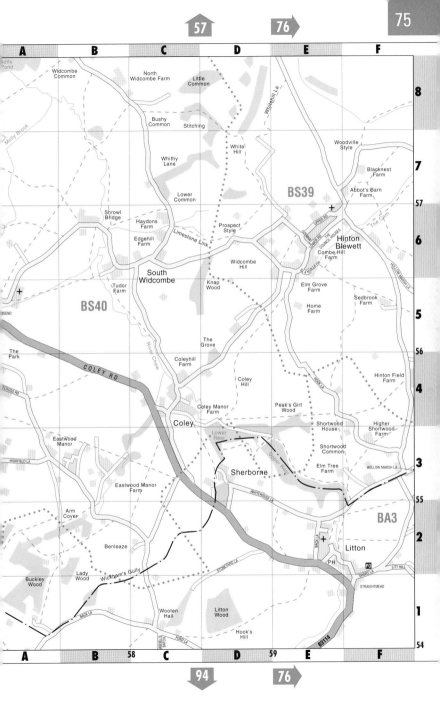

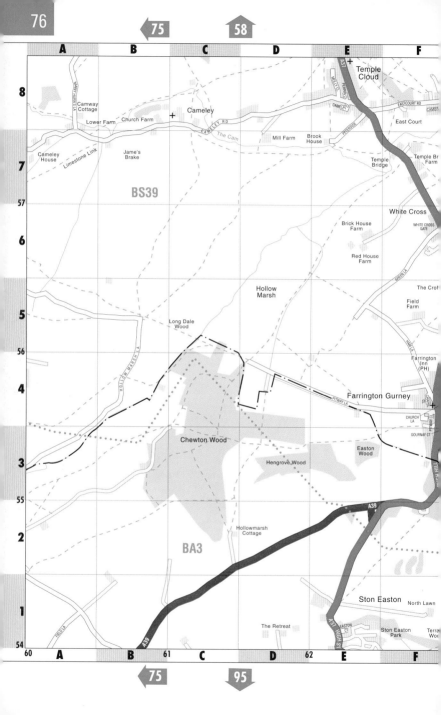

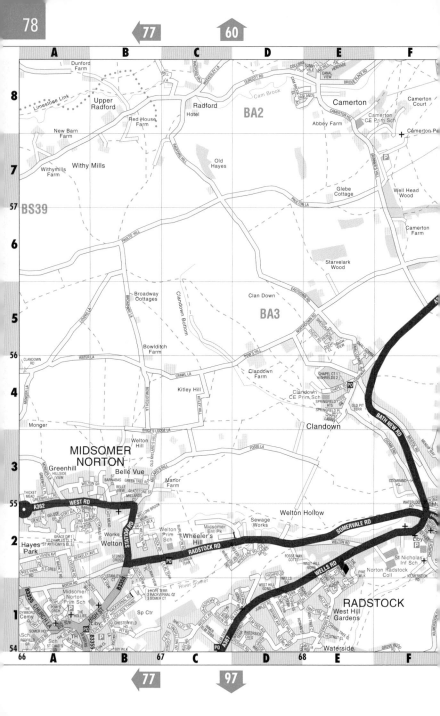

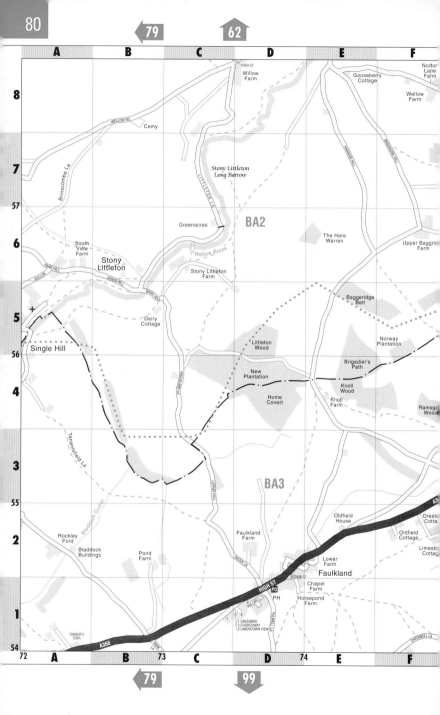

63

82

New Town

| A | B | C | D | E | F |

8

Prestick Wood

Cleaves Wood

Norton Barn

B3110

Tait Wood

Tuckson Wood

Norwood Wood

7

Lower aggridge Farm

57

Breach Brake

Kingsfield Brake

Hinton Field

Norwood Farm

BA2

Ring Wood

6

Norton Brook

New ntation

Hassage Wood

Rainbow Brake

Mast

Wr Twr

5

Broadlands

BATH RD

Norton Ho

A366

FARLEIGH RD

BRUTON LA

Hassage Cottage

Sewage Works

B3110

THADDOCK LA

56

THE BATTLE

SHEVER'S LA

PO

BELL HILL

CHURCH ST

PH

THE PLAIN

Norton St Philip

Hassage

BA3

Mount Pleasant Farm

SPRINGFIELD

ST PHILIP

PARSONAGE LA

RUBORNS

Norton St Philip CE Prim Sch

B3110 HIGH ST TOWN END

ORCHARD CL

COURT FARM LA

TELLISFORD LA

4

Vicarage

CHATLEY FURLONG

FROME RD

Watery La

Tucker's Grave Inn (PH)

Tucker's Grave Bottom

WELLS RD

Southfield Farm

B3110

3

Bingwell Farm

MIDDLE LA

55

Chickwell New Farm

2

CROCKERTON LA

Marrow Pole La

Peart Farm

Chickwell Farm

ROW LA

1

HAMMER LA

54

| A | B | C | D | E | F |

76

77

100

82

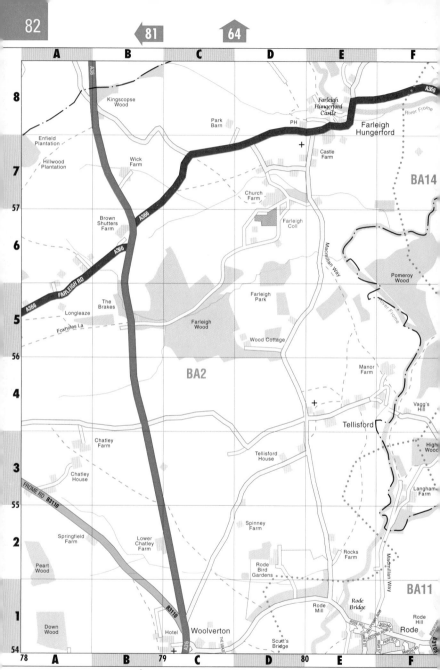

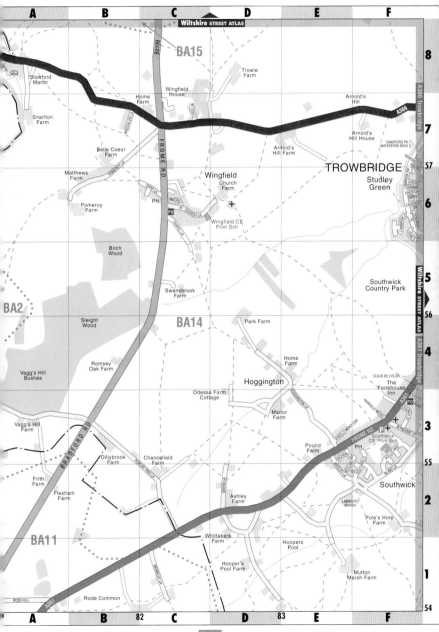

BA15

Stowford Manor

Snariton Farm

Home Farm

Wingfield House

Trowle Farm

Arnold's Hill

A366 Trowbridge

A366

8

Belle Coeur Farm

FROME RD

Arnold's Hill House

SANDFORD PK 1
WATERFORD BECK 2

Arnold's Hill Farm

7

Matthews Farm

POMEROY LA

Wingfield
Church Farm

TROWBRIDGE

Studley Green

57

Pomeroy Farm

PIGG LA

PH

PO

CHURCH LA

Wingfield CE Prim Sch

KINGS CHASE
SHERBORNE GDNS

6

CHAPEL LA

Birch Wood

Swansbrook Farm

Southwick Country Park

Wiltshire STREET ATLAS

A361 Trowbridge

5

BA2

Sleight Wood

BA14

Park Farm

56

Vagg's Hill Bushes

Romsey Oak Farm

BRADFORD RD

Home Farm

Hoggington

HOGGINGTON LA

FLEUR DE LYS DR
The Farmhouse Inn

FAIRFIELD

PO

4

Vagg's Hill Farm

Dillybrook Farm

POPLAR TREE LA

Chancefield Farm

Odessa Farm Cottage

Manor Farm

FROME RD

Southwick CE Prim Sch

PH

WYNSOME ST

3

Frith Farm

Flexham Farm

GREEN LA

Pound Farm

Southwick

55

BA11

Ashley Farm

Whittakers Farm

Hooper's Pool Farm

Hoopers Pool

LAMBERTS MARSH

Pole's Hole Farm

2

MONKS LA

Mutton Marsh Farm

1

RODE HILL
A361

Rode Common

54

	A	B	C	D	E	F

8

7

53

6

5

52

4

3

51

2

1

50

Unity Farm

SHRUBBERY CL

HERON PK

Hurn Farm

Mead Farm

Berrow Manor

Caravan Park

Rose Farm

Westcroft Nurseries

TA8

Berrow

Caravan Park

PH

MANOR CT

MANOR RD

PINNOCKSCROFT

NAGE RD

LITTLE PEN

PENMOOR

CHURCH HOUSE

SABLE ACRES

FAIRWAY CL

ROSE TREE

PADDOCK

ROSENEATH A

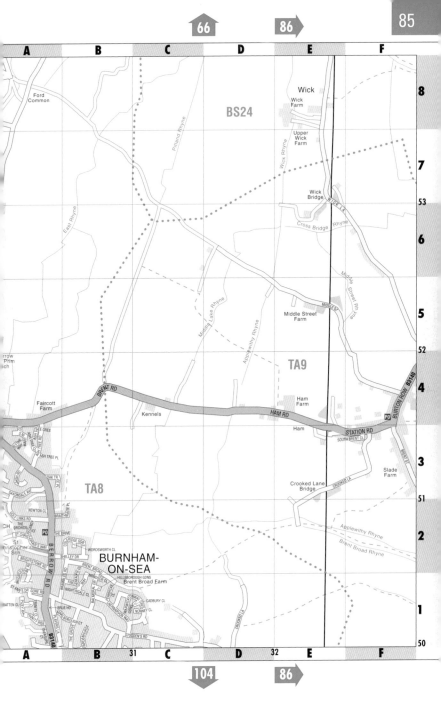

A　B　C　D　E　F

8

Ford
Common

Wick

Wick
Farm

BS24

Upper
Wick
Farm

7

Pitland Rhyne

Wick Rhyne

Wick
Bridge

53

Cross Bridge Rhyne

6

East Rhyne

Middle Street Rhc

Middle Street Rha

5

Middle Lake Rhyne

Applewithy Rhyne

Middle Street
Farm

52

rrow
Prim
ich

TA9

MIDDLE RD

Breat RD

Faircott
Farm

4

Kennels

HAM RD

Ham
Farm

BURTON ROW B3140

PO

Ham

STATION RD
SOUTH BRENT CL

BRENT ST

Slade
Farm

3

BERROW RD

TA8

OAK TR LN

NEWTON CL

THE
ORCHDS

PO

THE DRIVE

WORDSWORTH CL

SHELLEY DR

BURNHAM-
ON-SEA

HILLSBOROUGH GDNS

Brent Broad Farm

Crooked Lane
Bridge

CROOKED LA

Applewithy Rhyne

Brent Broad Rhyne

51

2

BS3140

CADBURY CL

NUNNEY CL.

SLODDEN'S RD

CROOKED LA

1

50

A　B　31　C　D　32　E　F

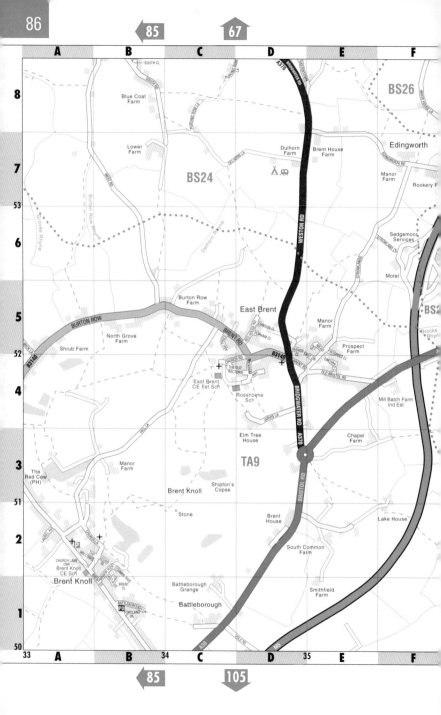

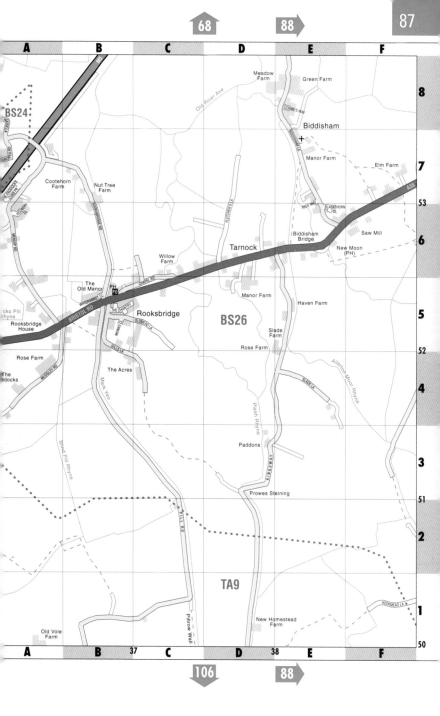

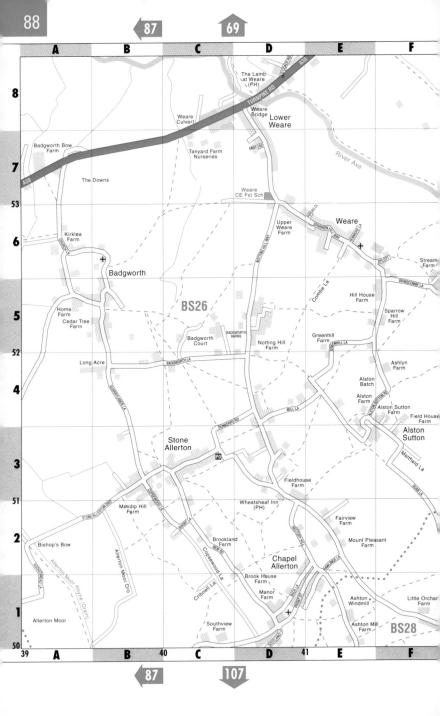

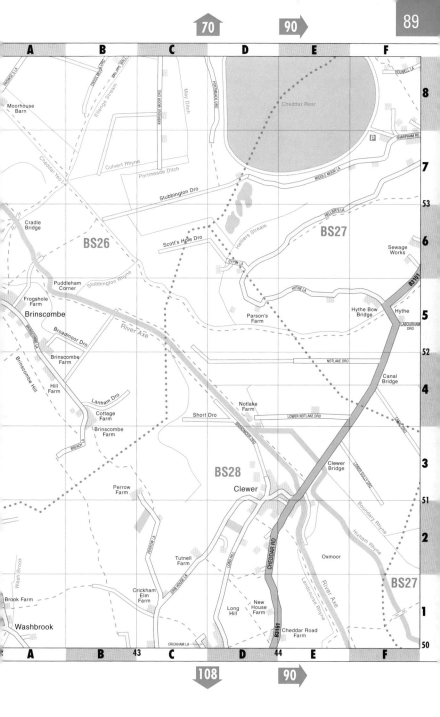

A B C D E F

8

Moorhouse
Barn

HOLWELL LA

Cheddar Rear

P SHARPHAM RD

CROSS MOOR DRO

DRELIPS WELL

Ellenge Stream

OLD MOOR DROVE

May Ditch

PORTMEADE DRO

Culvert Rhyne

MIDDLE MOOR LA

7

Cheddar Yeo

Portmeade Ditch

53

Stubbington Dro

HELLIER'S LA

Cradle
Bridge

BS26

Scott's Hole Dro

Helliers Stream

BS27

Sewage
Works

6

Puddleham
Corner

Stubbington Rhyne

GYPSY LA

Frogshole
Farm

Brinscombe

HYTHE LA

Parson's
Farm

Hythe Bow
Bridge

Hythe

5

B3151

Broadmoor Dro

River Axe

LABOURHAM DRO

BRINSCOMBE LA

Brinscombe
Farm

NOTLAKE DRO

52

Brinscombe Hill

Hill
Farm

Lanham Dro

Canal
Bridge

4

Cottage
Farm

Short Dro

Notlake
Farm

LOWER NOTLAKE DRO

BROADMOOR DRO

CANAL DRO

Brinscombe
Farm

BREACH

BS28

Clewer
Bridge

Clewer

LOWER BAILEY DRO

3

Perrow
Farm

Boundary Rhyne

51

Hexham Rhyne

BS27

2

Wash Brook

Tutnell
Farm

PERROW LA

DIBB HILL

LONG HILL

CHEDDAR RD

Oxmoor

River Axe

Landscouse Rhyne

DIBB HOUSE LA

Brook Farm

Crickham
Elm
Farm

Long
Hill

New
House
Farm

1

Washbrook

B3151

Cheddar Road
Farm

CRICKHAM LA

50

A B 43 C D 44 E F

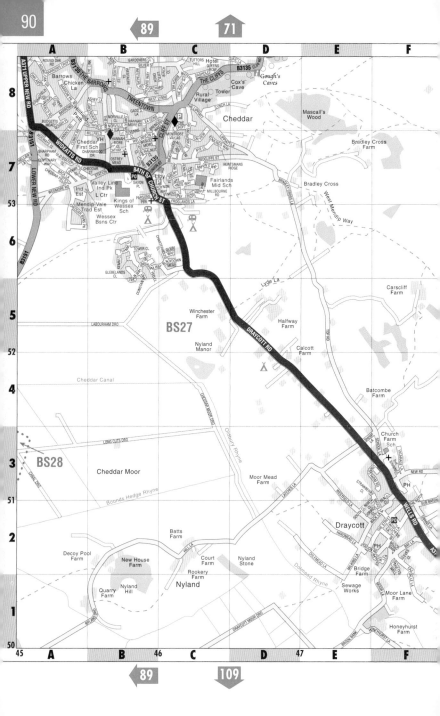

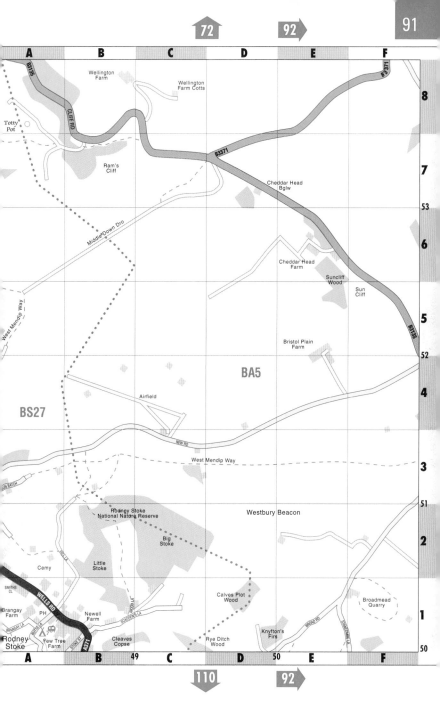

A B C D E F

8

7

53

6

5

52

4

3

51

2

1

50

Wellington Farm

Wellington Farm Cotts

B3135

CLIFF RD

Totty Pot

Ram's Cliff

B3371

B3371

Cheddar Head Bglw

Middle Down Dro

Cheddar Head Farm

Suncliff Wood

Sun Cliff

West Mendip Way

Bristol Plain Farm

B3135

BA5

BS27

Airfield

NEW RD

West Mendip Way

Westbury Beacon

Rodney Stoke National Nature Reserve

Big Stoke

Calves Plot Wood

Broadmead Quarry

SUN BATCH

Cemy

Little Stoke

STALL LA

STOKE WOOD LA

Knytton's Firs

BROAD RD

FENNING LA

SMITHS CL

WELLS RD

Brangay Farm

PH

Newell Farm

SCADDENS LA

Cleaves Copse

Rye Ditch Wood

Rodney Stoke

Yew Tree Farm

BRANGAY LA

STOKE ST

A371

A B C D E F

49 50

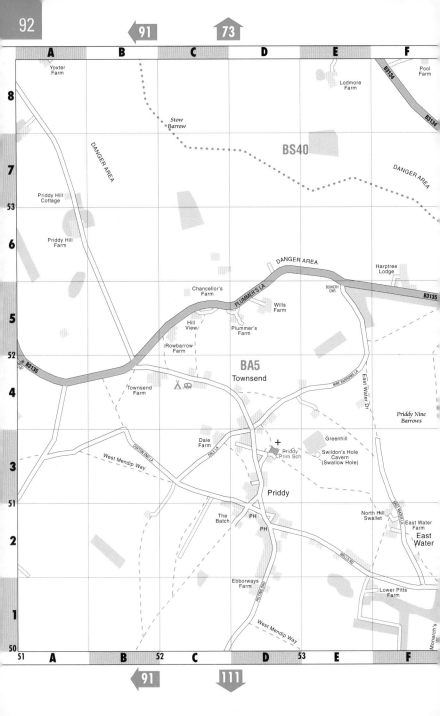

A   B   C   D   E   F

Monarch's Way

Devil's
Punch Bowl

Wurt Pit
(dis)

Roadside
Clump

Greendown Batch

8

Swallet
Farm

Mast

Nett Wood
Farm

Hill
Grange

Big
Clump

Niver
Hill

Hill
Farm

BS40

7

Castle of Comfort
(PH)

53

Priddy
Circles

Castle
Farm

OLD BRISTOL RD

Bendall's
Grove

The Belt

Eaker Hill
Farm

West
End

Wigmore
Farm

Monarch's Way

BA3

6

ranmore
View

Miners' Arms

B3134

Eaker
Hill

5

Red Quarr
Farm

52

TOR HOLE BOTTOM

4

BA5

P

North Hill

Monarch's Way

Priddy
Mineries

Bendalls
Farm

B3135

51

Stockhill

2

nder Barrow
Farm

Nursery

Cuckoo
Cleeves

Tower
Hill

1

Hunters Lodge
Inn

HILLGROVE RD

Ash
Plantation

A   B   55   C   D   56   E   F   50

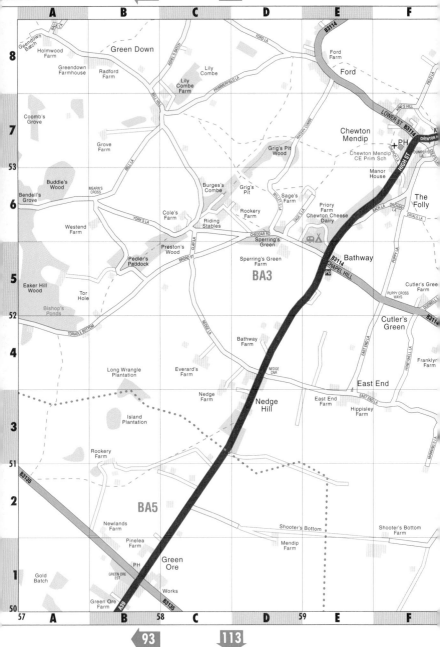

8

Greendown Batch
Holmwood
Green Down
Greendown Farmhouse
Radford Farm
Lily Combe
Lily Combe Farm
PINNARMEAD LN
FORD LA
ASHE'S BATCH
B3114
Ford Farm
Ford

7

Coomb's Grove
BELL LA
Grove Farm
Chewton Mendip
PH
LOWER ST B3114
LOWE'S HILL
B3114
CHEWTON H

53

Buddle's Wood
Bendell's Grove
MEARN'S CROSS
WATERY COMBE
Grig's Pit Wood
Chewton Mendip CE Prim Sch
Manor House
HIGH ST
BUMPER DROL LA

6

Westend Farm
YORK'S LA
Cole's Farm
Burges's Combe
Grig's Pit
Sage's Farm
Rookery Farm
Priory Farm
Chewton Cheese Dairy
BELL'S LA
SAGE'S LA
BIKA LA
ORCHARD LA
The 'Folly
DRIALS LA

Bathway

Preston's Wood
Pedler's Paddock
Riding Stables
CHEDDAR RD
Sperring's Green
CLAY LA
BROAD ST
B3114
CHAPEL HILL
PO
PUPPY LA
PUPPY CROSS WAYS
Cutler's Gree Farm
DUXWELL LA
B3114

5

Eaker Hill Wood
Bishop's Ponds
Tor Hole
Sperring's Green Farm
BA3

Cutler's Green

52

TORHOLE BOTTOM
HEDGE LA
EAST END LA
HONEYMELLA LA

4

Long Wrangle Plantation
Everard's Farm
Bathway Farm
NEDGE CNR
Nedge Farm
Nedge Hill
East End Farm
East End
HIPPISLEY Farm
EAST END LA
Franklyn Farm

3

Island Plantation
Rookery Farm
Nedge Farm
Shooter's Bottom
Shooter's Bottom Farm
MANNING LA

51

B3135
BA5

2

Newlands Farm
Pinelea Farm
Shooter's Bottom
Mendip Farm

1

Gold Batch
PH
GREEN ORE EST
Green Ore
Green Ore Farm
A39
B3135
Works

50

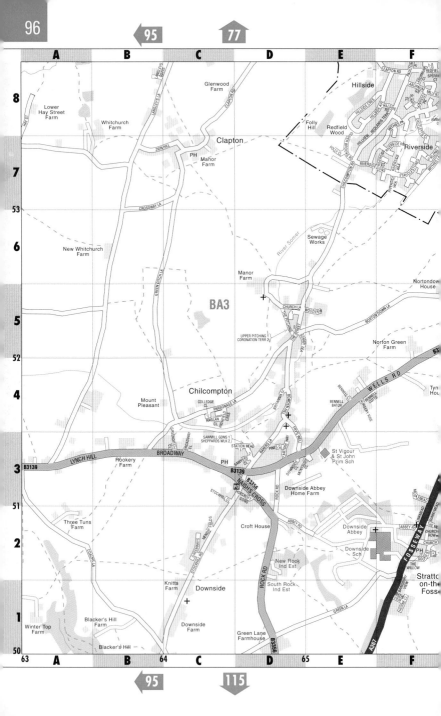

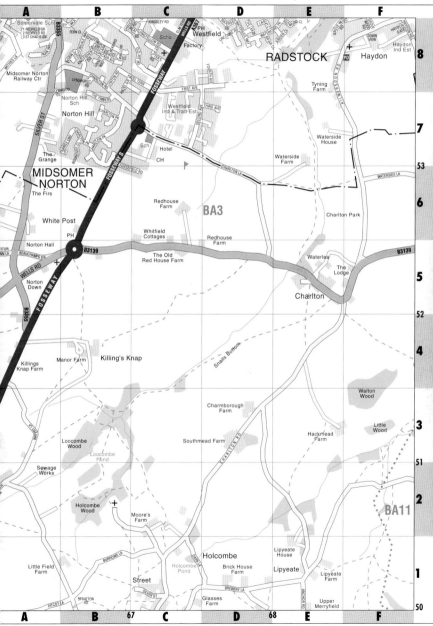

A B C D E F

8

Haydon House

Huish House

Upper Lentney Farm

Upper Lentney Farm Cottage

Peak's Wood

Haywood Wood

Haywood Farm

FROME RD A362

TERRY HILL

FROME RD

A366

AMMERDOWN TERR

7

Lentney Farm

KYSBURY LA

BA3

Lower Knobsbury

Upper Knobsbury

KNOBSBURY HILL

B3139

Terry Hill Plantation

53

WATERSIDE LA

Tyning Farm

Home Farm

Nap Wood

6

Kilmersdon CE Prim Sch

AMES LA

Sewage Works

Gagman Coppice

Ammerdown House

B3139 KILMERSDON HILL

FOSSE WAY

Kilmersdon

Ammerdown Park

Coldbath Plantation

5

Manor Farm

SILVER ST

P

Ammerdown Bridge

Hatchet Hill Coppice

The Colur

52

Walton Farm

Wedingham Copse

Beatle's Wood

Babington Wood

Batch Farm

NEW RD

HATCHET HILL

Kingsdown Wood

Mells Do Farm

4

HAMES LA

South View

Upton's Piece

3

Lowerfield Farm

Babington Park

Cornish's Grave

Works

Works

Jericho Bridge

51

Babington

Babington House

BA11

Lodge

2

Cherry Garden Farm

LUCKINGTON CROSS

Newbury House

CHARITY LA

White Cottage

Edney's Farm

1

Luckington Manor Farm

DARK LA

Newbury Farm

HAMES LA

BA3

BA3

Works

50

Newbury

69 A B 70 C D 71 E F

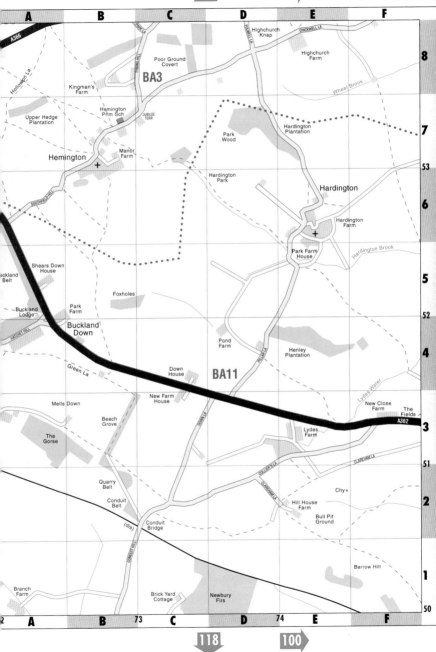

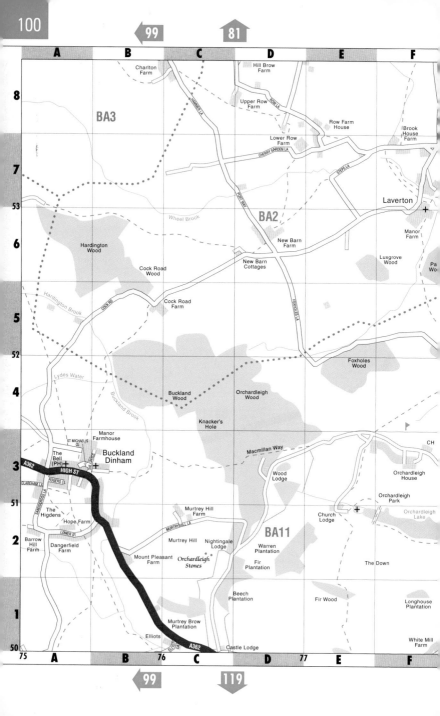

A | B | C | D | E | F

8

BA3

Charlton Farm

Hill Brow Farm

Upper Row Farm

HARNET LA

ROW LA

Row Farm House

Brook House Farm

Lower Row Farm

CHERRY GARDEN LA

7

53

Wheel Brook

BA2

Laverton

STEPS LA

Manor Farm

6

Hardington Wood

New Barn Farm

Luxgrove Wood

Pa Wo

Cock Road Wood

New Barn Cottages

5

Hardington Brook

COCK RD

Cock Road Farm

FOXHOLES LA

52

Foxholes Wood

4

Lydes Water

Buckland Brook

Buckland Wood

Orchardleigh Wood

Knacker's Hole

3

A362

St MICHAEL'S CL

The Bell (PH)

HIGH ST

Manor Farmhouse

Buckland Dinham

Macmillan Way

Wood Lodge

CH

Orchardleigh House

CLAREHAM LA

ROGERS CL

SANDPITS LA

51

The Higdens

Hope Farm

LOWER ST

Church Lodge

Orchardleigh Park

Orchardleigh Lake

2

Barrow Hill Farm

Dangerfield Farm

Murtrey Hill Farm

MURTREY HILL LA

Murtrey Hill

Mount Pleasant Farm

Nightingale Lodge

Orchardleigh Stones

BA11

Warren Plantation

Fir Plantation

The Down

1

Beech Plantation

Fir Wood

Longhouse Plantation

Murtrey Brow Plantation

Elliots

A362

Castle Lodge

White Mill Farm

50

75 | A | B | 76 | C | D | 77 | E | F

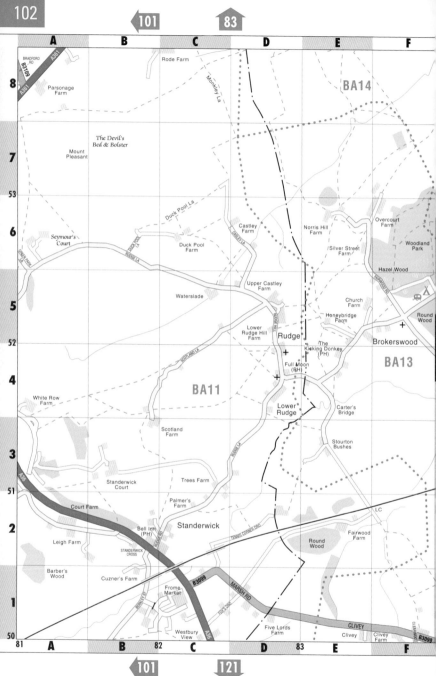

A B C D E F

BRADFORD RD
B3109

8 Parsonage Farm

Rode Farm

BA14

Monkley La

7 Mount Pleasant

The Devil's Bed & Bolster

53

6 Seymour's Court

Duck Pool La

Castley Farm

Norris Hill Farm

Overcourt Farm

Silver Street Farm

Woodland Park

Hazel Wood

Duck Pool Farm

LONG PARK RD

ROUDE LA

DUCK POOL

DULEY LA

5 Waterslade

Upper Castley Farm

Church Farm

Honeybridge Farm

Round Wood

52 Lower Rudge Hill Farm

RUDGE HILL

Rudge

The Kicking Donkey (PH)

Brokerswood

FARWOOD RD

BA13

4 BA11

Full Moon (PH)

White Row Farm

SCOTLAND LA

Lower Rudge

Carter's Bridge

3 Scotland Farm

Trees Farm

RUDGE LA

Stourton Bushes

51

A36

Standerwick Court

Palmer's Farm

LC

2 Court Farm

Bell Inn (PH)

Standerwick

TENNIS CORNER DRO

Round Wood

Fairwood Farm

Leigh Farm

STANDERWICK CROSS

RUDGE RD

Barber's Wood

Cuzner's Farm

Frome Market

MARSH RD

B3099

CLEVANWOOD

1 BEXLEY RD

FOX'S DRO

CLIVEY

Clivey

Clivey Farm

B3099

50 Westbury View

A36

Five Lords Farm

81 A B 82 C 83 D E F

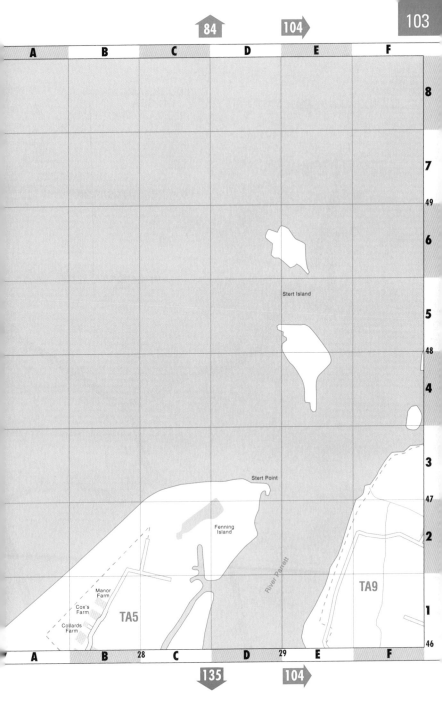

A   B   C   D   E   F

8

7

49

6

Stert Island

5

48

4

3

Stert Point

47

Fenning
Island

2

River Parrett

TA9

TA5

Manor
Farm

Cox's
Farm

Collards
Farm

1

46

A   B   28   C   D   29   E   F

A B C D E F

8

BURNHAM-
ON-SEA

1 SIDMOUTH CL
2 MEADOWCROFT DR
3 WEDMORE CL
4 BUCKLAND CL
5 WILTON CL
6 FROBISHER CL
7 AVEBURY CL
8 EXBURY CL
9 DYRHAM CL
10 COWAN CL
11 VINCENT CL
12 HOWARD CL
13 MADDEN CL
14 DEWAR CL
15 BURNETT CL
16 BERESFORD CL

Edithmead
Bridge

Inner
Farm

Edithmea

Homestead

GROVE HO 1
PORTLAND RD 2
HOMELANE HO 3
BEAUPORT CT 4

BELFIELD CT
ATLANTA KEY

BLENCATHARA CT

THE GROVE

Cemy

7

STEART CT 1
CHURCHLANDS CT 2
VICARAGE CT 3
KINVER TERR 4
RAVENSWORTH TERR 6
MANOR CT 7

REGENT ST 1
GEORGE ST 2

War
Memorial
Liby

LOVE LA

Jun
Sch

Westmans
Est

Chestnut
Farm

49

Supermarket

Burnham
Level

TA8

1 NOEL COWARD CL
2 SHAW PATH
3 RATTIGAN CL
4 AYCKBOURN CL
5 ARCHER CL
6 BRIAR CT

COTTAGE ROW 1
SOUTH TERR 2
PHOENIX TERR 3
SUMMERVILLE TERR 4
JUBILEE ST 5
AUTUMN CL 6
DUIM-ACE 7
CLOISTERS CROFT 8
ELIZABETH CT 9
KNIGHTSTONE CT 10
BISHOP'S PATH 11

Prim
Sch

6

HIGHBRIDGE RD

Mill
Mound

BT
Radio Sta

Worston
Bridge

Worston
House

Forge Rhyne

Mast

5

Holiday
Camp

Playing
Field

Sports
Ctr

King Alfred
Sch

Worston
Mdw

48

Caravan
Park

BURNHAM RD

BRISTOL RD

Apex
Leisure Park

Bristol
Bridge

Isleport
Bsns Pk

Abatte

4

CHURCH ST

Cemy

B3139

Morlands
Ind Pk

Jun
Sch

Inf
Sch

Liby

1 KENNEDY CL
2 FAIRFORD CL

HIGHBRIDGE

TYLERS
END

Brue Pill

Sewage
Works

Depot

3

New-Clyce
Bridge

General
Higgins Ho

Alstone Wildlife
Park

VICTORIA PL 1
HOPE COTTS 2
RIVERBED HO 3
QUANTOCK VIEW 4

MARKET ST WALROW

MARK RD

B3139

Brue
Bridge

Highbridge

River Brue

Brue
Farm

B31

47

Walrow
Ind Est

2

Sewage
Works

Alstone Court
Farm

Alstone

TA9

PH

North Rhyne

Maundril's
Farm

1

MAIN RD

West Huntspill
Com Prim Sch

Mill
Farm

Brent
Farm

46

Hotel

A38

NEWBRIDGE DR

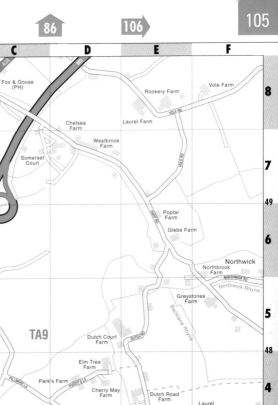

A | B | C | D | E | F

8

White Cross
Fox & Goose (PH)
WHITE CROSS
White Cross Farm
Rookery Farm
Vole Farm
VOLE RD
Chelsea Farm
Laurel Farm
Westbrook Farm
Somerset Court

7

B3140
BRISTOL RD
Ashland Farm
A38
22

49

Im Tree Farm
6
Poplar Farm
Glebe Farm
The Elms
uthport Farm
Northwick
Northbrook Farm
NORTHWICK RD

Oak Tree Farm
BURNHAM MOOR LA
BRENT RIVER (DRAIN)
Eastern Rhyne
Greystones Farm
Backlane Rhyne
Northwick Rhyne

TA9
5

Dutch Court Farm
DUTCH RD
PILLMORE LA
48

Isleport Farm
Elm Tree Farm
Park's Farm
PILLMORE LA
PUDDY'S LA
Cherry May Farm
Dutch Road Farm
4

Magnolia House
Laurel Farm
B3139
MARK CSWY
POPLAR LA
Causeway Farm

Watchfield Lawn
Rich's Farmhouse Cider Farm
Watchfield House
Upper Southwick Farm
3

Monkton House Farm
SOUTHWICK RD
PH
MARK RD
MARK RD
Elmwood Farm
Watchfield
Windmill
Manor Farm
Southwick
47

Walrow Farm
Grange Farm
Westhill Rhyne
Walrow
B3139
Elmside
Southwick Farm
2

Newbridge La
Bay Tree Farm
WESTHILL LA
B3141
Ash Tree Farm
CHURCH RD
Westhill Rhyne

Babb's Farm
Heath House Farm
HACK MEAD LA
1

Westhill Farm
Caravan Park
Malthouse Farm
NEWMANS LA
B3141
River Brue

46

A | B | 34 | C | D | 35 | E | F

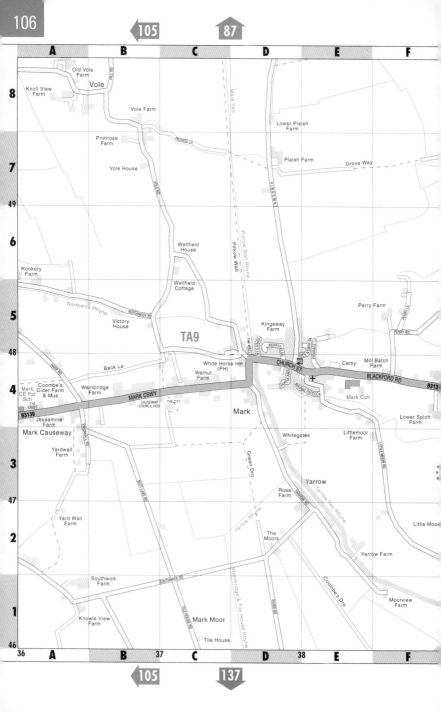

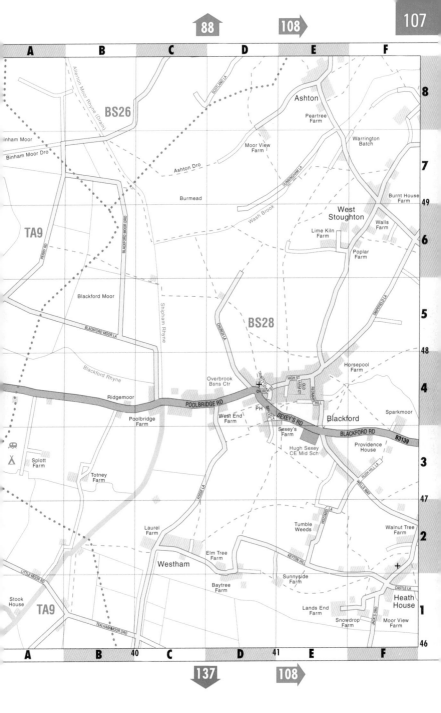

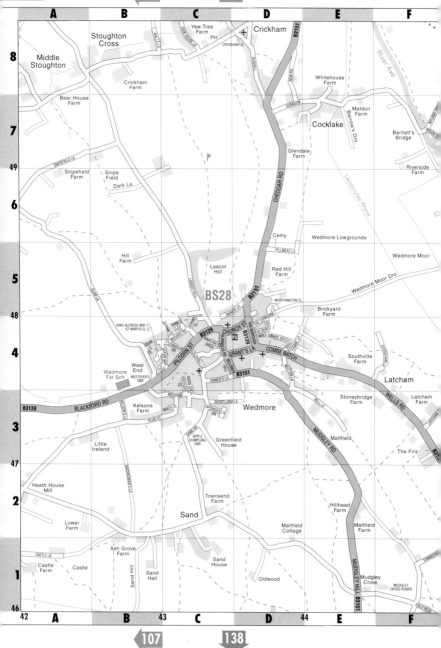

Crickham

Middle Stoughton

Stoughton Cross

Yew Tree Farm

PH

Crickham Farm

Bear House Farm

Whitehouse Farm

Maldon Farm

Barrow's Dro

Cocklake

Bartlett's Bridge

Snipefield La

Snipefield Farm

Snipe Field

Dark La

Glendale Farm

Riverside Farm

River Axe

Landcourse Rhyne

Hill Farm

Lascot Hill

Cemy

Wedmore Lowgrounds

Wedmore Moor

Red Hill Farm

Pillmead La

Dark La

Lascot Hill

BS28

Worthington Cl

Wedmore Moor Dro

Brickyard Farm

King Alfreds Way 1
St Marys Cl 2

Dame's La

Church St

The Lynch

Combe Batch

Southville Farm

Pilcorn St

Grant's La

Combe Batch

Latcham

West End

Wedmore Fst Sch

Westover's Cnr

Dando's La

Wells Rd

Latcham Farm

Blackford Rd

Kelsons Farm

Birch Cl

Shortland La

Springfield Dri

Wedmore

Stoneybridge Farm

B3139

Plud St

Mudgley Rd

Maltfield

The Firs

Little Ireland

Apple Dumpling Cnr

Greenfield House

Heath House Mill

Townsend Farm

Hillhead Farm

Lower Farm

Sand

Maltfield Cottage

Maltfield Farm

Castle La

Ash Grove Farm

Sand Hill

Sand Hall

Sand House

Oldwood

Mudgley Hill

Castle Farm

Castle

Mudgley Cross

Mudgley Cross Roads

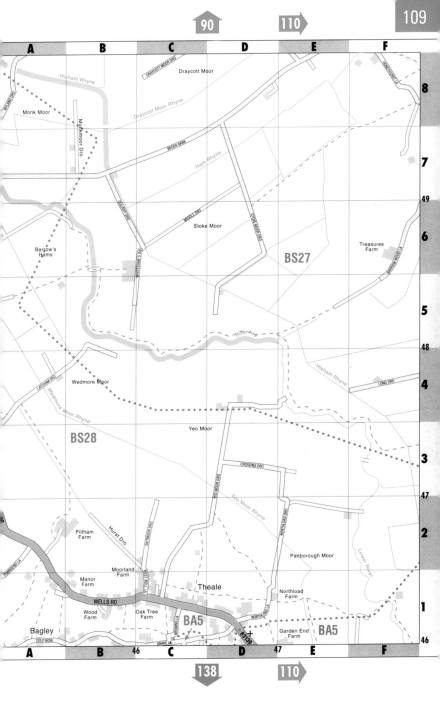

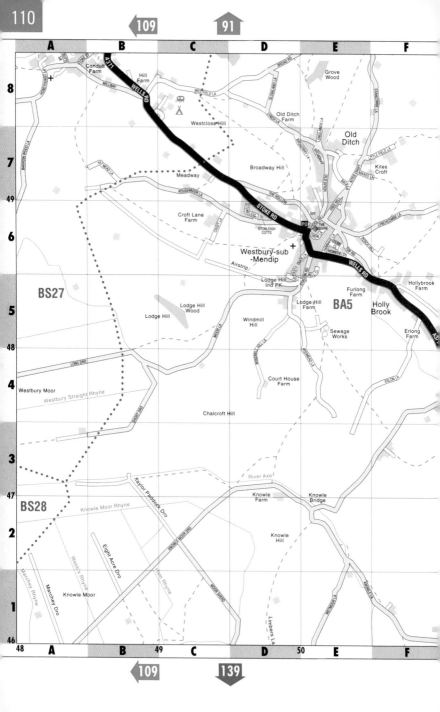

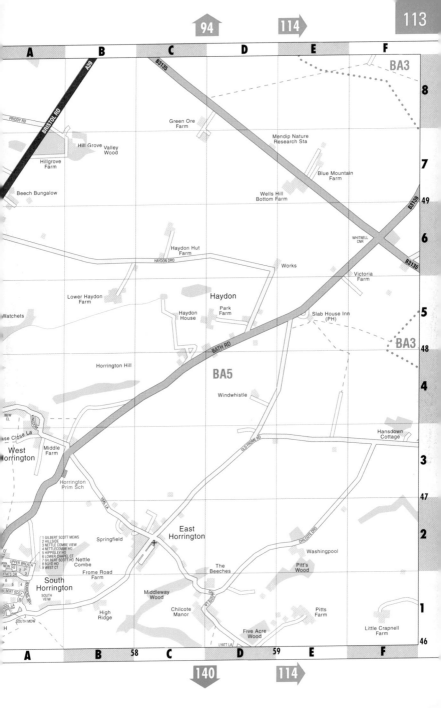

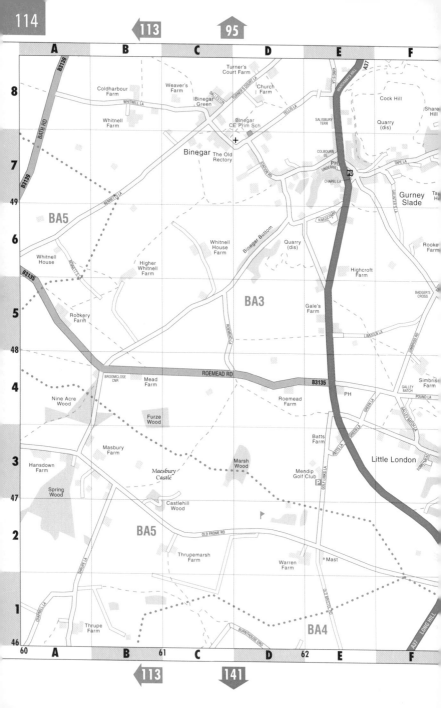

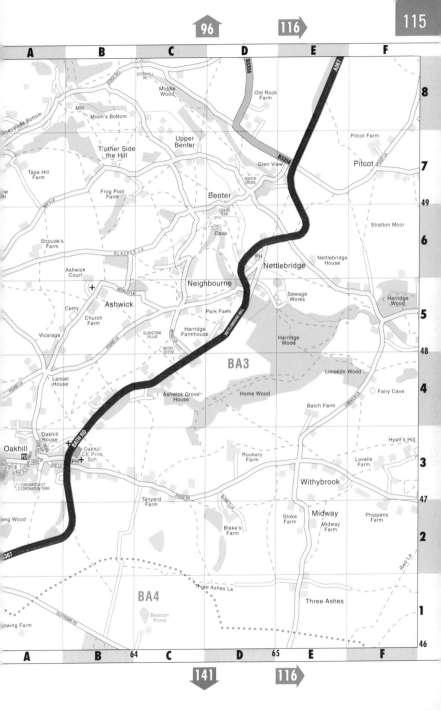

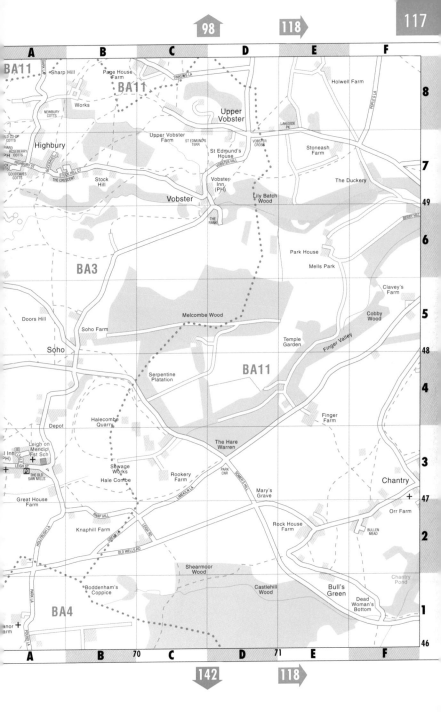

A **B** **C** **D** **E** **F**

BA11

Sharp Hill

Page House Farm

TINKENS LA

Holwell Farm

8

BA11

Works

NEWBURY COTTS

Upper Vobster

LAKESIDE PK

OLD CO-OP COTTS

Upper Vobster Farm

ST EDMUNDS TERR

VOBSTER CROSS

ROSEBERRY COTTS

Highbury

St Edmund's House

Stoneash Farm

PH

GOODEAVES COTTS

HIGHBURY ST

VOBSTER HILL

7

THE CRESCENT

STOCK HILL CT

Stock Hill

Vobster Inn (PH)

The Duckery

Vobster

Lily Batch Wood

49

THE PARK

BERRY HILL

6

Park House

BA3

Mells Park

Clavey's Farm

Doors Hill

Melcombe Wood

Cobby Wood

5

Soho Farm

Temple Garden

Finger Valley

Soho

48

BA11

Serpentine Platation

4

Finger Farm

Halecombe Quarry

Depot

The Hare Warren

3

Leigh on Mendip Fst Sch

Sewage Works

Rookery Farm

PARK CNR

Chantry

I Inn (PH)

SOMER HILL

PO

THE OLD SAW MILLS

Hale Combe

Mary's Grave

47

Great House Farm

Orr Farm

LINDENS LA

Knaphill Farm

KNAP HILL

LEIGH RD

Rock House Farm

BULLEN MEAD

2

GREAM DR

HOLY WELL LA

OLD WELLS RD

Shearmoor Wood

Bull's Green

Chantry Pond

BA4

Boddenham's Coppice

Castlehill Wood

Dead Woman's Bottom

1

PARK LA

PODILL

anor Farm

46

A **B** 70 **C** **D** 71 **E** **F**

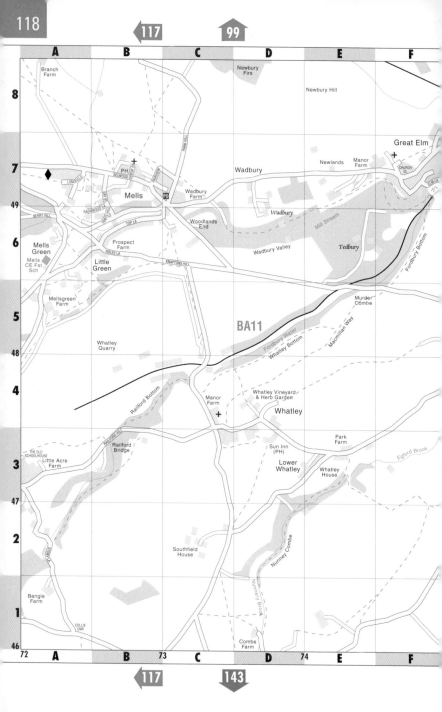

A B C D E F

8 Branch Farm

Newbury Firs

Newbury Hill

7 Great Elm

PH
BELWOOD ST

LONGMEAD

Mells

Wadbury

Newlands

Manor Farm

CHURCH CL

ELM LA

49 PO

Wadbury Farm

RASHWOOD LA

FRENCH

Wadbury

Mill Stream

Woodlands End

Fordbury Bottom

6 Mells Green

TOP LA

Prospect Farm

Wadbury Valley

Tedbury

Mells CE Fst Sch

HOLES LA

Little Green

KNAPTONS HILL

Murder Combe

5 Mellsgreen Farm

BA11

Fordbury Water

Whatley Bottom

Macmillan Way

48 Whatley Quarry

4 Railford Bottom

Manor Farm

Whatley Vineyard & Herb Garden

Whatley

Park Farm

Eglord Brook

3 THE OLD SCHOOLHOUSE

Little Acre Farm

RAILFORD HILL

Railford Bridge

Sun Inn (PH)

Lower Whatley

Whatley House

47

2 A MELLS

Southfield House

Nunney Combe

Nunney Brook

1 Bangle Farm

COLLIE CNR

Combe Farm

46

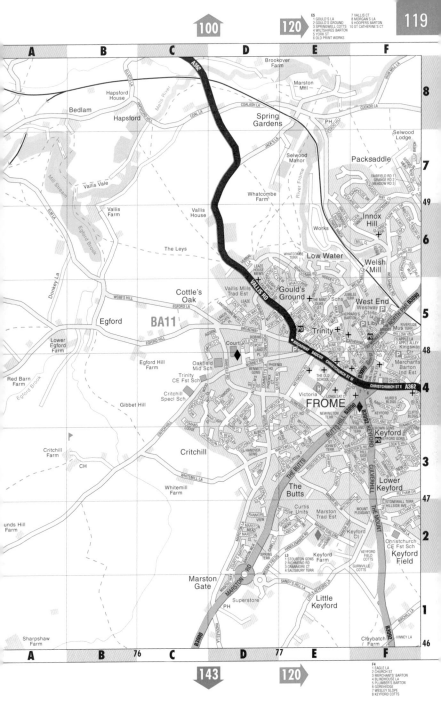

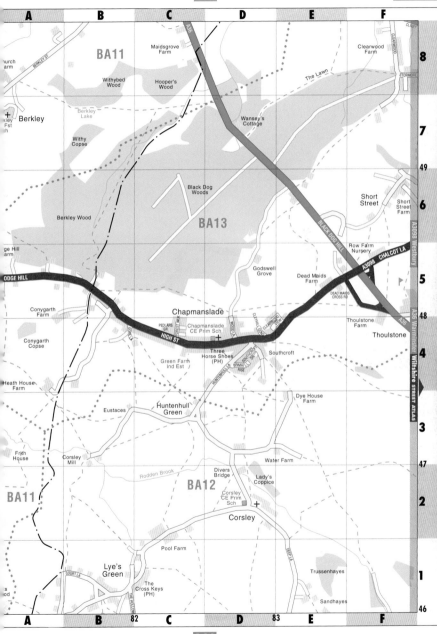

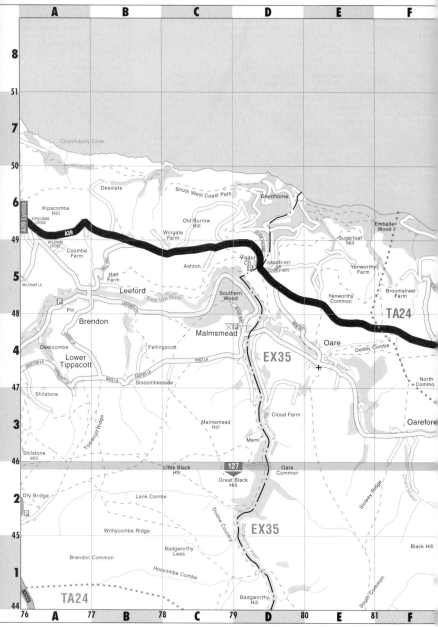

A   B   C   D   E   F

8

51

7

50

6

Countisbury Cove

Desolate

South West Coast Path

Glenthorne

Kipscombe Hill

KIPSCOMBE CROSS

A39 Lynton

A39

49

WILSHAM CROSS

Old Burrow Hill

Wingate Farm

Embelle Wood

Coombe Farm

Sugarloaf Hill

Yenworthy Farm

5

WILSHAM LA

Half Farm

Ashton

Visitor Ctr

COSGATES FEET OR COUNTY GATE

Broomstreet Farm

Leeford

East Lyn River

Southern Wood

Yenworthy Common

TA24

48

P

PH

Brendon

Malmsmead

Oare

Deddy Combe

4

Deercombe

Fellingscott

POST LA

EX35

Oare Water

Lower Tippacott

GRATTON LA

BALE LA

EASTER LA

Slocombeslade

North Commo

47

Shilstone

Tippacott Ridge

Malmsmead Hill

Cloud Farm

Oarefore

3

Shilstone Hill

Meml

46

Little Black Hill

127

Great Black Hill

Oare Common

Stowey Ridge

2

Dry Bridge

P

Lank Combe

Doone Country

EX35

Black Hill

45

Withycombe Ridge

Badgworthy Lees

Brendon Common

Hoccombe Combe

1

B3223

TA24

Badgworthy Hill

South Common

Chalk Water

44

76   A   77   B   78   C   79   D   80   E   81   F

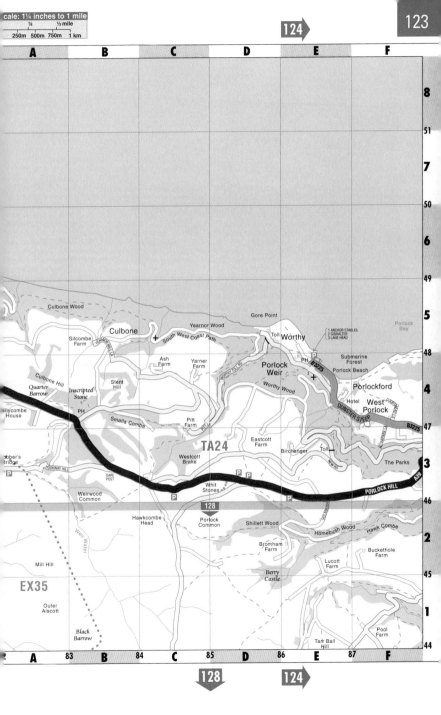

Scale: 1¼ inches to 1 mile

¼   ½ mile

250m   500m   750m   1 km

Greenaleigh Point

Burgundy Chapel (remains of)

Greenaleigh Farm

North Hill Woodland Trail

orth Hill

North Hill 1

Moor Wood

Beacon IRB Sta

Bratton Ball

CULVECLIFFE

Higher Town

Harbour

200

201

MINEHEAD

Madbrain Sands

Warren Point

Woodcombe

Bratton LA

WHITECROSS

THE PARKS

Sch

Minehead

The Strand

CH

Bratton Court

Cemy

Liby

WARREN RD

LC

Bratton

PORLOCK RD

Periton

West Somerset Rly

Holiday Village

Great Headon Plantation

Hotel

Higher Hopcott

TA24

Periton

TOWNSEND RD

HAYFIELD RD

Alcombe

Coll

BIRCHAM RD

The Old Manor

Works

Periton Hill

Hopcott Common

MacCullam Way West

Calins

STAUNTON

Penny Hill

Ellicombe

Marsh Street

Dunster

LC

LC

 vington ommon

Staunton Plantation

Hagley

Alcombe Common

Aldersmead

Conygar Tower

MARSH LA

Loxhole Bridge

A39

130

131

For full street detail of the highlighted areas see pages 200 and 201.

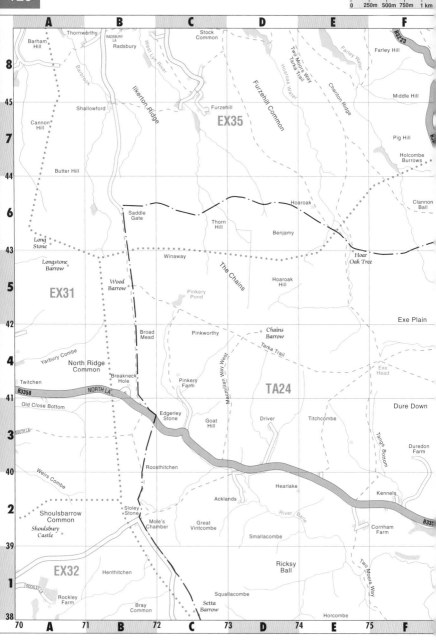

Scale: 1¼ inches to 1 mi

0   ¼   ½ mile
0 250m 500m 750m 1 km

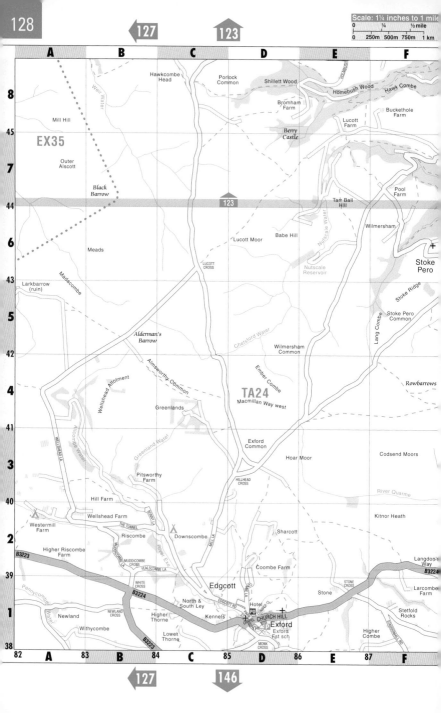

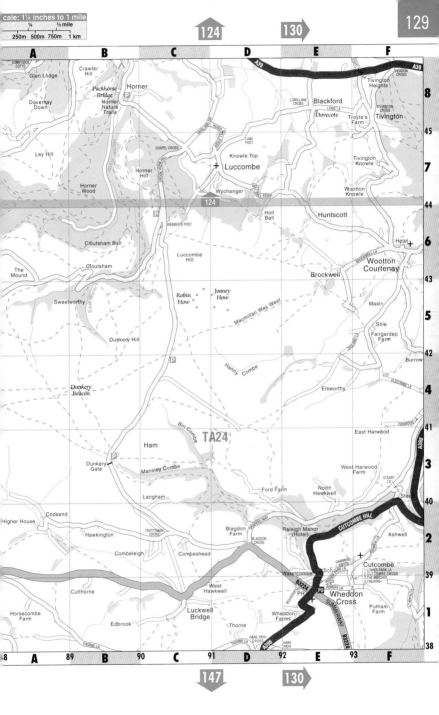

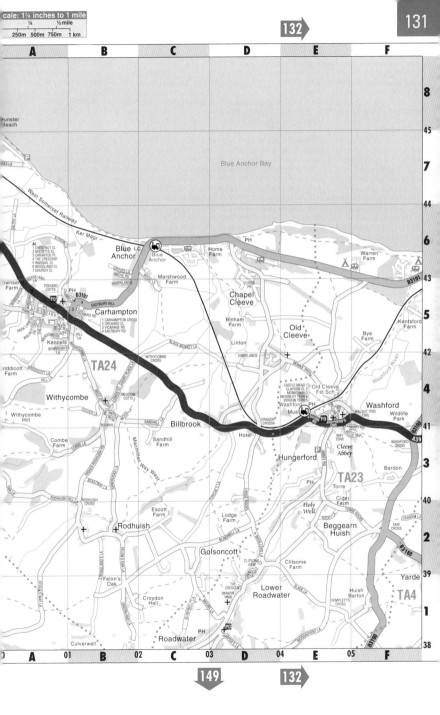

Scale: 1¼ inches to 1 mile

0   ¼   ½ mile
0   250m 500m 750m 1 km

A | **B** | **C** | **D** | **E** | **F**

8

45

7

44

202

WATCHET

6

43

B3191

Mill

St Decumans

WEST ST

PO

Watchet

BRENDON RD

DONIFORD RD

Doniford
Beach Hall

Doniford

Holiday
Park

The Belt

St Audrie's
Bay

Holiday
Village

Perry
Farm

The Home
Farm

St Audrie's
House

Stowborrow
Hill

A39

5

Five Bells

TA23

Liddymore
Farm

Rydon
Farm

West wood

42

WASHFORD HILL

B3190

B3191 FIVE BELLS

202

Williton

Wibble
Farm

STAPLE CL
BRACKEN EDGE

West
Quantoxhead

PO

PH

4

B3190

SMITHS LA

Sch

High
Bridge

Staple
Plantation

P

Williton
& District

LONG ST

Williton

PRIEST ST BANK

West Somerset Railway

Castle Hill

Torweston
Farm

TA4

Weacombe

A39

PO

Mus

TOWER HILL

A358

Sampford
Brett

Lower
Weacombe

3

41

202

Stream

Orchard
Wyndham

Woolston

Bicknoller
Hill

Bicknoller

GATCHELLS LA

Trendle
Ring

40

Black
Down
Wood

Capton

Macmillan Way West

CAPTON
CROSS

YELLOW
WOOD
CROSS

PH

Lower
Weacombe

Quantox
Moor
Farm

Chilcombe

2

B3188

Yarde

Woodford

Cemy

WOODFORD
GOITS

NETTLE LA

Lower
Yellow

Vellow Wood
Farm

Newton

Culverhays

HALSWAY HILL

A39

39

38

B3188

BEECH TREE
CROSS

COMBECROSS LA

Rowdon
Cross

VELLOW WOOD LA

ESCOTT LA

VELLOW LA

CULVERHAYS LA

COOKLEY LA

Yard Farm

06 **A** **07** **B** **08** **C** **09** **D** **10** **E** **11** **F**

For full street detail of the
highlighted area see page 202.

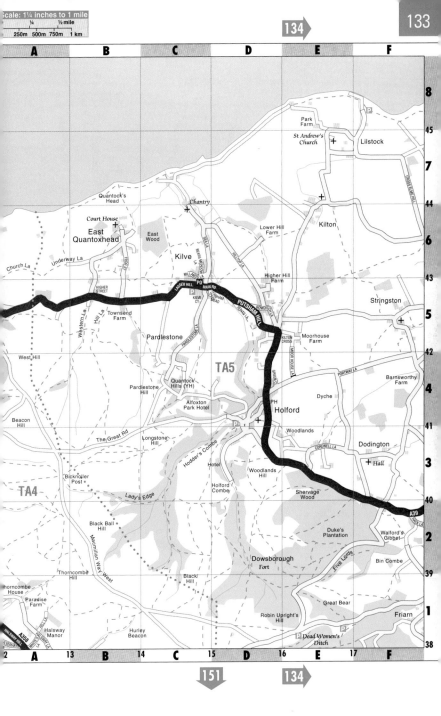

A   B   C   D   E   F

8

45

Park Farm

St Andrew's Church

Lilstock

7

Quantock's Head

Chantry

44

Lower Hill Farm

Kilton

Court House

East Quantoxhead

East Wood

Kilve

Higher Hill Farm

6

43

Higher Street

P O

Kilve Ct.

Stringston

Church La

Underway La

Townsend Farm

Ladder Hill

Main Rd

Cutsham Head

PUTSHAM HILL

5

42

West Hill

Pardlestone

TA5

Moorhouse Farm

Kilton Cross

Barnsworthy Farm

Pardlestone Hill

Quantock Hills (YH)

Dyche

Portway La

4

41

Beacon Hill

Alfoxton Park Hotel

P

PH

Holford

Woodlands

Cornwell La

Dodington

The Great Rd

Longstone Hill

Hodder's Combe

Hotel

Woodlands Hill

Hall

3

TA4

Bicknoller Post

Lady's Edge

Holford Combe

Shervage Wood

A39

40

Black Ball Hill

Duke's Plantation

Walford's Gibbet

Bin Combe

2

Thorncombe Hill

Macmillan Way West

Black Hill

Dowsborough Fort

Five Lords

39

Thorncombe House

Paradise Farm

Hurley Beacon

Robin Upright's Hill

Great Bear

Friarn

1

A358

Halsway Manor

Dead Women's Ditch

P

38

2   A   13   B   14   C   15   D   16   E   17   F

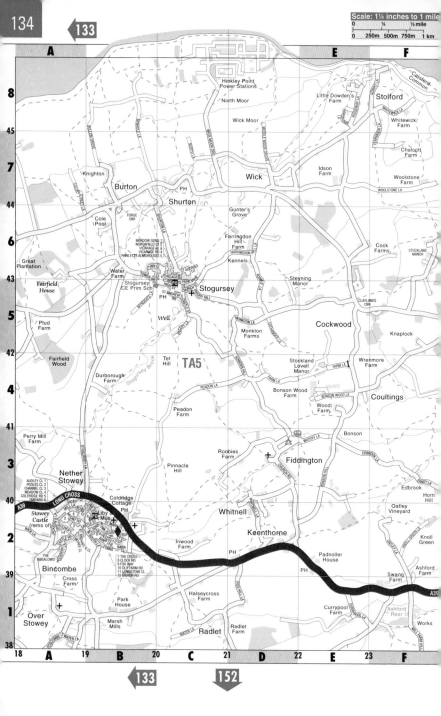

Scale: 1¼ inches to 1 mile

¼ ½ mile
250m 500m 750m 1 km

| A | B | C | D | E | F |

8

Steart

The Island

TA9

45

Wall Common

7

Marsh Farm

Yearsley Farm

44

CADWELL S LA

TOWER LA

STRETCHES LA

Dodds Farm

Stretcholt

6

Stockland Bristol

TA6

MOUNT VIEW TERR

MANOR PK

Cobb's Leaze Rhyne

HAM LA

CHAPEL RD

QUEENS WAY

MANOR RD

Otterhampton

Hill House

GAUNTS RD

Pawlett Hill

43

White House Rhyne

WHITE HOUSE RD

Pawlett Prim Sch

Hill Farm

Combwich

PH

Gaunt's Farm

Pawlett Hams

MONMOUTH FARM CL 1
OLD MAIN RD 2
SCOT CL 3
GRANGE WAY 4

5

WITHYCOMBE HILL

Otterhampton Prim Sch

PO

Combwich Reach

VICARAGE LA

QUANTOCK RD

1 NURSERY CL
2 FENDER CL
3 RIVER VIEW
4 MARTYN CL
5 HARBOUR VIEW
6 HARBOUR CT
7 KILN CL

42

BROOKSIDE RD

ESTUARY PK

WITHYCOMBE VILLAS

TA5

River Parrett

4

here Manor Farm

Bolham House

Putnell Farm

River Parrett Trail

Hallicks Farm

41

Castle Hill Quarry

Rodway Farm

Fort

Cannington Quarry

Shark's La

Cannington Brook

Dairy House Farm

3

Cannington Park

STRADLINGS HILL

CHINEHORN DRO

Rodway

STRAIGHT DRO

40

SANDY LA

PARK LA

Cannington

Cannington CE Prim Sch

1 SCHOOL FIELDS
2 RYDON CRES
3 SOUTHBROOK

Bower Hill

Withiel Farm

Cannington Coll

Cemy

PO

Vst Ctr

GDNS

Perry Court Farm

Manor Farm

MEADOW CL 1
SQUARES RD 2

Chilton Trinity

2

more Sec Tech Sch

WITHIEL DR

Perry Moor

ANDREWS RD

CHILTON LA

39

OAK TREE

ORCHARD

BROWNINGS

Sewage Works

208

Blackmore Farm

MAIN RD

The Grange

Bradley Green

Perry Green

Barton Farm

Chilton Trinity Sch

208

BLACKMORE LA

PH

Chiltern Trivett

NEW RD

QUANTOCK RD

HILSTONE

CHARLYNCH LA

B3339

208

TA6

WESTERN WAY

BLAKES LA

CHILTON LA

1

38

| A | 25 | B | 26 | C | 27 | D | 28 | E | 29 | F |

153 ◀ 136 ▶

For full street detail of the highlighted area see page 208.

B2
1 TOLL HOUSE RD
2 HENRY ROGERS HO
3 CLIFFORD LODGE
4 LOVERS WLK
5 CHURCH ST
6 BROOK LA
7 DUKE AVE
8 TEALS ACRE
9 HAWKERS CL

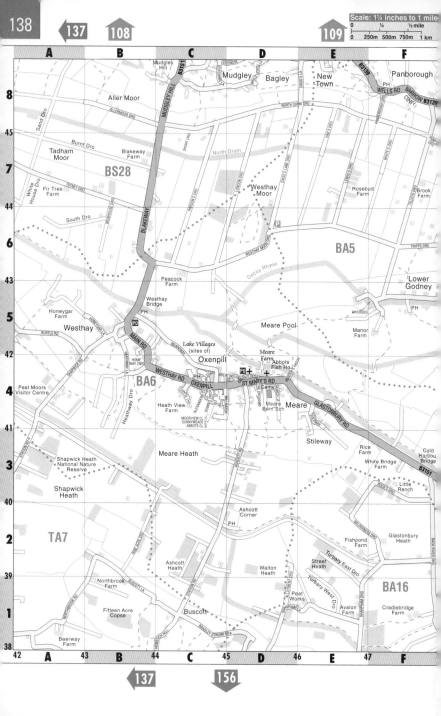

138

137 108

109

Scale: 1¼ inches to 1 mile
0   ¼   ½ mile
0   250m 500m 750m 1 km

A   B   C   D   E   F

8 Mudgley Hill
Mudgley   Bagley   New Town   Panborough
B3151
MUDGLEY HILL
WELLS RD   PH   BARROW CSWY
B3139
Aller Moor
ALLERMOOR DRO
NORTH CHINE DRO

45 Sand Dro
Burnt Dro
Blakeway Farm
North Drain

7 Tadham Moor
BS28
Westhay Moor
Rosebud Farm
Brook Farm

44 White House Dro
Fir Tree Farm
TOTNEY DRO
South Dro

6 Honeygar Farm
Peacock Farm
Westhay Bridge
BLAKEWAY
WESTHAY MOOR DRO
Decoy Rhyne
BA5
TRIPPS DRO

43 Lower Godney
RIVERSIDE
PH

5 Honeygar Farm
Westhay
BURTLE RD
PH
PO
MAIN RD
Lake Villages (sites of)
Meare Pool
Manor Farm

42 HOME WAY CNR
Oxenpill
Meare Farm
Abbots Fish Ho.

4 Peat Moors Visitor Centre
BA6
Heathway Dro
WESTHAY RD
PH
OXENPILL
ST MARY'S RD
Cemy
Meare Prim. Sch
Meare
GLASTONBURY RD
Heath View Farm

41 MOORVIEW CL 1
SUNNYMEADE 2
ABBOTS CL 3
Stileway

3 Shapwick Heath National Nature Reserve
Meare Heath
Rice Farm
White Bridge Farm
Cold Harbour Bridge
B3151

40 Shapwick Heath
Little Ranch

2 TA7
Ashcott Corner
PH
Fishpond Farm
Glastonbury Heath
Street Heath
Turbary East Dro
BA16

39 Northbrook Farm
Ashcott Heath
Walton Heath
Turbary West Dro
Peat Works
Avalon Farm
Cradlebridge Farm

1 Fifteen Acre Copse
Buscott

38 Beerway Farm

42 A   43 B   44 C   45 D   46 E   47 F

Scale: 1¼ inches to 1 mile

¼ ½ mile

250m 500m 750m 1 km

110

111

140

139

A B C D E F

8

B3139 Bleadney

WELLS RD

Worth Burcott

Wookey

B3139

A371 PORTWAY A371

Sewage Works

203

45

Henton Yarley Somerlaeze

7

Ben Knowle Hill

1 HOLMLEA
2 DUMMS LA
3 BUTTICE LA
4 DOCTOR'S HILL
5 BUXTONS CL
6 MARY BROWN DAVIS LA
7 VICARAGE LA

Hay Hill

Coxley Wick

Kewn Brook

GLASTONBURY RD

203

Godney Moor

Hembury Hill Callow Hill

Castle

Hurn Farm

Melsbury Farm

Upper Coxley

44

Coxley

A38

6

BA5

North Moor

Fenny Castle Hill

Melsbury

Coxley Vineyard

Hartirs

Pill Moor

Upper Godney

PO

Garslade Farm

43

Keen Hall Farm

Harter's Hill

Godney

Lower Crannel Farm

Polsham

5

42

River Sheppey

Southway

WELLS RD

Inn

Batch Farm

Upper Crannel Farm

Crannel Moor

Queen's Sedge Moor

4

BA6

East Backwear

Long Run

UPPER CRANNEL DRO

BA4

Hartlake Bridge

Hartlake Farm

41

206

West Backwear

Backwear Farm

Common Moor

CRAB TREE DRO

Tin Bridge RDBT

A39

Hearty Moor

3

Coldharbour Farm

Rifle Range

LOWERSIDE LA

Wells Road Trad Est

Brindham

BA6

MEARE RD

Mill Stream

New Close Rhyne

Lower New Close

Higher New Close

Cemy

GLASTONBURY

Wick

Stone Down Hill

Norwood Park

40

2

B5151

206

PO

SANDPITS TRD

New Close Farm

MANOR HOUSE RD

Mus

BA16

Beckery

Libry

Schs

Schs

TH

Abbey

Dove Town

Bushy Coombe

Chalice Well

Glastonbury Tor

STONE DOWN LA

39

East Street

1

River Brue

Cradle Bridge

Sewage Works

A39

A361 STREET RD

BERE LA

Northover

WIRRAL PARK RDBT

Edgarley

EDGARLEY RD

A361

38

A 49 B 50 C 51 D 52 E 53 F

157

140

For full street detail of the highlighted areas see pages 203 and 206.

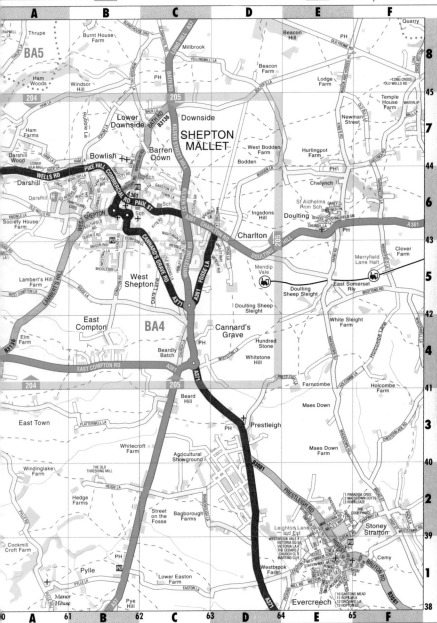

Scale: 1¼ inches to 1 mile

¼   ½ mile

250m 500m 750m 1 km

BA5

Thrupe

Burnt House Farm

Millbrook

YELLINGMILL LA

Beacon Hill

PH

Quarry

Ham Woods

Windsor Hill

BACK LA

PH

Beacon Farm

Lodge Farm

LONG CROSS OLD WELLS RD

WATERLIP

204

205

45

Lower Downside

Downside

SHEPTON MALLET

West Bodden Farm

Hurlingpot Farm

Newman Street

Temple House Farm

BA LA

7

Ham Farms

Rubble La

Barren Down

Bodden

BODDEN LA

PH

Chelynch

CHELYNCH RD

44

Darshill Wood

Bowlish

PIKE HILL

COMMERCIAL RD

Sch

GARSTON ST

TOWN LA

KILVER ST

St Aldhelms Prim Sch

CAREY CL

CHELYNCH

Chelynch

6

Darshill

WELLS RD

Sch

PAUL ST

A361

Sch

CHARLTON RD

Ingsdons Hill

Doulting

CHURCH LA

PH

COPSEFIELD DR

A361

Society House Farm

KNOWLE LA

WEST SHEPTON

QUEEN'S RD

Charlton

205

43

OLD WELLS RD

MASON WAY

COMPTON RD

CANNARD'S GRAVE RD

WHITSTONE LA

FOSSE LA

DOULTING

HILL

Mendip Vale

East Somerset Rly

Merryfield Lane Halt

Clover Farm

MERRYFIELD LANE

5

Lambert's Hill Farm

WEST COMPTON LA

LAMBERT'S HILL

FOSSE LA

West Shepton

A371

COCKHILL

CREEK LA

Doulting Sheep Sleight

Doulting Sheep Sleight

East Somerset Rly

HOLCOMBE LANE

42

B3136

East Compton

BA4

Cannard's Grave

White Sleight Farm

4

Elm Farm

EAST COMPTON RD

A361

A371

Beardly Batch

PH

WHITSTONE LA

Hundred Stone

Whitstone Hill

204

205

Farncombe

Holcombe Farm

41

East Town

PLATTERWELL LA

Beard Hill

PH

Prestleigh

Maes Down

3

Whitecroft Farm

Agricultural Showground

Maes Down Farm

CHESTERBLADE RD

40

Windinglake Farm

THE OLD THRESHING MILL

HEDGE LA

B3081

PRESTLEIGH RD

1 PARADISE CRES
2 MAESDOWN COTTS
3 ROEBLEAZE

2

Hedge Farms

PYLLE RD

Street on the Fosse

Bagborough Farms

Leighton Lane Ind Est

THE COURTYARDS

Stoney Stratton

WESTCOMBE LA

Cockmill Croft Farm

PH

PO

Pylle

PYLLE LA

Lower Easton Farm

EASTON LA

Westbrook Farm

WESTBROOK VALE
VICTORIA SQ
VICTORIA LA
THE CEDARS
CHURCH CL
MARTINS CL

STATION RD

BRUTON RD

Cemy

B3081

39

1

Manor House

Pye Hill

10 GARTONS MEAD
11 ROPE WLK
12 ORCHARD LA
13 HOPTON CL

Evercreech

38

For full street detail of the highlighted area see pages 204 and 205.

A   61   B   62   C   63   D   64   E   65   F

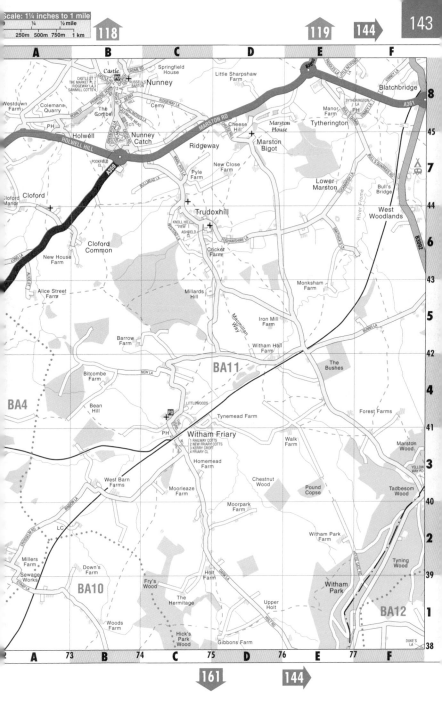

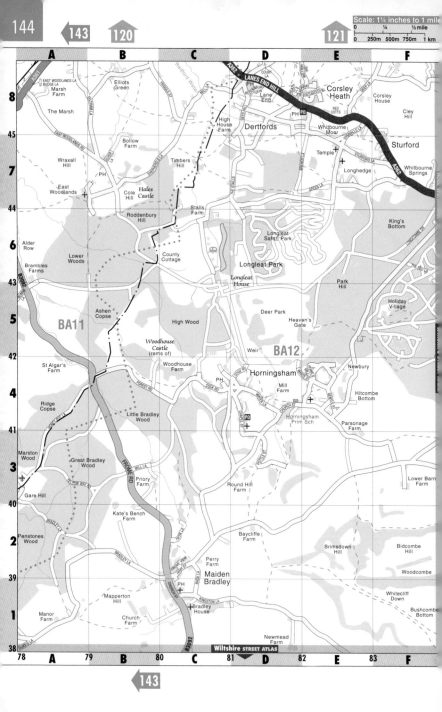

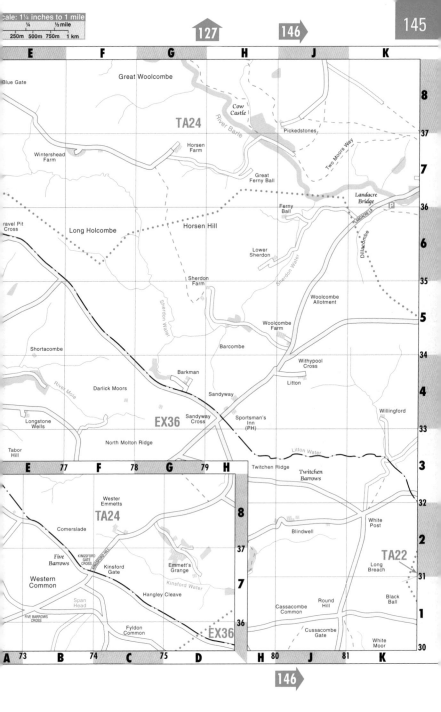

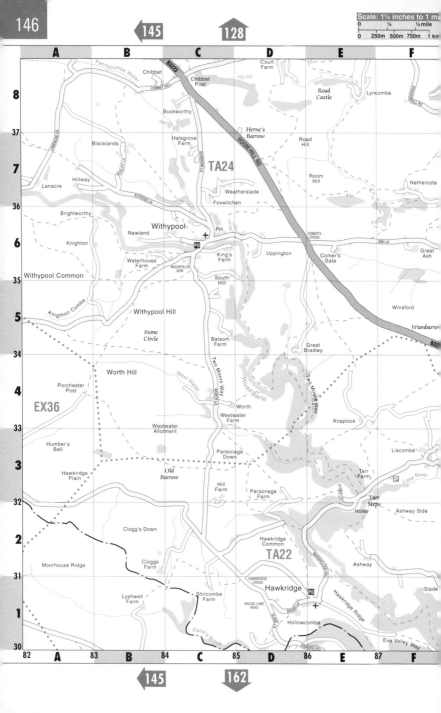

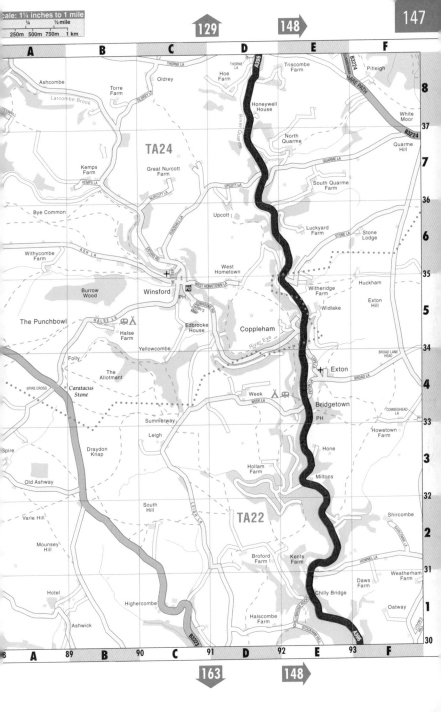

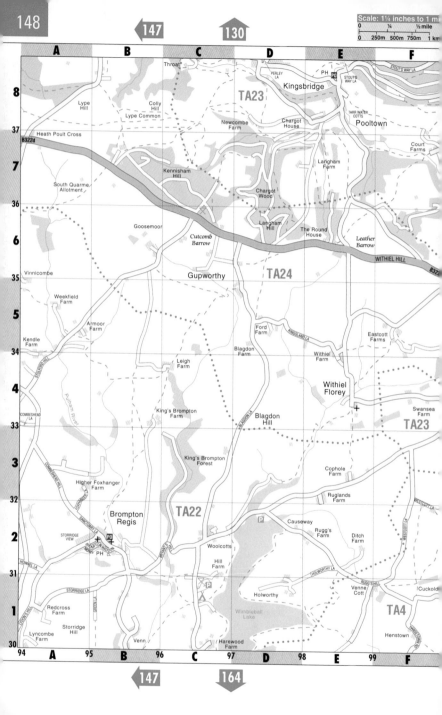

Scale: 1¼ inches to 1 mi

0   ¼   ½ mile
0   250m 500m 750m 1 km

A **B** **C** **D** **E** **F**

Throat

PERLEY LA

Kingsbridge

PH
PO
STOUT'S WAY LA

STOUT'S WAY LA

8

TA23

TARR WATER COTTS

Poottown

Lype Hill

Colly Hill

Lype Common

Newcombe Farm

Chargot House

Court Farms

37

B3224   Heath Poult Cross

Langham Florey

7

Kennisham Hill

South Quarme Allotment

Chargot Wood

36

Goosemoor

Cutcomb Barrow

Langham Hill

The Round House

Leather Barrow

6

WITHIEL HILL

B322

35

Vinnicombe

Gupworthy

TA24

Weekfield Farm

Ford Farm

Eastcott Farms

5

Armoor Farm

KINGSLAND LA

Withiel Farm

Kendle Farm

Blagdon Farm

Withiel Florey

34

STORRIDGE HILL

Leigh Farm

Swansea Farm

4

COMBESHEAD LA

Pulham River

King's Brompton Farm

Blagdon Hill

TA23

33

BLAGDON LA

King's Brompton Forest

Cophole Farm

3

Higher Foxhanger Farm

WESTCOTT LA

Ruglands Farm

32

CARNSHEAD LA

Brompton Regis

TA22

Causeway

Rugg's Farm

Ditch Farm

SANCTUARY LA

P

2

STORRIDGE VIEW

PO
PH

BRIDGES LA

Woolcotts

Rugg's Farm

HOLWORTHY LA

Venne Cott

Cuckold

31

HOWNEL LA

STORRIDGE LA

Hill Farm

P

Holworthy

RUGG'S HILL

TA4

1

Redcross Farm

GREEN LA

Storridge Hill

P

Wimbleball Lake

Henstown

Lyncombe Farm

Venn

Harewood Farm

30

94 **A** 95 **B** 96 **C** 97 **D** 98 **E** 99 **F**

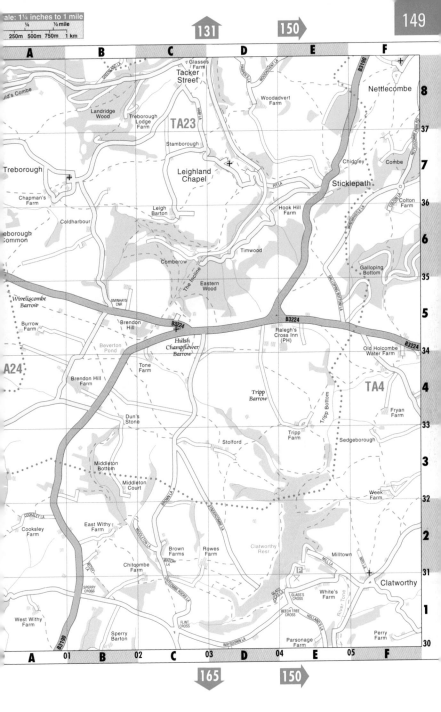

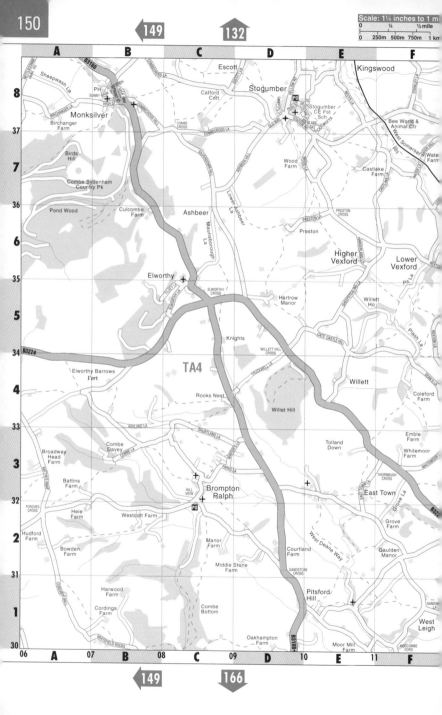

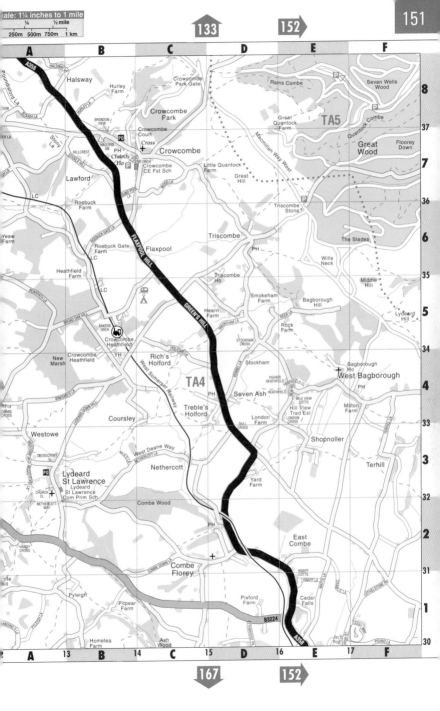

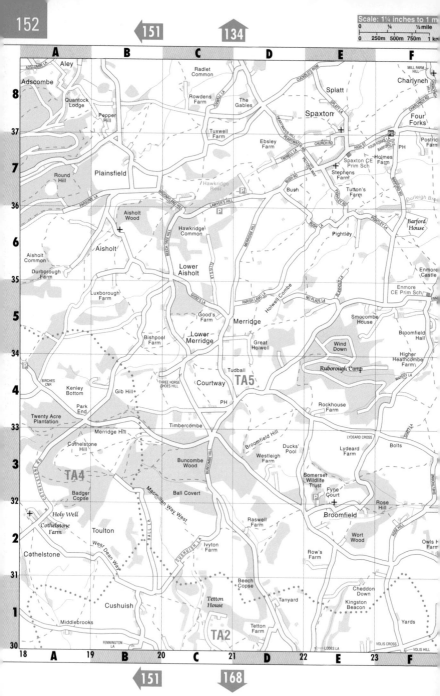

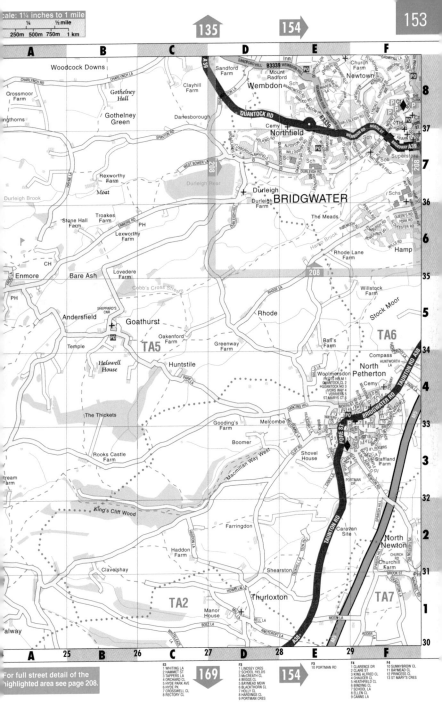

Scale: 1¼ inches to 1 mile
¼   ½ mile
250m 500m 750m 1 km

135   154

For full street detail of the highlighted area see page 208.

169   154

E3
1 WHITING LA
2 HAMMET ST
3 TAPPERS LA
4 ORCHARD CL
5 HYDE PARK AVE
6 HYDE PK
7 CROSSWELL CL
8 RECTORY CL

F3
1 LINDSEY CRES
2 SCHOOL FIELDS
3 McCREATH CL
4 BEGGS CL
5 BAYMEAD MDW
6 BLACKTHORN CL
7 HOLLY CL
8 HARDINGS CL
9 PORTMAN CRES

F3
10 PORTMAN RD

F4
1 CLARENCE DR
2 CLARE ST
3 KING ALFRED CL
4 CHAUCER CL
5 HEATHFIELD CL
6 BINDING CL
7 SCHOOL LA
8 ELLEN CL
9 CANNS CL

F4
10 SUNNYBROW CL
11 BAYMEAD CL
12 PRINCESS CL
13 ST MARY'S CRES

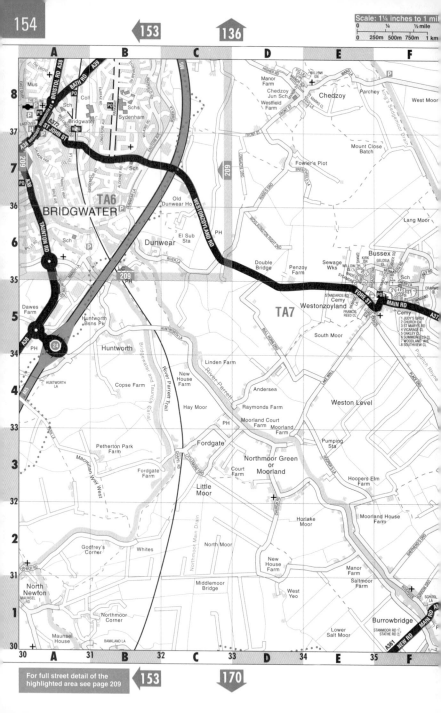

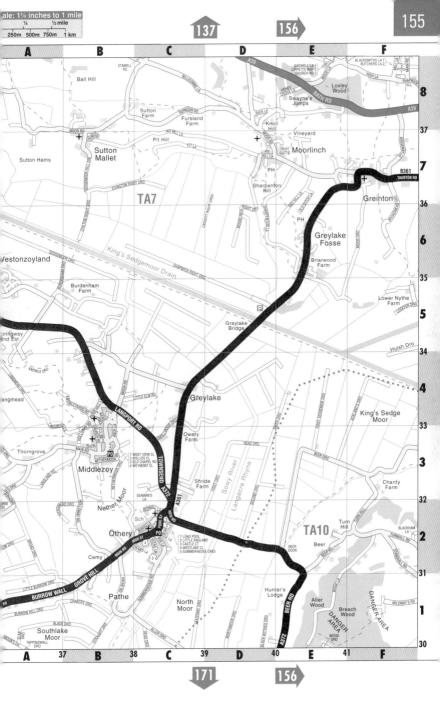

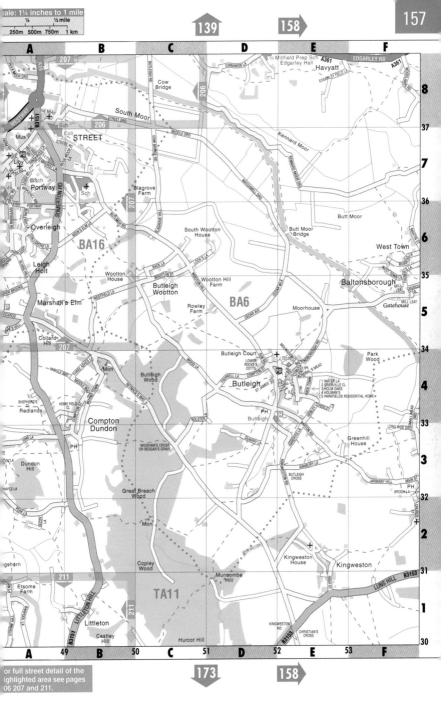

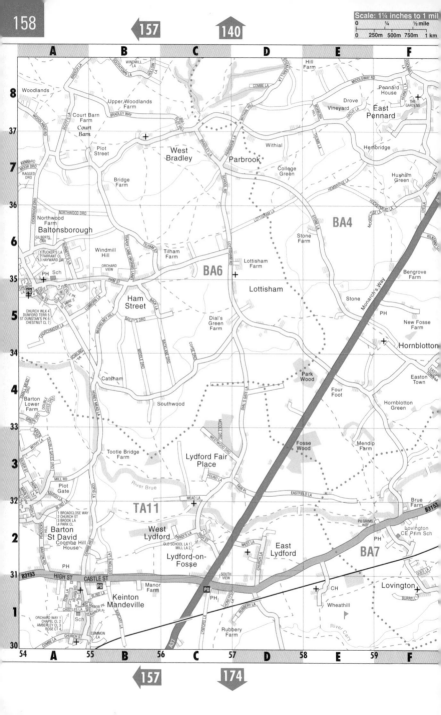

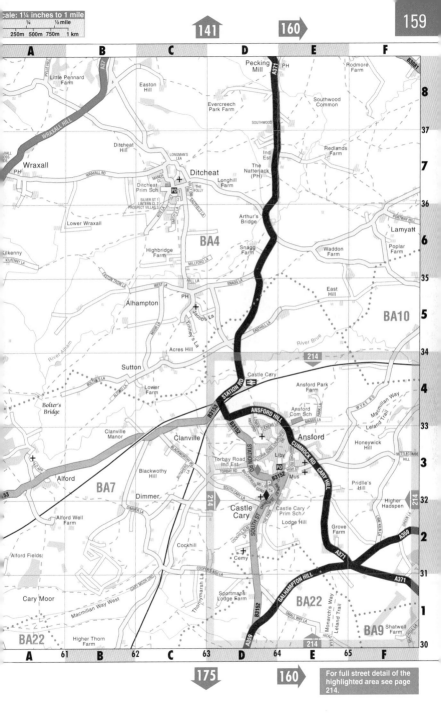

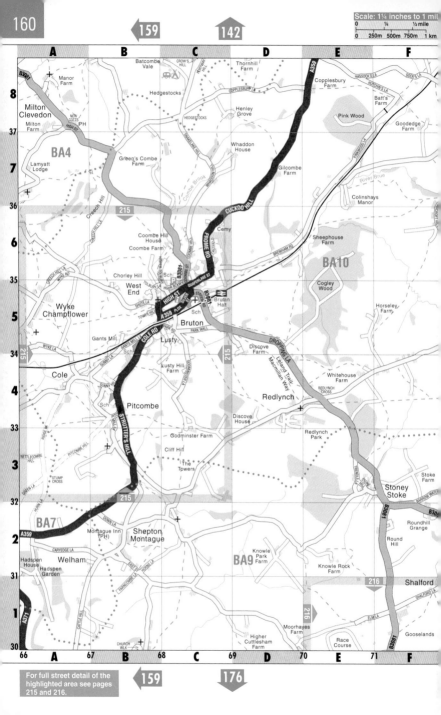

Scale: 1¼ inches to 1 mile
0   ¼   ½ mile
0   250m 500m 750m   1 km

A   B   C   D   E   F

B3081
Manor Farm
Milton Clevedon
Milton Farm
PH
NEW COTT
HIGH RD
8
37
BA4
Lamyatt Lodge
7
Creech Hill
SHEEP HILL LA
215
36
CREECH HILL LA
WYKE RD
6
Wyke Champflower
WYKE LA
35
West End
Chorley Hill
HIGH ST
Sch
Sch
A359
PLOX
TOWER HILL
5
Gants Mill
COLE RD
34
215
Cole
Lusty
SUNNY LA
DANIEL MEADE
Sch
4
Pitcombe
SUNNY LA
STRUTTER'S HILL
Lusty Hill Farm
33
RIDGE LA
NETTLECOMBE HILL
PITCOMBE HILL
Godminster Farm
Cliff Hill
The Towers
3
STUMP CROSS
GREEN LA
COLE LA
215
32
BA7
Montague Inn (PH)
Shepton Montague
DOWN LA
A359
Welham
CARYEDGE LA
EAST END
Hadspen House
Hadspen Garden
2
31
CATTLE HILL
FARNDGROVE LA
1
A371
CHURCH WLK
30
66   A   67   B   68   C   69   D   70   E   71   F

Batcombe Vale
CROW'S HILL
Thornhill Farm
Hedgestocks
HEDGESTOCKS
COPPLESBURY LA
Henley Grove
Whaddon House
SHEPLAKE HILL
Combe Brook
Coombe Hill House
Coombe Farm
B3081
Cemy
FROME RD
CUCKOO HILL
Gilcombe Farm
A359
Copplesbury Farm
HASSOCK'S LA
HUTCHIN'S LA
DOCK'S LA
Batt's Farm
Pink Wood
Goodedge Farm
River Brue
Colinshays Manor
BA10
Sheephouse Farm
BRENHAM RD
PINFORD LA
Cogley Wood
Horseley Farm
Bruton Halt
Bruton
PARK WALL
Discove Farm
DROPPING LA
Leland Trail Macmillan Way
Discove House
REDLYNCH CROSS
Redlynch
Whitehouse Farm
Redlynch Park
215
Stoney Stoke
Stoke Farm
Roundhill Grange
B3081
B3092
Round Hill
BA9
Knowle Park Farm
Knowle Rock Farm
216
Shalford
216
Moorhayes Farm
Higher Cuttlesham Farm
ELM LA
SHALFORD LA
B3081
Race Course
Gooselands

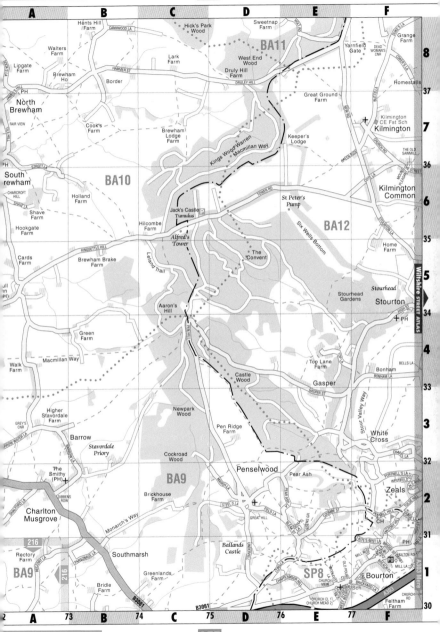

cale: 1¼ inches to 1 mile

¼   ½ mile

250m 500m 750m 1 km

143

A 73 **B** 74 **C** 75 **D** 76 **E** 77 **F**

Hents Hill Farm
CANNWOOD LA
Hick's Park Wood
Sweetnap Farm
Grange Farm

Walters Farm
Lark Farm
West End Wood
Yarnfield Gate
DEAD WOMAN'S CNR

Lipgate Farm
HAMMER ST
Druly Hill Farm
Homestalls

Brewham Ho
Border
DRULEY HILL
BA11

North Brewham

FAIR VIEW
Great Ground Farm
Kilmington CE Fst Sch
Kilmington

Cook's Farm
Brewham Lodge Farm
Keeper's Lodge
THE OLD SAWMILL

South rewham
BA10
Kings Wood Warren
Macmillan Way
Kilmington Common

CHARCROFT HILL
Holland Farm
Jack's Castle Tumulus
St Peter's Pump

Shave Farm
Hilcombe Farm
LOWER RD
BA12
Home Farm

Hookgate Farm
Alfred's Tower
Six Wells Bottom

Cards Farm
KINGSETTLE HILL
The Convent
Stourton

Brewham Brake Farm
Leland Trail

Walk Farm
Macmillan Way
Aaron's Hill
Stourhead Gardens
Stourhead
Stourton
PH

Green Farm
Top Lane Farm
BELLS LA
Bonham
BONHAM LA

GREY'S CNR
Castle Wood
Gasper
GASPER ST

Higher Stavordale Farm
Newpark Wood
Pen Ridge Farm

Barrow
Stavordale Priory
Cockroad Wood
White Cross

The Smithy (PH)
BA9
Penselwood
Pear Ash
CHAPEL LA

CIBBENS ROW
Brickhouse Farm
Zeals

Charlton Musgrove
Monarch's Way
Great Hill
CH

216
Rectory Farm
Ballands Castle
PH

BA9
Southmarsh
SP8
PO
Bourton

Bridle Farm
Greenlands Farm
CHURCH VIEW
CHURCH CL
CHURCH MEAD 2
Feltham Farm
B3061

A 73 **B** 74 **C** 75 **D** 76 **E** 77 **F**

177

Wiltshire STREET ATLAS

For full street detail of the highlighted area see page 216.

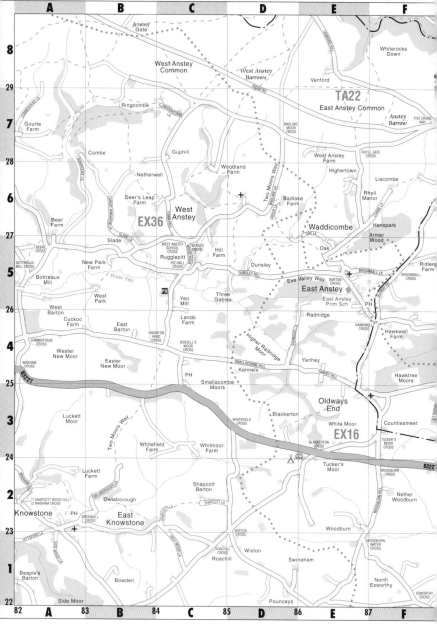

0   ¼   ½ mile
0   250m 500m 750m   1 km

A   **B**   **C**   **D**   **E**   **F**

Anstey
Gate

West Anstey
Common

West Anstey
Barrows

Whiterocks
Down

RIDGE RD

Venford

8

29

TA22

East Anstey Common

Anstey
Barrow

FIVE CROSS
WAY

Gourte
Farm

Ringcombe

7

Combe

Guphill

West Anstey
Farm

RHYLL GATE
CROSS

Highertown

Liscombe

28

Netherwell

Woodland
Farm

Badlake
Farm

Rhyll
Manor

Deer's Leap
Farm

West
Anstey

EX36

6

Beer
Farm

Henspark

Waddicombe

Armer
Wood

27

Slade

BEERE
CROSS

West Anstey
School
Cross

Wood's
Cross

Hill
Farm

Oak

Ridler's
Farm

BROADMBALL LA

BROOMBALL
CROSS

New Park
Farm

Rugglepitt

YEO MILL
CROSS

Dunsley

Dunsley Hill

Exe Valley Way

East Anstey

Barton
Cross

PH

BOTTREAUX
MILL CROSS

5

Bottreaux
Mill

River Yeo

West
Park

Yeo
Mill

Three
Gables

East Anstey
Prim Sch

26

West
Barton

Cuckoo
Farm

Lands
Farm

Radnidge

Hawkwell
Farm

HAWKWELL
CROSS

Hawkwell

East
Barton

HIGHATON
HEAD
CROSS

BUSSELL'S
MOOR
CROSS

Higher Radnidge
Moor

Yanhey

SOMMERTAUN
CROSS

4

Wester
New Moor

Easter
New Moor

Smallacombe Hill

Kennels

TARGEY HILL

Hawktree
Moors

WADHAM
CROSS

PH

25

Smallacombe
Moors

Oldways
End

Luckett
Moor

Whitefield
Cross

Blackerton

White Moor

EX16

Countiesmeet

TUCKER'S
MOOR
CROSS

3

Two Moors Way

Whitefield
Farm

Whitmoor
Farm

Blackerton
Cross

24

Tucker's
Moor

WOODBURN
CROSS

B322

Luckett
Farm

OWLABOROUGH LA

Shapcott
Barton

SHAPCOTT LA

Nether
Woodburn

2

1 SHAPCOTT WOOD HILL
2 WADHAM CROSS

Owlaborough

Knowstone

PH

GREENHILL
CROSS

East
Knowstone

MOLY MOOR LA

WISTON
CROSS

Woodburn

WOODBURN
WATER
CROSS

23

HITTSFORD LA

SIDE MOOR LA

Roachill

ROACHILL
CROSS

Wiston

Swineham

Beaple's
Barton

1

Bowden

North
Esworthy

ESWORTHY
CROSS

22

Side Moor

Pounceys

82   **A**   **83**   **B**   **84**   **C**   **85**   **D**   **86**   **E**   **87**   **F**

163
148

Scale: 1¼ inches to 1 mile

| 0 | ¼ | ½ mile |
| 0 | 250m | 500m | 750m | 1 km |

A B C D E F

8

Lyncombe Farm

Hartford Bottom

Hartford

West Hill Wood

Upton Farm

Hayne Farm

St James Church (rems of)

EASTMOOR LA

29

River Haddeo

Hadborough

Upton

B3190

Clammer

Haddon Hill

P

TA4

7

HADDON LA

Haddon Farm

HADDON HILL

Blindwell Farm

BLINDWELL

28

Chapple Farm

Frogwell Farm

Surridge Farm

South Haddon

HADDON LA

FROGWELL CROSS

6

Bury

DYEHOUSE CNR

Leigh Barton

Skilgate

PITSHAM LA

CROFT LA

GAMBLYN CROSS

27

TA22

Withywine Farm

WITHYWINE LA

Gamblyn Farm

Combeland

Brockhole Farm

Skilgate Wood

DOWNHOUSE ROCK LA

HONE CROSS

5

COMBELAND LA

Haynes Down Farm

QUARTLEY HILL

26

Warmore

Willishayes

HAYNE CROSS

Hayne Farm

Timewell

Morebath Manor

Coombe

East Combe

Quartley Farm

East Holcombe

4

Burston

MOOR LA

BUSTON LA

MORRELL'S CROSS

TIMEWELL HILL

Claypits

COURT LA

Court

COMBE CROSS

25

ASHTOWN CROSS

Morebath

Loyton

HOOPERS CROSS

Eastwoods

Shillingford Fst Sch

B3222

Ashtown Farm

Keens

Westwoods

Hayne Barton

Lower Rill

Great Ri Farm

3

Surridge Farm

Moore Farm

Bell Brook

BONNY CROSS

FIRWAY CROSS

HUKELEY HEAD CROSS

PH

BICKHAM LA

Shillingford

24

BLIGHTS HILL

Blight's Farm

LOWER LODFIN

CHILTERN CROSS

Hukeley Farm

RACKENFORD LA

FORDMILL CROSS

Doddiscombe

South Hayne Farm

2

Coldharbour Farm

Exe Valley Way

Lodfin Farm

Holwell Farm

Chapel (rems of)

Sunderleigh

Borough House

Zeal Farm

23

BONES LA

Birchdown

River Batherm

FORD RD

Pipshayne

1

Rows Farm

HIGH CROSS

Gumbland

B3227

HIGH ST

Libb

SCHOOL LA

SOUTH MOLTON RD

Bampton

Bampton Prim Sch

A TIVERTON RD B C D E F

94 95 96 97 98 99

163

B1
1 WINIFRED CLIFF CT
2 MEADOW VIEW
3 BALL HILL LA
4 MARKET CL
5 LORDS MEADOW LA
6 BARNHAY
7 CHURCH TERR
8 NEWTON SQ
9 FORE ST
10 MARY LA
11 SILVER ST
12 BOURCHIER DR
13 BOURCHIER CL
C1
1 TIVERTON RD
2 BRITON ST
3 NEW BLOGS

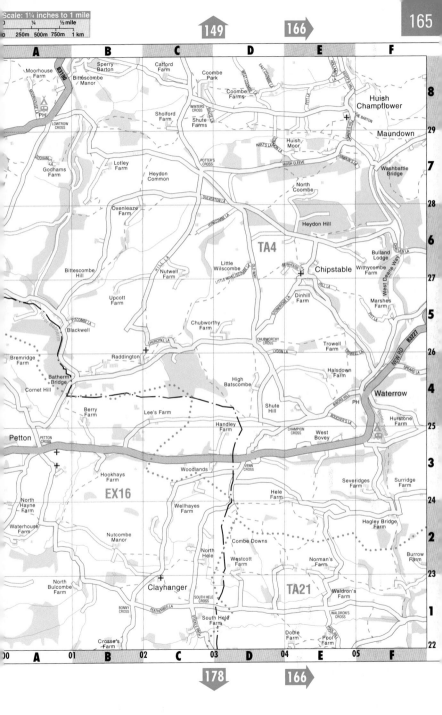

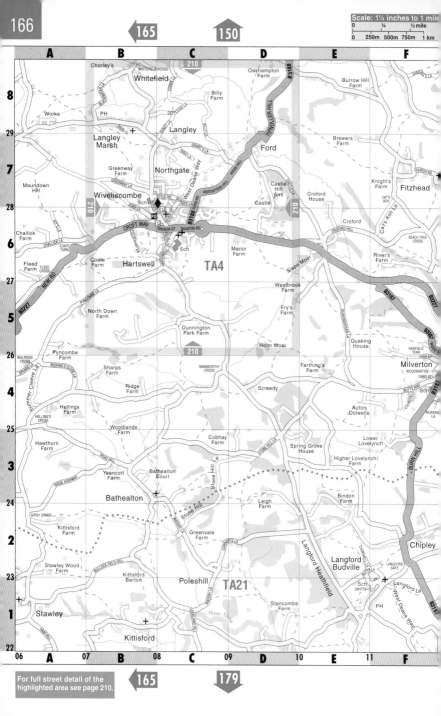

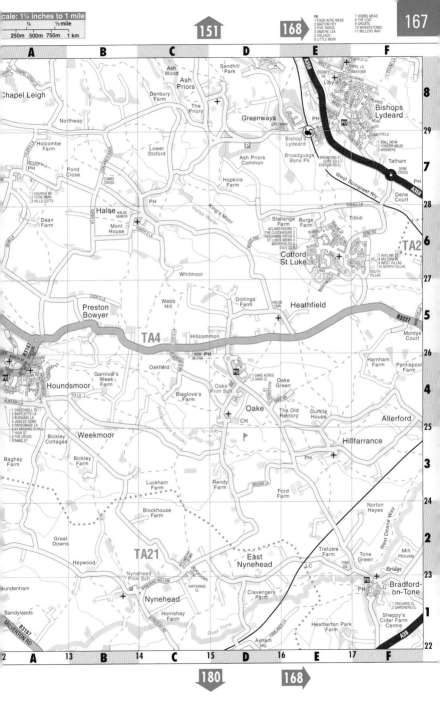

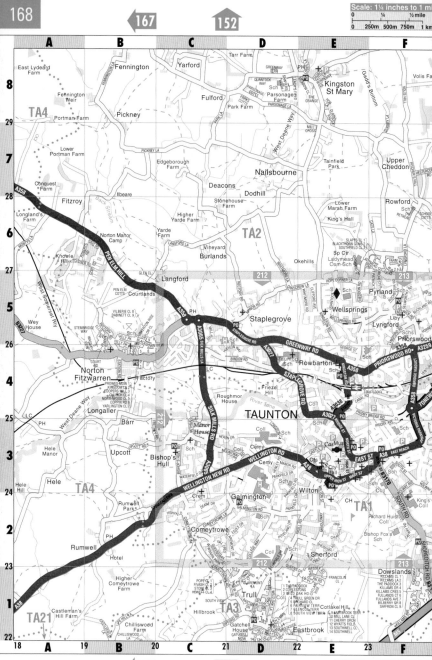

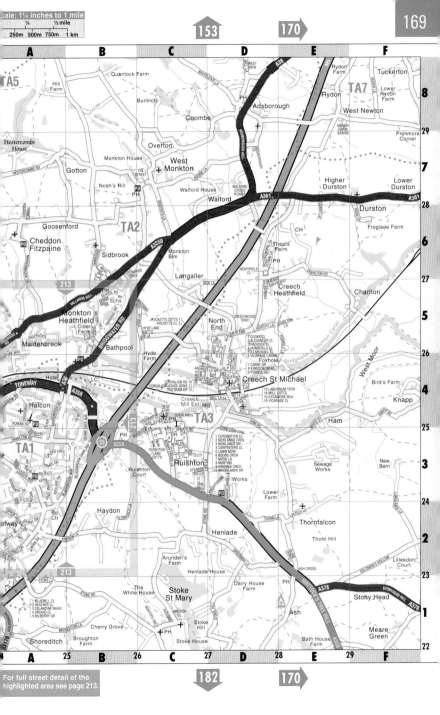

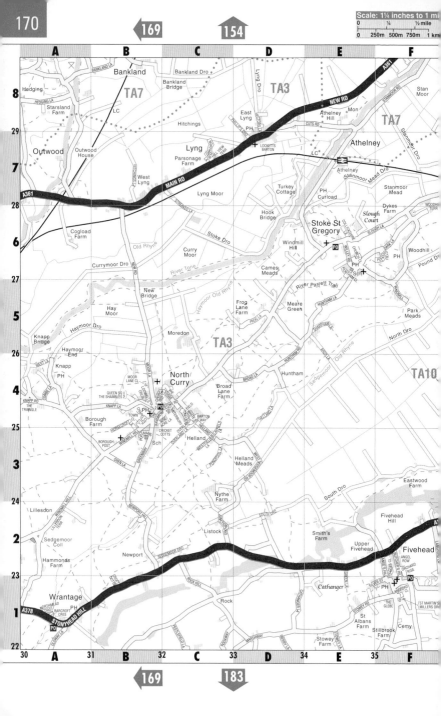

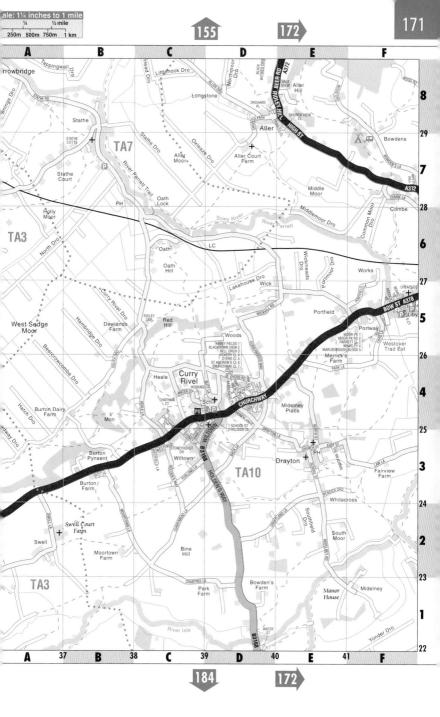

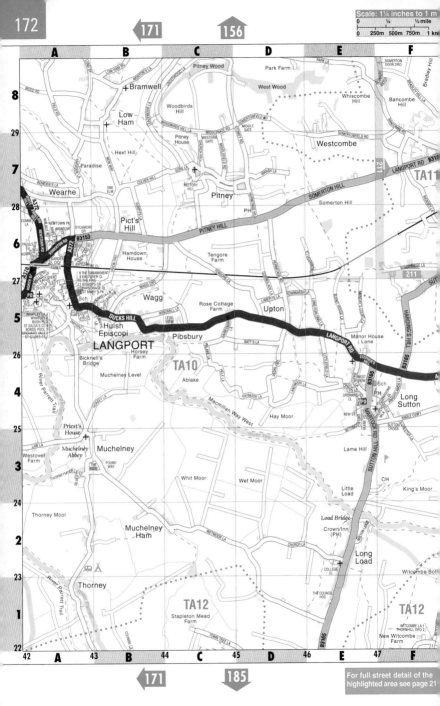

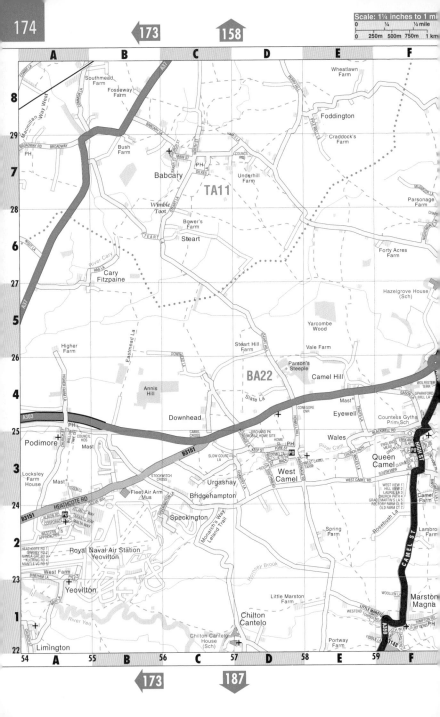

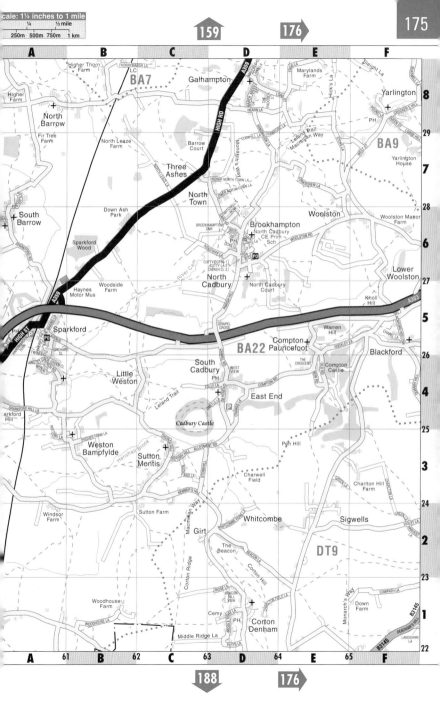

Scale: 1¼ inches to 1 mile

¼   ½ mile

250m 500m 750m 1 km

A   B   C   D   E   F

Higher Thorn Farm
THORNY MARSH LA
LC
BA7
Galhampton
Maryland's Farm
Sleight La
Yarlington

Higher Farm
North Barrow
HEARN LA
Hick's La
PH
BA9

Fir Tree Farm
North Leaze Farm
THE PADDOCK
LONG LA
Yarlington House

Three Ashes
Barrow Court
HIGH RD
Monarch's Way
Leland Trail
Macmillan Way

North Town
HIGHER NORTH TOWN LA
LOWER NORTHTOWN LA
ONSREW LA

South Barrow
Down Ash Park
North Cadbury
Brookhampton
Woolston
Woolston Manor Farm

Sparkford Wood
Brookhampton CNR
PH
North Cadbury CE Prim Sch
PO
WOOLSTON RD
Lower Woolston

River Cam
RIDGE HALL LA
CUTTY COTE
CUTTY LA
CATASH CL 3
North Cadbury
North Cadbury Court
Knoll Hill

Haynes Motor Mus
Woodside Farm
A303

A359
CHAPEL CROSS
Warren Hill
Compton Pauncefoot
BA22
Blackford

Sparkford
PO
HIGH ST
South Cadbury
WEST VIEW
PH
Compton Castle
Compton Rd
THE CRESCENT

ORCHARD LA
GREEN CL
Little Weston
FOLLY LA
East End
HOOKEY LA
CHANEL LA

SPARKFORD HILL LA
Leland Trail
CHAPEL LA
arkford Hill

RECTORY LA
Cadbury Castle
Pen Hill

Weston Bampfylde
Sutton Montis
Henshall Brook
ALLOTMENT RD
Charwell Field
Charlton Hill Farm

Windsor Farm
Sutton Farm
KEMBER'S HILL
Macmillan Way
Girt
Whitcombe
Sigwells

WHITCOMBE LA
The Beacon
BEACON LA
DT9

Corton Ridge
Corton Hill
Woodhouse Farm
RIDGE LA
BEACON HILL VIEW
Cemy
Corton Denham
Monarch's Way
Down Farm
COWPATH LA

WOODHOUSE LA
Middle Ridge La
PH
PUTTS LA
OAKHAM HILL
LANDSHIRE LA
B3145

A   61   B   62   C   63   D   64   E   65   F

29 8
7
28 6
27 5
26 4
25 3
24 2
23 1
22

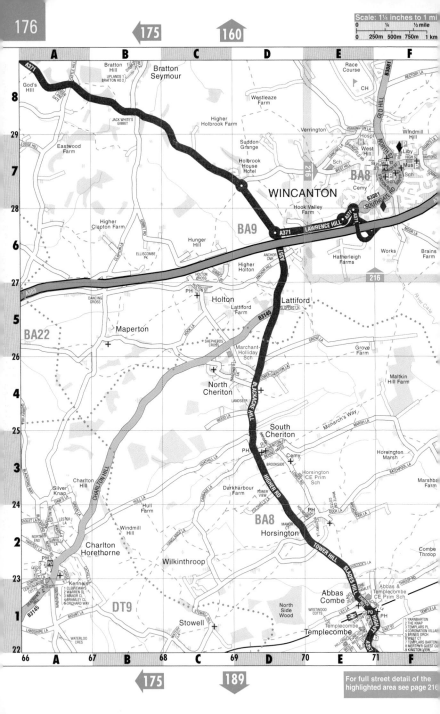

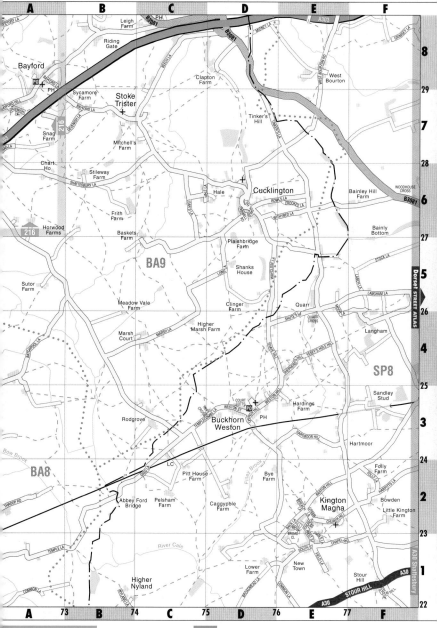

Scale: 1¼ inches to 1 mile

¼ mile   ½ mile
250m 500m 750m 1 km

A 73   **B** 74   **C** 75   **D** 76   **E** 77   **F**

8
29
7
28
6
27
5
26
4
25
3
24
2
23
1
22

Dorset STREET ATLAS

Leigh Farm
PH
B3081
Riding Gate
Bayford
PO
PH
BAYFORD HILL
DEVENISH
Snag Farm
Chart Ho
Sycamore Farm
BAYFORD LA
Stileway Farm
SHAFTESBURY LA
Frith Farm
Horwood Farms
216
Sutor Farm
BAYCROFT LA
Bow Brook
BA8
THROOP RD
Clapton Farm
Stoke Trister
Mitchell's Farm
BEER LA
Baskets Farm
LONG LA
Meadow Vale Farm
Marsh Court
MARSH LA
Hale
Frith Farm
BEAR'S LA
Higher Marsh Farm
Clinger Farm
Rodgrove
CHURCH LA
Abbey Ford Bridge
Pelsham Farm
Pitt House Farm
Caggypble Farm
TEMPLE LA
Higher Nyland
COMMON LA
River Cale
A303
B3081
MONET LA
Tinker's Hill
Clapton Farm
WEST BOURTON RD
West Bourton
Cucklington
ROWL'S LA
CROOKED LA
WITHYBED LA
Plaishbridge Farm
Shanks House
WHITESTONE LA
Quarr
QUARR CROSS
SHUTE'S LA
BAILEY HILL
SHEPHERDS CHILL
JESSE'S HOLE HILL
Court Cotts
PO
WESTON HILL
PH
Hardings Farm
HARTMOOR HILL
Bye Farm
Filley Brook
LC
ORCHARD
BROAD CL
SOUTH ST
REED LA
Lower Farm
BROADMEAD LA
New Town
BARTON HILL
Kington Magna
CHURCH HILL
CHAPEL HILL
Stour Hill
A30
STOUR HILL
A30 Shaftesbury
Bailey Hill Farm
WOODHOUSE CROSS
B3081
Bainly Bottom
STOCK LA
LANGHAM LA
Langham
SP8
Sandley Stud
Folly Farm
Hartmoor
Bowden
Little Kington Farm

BA9

For full street detail of the highlighted area see page 216.

Scale: 1¼ inches to 1 mi

0 ¼ ½mile
0 250m 500m 750m 1 km

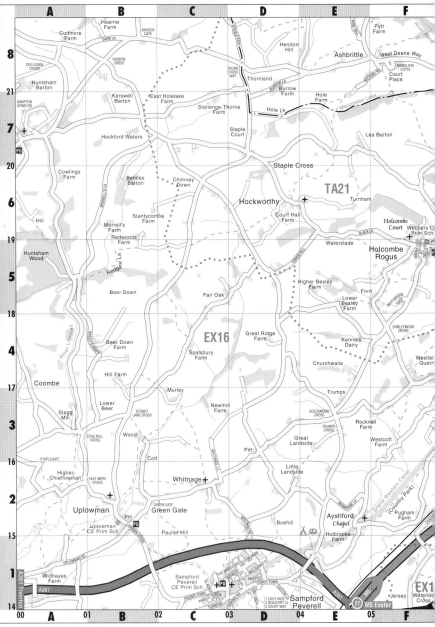

A | **B** | **C** | **D** | **E** | **F**

Cudmore Farm
Hearne Farm
DARK LA
BRODEN GATE

DOG DOWN CROSS
HENDON CROSS

Huntsham Barton
Kerswell Barton
East Holelake Farm

BAMPTON DOWN RD
PO

Hockford Waters
Stallenge-Thorne Farm
Staple Court

THORN CROSS WAY
Thornland
Heniton Hill
Burrow La
Hole La
Ashbrittle
West Deane Way
Pytt Farm
BOWCLIFFE COTTS
Court Place

Hole Farm
Marcombe Lake

Cowlings Farm
Bences Barton
Chimney Down
Staple Cross

TA21

Hill
Morrell's Farm
Slantycombe Farm
Hockworthy
Court Hall Farm
Turnham

MORRELL'S LA
Redwoods Farm
Waterslade
Holcombe Court
Webbers C Prim Sch

Huntsham Wood
REDGATE LA
Holcombe Rogus

BLACK LA

Beer Down
Fair Oak
Higher Besley Farm
Lower Besley Farm
Ford
WHITBROOK TREE

River Lowman
BALL'S LA MP
Beer Down Farm
Spalsbury Farm
Great Ridge Farm
EX16
Kennels Dairy
DURLEYMOOR CROSS

Hill Farm
Churchwalls
Westlei Quarr

Coombe
Lower Beer
Murley
Newmill Farm
Trumps

Stagg Mill
STONEY LANE CROSS
GOLDSMOOR CROSS
TRUMPS CROSS
Rocknell Farm

STAG MILL CROSS
Wood
Cott
Great Landside
Westcott Farm

STAPLEGATE
Pitt
Little Landside

Higher Chieflowman
EAST MERE CROSS
Whitnage
WHITNAGE LA

Uplowman
PH
PO
Green Gate
GREEN GATE
Boehill
Ayshford Chapel
Pugham Farm

GREEN CROSS
Paullet Hill
Holbrooke Farm

Uplowman CE Prim Sch

Grand Western Canal (Country Park)

Widhayes Farm
UPLOWMAN RD
HIGHER TOWN
Sampford Peverell CE Prim Sch
THE BUTTLANDS
FORELANDS
FAIRFIELD
LOWER TOWN
27
M5 Exeter
Jersey
EX1
Waterloo Cross

A361 Tiverton
A361
HIGHER TOWN
PAULL RD
TURNPIKE
COLE RD
FADWAYS RD
Sampford Peverell
A361
M5

1 COOT HIDE
2 BEAUFORT CL
3 COURT WAY

Grand Western Canal

A | **B** | **C** | **D** | **E** | **F**
00 | 01 | 02 | 03 | 04 | 05

8
21
7
20
6
19
5
18
4
17
3
16
2
15
1
14

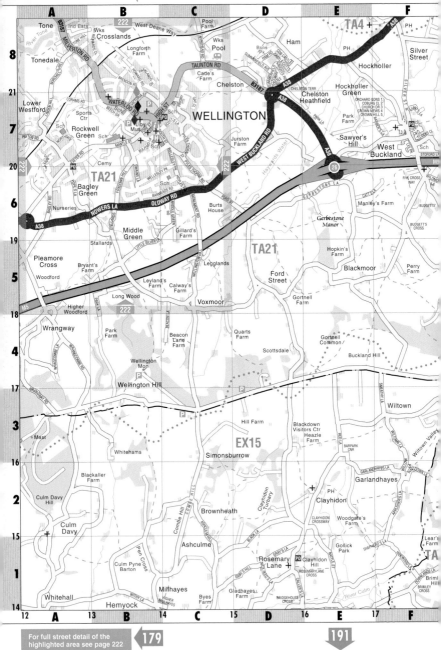

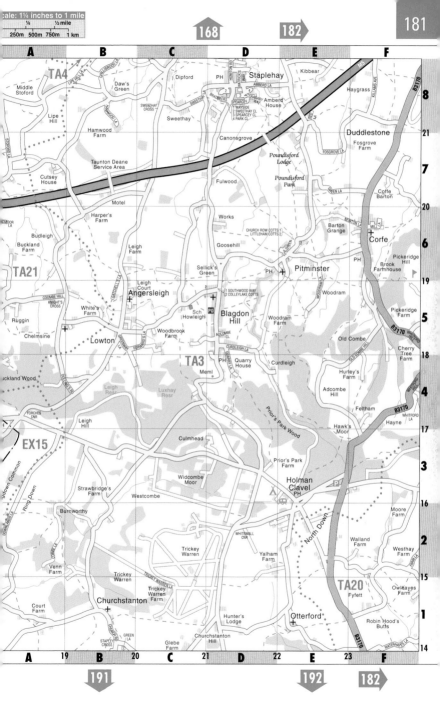

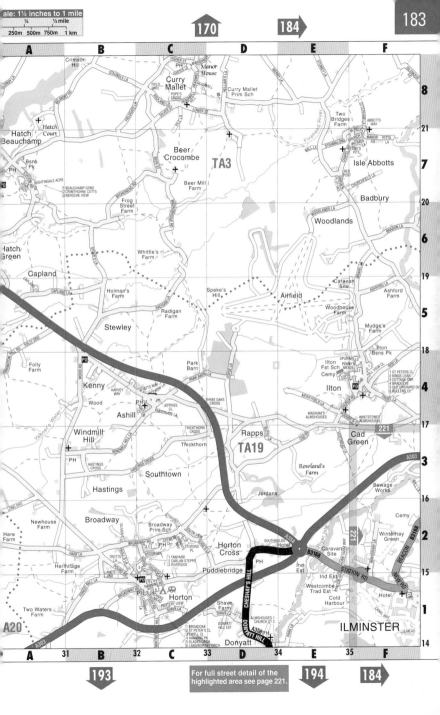

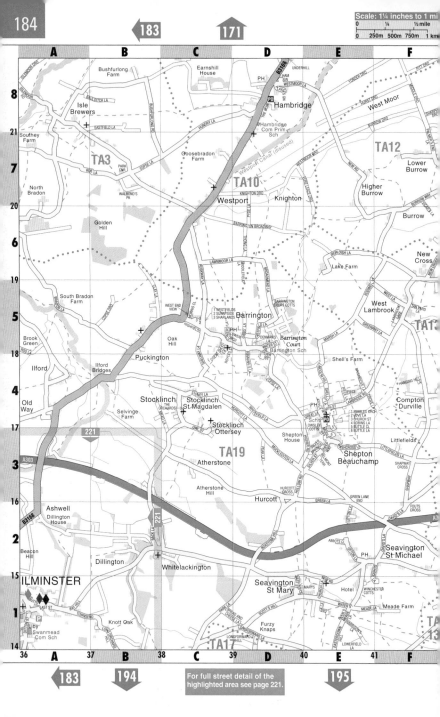

184

183

171

Scale: 1¼ inches to 1 mi
0   ¼   ½ mile
0   250m 500m 750m   1 km

A   B   C   D   E   F

UNDERHILL

B3168

Bushfurlong
Farm

Earnshill
House

HAM
IGN
WESTMOOR LA

PITT DRO

8

Isle
Brewers

BALLDITCH LA

EASTFIELD LA

PH

PO

HAM

Hambridge

West Moor

YONDER DRO

21

Southey
Farm

TA3

GEORGE LA

PARK
CNR

HUNGRY LA

Goosebradon
Farm

Hambridge
Com Prim
Sch

Westport Canal (disused)

HURST DRO

BURROW DRO

TA12

7

North
Bradon

ROE LA

WALROND'S
PK

Knighton DRO

TA10

Westport

Knighton

WESTMOOR DRO

NEW RD

Higher
Burrow

Lower
Burrow

BURROW WAY

20

BARRINGTON BROADWAY

THORNE LA

Burrow

6

Golden
Hill

LAWNMOOR LA

MIDDLEFIELD

BRACKNELL LA

IRON DISH LA

Lake Farm

New
Cross

19

South Bradon
Farm

BRADON LA

WEST END
VIEW

FIVE LANES DRO

BARRINGTON
COURT COTTS

1 WESTFIELDS
2 SUNNYSIDE
3 SHARLANDS

Barrington

West
Lambrook

TAN YARD LA

LAMBROOK

TA1

5

Brook
Green

Ilford

B3168

Ilford
Bridges

Oak
Hill

HIGHFIELD LA

PH

DENMANS

WATER ST

Barrington
Court
Barrington Sch

MARSH LA

GREENWAY LA

18

Old
Way

Puckington

LONG RD

ROTYE ST

CODE LA

Shell's Farm

HANGING HILL LA

4

Stocklinch

THE
ORCHARDS

STONEY LA

Stocklinch
St Magdalen

Selvinge
Farm

OKE ST

DITCHFIELD LA

Stocklinch
Ottersey

HURCOTT LA

MIDDLE LA

GREAT LA

PH

PO
Sch

1 PEBBLES ORCH
2 HOVE LA
3 CHURCH ST
4 ROBINS LA
5 BUTTLE LA
6 BUTTLE LA

LAMBROOK RD

LITTLEFIELDS

Compton
Durville

17

TA19

PEAK LA

Atherstone

MIDDLE MOOR LA

Shepton
House

OWSLEY
COTTS

Shepton
Beauchamp

SHAPWAY
CROSS

3

Atherstone
Hill

HURCOTT
CROSS

Hurcott

GREEN LA

GREEN LANE
END

A303

16

Ashwell

Dillington
House

B3168

BACK LA

221

WILLOW RD

ABBOTS CL

FOUTS
CROSS

A303

2

Beacon
Hill

Dillington

221

Whitelackington

STOUT LA
PH

Seavington
St Michael

15

ILMINSTER

EAST ST

TOWNSEND

Knott Oak

Seavington
St Mary

ST MARYS
CL

SCOTT'S HILL

Hotel

WATER ST

WINCHESTER
COTTS

MEADE LA

Meade Farm

1

Sch

Liby
Swanmead
Com Sch

LONGFORWARD
HILL

Furzy
Knaps

LOWERFIELD
LA

TA
13

TA17

14

36   A   37   B   38   C   39   D   40   E   41   F

183

194

For full street detail of the
highlighted area see page 221.

195

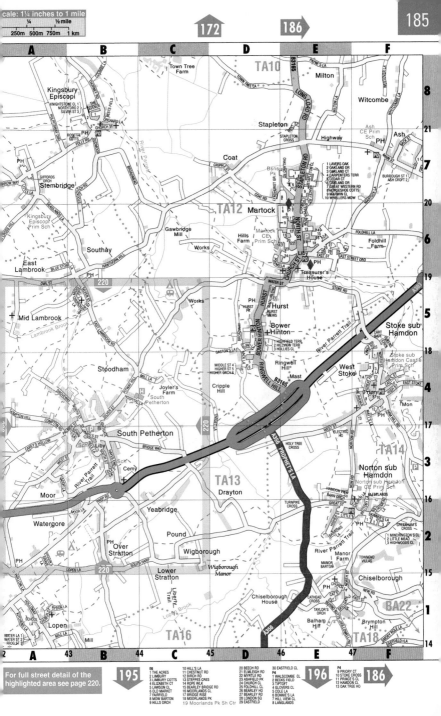

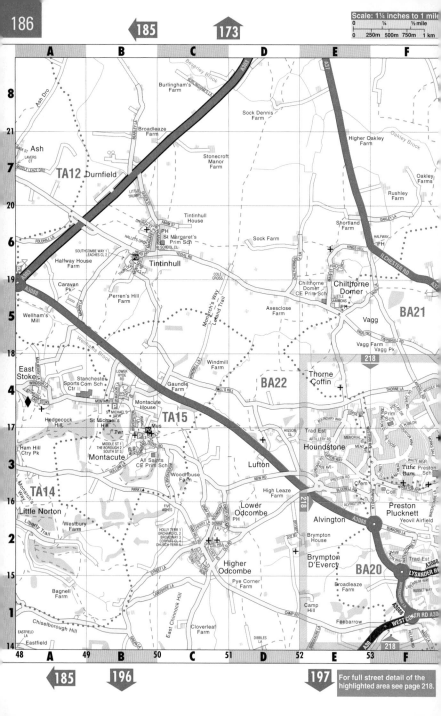

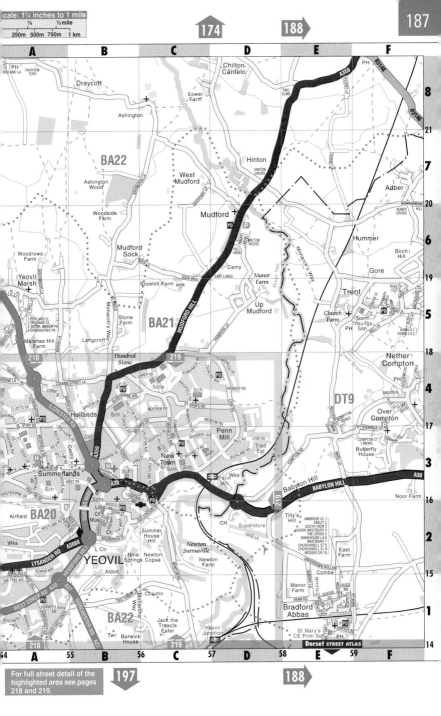

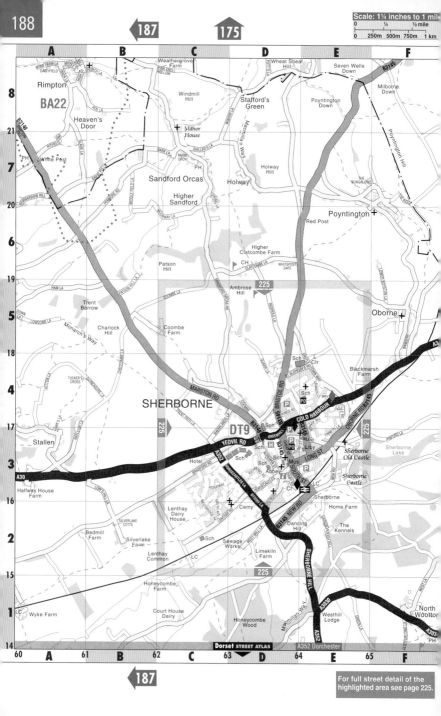

Scale: 1¼ inches to 1 mile

0   ¼   ½ mile
0   250m 500m 750m 1 km

A   B   C   D   E   F

8

Rimpton

BA22

Heaven's
Door

21

PH   Whitle Post

Weathergrove
Farm

Windmill
Hill

Manor
House

Wheat Sheaf
Hill

Stafford's
Green

Seven Wells
Down

B3145

Milborne
Down

Poyntington
Down

7

Sandford Orcas

Higher
Sandford

Holway
Hill

Holway

Poyntington Hill

THE
BUNGALOWS

20

Red Post

Poyntington

6

Patson
Hill

Higher
Clatcombe Farm

CH   WHITEPOST
GATE

Ambrose
Hill   225

Oborne

19

Trent
Barrow

Coombe
Farm

Charlock
Hill

Monarch's Way

5

TUCKER'S
CROSS

Sch   Ctr

Blackmarsh
Farm

18

MARSTON RD

SHERBORNE

225

DT9

YEOVIL RD

Sch

Hotel

Sch

Cold Harbour

P
PO

Sch

Sch

P
PO

H

P
PO

Licty

Mus

Abbey

Long St

P

Sherborne
Old Castle

Sherborne
Lake

Sherborne
Castle

4

Stallen

17

3

Halfway House
Farm

16

Bedmill
Farm

Silverlake
Farm

SILVERLAKE
COTTS

Lenthay
Dairy
House

Lenthay
Common

LC

Sch

Sewage
Works

Limekiln
Farm

225

Cemy

B3145 NEW RD

Dancing
Hill

Sherborne

Home Farm

The
Kennels

2

15

Honeycombe
Farm

Sherborne Hill

1

LC   Wyke Farm

Court House
Dairy

Honeycombe
Wood

Macmillan Way

A3030

Westhill
Lodge

North
Wootton

A303

PH

14

A30   A352   A3145   Dorset STREET ATLAS   A352 Dorchester   A303

60   A   61   B   62   C   63   D   64   E   65   F

**For full street detail of the
highlighted area see page 225.**

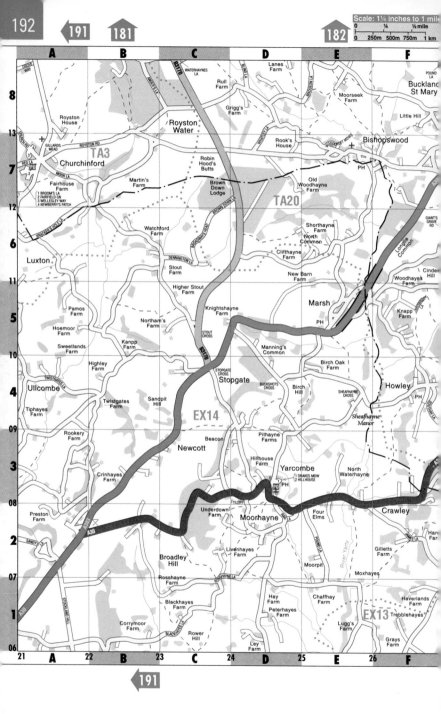

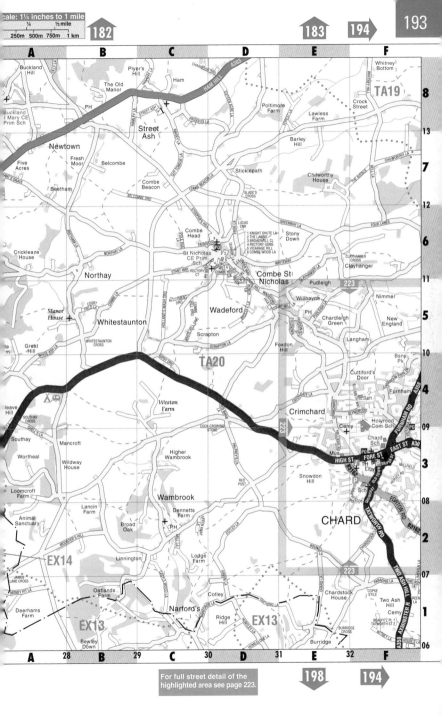

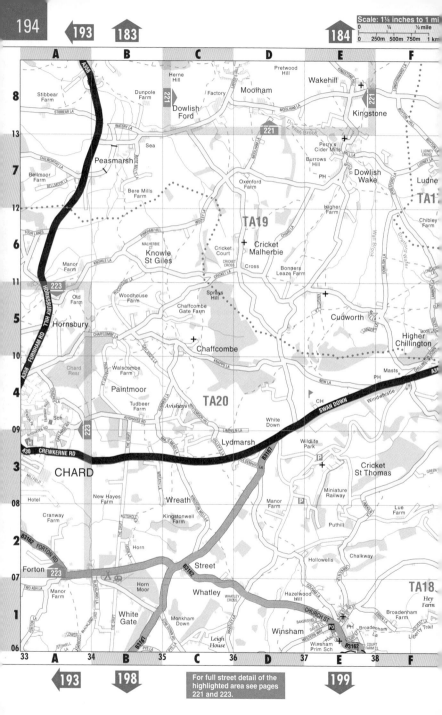

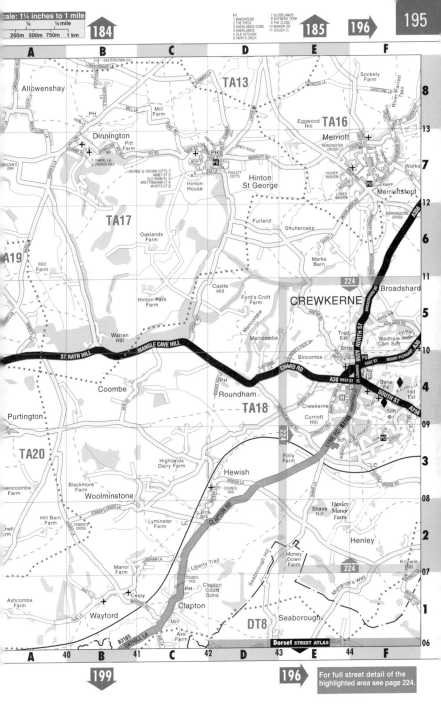

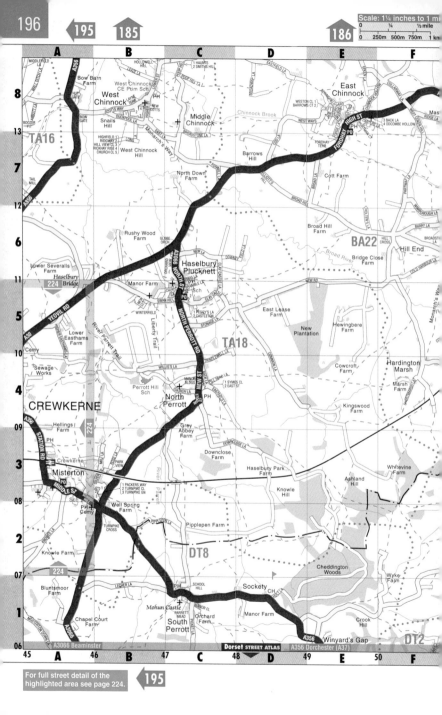

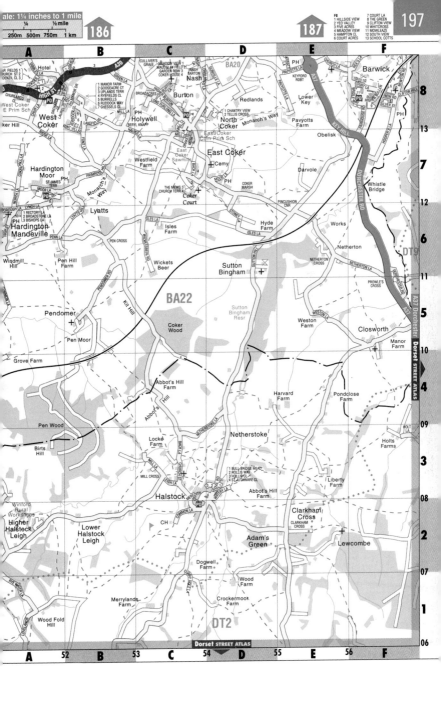

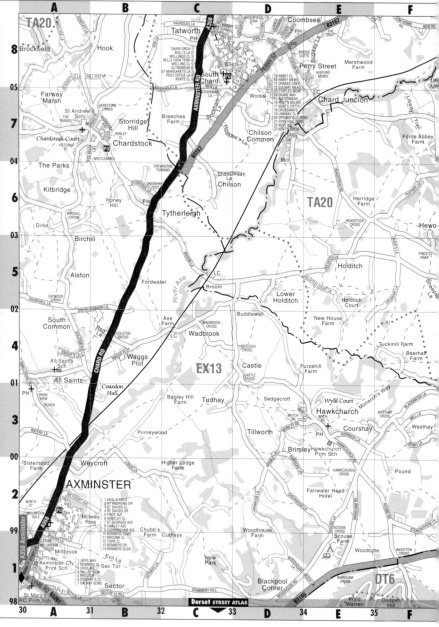

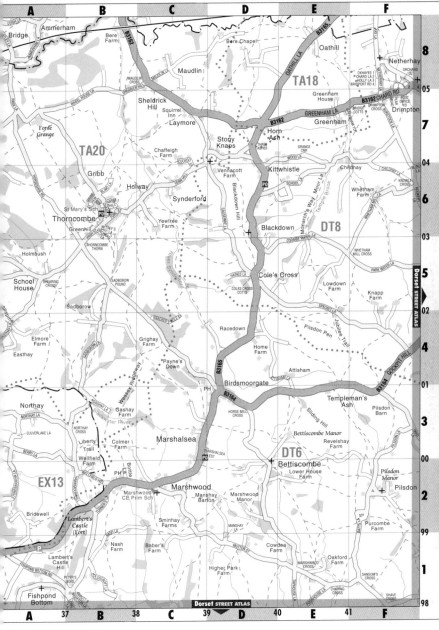

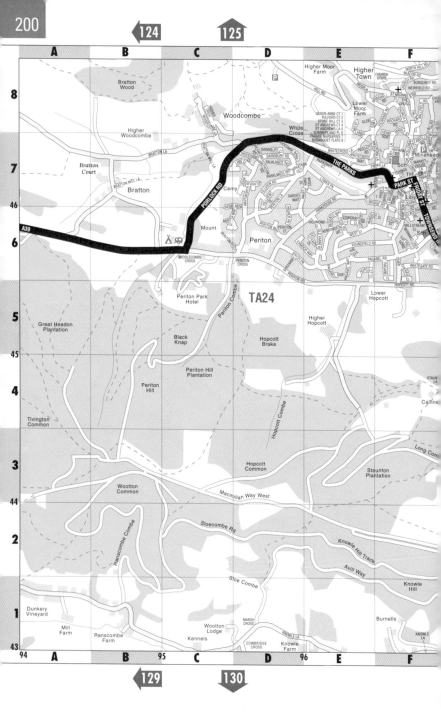

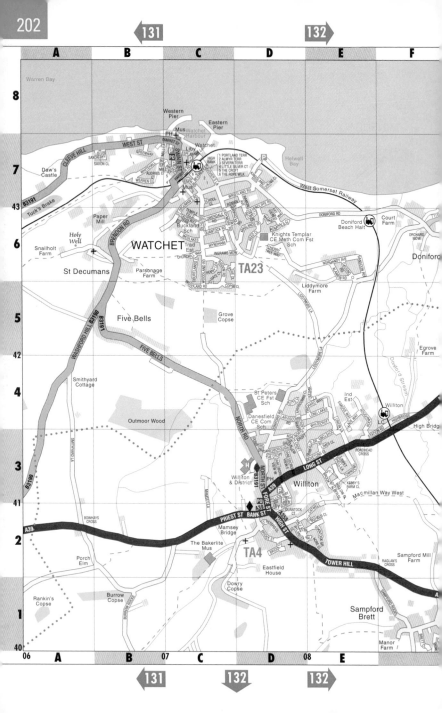

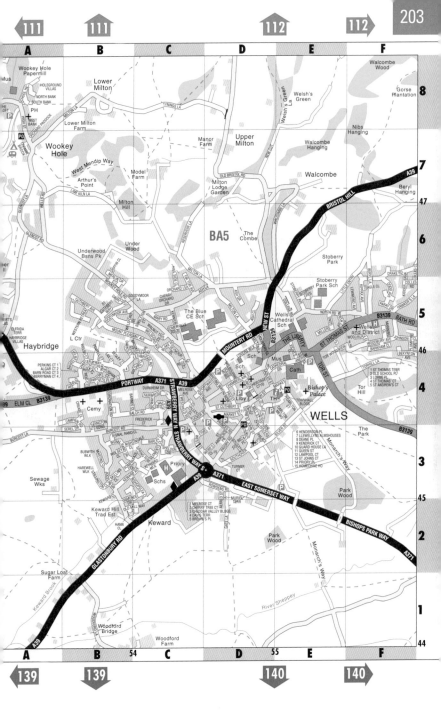

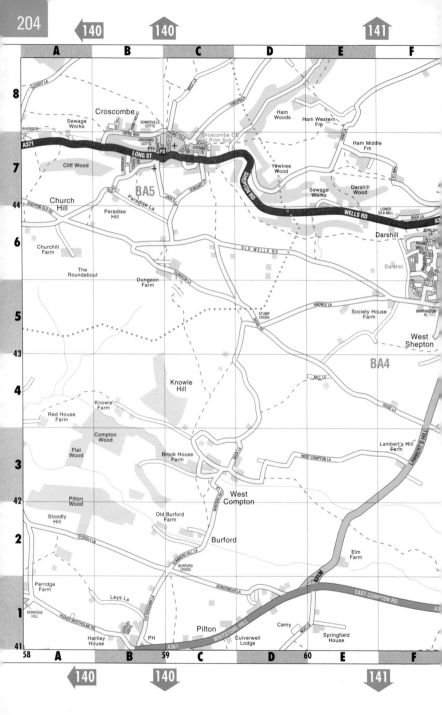

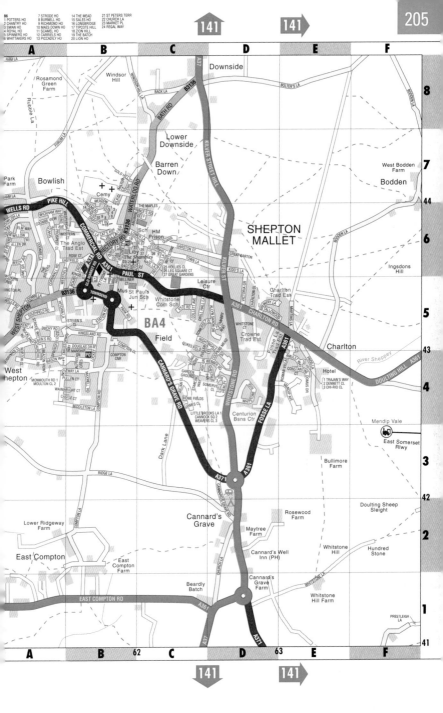

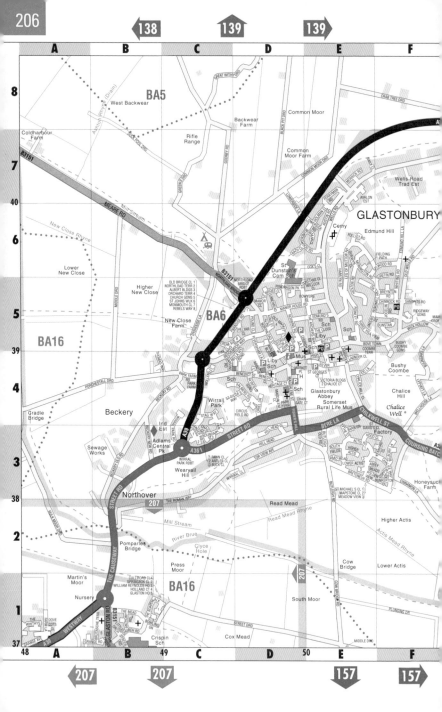

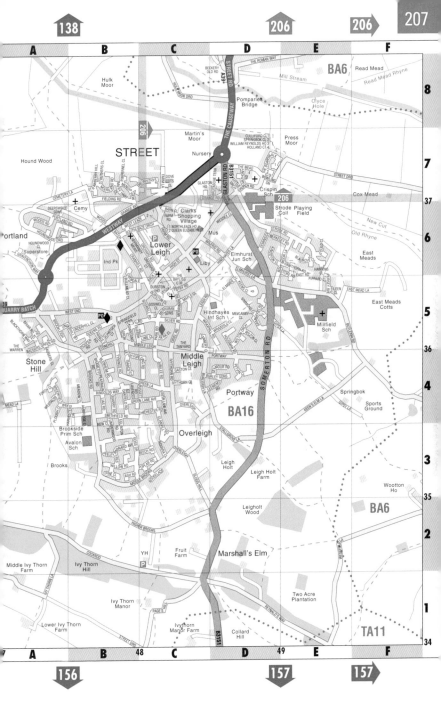

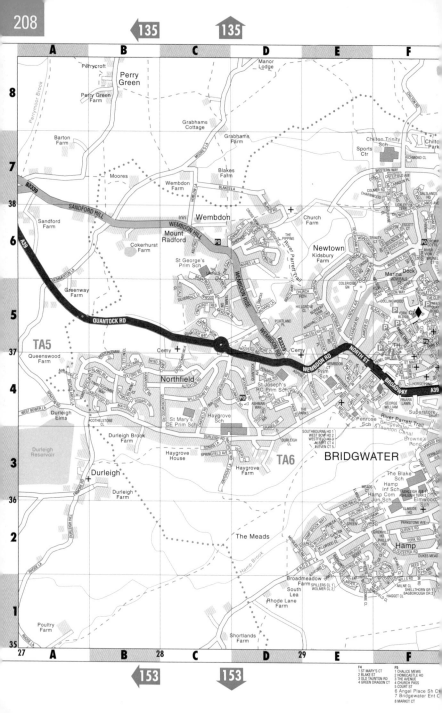

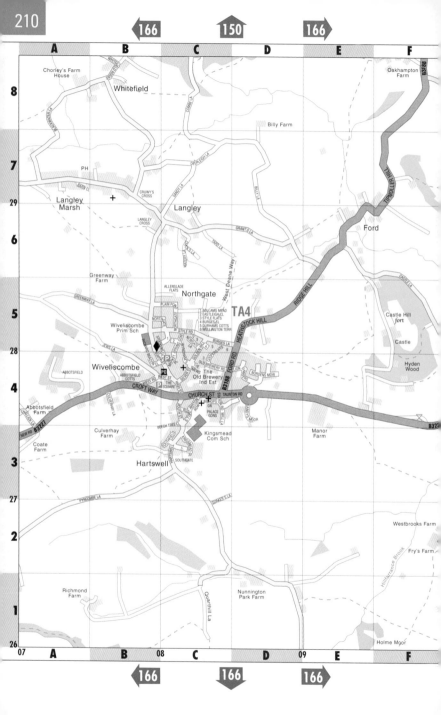

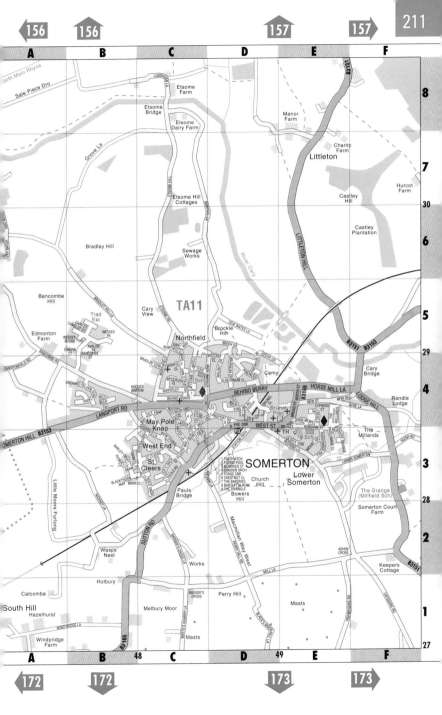

168 168

A B C D E F

8 Langford
A358
Langford

Rag Hill
Mills
Staplegrove Farm
Staplegrove
Whitmore Farm
Wellsprings
Wellsprings Prim Sch

7 PH
Langford Bridge
B3221
A358
A3065
Westerkirk
STAPLEGROVE RD
TA2

26 Taunton Trad Est
Yarlington
B3221
Somerset Nuffield
Sch
Larkspur
Rowbarton
GREENWAY RD

6 The Apple Bsns Ctr
Bsns Pk
Bindon Rd
Livingstone Way
Taunton Sch
Cyril St
STAPLEGROVE RD
KINGSTON RD

5 West Deane Way
Roughmoor House
River Tone
Frieze Hill
Cemy
TAUNTON
North Town
Belvedere Trad Est
Taunton

25 SILK MILLS RD
Longrun Farm
Somerset Coll of Art & Tech
Northfield
A3027
North St
Cty Crick
Arts Ctr

4 Manor House
Hospice
Bishop's Hull Prim Sch
Bishop's Hull
The Castle Sch
Tangier Superstore
Castle Mus
EAST ST A38

3 A3065
WELLINGTON RD
Cemy
TA Ctr
Coll
Cemy
A38
City Hall
Lib
UPPER HIGH ST

24 A38 STONEGALLOWS
WELLINGTON NEW RD
Wks
Taunton & Somerset Musgrove Park
TA1
Parkfield Prim Sch
Wilton
CH

2 Comeytrowe Orch
Copper Beeches
Galmington
Haseley Cl
Vivary Park
Haines Hill
Vivary Park

1 Comeytrowe Manor
Hofts Bridge
TA4
Comeytrowe
Sports Gd
Queens Coll
Sherford
Sherford Bridge Farm

23
20 A 21 B C 22 D E F

168 168

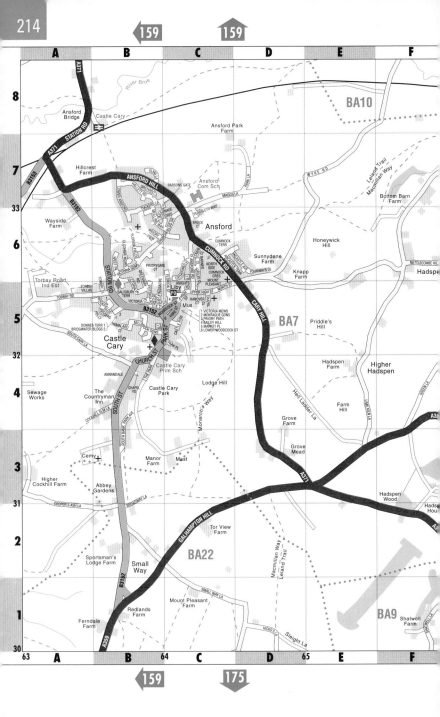

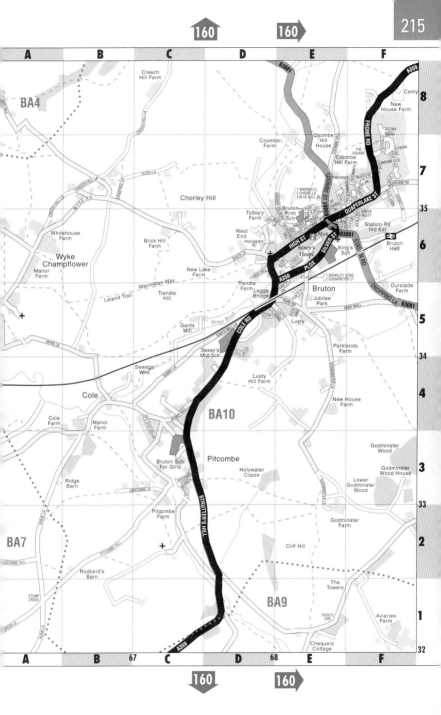

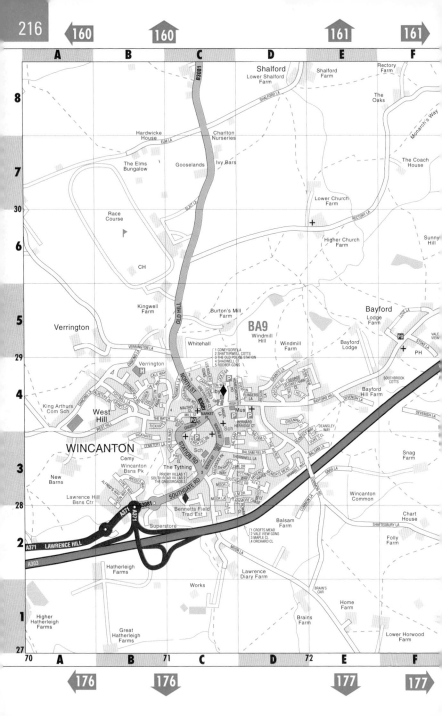

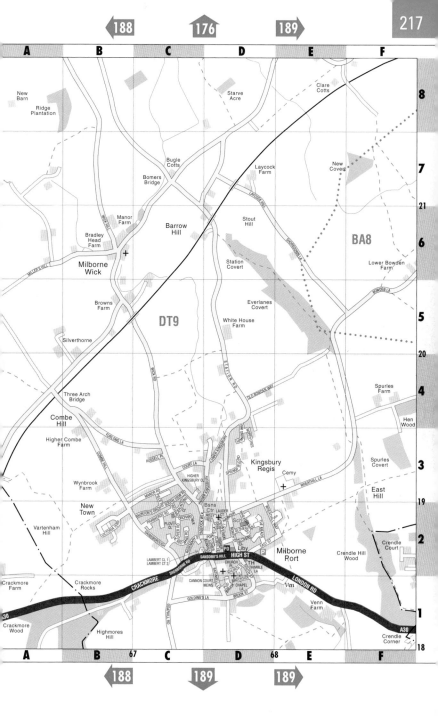

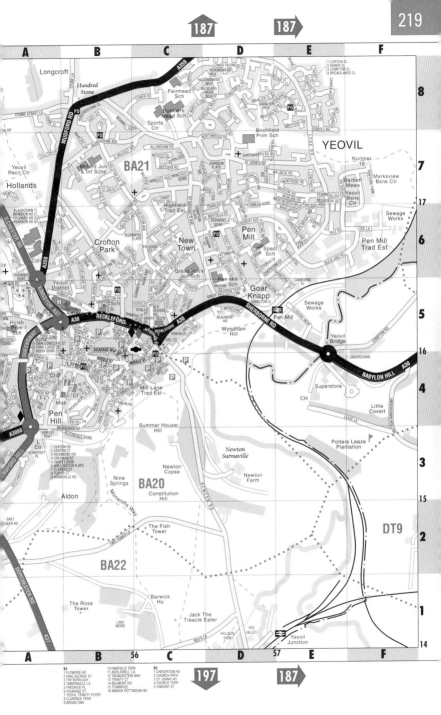

A | B | C | D | E | F

8

Longcroft
Hundred Stone
1 CORTON CL
2 ADBER CL
3 COMPTON CL
4 BROADLANDS CL
Fairmead Sch
Bucklers Mead Sch
Sports Ctr
LOWER FAIRMEAD RD
HERONSMEAD
FALCONSMEAD
BUCKLERS MEAD
CAVALIER CL
CAVALIER WLK

Yeovil Recn Ctr
Hollands
Mudford Jun & Inf Schs
BA21
Birchfield Prim Sch
CHATSWORTH RD
ST JOHN'S RD
JOHNSTON FLATS
THE HOLLIES
ALLINGHAM RD
WELBECK RD
WINTROSE RD
YEOVIL
Number 15
Marksview Bsns Ctr
Bartlett Mews
Yeovil Bsns Ctr

7

BLACKDOWN
BRANDON HO 2
ORCHARD HO 4
PEARSON HO 4
Coll
Highfield Trad Est
Crofton Park
New Town
Elizabeth Flats
FIELDING
Pen Mill
MAYFIELD RD
DERWENT GDNS
ROSEBERY AVE
Spec Sch
Pen Mill Trad Est
Sewage Works

17

6

Yeovil District
Grass Royal Jun Sch
Pen Mill Marine Sch
Goar Knapp
Pen Mill
Sewage Works
CAMBORNE PL
COMPTON RD

KINGSTON
Huish Prim Sch
QUEENSWAY
RECKLEFORD
A30
KIDDLES
RYALLS
DAMPIER
PERRY
SCHOOL
CHARLTON CL
WYNDHAM
BEAUMONT
SHERBORNE RD
Pen Mill
Yeovil Bridge
UNDERDOWN
BABYLON HILL
A30

5

16

1 SEATON RD
2 SEATON RD
3 RICHMOND HO
4 ORCHARD ST
5 SWIFT LODGE
6 WELLINGTON FLATS
7 CLARKES CT
8 TUDOR CT
9 HOMEVILLE HO
Mus
Pen Hill
L Ctr
SOMERSET PL
BRUNSWICK ST
ALTONDALE GDNS
Summer House Hill
Wyndham Hill
Superstore
CH
Little Covert
Potters Leaze Plantation

4

A3088
Nine Springs
Aldon
Monarchs Way
Newton Copse
Constitution Hill
BA20
Newton Surmaville
Newton Farm

3

EAST COKER RD
The Fish Tower
15

2

DORCHESTER RD
A37
BA22
The Rose Tower
Barwick Ho
Jack The Treacle Eater
LAKE MEWS
HILLSIDE VIEW
YEO VALLEY
Yeovil Junction
DT9

1

14

A | B | 56 | C | D | 57 | E | F

B4
1 FLOWERS HO
2 KING GEORGE ST
3 THE BOROUGH
4 TABERNACLE LA
5 FREDRICK PL
6 VICARAGE ST
7 YEOVIL TRINITY FOYER
8 CLARENCE TERR
9 BROAD OAK

10 HARFIELD TERR
11 ADDLEWELL LA
12 TAUNGSSTEIN WAY
13 TRINITY CT
14 BELMONT HO
15 TOWNRISE
16 MARSH POTTISTON HO

B5
1 CHEVERTON HO
2 CHURCH PATH
3 ST JOHNS HO
4 CHURCH TERR
5 VINCENT ST

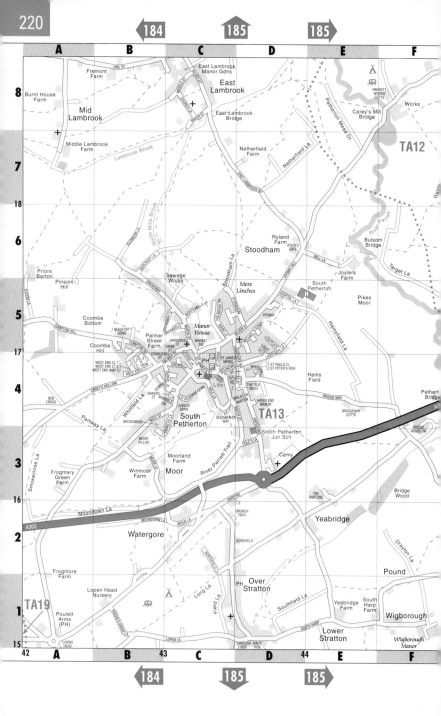

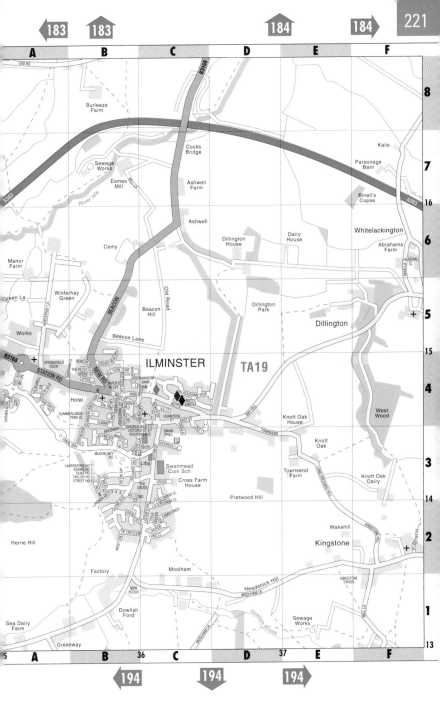

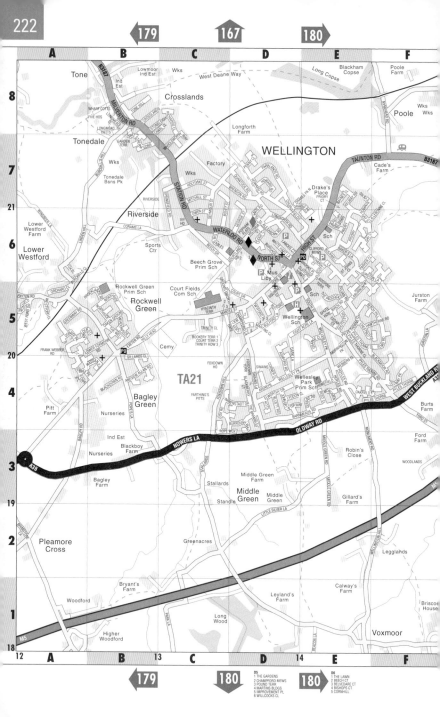

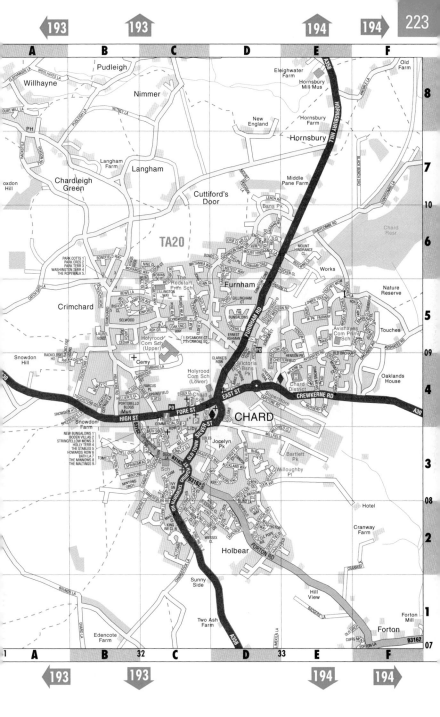

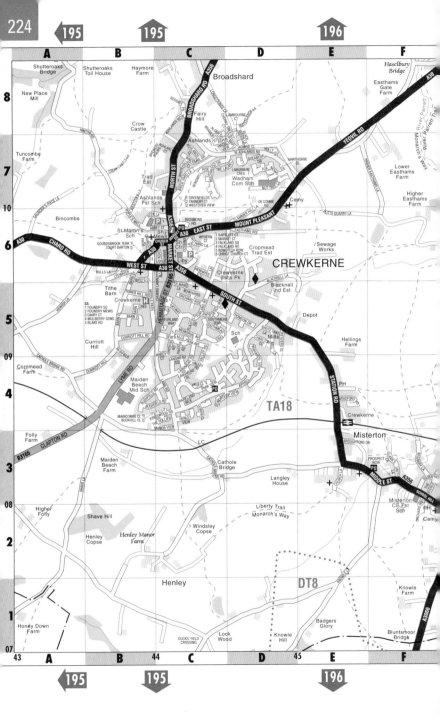

195 195 196

CREWKERNE

TA18

DT8

Broadshard

Misterton

Henley

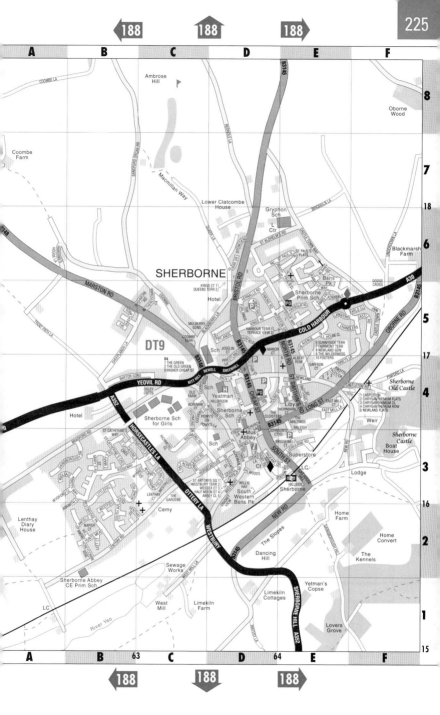

SHERBORNE

DT9

D4
1 THE GREEN
2 THE OLD GREEN
3 HIGHER CHEAP ST

1 CASTLETON
2 CHRYSANTHEMUM TERR
3 CHRYSANTHEMUM CL
4 CHRYSANTHEMUM ROW
5 NEWLAND FLATS

6 SUNNYSIDE TERR
7 FAIRMONT TERR
8 NEWLAND GDN
9 THE WILDERNESS
10 FOSTERS

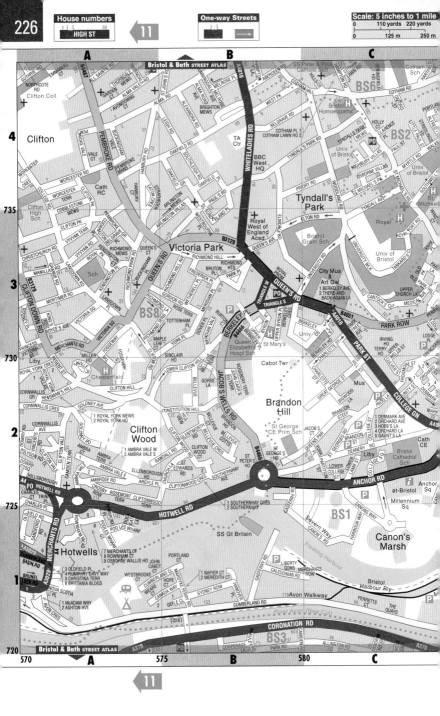

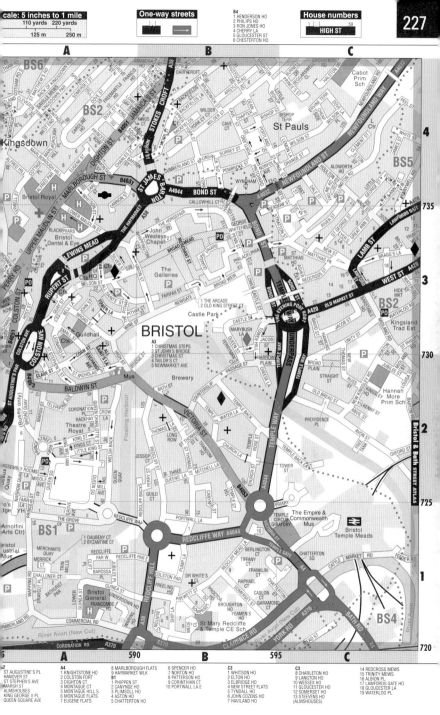

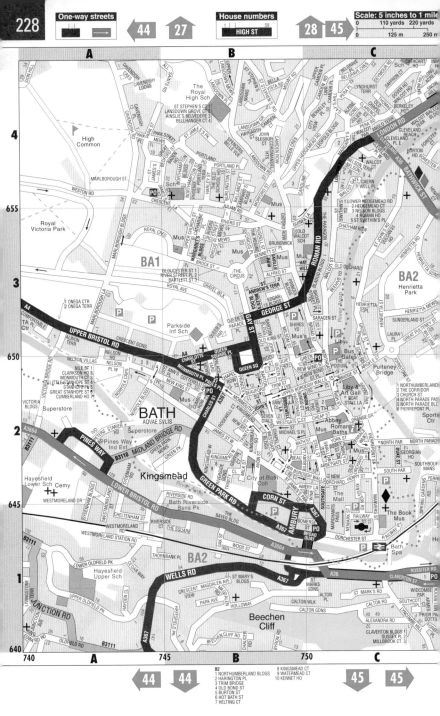

Index

Church Rd 6 Beckenham BR2.........**53** C6

Place name
May be abbreviated
on the map

Location number
Present when a number
indicates the place's
position in a crowded
area of mapping

Locality, town or village
Shown when more than
one place has the same
name

Postcode district
District for the indexed
place

Page and grid square
Page number and grid
reference for the standard
mapping

Public and commercial buildings are highlighted in magenta. Places of interest are highlighted in blue with a star ★

Abbreviations used in the index

Acad	**Academy**	Comm	**Common**	Gd	**Ground**	L	**Leisure**	Prom	**Promenade**
App	**Approach**	Cott	**Cottage**	Gdn	**Garden**	La	**Lane**	Rd	**Road**
Arc	**Arcade**	Cres	**Crescent**	Gn	**Green**	Liby	**Library**	Recn	**Recreation**
Ave	**Avenue**	Cswy	**Causeway**	Gr	**Grove**	Mdw	**Meadow**	Ret	**Retail**
Bglw	**Bungalow**	Ct	**Court**	H	**Hall**	Meml	**Memorial**	Sh	**Shopping**
Bldg	**Building**	Ctr	**Centre**	Ho	**House**	Mkt	**Market**	Sq	**Square**
Bsns, Bus	**Business**	Ctry	**Country**	Hospl	**Hospital**	Mus	**Museum**	St	**Street**
Bvd	**Boulevard**	Cty	**County**	HQ	**Headquarters**	Orch	**Orchard**	Sta	**Station**
Cath	**Cathedral**	Dr	**Drive**	Hts	**Heights**	Pal	**Palace**	Terr	**Terrace**
Cir	**Circus**	Dro	**Drove**	Ind	**Industrial**	Par	**Parade**	TH	**Town Hall**
Cl	**Close**	Ed	**Education**	Inst	**Institute**	Pas	**Passage**	Univ	**University**
Cnr	**Corner**	Emb	**Embankment**	Int	**International**	Pk	**Park**	Wk, Wlk	**Walk**
Coll	**College**	Est	**Estate**	Intc	**Interchange**	Pl	**Place**	Wr	**Water**
Com	**Community**	Ex	**Exhibition**	Junc	**Junction**	Prec	**Precinct**	Yd	**Yard**

Index of localities, towns and villages

A

Abbots Leigh	11 A8
Alhampton	159 C5
Aller	171 D8
Allerford	124 C4
Alweston	189 A1
Angersleigh	181 C5
Ash	185 F7
Ashbrittle	178 E8
Ashcott	156 B8
Ashill	183 B4
Avonmouth	4 B8
Axbridge	70 B1
Axminster	198 B2

B

Babcary	174 C7
Backwell	19 B6
Baltonsborough	158 A6
Bampton	163 C1
Banwell	51 B3
Barrington	184 D5
Barrow Gurney	20 E5
Barton St David	158 A2
Barwick	197 F8
Batcombe	142 D1
Bath	44 E8

Bath	228 A2
Bathampton	28 F1
Batheaston	28 F4
Bathford	29 C1
Bawdrip	136 E2
Beckington	101 E4
Berkley	121 A7
Berrow	84 E5
Bicknoller	132 F2
Biddisham	87 E8
Binegar	114 C7
Bishop Sutton	57 D3
Bishops Lydeard	167 F8
Bitton	25 E8
Blagdon	54 E2
Blagdon Hill	181 D5
Blatchbridge	143 F8
Bleadney	139 A8
Bleadon	67 C7
Blue Anchor	131 B6
Bourton	161 F1
Bradford Abbas	187 E1
Bradford on Tone	167 F1
Bratton Seymour	176 C8
Brean	65 F5
Brendon	122 A4
Brent Knoll	86 A1
Bridgehampton	174 A6
Bridgwater	208 E3
Bristol	22 E6
Bristol	227 B3

Broadway	183 B2
Brockley	18 C2
Brompton Ralph	150 C3
Brompton Regis	148 B2
Brushford	163 D4
Bruton	160 C5
Bruton	215 E5
Buckhorn Weston	177 D3
Buckland Dinham	100 B3
Buckland St Mary	182 F8
Burcott	139 E8
Burlescombe	179 B3
Burnham-on-Sea	104 D8
Burrington	53 F3
Burrowbridge	154 F1
Burtle	137 D6
Butleigh	157 D4

C

Camerton	78 E8
Cannington	135 C2
Carhampton	131 B5
Castle Cary	159 D2
Castle Cary	214 B5
Catcott	137 D2
Chantry	117 F3
Chapel Leigh	167 A8
Chapmanslade	121 C5
Chard	193 E2

Chard	223 D4
Chard Junction	198 E7
Chardstock	198 B7
Charlcombe	27 E3
Charlton Adam	173 F7
Charlton Horethorne	176 B2
Charlton Mackrell	173 E7
Cheddar	90 D8
Chedzoy	154 E8
Chesterblade	142 A4
Chew Magna	39 C4
Chew Stoke	56 D8
Chewton Mendip	94 E7
Chilcompton	96 C4
Chilthorne Domer	186 E5
Chilton Polden	137 B2
Chilton Trinity	135 F2
Chipstable	165 E6
Chiselborough	185 F1
Churchill	52 F5
Churchill Green	52 D5
Churchinford	192 A7
Churchstanton	181 B1
Clapton	195 C1
Clapton in Gordano	8 E8
Clatworthy	149 F1
Claverham	17 E1
Clayhanger	165 C1
Cleeve	35 C8
Clevedon	6 B3

Clutton	58 E3
Cold Ashton	12 F6
Coleford	116 F7
Colerne	29 F8
Combe St Nicholas	193 D6
Comwich	135 B5
Compton Bishop	69 A3
Compton Dando	41 D6
Compton Dundon	157 B4
Compton Martin	74 A7
Congresbury	34 E4
Corfe	181 F6
Corsley Heath	144 E8
Corston	43 B7
Cossington	136 F3
Cotford St Luke	167 E6
Coultings	134 F4
Coxley	139 F6
Cranmore	142 B6
Creech St Michael	169 D4
Crewkerne	195 E5
Crewkerne	224 D6
Cricket St Thomas	194 E3
Croscombe	140 E7
Crowcombe	204 B8
Crowcombe	151 C7
Cucklington	177 D6
Culverhays	132 F1
Curland	182 D4
Curry Mallet	183 C8
Curry Rivel	171 C4

D

Dinder 140 D7
Dinnington 195 B7
Ditcheat 159 C7
Donyatt 183 D1
Doulting 141 E6
Downhead 142 C8
Doynton 12 A8
Draycott 90 E2
Drayton 171 E3
Drimpton 199 F7
Dulverton 163 E6
Dundry 21 D2
Dunkerton 61 E4
Dunster 130 F6
Dunster 201 E2

E

East Anstey 162 E5
East Brent 86 D5
East Chinnock 196 E8
East Coker 197 D7
East Harptree 74 E4
East Huntspill 136 E7
East Lambrook 220 C8
East Pennard 140 B1
East Quantoxhead 133 B6
Easton 111 A4
Easton-in-Gordano 4 A4
Edington 137 C3
Edingworth 86 F7
Emborough 95 C3
Enmore 153 A6
Evercreech 141 E1
Exford 128 D1

F

Failand 10 C3
Farmborough 59 F5
Farrington Gurney 77 A3
Faulkland 80 E2
Felton 37 C8
Filehead Magdalen 198 F8
Fitzhead 166 F7
Fivehead 170 F2
Flax Bourton 19 F7
Freshford 64 B5
Frome 119 E4

G

Galhampton 175 D8
Glastonbury 139 D2
Glastonbury 206 F6
Goathurst 153 B5
Golsoncott 131 D2
Great Elm 118 F7
Greenham 179 B7
Gurney Slade 114 F7

H

Halse 167 B6
Halstock 197 C3
Hambridge 184 D8
Hardington
  Mandeville 197 A6
Haselbury Plucknett ... 196 C6
Hatch Beauchamp 183 A7
Hawkridge 146 D1
Hemington 99 B7
Hemyock 180 B1
Henstridge 190 A6
Hewish 33 C5
High Ham 156 A2
High Littleton 59 C1
Highbridge 104 E3
Higher Chillington ... 194 F5
Higher Odcombe 186 C2
Higher Vexford 150 E6
Hinton Blewett 75 F6
Hinton Charterhouse ... 63 F1
Hinton St George 195 D7

Hockworthy 178 D6
Holcombe 116 C8
Holcombe Rogus 178 F5
Holford 133 D4
Holman Clavel 181 E3
Holton 176 C5
Holywell Lake 179 E7
Horningsham 144 D4
Horrington 113 A1
Horsington 176 D2
Horton 183 C1
Houndstone 218 A6
Huish Champflower 165 F8
Hutton 49 E2

I

Ilchester 173 E1
Ilminster 184 A1
Ilminster 221 C4
Ilton 183 E4
Isle Abbotts 183 F7

K

Keenthorne 134 D2
Keinton Mandeville ... 158 B1
Kelston 26 C3
Kenn 16 F7
Keynsham 24 E3
Kilmersdon 98 B5
Kilmington 161 F7
Kilve 133 C6
Kingsbridge 148 E8
Kingsbury Episcopi ... 185 A8
Kingsdon 173 E4
Kingsdown 29 F3
Kingston Seymour 16 C2
Kingston St Mary 168 D8
Kington Magna 177 E2
Kingweston 157 E2
Knole 173 A4
Knowstone 162 A2

L

Langford 53 C5
Langford Budville ... 166 E4
Langport 172 B5
Langridge 27 F7
Laverton 100 F7
Leigh upon Mendip ... 116 F3
Leigh Woods 11 D6
Limpley Stoke 64 A6
Litton 75 F2
Locking 50 A4
Long Ashton 11 A1
Long Sutton 172 F4
Lopen 185 A1
Lovington 158 F1
Loxton 68 C4
Lydeard St Lawrence .. 151 B3
Lydford-on-Fosse 158 C2
Lympsham 67 B1
Lyng 170 C7

M

Mackham 191 A4
Maiden Bradley 144 C1
Mark 106 D4
Marksbury 42 B1
Marnhull 190 F5
Marsh 192 E5
Marshfield 13 E8
Marshwood 199 C2
Marston Magna 174 F1
Martock 185 D6
Meare 138 D4
Mells 118 B7
Merriott 195 E7
Middlezoy 155 B3
Midford 63 C6
Midsomer Norton 78 B3
Milborne Port 189 C5
Milborne Port 217 E2
Millmoor 179 E1

Milton Clevedon 160 A8
Milverton 166 F4
Minehead 125 D3
Minehead 201 A8
Monksilver 158 B8
Monkton Combe 45 F1
Monkton Farleigh 46 F7
Monkton Heathfield .. 213 E8
Montacute 186 B3
Moorlinch 155 E7
Mudford 187 D6
Mudgley 138 D8

N

Nailsea 8 E3
Nether Compton 187 F4
Nether Stowey 134 A3
Newton St Loe 43 D6
North Brewham 161 A7
North Cadbury 175 D6
North Curry 170 C4
North End 17 F3
North Newton 153 F2
North Perrott 196 C4
North Petherton 153 F4
North Wootton 140 C4
Norton Fitzwarren .. 168 B4
Norton St Philip 81 F4
Norton sub Hamdon .. 185 F3
Nunney 143 C8
Nynehead 167 C1

O

Oake 167 D4
Oakhill 115 A3
Oldways End 162 E3
Othery 155 B2
Oxenpill 138 C4

P

Panborough 138 F8
Parbrook 158 D7
Paulton 77 F5
Pawlett 136 A5
Peasedown St John .. 79 C8
Penselwood 161 D2
Pensford 40 C4
Pill 4 C4
Pilton 140 F4
Pitcombe 215 D3
Pitminster 181 E6
Pitney 172 C7
Podimore 174 A3
Porlock 124 A4
Portbury 3 E3
Portishead 2 B4
Poyntington 188 E6
Priddy 92 D3
Priston 61 B5
Publow 40 F5
Puriton 136 C4
Purse Caundle 189 D4
Purtington 195 A4
Pylle 141 B1

Q

Queen Camel 174 F3

R

Radsbury 126 B8
Radstock 78 E1
Rawridge 191 F1
Redhill 36 D3
Rimpton 188 A8
Rockwell Green 222 B5
Rode 101 F8
Rodhuish 131 B2
Rodney Stoke 91 A1
Rooksbridge 87 C5
Rowberrow 53 A1
Rudge 102 D5

Ruishton 169 C3
Runnington 179 F8

S

Saltford 25 D2
Sampford Arundel ... 179 E5
Sampford Brett 132 C3
Sampford Peverell ... 178 E1
Sandford 52 A3
Sandford Orcas 188 C7
Seaborough 195 E1
Seavington 184 D1
Shapwick 137 F1
Shepton Beauchamp .. 184 E3
Shepton Mallet 141 C7
Shepton Mallet 205 D6
Shepton Montague ... 160 B2
Sherborne 188 C4
Sherborne 225 C6
Shillingford 164 E2
Shipham 70 F7
Shirehampton 4 E7
Shockerwick 29 F5
Shoulsbarrow
  Common 126 A2
Simonsbath 127 B2
Skilgate 164 E6
Somerton 173 B6
Somerton 211 D3
South Cadbury 175 C4
South Cheriton 176 D3
South Perrott 196 C1
South Petherton ... 220 C4
Southstoke 62 E7
Southwick 83 F2
Sparkford 175 A5
Spaxton 152 E8
Stalbridge 190 C4
Standerwick 102 C2
Stanton Drew 39 F1
Staple Fitzpaine .. 182 C5
Staplegrove 212 C8
Staplehay 181 D8
Star 52 D1
Stawell 137 A1
Sticklepath 149 E7
Stocklinch 184 C4
Stogumber 150 D8
Stogursey 134 C5
Stoke St Gregory .. 170 E6
Stoke St Mary 169 C1
Stoke St Michael .. 116 B2
Stoke sub Hamdon .. 185 F5
Stoke Trister 177 B7
Stolford 134 F8
Ston Easton 95 B8
Stoney Stratton ... 141 F2
Stopgate 192 C4
Stourton 161 F5
Stourton Caundle .. 189 F2
Stratton-on-the-Fosse . 96 F2
Street 157 B7
Street 207 B7
Sutton Mallet 155 B7

T

Tatworth 198 C8
Taunton 168 D4
Taunton 212 D5
Temple Cloud 58 E1
Templecombe 176 E1
Theale 109 D1
Thorncombe 199 B6
Thurloxton 153 D1
Tickenham 7 F4
Timberscombe 130 C4
Timsbury 60 B1
Tintinhull 186 C6
Trent 187 E5
Trowbridge 83 F6
Trudoxhill 143 C6

U

Ubley 55 E1
Uplowman 178 B2

Uppottery 191 F2
Upper Swainswick ... 28 B5
Upton 164 F6
Upton Cheyney 26 B8
Upton Noble 142 F2

V

Vobster 117 C4

W

Walton 156 E4
Wanstrow 142 F4
Washford 131 F4
Watchet 132 B6
Watchet 202 B6
Watchfield 105 D2
Waterrow 165 F4
Wedmore 108 D2
Wellington 180 C2
Wellington 222 D4
Wellow 62 D1
Wells 110 A2
Wembdon 208 C4
West Anstey 162 C6
West Bagborough .. 151 E6
West Buckland 180 F1
West Camel 174 D1
West Chinnock 196 B8
West Coker 197 A4
West Harptree 74 E1
West Huntspill ... 136 A4
West Monkton 169 C4
West Pennard 140 B8
West Quantoxhead . 132 E1
Westbury sub Mendip 110 D6
Westcombe 142 B4
Western Common ... 145 B8
Westhay 138 B7
Westleigh 179 A4
Weston 27 B6
Weston-super-Mare . 48 C4
Westonzoyland ... 154 E1
Westwood 64 E1
Whatley 118 D3
Wheddon Cross 129 E3
Whitchurch 23 D1
White Cross 76 F7
Wick St Lawrence .. 32 B7
Williton 202 D2
Wincanton 176 D3
Wincanton 216 B4
Winford 37 F7
Wingfield 83 D8
Winscombe 69 F7
Winsford 147 C4
Winsham 194 E8
Winsley 64 D2
Witham Friary 143 C2
Withypool 146 C4
Wiveliscombe 166 B8
Wiveliscombe 210 B1
Wookey 139 E3
Wookey Hole 203 A7
Woolavington 136 F7
Woolley 27 A2
Woolminstone 195 B8
Wootton Courtenay . 129 F7
Wrantage 170 A4
Wraxall 9 C1
Wrington 35 E3

Y

Yarcombe 192 C2
Yarley 139 C2
Yatton 34 C4
Yenston 189 F7
Yeovil 187 B6
Yeovil 218 F2
Yeovilton 174 A7

Z

Zeals 161 A5

5

5c Bsns Ctr BS21 . . . . .6 B1

A

Abbas & Templecombe CE
Prim Sch BA8 . . . . .176 E1
Abbey Cl
Curry Rivel TA10 . . . . .171 D4
Keynsham BS31 . . . . .24 F6
Sherborne DT9 . . . . .225 D3
Tatworth TA20 . . . . .198 D8
Wookey BA5 . . . . .139 D8
Abbey Ct BA2 . . . . .45 B7
Abbey Fields TA10 . . . . . .171 D4
Abbey Gn BA1 . . . . .228 C2
Abbey Hill Dro TA3 . . . . . .182 E5
Abbey La BA3 . . . . .64 A4
Abbey Meads BA6 . . . . . .206 E3
Abbey Mews TA20 . . . . . .198 D8
Abbey Pk BS31 . . . . .24 F6
Abbey Rd Bristol BS9 . . . . . . .5 F7
Chilcompton BA3 . . . . .96 D2
Sherborne DT9 . . . . .225 D4
Stratton-on-the-Fosse BA3 . .96 F2
Washford TA23 . . . . .131 E3
Yeovil BA21 . . . . .218 D6
Abbey St Bath BA1 . . . . . .228 C2
Crewkerne TA18 . . . . .224 C6
Hinton St George TA17 . . . .195 C7
Abbey View Bath BA2 . . . . .45 B5
Radstock BA3 . . . . .79 A3
Abbey View Gdns BA2 . . . .45 B5
Abbeygate St BA1 . . . . . .228 C2
Abbeywood Dr BS9 . . . . .5 C5
Abbot's Cl BS22 . . . . .32 A3
Abbots Cl Bristol BS14 . . . .23 A3
Burnham-On-Sea TA8 . . . . .104 B6
Ilminster TA19 . . . . .221 B3
Oxenpill BA6 . . . . .138 C4
Seavington TA19 . . . . .184 E2
Abbots Ct BA6 . . . . .206 D4
Abbots Fish Ho* BA6 . . .138 D4
Abbots Horn BS48 . . . . .8 D2
Abbots Leigh Rd BS8 . . . . .11 C7
Abbots Meade BA21 . . . .218 D5
Abbots Way
Minehead TA24 . . . . .200 C6
Pilton BA4 . . . . .140 E3
Sherborne DT9 . . . . .225 B3
Yeovil BA21 . . . . .218 D6
Abbotsbury Rd BS48 . . . . . .8 D1
Abbotsfield TA4 . . . . .210 A4
Abbotsfield Cotts TA4 . . .210 B4
Abbott La TA16 . . . . .196 A8
Abbott's Wootton La
DT6 . . . . .199 B1
Abbotts Farm Cl BS39 . . . .77 D5
Abbotts Rd BA22 . . . . .173 D1
Abbotts Way TA3 . . . . .183 F7
Abels La DT9 . . . . .187 F5
Aberdeen Rd BS6 . . . . . . .226 B4
Abingdon Gdns BA2 . . . . . .62 D8
Abingdon St TA8 . . . . .104 B6
Abington Cross TA24 . . . .124 B4
Ablake La TA10 . . . . .172 C5
Ableton Wlk BS9 . . . . .5 C5
Abon Ho BS9 . . . . .5 C4
Acacia Ave BS23 . . . . .49 B8
Acacia Ct BS31 . . . . .24 C4
Acacia Dr BA11 . . . . .120 C7
Acacia Gdns TA2 . . . . . . .213 E7
Acacia Gr BA2 . . . . .44 C3
Acacia Rd BA3 . . . . .78 E1
Accommodation Rd BS24 .66 E6
Acer Dr BA21 . . . . .218 C7
Ackland's Dro TA10 . . . . .155 F4
Acland Round TA4 . . . . . .167 E6
Acombe Cross TA3 . . . . . .191 E8
Aconite Cl BS22 . . . . .32 B5
Acorn Cl Frome BA11 . . . .119 D5
Highbridge TA9 . . . . .104 D4
Acorn Gr BS13 . . . . .21 E6
Acre La TA11 . . . . .211 F4
Acreman Ct DT9 . . . . .225 C4
Acreman Pl DT9 . . . . .225 D3
Acreman St DT9 . . . . .225 D4
Acres Ct BA22 . . . . .197 F8
Acres The 1 TA12 . . . . . . .185 E6
Acresbush Cl BS13 . . . . . . .22 A5
Actis Rd BA6 . . . . .206 E3
Adam St TA8 . . . . .104 B6
Adam's La TA5 . . . . .134 D6
Adams Cl Highbridge TA9 .104 C2
Peasedown St John BA2 . . . .79 D8
Adams Ct 5 BS8 . . . . .11 F6
Adams Ho TA19 . . . . .221 B3
Adams Mdw TA19 . . . . . . .221 A4
Adastral Rd BS24 . . . . .50 D4
Adber Cl BA21 . . . . .219 E8
Adber Cross DT9 . . . . .187 F6
Adcombe Cl TA3 . . . . .181 D5
Adcombe Rd TA2 . . . . .213 B8
Adder La TA7 . . . . .169 F8
Adderwell BA11 . . . . .120 A3
Adderwell Cl BA11 . . . . . .120 A3
Addicott Rd BS23 . . . . .48 E6
Addiscombe Rd
Bristol BS14 . . . . .23 B5
Weston-Super-Mare BS23 . . .48 E4
Addison Gr TA2 . . . . .212 E6
Addlewell La 11 BA20 . . .219 B4
Adlams Central Pk BA6 . .206 B3
Admiral Blake Mus* TA6 209 A4
Admiral's Mead BA6 . . . .157 E4
Admiral's Wlk BS20 . . . . . . .2 B5
Admirals Cl
Sherborne DT9 . . . . .225 E5
Watchet TA23 . . . . .202 D6
Admirals Ct TA6 . . . . .208 F5
Admiralty Way TA1 . . . . .213 C5
Adsborough Hill TA2 . . . .169 D7
Adsborough La TA2 . . . . .169 D7
Adscombe Ave TA6 . . . . .209 C6
Adscombe La TA5 . . . . . . .134 A1
Aelfric Mdw BS20 . . . . .2 F4
Ainslie's Belvedere BA1 .228 B4
Ainstey Dr BA22 . . . . .175 A4
Airey Hos TA13 . . . . .220 D1
Airport Rd BS14 . . . . .23 A8
Airport Rdbt BS24 . . . . .49 E7
Aisecome Way BS22 . . . . .49 C6
Akeman Cl BA21 . . . . .218 D7
Akeman Way BS11 . . . . .4 C8
Alamein Rd TA23 . . . . . . .202 E6
Alard Rd BS4 . . . . .22 F7
Alastair Cl BA21 . . . . .218 F7
Alastair Dr BA21 . . . . .218 F7
Albany BS23 . . . . .30 F1
Albany Cl DT9 . . . . .225 E6
Albany Rd BA2 . . . . .44 C6
Albemarle Rd TA1 . . . . . .212 F5
Albemarle Row 9 BS8 . . .11 F6
Albert Ave
Peasedown St John BA2 . . . .79 C7
Weston-Super-Mare BS23 . . .48 E6
Albert Bldgs BA6 . . . . . . .206 D5
Albert Cl BA21 . . . . .218 E7
Albert Ct Bridgwater TA6 . .208 E4
14 Taunton TA1 . . . . .213 A4
Weston-Super-Mare BS23 . . .48 E6
Albert Pl Bath BA2 . . . . .45 C1
Portishead BS20 . . . . .2 D4
Albert Quadrant BS23 . . . .48 E8
Albert Rd Clevedon BS21 . . . .6 C3
Keynsham BS31 . . . . .24 E5
Portishead BS20 . . . . .2 D5
Weston-Super-Mare BS23 . . .48 E6
Albert Row DT9 . . . . .225 E4
Albert St TA6 . . . . .208 E4
Albert Terr BA2 . . . . .44 C6
Albion Cl TA6 . . . . .209 B5
Albion Pl 16 Bristol BS2 . .227 C3
Frome BA11 . . . . .119 D3
Albion Rd BA22 . . . . .174 A2
Albion Terr BA1 . . . . .228 A3
Alburys BS40 . . . . .35 D3
Alcombe Cross TA24 . . . .201 B5
Alcombe Rd TA24 . . . . . . .201 A5
Aldeburgh Pl BA14 . . . . . . .83 F6
Alder Cl
North Petherton TA6 . . . . . .153 F3
Taunton TA1 . . . . .213 D1
Williton TA4 . . . . .202 E3
Alder Gr Crewkerne TA18 .224 C7
Yeovil BA20 . . . . .218 E2
Alder Terr BA3 . . . . .78 E2
Alder Way BA2 . . . . .62 D8
Alder Wlk BA11 . . . . .120 B7
Aldercombe Rd BS9 . . . . . . .5 C8
Alderdown Cl BS11 . . . . . . .5 A8
Alderley Rd BA2 . . . . .44 B4
Alderney Rd TA6 . . . . . . .209 C3
Aldondale Gdns BA20 . . .219 B3
Aldwick Ave BS13 . . . . .22 C3
Aldwick La BS40 . . . . .54 C7
Aldworth Ho BS2 . . . . . . .227 C4
Alec Ricketts Cl BA2 . . . . .43 F5
Alexander Bldgs 12 BA1 . . .28 B1
Alexander Cl TA3 . . . . . . .169 D5
Alexander Ho 5 BS23 . . . . .48 F4
Alexander Mews BS23 . . . .48 E7
Alexander Pl BA3 . . . . .64 C6
Alexander Way BS49 . . . . .34 B7
Alexanders Cl BA6 . . . . . .138 C4
Alexandra Ct BS21 . . . . .6 C4
Alexandra Gdns TA24 . . .201 A6
Alexandra Par BS23 . . . . . .48 E7
Alexandra Pk BS39 . . . . . . .77 F5
Alexandra Pl BA2 . . . . .45 C1
Alexandra Rd Bath BA2 . .228 C1
Bridgwater TA6 . . . . .208 E5
Bristol BS8 . . . . .226 B4
Bristol, Highridge BS13 . . . . .21 F7
Clevedon BS21 . . . . .6 C4
Frome BA11 . . . . .119 F4
Minehead TA24 . . . . .201 A6
Wellington TA21 . . . . .222 D6
Yeovil BA21 . . . . .219 D6
Alexandra Terr BS39 . . . . .77 E5
Alford La BA4,BA7 . . . . . .159 B4
Alfoxton Rd TA6 . . . . .208 C4
Alfred Cres BA4 . . . . .205 B4
Alfred Ct BS23 . . . . .48 E7
Alfred Hill BS2 . . . . .227 A4
Alfred Par BS2 . . . . .227 A4
Alfred Pl BS2 . . . . .226 C4
Alfred St Bath BA1 . . . . . .228 B3
Taunton TA1 . . . . .213 B4
Wells BA5 . . . . .203 D3
Weston-Super-Mare BS23 . . .48 E8
Alfred's Twr* BA10 . . . . .161 C6
Alfred's Way BA9 . . . . . . .216 B3
Algar Ct BA5 . . . . .203 B4
Alice St BA11 . . . . .143 A6
Alison Gdns BS48 . . . . .19 A7
All Hallows Prep Sch
BA4 . . . . .142 C6
All Saints CE Prim Sch
TA15 . . . . .186 B3
All Saints East Clevedon CE
Prim Sch BS21 . . . . .6 F4
All Saints La BS21 . . . . .6 F4
All Saints Rd BA1 . . . . . . .228 B4
All Saints Sch EX13 . . . . .198 A4
All Saints' La BS1 . . . . . .227 A2
All Saints' Rd Bristol BS8 .226 A4
Weston-Super-Mare BS23 . . .30 E1
All Saints' St BS1 . . . . . . .227 A3
All Saints' Terr TA6 . . . . .209 B4
Allandale Rd TA8 . . . . . . .104 A8
Allanmead Rd BS14 . . . . . .23 B8
Allen Dr BA4 . . . . .205 A6
Allen Rd TA6 . . . . .208 F1
Allens La Shipham BS25 . . . .70 F8
Wells BA5 . . . . .112 E1
Allenslade Flats TA4 . . . .210 C5
Aller BS24 . . . . .49 B2
Aller Dro Aller TA10 . . . . .171 D8
NonRoady TA7 . . . . .155 C1
Aller Par BS24 . . . . .49 B2
Allermoor Dro BS28 . . . . .138 B8
Allerpark La TA24 . . . . . .123 F3
Allerton Cres BS14 . . . . . . .23 B4
Allerton Gdns BS14 . . . . . .23 B5
Allerton Rd
Bridgwater TA6 . . . . .209 B7
Bristol BS14 . . . . .23 B4
Allingham Rd BA21 . . . . .219 C7
Allington Cl TA1 . . . . . . .213 E4
Allington Gdns BS48 . . . . .18 C8
Allington Rd BS3 . . . . . . .226 C1
Allotment Dro
Combe St Nicholas TA20 . . .193 C5
Glastonbury BA16 . . . . .138 D1
Allotment Rd BA22 . . . . . .175 C3
Allshire La EX16 . . . . .162 F3
Allyn Saxon Dr BA4 . . . . .205 D5
Alma Rd BS8 . . . . .226 B4
Alma Road Ave BS8 . . . . .226 B4
Alma St Taunton TA1 . . . . .213 A3
Weston-Super-Mare BS23 . . .48 E7
Alma Vale Rd BS8 . . . . . . .226 A4
Almond Cl BS22 . . . . .32 A1
Almond Tree Cl TA6 . . . . .209 D4
Almshouse La BA22 . . . . .173 E1
Almshouses
5 Bristol BS1 . . . . .227 A2
Donyatt TA19 . . . . .183 D1
Marshfield SN14 . . . . .13 E8
Almyr Terr TA23 . . . . .202 C7
Alpha Ho TA9 . . . . .104 E3
Alpine Cl BS39 . . . . .77 F4
Alpine Gdns BA1 . . . . . . .228 C4
Alpine Rd BS39 . . . . .77 F4
Alston Cl TA1 . . . . .212 C1
Alston Sutton Rd BS26 . . . .88 F4
Alstone Gdns TA9 . . . . . . .104 C2
Alstone La TA9 . . . . .104 C2
Alstone Rd TA9 . . . . .104 C2
Alstone Wildlife Pk*
TA9 . . . . .104 C3
Alton Pl BA2 . . . . .228 C1
Alverstoke BS14 . . . . .22 F7
Alveston Wlk BS9 . . . . .5 B7
Alvington La BA22 . . . . . .218 B5
Alweston DT9 . . . . .189 A1
Ambares Ct BA3 . . . . .96 F8
Amber Mead TA1 . . . . . . .213 D3
Amberd La TA3 . . . . .181 D8
Amberey Rd BS23 . . . . .48 F5
Amberlands Cl BS48 . . . . .19 A7
Amberley Cl
Keinton Mandeville TA11 . .158 A1
Keynsham BS31 . . . . .24 E4
Amberley Gdns 3 BS48 . . .8 D1
Ambleside Rd BA2 . . . . . . .44 C2
Ambra Ct BS8 . . . . .226 A2
Ambra Terr BS8 . . . . .226 A2
Ambra Vale BS8 . . . . .226 A2
Ambra Vale E BS8 . . . . . .226 A2
Ambra Vale S BS8 . . . . . .226 A2
Ambra Vale W BS8 . . . . . .226 A2
Ambridge BA16 . . . . .207 B4
Ambrose Cl DT9 . . . . .187 E1
Ambrose Rd BS8 . . . . .226 A2
Ambury BA1 . . . . .228 B1
Amercombe Wlk BS14 . . . .23 D7
American Mus in Britain*
BA2 .46 A5
Amery La BA1 . . . . .228 C2
Ames La BA3 . . . . .98 B6
Amesbury Dr BS24 . . . . . . .67 B6
Ammerdown Terr BA3 . . . .98 F7
Ammerham La TA20 . . . . .199 A8
Amor Pl TA1 . . . . .212 D2
Amory Rd TA22 . . . . .163 D6
Amulet Way BA4 . . . . .205 E4
Ancastle Ave BA7 . . . . . . .214 D6
Ancastle Terr BA7 . . . . . . .214 C6
Anchor Cl BA3 . . . . .116 E8
Anchor Cnr BA9 . . . . .176 D6
Anchor Hill BA9 . . . . .176 D6
Anchor Rd Bathford BA1 . . .27 B1
Bristol BS1 . . . . .226 C2
Coleford BA3 . . . . .116 E8
Anchor Sq BS1 . . . . .226 C2
Anchor St TA23 . . . . .202 C7
Anchor Stables TA24 . . . .123 E4
Anchor Way BS20 . . . . .4 D4
Ancliff Sq BA15 . . . . .64 E4
Ander's La TA3 . . . . .192 B8
Andereach Cl BS14 . . . . . . .23 B8
Andersfield Cl TA6 . . . . . .208 A4
Andrew Allan Rd TA21 . . .222 B4
Andrew's Hill TA22 . . . . .163 D6
Andrew's Hill Cross
TA22 . . . . .163 C6
Andruss Dr BS41 . . . . .21 D2
Angel Cres TA6 . . . . .208 F5
Angel La BA9 . . . . .216 C4
Angel Place Sh Ctr 6
TA6 . . . . .208 F5
Angel Row TA3 . . . . .170 F2
Angela Cl TA1 . . . . .212 D2
Anglesey Cotts DT10 . . . .190 B4
Anglo Terr BA1 . . . . .228 C4
Anglo Trad Est The BA4 . .205 B6
Angwin Cl BA4 . . . . .205 B6
Animal Farm Ctry Pk*
TA8 .66 B2
Annaly Rd BS27 . . . . .90 A7
Annandale BA7 . . . . .214 B4
Annandale Ave BS22 . . . . .31 E1
Ansford Com Sch BA7 . . .214 C7
Ansford Hill BA7 . . . . . . .214 B7
Ansford Rd BA7 . . . . .214 C6
Anson Cl BS31 . . . . .25 D2
Anson Rd Locking BS24 . . . .50 B5
Weston-Super-Mare BS22 . . .31 D4
Anson Way TA6 . . . . .208 F5
Anthony Rd BA16 . . . . . . .207 D7
Antler Cl BA6 . . . . .206 C3
Antona Ct BS11 . . . . .4 D7
Antona Dr BS11 . . . . .4 D7
Anvil Rd BS49 . . . . .17 F1
Anvil St BS2 . . . . .227 C2
Apex Dr TA9 . . . . .104 C4
Aplins Cl TA19 . . . . .221 B3
Apple Alley BA11 . . . . . . .119 F5
Apple Bsns Ctr The TA2 .212 B6
Apple Cl TA19 . . . . .194 E7
Apple Dumpling Cnr
BS28 . . . . .108 C3
Apple La BA11 . . . . .119 F5
Apple Tree Cl TA6 . . . . . . .209 D4
Apple Tree Dr BS25 . . . . . .70 A8
Appleby Wlk BS4 . . . . .22 D7
Applecroft BA2 . . . . .79 E6
Appledore 4 BS22 . . . . . . .31 F2
Appledore Cl BS14 . . . . . . .23 B8
Applehayes La EX15 . . . . .180 F2
Appletree Ct BS22 . . . . . . .32 B2
Appletree Mews BS22 . . . .32 B2
Appley Cross TA21 . . . . . .179 B8
Appsley Cl BS22 . . . . .31 C1
Apricot Tree Cl TA6 . . . . .209 D5
Apsley Rd BA1 . . . . .44 A7
Aquara Cl BA16 . . . . .207 C3
Arbutus Dr BS9 . . . . .5 C8
Arcade The 2 BS1 . . . . . .227 B3
Arch Cl BS41 . . . . .10 F1
Arch La TA3 . . . . .170 E4
Archbishop Cranmer CE Com
Prim Sch TA1 . . . . .213 A4
Archer Ct BS21 . . . . .6 D4
Archer Dr TA8 . . . . .104 C6
Archer Wlk BS14 . . . . .23 E6
Archers Way The BA6 . . . .206 E5
Arches The BA2 . . . . .44 A6
Archgrove BS41 . . . . .10 F1
Archstone Ave TA5 . . . . . .135 F2
Archway St BA2 . . . . .45 B5
Arden Cl BS22 . . . . .31 F3
Ardern Cl BS9 . . . . .5 B8
Ardmore BS8 . . . . .11 D7
Ardwyn TA21 . . . . .222 D4
Argyle Ave BS23 . . . . .48 F4
Argyle Pl BS8 . . . . .226 A2
Argyle Rd Bristol BS2 . . . .227 B4
Clevedon BS21 . . . . .6 D6
Argyle St BA2 . . . . .228 C2
Argyle Terr BA2 . . . . .44 C6
Arlington Cl
Bridgwater TA6 . . . . .209 A2
Yeovil BA21 . . . . .218 C7
Arlington Mans BS8 . . . . .226 B4
Arlington Rd BA2 . . . . .44 D5
Arlington Villas BS8 . . . .226 B3
Armada Ho BS2 . . . . .227 A4
Armada Pl BS1 . . . . .227 B4
Armada Rd BS14 . . . . .23 A6
Armes Ct BA2 . . . . .228 C1
Armoury Rd BA22 . . . . . .218 A6
Armstrong Rd BA11 . . . . .120 B5
Armtech Row BA22 . . . . .218 B6
Arnewood Gdns BA20 . . .218 F2
Arnold Cl TA2 . . . . .212 F7
Arnold Noad Cnr BA14 . . .83 E3
Arnold's Way BS49 . . . . . . .17 A2
Arnolfini (Arts Ctr) BS1 .227 A1
Arnor Cl BS22 . . . . .32 A4
Arrowfield Cl BS14 . . . . . .23 A2
Artemesia Ave BS22 . . . . .49 E8
Arthurswood Rd BS13 . . . .22 A4
Artillery Rd BA22 . . . . . . .218 A6
Arun Gr TA1 . . . . .213 D4
Arundel Cl BS13 . . . . .22 B5
Arundel Rd Bath BA1 . . . . .28 A1
Clevedon BS21 . . . . .6 D3
Yeovil BA21 . . . . .219 E6
Arundel Wlk BS31 . . . . . . .24 D5
Arundell Ct BS23 . . . . .48 E8
Arundell Rd BS23 . . . . .30 E1
Arundells Way TA3 . . . . .169 D4
Ascension Ho BA2 . . . . . . .44 D4
Ash Brook BS39 . . . . .59 D1
Ash CE Prim Sch TA12 . . .185 F7
Ash Cl Bridgwater TA6 . . . .209 D4
Wells BA5 . . . . .203 D5
Winscombe BS25 . . . . .52 A1
Ash Cres TA1 . . . . .212 B2
Ash Croft TA12 . . . . .185 F7
Ash Cross TA3 . . . . .169 E2
Ash Ct BS14 . . . . .23 A6
Ash End BA8 . . . . .189 F7
Ash Gr Bath BA2 . . . . .44 C4
Chard TA20 . . . . .223 C5
Clevedon BS21 . . . . .6 E4
Ash Gr *continued*
Minehead TA24 . . . . .200 D7
Shepton Mallet BA4 . . . . . .205 C4
Wells BA5 . . . . .203 D5
Weston-Super-Mare BS23 . . .48 E2
Ash Grove Way TA6 . . . . .209 D7
Ash Hay Dro BA5 . . . . . . .139 C6
Ash Hayes Dr BS48 . . . . . . .8 E1
Ash Hayes Rd BS48 . . . . . . .8 F1
Ash Ho TA8 . . . . .65 F2
Ash La
Shepton Beauchamp TA19 .184 E4
Wells BA5 . . . . .203 C5
Winsford TA24 . . . . .147 B6
Ash Moor Dro BA5 . . . . . .139 C6
Ash Rd Banwell BS29 . . . . .50 E4
Street BA16 . . . . .207 B3
Ash Tree Cl Bleadon BS24 . .67 C6
Burnham-On-Sea TA8 . . . . . .85 A3
Ash Tree Cres TA8 . . . . . . .85 A3
Ash Tree Ct BA3 . . . . .78 E1
Ash Tree Pl TA8 . . . . .85 A3
Ash Tree Rd TA8 . . . . .85 A3
Ash Trees TA9 . . . . .86 C5
Ash Wlk BA8 . . . . .190 A6
Ashbeer Hill TA4 . . . . . . .150 D7
Ashbourne Cres TA1 . . . .213 D3
Ashbrooke House Sch
BS23 . . . . .48 D6
Ashbury Dr BS22 . . . . .31 B2
Ashcombe Ct
Ilminster TA19 . . . . .221 B4
Weston-Super-Mare BS23 . . .48 F7
Ashcombe Gdns BS23 . . . .49 A8
Ashcombe La
Alweston DT9 . . . . .189 B2
Ilminster TA19 . . . . .221 B4
Ashcombe Park Rd BS23 .31 A1
Ashcombe Prim Sch
BS23 . . . . .49 A7
Ashcombe Rd BS23 . . . . . .48 F7
Ashcott BS14 . . . . .22 F7
Ashcott Cl TA8 . . . . .104 C6
Ashcott Dr TA8 . . . . .104 C6
Ashcott Pl TA8 . . . . .104 C6
Ashcott Prim Sch TA7 . . .156 B8
Ashcott Rd BA6 . . . . .138 D3
Ashcroft Chard TA20 . . . .223 D2
Weston-Super-Mare BS24 . . .49 B2
Ashcroft Ave BS31 . . . . . . .24 D5
Ashcroft Rd BS9 . . . . .5 C7
Ashculm Hill EX15 . . . . . .180 C2
Ashdene Rd BS23 . . . . .49 A8
Ashdown Ct BS9 . . . . .5 F8
Ashdown Rd BS20 . . . . .2 A6
Ashel's Batch BA3 . . . . . . .94 C8
Ashen Cross TA11 . . . . . . .211 E2
Asher La BS2 . . . . .227 C3
Ashes La BA3 . . . . .64 A4
Ashey La Burrington BS40 . .54 A5
Cheddar BS27 . . . . .90 B8
Ashfield TA20 . . . . .223 D2
Ashfield Cl BA11 . . . . . . .143 C6
Ashfield Pk 23 TA12 . . . . .185 E6
Ashford Cl
Bridgwater TA6 . . . . .208 E2
Milverton TA4 . . . . .167 A4
Ashford Dr BS24 . . . . .49 A1
Ashford Gr BA21 . . . . . . .219 B7
Ashford La TA19 . . . . .183 F5
Ashford Rd Bath BA2 . . . . .44 D4
Redhill BS40 . . . . .36 E4
Taunton TA1 . . . . .212 C2
Wellington TA21 . . . . .222 D4
Ashgrove BA2 . . . . .79 D8
Ashgrove Ave BS8 . . . . . . .11 B7
Ashgrove Ct BA2 . . . . .79 D8
Ashill Cl TA1 . . . . .212 E1
Ashington La BA21 . . . . .187 B7
Ashland Ct TA18 . . . . .224 C7
Ashland La TA4 . . . . .150 B4
Ashland Rd BS13 . . . . .22 A4
Ashlands Cl TA18 . . . . . . .224 C7
Ashlands Fst Sch TA18 . .224 C7
Ashlands Mdw TA18 . . . .224 C8
Ashlands Rd TA18 . . . . . .224 D7
Ashlea Pk TA9 . . . . .136 E8
Ashleigh Ave TA6 . . . . . . .209 A3
Ashleigh Cl Paulton BS39 . .77 E6
Weston-Super-Mare BS23 . . .49 A8
Ashleigh Cres BS49 . . . . . .34 B8
Ashleigh Gdns TA1 . . . . .212 E5
Ashleigh Rd
Weston-Super-Mare BS23 . . .49 A8
Yatton BS49 . . . . .34 B8
Ashleigh Terr TA6 . . . . . .209 A3
Ashley Ave Bath BA1 . . . . .44 C7
Burnham-On-Sea TA8 . . . . .104 B6
Ashley Cl BS25 . . . . .70 A7
Ashley La BA15 . . . . .64 F7
Ashley Rd Bathford BA1 . . .29 E3
Clevedon BS21 . . . . .6 B1
Taunton TA1 . . . . .212 D3
Ashley Terr BA1 . . . . .44 C7
Ashman Way TA6 . . . . . . .208 D4
Ashmans Ct BA1 . . . . .44 B6
Ashmans Gate BS39 . . . . . .77 E5
Ashmans Yd BA1 . . . . .44 B6
Ashmead
Temple Cloud BS39 . . . . . . .58 E1
Yeovil BA20 . . . . .218 C2
Ashmead Rd BS31 . . . . . . .25 B5
Ashmead Road Ind Est
BS31 . . . . .25 B5
Ashmead Way 8 BS1 . . . . .11 F5

Ashmoor Dro BA5 .....139 B6
Ashton Ave BS1 .....226 A1
Ashton Cl
  Ashill TA19 .....183 C4
  Clevedon BS21 .....6 B1
Ashton Court Est* BS41 .....11 C4
Ashton Cres BS48 .....8 D1
Ashton Ct TA1 .....212 C1
Ashton Dr BS3 .....11 F2
Ashton Gate Trad Est BS3 .....11 E3
Ashton Gate Underpass BS3 .....11 F3
Ashton Hill BA2 .....43 A7
Ashton Rd
  Bridgwater TA6 .....208 F2
  Bristol, Ashton Gate BS3 ...11 F4
  Bristol, Bower Ashton BS3 ...11 D3
Ashton Vale Prim Sch BS3 .....11 E3
Ashton Vale Rd BS3 .....11 E3
Ashton Vale Trad Est BS3 .....11 F1
Ashton Way BS31 .....24 E6
Ashton Windmill* BS28 .....88 E1
Ashtown Cross BS28 ...164 A3
Ashtree Rd BA11 .....120 A6
Ashwell Cl BS48 .....9 A2
Ashwick Cl BS14 .....23 E6
Ashwell La
  Glastonbury BA6 .....139 D1
  Wheddon Cross TA24 ...129 F2
Ashwicke BS14 .....23 A6
Ashwood BS40 .....74 F4
Ashwood Dr BA21 .....219 E8
Askwith Cl DT9 .....225 B3
Asney Rd BA16 .....156 E7
Aspen Cl BA11 .....120 B7
Aspen La TA6 .....208 C4
Aspen Park Rd
  BS22 .....49 E8
Aspen Way TA18 .....224 D7
Aspley Cl BA1 .....44 B7
Asquith St TA2 .....212 E6
Assembly Rooms La
  BS1 .....227 A2
Aston Ho 6 BS1 .....227 B1
at-bristol* BS1 .....226 C1
Athelney Sta TA3 .....170 F7
Athelney Way BA21 ...218 D6
Athlone Rd TA6 .....209 A2
Atholl Cl BS22 .....31 F3
Atkin's Gate TA13 .....220 D6
Atkins Cl BS14 .....23 E6
Atlanta Key TA8 .....104 A8
Atlantic Cres TA8 .....104 B5
Atlantic Ct BS23 .....30 C1
Atlantic Rd
  Bristol BS11 .....4 C8
  Weston-Super-Mare BS23 ...30 C1
Atlantic Rd S BS23 .....30 C1
Atlantic Way BA22 .....174 A2
Atlay Ct BS49 .....17 B1
Attewell Ct BA2 .....44 F4
Attisham La DT6 .....199 D4
Atyeo Cl TA8 .....104 C8
Aubrey Meads BS30 ...25 E8
Auckland Cl BS23 .....48 F3
Auckland Way TA20 ...223 D3
Audley Ave BA1 .....44 D7
Audley Cl Bath BA1 ....44 D7
  Nether Stowey TA5 .....134 A2
Audley Gr BA1 .....44 C7
Audley Park Rd BA1 .....44 C7
Audries Ct TA23 .....202 B7
Augustine's Cl BS20 .....1 E4
Austen Dr BS22 .....32 B4
Austin Cl BA11 .....119 F2
Austin Rd BA6 .....206 E6
Autumn Mews BS24 .....50 A8
Avalon Bldgs BA6 .....206 D5
Avalon Cl BS49 .....17 A1
Avalon Est BA6 .....206 E7
Avalon Ho BS48 .....8 C1
Avalon Pk TA11 .....211 B5
Avalon Rd
  Bridgwater TA6 .....209 D5
  Highbridge TA9 .....104 E4
Avalon Sch BA16 .....207 B4
Avebury Cl TA8 .....104 D8
Avebury Dr TA6 .....209 D5
Avebury Rd BS3 .....11 F2
Aveline Ct TA4 .....167 F6
Avening Cl BS48 .....19 A8
Avenue Pl BA2 .....45 B1
Avenue Rd BA11 .....120 A4
Avenue The
  Backwell BS48 .....19 A7
  Bath, Claverton Down BA2 ...45 E5
  Bath, Combe Down BA2 ...45 C1
  Bicknoller TA4 .....132 F4
  3 Bridgwater TA6 .....208 F5
  Bristol, Sneyd Park BS9 ...5 E3
  Chard DT10 .....193 F7
  Clevedon BS21 .....6 C3
  Crewkerne TA18 .....224 F3
  Keynsham BS31 .....24 E6
  Kingsbury Episcopi TA12 ...185 B8
  Langport TA10 .....172 A6
  Minehead TA24 .....201 A7

Avenue The continued
  Sherborne DT9 .....225 E5
  Sparkford BA22 .....175 A5
  Stoke sub Hamdon TA14 ...185 F4
  Taunton TA1 .....212 E5
  Timsbury BA2 .....60 B2
  Wincanton BA9 .....216 D3
  Winscombe BS25 .....70 C8
  Yatton BS49 .....34 B8
  Yeovil BA21 .....219 B5
Averill Cl BS21 .....6 D4
Avill Cres TA1 .....213 C4
Avishayes Com Prim Sch TA20 .....223 C5
Avishayes Rd TA20 .....223 E4
Avon & Somerset Pol HQ BS20 .....2 A4
Avon Cl Keynsham BS31 ...24 F6
  Taunton TA1 .....212 D2
  Weston-Super-Mare BS23 ...48 F2
  Yeovil BA21 .....219 D6
Avon Cres BS1 .....226 A1
Avon Ct BA1 .....29 A4
Avon Gorge Ind Est BS11 ...4 C7
Avon Gorge Nature Reserve* BS8 .....11 E7
Avon Gr BS9 .....5 D2
Avon Hts BA3 .....64 C6
Avon La BS31 .....25 F5
Avon Mill La BS31 .....24 F6
Avon Pk BA1 .....44 A7
Avon Prim Sch BS11 .....4 D8
Avon Rd Bristol BS13 ...22 A6
  Keynsham BS31 .....24 F6
  Pill BS20 .....4 C5
Avon Riverside Est BS11 ...4 C7
Avon Ski Ctr* BS25 .....52 C3
Avon St Bath BA1 .....228 B2
  Bristol BS2 .....227 C2
Avon Vale BS9 .....5 E4
Avon Valley Ctry Pk* BS31 .....25 D6
Avon Valley Rly* BS30 ...25 D6
Avonbank Ind Est BS11 ...4 B7
Avonbridge Trad Est BS11 ...4 C8
Avoncliff Halt BA15 .....64 F5
Avondale Bldgs BA1 ...28 B2
Avondale Ct BS9 .....5 D3
Avondale Ho TA6 .....209 A2
Avondale Pl BA1 .....28 F3
Avondale Rd BA1 .....44 B6
Avondowns Ct BS8 .....226 A4
Avonleaze BS9 .....5 B5
Avonmouth CE Prim Sch BS11 .....4 C8
Avonmouth Rd BS11 .....4 C8
Avonwood Cl BS11 .....4 C6
Awkward Hill BS40 .....55 D5
Axbridge CE First Sch BS26 .....70 C1
Axbridge Cl
  Burnham-On-Sea TA8 ...104 C8
  Nailsea BS48 .....18 E8
Axbridge Moor Dro BS26 ...70 C1
Axbridge Mus* BS26 ...70 C2
Axbridge Rd Bath BA2 ...45 B2
  Cheddar BS27 .....70 F2
Axe Cl BS23 .....49 A5
Axe La Clapton DT8 .....195 C1
  Drimpton DT8 .....199 F8
Axe Rd Bridgwater TA6 ...209 B3
  Wookey BA5 .....139 D8
Axe Valley Sch The EX13 .....198 A1
Axeford TA20 .....198 E8
Axeford Mdws TA20 ...198 E8
Axford Way BA2 .....79 D8
Axis BS14 .....22 D5
Axminster Cty Prim Sch EX13 .....198 A1
Axminster Rd TA20 .....198 C7
Ayckbourn Cl TA8 .....104 C6
Aycote Cl BS22 .....31 C2
Ayford La SN14 .....13 F4
Aylands Rd TA1 .....212 D3
Aylmer Cres BS14 .....23 B6
Ayr St BA2 .....44 D6
Azalea Rd BS22 .....32 A5

B

Babcary La BA22 .....174 B8
Babwell Rd BA9 .....177 D6
Babylon Hill
  Sherborne DT9 .....188 A3
  Yeovil BA21 .....219 F4
Babylon View BA3 .....95 F1
Back La Axbridge BS26 ...70 C2
  Axbridge BS26 .....88 D1
  Baltonsborough BA6 .....158 B5
  Batcombe BA4 .....142 C2
  Bradford Abbas DT9 .....187 F1
  Cheddar BS27 .....90 A7
  Chewton Mendip BA3 ...95 A8
  Chewton Mendip BA3 ...94 F6
  Curry Rivel TA10 .....171 D3
  Draycott BS27 .....90 F2
  East Chinnock BA22 .....196 E8
  East Coker BA22 .....197 C7
  Halstock BA22 .....197 C3
  Ilchester BA22 .....173 E1
  Ilminster TA19 .....221 F6
  Keynsham BS31 .....24 E6
  Kingston Seymour BS21 ...16 A5

Back La continued
  Kington Magna SP8 .....177 E2
  Litton BA3 .....75 E2
  Maiden Bradley BA12 ...144 C2
  Marshfield SN14 .....13 F8
  Martock TA12 .....185 D4
  Middlecombe TA7 .....155 B3
  Montacute TA15 .....186 B3
  Moorlinch TA7 .....155 D8
  North Perrott TA18 .....196 C4
  Pill BS20 .....4 C5
  Pilton BA4 .....204 D3
  Rimpton BA22 .....188 A8
  Rowberrow BS25 .....53 A1
  Shepton Mallet, Darshill BA4 .....204 F6
  Shepton Mallet, Downside BA4 .....205 C8
  Sherborne DT9 .....225 D4
  Stoney Stratton BA4 .....141 F2
  Street BA16 .....207 D6
  Street BA6 .....157 C6
  Westbury Sub Mendip BA5 ...110 E7
Back Of Kingsdown Par BS6 .....227 A4
Back River Dro BA16 ...138 F2
Back St Ash TA12 .....186 A7
  Bampton EX16 .....164 B1
  Bradford On Tone TA4 ...167 F1
  Long Sutton TA10 .....172 E4
  Martock TA12 .....185 F7
  Wanstrow BA11 .....142 G6
  West Camel BA22 .....174 F3
  Weston-Super-Mare BS23 ...48 E7
  Winsham TA20 .....194 E1
Back Stoke La BS9 .....5 F6
Back Town BA6 .....157 E4
Back Way TA4 .....150 B8
Backfields BS2 .....227 B4
Backfields La BS2 .....227 B4
Backfields La BS2 .....227 B4
Backlane Dro BA6 .....158 C5
Backways La TA21 .....179 F6
Backwell Bow BS48 .....9 C1
Backwell CE Sch BS48 ...19 C5
Backwell Com Sch BS48 ...19 B8
Backwell Comm BS48 ...19 B8
Backwell Hill Rd BS48 ...19 F5
Backwell Wlk BS13 .....21 F8
Bacon Dr TA1 .....213 D3
Badcox BA11 .....119 E4
Baden Ho BA1 .....228 B4
Badenham Gr BS11 .....4 F8
Badger Hts BA22 .....218 B5
Badger Pk TA24 .....201 C4
Badger Rise BS20 .....2 A4
Badger's Cross
  Oakhill BA3 .....114 F5
  Somerton TA11 .....211 C2
Badger's Cross La TA11 ...211 C2
Badgers Cl Street BA16 ...207 A5
  Taunton TA1 .....212 B3
Badgers Folly BA2 .....44 C5
Badgers Green Rd BA16 ...207 A5
Badgers Hill BA11 .....120 A5
Badgers Way BS24 .....49 F8
Badgers' La TA20 .....223 E1
Badgworth Barns BS26 ...88 D5
Badgworth La BS26 .....88 C4
Badlake La EX36 .....162 D6
Badlake Moor Cross TA22 .....162 D7
Badman Cl BS39 .....77 D5
Badminton Gdns BA1 ...44 C8
Bagber Cross BA8 .....176 F1
Bagber Cross La TA11 ...211 D2
Bagborough Dr TA6 ...208 D2
Bagborough La BA4 .....141 C2
Bagborough Rd TA2 ...212 F7
Baggridge Hill BA2 .....80 F7
Baggs La BS27 .....90 F2
Bagley Rd TA11 .....222 A3
Bagnell Cl BS14 .....23 E5
Bagnell Rd BS14 .....23 E5
Bailbrook Coll BA1 .....28 D2
Bailbrook Ct BA1 .....28 C3
Bailbrook La BA1 .....28 D3
Baildon Cres BS23 .....49 A4
Baildon Ct 2 BS23 .....49 A4
Baildon Rd BS23 .....49 A4
Bailey Cl BS22 .....49 E8
Bailey Hill BA7 .....214 C5
Bailey St TA6 .....209 B5
Bailey's Barton BA15 ...64 E3
Bailey's Knapp EX16 ...178 B4
Bailey's La BA4 .....142 B1
Bailey's Gate TA4 .....167 F6
Bailiffs Cl BS26 .....70 C1
Bailiffs' Wall BS26 .....70 B1
Baily Cl BA6 .....206 E7
Bainsbury View BA3 .....95 F1
Bakehouse La TA16 ...195 F7
Bakehouse La DT9 .....187 E1
Baker Cl 9 BS21 .....6 B1
Baker St Babcary TA11 ...174 C7
  Frome BA11 .....119 E5
  Weston-Super-Mare BS23 ...48 E8
Baker's Bldgs BA3 .....35 D2
Baker's Cross TA3 .....171 D7
Baker's La
  Churchinford TA3 .....191 D7
  Wellington TA21 .....222 E6
Bakeries The TA1 .....213 A4
Bakelie Mus The* TA4 .....202 C2
Bakers Cl TA1 .....212 A3
Bakers Ct TA13 .....220 C4
Bakers La
  Barrington TA19 .....184 C5

Bakers La continued
  Chilcompton BA3 .....96 D3
  Langford BS40 .....53 C8
Bakers Orch TA4 .....151 B5
Bakers Par BA2 .....60 B2
Bakersfield TA20 .....194 E1
Bakery La BA4 .....140 F3
Balch Rd BA5 .....203 C4
Baldwin Rd TA1 .....213 B5
Baldwin St BS1 .....227 A2
Ball La Doulting BA4 .....141 F7
  Isle Abbotts TA3 .....183 C5
  Spaxton TA2/TA5 .....152 B2
Ball The Dunster TA24 ...201 E2
  Minehead TA24 .....200 F8
Ball's Hill BA22,TA15 ...186 C4
Ball's La TA5 .....153 E4
Ballance St BA1 .....228 B4
Ballfield Rd TA24 .....200 F8
Ballhill La 3 EX16 .....164 B1
Balls Barn La BS24 .....33 A2
Balmoral Dr TA8 .....85 B1
Balmoral Ho TA6 .....209 C4
Balmoral Rd
  Keynsham BS31 .....24 C4
  Yeovil BA21 .....219 E6
Balsam Cl BA9 .....216 D3
Balsam Fields BA9 .....216 D3
Balsam La BA9 .....216 E3
Balsam Pk BA9 .....216 C3
Baltic Pl BS20 .....4 D4
Baltonsborough CE Prim Sch BA6 .....158 A6
Baltonsborough Rd BA6 ...157 E4
Bamfield BS14 .....23 A6
Bampton 4 BS22 .....31 F2
Bampton Cl Bristol BS13 ...22 B5
Bampton Down Rd EX16 .....178 A7
Bampton Prim Sch EX16 .....164 B1
Bampton St TA1 .....200 F6
Banbury La BA6 .....157 E3
Bancks St TA24 .....200 F7
Bancombe Cl TA11 .....211 B5
Bancombe Rd TA11 .....211 A4
Banfield Cl BS11 .....5 A8
Bangrove Wlk BS11 .....4 E8
Banister Gr BS4 .....22 D7
Banjup BA22 .....174 F6
Bank Sq TA22 .....163 D6
Bank St Highbridge TA9 ...104 D3
  Williton TA4 .....202 D2
Banking St TA18 .....224 C6
Bankland La TA7 .....154 B1
Banks Cl BS21 .....16 B6
Bannerdown Cl BA1 .....29 B4
Bannerdown Dr BA1 .....29 C5
Bannerdown Rd BA1 ...29 C5
Bannerleigh La BS8 .....11 E6
Bannerleigh Rd BS8 .....11 E6
Bannerson Rd TA5 .....134 B2
Bantock Cl BS4 .....22 D6
Bantry Rd BS4 .....22 E8
Banwell Cl Bristol BS13 ...22 A8
  Keynsham BS31 .....25 A2
  Taunton TA1 .....213 D4
Banwell Prim Sch BS29 ...51 B3
Banwell Rd
  Banwell BS26,BS29 ...68 D8
  Bath BA2 .....62 D8
  Locking BS24 .....50 B8
  Winscombe BS25,BS29 ...51 E1
Banyard Rd BS20 .....3 E5
Barbary Cl BA8 .....176 D3
Barber's La TA21 .....179 F6
Barbers Mead TA2 .....212 B6
Barberry Farm Rd BS49 ...17 B1
Barbers Mead TA2 .....213 C7
Barbour Gdns BS13 .....22 D3
Barbour Rd BS13 .....22 D3
Barcroft Cres TA3 .....170 A1
Barcroft La TA13 .....220 B6
Bardel Ct BA22 .....218 B6
Barford Cl TA5 .....152 F7
Barford Rd TA5 .....152 F7
Barham Ct BA22 .....218 A5
Barhams Cl TA6 .....209 A7
Barkham BA5 .....203 F5
Barle Cl TA1 .....213 D4
Barley Cl BA5 .....203 C3
Barley Croft Bristol BS9 ...5 F5
  Somerton TA11 .....211 B3
Barley Cross BS22 .....32 A5
Barlinch Cl TA2 .....213 B7
Barlynch Ct BA21 .....218 D6
Barn Cl Crewkerne TA18 ...224 B5
  Frome BA11 .....119 D3
  Nether Stowey TA5 .....134 B2
  Somerton TA11 .....211 B3
Barn End TA4 .....150 F8
Barn Gn BA6 .....206 D3
Barn Hill BA2 .....79 F5
Barn La Oulton BS39 .....59 A7
Barn Mead TA21 .....222 F5
Barn Orch TA14 .....185 E3
Barn Pool BS25 .....70 F8
Barn Rd BA5 .....203 B4
Barn St TA18 .....224 B6

Barnabas Cl BS26 .....70 D2
Barnaby Cl BA3 .....78 B2
Barnard Ave BA16 .....207 B3
Barnard Wlk BS31 .....24 D4
Barnard's Cl BS49 .....34 C7
Barnes Cl
  Castle Cary BA7 .....214 C6
  Wells BA5 .....203 B4
Barnes Close Mead TA22 .....163 D6
Barnet Cl BA21 .....218 E7
Barnetts Well BS27 .....90 F2
Barnfield Way BA1 .....29 B3
Barnhay 6 EX16 .....164 B1
Barnmeads Rd TA21 ...222 E4
Barns Cl
  Barrow Gurney BS48 .....20 C4
  Nailsea BS48 .....8 C1
Barns Close Ind Est TA22 .....163 D6
Barnsclose TA22 .....163 D6
Barnsclose N TA22 .....163 D6
Barnsclose W TA22 .....163 D6
Barnstaple Ct BS4 .....22 E8
Barnstaple Rd BS4 .....22 E8
Barnstaple Wlk BS4 .....22 F8
Barossa Pl BS1 .....227 A1
Barpark Cnr EX15 .....180 E3
Barpool La TA11 .....211 D6
Barrack's La BS11 .....4 D8
Barracks Cl BA22 .....218 B7
Barrie Way TA8 .....104 C6
Barrington Broadway TA10 .....184 D6
Barrington Cl TA1 .....212 C1
Barrington Court Cotts TA19 .....184 D5
Barrington Ct* TA19 ...184 D5
Barrington Hill Nat Nature Reserve* TA19 .....182 F4
Barrington Pl BA4 .....204 F5
Barrington Rd TA8 .....104 C8
Barrington Sch TA19 ...184 D5
Barrow Court La BS19 ...20 B5
Barrow Cswy BA5 .....138 E8
Barrow Ct BS21 .....7 F4
Barrow Dr TA1 .....213 E5
Barrow Hill
  Stalbridge DT10 .....190 B4
  Stourton Caundle DT10 ...189 F10
Barrow Hill Cres BS11 ...4 C7
Barrow Hill Rd BS11 .....4 C8
Barrow Hospl
  Barrow Gurney BS48 .....20 F6
  Dundry BS48 .....21 A6
Barrow La
  North Wootton BA4 .....140 A4
  Pilton BA4 .....140 F3
  Wincanton BA9 .....161 B3
  Winford BS40 .....37 F5
Barrow Lea DT10 .....190 B4
Barrow Pk BS27 .....90 A8
Barrow St Bath BA2 .....44 C1
  Barrow St BS48 .....20 D5
Barrow Stile BA4 .....140 F3
Barrow Water La BA9 ...161 A3
Barrow Wood La BS27 ...110 A7
Barrowmead Dr BS11 ...4 F7
Barrows Cl TA6 .....208 E2
Barrows Croft BS27 .....90 A8
Barrows Ct BA22 .....196 E8
Barrows La TA14 .....185 E2
Barrows Rd BS27 .....90 A8
Barrows The
  Cheddar BS27 .....90 A8
  Weston-Super-Mare BS22 ...49 C7
Barry Cl BS24 .....49 A1
Barry La BA22 .....196 F6
Barrymore Cl TA10 .....172 A6
Barstable Ho BS2 .....227 C3
Bartec 4 BA20 .....218 C3
Bartholomew Row BA2 ...60 B2
Bartlett Cl Frome BA11 ...120 C6
  Taunton TA1 .....212 B1
Bartlett Ct
  Crewkerne TA18 .....224 C6
  Yeovil BA20 .....218 D3
Bartlett Mews BA21 ...219 F7
Bartlett Pk Chard TA20 ...223 C3
  Yeovil BA20 .....218 D3
Bartlett St BA1 .....228 B3
Bartletts La TA4 .....167 A4
Bartletts Pl BA21 .....218 D5
Bartletts Row TA11 .....211 D4
Bartletts Way BS24 .....49 B2
Barton Cl Berrow TA8 .....84 F5
Barton Cross EX16 .....162 E5
Barton Dro BS25 .....69 D5
Barton Gdns DT9 .....225 B4
Barton Gn TA1 .....168 D1
Barton Hey 2 TA4 .....167 F8
Barton Hill SP8 .....177 E2
Barton Rd
  Barton St David TA11 ...158 A2
  Berrow TA8 .....84 F4
  Bristol BS2 .....227 C3
  Butleigh BA6 .....157 E3
  Minehead TA24 .....201 B4
  Wincanton BA9 .....216 B3
Barton St Bath BA1 .....228 B2
Barton The Bleadon BS24 ...67 C6
  Corston BA2 .....43 A7
  Huish Champflower TA4 ...165 E8
  Norton St Philip BA2 .....81 F4
Barton Villas BA3 .....116 F6

Barton Way TA3 . . . . 170 C4
Barton Wlk BA11 . . . . . . 119 D2
Bartons The
  Bishops Lydeard TA4 . . . . 167 E8
  South Petherton TA13 . . . 220 E3
Barwick & Stoford Com Prim
  Sch BA22 . . . . 197 E8
Barwick Ho BS11 . . . . 4 E7
Basketfield La BA6 . . . . . 139 D1
Bat Alley DT10 . . . . 190 F5
Batallers La TA23 . . . . . . 131 D2
Batchelors Bax BS24 . . . . . 66 F2
Batch Cl TA7 . . . . 136 C4
Batch La Clutton BS39 . . . . 58 F3
  Lympsham BS24 . . . . 66 F3
Batch Rd TA7 . . . . 136 B5
Batch The Ashcott TA7 . . . 156 B7
  Backwell BS48 . . . . 19 D1
  Batheaston BA1 . . . . 28 F3
  Blagdon BS40 . . . . 55 B8
  Burrington BS40 . . . . 54 B3
  Chew Magna BS40 . . . . . . 39 B3
  Churchill BS25 . . . . 52 F4
  Draycott BS27 . . . . 90 F2
  Farmborough BA2 . . . . . . 60 A6
  Hinton Charterhouse BA2 . . 63 E1
  Saltford BS31 . . . . 25 F3
  🔟 Shepton Mallet BA4 . . 205 B6
  Wincanton BA9 . . . . 216 B4
  Yatton BS49 . . . . 34 B7
Batchpool La BA8 . . . . . . 176 F3
Bath Abbey* BA1 . . . . . . 228 C2
Bath Bridge Bsns Pk
  TA6 . . . . 209 B6
Bath Cl BA6 . . . . 206 D6
Bath Foyer The BA2 . . . . . 44 A6
Bath Hill Keynsham BS31 . . 24 F5
  Wellow BA2 . . . . 62 D2
Bath House Ct TA1 . . . . . 212 E3
Bath La TA20 . . . . 223 C3
Bath Meadow Dr TA22 . . 163 E6
Bath New Rd BA3 . . . . 78 F4
Bath Old Rd BA3 . . . . 78 F4
Bath Pl TA1 . . . . 212 F3
Bath Postal Mus* BA1 . . 228 C3
Bath Race Course* BA1 . . 12 B6
Bath Rd Ashcott TA7 . . . . 156 B7
  Beanacre BA12 . . . . 136 D2
  Beckington BA11 . . . . . . 101 D5
  Bitton BA1,BA2,BS30 . . . . 25 F7
  Bitton BS30 . . . . 25 D8
  Blagdon BS40 . . . . 55 B1
  Bridgwater TA6 . . . . 209 C7
  Bristol BS2 . . . . 227 C2
  Farmborough BA2 . . . . . . 59 E5
  Frome BA11 . . . . 120 A7
  Horrington BA3,BA5 . . . . 113 D5
  Kingsdown SN13 . . . . . . 29 F5
  Moorlinch TA7 . . . . 155 E8
  Norton St Philip BA2 . . . . 81 E5
  Oakhill BA3 . . . . 115 B3
  Paulton BS39 . . . . 77 F6
  Peasedown St John BA2 . . 79 C7
  Saltford BS31 . . . . 25 D3
  Shepton Mallet BA4 . . . . 141 G8
  Stawell TA7 . . . . 137 B1
  Wells BA5 . . . . 112 E1
Bath Riverside Bsns Pk
  BA2 . . . . 228 A1
Bath Small Sch BA1 . . . . . 28 C2
Bath Spa Sta BA1 . . . . . . 228 C1
Bath Spa Univ Coll BA1 . . 27 E1
Bath Spa University Coll
  BA2 . . . . 43 B5
Bath Sq TA20 . . . . 223 C3
Bath St Bath BA1 . . . . . . 228 C2
  Bristol BS1 . . . . 227 B2
  Chard TA20 . . . . 223 C3
  Cheddar BS27 . . . . 90 B7
  Frome BA11 . . . . 119 F4
Bath View BA3 . . . . 96 F1
Bathampton La BA2 . . . . . 28 E1
Bathampton Prim Sch
  BA2 . . . . 28 F2
Batheaston CE Prim Sch
  BA1 . . . . 28 F4
Bathford Hill Bathford BA1 . 29 B2
  Compton Dando BS39 . . . . 41 E5
Bathford Prim Sch BA1 . . 29 C2
Bathurst Cl TA6 . . . . 104 D8
Bathurst Par BS1 . . . . . . 227 A1
Bathurst Rd BS22 . . . . . . 49 C8
Bathwell La DT9 . . . . 217 D1
Bathwick Hill BA2 . . . . . . 45 C6
Bathwick Rise BA2 . . . . . . 45 B7
Bathwick St BA1,BA2 . . . . 228 C4
Batstone Cl BA1 . . . . 28 B2
Batt's La TA10 . . . . 172 D5
Battery La BS20 . . . . 2 D7
Battery Rd BS20 . . . . 2 D6
Battin's Knap TA4 . . . . . . 150 A3
Battle La BS40 . . . . 39 A3
Battle St EX15 . . . . 180 E1
Battleborough La TA9 . . . . 86 B1
Batts La Marshwood DT6 . . 199 F2
  Oakhill BA3 . . . . 114 E3
Batts Pk TA1 . . . . 212 E1
Battson Rd BS14 . . . . 23 E4
Bauldicth La TA3 . . . . 184 B8
Baunton's Orch DT9 . . . . 217 C2
Bauntons Cl DT9 . . . . . . 217 C2
Bawden Cl TA7 . . . . 136 E4
Bawdrip La TA7 . . . . 136 E2
Bawler's La TA10 . . . . . . 171 C3
Bay Hill TA19 . . . . 221 D4
Bay La BS27 . . . . 90 F2
Bay Rd Clevedon BS21 . . . . 6 D6

Bay Rd *continued*
  Porlock TA24 . . . . 124 A4
Bay Tree Rd Bath BA1 . . . . 28 B2
  Clevedon BS21 . . . . 6 E1
Bay Tree View BS22 . . . . . 31 D1
Bay View TA23 . . . . 202 D6
Bay View Gdns TA8 . . . . 104 B5
Bay's La BS3 . . . . 115 A7
Bayer Bldg The BA2 . . . . 228 B1
Bayford Hill BA9 . . . . . . 216 E4
Bayford La BA9 . . . . 177 B7
Bayford Rd BA9 . . . . 209 C6
Bayliss Cir The BA16 . . . . 207 C5
Baymead Cl 🔟 TA6 . . . . 153 F4
Baymead La TA6 . . . . 153 F3
Baymead Mdw 🔼 TA6 . . 153 F3
Bays The BS27 . . . . 222 E7
Baytree Cl BS22 . . . . 31 D1
Baytree Rd BS22 . . . . 31 C1
Baytree Sch BS22 . . . . . . 49 C8
Baytree View BS22 . . . . . . 31 D1
Baze La EX35 . . . . 122 B4
Bazelands Hill BA8 . . . . . 190 B7
Beach Ave BS21 . . . . 6 C2
Beach Ct BS23 . . . . 48 D6
Beach End Rd BS23 . . . . . 48 C2
Beach Hill BA2 . . . . 62 F6
Beach Mews BS21 . . . . 6 C4
Beach Rd
  Weston-Super-Mare BS22 . . 31 A5
  Weston-Super-Mare BS23 . . 48 D6
Beach Rd E BS20 . . . . 2 D6
Beach Rd W BS20 . . . . 2 C6
Beach The BS21 . . . . 6 C4
Beach Tree Cross TA4 . . . 166 F6
Beachley Wlk BA1 . . . . . . 44 D7
Beacon TA19 . . . . 221 B5
Beacon Hill View DT9 . . . 175 D1
Beacon La
  Charlton Horethorne DT9 . 175 D2
  Wellington TA21 . . . . . . 180 C4
Beacon Rd Bath BA1 . . . . . 28 A1
  Minehead TA24 . . . . 200 F8
Beacon View
  Coleford BA3 . . . . 116 E7
  Shepton Mallet BA4 . . . . 205 A4
Beaconfield Ho TA6 . . . . 209 A2
Beaconfield Rd BA20 . . . . 218 E1
Beaconsfield Rd
  Clevedon BS21 . . . . 6 E3
  Weston-Super-Mare BS23 . . 48 E7
Beaconsfield Way BA11 . . 120 B7
Beadon La TA4 . . . . 166 E7
Beadon Rd TA1 . . . . 213 C5
Beale Cl TA4 . . . . 23 E6
Beale Way TA8 . . . . 104 D5
Bean Acre The BS11 . . . . . 4 D8
Bearbridge Rd BS13 . . . . . 21 F4
Beard's Yd TA10 . . . . . . 171 F5
Bearley Bridge Rd 🔟
  TA12 . . . . 185 E6
Bearley Ho 🔟 TA12 . . . . 185 E6
Bearley La BA22 . . . . 186 B2
Bearley Rd 🔟 TA12 . . . . 185 E6
Bears Meadow La TA5 . . . 133 C6
Beasley Ct TA20 . . . . 223 B5
Beastway La TA24 . . . . . . 131 B3
Beatty Way TA8 . . . . 104 C7
Beau La BA4 . . . . 228 B2
Beauchamp Gdns BA3 . . . 183 A7
Beauchamps Dr BA3 . . . . . 97 A5
Beaufitz Pl TA20 . . . . . . 193 F1
Beauford Sq BA1 . . . . . . 228 B2
Beaufort Ave BA2 . . . . 78 A2
Beaufort Bldgs 🔽 BA1 . . 11 F7
Beaufort Ct Locking BS24 . . 50 C3
  Sampford Peverell EX16 . . 178 D1
Beaufort Ct
  Burnham-On-Sea TA8 . . . . 85 A1
  Clevedon BS21 . . . . 6 C5
  Ilchester BA22 . . . . 173 E2
Beaufort E BA1 . . . . 28 C1
Beaufort Gdns
  🔼 Nailsea BS48 . . . . . . 8 D1
  South Petherton TA13 . . . 220 B5
Beaufort Mews 🔼 BA1 . . 28 C1
Beaufort Pl BA1 . . . . 28 C1
Beaufort Rd Taunton TA1 . 212 E5
  Weston-Super-Mare BS23 . . 48 E5
Beaufort Villas 🔼 BA1 . . 28 B1
Beaufort W BA1 . . . . 28 B1
Beauley Rd BS3 . . . . 226 B1
Beaulieu Dr BA21 . . . . . . 218 D6
Beaumont Cl BS23 . . . . . . 48 F4
Beaumont Ho BA21 . . . . . 219 D5
Beavor La EX13 . . . . 198 A1
Beck's La BA11 . . . . 116 D6
Beckery New Rd BA6 . . . . 206 B3
Beckery Old Rd BA6 . . . . 206 B3
Beckery Rd BA6 . . . . 206 B4
Becket Dr BS22 . . . . 32 A3
Becket Pl BA5 . . . . 203 D3
Becket Prim Sch BS22 . . . . 32 A2
Becket Rd BS22 . . . . 32 A4
Becket's La BS48 . . . . 18 E8
Beckford Cl BA2 . . . . 45 B7
Beckford Rd BA2 . . . . 45 B7
Beckland's Twr* BA1 . . . . 22 F4
Beckhampton Rd BA2 . . . . 44 D5
Beckington BS24 . . . . 49 A2
Beckington CE Fst Sch
  BA11 . . . . 101 E4
Beckington Bsns Pk BS23 . . 49 A6
Becks Field 🔼 TA14 . . . . 185 F4

Beckworth Cl TA6 . . . . . . 209 C3
Bector La BA3 . . . . 116 C4
Bedford Cl TA6 . . . . 209 C3
Bedford Ct TA6 . . . . 41 B1
Bedford Ct BA1 . . . . 45 B8
Bedford Rd Wells BA5 . . . 112 C1
  Weston-Super-Mare BS23 . . 48 E4
  Yeovil BA21 . . . . 219 D8
Bedford St BA1 . . . . 45 B8
Bedminster Down Sch
  BS13 . . . . 21 F7
Bedwell La TA7 . . . . 155 C2
Bedwin Cl BS20 . . . . 1 F4
Bee World & Animal Ctr*
  TA4 . . . . 150 F8
Beech Ave Bath BA2 . . . . . 45 E5
  Shepton Mallet BA4 . . . . 205 A6
Beech Cl Doulting BA4 . . . 141 E6
  Shipham BS25 . . . . 70 F8
  Taunton TA2 . . . . 212 F8
Beech Ct Bristol BS14 . . . . 23 A5
  Frome BA11 . . . . 120 B7
  Taunton TA1 . . . . 212 E3
  🔼 Wellington TA21 . . . 222 D6
Beech Dr Bridgwater TA6 . . 209 D5
  Nailsea BS48 . . . . 9 A3
  Shipham BS25 . . . . 70 E8
Beech Gr Bath BA2 . . . . . . 44 D4
Beech Grove Prim Sch
  TA21 . . . . 222 C6
Beech Hill TA21 . . . . 222 F5
Beech La Axminster EX13 . 198 E1
  Stoke Trister BA9 . . . . . 177 C8
Beech Rd
  Bridgwater TA6 . . . . 209 D5
  🔼 Martock TA12 . . . . . 185 E6
  Saltford BS31 . . . . 25 E3
  Shipham BS25 . . . . 70 E8
  Street BA16 . . . . 207 C3
  Yatton BS49 . . . . 34 C8
Beech Terr BA3 . . . . 78 E1
Beech Tree La TA3 . . . . . 130 D1
Beech Tree CI TA4 . . . . . 210 C4
Beech Tree Cross
  Clatworthy TA4 . . . . . . 149 E1
  Dulverton TA22 . . . . . . 163 C7
  Monksilver TA4 . . . . . . 132 B1
Beech Tree Hill TA5 . . . . 152 C6
Beech Way BA4 . . . . 141 E1
Beechcroft BS41 . . . . 21 D2
Beechen Cliff Boys' Sch
  BA2 . . . . 45 A4
Beechen Cliff Rd BA2 . . . . 228 B1
Beeches The Bath BA2 . . . . 44 D1
  Langport TA10 . . . . 172 A6
  Sandford BS25 . . . . 52 B4
  Wheddon Cross TA24 . . . 129 E1
Beechfield Cl BS41 . . . . . . 5 C8
Beechfield Gr BS9 . . . . . . 5 C8
Beechfield Inf Sch TA9 . . 104 D4
Beeching Cl TA20 . . . . . . 223 E6
Beechmont Cl BS24 . . . . . . 48 F1
Beechmont Dr BS24 . . . . . 49 A1
Beechmount Ct BS14 . . . . 23 B8
Beechmount Gr BS14 . . . . 23 B8
Beechwood
  Bridgwater TA6 . . . . 208 E2
  Yeovil BA20 . . . . 218 F2
Beechwood Ave
  Frome BA11 . . . . 120 A5
  Locking BS24 . . . . 50 A5
Beechwood Cl
  Bristol BS14 . . . . 23 C8
  Frome BA11 . . . . 120 A5
Beechwood Dr
  Crewkerne TA18 . . . . . . 224 C7
  Portishead BS20 . . . . 1 E5
Beechwood Rd Bath BA2 . . 45 B1
  Easton-in-G BS20 . . . . . . 4 A4
  Nailsea BS48 . . . . 8 D2
  Portishead BS20 . . . . 1 E5
Beehive Yd BA1 . . . . 228 C3
Beek's La SN14,BA1 . . . . . 13 D5
Beer Door TA10 . . . . 155 E2
Beer Dro TA10 . . . . 155 E2
Beer La
  Burlescombe EX16 . . . . . 179 B2
  Dulverton TA22 . . . . . . 163 B5
Beer Rd TA10 . . . . 155 E2
Beer St Curry Mallet TA3 . 183 C7
  Yeovil BA20 . . . . 219 A4
Beere Cross EX36 . . . . . . 162 A5
Bees Ho BS21 . . . . 6 C2
Beetham La TA20 . . . . . . 193 B6
Beggar Bush La BS8 . . . . . 11 B6
Beggarswell Cl BA22 . . . . 227 C4
Beggs Cl 🔼 TA6 . . . . . . 153 F3
Behind Berry TA11 . . . . . 211 D4
Behind Butts TA11 . . . . . 185 E1
Behind Hayes BA8 . . . . . . 176 D2
Bekynton Ave BA5 . . . . . 203 F4
Belcombe Dro TA10 . . . . 193 B7
Belfast Wlk BS4 . . . . 22 E8
Belfield Cl TA8 . . . . 104 A8
Belgrave Cres BA1 . . . . . 228 C4
Belgrave Pl Bath BA1 . . . . 228 C4
  Bristol BS8 . . . . 226 A3
  Taunton TA1 . . . . 212 F6
Belgrave Rd Bath BA1 . . . 228 B4
  Weston-Super-Mare BS22 . . 49 B8
Belgrave Terr 🔼 BA1 . . . 28 A1
Bell Barn Rd BS9 . . . . 5 D6
Bell Cl Bridgwater TA6 . . . 208 F6
  Farmborough BA2 . . . . . . 59 F6
  Westbury Sub Mendip BA5 . 110 E6

Bell Hill
  Chewton Mendip BA3 . . . . 94 B7
  Norton St Philip BA2 . . . . 81 E4
Bell La Bristol BS1 . . . . . 227 A3
  Chard TA19,TA20 . . . . . 193 F7
  Chewton Mendip BA3 . . . . 94 B7
  Cossington TA7 . . . . 137 A3
Bell Orch TA10 . . . . 171 D4
Bell Sq BS40 . . . . 54 E3
Bell Wlk BS40 . . . . 35 E2
Bella View Gdns BA6 . . . . 206 D4
Bella Vista Rd BA1 . . . . . 228 B4
Bellamy Ave BS13 . . . . . . 22 C4
Belland Dr BS14 . . . . 22 F4
Belle View BA3 . . . . 78 B3
Belle View Terr TA20 . . . . 198 C8
Belle Vue TA23 . . . . 131 E3
Bellevue BS8 . . . . 226 B2
Bellevue Cotts BS8 . . . . . 226 B2
Bellevue Cres BS8 . . . . . . 226 B2
Bellevue Ct Bristol BS8 . . . 226 B2
  Clevedon BS21 . . . . 6 D4
Bellevue Mans BS21 . . . . . 6 D4
Bellevue Rd BS21 . . . . 6 D4
Bellevue Terr BS8 . . . . . . 226 B2
Bellfield BA3 . . . . 117 A3
Bellhanger Ct BA1 . . . . . . 28 B4
Bellhorse La BS40 . . . . . . 74 C5
Bellifants BA2 . . . . 60 A6
Bellman's Cross BA8 . . . . 190 B7
Bellmoor La TA19 . . . . . . 194 A7
Bellotts Rd BA2 . . . . 44 C6
Belluton La BS39 . . . . 40 E5
Belluton Terr BS39 . . . . . . 40 D5
Belmont Cl TA6 . . . . 208 B4
Belmont Dr Failand BS8 . . . 10 B3
  Taunton TA1 . . . . 212 E2
Belmont Hill BS48 . . . . . . 10 B1
Belmont Ho 🔼 BA20 . . . 219 B4
  Hatch Beauchamp TA3 . . . 183 A8
  Taunton TA1 . . . . 212 C3
  Winscombe BS25 . . . . . . 70 A8
Belmont Terr TA19 . . . . . 184 E3
Belmore Gdns BA2 . . . . . . 44 B3
Belstone Wlk BS4 . . . . . . 22 C8
Belton Ct BA1 . . . . 27 B2
Belton Rd BS20 . . . . 2 A6
Belvedere 🖪 TA21 . . . . . 222 D6
Belvedere Cres TA11 . . . . 135 B2
Belvedere Grange TA11 . . 211 E3
Belvedere Rd
  Taunton TA1 . . . . 212 F5
  Yeovil BA21 . . . . 219 E7
Belvedere Trad Est TA1 . . 212 E5
Belvoir Rd BA2 . . . . 44 D5
Bemberry Bank TA24 . . . . 130 A8
Ben Travers Way TA8 . . . 104 C6
Bences Cl SN14 . . . . 13 F8
Bench La TA20 . . . . 193 D5
Benches La BS40 . . . . 37 D3
Benedict Ct BA6 . . . . 206 D6
Benedix Rd TA6 . . . . 134 B8
Bennell Batch BA3 . . . . . . 96 E4
Bennell Cl BA3 . . . . 96 E4
Bennell Cotts BA3 . . . . . . 96 E4
Bennett Gdns BA11 . . . . . 119 E4
Bennett La BA1 . . . . 28 A1
Bennett Rd TA9 . . . . 104 F4
Bennett St BA1 . . . . 228 B3
Bennett Way BS1,BS8 . . . . 11 F5
Bennetts La TA5 . . . . 204 B7
Bennett's Rd BA1 . . . . 28 C3
Bennetts Field Trad Est
  BA9 . . . . 216 C2
Bennetts La BA3,BA5 . . . . 114 B7
Benville Ave BS9 . . . . 5 C8
Bere La BA6 . . . . 206 E4
Bere Mills La TA19 . . . . . 194 B7
Beresford Cl
  Burnham-On-Sea TA8 . . . 104 C7
Beresford Gdns BA1 . . . . . 27 A3
Berkeley Ave Bristol BS8 . . 226 C3
  Midsomer Norton BA3 . . . . 78 A2
Berkeley Cres
  Bristol BS8 . . . . 226 B3
  Weston-Super-Mare BS23 . . 48 C2
Berkeley Ct BA2 . . . . 45 B5
Berkeley Gdns
  Bruton BA10 . . . . 215 E6
  Keynsham BS31 . . . . 24 E4
Berkeley Ho Bath BA1 . . . 228 C3
  Bristol BS1 . . . . 226 C3
Berkeley Pl Bath BA1 . . . . 228 C4
  Bristol BS8 . . . . 226 B3
Berkeley Rd Street BA16 . . 207 E6
  Yeovil BA20 . . . . 219 A4
Berkeley Sq BS8 . . . . 226 C3
Berkeley Ave BS8 . . . . . . 226 B3
Berkley Cross BA11 . . . . . 121 A7
Berkley Ct BA11 . . . . 121 A7
Berkley Ho BA11 . . . . . . 120 B6
Berkley La BA11 . . . . 101 D3
Berkley Rd BA11 . . . . . . 120 D6
Berkley St BA11 . . . . 120 D8
Berlington Ct BS1 . . . . . . 227 B1

Bernard Cres TA24 . . . . . 200 F6
Bernard Herridge Ct
  BA9 . . . . 216 D4
Bernard Ireland Ho BA1 . . 27 B1
Bernard Taylor Homes 🔟
  TA1 . . . . 213 A4
Berners Cl BS4 . . . . 22 D7
Berrow CE Prim Sch TA8 . 84 F4
Berrow Lodge 🔽 BS23 . . 48 E5
Berrow Rd TA8 . . . . 85 A2
Berry Cl TA6 . . . . 208 E2
Berry Hill Mells BA11 . . . 118 A6
  Nunney BA11 . . . . 143 B8
Berry La EX13 . . . . 198 F3
Berrydale Ave TA6 . . . . . 208 E6
Berryman Cl BA4 . . . . . . 205 A5
Berryman Ct BA5 . . . . . . 203 B4
Bertha Terr TA9 . . . . 104 D3
Berwick Cl TA1 . . . . 212 C1
Beryl Gr BS14 . . . . 23 C8
Beryl Knapp BA22 . . . . . . 197 B8
Beryl La BA5 . . . . 203 F6
Besley St BA5 . . . . 203 B4
Bests Field TA12 . . . . 185 B8
Beverley Cl Frome BA11 . . 119 D3
  Taunton TA2 . . . . 212 C6
Beverley Dr TA23 . . . . . . 202 C7
Beverley Gdns BS9 . . . . . . 5 D7
Bewdley Rd BA2 . . . . 45 B4
Bewley Ct TA20 . . . . 223 B4
Bexes La TA20 . . . . 223 B5
Bibors Hill TA4 . . . . 165 E4
Bibury Cl BS48 . . . . 9 A1
Bibury Ho BA1 . . . . 27 B2
Bickenhall La TA3 . . . . . . 182 F6
Bickfield La BS40 . . . . 74 B8
Bicking's Close La TA4 . . 166 A4
Bicknell Gdns BA21 . . . . . 219 B8
Bidbrooke La EX36 . . . . . 162 A6
Biddiscombe Cl TA6 . . . . 208 C1
Biddisham Cl 🔟 BS48 . . . 8 E1
Biddisham La BS26 . . . . . . 87 E7
Biddle St BS49 . . . . 34 B7
Bideford Cres BS4 . . . . . . 22 F8
Bideford Rd BS22 . . . . 31 F2
Bifield Cl BS14 . . . . 23 E5
Bifield Gdns BS14 . . . . . . 23 E5
Bifield Rd BS14 . . . . 23 F5
Big Tree Cl BS26 . . . . 69 C3
Bignal Rand Cl BA5 . . . . . 203 B3
Bignal Rand Dr BA5 . . . . 203 B3
Bignell Cl BS25 . . . . 69 F8
Bigwood La BS1 . . . . 226 C2
Bilberry Cl BS9 . . . . 5 C8
Bilberry Gr TA1 . . . . 168 F1
Bilbie Cl BS40 . . . . 56 E8
Bilbie Rd Chew Stoke BS40 . 56 E8
  Weston-Super-Mare BS22 . . 32 B3
Bilbury La Bath BA1 . . . . 228 B2
  Glastonbury BA6 . . . . . . 206 F3
Billand Cl BS13 . . . . 21 E3
Billet St TA1 . . . . 212 F3
Billetfield TA1 . . . . 212 F3
Billicombe La TA7 . . . . . . 155 C8
Billing's Hill BS28 . . . . . . 108 C4
Billy La TA4 . . . . 210 D7
Bince's Lodge La BA3 . . . . 78 B3
Binces La BA2 . . . . 42 E3
Bincombe Dr TA18 . . . . . 224 C7
Bincombe Rd TA6 . . . . . . 209 C4
Binding Cl 🔟 TA6 . . . . . 153 F4
Bindon La BA11 . . . . 143 B2
Bindon Rd TA2 . . . . 212 C6
Bindwell La BA22 . . . . . . 197 F3
Binegar CE Prim Sch
  BA3 . . . . 114 D8
Bineham Ct TA10 . . . . . . 173 B4
Bineham La
  Ilchester BA22 . . . . 173 F2
  Yeovilton BA22 . . . . 174 A2
Binford Pl TA6 . . . . 209 A5
Bishop Cross TA4 . . . . . . 151 A4
Binhay Rd BS49 . . . . 34 C7
Binley Gr BS14 . . . . 23 D5
Binmead Gdns BS13 . . . . . 22 B4
Binnings The BS27 . . . . . . 90 F3
Birbeck Rd BS9 . . . . 5 E5
Birch Ave Bleadon BS24 . . . 67 C6
  Clevedon BS21 . . . . 6 E4
  Taunton TA1 . . . . 212 C5
Birch Hill TA27 . . . . 90 C8
Birch Ho TA8 . . . . 65 F2
Birch Rd TA21 . . . . 222 E6
Birch Hill 🔼
  🔼 Martock TA12 . . . . . 185 E6
  Radstock BA3 . . . . 78 E1
  Wellington TA21 . . . . . . 222 E5
Birch La BA2 . . . . 81 E4
Birch WIk BA11 . . . . 120 B7
Bircham Cl TA6 . . . . 208 C4
Birch La TA6 . . . . 204 C4
Bircham Rd
  Minehead TA24 . . . . 201 B5
  Taunton TA2 . . . . 213 A8
Birchanger La TA4 . . . . . 150 A8

Birchdale BA20 ....218 D2
Birchdale Rd BS14 ....23 A8
Birches Cnr TA4 ....152 A4
Birches The BS48 ....9 A2
Birchfield Prim Sch
BA21 ....219 D7
Birchfield Rd BA21 ......219 D8
Birchill Cross EX13 ......198 A6
Birchill La BA11 ....120 A1
Birchwood Rd BA23 .....49 A7
Birchwood Cl BA12 .....144 E8
Birchwood La BS39 ....40 F2
Bird's Cl TA18 ....224 B6
Birdcombe Cl BS48 ....8 E3
Birdlip Cl BS48 ....9 A1
Birdwell La BS41 ....10 F1
Birdwell Prim Sch BS41 .21 A8
Birdwell Rd BS41 ....10 F1
Birkbeck Ct BS23 ....48 D7
Birkett Rd BS23 ....30 B1
Birnbeck Rd BS23 ....30 C1
Biscombe Cross TA3 ....191 B8
Bisdee Rd BS24 ....49 D2
Bishop Ave BS22 ....32 A3
Bishop Cl TA20 ....223 B5
Bishop Fox Dr TA1 ......213 A2
Bishop Fox's Sch TA1 ...213 A1
Bishop Henderson CE Prim
Sch
Coleford BA3 ....116 E8
Taunton TA1 ....212 C2
Bishop Rd TA5 ....134 B2
Bishop St Bristol BS2 ...227 B4
Faulkland BA3 ....80 D2
Bishop Sutton Cty Prim Sch
BS39 ....57 D4
Bishop Terr BS2 ....227 C4
Bishop's Hill TA21 ......179 B7
Bishop's Hull Hill TA1 ..212 B4
Bishop's Hull Prim Sch
TA1 ....212 B4
Bishop's Hull Rd TA1 ...212 A3
Bishop's La DT9 ....187 E1
Bishop's Lydeard Sta
TA4 ....167 E2
Bishop's Mead TA2 .....212 E8
Bishop's Pal* BA5 ....203 E4
Bishop's Path TA8 ......104 B6
Bishops Cl BS39 ....5 E3
Bishops Cove BS13 ....21 F5
Bishops Ct TA21 ....222 D6
Bishops Dr TA10 ....172 A5
Bishops Gn TA4 ....210 C4
Bishops Knoll BS9 ....5 C3
Bishops La BA22 ....197 A6
Bishops Lydeard Prim Sch
TA4 ....167 E8
Bishops Mead BA9 ......35 A8
Bishops Park Way BA5 ..203 F2
Bishops Rd BS49 ....35 A8
Bishops Wlk BA22 ......173 D1
Bishopsland BS45 ......203 C3
Bishopston TA15 ....186 B4
Bishopsworth CE Jun Sch
BS13 ....21 F6
Bishopsworth Rd BS13 ..22 A7
Bishport Ave BS13 ......22 C3
Bishport Cl BS13 ....22 B4
Bishport Gn BS13 ....22 C3
Bitham Wlk TA7 ....136 E3
Bittern Cl BS22 ....31 F1
Bittlemead BS13 ....22 D4
Black Bench Dro TA20 ..223 F7
Black Dog Hill BA13 ....121 E6
Black Dro TA7 ....155 A1
Black La Axbridge BS26 ..70 E2
Hemyock EX15 ....180 D2
Holcombe Rogus TA21 ..178 E6
Black Mere BA22 ....218 B5
Black Mixen La TA18 ...224 C7
Black Monkey La TA24 ..131 C5
Black Pit Dro BA6 ......206 D8
Black Withies Dro TA10 ..155 D1
Black's Moor Hill La
TA11 ....173 A5
Blackacre BS14 ....23 C4
Blackacre Hill BA8 .....176 D4
Blackaller La EX16 .....163 C1
Blackberry Ct TA21 ....222 D4
Blackberry Dr BS22 .....32 A2
Blackberry La
Portishead BS20 ....1 F5
Sherborne DT9 ....225 D5
Winsley BA3,BA15 ......64 C8
Blackbird Cl BA3 ....97 B8
Blackbird Way BA11 ...120 B6
Blackbrook Park Ave
TA1 ....213 E4
Blackbrook Prim Sch
TA1 ....213 D3
Blackbrook Rd TA1 ....213 E5
Blackbrook Way TA1 ...213 E3
Blackdown BA21 ....219 A6
Blackdown Ct BS14 .....23 B5
Blackdown Mead BS27 ..90 C6
Blackdown Rd
Bridgwater TA6 ....209 D4
Portishead BS20 ....2 F5
Rockwell Green TA21 ...222 B4
Taunton TA2 ....213 B8
Blackdown View
Curry Rivel TA10 ....171 D4
Ilminster TA19 ....221 C4
Norton Fitzwarren TA2 ..168 B4

Blackdown View continued
Nynehead TA21 ....167 C2
Sampford Peverell EX16 ..178 C1
Blackdown Visitors Ctr*
EX15 ....180 D3
Blacker's La BA3 ....116 E8
Blackerton Cross EX16 ..162 E3
Blackey La BA3 ....115 B6
Blackford Hollow BA22 ..175 F5
Blackford Moor Dro
BS26,BS28 ....107 B6
Blackford Moor La TA9,
BS28 ....107 B5
Blackford Rd
Charlton Horethorne DT9 ..176 A2
Mark TA9 ....106 F4
Wedmore BS28 ....108 A3
Blackford Way DT9 ....176 A3
Blackfriars BS1 ....227 A3
Blackfriars Rd BS48 ......8 B1
Blackham La TA10 .....155 F2
Blackhayes La EX14 ....192 C1
Blackland Dro TA20 ...194 A1
Blackland La TA10 .....194 B1
Blacklands TA6 ....208 F5
Blackmoor Clevedon BS21 ..6 C1
Langford BS40 ....53 C6
8 Weston-Super-Mare
BS22 ....31 F2
Blackmoor Cl BS40 .....53 C6
Blackmoor La 6 BA10 ..196 A6
Blackmoor Rd
Abbots Leigh BS8 ....4 E2
Taunton TA2 ....213 B7
Wellington TA21 ....222 F4
Blackmoors La BS3 .....11 E4
Blackmore Chase BA9 ..216 D3
Blackmore Dr BA2 ......44 C5
Blackmore La TA5 .....135 B1
Blackmore Rd DT10 ...190 B4
Blacknell Ind Est TA18 ..224 D5
Blacknell La TA18 ......224 D6
Blackrock La
Pensford BS14,BS39 ....40 E7
Publow BS39 ....40 E7
Blacksmith La BA1 .....28 B6
Blacksmith's La BA1 ...26 B3
Blacksmiths La TA7 ....155 F8
Blackthorn Cl
Bridgwater TA6 ....209 C3
Blackthorn Dr BS20 .....2 C5
6 North Petherton TA6 ..153 F3
Blackthorn Gdns
Taunton TA2 ....168 F6
Weston-Super-Mare BS22 ..32 A1
Blackthorn Rd BS13 ....22 D8
Blackthorn Sq BS21 .....6 D1
Blackthorn Terr BS22 ...32 A1
Blackthorn Way
Nailsea BS48 ....9 A2
Somerton TA11 ....211 B3
Street BA16 ....207 A5
Blackthorne Cl BA22 ...173 E2
Blackwater La
Axminster EX13 ....198 F3
Wiveliscombe TA4 .....210 A8
Blackwell Rd BA22 .....174 F3
Blackworthy Rd BA7 ...159 C3
Bladen Cl BS20 ....2 E4
Bladud Bldgs BA1 ......228 C3
Blagdon Cl BS27 ....48 F1
Blagdon Cres TA1 ......212 D1
Blagdon Cross TA1 ....129 D2
Blagdon La Blagdon BS40 ..54 F6
Brompton Regis TA22,
TA24 ....148 D4
Blagdon Pk BA1 ....44 A4
Blagdon Prim Sch BS40 ..54 F2
Blagdon Wlk BA11 ....120 D7
Blagrove Cl Bristol BS13 ..22 C2
Street BA16 ....207 C6
Blagrove Cres BS13 ....22 C3
Blagrove Hill BA6 ......157 C6
Blagrove's Rd TA4 .....167 C4
Blaisdon BS22 ....49 F7
Blaise Wlk BS9 ....5 C6
Blake End BS22 ....31 E4
Blake Gn TA7 ....156 B7
Blake Ind Est TA6 .....209 A3
Blake Pl TA6 ....209 A5
Blake Rd
6 Crewkerne TA18 ....224 C5
Wells BA5 ....203 C5
Blake St
2 Bridgwater TA6 .....208 F4
Taunton TA1 ....213 B4
8 Blake's Cres TA9 ....104 E5
Blake's La TA5,TA6 ....208 C7
Blakeney Gr BS48 ....18 C8
Blakes La TA5,TA6 ....208 C7
Blakes Rd TA6 ....208 D6
Blakeway BS28 ....138 B6
Blandford Cl BS48 ......8 E1
Blaxhold La TA5 ....148 A8
Bleadon Hill BS23,BS24 ..67 A8
Bleadon Mill BS24 ......67 C5
Bleadon Rd BS24 ....67 B7
Bleak St BA9 ....161 E2
Blencathara Ct TA8 ...104 A8
Blenheim Cl
Peasedown St John BA2 ..79 D7
Weston-Super-Mare BS22 ..32 A4
Blenheim Gdns BA1 ....28 A2
Blenheim Mews TA24 ..200 F7

Blenheim Rd
Bridgwater TA6 ....209 D7
Minehead TA24 ....201 A7
Street BA16 ....207 B4
Taunton TA1 ....213 D5
Yeovil BA21 ....219 D7
Blenheim View TA24 ...201 A7
Blenheim Way BS20 .....2 E5
Blights Hill EX16,TA22 ..163 F3
Blind La
Barton St David TA11 ..158 A2
Bath BA1 ....27 C2
Buckland St Mary TA20 ..182 A1
Chard TA20 ....223 D2
Chew Stoke BS40 ....56 E8
Congresbury BS49 ....34 F6
Drimpton DT8 ....199 F6
Isle Abbotts TA3 ....183 F8
Keinton Mandeville TA11 ..158 B1
Martock TA12 ....185 D5
Peasedown St John BA2 ..61 A4
Southwick BA14 ....83 F7
Thorncombe TA20 ....22 C6
Blindhouse La 4 BA11 ..119 F4
Blindwell La
Golsoncott TA23,TA24 ..131 C1
Skilgate TA4 ....164 E6
Bloom Row TA6 ....209 D5
Bloomfield BS24 ....67 A8
Bloomfield Ave Bath BA2 ..44 E4
Timsbury BA2 ....60 B3
Bloomfield Cl
Taunton TA1 ....213 C5
Timsbury BA2 ....60 B2
Bloomfield Cotts BA2 ...79 C7
Bloomfield Cres BA2 ....44 D2
Bloomfield Dr BA2 .....44 D2
Bloomfield Gr BA2 ......44 E3
Bloomfield Pk BS20 .....39 B5
Bloomfield Park Rd BA2 ..60 B3
Bloomfield Rd Bath BA2 ..44 E3
Timsbury BA2 ....60 B3
Bloomfield Rise BA2 ....44 D2
Bloomfield Rise N BA2 ..44 D2
Bloomfield Terr BA2 ....79 C7
Blossom Cl TA6 ....209 C5
Blue Anchor Sta TA24 ..131 C6
Blue Bull Ch BA10 .....215 E6
Blue CE Sch The BA5 ...203 C5
Blue Stone La TA13 ....185 B6
Blue Water Dr BS24 .....50 D3
Bluebell Cl Bristol BS9 ...5 F6
Taunton TA1 ....213 C1
Bluebell Rd
Houndstone BA22 ......218 B5
Weston-Super-Mare BS22 ..32 A6
Blueberry Way BS22 ....31 F1
Bluett Rd TA21 ....222 D4
Blythe Cl TA1 ....212 D1
Blythe Gdns BS22 ....32 A3
Blythe Way TA8 ....85 A3
Boards La BA5 ....204 C7
Boards Rd TA6 ....209 D6
Boardwalk The BA16 ..207 D7
Boarpath La TA4 ....151 A5
Boat La BS24 ....67 C3
Boat Stall La BA2 ......228 C2
Bobbin La BA15 ....64 E6
Bobbin Pk BA15 ....64 F3
Bodden La BA4 ....205 E6
Boden St TA20 ....223 C3
Boden Villas BA7 ....223 C3
Bodmin Rd TA2 ....213 A8
Bodmin Wlk BS4 ....22 F8
Boffa La TA2 ....153 D1
Bofors Pk BA22 ....218 A6
Bollams Mead TA4 ....210 C5
Bolster La BA6 ....157 C4
Bolter's La
Alhampton BA4,BA7 ...159 B4
Shepton Mallet BA4 ...141 D8
Bolton Cl TA9 ....104 F4
Bond St Bridgwater TA6 ..208 F5
Bristol BS1 ....227 B3
Houndstone BA22 ......218 B5
Yeovil BA20 ....219 B4
Bond's La TA20 ....124 A3
Bondfield Way TA20 ...223 B6
Bondip Hill BA22,TA11 ..173 D3
Bonds Cl TA20 ....223 D2
Bonds Pool TA10 ......172 A5
Bonfire Cl TA20 ....223 C2
Bonfire La TA11 ....173 F7
Bonham La BA2 ....161 F4
Bonhill Rd BS39 ....57 D5
Boniface Wlk TA6 .....104 B6
Bonners Cswy EX13 ...198 A2
Bonners Dr EX13 ....198 A2
Bonners Glen EX13 ....198 A1
Bonnie's La 8 TA14 ...185 F4
Bonning's La TA14 ....184 D4
Bonniton La TA24 ......124 B3
Bonniton New Rd TA24 ..201 D1
Bonny Cross
Bampton EX16 ....164 B3
Clayhanger EX16 ....165 B1
Bonny La TA24 ....134 D4
Bonson Hill TA5 ....134 B2
Bonson Wood La TA5 ..134 B2
Boobery EX16 ....178 D1
Book Mus The* BA1 ...228 C1
Boome La TA2 ....169 C3
Boons Orch TA3 ....169 C3
Booth Way TA6 ....208 F6
Boozer Pit TA16 ....195 F8

Borden Gate EX16 .....178 B8
Bordesley Rd BS14 .....23 A3
Boreal Way BS24 ....49 F8
Boreland La BA22 .....187 A8
Borgie Pl BS22 ....31 F3
Borleyton Wlk BS13 ....21 F4
Borough Mall The BS28 ..108 D4
Borough Post TA3 .....170 B3
Borough The
Montacute TA15 ....186 B3
Wedmore BS28 ....108 D4
3 Yeovil BA20 ....219 B4
Borver Gr BS13 ....22 B4
Bosanquet Flats TA24 ..200 F7
Bossington Dr TA2 ....213 B8
Bossington La TA24 ...124 B4
Boswell Rd BA15 ....64 F3
Botham Cl BS22 ....32 A4
Bottreaux Mill Cross
EX36 ....162 A5
Boucher's La TA4 ......165 E4
Boulevard BS23 ....48 E8
Boulters Rd BS13 ....22 C4
Boundaries The BS24 ..67 B1
Boundary Ave
Frome BA11 ....120 B5
Houndstone BA22 ......218 B7
Boundary Cl
Holcombe BA3 ....116 C8
Midsomer Norton BA3 ..97 B7
Weston-Super-Mare BS23 ..48 E3
Yeovil BA21 ....218 E7
Boundary Rd
Houndstone BA22 ......218 A5
Weston-Super-Mare BS24 ..50 A7
Boundary Way
Glastonbury BA6 ....206 C3
Houndstone BA22 ......218 A7
Boundhay BA22 ....186 C2
Bounds La TA20 ....223 A1
Bourchier Cl BS20 .....11 A1
Bourchier Dr 12 EX16 ..164 B1
Bourchier Gdns BS13 ..22 A4
Bourne Gr TA1 ....213 D4
Bourne La Blagdon BS40 ..54 C4
Burrington BS40 ....54 B4
Bournville Inf Sch BS23 ..49 A4
Bournville Jun Sch BS23 ..48 F5
Bourton Combe BS48 ..19 F7
Bourton La
Compton Bishop BS26 ..69 E3
Weston-Super-Mare BS22 ..32 D4
Bourton Mead
Flax Bourton BS48 ....19 F8
Long Ashton BS41 ......11 A1
Bourton Wlk BS13 ......22 A8
Bourtonbridge Dro BA5 ..139 F5
Bouverie Cl TA24 ....200 F6
Bouverie Rd TA6 ....208 D5
Bove Moor La BA16 ...207 E6
Bove Town BA6 ....206 E5
Bovet Cl TA1 ....212 B1
Bovet St TA21 ....222 D6
Bow Gate TA18 ....196 A8
Bow St TA10 ....171 F5
Bowden Cl BS9 ....5 C8
Bowden Hill BA3 ....96 D4
Bowden La
Milborne Port BA8 .....217 F5
Rodhuish TA24 ....130 F3
Yenston BA8 ....189 D7
Bowden Rd BA8 ....189 D8
Bowden Way BS14 .....23 B5
Bowdens La BA22 ......164 E3
Bowditch Row TA18 ..224 C6
Bowen Rd BS24 ....50 C5
Bower Ashton Terr BS3 ..11 F4
Bower Gdns TA6 ....209 C5
Bower Hinton TA12 ...185 D5
Bower La TA6 ....209 C6
Bower Manor Sh Ctr
TA6 ....209 D6
Bowerhayes La TA24 ..131 A5
Bowerings Rd TA6 .....208 E2
Bowerleaze BS9 ....5 B6
Bowermead La BA4 ...204 C1
Bowery Cnr BA5 ....92 E5
Bowfell Cl TA1 ....212 B1
Bowhayes TA18 ....224 C5
Bowhays Cross TA4 ...202 A2
Bowlditch La BA3 ....78 B4
Bowleaze BA21 ....218 D6
Bowling Gn BA10 ......207 D7
Bowlish Inf Sch BA4 ...205 A6
Bowlish La BA4 ....205 A6
Bowmont Gr TA1 ......213 D3
Bowns Cl BA21 ....141 E1
Bowood Rd TA2 ....213 A6
Bowring Cl Bristol BS13 ..22 C3
Coxley BA5 ....139 E6
Bowyers Cl BA6 ....204 C1
Box Bush La BS24 ....33 C1
Box Rd BA1 ....29 C3
Box Wlk BS31 ....24 C4
Boxbury Hill BS39 ......77 F3
Boxbush Hill BA4 .....158 E8
Boxstone Hill TA19 ...184 D2
Boyce Cl BA2 ....43 F5
Boyce's Ave BS8 ......226 A3
Boyd Cl BS30 ....25 E8
Boyd Rd BS31 ....25 E3
Boyle Cl DT10 ....190 B4
Boyton Hill TA19 ......194 F8
Boyton La TA19 ....194 F7
Bracey Rd TA12 ....185 E6
Bracken Edge TA4 .....132 C4

Bracken Way TA20 ....223 F5
Brackenwood Gdns*
BS20 ....1 F5
Brackenwood Rd BS21 ..6 E6
Bracton Dr BS14 ....23 A5
Bradbeers TA3 ....181 D8
Bradfield Cl TA6 ....208 E1
Bradfield Way TA20 ...223 C3
Bradford Cl Clevedon BS21 ..6 C1
Taunton TA1 ....168 D1
Bradford Pk BA2 ....45 A2
Bradford Rd Bath BA2 ..45 A1
Bathford BA1 ....29 B2
Crewkerne TA18 ....224 E4
Rode BA11 ....101 F8
Sherborne DT9 ....225 B3
Wingfield BA11,BA14 ...83 B3
Winsley BA15 ....64 B5
Winsley BA15 ....64 E7
Bradley Ave BS11 ....4 E6
Bradley Cres BS11 ......4 E6
Bradley Cross La BS27 ..90 D7
Bradley Hill La TA11 ..211 B5
Bradley La Ashcott TA7 ..156 B7
Maiden Bradley BA11,
BA12 ....144 B2
Parbrook BA6 ....158 C7
Bradley Rd BS20 ....3 E5
Bradley Stream Rd
BA16,TA7 ....138 C1
Bradley View TA11 ....211 C4
Bradley Way BA6 ......158 B8
Bradley Way TA11 ....183 F4
Bradney La BA22 ......136 D1
Bradon La
Isle Abbotts TA3 ....183 F6
Stocklinch TA19 ....184 A5
Bradville Gdns BS41 ...20 F8
Brae Rd BS25 ....70 B8
Brae Rise BS25 ....70 A8
Bragg's La BS22 ....227 C3
Braikenridge Cl BS21 ...6 C1
Brains La BA22 ....175 A5
Brainsfield BS9 ....5 F6
Braithwaite Pl TA8 .....85 A2
Braithwaite Way BA11 ..120 C6
Brakewell Gdns BS14 ..23 A4
Bramble Dr Bristol BS9 ..5 C4
South Petherton TA13 ..220 C4
Bramble Hill BA16 .....156 D6
Bramble La Bristol BS9 ..5 C4
Haselbury Plucknett TA18 ..196 C5
Bramble Pk TA1 ....213 C2
Bramble Rd BS22 ......31 E3
Bramble Way BA2 .....45 B1
Brambles Rd TA8 ....85 B1
Brambles The
Hinton Charterhouse BA2 ..63 E1
Keynsham BS31 ....24 D3
Wellington TA21 ....222 D4
Bramblewood BS49 ....17 B1
Bramley Cl
Charlton Horethorne DT9 ..176 A2
Crewkerne TA18 ....224 C7
Locking BS24 ....50 A5
Peasedown St John BA2 ..79 D7
Pill BS20 ....4 C4
Sandford BS25 ....52 A4
Yatton BS49 ....34 B7
Bramley Dr Backwell BS48 ..19 A5
Frome BA11 ....120 C6
Bramley Rd Street BA16 ..207 B4
Taunton TA1 ....213 D5
Bramleys The
Nailsea BS48 ....18 B8
Portishead BS20 ....2 F5
Brampton Ho BS20 .....2 E4
Brampton Way BS20 ....2 E4
Bramshill Dr BS22 .....31 F3
Branch Rd BA2 ....63 F2
Branche Gr BS13 ....22 D3
Branches Cross BA10 ..35 E3
Brandon Ho Bristol BS8 ..226 B2
Brandon La TA4 ....219 A6
Brandon St BS1 ....226 C2
Brandon Steep BS1 ...226 C2
Brangay La BS27 ....91 A1
Brangwyn Sq BS22 .....31 F2
Brankscome Ave TA6 ..209 B5
Bransby Way BS24 .....50 A8
Branscombe Rd BS9 ....5 C4
Branscombe Wlk BS20 ..1 F3
Brantwood Rd TA6 ....208 C5
Brassknocker Hill BA2 ..45 F2
Brassmill Ent Ctr BA1 ..44 A7
Brassmill La BA1 ....44 A7
Brassmill Lane Trad Est
BA1 ....44 A7
Bratton La TA24 ....200 D7
Bratton Ho BA24 ......176 B8
Bratton La TA24 ....200 D7
Bratton Mill La
Minehead TA24 ....200 B7
Minehead TA24 ....200 C7
Bratton Rd BA4 ....141 B2
Bray Cl EX16 ....179 B3
Braysbridge BA21 ......90 C7
Braysdown Cl BA2 ......79 B6
Braysdown La BA2 ......79 A5
Breach Cl SP8 ....161 F1
Breach Cl SP8 ....179 F5
Breach Furlong La
TA10 ....156 A1
Breach Hill TA3 ....179 F5
Breach Hill La BS40 ....56 C6
Breach La Axbridge BS26 ..89 B3
Corsley Heath BA12 ...144 E7

Breach La continued
Kington Magna SP8 ...177 E2
Nailsea BS48 ...17 F7
Wanstrow BA4 ...142 E4
Breaches The BS20 ...4 B5
Bread & Cheese La
TA19 ...184 C1
Bread St BA4 ...140 F3
Bream Court Ho TA8 ...65 F3
Bream Ct TA8 ...65 F3
Brean Down Ave BS23 ...48 E4
Brean Down Rd TA8 ...47 F1
Brean Rd BS24 ...66 F1
Brecon View BS24 ...49 A1
Bree BS22 ...32 A4
Breech La BA5 ...158 A8
Bremis Rd TA24 ...201 E3
Brendon Ave BS23 ...48 F8
Brendon Cl TA23 ...131 D2
Brendon Gdns 2 BS48 ...8 E1
Brendon Rd
Bridgwater TA6 ...208 F6
Portishead BS20 ...2 A5
Watchet TA23 ...202 B6
Wellington TA21 ...222 D7
Brendon View TA4 ...151 B7
Brendon Way
Bridgwater TA6 ...208 F6
Cheddar BS27 ...90 C8
Brendons TA4 ...167 E8
Brendons The EX16 ...178 D1
Brent Broad TA8 ...85 B2
Brent Cl Brent Knoll TA9 ...86 B1
Weston-Super-Mare BS24 ...49 B2
Brent Knoll CE Sch TA9 ...86 A2
Brent Rd
Burnham-On-Sea TA8, TA9 ...85 B4
Cossington TA7 ...136 F3
East Brent TA9 ...86 C5
Brent St TA9 ...86 A2
Brentsfield La TA7 ...154 E7
Breowen Cl TA19 ...221 B4
Brereton Rd TA24 ...201 B6
Bretonaux Rd BA6 ...206 E3
Brett Cl TA4 ...202 F1
Brettingham Ct TA17 ...195 C7
Brewery Bglws TA18 ...224 C7
Brewery Hill BS30 ...25 F7
Brewery La Holcombe BA3 ...97 D1
Ilminster TA19 ...221 B4
Oakhill BA3 ...115 A3
Shepton Mallet BA4 ...205 D5
Brewham Rd BA10 ...160 D6
Brewhouse Theatre & Arts
Ctr TA1 ...212 F4
Briant Rd BA6 ...206 F5
Briant Cl TA1 ...212 B1
Briar Cl
Burnham-On-Sea TA8 ...104 C6
Frome BA11 ...120 B7
Nailsea BS48 ...9 A2
Radstock BA3 ...97 D8
Yeovil BA21 ...219 E8
Briar Ct
Burnham-On-Sea TA8 ...104 C6
Pill BS20 ...4 C4
Briar Mead BS49 ...17 A1
Briar Rd Hutton BS24 ...49 E3
Street BA16 ...207 A5
Briarfield BA22 ...173 E2
Briars Ct BA2 ...44 D1
Briars The Backwell BS48 ...18 F7
Yeovil BA20 ...218 C2
Briarwood BS9 ...5 F6
Briary Rd BS20 ...2 C5
Brick Cotts BA3 ...117 A7
Brick St BS2 ...227 C3
Brick Yard La TA18 ...224 C7
Bricklin La DT9 ...225 E7
Brickyard La
Bourton SP8 ...161 F1
Wanstrow BA4 ...142 F5
Biddicott La TA24 ...131 A4
Bridewell La Bath BA1 ...228 B2
Hutton BS24, BS26, BS29 ...50 D1
Shapwick TA7 ...137 F1
Bridewell St BS1 ...227 A3
Bridge Bldgs BS39 ...77 B3
Bridge Cl Evercreech BA4 ...141 E2
Whitchurch BS14 ...23 C4
Williton TA4 ...202 D2
Bridge Cotts
Chard Junction TA20 ...198 D8
Drimpton DT8 ...199 F7
Bridge Farm Cl BS14 ...23 A3
Bridge Farm Inf Sch
BS14 ...23 A4
Bridge Farm Jun Sch
BS14 ...23 A4
Bridge Gdns BA2 ...60 A6
Bridge Hill BA4 ...142 F4
Bridge Rd Bath BA1 ...28 C1
10 Clevedon BS21 ...6 C2
Weston-Super-Mare BS23 ...48 F6
Bridge House Pk TA13 ...220 F4
Bridge Pl BS20 ...187 F4
Bridge Place Rd BA2 ...78 E8
Bridge Rd Bath BA22 ...44 C5
Bleadon BS24 ...67 B6
Leigh Woods BS8 ...11 E6
Weston-Super-Mare BS23 ...48 F6
Bridge Rise 17 TA12 ...185 E6
Bridge St
Bourton SP8 ...161 F1
Bristol BS1 ...227 A2
Dulverton TA22 ...163 D6
Frome BA11 ...119 F5

Bridge St continued
Taunton TA1 ...212 F4
Williton TA4 ...202 D2
Bridge Terr EX16 ...164 B1
Bridge The Frome BA11 ...119 F5
Taunton TA1 ...212 F4
Bridge Valley Rd BS8 ...11 E8
Bridge Way TA13 ...220 E4
Bridgehouse Cross
EX15 ...180 D1
Bridges Mead TA24 ...201 E3
Bridgewater Ent Ctr 7
TA6 ...208 F5
Bridgeway Cotts TA13 ...220 E4
Bridgewell Ct DT9 ...225 E3
Bridgwater TA6 ...208 F4
Bridgwater Bldgs BA7 ...214 B5
Bridgwater Coll TA6 ...209 B5
Bridgwater Ct BS24 ...49 A3
Bridgwater General Hospl
TA6 ...208 D5
Bridgwater Rd
Dundry BA1,BS13,BS48 ...21 C6
East Brent TA9 ...86 D4
Lympsham BS24 ...67 C5
North Petherton TA6 ...153 F4
Taunton TA1 ...213 D5
Weston-Super-Mare BS23,
BS24 ...48 F2
Winscombe BS25 ...70 A5
Bridgwater Sta TA6 ...209 B4
Bridle Way BA22 ...197 F8
Bridport Rd DT8 ...199 F8
Briercliffe Rd BS9 ...5 D7
Briery Leaze Rd BS14 ...23 A4
Brigadier Cl BA22 ...218 A5
Brighton Mews BS8 ...226 B4
Brighton Rd BS23 ...48 E6
Brighton St BS2 ...227 B4
Brigstocke Rd BS2 ...227 B4
Brimble Cotts DT10 ...189 F1
Brimbleworth La BS22 ...32 C3
Brimclose Rd TA17 ...195 B7
Brimgrove La TA19 ...184 E4
Brimhill Rise BA13 ...121 D4
Brimley Cross BS15 ...180 F1
Brimley Hill EX13 ...198 D2
Brimley Rd EX13 ...198 D3
Brimridge Rd BS25 ...70 A8
Brimstone La
Rockwell Green TA21 ...222 A2
Sampford Arundel TA21 ...179 F6
Sampford Peverell EX16 ...178 E2
Brincil Hill TA11 ...173 D4
Brindham La BA6 ...206 F8
Brindle Cl TA2 ...212 C7
Brines Orch BA8 ...176 E1
Brinmead Wlk BS13 ...21 F3
Brinscombe La BS26 ...89 A5
Brinsea Batch BS49 ...52 E8
Brinsea La BS49 ...52 F8
Brinsea Rd BS49 ...34 E2
Briscoes Ave BS13 ...22 D4
Brislington Sch BS4 ...23 F8
Bristol Cathedral Sch
BS1 ...226 C2
Bristol City Flagd Gd BS3 ...11 F3
Bristol Dental Hospl
BS1 ...227 A3
Bristol Gate BS8 ...11 F5
Bristol General Hospl
BS1 ...227 A1
Bristol Gram Sch BS8 ...226 C3
Bristol Harbour Rly*
BS1 ...226 C1
Bristol Hill BA5 ...203 B6
Bristol Homeopathic Hospl
BS8 ...226 C4
Bristol Ind Mus BS1 ...227 A1
Bristol Rd
Bridgwater TA6 ...209 B7
Chew Stoke BS40 ...56 E8
Chewton Mendip BA5 ...113 A8
Churchill BS25 ...53 A5
Congresbury BS49 ...34 D5
Farrington Gurney BS39 ...76 F5
Highbridge TA9 ...104 F4
Horrington BA5 ...112 F6
Keynsham BS31 ...24 E6
Newton St Loe BA2 ...43 D7
Paulton BS39 ...77 F7
Pensford BS39 ...40 D6
Portishead BS20 ...2 E4
Puriton TA6 ...136 B3
Radstock BA3 ...78 F3
Rooksbridge BS26,TA9 ...87 B5
Sherborne DT9 ...225 D5
Weston-Super-Mare BS22 ...32 C2
Whitchurch BS14 ...23 D3
Winscombe BS25 ...70 C8
Wraxall BS48 ...9 D4
Bristol Rd Lower BS23 ...30 E1
Bristol Royal Infmy BS2 ...227 A4
Bristol Temple Meads Sta
BS1 ...227 C1
Bristol View BA2 ...62 C8
Bristol Zoo Gdns* BS8 ...5 F1
Britannia Cl BA3 ...96 D4
Britannia Way
Chard TA20 ...223 C6
Clevedon BS21 ...6 C1
Briton St 2 EX16 ...164 C1
Brittan Pl BS20 ...3 E3

Brittania Bldgs BS8 ...226 A1
Britten's Cl BS39 ...77 F6
Britten's Hill BS39 ...77 F6
Brittons Ash TA2 ...213 F8
Brittons Pass SN14 ...13 F8
Broad Cl
Kington Magna SP8 ...177 E1
Wells BA5 ...112 E1
Broad Dro
Burrowbridge TA7 ...155 A2
North Wootton BA4 ...140 A3
Broad Hill BA22 ...196 D7
Broad La
East Chinnock BA22 ...196 E7
Hawkridge TA22 ...146 D1
North Curry TA3 ...170 D4
Winsford TA22 ...147 F4
Broad Lane Head
Hawkridge TA22 ...146 D1
Winsford TA22 ...147 F4
Broad Mead La BS40 ...38 A3
Broad Oak 2 BA20 ...219 B4
Broad Oak Hill TA4 ...151 B5
Broad Oak Rd BS13 ...21 F4
Broad Oaks BS8 ...11 E6
Broad Path EX16 ...179 A1
Broad Plain BS2 ...227 C2
Broad Quay Bath BA1 ...228 C1
Bristol BS1 ...227 A2
Broad Rd Blagdon BS40 ...72 D8
Rodney Stoke BA5 ...91 E1
Broad St Bath BA1 ...228 C3
Bristol BS1 ...227 A3
Charlton Adam TA11 ...173 F7
Chewton Mendip BA3 ...94 C5
Churchinford TA3 ...191 D7
Congresbury BS49 ...34 D4
Somerton TA11 ...211 E4
Stoney Stratton BA4 ...141 F2
Wells BA5 ...203 D4
Wrington BS40 ...35 D2
Broad Stones BA15 ...46 E7
Broad Street Pl BA1 ...228 C3
Broad Way TA12 ...185 D5
Broad Weir BS1 ...227 B3
Broadacres BA22 ...197 C8
Broadbridge Rd TA3 ...183 C6
Broadbury Rd BS4 ...22 E8
Broadclose Way TA11 ...158 A2
Broadcroft BS40 ...38 F3
Broadcroft Ave BS49 ...17 F1
Broadcroft Cl BS49 ...17 F1
Broadenham La TA20 ...194 E1
Broadfield Rd BS4 ...23 A8
Broadguage Bsns Pk
TA4 ...167 E7
Broadlands BA5 ...110 E7
Broadhurst Gdns TA8 ...104 B5
Broadlands BS21 ...6 F3
Broadlands Ave
Keynsham BS31 ...24 D6
North Petherton TA6 ...153 F4
Broadlands Cl BA21 ...219 E8
Broadlands Ct TA1 ...212 E2
Broadlands Dr BS11 ...5 A8
Broadlands Rise TA1 ...212 E2
Broadlands Sch BS31 ...24 D6
Broadlands Way TA1 ...212 E2
Broadlawn TA6 ...136 E4
Broadleas BS13 ...22 C7
Broadmeade Bristol BS11 ...4 E7
Yeovil BA21 ...218 C6
Broadleaze Way BS25 ...51 F2
Broadly Gdns TA2 ...213 E8
Broadmead Bristol BS1 ...227 B3
Kingsbury Episcopi TA12 ...185 B7
South Petherton TA13 ...220 B4
Broadmead Dro TA7 ...155 F6
Broadmead La
Barrington TA19 ...184 D6
Catcott TA7 ...137 D2
Edington TA7 ...137 C3
Keynsham BS31 ...25 A6
Kington Magna SP8 ...177 D1
Norton Sub Hamdon TA14 ...185 F2
Broadmead Rd BA21 ...219 E8
Broadmoor Dro BS28 ...89 D3
Broadmoor La Bath BA1 ...27 A3
Horsington BA8 ...176 E2
Broadmoor Pk BA1 ...27 B2
Broadmoor Vale BA1 ...27 A3
Broadoak TA19 ...183 C2
Broadoak Com Sch BS23 ...48 E3
Broadoak Hill BS41 ...21 F2
Broadoak Rd
Bridgwater TA6 ...209 D5
Langford BS40 ...53 A5
Weston-Super-Mare BS23 ...48 D3
Broadoak Wlk BS13 ...22 D5
Broadstone TA7 ...154 E6
Broadstone La
Hardington Mandeville
BA22 ...197 A6
Kington Seymour BS21 ...15 F3
West Chinnock TA18 ...196 C7
Broadstone Wlk BS13 ...22 D5
Broadway Bath BA2 ...208 F4
Charlton Adam TA11 ...174 A7
Chilcompton BA3 ...96 C3
Chilton Polden TA7 ...137 B2
Frome BA11 ...119 D5
Locking BS24 ...50 D4
Merriott TA16 ...195 F7
Saltford BS31 ...25 D3

Broadway continued
Shipham BS25 ...70 E8
Weston-Super-Mare BS24 ...49 A2
Broadway Ave TA7 ...137 B2
Broadway Cl BA3 ...96 C3
Broadway Hill TA19 ...183 B1
Broadway La
Castle Cary BA22 ...214 B3
East Chinnock BA22 ...196 D8
Midsomer Norton BA3 ...78 B5
Westbury Sub Mendip
BA5 ...110 D7
Broadway Prim Sch
TA19 ...183 C2
Broadway Rd
Bristol, Bishopsworth BS13 ...21 F5
Charlton Adam TA11 ...173 F7
Horton TA19 ...183 C2
Broadways Head EX14,
TA20 ...192 C6
Broadwell Cl BA20 ...193 D6
Broadwood Rd TA24 ...130 D4
Brock Cl BA7 ...214 C6
Brock End BS20 ...1 F3
Brock St BA1 ...228 B3
Brockhole La
Dinnington TA17 ...195 B8
Tatworth EX13,TA20 ...198 B7
Brockle Cl TA11 ...211 C2
Brockley Cl Nailsea BS48 ...8 D1
Weston-Super-Mare BS24 ...48 F1
Brockley Combe Rd
BS48 ...19 B1
Brockley Cres BS24 ...48 F1
Brockley La BS48 ...18 D4
**Brockley Mini Farm (Open
Farm)*** BS48 ...35 F7
Brockley Rd BS31 ...25 D2
Brockley Way BS49 ...18 B3
Brockley Wlk BS13 ...22 A8
Brocks La BS41 ...10 F3
Brockway BS48 ...8 F2
Brockwell La TA24 ...129 F6
Brockwood BA15 ...64 F7
Brocole La TA20 ...193 D5
Broderip 7 ...136 F3
Bromes La TA3 ...183 F7
Bromley Rd BS39 ...39 F1
Bromley Sq BS49 ...34 E3
Brompton Mdws TA22 ...148 B2
Brompton Rd BS24 ...49 A2
Brook Bank Draycott BS27 ...90 F2
Rodney Stoke BS27 ...109 C7
Brook Cl Long Ashton BS41 ...11 B1
Minehead TA24 ...200 F7
North Petherton TA6 ...153 E3
Brook Cotts BA2 ...43 B7
Brook Gate BS3 ...11 E1
Brook La
Barton St David BA6 ...157 F3
Catcott TA7 ...137 D2
Henstridge BA8 ...190 A6
Brook Rd Bath BA2 ...44 D6
Williton TA4 ...202 E3
Brook St Bampton EX16 ...164 B1
Cannington TA5 ...135 B2
Milborne Port DT9 ...217 D1
Minehead TA24 ...201 B5
North Newton TA7 ...153 F1
Timberscombe TA24 ...130 B5
Brook Street Mews
TA24 ...201 B5
Brookdale Rd BS13 ...22 B6
Brooke Rd Berrow TA8 ...84 F4
Taunton TA1 ...213 B4
Brookes Cl BA5 ...203 C5
Brookfield Pk BA1 ...27 B2
Brookfield Way BA16 ...207 A4
Brookfield Wlk BS21 ...6 F3
Brookfields BA7 ...214 B5
Brookhampton Cnr
BA22 ...175 D6
Brookland Rd
Langport TA10 ...172 A6
Weston-Super-Mare BS22 ...49 B7
Brookland Way 8 BA8 ...190 A6
Brooklands
Bridgwater TA6 ...209 C5
Peasedown St John BA2 ...61 D3
Brooklands Rd BA21 ...222 B5
Brookleaze BS9 ...5 C5
Brookleaze Bldgs BA1 ...28 B2
Brookleigh BA16 ...207 A5
Brooklyn BS40 ...35 D2
Brooklyn Rd Bath BA1 ...28 C2
Bristol BS13 ...22 B8
Brooklyn Terr BA5 ...139 D8
Brooks Hill LS15 ...179 C1
Brooks La BS41 ...10 F1
Brooks Pl TA21 ...222 C6
Brooks Rd BA16 ...207 C4
Brookside
Paulton BA19 ...183 C2
Milborne Port DT9 ...217 D1
Paulton BS39 ...77 F6
Pill BS20 ...4 D3
South Cheriton BA8 ...176 D3
Weston-Super-Mare BS24 ...197 A8
Brookside Cl
Batheaston BA1 ...28 F5
Paulton BS39 ...77 F6
Brookside Dr BA2 ...59 F6
Brookside Rd BS4 ...23 D8
Brookside Prim Sch
BA16 ...207 B4

Brookside Rd BS13 ...135 B5
Brookview Wlk BS13 ...22 B7
Broom Cl EX13 ...198 A1
Broom Farm Cl BS48 ...18 E8
Broom Hill La BS39 ...77 E8
Broom La
Chardstock EX13 ...198 C5
Oake TA4 ...167 D3
Broom's La TA3 ...191 F7
Broomball Cross TA22 ...162 F5
Broomball La EX16 ...162 E5
Broomclose Cnr BA3 ...114 B4
Broomfield Ho TA2 ...212 C7
Broomground BA15 ...64 E7
Broomhill La BS39 ...58 E3
Broomyland Hill TA5 ...152 C7
Brottens Rd
Cranmore BA4 ...142 A5
Doulting BA4 ...141 F5
Brougham Hayes BA2 ...44 D6
Brougham Pl BA1 ...28 B2
Broughton Cl
Taunton TA11 ...213 C2
Walton BA16 ...156 F7
Broughton Ho BS1 ...227 B1
Broughton La TA3 ...169 B1
Broughtons Dr TA18 ...224 E3
Brow Hill BA2 ...28 F3
Brow The Bath BA2 ...44 B5
Bath, Monkton Combe BA2 ...45 C1
Brown Down La TA20 ...192 C7
Brown La TA4,TA20 ...149 C3
Brown's Pl BA5 ...203 C4
Brownes Hill BS39 ...58 C6
Brownings Rd WS5 ...135 B2
Brownlow Rd BS23 ...48 E4
Browns Cl BS28 ...109 C1
Browns La BS28 ...109 C1
Browns Rd TA24 ...169 C5
Broxholme Wlk BS11 ...4 F8
Brue Ave Bridgwater TA6 ...209 B3
Bruton BA10 ...215 F7
Brue Bsns Pk TA9 ...136 E8
Brue Cl Bruton BA10 ...215 F7
Weston-Super-Mare BS23 ...49 A5
Bruce Cres TA8 ...104 B5
Brue Ho TA8 ...85 A1
Brue Way TA9 ...104 F3
Bruelands BA10 ...215 F7
Bruford Cl TA1 ...212 E3
Brummel Way BS39 ...77 C6
Brunel Cl Somerton TA11 ...211 D4
Weston-Super-Mare BS24 ...48 F1
Brunel Ct TA6 ...208 F6
Brunel Ho BA2 ...44 A6
Brunel Lock Rd BS1 ...11 F5
Brunel Prec TA11 ...211 D4
Brunel Rd Bristol BS13 ...22 A8
Nailsea BS48 ...8 B1
Brunel Way
Bristol BS1,BS3 ...11 F4
Frome BA11 ...120 C7
Minehead TA24 ...201 B6
Brunel's Way TA9 ...104 C5
Brunnell's Knap DT10 ...190 A1
Brunswick Pl Bath BA1 ...228 B3
10 Bristol BS1 ...11 F5
Brunswick Sq BS2 ...227 B4
Brunswick St 1 Bath BA1 ...28 B1
Bristol BS2 ...227 B4
Yeovil BA20 ...219 A4
Brushford Cross TA22 ...163 E4
Brushford New Rd TA22 ...163 E4
Brutasche Terr BA16 ...207 D7
Bruton BS24 ...49 A2
Bruton Ave Bath BA2 ...44 F4
Portishead BS20 ...2 F4
Bruton Avenue Garages
BA2 ...44 F4
Bruton Cl BS48 ...18 E8
Bruton Hatt BA10 ...215 E6
Bruton La BA4 ...142 F2
Bruton Pl BS8 ...226 B3
Bruton Prim Sch BA10 ...215 E6
Bruton Rd BA4 ...141 F1
Bruton Sch For Girls
BA10 ...215 C3
Brutton Way Chard TA20 ...223 B3
Bryant Ave BA3 ...78 D1
Bryant Gdns BS21 ...6 C1
Bryant's Hill TA22 ...148 C2
Bryer Cl Bridgwater TA6 ...208 E1
Chard TA20 ...223 D3
Brymore Cl BA21 ...219 D6
Brymore Sec Tech Sch
TA5 ...135 A2
Brympton Ave BA22 ...186 D2
Brympton Way BA20 ...218 D3
Bubwith Cl TA20 ...223 D3
Bubwith Rd TA20 ...223 D3
Buces Rd TA1 ...212 B1
Buck Cl BA6 ...206 C3
Buckers Mead Sch
BA21 ...219 C8
Buckhill TA24 ...131 B4
Buckhill Cl TA18 ...224 D3
Buckingham Cl TA6 ...209 A2
Buckingham Pl BS8 ...226 A3
Buckingham Rd BS24 ...49 B2
Buckingham St BS3 ...226 A4
Buckland Cl TA8 ...104 C8
Buckland Gn BS22 ...32 A5
Buckland La BA22 ...175 C3

Buckland Rd
Shepton Mallet BA4 ......205 A5
Taunton TA2 ....213 B8
Yeovil BA21 ....219 C6
Buckland Sch TA23 ......202 C6
Buckland St Mary CE Prim
Sch TA20 ....193 A8
Bucklands Batch BS48 ...18 F8
Bucklands Dr BS48 ....19 A8
Bucklands End BS48 ......19 A8
Bucklands Gr BS48 ....18 F8
Bucklands La BS48 ....18 F8
Bucklands View BS48 .....19 A8
Buckle Pl BA22 ....218 B6
Bucklers Mead Rd
BA21 ....219 D8
Bucklers Mead Wlk
BA21 ....219 D8
Buckshots Cross EX14 ...192 D4
Buckwell TA21 ....222 E6
Bude Cl BS48 ....9 B1
Budge La BA11 ....144 A8
Budgett's Cross TA21 ...180 F6
Budgetts TA21 ....180 F6
Bughole La TA21 ....179 E8
Bugle Ct 11 BA8 ....190 A6
Building of Bath Mus*
BA1 ....228 C3
Bulford TA21 ....222 D5
Bulford La TA21 ....222 D5
Bull Bridge Mead BA22 .197 D3
Bull Horn Dro TA7 ......154 D5
Bull La BS20 ....4 C4
Bull Mdw TA4 ....167 F7
Bull Plot Hill BA6 .....158 C8
Bull St TA1 ....169 D4
Bull's Hill BA2 ....62 E1
Bull's La Tatworth TA20 ..198 C8
Upton Noble BA4 ....142 F2
Bull's Quarr BA21 .....143 F8
Bull's Quarries Rd BA11 143 F7
Bullen Mead BA11 ......117 F2
Bullens Cl TA1 ....183 F4
Buller Ave BA22 ....218 A6
Bullmead Cl BA16 ......207 B5
Bullmead La BA11 ......143 C7
Bullock Field Hill TA6 .166 B2
Bullocks La BS21 ....16 C4
Bullon Dro TA5 ....134 B7
Bulls La TA18 ....224 B6
Bulwarks La BA6 ....206 F4
Bumper's Batch BA2 .....63 A8
Buncombe Hill TA5 .....152 C3
Bunford Hollow Rdbt
BA20 ....218 D1
Bunford La BA20 ....218 C4
Bungalows The
Axbridge BS26 ....70 C2
Chard TA20 ....223 D5
Nether Stowey TA5 ....134 A2
Poyntington DT9 ....188 A8
Bungay's Hill BA3,BS39 ..59 E1
Bunker Military Mus The*
TA9 ....104 D3
Bunns La Frome BA11 ...143 F5
Horningsham BA11 .....144 A5
Bunting Ct BS22 ....31 E1
Burch's Cl TA1 ....212 C2
Burchill BS39 ....58 F3
Burchill's Hill TA21 ...222 B7
Burchills Cl TA21 ......212 B1
Burcott La Coxley BA5 .139 E7
Wells BA5 ....203 A3
Burcott Rd BA5 ....203 B3
Burdenham Dro TA7 ....155 A6
Burfoot Rd BS14 ....23 E4
Burfoote Gdns BS14 .....23 E4
Burford Cl Bath BA1 ....44 B3
Portishead BS20 ....2 B5
Burford Cross BA4 .....204 C2
Burford Gr BS11 ....4 F5
Burgage TA21 ....222 D6
Burgage La TA4 ....167 A4
Burgage Rd TA5 ....134 C6
Burge Cres TA4 ....167 E6
Burge's Hill BA3 ....116 B1
Burge's La BA3 ....116 B1
Burges Cl Marnhull DT10 190 F4
Wiveliscombe TA4 ....210 C5
Burges La TA4 ....210 C5
Burgess Cl TA1 ....212 B1
Burgess La BA6 ....157 F6
Burgis Rd BS14 ....23 D6
Burgundy Rd TA24 .....201 A8
Burleigh Gdns BA1 .....44 A8
Burleigh La BA16 ......207 C4
Burlescombe CE Prim Sch
EX16 ....179 A3
Burley Gdns BA16 .....207 D4
Burlingham's La BA22 ..186 C8
Burlington Rd
Midsomer Norton BA3 ...78 C2
Portishead BS20 ....2 E7
Burlington St Bath BA1 .228 B4
15 Weston-Super-Mare
BS23 ....48 E8
Burn Hill TA4,TA21 .....166 F7
Burnbush Cl BS14 ....23 E6
Burnbush Prim Sch BS14 .23 D5
Burnell Dr BS2 ....227 C4
Burnell Ho **3** BA4 ....205 B6
Burnett Bsns Pk BS31 ...25 E1
Burnett Hill TA8 ....104 C7
Burnett Hill BS31 ......42 B8
Burnett Ind Est BS40 ...35 E1

Burnett's La BA6 .....158 A6
Burnham CI BS24 ....48 F1
Burnham Dr BS24 ....48 F1
Burnham Moor La TA9 ..105 B5
Burnham Rd Bath BA2 ....44 C6
Bristol BS11 ....4 D6
Highbridge TA9 ....104 D4
Burnham-on-Sea Inf Sch
TA8 ....104 C8
Burns Rd TA1 ....213 C4
Burnshill Dr TA2 ......212 A7
Burnt House Cotts BA2 ..62 C8
Burnt House La
Long Sutton TA10 ......172 E5
Stoke St Michael BA3 ..116 C2
Burnt House Rd BA2 ....62 D8
Burnthouse Dro BA5 ...141 B8
Burrell La BA7 ....158 F1
Burrells BA22 ....197 B8
Burridge Cross TA20 ...193 E1
Burrington Ave BS24 ...49 E2
Burrington CE Prim Sch
BS40 ....53 F3
Burrington Cl Nailsea BS48 .8 E1
Weston-Super-Mare BS24 .49 E1
Burrington Coombe*
BS40 ....54 A1
Burrington La BS40 ....54 A3
Burrington Wlk BS13 ...22 A8
Burrough St TA12 ......185 F7
Burrough Way TA21 ....222 D4
Burroughes Ave BA21 ..218 A6
Burrow Dro
Burrowbridge TA7 .....154 F1
Hambridge TA12 ....184 F8
Burrow Hill Dro TA7 ...155 A1
Burrow La
Ashbrittle TA21 ....178 D8
High Ham TA10 ....156 A1
Burrow Rocks TA4 .....202 B1
Burrow Wall TA7 ......155 A1
Burrow Way
Hambridge TA12 ....184 F8
Kingsbury Episcopi TA12 185 A7
Burrowfield Cl BA10 ...215 F7
Burrowfields BA10 ....215 F7
Burston La BA3 ....97 B1
Burstock La EX16 ......164 A4
Burt's Hill BA4 ....142 F3
Burtle Rd Burtle TA7 ...137 D6
East Huntspill TA9 ....136 F4
Westhay BA6 ....138 A5
Burton Cl BS1 ....227 B1
Burton Ct BS8 ....226 B3
Burton La BA22 ....197 C8
Burton Pl TA1 ....212 E3
Burton Row TA7 ....137 B3
Burton Row TA5 ....86 A5
Burton St **5** Bath BA1 228 B2
Marnhull DT10 ....190 F6
Burtonhayes DT10 .....190 F6
Burwalls Rd BS8 ....11 F6
Bury The BS24 ....50 A3
Buscott La TA7 ....138 B1
Bush La TA5 ....152 E6
Bush Pl TA10 ....172 E5
Bush Rd TA5 ....152 D7
Bushfield Rd TA18 .....224 B4
Bushfurlong Rd TA3 ...184 B8
Bushs Orch TA11 ......221 A4
Bushy Coombe Gdns
BA6 ....206 F5
Bushy Cross La TA3 ...169 C3
Bushy Thorn Rd BS40 ...56 E3
Business Pk The BS13 ...22 E3
Bussell's Moor Cross
EX36 ....162 C4
Bussex Sq TA7 ....154 F6
Butcher's Hill TA3 ....170 F2
Butcher's La TA5 ......134 A2
Butchers La
Castle Cary BA7 ....159 C3
Shapwick TA7 ....155 F8
Butcombe BS40 ....49 A2
Butcombe La BS40 ......55 B7
Butcombe Wlk BS14 ....23 B5
Butham La
Chew Magna BS40 ......39 A4
Chew Magna BS40 ......39 B4
Butlass Cl BS39 ....59 D1
Butleigh CE Prim Sch
BA6 ....157 E3
Butleigh Cl TA6 ....209 D4
Butleigh Cross BA6 ...157 E3
Butleigh Dro
Ashcott TA7,BA16 .....156 C5
Walton BA16 ....156 D6
Butleigh Hospl BA6 ...157 D4
Butleigh Old Rd BA6 ..206 E3
Butleigh Rd
Glastonbury BA6 ......206 E3
Street BA16 ....207 E5
Butler's Gdns BA11 ...120 A4
Butlers Cl BA6 ....206 E5
Butt La TA10 ....171 D4
Butt Lake Rd TA9 .....106 B3
Butt's Batch BS40 ......35 D1
Butterlciffe Rise BA1 ...143 E1
Butterfield Pk BS21 .....6 C1
Butterfly Ho DT9 .....187 F3
Buttermere Rd BS23 ....49 A5
Butterworth Ct BS4 ....22 D7
Buttice La BA5 ....111 B1
Buttle La TA19 ....184 E4
Buttle's Cross TA3 ....191 F7

Buttle's La TA3 ......191 E6
Button Cl BS14 ....23 A6
Button St TA11 ....119 D5
Butts TA19 ....221 C4
Butts Batch BS26 ....69 B3
Butts Castle TA1 ......221 C4
Butts Cl Marnhull DT10 190 F5
Williton TA4 ....202 D4
Butts Cnr TA6 ....153 F4
Butts Hill BA11 ....119 E3
Butts La Ilton TA19 ...183 D3
Kilmington BA12 ......161 F7
Langford Budville TA21 166 F2
Rodney Stoke BS27 .....91 A1
Butts Orch BA40 ....35 D1
Butts Quarry La TA18 ..224 C6
Butts The BA11 ....119 E3
Butts Way TA4 ....166 F4
Buxtons Cl **6** BA5 ...139 D8
Byfield BA2 ....45 B1
Byfields BS21 ....16 C8
Byron Cl BS24 ....50 A4
Byron Ct BS23 ....48 F8
Byron Pl BS8 ....226 B3
Byron Rd Bath BA2 .....44 F4
Locking BS24 ....50 A4
Taunton TA1 ....213 C3
Weston-Super-Mare BS23 49 A5
Byzantine Ct BS1 ......227 A1

C

Cabbage La BA8 ....176 C3
Cabell Ct BA11 ....119 D2
Cabell Rd BA11 ....119 E2
Cabot Cl BS31 ....25 D2
Cabot Prim Sch BS2 ...227 C4
Cabot Rise BS20 ....2 A5
Cabot Twr* BS8 ....226 B2
Cabot Way Bristol BS8 ..11 F5
Pill BS20 ....4 D3
Weston-Super-Mare BS22 32 A3
Cadstand BS20 ....2 D6
Cad Rd Ilminster TA19 .221 A8
Ilton TA19 ....183 E3
Cadbury Camp La BS20 ..8 C6
Cadbury Camp La W BS21 .7 C5
Cadbury Castle* BA22 ..175 C4
Cadbury Cl BA11 ......120 C6
Cadbury Farm Rd BS49 ..34 C7
Cadbury Halt BS20 .....1 F1
Cadbury Ho BS20 ....2 A4
Cadbury La BS20 ....2 A4
Cadbury Rd
Keynsham BS31 ....25 A2
Portishead BS20 ....2 A4
Cadbury Sq BS49 ....34 C3
Cadby Ho BA2 ....44 A6
Cadogan Rd BS14 ....23 A8
Cadwell's La TA9 .....136 A8
Caern Well Pl BA1 ....228 C4
Caernarvon Rd BS31 ....24 D4
Caernarvon Way TA8 ...85 B1
Cairn Cl BS48 ....9 A1
Cala Trad Est BS3 .....11 F3
Calder Cl BS31 ....25 A4
Calder Cres TA1 ......213 D4
Cale Cl DT10 ....190 C4
Cale Way TA4 ....216 B4
Caledonia Mews BS8 ..11 F6
Caledonia Pl BS8 ......11 F7
Caledonian Rd Bath BA2 44 D6
Bristol BS1 ....226 B1
Caller's La EX15 ......180 D1
Callins Cl TA24 ....201 A5
Callins View TA24 ....201 A5
Callow Hill BA5 ......139 C7
Callowhill Ct **4** BS1 227 B3
Calluna Cl BS22 ....32 A5
Calton Gdns BA2 ......228 C1
Calton Rd BA2 ....228 C1
Calton Wlk BA2 ....228 B1
Calvados Rd TA1 ......213 C3
Calway Rd TA1 ....213 B2
Cam Brook Cl BA2 ......78 D8
Camberley Rd BS4 ......22 D8
Camberley Wlk BS22 ...49 E8
Camborne Gr BA21 ....219 E5
Camborne Pl BA21 ....219 E5
Camborne St BA21 ....219 E5
Cambridge Cl BA20 ...218 D5
Cambridge Gr BS21 .....6 D5
Cambridge Pl BS23 ....48 D8
Cambridge St BA20 ...223 D4
Cambridge Terr Bath BA2 45 B5
11 Taunton TA2 .....213 A8
Cambrook Ho BS39 .....76 F8
Camden Cres BA1 .....228 B4
Camden Ct BA1 ....228 B4
Camden Rd Bath BA1 ...28 A1
Bristol BS3 ....226 B1
Somerton TA11 ....211 C4
Camden Row Bath BA1 .228 B4
Camden Terr Bristol BS8 226 A2
Weston-Super-Mare BS23 48 D8
Camel Cross TA4 ......167 B1
Camel St TA11 ....173 F7
Cameley CE Prim Sch
BS39 ....58 E1
Cameley Gn BA2 ....44 A6
Cameley La BS39 ....58 D1
Cameley Rd BS39 ....76 C8
Camelot Ct TA11 ......211 B5
Cameroons Cl BS31 ....24 E4

Camerton CE Prim Sch
BA2 ....78 E8
Camerton Cl BS31 ......25 E3
Camerton Hill BA2 .....78 E8
Camerton Rd BA2 ......78 E8
Camp Rd Bristol BS8 ...11 F7
Weston-Super-Mare BS23 30 C1
Yeovil BA22 ....186 D1
Camp Rd N BS23 ....30 B1
Camp View BS48 ....8 D2
Campania BA22 ....219 D7
Campion Dr
Houndstone BA22 ......218 B5
Taunton TA1 ....213 C1
Campion Gdns TA20 ...223 D5
Campion Wlk BS4 .....22 D6
Campkin Rd BA5 ......203 B4
Camplins BS21 ....6 C1
Camvale BA2 ....78 B8
Camview BS39 ....77 D6
Canada Coombe BA24 ...50 A1
Canada Way BS1 ......226 B1
Canal Cl TA21 ....222 B8
Canal Dro BS27,BS28 ...90 A3
Canal Rd TA1 ....212 F5
Canal Terr
Bathampton BA2 ....28 F1
Taunton TA1 ....212 F5
Canal View TA6 ....209 A4
Canal Way TA19 ....221 A3
Canberra BS24 ....50 B6
Canberra Rd BS23 .....48 F3
Canford La BS9 ....5 E8
Canford Rd BS9 ....5 F8
Cann St TA1 ....212 E3
Cannard's Grave Rd
BA4 ....205 C4
Cannington CE Prim Sch
TA5 ....135 C2
Cannington Coll TA5 ..135 B2
Cannington Coll (Yeovil Ctr)
BA20 ....218 C5
Cannington College Gdns*
TA5 ....135 C2
Cannington Countryside Vst
Ctr* TA5 ....135 B2
Cannock Sq BA4 ......205 C4
Cannon Cl TA6 ....209 B5
Cannon Court Mews
DT9 ....217 D1
Cannon St BS1 ....227 A4
Cannons Gate BS21 ....16 C8
Canns La
9 North Petherton TA6 153 F4
Puriton TA7 ....136 C4
Cannwood La BA10 ....161 B8
Canon St TA1 ....213 A4
Canon's Rd BS1 ......226 C1
Canons Cl BA2 ....44 B2
Canons Gate BA22 ....173 E1
Canons Rd BS1 ....226 C2
Canons Way BS1 ......226 C1
Canons Wlk BS22 ......31 D2
Cantell Gr BS14 ....23 F5
Canterbury Cl BS22 ...32 B3
Canterbury Dr TA3 ...170 C4
Canterbury Rd BA2 ....44 D5
Cantock's Cl BS8 .....226 C3
Canvin Ct TA11 ....211 B5
Canworth Way TA6 ...209 C3
Canynge Ho **2** BS1 ...227 B1
Canynge Rd BS8 ....11 F8
Canynge Sq BS8 ....11 F8
Canynge St BS1 ......227 B2
Capell Cl BS22 ....49 B8
Capenor Cl BS20 ....2 C4
Capes Cl TA6 ....209 A5
Capland Ct TA3 ....183 A8
Capland La TA3 ......183 A8
Caple La BA40 ....56 B5
Capton TA4 ....132 C2
Capton Cross TA4 ....132 C2
Carantoc Pl **1** TA24 131 A5
Caraway Cl TA20 .....223 F5
Caray Gr TA3 ....169 D4
Carberry View BS24 ...50 A8
Cardigan Cres BS22 ...49 C8
Cardiff Cl BS13 ....22 A8
Cardinal Cl BA2 ....62 D8
Carditch Dro BS49 ....52 B8
Carey Cl BA4 ....141 E6
Carey Developments 1
.... 6 C1
Carey's Cl BS21 ....6 F3
Carey's Hollow TA13 ..220 B4
Careys Mead BA11 ....116 F7
Carhampton Cross
TA24 ....131 A5
Carice Gdns BS21 .....16 D8
Carisbrooke Gdns BA20 218 F5
Carisbrooke Rd BS4 ...22 D7
Carlan Stepps TA19 ...183 C2
Carlingford Terr BA3 ...79 A2
Carlingford Terrace Rd
BA3 ....79 A2
Carlow Rd BS4 ....22 E8
Carlton Cl BS39 ....58 F3
Carlton Ct BS9 ....5 F8
Carlton Dr TA6 ....209 D7
Carlton Mead TA3 ....181 D4
Carlton Mews BA5 ....203 E4
Carlton St BS23 ......48 D7
Caroline Bldgs BA2 ...45 B5
Caroline Cl BS31 ......24 C4
Caroline Ho BS2 ......227 A4
Caroline Pl BA1 ......228 B4

Carpenters Cl TA3 ...169 C3
Carpenters Ho TA19 ..221 B3
Carpenters La BS31 ....24 E5
Carpenters Terr TA12 .185 E7
Carr Ho BA2 ....44 A6
Carraway La DT10 ....190 F5
Carre Gdns BS22 ....31 F4
Carrick Ho **7** BS8 ...11 F6
Carriels Ho **12** BA4 .205 B6
Carrier's La TA21 ....166 C2
Carrington Way BA9 ..216 C4
Cart Gate TA14 ......185 F5
Carter Rd BS39 ....77 D5
Carters La BA22 ......196 E8
Carters Way BA3 ......96 D3
Carvers Rd TA6 ......209 A5
Cary Ct TA11 ....81 B5
Cary Hill Castle Cary BA7 214 D5
Kingsdon BA11 ....173 E5
Cary Moor Dro BA7 ...159 C2
Cary Rd BA22 ....175 D6
Cary Way Kingsdon TA11 173 D5
Somerton TA11 ....211 C5
Caryedge La BA7 ......160 A2
Cashford Gate TA2 ...213 C7
Casion Ct BS1 ....227 B1
Casley La BA11 ....102 D6
Cassino Rd TA23 .....202 E6
Cassis Cl TA8 ....104 C5
Castlake La TA4 ......150 F7
Castle Batch Prim Sch
BS22 ....32 A5
Castle Cary Mus* BA7 214 C5
Castle Cary Prim Sch
BA7 ....214 C4
Cary Cl **7** BA4 .....214 B8
Castle Cl BS48 ....18 F7
Castle Cnr BA11 ......101 D3
Castle Cotts TA21 ....180 D8
Castle Cross EX13 ....198 D4
Castle Ct NonRoady TA7 155 C2
Shepton Mallet BA4 ..205 A4
Castle Farm La BA1 ...21 B2
Castle Field Ind Est
TA6 ....209 A6
Castle Gdns BA2 ....44 E3
Castle Gn TA1 ....212 F4
Castle Hill Banwell BS29 51 C2
Dunster TA24 ....201 E2
Nether Stowey TA5 ...134 A2
Nunney BA11 ....143 B8
Castle La Cranmore BA4 142 A6
South Cadbury BA22 ..175 D4
Wedmore BS28 ....108 A1
West Pennard BA6 ....140 C1
Wiveliscombe TA4 ...210 F6
Yarley BA5 ....139 D7
Castle Mead TA23 ....131 E4
Castle Moat TA6 .....208 F5
Castle Prim Sch BS31 ..25 D4
Castle Rd Clevedon BS21 ..6 E6
Sherborne DT9 ....225 E3
Taunton TA1 ....180 D8
Weston-Super-Mare BS22 31 E3
Castle Rise BA7 ......214 C5
Castle Sch The TA1 ...212 D4
Castle St Bampton EX16 164 B1
Bridgwater TA6 ....208 F5
Bristol BS1 ....227 B3
Frome BA11 ....119 E5
Keinton Mandeville TA11 158 B1
Nether Stowey TA5 ...134 A2
Stogursey TA5 ....134 C5
Stoke sub Hamdon TA14 185 F4
Taunton TA1 ....212 E4
Castle Town Way DT9 .225 E6
Castle View Cotts TA3 .182 D4
Castle View Rd BS21 ...6 E6
Castle Way TA1 ....212 D4
Castle Wood La TA3,EX13,
TA20 ....193 C1
Castlefield La TA4 ...168 B1
Castlemans Rd TA1 ...212 B1
Castleton
Haselbury Plucknett TA18 196 C5
Sherborne DT9 ....225 E4
Castleton Rd DT9 ....225 F4
Castlewood Cl BS21 ....6 D4
Caswell Hill BS20 ....3 B1
Caswell La BS20 ....3 B2
Cat La Stalbridge DT10 .190 A1
Stourton Caundle DT10 189 F1
Cat St TA14 ....185 F1
Cat's Ash BA4 ....166 F7
Cat's Ash TA4 ....205 B6
Catash Cl BA22 ....175 D6
Catch Gate La TA20 ..223 A5
Catch Rd BA11 ....143 B7
Catcott Broad Dro TA7 137 C2
Catcott Ph TA7 ....137 D2
Catcott Right Dro TA7 .155 C6
Catemead BS21 ....16 C8
Cater Rd BS13 ....22 B6
Cathanger La
Fivehead TA3 ....170 D1
Stogursey TA5 ....134 D5
Catharine Pl BA1 ....228 B3
Cathay La BS27 ....90 B7
Cathcart Ho BA1 ....28 A1
Cathead Cross TA14 ..185 E1
Cathedral Church of the Holy
& Undivided Trinity*
BS1 ....226 C2
Cathedral Gn BS1 .....203 E4
Cathedral Gram Sch
BS1 ....226 C2

Catherine Hill BA11 .... 119 F5
Catherine St
Avonmouth BS11 .... 4 C8
East Huntspill TA9 .... 136 D8
Frome BA11 .... 119 E5
Catherine Way BA1 .... 29 A5
Catherines Cl BA7 ...... 214 C6
Catherson Cl BA11 ...... 119 D3
Cathill La DT9 .... 176 A2
Cathole Bridge Rd TA18 ..224 A4
Catley Gr BS41 .... 11 B2
Catmoor Cross EX13 ..... 198 A5
Cats La Minehead TA24 ... 201 A6
Taunton TA2 .... 168 F6
Cats' Castle Hill TA4 .... 150 E5
Catsgore Rd TA11 .... 173 C5
Catt's La TA21 .... 180 E6
Cattle Hill
Bratton Seymour BA9 ..... 176 A8
Shepton Montague BA7 ... 160 A1
Cattle Market Rd BS1 .... 227 C1
Catwell TA4 .... 202 E2
Caulfield Rd BS22 .... 32 B4
Caundle La
Stalbridge DT10 .... 190 A3
Stourton Caundle DT10 .. 189 F1
Causeway Nailsea BS48 ....8 B3
Woolavington TA7,TA9 ... 136 E6
Causeway Cl TA7 .... 136 E4
Causeway Council Hos
TA9 .... 106 B4
Causeway La DT8 .... 199 D6
Causeway Terr TA23 .... 202 C6
Causeway The
Congresbury BS49 .... 34 D4
Nailsea BS20 .... 8 F8
Street BA16 .... 207 D8
Yatton BS49 .... 34 C7
Causeway View BS48 .... 8 C2
Cautletts Cl BA3 .... 96 F8
Cavalier Cl BA21 .... 219 D8
Cavalier Way
Wincanton BA9 .... 216 C3
Yeovil BA21 .... 219 E8
Cavalier Wlk BA21 ..... 219 D8
Cave Ct BS2 .... 227 B4
Cave St BS2 .... 227 B4
Cavell Ct BS21 .... 6 C1
Cavendish Cl BS31 .... 25 D2
Cavendish Cres BA21 .... 228 A4
Cavendish Ct BA22 ..... 173 E2
Cavendish Dr BA14 ...... 83 F6
Cavendish Gdns BS9 ....5 C4
Cavendish Lodge BA1 ...228 A4
Cavendish Pl BA1 .... 228 A4
Cavendish Rd BA1 ...... 228 A4
Caveners Ct BS22 .... 31 B1
Caversham Dr BS48 .... 9 A2
Cawley Ave EX13 .... 198 A2
Caxton Rd BA3 .... 120 A3
Cecil Rd Bristol, Clifton BS8 .11 F8
Weston-Super-Mare BS23 ..30 E1
Cecil St BA20 .... 219 B5
Cecil Terr TA6 .... 209 B4
Cedar Ave Butleigh BA6 ..157 D5
Weston-Super-Mare BS22 ..31 C1
Cedar Cl Brent Knoll TA9 ..86 B2
Bridgwater TA6 .... 209 C3
Chard TA20 .... 223 B5
Long Ashton BS41 .... 10 F1
Taunton TA1 .... 213 D2
Cedar Ct
Bristol, Westbury on Trym
BS9 .... 5 D7
Bristol,Combe Dingle BS9 ..5 D7
Bristol,Sneyd Park BS9 .... 5 C4
Martock TA12 .... 185 E7
Wellington TA21 .... 222 E5
Cedar Dr BS31 .... 24 D4
Cedar Fields BA22 ...... 197 A8
Cedar Gr Bath BA2 .... 44 D3
Bristol BS9 .... 5 D5
Somerton TA11 .... 211 D4
Yeovil BA21 .... 218 E6
Cedar Pk BS9 .... 5 D5
Cedar Row BS11 .... 4 F6
Cedar Terr BA3 .... 78 D1
Cedar Way Bath BA2 .... 228 A1
Nailsea BS20 .... 9 A2
Portishead BS20 .... 2 C4
Cedar Wlk BA6 .... 157 E5
Cedarhurst Rd BS20 ..... 1 E4
Cedarn Ct BS22 .... 31 B4
Cedars The
Chew Stoke BS40 .... 56 D8
Evercreech BA4 .... 141 C1
Cedern Ave BS24 .... 50 C3
Cedric Rd BA1 .... 44 C8
Cefn Ct TA24 .... 201 B4
Celandine Mead TA1 .... 169 A1
Celandine Rd BA22 ..... 218 A5
Celtic Way BA6 .... 138 B4
Cemetery La Street BA16 .207 A7
Wincanton BA9 .... 216 B3
Centenary Cotts DT9 .... 176 A1
Centenary Gdns BA8 .... 190 A6
Centenary Way BS27 ..... 90 A7
Central Acre BA20 ...... 219 B4
Central Ave BA22 .... 219 D4
Central CE Jun Sch
BA5 .... 203 C3
Central Pk BS14 .... 23 B7
Central Rd BA20 .... 219 B5
Central Way BS21 .... 6 E1
Centre Dr BS29 .... 50 E4
Centre Rd TA7 .... 137 C2
Centre The
Keynsham BS31 .... 24 F5

Centre The continued
Weston-Super-Mare BS23 ..48 E7
Centurion Bsns Ctr BA4 ..205 D4
Cerdic Cl TA20 .... 223 E4
Cerdic Terr TA20 .... 223 D4
Cerney Gdns BS48 .... 9 A2
Cerney La BS11 .... 4 E6
Chackrell La
Sampford Peverell EX16 ..178 F2
Westleigh EX16 .... 179 A2
Chad's Hill TA5 .... 135 B2
Chadleigh Gr BS4 .... 22 D7
Chaffcombe La TA20 .... 194 B5
Chaffcombe Rd TA20 ....223 E6
Chaffeymoor Hill SP8 .. 161 E1
Chaffinch Ave BA11 .... 120 B6
Chaffinch Cl TA1 .... 212 B4
Chaffinch Dr BA3 .... 97 B8
Chaffins The BS21 .... 6 D3
Chain Gate Ct BA6 ...... 206 D4
Chains Rd EX16 .... 178 C1
Chalcombe Rocks La
TA4 .... 164 E5
Chalcot La BA13 .... 121 F5
Chalcroft Wlk BS13 ..... 21 E4
Chalfield Cl BS31 .... 25 A2
Chalfont Rd BS22 .... 49 C8
Chalice Cl BA6 .... 206 E4
Chalice Ct BA6 .... 206 E4
Chalice Mews [1] TA6 ...208 F5
Chalice Way BA6 .... 206 F3
Chalice Well * BA6 ..... 206 F4
Chalk Farm Cl BS39 .... 40 A7
Chalks The BS40 .... 39 B3
Challenger Way BA22 ...218 B6
Challick La
Chipstable TA4 .... 165 F6
Wiveliscombe TA4 ...... 166 A6
Challoner Ct BS1 .... 227 A1
Challow Dr BS22 .... 31 B2
Chamberlain Ho TA1 ....212 D5
Chamberlain St BA5 .... 203 D4
Chamberlin Ave TA6 .... 209 C6
Champford La TA21 ..... 222 D5
Champford Mews [2]
TA21 .... 222 D5
Champion Cross TA4 .... 165 E3
Champney Rd BA11 .... 120 A7
Chancel Cl Bristol BS9 ....5 D3
Nailsea BS48 .... 8 D1
Chancellor Cl BA14 .... 156 D7
Chancellor Rd BA16 .... 156 D7
Chancellor's Pound Sch ..36 D3
Chandag Inf Sch BS31 ... 25 A4
Chandag Jun Sch BS31 .. 25 A4
Chandag Rd BS31 .... 25 A4
Chandler Cl BA1 .... 27 B1
Chandlers Ct BS20 ...... 225 E5
Chandlers La TA7 .... 137 C3
Chandos Ct BS23 .... 48 D6
Chandos Rd BS31 .... 24 F7
Chandos St TA6 .... 208 F5
Change La TA4 .... 164 D6
Channel Cl TA5 .... 134 A2
Channel Ct
Burnham-On-Sea TA8 ....104 B5
Weston-Super-Mare BS22 ..31 B3
Channel Dash Rd BA22 ..173 E2
Channel Hts BS24 .... 48 F1
Channel Rd BS21 .... 6 E5
Channel View Cres BS20 ..2 B5
Channel View Rd BS20 .... 2 B5
Channells La TA19 ...... 183 C1
Channing Cl TA8 .... 104 B5
Chantry Cl Nailsea BS48 ..8 C1
Taunton TA2 .... 213 B7
Chantry Ct TA11 .... 211 C3
Chantry Dr BS22 .... 32 A4
Chantry Dro TA7 .... 155 B1
Chantry Gdns BA14 ...... 83 F3
Chantry Ho [9] BA4 .... 205 B6
Chantry La BA22 .... 174 D3
Chantry Mead Rd BA2 ... 44 E3
Chantry The BS26 .... 87 B5
Chantry View BA20 .... 197 D8
Chapel Barton BS48 ...... 8 C2
Chapel Cl
Castle Cary BA7 .... 214 C5
Chew Stoke BS40 .... 56 E8
Chilton Polden TA7 ..... 137 B2
Farrington Gurney BS39 ..74 F4
Keinton Mandeville TA11 ..158 A1
Nailsea BS48 .... 8 E2
North Curry TA3 .... 170 B4
Winford BS40 .... 38 A6
Chapel Cross
North Cadbury BA22 .... 175 D5
Thorncombe TA20 ...... 199 B6
Chapel Ct Bath BA1 ..... 228 B2
Radstock BA3 .... 78 E4
Clevedon BS21 .... 6 D3
Chapel Field BA2 .... 62 D1
Chapel Forge Cl TA7 ... 136 B8
Chapel Hill Ashcott TA7 ..156 B8
Backwell BS48 .... 19 D7
Chewton Mendip BA3 ... 94 E5
Clevedon BS21 .... 6 D3
Wrington BS40 .... 35 D2
Cleeve BS49 .... 35 B7

Chapel La continued
Dinnington TA17 .... 195 B7
East Huntspill TA9 ...... 136 E8
Gurney Slade BA3 .... 114 C7
Holcombe BA3 .... 116 C8
Milborne Port DT9 ...... 217 D2
North Cadbury BA22 .... 175 D6
Oxenpill BA6 .... 138 C4
Penselwood BA9 .... 161 C2
South Cadbury BA22 .... 175 F5
Sparkford BA22 .... 175 A6
Winford BS40 .... 38 A6
Wingfield BA14 .... 83 C6
Yenston BA8 .... 189 F7
Yeovil Marsh BA21 ...... 187 A5
Zeals BA12 .... 161 F3
Chapel Lawns BA3 .... 78 E4
Chapel Leigh La TA4 .... 167 A8
Chapel Rd
Bridgwater TA7 .... 154 C3
Bristol, Bishopsworth BS13 ..22 A6
Isle Abbotts TA3 .... 183 E7
Pawlett TA6 .... 135 F6
Radstock BA3 .... 78 E4
Rooksbridge BS26 .... 87 A5
South Cadbury BA22 .... 175 D4
Chapel Row Bath BA1 ...228 B2
Bathford BA1 .... 29 C2
Dunster TA24 .... 201 D2
Pill BS20 .... 4 C4
Chapel St
Bridgwater TA6 .... 209 A5
Burnham-On-Sea TA8 ... 104 A7
Dulverton TA22 .... 163 D6
Exford TA24 .... 128 D1
Horningsham BA12 ...... 144 D4
Upton Noble BA4 .... 142 F2
Chapel Wlk BA2 .... 60 C2
Chapel Yd BA7 .... 214 B4
Chapelfield BA3 .... 115 A3
Chapman Cl TA1 .... 212 C1
Chapmans Cl
Frome BA11 .... 119 F6
[2] Wookey BA5 .... 139 D8
Chapmanslade CE Prim Sch
BA13 .... 121 D4
Chapter St BS2 .... 227 B4
Charbury Wlk BS11 .... 4 E5
Charcroft Hill BA10 .... 160 F6
Chard & District Hospl
TA20 .... 223 C4
Chard Cl BS48 .... 18 F8
Chard Ct BS14 .... 23 B6
Chard La Chard TA20 ... 223 B1
Drimpton DT8 .... 199 F8
Tminster TA19 .... 194 D6
Tatworth EX13,TA20 ... 193 E1
Woolminstone TA18,TA20 ..195 B2
Chard Mus* TA20 ...... 223 B4
Chard Rd Axminster EX13 ..198 B4
Cricket St Th TA20 ..... 194 E1
Crewkerne TA18 .... 224 A6
Drimpton DT8 .... 199 F7
Chard Sch TA20 .... 223 C4
Chard St
Chardstock EX13 .... 198 B7
Thorncombe TA20 ...... 199 B6
Chardstock Ave BS9 ..... 5 D8
Chardstock La TA20 .... 223 C2
Chardyke Dr BS39 .... 58 E1
Charing Cross DT6 ...... 199 F1
Charity La BA11 .... 143 C1
Charlcombe La BA1 ...... 27 F3
Charlcombe Rise BA1 ... 27 F2
Charlcombe View Rd
BA1 .... 28 A2
Charlcombe Way BA1 ... 27 F2
Charlecombe Ct BS9 ...... 5 F6
Charlcombe Rd BS9 ...... 5 F6
Charles Cres TA1 ...... 213 D4
Charles Cl BS8 .... 226 A2
Charles Pl BS8 .... 226 A2
Charles Rd Frome BA11 ..119 F3
Yeovil BA21 .... 219 D6
Charles St Bath BA1 .... 228 B2
Bristol BS1 .... 227 A4
Charlcombe Rd La TA8 ..104 B8
Charlock Cl BS22 .... 49 D7
Charlock Rd BS22 .... 49 D7
Charlotte St Bath BA1 ...228 B2
Bristol BS1 .... 227 A4
Charlotte St S BS1 ..... 226 C2
Charlton Ave BS23 ...... 48 D4
Charlton Cl
Bridgwater TA6 .... 209 C4
Crewkerne TA18 .... 224 D5
Shepton Mallet BA4 .... 205 D5
Charlton Dro BS28 .... 9 C7
Charlton Field La DT9 ..175 D1
Charlton Hill DT9,BA8 .. 176 B3
Charlton La
Charlton Horethorne DT9 ..175 E3
Creech St Michael TA3 .. 169 E5
Charlton Mackrell CE Prim
Sch TA11 .... 173 E7
Charlton Pk
Keynsham BS31 .... 24 D5
Midsomer Norton BA3 ... 97 B7
Charlton Rd
Creech St Michael TA3 .. 169 E6
Holcombe BA3 .... 116 F7
Keynsham BS31,BS14 ... 24 D5
Midsomer Norton BA3 ... 97 B8
Shepton Mallet BA4 .... 205 D5

Charlton Rd continued
Weston-Super-Mare BS23 ..48 D4
Charlton Trad Est BA4 ..205 E5
Charlton View BS20 ...... 2 C5
Charlynch La TA5 .... 153 B8
Charlynch Rd TA5 ...... 153 A8
Charmoor Dro TA20 .... 182 F1
Charmoor La TA20 ..... 182 F1
Charmouth Rd BA1 ...... 44 B7
Charnwood Cl TA6 ..... 208 F7
Charnwood Dr BS27 ..... 90 B7
Charnwood Rd BS14 .... 23 B4
Charter Ho TA1 .... 209 A4
Charter Rd BS22 .... 49 B8
Charter Way BA5 ...... 203 B4
Charter Wlk Bristol BS14 ..23 A6
Taunton TA1 .... 213 C5
Charterhouse Cl
Cheddar BS27 .... 90 C6
Nailsea BS48 .... 8 F1
Charterhouse Dr BA11 ..120 C7
Chartley BS9 .... 5 D2
Chase La BA6 .... 206 C3
Chasey's Dro BA6 ...... 139 C4
Chatham Ave TA6 ...... 208 E6
Chatham Ct TA10 .... 171 C4
Chatham Pk BA2 .... 45 C6
Chatham Pl TA10 .... 171 C4
Chatham Row BA1 ...... 228 C3
Chatley Furlong BA2 .... 81 F3
Chatsworth Rd BA21 ... 219 D7
Chatterton Gn BS14 ..... 22 F3
Chatterton Ho [5] BS1 ..227 B1
Chatterton Rd BS1 ..... 227 B1
Chatterton Sq BS1 ..... 227 C1
Chaucer Cl [4] TA6 .... 153 F4
Chaucer Rd Bath BA2 ... 44 F4
Midsomer Norton BA3 ... 97 B8
Chaundey Gr BS13 ...... 22 B5
Cheap Side TA1 .... 212 F3
Cheap St Bath BA1 ..... 228 C2
Frome BA11 .... 119 F5
Sherborne DT9 .... 225 D4
Cheapside Bristol BS2 .. 227 C4
Langport TA10 .... 171 F5
Cheats Rd TA3 .... 169 C3
Checcombe La DT9 ..... 188 B4
Checkridge La EX13 .... 198 D2
Chedburn Cl [5] BS21 .... 6 F3
Cheddar Bsns Pk BS27 ...90 A6
Cheddar Cl
Burnham-On-Sea TA8 ... 104 C8
Frome BA11 .... 120 C7
Nailsea BS48 .... 18 F8
Cheddar Fields BS27 ..... 90 A7
Cheddar First Sch BS27 .. 90 B7
Cheddar Gorge Rural
Village* BS27 .... 90 C8
Cheddar Gr BS13 .... 22 A8
Cheddar Grove Prim Sch
BS13 .... 22 A8
Cheddar Moor Dro BS27 ..90 C4
Cheddar Rd Axbridge BS26 ..70 E2
Chewton Mendip BA3 ... 94 D6
Wedmore BS28 .... 108 D6
Cheddar Valley Bldgs
BA5 .... 203 C3
Cheddar YH* BS27 ...... 90 B7
Cheddon Fitzpaine CE Prim
Sch TA2 .... 168 F6
Cheddon Lawns TA2 .... 169 A6
Cheddon Rd TA2 .... 212 F7
Chedworth Cl BA2 ...... 45 F3
Chedzoy Jun Sch TA7 .. 154 D8
Chedzoy La TA7 .... 209 E7
Cheek's La BA10 .... 215 E6
Cheese Hill BA11 ...... 143 D8
Cheese La BS2 .... 227 B2
Chelmer Cl TA1 .... 213 D4
Chelmer Gr BS31 .... 24 F4
Chelscombe BA1 .... 27 B1
Chelsea Cl BS31 .... 25 A5
Chelsea Rd BA1 .... 44 C7
Chelsfield BS48 .... 19 A7
Chelston Ave BS22 ..... 219 B7
Chelston Rd BA4 .... 141 E1
Chelston Terr TA21 .... 180 D8
Chelswood Ave BS22 ... 49 C8
Chelswood Gdns BS22 ..49 D8
Cheltenham St BA2 .... 228 A1
Chelvey Batch BS48 .... 18 F3
Chelvey La BS48 .... 18 E4
Chelvey Rd BS48 .... 18 C3
Chelvey Rise BS48 ...... 9 A1
Chelwood BS13 .... 22 D3
Chelwood Rd BS31 ..... 48 F8
Chelynch Pk BA4 .... 141 E6
Chelynch Rd BA4 ...... 141 E7
Chepstow Ave TA6 ..... 209 A2
Chepstow Pk BS21 ..... 209 A4
Chepstow Rd BS4 .... 22 D8
Chepstow Wlk BS31 .... 24 D5
Cheriton TA24 .... 200 F6
Cherford Rd BS48 .... 9 A2
Cherington Rd BS48 ...... 9 A2
Cheriton Cl BA8 .... 176 D3
Cherry Ave BS21 .... 6 E2
Cherry Cl Bridgwater TA6 ..209 C3

Cherry Cl continued
Yatton BS49 .... 34 B8
Cherry Garden La BA2 .. 100 D7
Cherry Gr Frome BA11 ..119 E3
Taunton TA2 .... 212 F6
Cherry La [4] Bristol BS1 ..227 B4
Higher Odcombe BA22 ..186 C2
Cherry Orch TA3 .... 168 D1
Cherry Orchard Dr BA3 .203 C5
Cherry Pie La BA22 .... 175 A5
Cherry Rd
Long Ashton BS41 ...... 10 F1
Nailsea BS48 .... 8 D1
Cherry Tree Cl
Keynsham BS31 .... 24 C4
Radstock BA3 .... 78 E1
Cherry Tree Ct
Crewkerne TA18 .... 224 D8
Wells BA5 .... 203 C3
Cherry Tree Dr BA20 .. 218 D2
Cherry Tree La TA1 .... 212 F1
Cherry Tree Way TA23 .202 D6
Cherrywood Rd BS22 ... 31 F2
Cherrywood Rise BS22 . 31 F2
Chervil Cl TA7 .... 136 E4
Cherwell Rd BS31 ...... 25 A4
Chescombe Rd BS49 .... 34 B7
Chesham Rd N BS22 ... 49 B8
Chesham Rd S BS22 ... 49 B8
Cheshay's Hill TA19 ... 183 D1
Cheshire Cl BS20 .... 1 E3
Chesle Way BS20 .... 1 E3
Cheslefield BS20 .... 1 E3
Chessell La BA4 .... 140 C4
Chessel Rd BA22 ...... 197 B8
Chessels La TA11 ...... 211 C5
Chessington Ave BS14 . 23 B5
Chester Cl BS24 .... 50 A8
Chester Cres BS13 ..... 22 B8
Chester Terr TA20 ..... 223 D4
Chesterblade Rd
Chesterblade BA4 ...... 142 A4
Evercreech BA4 .... 141 F3
Chesterfield Cl BS29 ... 50 F3
Chesterfield Rd BS6 .... 78 F1
Chesterfield Hospl BS8 .226 A2
Chesterton Dr BS48 ..... 9 A2
Chesterton Ho [6] BS2 .227 B4
Chestertons The BA2 ... 45 F8
Chestnut Ave
Axbridge BS26 .... 70 C2
Weston-Super-Mare BS22 .32 A1
Chestnut Chase BS48 .... 9 A3
Chestnut Cl
Baltonsborough BA6 .. 158 A5
Banwell BS29 .... 51 A3
Bridgwater TA6 .... 209 C4
Bristol BS14 .... 23 B5
Paulton BS39 .... 77 F6
Radstock BA3 .... 78 E1
Somerton TA11 .... 211 C3
Wellington TA21 ...... 222 E5
Chestnut Dr
Taunton TA1 .... 213 C1
Yeovil BA20 .... 218 F3
Chestnut Gr Bath BA2 .. 44 C4
Clevedon BS21 .... 6 E4
Chestnut Ho Brean TA8 . 65 F2
Bristol BS13 .... 22 D3
Chestnut Par BA4 ..... 205 D4
Chestnut Rd
Long Ashton BS41 ...... 11 B2
[1] Martock TA12 ..... 185 E6
Chestnut Way TA24 ... 201 A5
Chestnuts The
Cheddar BS27 .... 71 A1
Winscombe BS25 ...... 70 A7
Cheer's La BA3 .... 78 C7
Cheverton Ho [1] BA21 .219 B5
Chew Cotts BS31 .... 24 F5
Chew Hill BS40 .... 57 D4
Chew Hill BS40 .... 39 A4
Chew La BS40 .... 39 B2
Chew Magna Prim Sch
BS40 .... 39 B3
Chew Rd BS40 .... 38 D3
Chew St BS40 .... 39 A3
Chew Stoke CE Prim Sch
BS40 .... 56 D8
Chew Valley Sch BS40 . 38 F1
Chewton Cheese Dairy*
BA4 .... 94 E6
Chewton Cl BS14 ...... 23 B5
Chewton Hill BA3 ...... 95 A7
Chewton Mendip CE Prim
Sch BA3 .... 94 F7
Cheyne Rd BS9 .... 5 D6
Chibbet Hill TA24 ..... 146 D8
Chibbet Post TA24 .... 147 A8
Chichester Cl TA8 ..... 104 C8
Chichester Pl BA3 ..... 116 F3
Chichester Rd BA16 ... 207 C4
Chichester Way BS24 .. 50 A8

Chick's La TA14 .... 210 C6
Chicks La BA3 .... 95 D7
Chickwell La BA3 .... 81 A1
Chidgey Cl TA6 .... 208 F5
Chilcombe La TA4 .... 132 F1
Chilcompton Bsns Pk
TA6 ...... 133 B7
Chilcompton Bsns Pk BA3 ..96 F7
Chilcote Dro BA5 .... 113 E2
Chilcote La BA5 .... 113 D1
Chilcott Cross TA22 .... 163 A7
Chilcott La TA22 .... 163 A7
Childhay La DT8 .... 199 F6
Chilkwell St BA6 .... 206 E4
Chill Pits La EX13 .... 198 B8
Chillington Down TA19,
TA20 ...... 194 F4
Chilliswood Cres TA1 .... 212 B2
Chilliswood La
Staplehay TA3 .... 181 B8
Taunton TA3 .... 168 B1
Chillybridge Rocks
TA22 ...... 147 E1
Chillyhill La BS40 .... 38 F2
Chilpitts TA7 .... 136 F4
Chiltern Cl BS14 .... 23 B4
Chiltern Cross EX16 ...... 164 B2
Chilthorne Domer CE Prim
Sch BA22 ...... 186 E5
Chilthornehill La BA22 ..186 D6
Chilton Cantelo House (Sch)
BA22 ...... 174 C1
Chilton Cl TA6 .... 208 F7
Chilton Ct 7 BA1 .... 28 B1
Chilton Dro TA7 .... 137 C6
Chilton Gr BA21 .... 219 A7
Chilton Rd Bath BA1 ..... 28 B1
Bridgwater TA5,TA6 ..... 208 F8
Bristol BS4 .... 23 A8
Chilton Polden TA7 ...... 137 B8
Chilton Right Dro TA7 ...155 B6
Chilton St TA6 .... 208 F7
Chilton Trinity Sch TA6 ..208 F7
Chilworthy La TA19,TA20 .193 F7
Chimes The BS48 .... 18 C8
Chinehorn Dro TA5 ...... 135 F3
Chinnock Hollow BA22 ...196 E8
Chinnock Rd BA6 .... 206 F5
Chip La TA1 .... 212 E5
Chippel La DT10 .... 190 F5
Chipping Cross BS21 ..... 16 C8
Chistand Dr TA24 .... 129 C8
Chistles La TA11 .... 158 A1
Chitcombe Rocks La
TA4 ...... 149 C1
Chorwell La TA21 .... 166 E2
Chovel La BA11 .... 142 F6
Chowins Rd TA18 .... 224 C5
Christ Church CE Prim Sch
Bristol BS8 .... 226 B3
Weston-Super-Mare BS23 ..48 E8
Christ Church Ct BA11 ...119 F2
Christchurch CE Fst Sch
BA11 ...... 119 F2
Christchurch Cl 8 BS48 ..8 E2
Christchurch Path S 12
BS23 ...... 48 E8
Christchurch Rd BS8 ..... 226 A3
Christchurch St E BA11 ..119 F4
Christchurch St W BA11 .119 E4
Christian Cl BS22 .... 32 A3
Christian's Cross BA6 .... 157 E3
Christina Terr BS8 .... 226 A1
Christmas St 8 BS1 ...... 227 A3
Christmas Stps 8 BS1 ....227 A3
Christon Bwnell BS29 .....51 A1
Loxton BS26 .... 70 D7
Christon Terr BS23 .... 48 F2
Christopher Cl BA20 .....218 E5
Christopher Way BA4 ....205 A5
Chrysanthemum Cl DT9 .225 E4
Chrysanthemum Flats
DT9 ...... 225 E4
Chrysanthemum Row
DT9 ...... 225 E4
Chubbs Lawn TA18 .... 224 C5
Chubworthy Cross TA4 ..165 D5
Chur La BA22 .... 197 A8
Church Ave BS9 ....5 E4
Church Cl Bathampton BA2 .28 F2
Bathford BA1 .... 29 B2
Bourton SP8 .... 161 E1
Carhampton TA24 .... 131 A5
Clevedon BS21 ....6 A2
East Huntspill TA9 .... 136 E8
Evercreech BA4 .... 141 E1
Great Elm BA11 .... 118 F7
Lydeard St Lawrence TA4 .151 A3
Norton Fitzwarren TA2 ...168 B4
Portishead BS20 ....2 D5
Shapwick TA7 .... 137 F1
Stoke St Gregory TA3 ....170 E6
Stoke St Mary TA3 .... 169 C1
West Chinnock TA18 ..... 196 B8
Yatton BS49 .... 34 C7
Church Cnr BS24 .... 67 B5
Church Cotts
Monkton Combe BA2 ..... 63 E8
Redhill BA40 .... 43 B6
Church Ct
Midsomer Norton BA3 ....78 A1
Redhill BS40 .... 36 D3
Church Dr
Congresbury BS49 .... 34 D4
West Buckland TA21 ..... 180 F7

Church Farm Bsns Pk
BA2 ...... 43 A7
Church Farm Cl
Marksbury BA2 .... 42 B1
Stawell TA7 .... 137 A1
Church Farm Paddock
BS30 ...... 25 E7
Church Field La TA7 ......136 C4
Church Fields
Wellington TA21 .... 222 E6
Wincanton BA9 .... 216 C3
Church Gdns BA6 .... 206 D5
Church Hayes Cl BS48 ....18 E8
Church Hayes Dr BS48 ...18 E8
Church Hill
Beckington BA11 .... 101 E4
Buckhorn Weston SP8 ...177 D3
Charlton Adam TA11 ..... 173 F7
Combwich TA5 .... 135 B5
Dinnington TA17 .... 195 B7
Exford TA24 .... 128 D1
Freshford BA3 .... 64 B5
Kington Magna SP8 ...... 177 E2
Pitney TA10 .... 172 C7
Radstock BA3 .... 79 C3
South Cadbury BA22 .....175 C3
Stalbridge DT10 .... 190 B5
Templecombe BA8 .... 176 E1
Timsbury BA2 .... 60 B2
Church House Rd TA8 ....84 F5
Church La Axbridge BS26 .70 C2
Axbridge, Badgworth BS26 .88 A6
Backwell BS48 .... 19 C5
Baltonsborough BA6 ..... 158 A5
Bath BA2 .... 45 C4
Batheaston BA1 .... 28 F4
Bicknoller TA4 .... 132 F2
Bishop Sutton BS39 ......57 D4
Bitton BS30 .... 25 E7
Brent Knoll TA9 .... 86 A2
Bristol BS1 .... 227 B2
Bristol, Clifton Wood BS8 .226 B2
Carhampton TA24 .... 131 B5
Chew Stoke BS40 .... 56 D8
Chewton Mendip BA3 ....94 F7
Chilcompton BA3 .... 96 D5
Chilton Polden TA7 ...... 137 B8
Chiselborough TA14 ......185 E1
Churchill BS25 .... 52 D5
Clutton BS39 .... 58 E3
Coleford BA3 .... 116 F7
Compton Bishop BS26 ....69 B3
Compton Dando BS39 ....41 D6
Crewkerne TA18 .... 224 E3
Doulting BA4 .... 141 E6
Dulverton TA22 .... 163 D6
East Coker BA22 .... 197 E8
East Harptree BS40 ......74 E4
East Huntspill TA9 .... 136 E8
East Lambrook TA13 ..... 220 C8
Evercreech BA4 .... 141 E1
Farmborough BA2 .... 60 A6
Farrington Gurney BS39 ..77 A4
Flax Bourton BS48 .... 19 F7
Glastonbury BA6 .... 206 D5
Haselbury Plucknett TA18 .196 C5
Hatch Beauchamp TA3 ...182 E8
Horton TA19 .... 183 C2
Hutton BS24 .... 49 E2
Ilminster TA19 .... 221 C4
Kingston St Mary TA2 ....168 E8
Limpley Stoke BA3 .... 64 A5
Long Ashton BS41 .... 11 C2
Long Sutton TA10 .... 172 D2
Loxton BS26 .... 68 D4
Lympsham BS24 .... 67 B1
Lynford-on-Fosse TA11 ...158 D2
Meare BA6 .... 138 D4
Midsomer Norton BA3 ....78 A1
Nailsea BS21 ....8 C4
Nailsea BS48 .... 17 B1
North Perrott TA18 ...... 196 C4
Norton Sub Hamdon TA14 .185 F2
Paulton BS39 .... 77 E6
Portbury BS20 .... 3 E3
Rimpton BA22 .... 188 B8
Rode BA11 .... 101 F8
Ruishton TA3 .... 169 C4
Ruishton, Thornfalcon TA3 .169 E2
Saltford BS31 .... 25 E4
Shepton Mallet BA4 ..... 205 D2
Shepton Mallet, Cannards Grove
BA4 ...... 205 D2
Sherborne DT9 .... 225 E6
Smeaton-the-Fosse BA3 ..96 F2
Timsbury BA2 .... 60 B2
Wedmore BS28 .... 107 D5
West Pennard BA6 .... 140 B1
Westonzoyland TA7 ...... 154 F5
Wingfield BA14 .... 83 C6
Winsmoor BS25 .... 69 E6
Yatton BS49 .... 34 C7
Church La End BS48 ......19 F8
Church Lane Cnr TA9 .....86 A2
Church Leaze BS11 ....4 D6
Church Mdws BS14 ....23 D6
Church Mead SP8 .... 161 E1
Church Pass 7 TA6 ...... 208 F5
Church Path Aller TA10 ...171 D8
Bridgwater TA6 .... 208 E5
Crewkerne TA18 .... 224 B6
Meare BA6 .... 138 D4
Minehead TA24 .... 200 F8
Queen Camel BA22 ...... 174 F3
South Petherton TA13 ...220 C2
2 Yeovil BA20 .... 219 B5
Church Pl
Milborne Port DT9 ...... 217 D2

Church Pl continued
Pill BS20 .... 4 C4
Church Rd
Abbots Leigh BS8 .... 11 A8
Bath, Combe Down BA2 ..45 C1
Bath, Weston Park BA1 ...27 C1
Bawdrip TA7 .... 136 E2
Bitton BS30 .... 25 E7
Bradford Abbas DT9 ..... 187 E1
Brean TA8 .... 65 F4
Bridgwater, Moorland TA7 .154 D3
Bridgwater, North Newton
TA7 ...... 154 A2
Bristol, Bishopsworth BS13 .22 A6
Bristol, Sneyd Park BS9 ...5 D3
Chapel Leigh TA4 .... 167 A7
Churchinford TA3 .... 191 F8
Churchstanton TA3 ...... 181 B1
Coxley BA5 .... 139 E6
Dundry BS41 .... 21 D2
East Brent TA9 .... 86 C4
Easton-in-G BS20 .... 4 A4
Edington TA7 .... 137 C2
Fitzhead TA4 .... 166 F7
Ilton TA19 .... 183 E4
Keenthorne TA5 .... 134 D3
Kilmington BA12 .... 161 F7
Leigh Woods BS8 .... 11 D6
Lympsham BS24 .... 67 A1
Middlezoy TA7 .... 155 B3
Minehead TA24 .... 200 F8
North Curry TA3 .... 170 D4
North Newton TA7 .... 153 F2
Peasedown St John BA2 ..78 B8
Pensford BS39 .... 40 A7
Redhill BS40 .... 36 D3
Shapwick TA7 .... 137 D4
South Cadbury BA22 .....175 D4
Sparkford BA22 .... 175 A4
Spaxton TA5 .... 152 E7
Street BA16 .... 207 D7
Sutton Mallet TA7 .... 155 B8
Taunton TA3 .... 168 D1
Wembdon TA6 .... 208 D6
West Huntspill TA9 ...... 136 A8
Weston-Super-Mare BS22 .31 E2
Whitchurch BS14 .... 23 C4
Winford BS40 .... 38 A7
Winscombe BS25 .... 69 E7
Yatton BS49 .... 34 C7
Church Rd N BS20 .... 2 D5
Church Rd S BS20 .... 2 D4
Church Rise BS40 .... 38 A7
Church Row TA3 .... 96 F2
Church Row Cotts TA3 ...181 E6
Church Sq BS21 .... 58 E2
Midsomer Norton BA3 ....78 A1
8 Taunton TA1 .... 212 F4
Church St Babcary TA11 ..174 C7
Banwell BS29 .... 51 B3
Barton St David BA6 ..... 157 F2
Bath BA1 .... 228 C2
Bath, Weston park BA1 ...45 B4
Beckington BA11 .... 101 E4
Bishops Lydeard TA4 .....167 E8
Blagdon BS40 .... 54 F2
Bridgwater TA6 .... 209 A5
Bristol BS1 .... 227 B2
5 Cannington TA5 ...... 135 B2
Castle Cary BA7 .... 214 B4
Chard TA20 .... 223 C3
Cheddar BS27 .... 90 C8
Coleford BA3 .... 116 F7
Crewkerne TA18 .... 224 C6
Croscombe BA5 .... 204 C7
Dinder BA5 .... 140 D7
Donyatt TA19 .... 183 D1
Drayton TA10 .... 171 E3
Dunster TA24 .... 201 E2
2 Frome BA11 .... 119 F4
Halstock BA22 .... 197 C3
8 Henstridge BA8 ....190 A6
Highbridge TA9 .... 104 E4
Hinton St George TA17 ...195 C7
Horningsham BA12 ......144 D4
Ilchester BA22 .... 173 E1
Isle Abbotts TA3 .... 183 F7
Keinton Mandeville TA11 .158 A1
Kingsbury Episcopi TA12 .185 B8
Kington Magna SP8 ...... 177 E2
Lopen TA13 .... 185 A1
Maiden Bradley BA12 ...144 C1
Mark TA9 .... 106 D4
Martock TA12 .... 185 E6
Merriott TA16 .... 195 F7
Milborne Port DT9 ...... 217 D2
Minehead TA24 .... 200 F8
Minehead, Alcombe TA24 .201 B5
Norton St Philip BA2 .....81 E4
Nunney BA11 .... 143 B8
Paulton BS39 .... 77 D6
Pensford BS39 .... 40 A7
Podimore BA22 .... 174 A3
Radstock BA3 .... 79 C2
Shepton Beauchamp TA19 .184 E4
Southwick BA14 .... 83 F3
Stogursey TA5 .... 134 B5
Stoke St Michael BA3 ....116 A2
Taunton TA1 .... 213 B3
Timberscombe TA24 .....130 B5
Tintinhull BA22 .... 186 B6
Upton Noble BA4 .... 142 F2
Wedmore BS28 .... 108 C4
West Coker BA22 .... 197 A8

Church St continued
Wincanton BA9 .... 216 C4
Winsham TA20 .... 194 E1
Wiveliscombe TA4 ...... 210 C4
Woolavington TA7 ...... 136 E4
Woolley BA1 .... 27 F6
Yeovil BA20 .... 219 B5
Yeovilton BA22 .... 174 A1
Church Stps TA1 .... 200 F8
Church Terr
7 Bampton EX16 .... 164 B1
East Coker BA22 .... 197 C7
Higher Odcombe BA22 ...186 C2
4 Yeovil BA20 .... 219 B5
Church Tk SP8 .... 161 E1
Church Town BS48 ...... 19 C5
Church View
Bourton SP8 .... 161 E1
Chilton Trinity TA5 ...... 135 F2
Evercreech BA4 .... 141 E1
North Wootton BA4 ..... 140 C4
Wraxall BS48 ....9 B2
Church View Cl TA10 ....171 E8
Church Way TA7 .... 137 D2
Church Wlk
Baltonsborough BA6 .....158 A5
Bawdrip TA7 .... 136 E2
Bratton Seymour BA9 ...176 B8
Ilminster TA19 .... 221 C4
Long Sutton TA10 .... 172 F4
Marston Magna BA22 ....174 F1
Pill BS20 .... 4 C4
Wrington BS40 .... 35 D2
Churchdown Wlk BS11 ...4 E5
Churchfield La TA3 ....183 F7
Churchfields TA21 .... 222 D7
Churchill Ave BA7 .... 214 C6
Churchill Ave
Clevedon BS21 ....6 C2
Wells BA5 .... 112 E1
Churchill CE Prim Sch
Churchill BS25 .... 52 F4
Langford BS40 .... 53 A5
Churchill Cl
Burnham-On-Sea TA8 ...104 C5
6 Clevedon BS21 .... 6 C2
Wells BA5 .... 112 E1
Churchill Comm Sch
BS25 ...... 52 D5
Churchill Gate BS25 ..... 52 C5
Churchill Rd BS25 .... 52 C5
Churchill La
Axminster EX13 .... 198 A5
Chipstable TA4 .... 165 C5
Churchill Rd
Frome BA11 .... 119 D4
Shepton Mallet BA4 .....205 A5
Wells BA5 .... 112 E1
Weston-Super-Mare BS23 .49 A7
Churchill Way BA5 ...... 112 E1
Churchlands Way BS24 ..50 D8
Churchlands TA3 .... 106 D4
Churchlands Ct TA4 .....104 A7
Churchstanton Prim Sch
TA3 ...... 191 E8
Churchward Dr BA11 ....120 C6
Churchward Rd BS22 ....32 B3
Churchway
Curry Rivel TA10 .... 171 D4
Faulkland BA3 .... 80 D1
Churchway Cl TA10 ..... 171 D4
Churchwell Ct DT9 ...... 187 E1
Churchwell St DT9 ...... 187 E1
Churlands Cl BA22 ...... 197 A8
Churston Cl BS14 .... 23 A3
Cider Farm* TA4 .... 213 E7
Cinder Ash La TA18 .....195 D4
Cinnamon La BA6 .... 206 F3
Circle The BA2 .... 44 B3
Circular Rd BS9 .... 5 E2
Circus Field Rd BA6 .....206 D4
Circus Mews BA1 .... 228 B3
Circus Pl BA1 .... 228 B3
Circus The BA1 .... 228 B3
City Mus & Art Gal*
BS8 ...... 226 C3
City of Bath Coll BA1 ...228 B2
City Rd BS2 .... 227 B4
City The TA9 .... 104 E4
City View BA1 .... 228 C4
Clammer Hill La TA18 ...224 D6
Claremap Rd BS3 .... 11 E4
Clanders Batch BS40 ....54 D3
Clandown CE Prim Sch
BA3 ...... 78 E4
Clandown Rd BS39 ...... 77 F4
Clanfield DT9 .... 225 B2
Clanville TA20 .... 200 F7
Clanville Rd BA4 .... 200 F7
Clapton Court Gdns*
TA18 ...... 195 D1
Clapton Dro BS20 ....3 C3
Clapton Gate TA18 ..... 195 C2
Clapton La Holton BA9 ..176 B6
Portishead BS20 ....3 C3
Clapton Rd
Crewkerne TA18 .... 195 D2
Midsomer Norton BA3 ....77 D1
Clapton Wlk BS9 ....5 C5
Clare Gdns BA2 .... 44 D1
Clare St Bridgwater TA6 .208 F5

Clare St continued
Bristol BS1 .... 227 A2
2 North Petherton TA6 ..153 F4
Claredon Villas BA2 ..... 45 B5
Clareham La BA11 .... 99 D2
Claremont Bldgs BA1 ....28 A1
Claremont Cres BS23 ....30 B1
Claremont Ct TA1 .... 212 C1
Claremont Dr TA1 .... 212 C1
Claremont Gdns
Clevedon BS21 ....6 E1
Paulton BS39 .... 77 B7
4 Nailsea BS48 .... 8 D1
Claremont Gr TA6 .... 209 D6
Claremont La TA1 .... 212 C1
Claremont Pl 8 BA1 .....28 A1
Claremont Rd BA1 ...... 28 B1
Claremont Wlk BA1 ..... 28 A1
Clarence Dr 1 TA1 ...... 153 F4
Clarence Grove Rd BS23 .48 E5
Clarence Pl Bath BA1 ....44 B6
Bristol BS2 .... 226 C4
Clarence Rd BS1 .... 227 B1
Clarence Rd E BS23 .....48 E5
Clarence Rd N BS23 .....48 D5
Clarence Rd S BS23 .....48 D5
Clarence St Bath BA1 ....228 C4
Taunton TA1 .... 212 E4
Yeovil BA20 .... 219 A5
Clarence Terr Bath BA2 ..45 D5
Clarendon Rd Bath BA2 ..45 B5
Weston-Super-Mare BS23 .48 F8
Clark Cl
Woolavington TA7 ...... 136 E4
Wraxall BS48 ....9 B2
Clark's La TA18 .... 224 F3
Clarke's Cl TA20 .... 223 D4
Clarke's Row TA20 ..... 223 D4
Clarken Cl BS48 ....8 E1
Clarken Coombe BS41 ...11 B3
Clarkes Ct BA20 .... 219 A4
Clarkham Cross BA22 ...197 E2
Clarks Cl BA22 .... 218 A5
Clarks Rd TA6 .... 209 C4
Clarks Shopping Village
BA16 ...... 207 C6
Clarkson Ave BS22 ...... 31 C1
Clarkson Ho BA1 .... 228 A2
Clatcombe La DT9 ...... 188 D6
Clatworthy Dr BS14 .....23 A7
Claude Ave BA2 .... 44 C5
Claude Terr BA2 .... 44 C5
Claverham Cl BS49 ...... 34 D7
Claverham Dro BS49 ....17 D5
Claverham Pk BS49 ..... 34 F8
Claverton Bldgs BA2 ....228 C1
Claverton Ct BA2 .... 45 E4
Claverton Down Rd BA2 .45 F3
Claverton Dr BA2 .... 45 F3
Claverton Pumping Sta*
BA2 ...... 46 C3
Claverton Rd BS31 ...... 25 D3
Claverton Rd W BS31 ....25 D3
Claverton St BA2 .... 228 C1
Clay Castle TA18 .... 196 C5
Clay Castle La TA18 ..... 196 C5
Clay La Barrington TA19 .184 B5
Bitton BS30 .... 25 D8
Chewton Mendip BA3 ....94 C5
Higher Chillington TA19 .194 F5
Rode BA11 .... 101 F8
Westleigh EX16 .... 179 A1
Claydon Cl TA23 .... 131 E4
Claydon Gn BS14 .... 22 F3
Clayford La TA22 .... 163 C5
Clayford Rd TA22 .... 163 C5
Clayhanger Cross TA20 .193 E6
Clayhanger La
Chard TA20 .... 223 A8
Combe St Nicholas TA20 .193 E6
Clayhidon Crossway
EX15 ...... 180 E2
Claylands Cnr TA5 ...... 134 E5
Claypiece Rd BS13 ...... 22 A4
Clayton Cl
Houndstone BA22 .... 218 A6
Portishead BS20 ....2 E4
Clearwood BA13 .... 121 F8
Clearwood View BA13 ...121 A4
Cleavedale Cl BA22 .....174 F3
Cleeve Abbey* BA3 ..... 131 E3
Cleeve Dr BS49 .... 35 B8
Cleeve Gn BA2 .... 44 A6
Cleeve Gr BS31 .... 24 D5
Cleeve Hill
Compton Martin BS40 ...73 B8
Watchet TA23 .... 202 A7
Cleeve Hill Rd BS40 .....35 C7
Cleeve La TA24 .... 131 D5
Cleeve Pl BS48 ....9 A1
Cleeve Rd TA2 .... 213 B7
Cleeveleaze Rd BA22 ...45 C1
Cleeveways BA22 .... 176 A2
Clemence Rd BA16 ..... 207 D4
Clement St BS2 .... 227 C4
Clements Cl BA5 .... 203 C3
Cleve Ct 3 BS8 .... 11 F6
Cleve St TA20 .... 218 C6
Clevedon Com Sch BS21 .6 F3
Clevedon Craft Ctr* BS21 .7 A2
Clevedon Ct* BS21 ......7 B2
Clevedon Hospl BS21 ....6 C2
Clevedon Min Rly* BS21 .6 B3
Clevedon Pier* BS21 .....6 C4

Clevedon Rd
Midsomer Norton BA3 .....78 A2
Nailsea BS21 .....8 B4
Portishead BS20 .....2 D3
Weston-Super-Mare BS23 .....48 E6
Wraxall BS48 .....9 B4
Wraxall BS48 .....9 D6
Wraxall, Flax Bourton BS48 .....9 A2
Clevedon Terr BS6 .....227 A4
Clevedon Wlk BS4 .....8 E2
Cleveland Cl BA2 .....45 C6
Cleveland Pl BA1 .....228 C4
Cleveland Pl E BA1 .....228 C4
Cleveland Pl W BA1 .....228 C4
Cleveland Reach BA1 .....228 C4
Cleveland Row BA1 .....45 B8
Cleveland St TA1 .....212 E4
Clewson Rise BS14 .....22 E3
Cleyhill Gdns BA11 .....121 D4
Cliff Rd Cheddar BS27 .....71 E1
North Petherton TA6 .....153 E3
Weston-Super-Mare BS22 .....31 A2
Cliff St BS27 .....90 C8
Cliffe Dr BA1 .....64 A6
Clifford Ave TA2 .....212 E8
Clifford Cres TA2 .....212 E8
Clifford Gdns BS11 .....4 E6
Clifford Lodge 3 TA5 .....135 B2
Clifford Mews TA21 .....222 E6
Clifford Pk TA5 .....135 B2
Clifford Terr TA21 .....222 E6
Cliffs The BS27 .....90 C8
Clift House Rd BS3 .....11 F4
Clift House Spur BS3 .....11 F4
Clift Pl BS1 .....227 A1
Clifton Ave BS23 .....48 E5
Clifton Cl 1 Bristol BS8 .....11 F7
Yeovil BA21 .....219 E6
Clifton Cot BS8 .....226 A4
Clifton College Prep Sch
BS8 .....5 F1
Clifton Ct 11 BS21 .....6 C2
Clifton Down BS8 .....11 F7
Clifton Down Rd BS8 .....226 A3
Clifton High Sch BS8 .....226 A4
Clifton Hill Barwick BA22 .....197 F8
Bristol BS8 .....226 A2
Clifton Park BS8 .....11 F8
Clifton Pk BS8 .....226 A3
Clifton Rd Bristol BS8 .....226 A2
Weston-Super-Mare BS23 .....48 E5
Clifton St BS20 .....2 C2
Clifton Suspension Bridge*
BS8 .....11 F7
Clifton Vale BS8 .....226 A2
Clifton Vale Cl BS8 .....226 A2
Clifton View 8 BA22 .....197 F8
Clifton Wood Ct BS8 .....226 B2
Clifton Wood Rd BS8 .....226 B2
Cliftonwood Cres BS8 .....226 B2
Cliftonwood Terr BS8 .....226 A2
Clifts Bldgs BA11 .....119 F4
Clink Farm Ct BA11 .....120 C6
Clink Rd BA11 .....120 D6
Clink The TA6 .....209 A5
Clipper Cl TA6 .....209 C4
Clistview TA23 .....131 D2
Clive Rd BS14 .....23 C8
Cliwey BA13 .....102 E1
Clock Ho TA5 .....134 B2
Clockhouse Mews BS20 .....2 D6
Clockhouse The TA4 .....167 E6
Cloister The TA4 .....225 D4
Cloisters Croft TA8 .....104 B6
Cloisters The BA5 .....203 D3
Close The
Glastonbury BA6 .....206 E5
8 Merriott TA16 .....195 F7
Minehead TA24 .....201 B5
Wellington BA22 .....175 D6
Portishead BS20 .....1 F1
Closemead BA21 .....6 B1
Clotfurlong La DT9 .....188 F1
Clothier Mdws BA7 .....214 B6
Cloud Hill End Est BS39 .....77 A8
Cloudberry Cl TA20 .....223 F5
Clovelly Rd BS22 .....32 A2
Clover Cl Clevedon BS21 .....6 F3
Paulton BS39 .....77 E4
Clover Ct BS22 .....49 D7
Clover Mead TA1 .....213 C1
Clover Rd BS22 .....32 A6
Clover Way TA9 .....104 E4
Cloverton Dr TA6 .....209 D7
Clumber Dr BA11 .....119 F6
Clutton Hill BS39 .....59 B4
Clutton Prim Sch BS39 .....58 F4
Clyce Rd TA9 .....104 D3
Clyde Ave BS31 .....24 F4
Clyde Gdns BA2 .....44 B6
Clydesdale Cl BS14 .....23 A6
Clynder Gr BS21 .....6 E6
Coach House Mews
BS23 .....30 D1
Coach Rd TA24 .....124 A3
Coal Barton BA3 .....116 B8
Coal La BA11 .....119 C8
Coal Orch TA1 .....212 F4
Coalash La BA11 .....119 D8
Coalbridge Cl BS22 .....31 F2
Coaley Rd BS11 .....4 D5
Coalpit La
Chilcompton BA3 .....96 A3
Stoke St Michael BA3 .....116 B3
Coalpit Rd BA1 .....29 A4
Coape Rd BS14 .....23 F5

Coast Rd TA8 .....84 F7
Coastguard Cotts TA24 .....201 A8
Coat Rd TA12 .....185 D7
Coate Turn TA4 .....166 A6
Coates Est BS48 .....8 F3
Coates Gr BS48 .....9 A2
Coates Wlk BS4 .....22 D6
Cob Castle TA21 .....180 D8
Cobblestone Mews BS8 .....226 A4
Cobburn Dr BS13 .....21 F4
Cobley Croft BS21 .....16 C8
Cobthorn Way BS49 .....91 C8
Coburg Cl TA21 .....180 F7
Coburg Villas 13 BA1 .....28 A1
Cock & Yew Tree Hill
BS40 .....38 A2
Cock Rd
Buckland Dinham BA2,
BA11 .....100 B5
Horningsham BA12 .....144 C4
Cock-Crowing Stone
TA20 .....193 D4
Cockers Hill BS39 .....41 C5
Cockhill Elm La BA7 .....214 B4
Cockhill La BA22 .....175 D7
Cockland Hill
Holywell Lake TA21 .....179 C8
Langford Budville TA21 .....166 C1
Cockmill La BA4 .....140 A1
Cockpit Hill DT6,DT8 .....199 F4
Cockpit La BA4 .....142 C2
Cockrod BA6 .....207 B2
Cod La BA22 .....196 D7
Codrington Pl BS8 .....226 A2
Cogsall Rd BS14 .....23 F6
Coker Hill BA22 .....196 F8
Coker Hill La BA22 .....197 A7
Coker Ho BA22 .....197 C8
Coker Marsh BA22 .....197 D7
Coker Rd BS22 .....32 B2
Coker's La BA12 .....161 FB
Colbourn Cl BA3 .....114 E7
Colbourne Rd BA2 .....44 D1
Colchester Cres BS4 .....22 D7
Cold Harbour
Milborne Port DT9 .....217 D2
Sherborne DT9 .....225 E5
Cold Harbour La BA22 .....196 F6
Cold Nose BS28 .....138 D8
Cold Rd TA3 .....182 D6
Coldharbour Bsns Pk
TA5 .....225 E6
Coldharbour La BS23 .....48 D3
Coldhills La BA8 .....176 D2
Coldpark Gdns BS13 .....21 E5
Coldrick Cl BS14 .....22 F3
Coldridge Cottage*
TA5 .....134 B2
Cole Cl TA4 .....167 E6
Cole Cross BA22 .....186 C6
Cole La 5 TA4 .....185 F4
Cole Mead BA10 .....215 D5
Cole Rd BA10 .....215 D5
Cole's La
Chewton Mendip BA3 .....95 A6
South Petherton TA13 .....220 D3
Colehouse La BS21 .....16 C8
Colemead BS13 .....22 B5
Coleridge Cres TA1 .....213 B3
Coleridge Gdns TA8 .....85 B2
Coleridge Gn TA6 .....208 C5
Coleridge Rd
Bridgwater TA6 .....208 E6
Clevedon BS21 .....6 C3
Nether Stowey TA5 .....134 A2
Weston-Super-Mare BS23 .....49 A4
Coleridge Sq TA6 .....208 C6
Coleridge Vale Rd E 1
BS21 .....6 D2
Coleridge Vale Rd N 6
BS21 .....6 C2
Coleridge Vale Rd W 3
BS21 .....6 D2
Coles Cross Cotts DT8 .....199 D5
Coles Cross TA20 .....223 C3
Coles La EX13 .....198 B1
Coleshill Dr BS13 .....22 B5
Colesmore TA4 .....167 A4
Coley La TA3 .....194 F5
Coley Rd BS40 .....75 B4
Colham La TA20 .....194 E1
Colin Rd TA2 .....212 F7
Collards La TA2 .....213 A7
Collarway La BA22 .....196 F8
Colledge Cl BA3 .....96 C6
College BA22 .....196 E8
College Ct TA10 .....172 E2
College Fields BS8 .....11 FB
College Gn Bristol BS1 .....226 C2
Taunton TA1 .....212 D4
College Rd BA1 .....27 E1
Bristol, Clifton BS8 .....11 FB
Taunton TA1 .....212 D6
Wells BA5 .....203 E5
College Sq BS1 .....226 C2
College St Bristol BS1 .....226 C2
Burnham-On-Sea TA8 .....104 A7
College View
Taunton TA1 .....212 C2
8 Bath BA1 .....28 A1
College Way
Bridgwater TA6 .....209 C6
Taunton TA1 .....212 C1
Colles Cl BA5 .....203 F5
Colles Rd BA5 .....203 F5

Collett Ave BA4 .....205 C5
Collett Cl BS22 .....32 C4
Collett Way BA11 .....120 C7
Colley La TA6 .....209 B4
Colley Lane Ind Est TA6 .....209 B3
Colleylake Cotts TA3 .....181 C5
Collickshire La TA3 .....170 E6
Collie Cnr BA11 .....118 D8
Collier's La BA11 .....99 D2
Colliers Cl BA2 .....78 D8
Colliers La BA1 .....27 F4
Colliers Rise BA3 .....79 A3
Colliers Wlk 4 BS48 .....8 E2
Collingwood Cl
Saltford BS31 .....25 E2
Weston-Super-Mare BS22 .....31 E4
Collingwood Ct TA6 .....208 F5
Collins St BS11 .....4 B8
Collins' La TA11 .....173 F7
Collinson Rd BS13 .....22 B5
Collum La BS22 .....31 E6
Colman Rd TA1 .....212 B1
Colmer Rd
Bridgwater TA6 .....208 F7
Yeovil BA21 .....219 B6
Colne Gn BS31 .....25 A4
Colombo Cres BS23 .....48 E3
Colston Ave BS1 .....227 A2
Colston Cross EX13 .....198 B4
Colston Fort 2 BS2 .....227 A4
Colston Par BS1 .....227 B1
Colston St Bristol BS1 .....227 A3
Colston Yd BS1 .....227 A3
Colton La TA4 .....149 F7
Columbus Ho BA2 .....45 D8
Colyton 1 BS22 .....32 A2
Combe Ave BS20 .....2 C4
Combe Batch BS28 .....108 D4
Combe Batch Rise
BS28 .....108 D4
Combe Beacon La TA20 .....193 C7
Combe Cl Bicknoller TA4 .....132 E2
Combe Cross Haise TA4 .....167 B7
Monksilver TA4 .....150 C8
Shillingford EX16 .....164 D4
Combe Cross Wlk BS13 .....22 B3
Combe Down La TA4 .....151 C2
Combe Fields BS20 .....2 C6
Combe Gn BA5 .....204 B7
Combe Gr BA1 .....44 B8
Combe Hay La BA2 .....62 B6
Combe Hill
Barton St David TA11 .....158 A2
Combe St Nicholas TA20 .....193 D5
Hemyock EX15 .....180 C2
Milborne Port DT9 .....217 B3
Sherborne DT9 .....225 B1
Combe La TA20 .....198 C4
Combe Rd Bath BA2 .....45 B1
Portishead BS20 .....2 C5
Combe St TA20 .....223 C4
Combe Street La BA21 .....219 A4
Combe Street Lane Rdbt
BA21 .....218 F8
Combe Sydenham Country
Pk* TA4 .....150 A7
Combe Terr TA9 .....136 E8
Combe The BS40 .....53 F2
Combecross Hill TA4 .....150 B8
Combecross La
Monksilver TA4 .....150 B8
Stogumber TA4 .....150 C8
Combeland La TA22 .....164 A5
Combeland Rd TA24 .....201 B4
Combeshead TA4 .....148 A3
Combeshead La
Brompton Regis TA22 .....148 A4
West Anstey EX36 .....162 A7
Combeside BA2 .....45 A3
Comer Rd BS27 .....90 A7
Comer's Cross TA24 .....146 E6
Comeytrowe La TA1 .....212 A2
Comeytrowe Orch TA1 .....212 A2
Comeytrowe Rd TA1 .....212 B1
Comeytrowe Rise TA1 .....212 B2
Comfortable Pl BA1 .....228 A3
Commerce Way TA9 .....104 F2
Commercial Rd
Bristol BS1 .....227 A1
Shepton Mallet BA4 .....205 B6
Commercial Row TA20 .....223 C3

Common La
Charlton Adam TA11 .....174 A8
Churchill Green BS25 .....52 B5
Easton-in-G BS20 .....4 B2
Halstock BA22 .....197 C2
Hardington Mandeville
BA22 .....197 A5
Holcombe BA3 .....116 D7
Hush Champflower TA4 .....165 D7
Kington Magna SP8 .....177 E1
Marnhull DT10 .....190 A4
North Perrott TA18 .....196 D4
Templecombe BA8 .....184 D3
Wincanton BA9 .....216 D3
Yenston BA8 .....189 F8
Common Moor Dro BA6 .....206 E7
Common Rd BA9 .....216 E3
Compass Hill TA1 .....212 E3
Compass Rise TA1 .....212 E3
Compton Acres DT9 .....187 E4
Compton Cl
Taunton TA1 .....213 A6
Yeovil BA21 .....219 E8
Compton Cnr BA4 .....205 B5
Compton Ct Mews DT9 .....187 F3
Compton Dr BS9 .....5 C7
Compton Flats BA21 .....219 C6
Compton Gdns BA11 .....120 D7
Compton Gn BS31 .....24 E4
Compton Hill TA13 .....220 A5
Compton La BA4 .....205 B5
Compton Rd
Shepton Mallet BA4 .....205 B4
South Cadbury BA22 .....175 D4
South Petherton TA13 .....220 B5
Compton St TA11 .....173 E3
Compton Ave BS25 .....70 B8
Concorde Dr BS10 .....6 B1
Condell Cl TA6 .....208 C5
Condor Cl TA22 .....49 D8
Conduit Hill BA11 .....99 B1
Conegore Cnr BA22 .....179 D4
Conegore BS13 .....21 F6
Conference Ave BS20 .....2 F5
Conference Cl BS20 .....2 F4
Conifer Cl TA24 .....128 D1
Conifer Way BS24 .....49 F5
Coniston Ave BS9 .....5 F6
Coniston Cres BS23 .....48 F4
Coniston Gdns BA21 .....219 A7
Connaught Ho TA6 .....209 C5
Connaught Pl BS23 .....48 D8
Connaught Rd BS4 .....22 E8
Connection Rd BA2 .....44 A6
Connelly Dr BS28 .....108 C4
Constable Cl
Keynsham BS31 .....24 E4
Yeovil BA21 .....219 E8
Constable Dr BS22 .....31 F3
Constantine Ct BA4 .....205 C5
Constitution Hill
Bristol BS8 .....226 B2
Bath BA5 .....140 C8
Convocation Ave BA2 .....45 F5
Conway Cres TA8 .....85 C1
Conway Rd TA5 .....135 A3
Conygar Cl BS21 .....6 F5
Conygar View TA24 .....201 E3
Conygre Gn BA2 .....60 B2
Conygre Rd BS34 .....B
Cook Ave TA20 .....223 D3
Cook Cl BS28 .....108 D4
Cook Way TA2 .....212 C6
Cook's Folly Rd BS9 .....5 D3
Cook's La Banwell BS29 .....51 A4
Clevedon BS25 .....7 B2
Cranmore BA4 .....142 A6
Milverton TA4 .....167 B5
Stalbridge DT10 .....190 B2
Cooke's La TA10 .....156 B2
Cookley La TA4 .....150 F8
Cooks Bridle Path BS48 .....36 D8
Cooks Cl TA3 .....169 D5
Cooks Gdns BS48 .....9 A2
Cooks La DT9 .....225 D3
Cooksley La TA1 .....149 A2
Coomb End BA3 .....78 F3
Coomb Rocke BS9 .....5 D6
Coomband Ho BA3 .....78 F3
Coombe Bridge Ave BS9 .....5 D6
Coombe Brook BA5 .....203 A7
Coombe Cotts BA5 .....204 C6
Coombe Dale
Backwell BS48 .....37 A8
Bristol BS9 .....5 C6
Coombe Gdns BS9 .....5 E6
Coombe Hill
Ansersleigh TA21 .....181 A5
Bruton BA10 .....215 E7
Kingsbury Episcopi TA12 .....185 B8
Shepton Mallet BA4 .....205 A6
Coombe Lodge (Coll)
BS40 .....84 B2
Coombe Rd
Dinnington TA17 .....195 B7
Nailsea BS48 .....8 D1
Weston-Super-Mare BS23 .....30 E1
Coombe Side TA9 .....86 B2

Coombe St Bruton BA10 .....215 E7
Penselwood BA9 .....161 E2
Coombe Terr
Glastonbury BA6 .....206 E5
Compton BS9 .....225 C5
Coombe The
Blagdon BS40 .....54 C3
Compton Martin BS40 .....74 A6
Coombe View BA4 .....205 A6
Coombe Water La DT8 .....199 E5
Coombe's Cider Farm &
Mus* TA9 .....106 A4
Coombs' Way BS26 .....87 E8
Cooper Rd BS9 .....5 F7
Cooper's Ash La BA7,
BA22 .....214 A2
Cooperage La BS3 .....226 B2
Cooperage The BA11 .....119 F3
Coopers Hts TA1 .....210 C4
Coopers Mead BA4 .....205 D4
Coopers Mill TA2 .....168 B4
Coot Hide EX16 .....178 D1
Coots The BS14 .....23 E6
Copeland Dr BS14 .....23 B5
Copis La TA11 .....158 B3
Coplestons TA3 .....168 D1
Copley Gdns BS22 .....31 F2
Coppack Ho 7 BS21 .....6 C2
Copper Beech Rd TA11 .....173 D5
Copper Beeches TA1 .....212 A2
Copper Cl BS27 .....90 A8
Copperfield Dr BS22 .....31 F4
Coppern Way DT10 .....190 B4
Coppice Cl BA20 .....218 D2
Coppice End Cnr BS24 .....67 C2
Coppice The BS13 .....21 E4
Coppin Cl BA6 .....206 F3
Coppin Rd TA2 .....168 B4
Coppits Hill La
Yeovil BA21 .....218 D8
Yeovil Marsh BA21 .....187 A5
Copplesbury La BA4,
BA10 .....160 D8
Copse Cl Watchet TA23 .....202 C5
Weston-Super-Mare BS24 .....49 A1
Copse Cnr BS24 .....67 C2
Copse Dro
Baltonsborough BA6 .....158 C5
Barrington BA19 .....184 B5
Copse End BS25 .....51 F2
Copse La Ashill TA19 .....183 D4
Barrington TA19 .....184 D4
Hambridge TA3 .....184 B7
Ilton TA19 .....183 F4
Pilton BA4 .....140 F3
Copse Rd Clevedon BS21 .....6 C4
Houndstone BA22 .....218 B7
Keynsham BS31 .....25 C4
Copse Shoot La TA19 .....184 C5
Copse Stile TA20 .....193 F1
Copse The
Bridgwater TA6 .....209 D5
Dunpolton TA7 .....136 F3
Frome BA11 .....120 B6
Copseland BA2 .....45 D5
Copsewood La BS14 .....23 B5
Copthorne Cl BS14 .....23 B5
Coralberry Dr BS22 .....31 F1
Corams La TA21 .....222 B6
Cording's Ball TA4 .....150 A1
Corewell La TA5 .....133 E3
Corfe Cl BS48 .....8 D1
Corfe Cres BS31 .....24 E4
Corfe Rd BS4 .....22 D7
Corinthian Ct 9 BS1 .....227 B1
Cork Pl BA1 .....44 D7
Cork St Bath BA1 .....44 D7
Frome BA11 .....119 F5
Cork Terr BA1 .....44 D7
Corkscrew La
North Cadbury BA22 .....175 E7
Staplegrove TA2 .....212 D8
Corner Ho 2
Bridgwater TA6 .....209 D6
Stogursey TA7 .....136 F3
Corn St Bath BA1 .....228 B2
Cornborough Pl TA6 .....209 B5
Corner Cl TA2 .....222 D4
Corner Croft BS21 .....6 D1
Cornfields The BS14 .....21 F5
Cornhill Bridgwater TA6 .....208 F5
Shepton Mallet BA4 .....205 C6
8 Wellington TA21 .....222 D6
Cornhill Dr BS14 .....23 A6
Cornish Gr BS14 .....23 E6
Cornish Rd BS14 .....23 E6
Cornish Wlk BS14 .....23 E6
Cornishway E TA1 .....212 B3
Cornishway N TA1 .....212 B3
Cornishway S TA1 .....212 B3
Cornishway W TA1 .....212 B3
Cornlands EX16 .....178 A2
Cornlands La BS48 .....22 A5
Cornmoor Cres TA9 .....136 E7
Cornwall Rd BA4 .....205 A6
Cornwallis Ave
Bristol BS8 .....226 A2
Weston-Super-Mare BS23 .....31 F4
Cornwallis Cres BS8 .....11 F6
Cornwallis Gr BS8 .....226 A2
Coromandel Hts BA1 .....228 B4

Coronation Ave Bath BA2 44 C4
Keynsham BS31 24 D4
Yeovil BA21 218 F7
Coronation Cl
Ruishton TA3 169 C3
Wanstrow BA4 142 F4
Coronation Ct BA3 115 A3
Coronation Est BS23 48 F3
Coronation Ho TA6 209 C6
Coronation Pl BS1 227 A2
Coronation Rd
Banwell BS29 51 A3
Bath BA1 44 D7
Bleadon BS24 67 C6
Bridgwater TA6 208 E5
Bristol BS3 226 B1
Frome BA11 120 B5
Highbridge TA9 104 D4
Wells BA5 203 B4
Weston-Super-Mare BS22 31 E2
Coronation St TA20 223 C3
Coronation Terr
Chilcompton BA3 96 D5
Oakhill BA3 115 A3
Coronation Villas BA8 176 E1
Corondale Rd BS22 49 D8
Corporate Rd BA22 174 A2
Corporation St TA1 212 F3
Corpus Christi RC Prim Sch BS23 48 D6
Corrick Cl BS27 90 F2
Corridor The BA1 228 C2
Corsham Dr TA8 104 C8
Corsley CE Prim Sch BA12 121 D2
Corsley Wlk BS4 22 F8
Corston BS24 49 A2
Corston La BA2 43 A8
Corston View BA2 44 C2
Corston Wlk BS11 4 D7
Corton Cl BA21 219 E8
Cory Rd TA2 213 A8
Coryate Cl BA22 186 C2
Cosgates Feet or County Gate EX35 122 D5
Cossington La TA7 136 E3
Cossington Prim Sch TA7 136 F3
Cossington Rd BS4 22 F8
Cossins La TA18 224 C6
Costello Hill BA22 173 F2
Costiland Dr BS13 21 F6
Cote Cnr TA9 136 F7
Cote La BA12 161 F6
Cote Paddock BS9 5 F4
Cote Pk BS9 5 E6
Cotham Hill BS6 226 C4
Cotham Lawn Ho BS6 226 C4
Cotham Lawn Rd BS6 226 C4
Cotham Pl BS6 226 C4
Cotham Rd BS6 226 C4
Cotham Rd S BS6 227 A4
Cotham Sch BS6 226 C4
Cothelstone Cl TA6 208 B4
Cothelstone Rd TA4 151 F1
Cotlake Cl TA1 212 F1
Cotlake Rise TA1 168 E1
Cotleigh Crossing EX14 191 F1
Cotley La TA20 193 D2
Cotman Wlk 1 BS22 31 F2
Cotswold Cl BS20 2 E4
Cotswold Rd BA2 44 E4
Cotswold View BA2 44 B5
Cottage Cnr TA19 183 F4
Cottage La TA22 163 D6
Cottage Pl Bath BA1 28 B2
Bristol BS2 227 A4
Cottage Row TA8 104 A6
Cottages The BS40 35 D2
Cotterell Ct BA1 228 B2
Cottle Gdns BS14 23 F6
Cottle Rd BS14 23 F6
Cottles La
West Pennard BA6 140 B1
Winsley BA15 64 F6
Cotton Cnr 13 BA8 190 A6
Cotton Mead BA2 43 B7
Cotton's La TA11 158 B2
Coulson Dr BS22 32 B3
Coulson's Cl BS14 23 A3
Coulson's Rd BS14 23 A3
Council Hos
Babcary TA11 174 D7
Clapton TA18 195 C1
Crewkerne TA18 195 D3
Podimore BA22 174 A4
Wick St Lawrence BS22 32 B8
Council Hos The TA10 172 E1
Council Houses The
Blagdon BS40 55 B8
Hinton Blewett BS39 75 E6
Counterslip BS1 227 B2
Counterslip Gdns BS14 23 C6
Countess Gytha Prim Sch BA22 174 F3
County Wlk TA1 213 A3
Couple Cross TA24 130 B1
Coursing Batch BA6 206 F3
Court Acres 6 BA22 197 E8
Court Ash BA20 219 B5
Court Ave BS49 34 C7
Court Barton
Crewkerne TA18 224 B6
Ilminster TA19 221 C4
Court Cl Backwell BS48 19 C5
Court Cl *continued*
Portishead BS20 2 D4
Court Cotts SP8 177 D3
Court Dr Sandford BS25 52 B4
Wellington TA21 222 D5
Court Farm Cl TA20 194 E1
Court Farm Pk* BS29 50 F5
Court Farm Rd BS14 22 F3
Court Field La TA20 193 B5
Court Fields Com Sch TA21 222 C5
Court Gdns
Batheaston BA1 29 A4
Marston Magna BA22 174 F1
Yeovil BA21 218 E8
Court Gr TA7 136 C4
Court Hill
Compton Dando BS39 41 D5
Taunton TA1 212 D2
Court La Bampton EX16 164 D4
7 Barwick BA22 197 F8
Bathford BA1 29 B2
Clevedon BS21 7 A3
Corsley Heath BA12 121 B1
Milborne Port DT9 217 C3
Shipham BS25 70 F8
Court Mill La TA20 223 A8
Court Moors La TA21 179 E5
Court Pl BS22 31 F2
Court Place La TA24 131 B4
Court Rd
Norton Fitzwarren TA2 168 B4
Weston-Super-Mare BS22 31 A5
Court St
5 Bridgwater TA6 208 F5
Winsham TA20 194 E1
Court Terr TA21 222 C5
Court The TA24 131 A5
Court Way EX16 178 D1
Court's Barton BA11 119 D2
Court-de-Wyck CE Prim Sch BS49 17 F1
Courtenay Rd BS31 25 B2
Courtenay Wlk BS22 32 A3
Courteney Cres BS4 22 D7
Courtfield Langport TA10 172 A5
Milverton TA4 166 F4
Courtland Rd TA21 222 D6
Courtlands BS31 24 E5
Courtlands Cl TA23 202 C6
Courtlands La BS3 11 E4
Courtlands Unit BS4 22 D8
Courtmead BA2 62 F7
Courtmead La TA24 123 F4
Courtway Ave TA6 209 C4
Courtyard The
Dunster TA24 201 E2
East Harptree BS40 74 E6
Evercreech BA4 141 F2
3 Taunton TA1 212 F4
Coverdale Ct BA21 218 F6
Coveyhill La BA4 142 E5
Cow Bridge Rd BA6 157 C7
Cow Down Rd TA20 194 C1
Cowan Cl TA8 104 C7
Cowbridge Cross TA24 200 D1
Cowdray Cl TA24 200 E6
Cowdray Rd Bristol BS4 22 D7
Minehead TA24 200 E6
Cowen Cl TA18 224 C4
Cowl St BA4 205 B7
Cowleaze Dro TA3 169 D3
Cowleaze La BS40 74 C6
Cowler Wlk BS13 21 F4
Cowling Dr BS14 23 C5
Cowling Rd BS14 23 D5
Cowpath La DT9 176 A1
Cowslip La BS26 68 D3
Cox Hill DT10 190 E4
Cox Rd TA21 222 C4
Cox's Cl Bruton BA10 215 E5
Glastonbury BA6 206 E6
Cox's Dr BA6 158 A6
Cox's Gn BS40 35 E1
Cox's La TA4 167 C5
Coxbridge Dro BA6 158 A6
Coxland's Rock TA4 167 B7
Coxley Dr BA1 28 B2
Coxley Prim Sch BA5 139 E6
Coxley Vineyard* BA5 139 E6
Coxs Cl BA22 175 D6
Coxton End La BA5 92 B3
Coxway BS21 6 F2
Coxwithy La BA6 139 D1
Crab Tree Dro BA6 206 F8
Crabtree Cl BS41 21 D1
Crabtree La Bruton BA10 215 B7
Curry Rivel TA10 171 C1
Dundry BS41 21 D2
Crackmore DT9 217 C1
Craig Lea TA2 212 E7
Cranberry Wlk BS9 5 C8
Cranbourne Chase BS23 31 A1
Cranbourne Cl TA6 208 F6
Crancombe La TA7 136 D3
Crandale Rd BA2 44 D5
Crane Cotts BA4 142 B6
Crane Hill TA10,TA11 173 C4
Cranes Cl TA2 213 D7
Cranford Cl BS22 31 D1
Crangs La BA22 175 D4
Cranhill Rd Bath BA1 44 D8
Street BA16 207 B6
Cranleigh BA2 62 F8
Cranleigh Ct TA13 220 B4
Cranleigh Gdns
Bridgwater TA6 209 A4
Bristol BS9 5 E4
Cranleigh Rd BS14 23 B5
Cranmer Rd TA1 213 A4
Cranmore BS24 49 A2
Cranmore Ave BS31 24 E6
Cranmore Ct 3 BA11 119 E3
Cranmore Pl BA2 62 E8
Cranmore View BA11 119 D2
Cranmore West Sta BA4 142 A5
Cransey La
Bicknoller TA4 132 A2
Washford TA4,TA23 131 F2
Crantock Ave BS13 22 B8
Cranway La TA20 223 F2
Cranwell Cl TA7 154 F5
Cranwell Gr BS14 23 A5
Cranwell Rd BS24 50 C5
Cranwells Pk BA1 44 D8
Crapnell La BA5 140 F8
Crawford Cl 1 BS21 6 B1
Crawford La BA22 175 D7
Crawl La BA3 78 C4
Crawlic La TA4 151 E1
Crawter Dr TA24 124 A3
Craydon Gr BS14 23 D4
Craydon Rd BS14 23 D5
Craydon Wlk BS14 23 D5
Crease Cl BA5 203 B4
Crediton 5 BS22 32 A2
Creech Hill La BA10 215 A7
Creech Mill Est TA3 169 C4
Creech St Michael CE Prim Sch TA3 169 D4
Creechbarrow Rd TA1 213 C5
Creechberry Orch TA1 213 D5
Creeches La BA16 156 D7
Creechwood Terr TA3 169 D5
Creedwell Cl TA4 167 A4
Creedwell Orch TA4 167 A4
Creighton Cl BA5 140 C8
Crescent Gdns BA1 228 A3
Crescent La BA1 228 B4
Crescent The
Backwell BS48 19 A6
Bristol, Sea Mills BS9 5 C6
4 Carhampton TA24 131 A5
Coleford BA3 117 A2
Farrington Gurney BS39 77 B3
Golsoncott TA23 131 D1
Ilminster TA19 221 B2
Lympsham BS24 67 C5
South Cadbury BA22 175 E4
Stanton Drew BS39 39 F1
Taunton TA1 212 F3
Weston-Super-Mare BS22 31 B1
Yeovil BA20 219 A4
Crescent View BA2 228 B1
Crescent View Ct BS22 31 B1
Crescent Way TA1 212 F3
Creslands Ind Units BS24 49 A3
Cresswell Ave TA2 212 D7
Cresswell Cl BS22 32 A2
Crestfield Ave TA6 208 F7
Creswick Way TA8 104 C8
Creswicke Rd BS4 22 E7
Crewkerne Bsns Pk TA18 224 D6
Crewkerne Cl BS48 9 B1
Crewkerne Hospl TA18 224 B5
Crewkerne Rd TA20 223 E4
Crewkerne Sta TA18 224 E4
Crewkerne Turning EX13 198 C6
Crib Cl TA20 223 D6
Crib House La BS28 89 C1
Cribb's La BS40 36 D1
Crickback La BS40 39 A3
Cricket Cotts TA3 170 B3
Cricket Cross TA19 194 C6
Cricket Field Gn BS48 8 D2
Cricket La TA19,TA20 194 C6
Cricket St Thomas Wildlife Pk* TA20 194 E3
Cricket View DT9 225 D3
Crickham La BS28 108 D8
Cricklade Ct BS48 9 A1
Cridlake EX13 198 A1
Crimchard TA20 223 B5
Crimthorne Cotts TA3 183 A7
Cripple St TA12 185 D7
Crispin Sch BA16 207 D7
Critch Hill BA11 119 C3
Critchill Cl BA11 119 D3
Critchill Gr BA11 119 D3
Critchill Rd BA11 119 D3
Critchill Specl Sch BA11 119 C4
Crocker's Hill BA9 175 F8
Crockerne CE Prim Sch BS20 4 C4
Crockerne Dr BS20 4 C3
Crockerne Ho BS20 4 D4
Crockers Hill TA7 136 E4
Crocombe BA2 60 C3
Crocombe La BA2 60 C3
Croford Hill TA4 166 E6
Croft Cl BS30 25 D8
Croft Cotts
Moorlinch TA7 155 E7
Wrantage TA3 170 B1
Croft La Brushford TA22 163 C4
Skilgate TA4 164 E6
Westbury Sub Mendip BA5 110 C6
Croft Mdw TA4 202 F1
Croft Rd Bath BA1 28 B1
Holcombe BA3 116 C8
Croft The Backwell BS48 19 A7
Bath BA2 45 E1
Croft The *continued*
Cheddar BS27 90 C8
Clevedon BS21 6 F4
Hutton BS24 49 E3
Mark TA9 106 A4
Watchet TA23 202 C7
Westwood BA15 64 F3
Williton TA4 202 D3
Wookey Hole BA5 203 A8
Yeovil BA20 218 C2
Croft Way TA4 210 C4
Croftland La TA10 171 E2
Crofton Ave BA21 219 B6
Crofton Ct BA21 219 B5
Crofton Pk BA21 219 B5
Crofton Rd BA21 219 B6
Crofts Mead BA9 216 C2
Croftways TA4 202 D4
Cromer Ct BS21 6 D5
Cromer Rd BS23 48 E5
Cromwell Dr BS22 32 A4
Cromwell Rd
Bridgwater TA6 209 A2
Taunton TA1 213 B5
Yeovil BA21 219 D6
Crook Horn Hill TA24 129 C7
Crook's La BS22 31 A4
Crooked La
Burnham-On-Sea TA8 85 D1
Burnham-On-Sea TA9 85 E3
Cucklington SP8 177 E6
Rode BA11 101 E7
Cropmead Trad Est TA18 224 D6
Crosby Row BS8 226 A2
Croscombe BA5 204 D8
Croscombe CE Prim Sch BA5 204 C7
Croscombe Gdns BA11 120 D6
Cross TA19 221 C3
Cross Elms Hill TA5 133 F7
Cross Elms La BS9 5 E5
Cross Farm Cl TA24 201 A5
Cross Farm Rd BS27 90 F3
Cross Keys Cl TA2 212 A7
Cross La Axbridge BS26 70 A2
Brendon EX35 122 A4
Long Sutton TA10 172 F4
Cross Lanes BS20 4 C4
Cross Moor Dr BS26 70 B1
Cross Moor Dro BS26 69 E1
Cross Moor Rd BS26 70 B1
Cross Rd DT9 187 E1
Cross St
Burnham-On-Sea TA8 104 A7
Keynsham BS31 24 F7
Weston-Super-Mare BS23 48 E7
Cross The
Bradford Abbas DT9 187 E1
Buckland Dinham BA11 100 A3
East Harptree BS40 74 F4
9 Henstridge BA8 190 A6
Ilminster TA19 221 C3
Milverton TA4 167 A4
Minehead TA24 200 F8
Nether Stowey TA5 134 B2
Street BA16 207 D7
Cross View Rise TA6 208 D6
Cross Way DT9 187 E1
Cross Wlk BS14 23 A6
Crossacre TA6 208 D6
Crosscombe Dr BS13 22 C3
Crosscroft TA4 151 A3
Crosselm Rd BA4 143 A2
Crossfield Cl TA6 208 D6
Crossfields DT9 187 F4
Crossing Dro BS28 109 D3
Crossland La EX14 191 F2
Crosslands TA21 222 B8
Crossman Wlk BS21 6 F2
Crossmead TA7 136 E4
Crosspost La BA2 42 B4
Crossroads The BA9 216 C3
Crossway TA1 213 C5
Crossway La BA3 96 B7
Crossways Coleford BA3 116 F7
Tatworth TA20 198 D8
Crossways Rd TA6 209 B1
Crosswell Cl 7 TA6 153 E3
Crouds La TA10 172 E4
Crow Castle La TA18 224 B7
Crow La Ashill TA19 183 C4
Bristol BS1 227 A2
Broadway TA19 194 A8
Westbury Sub Mendip BA5 110 E6
Crow's Hill BA4 142 C1
Crow's La TA7 209 E6
Crowcombe CE Fst Sch TA4 151 C7
Crowcombe Heathfield Sta TA4 151 B5
Crowcombe Rd TA2 212 F8
Crowcombe Wlk TA6 208 C4
Crowe Hill BA3 64 B5
Crowe La BA3 64 B5
Crown Cl TA2 213 C6
Crown Gdns BA11 119 F3
Crown Glass Pl 5 BS48 8 E2
Crown Hill Bath BA1 27 C1
West Buckland TA21 180 F7
Winford BS40 38 A5
Crown Ho BS48 8 C1
Crown Ind Est TA2 213 C6
Crown La
Creech St Michael TA3 169 D6
South Petherton TA13 220 C4
Crown Mews TA21 180 F7
Crown Rd BA1 27 B1
Crown Wlk TA1 212 F3
Crowne Trad Est BA4 205 D5
Crowpill Cotts TA6 208 F6
Crowpill La TA6 208 F6
Crowshute Link TA20 223 C3
Crufts Mdw TA3 169 D4
Crusty La BS20 4 C5
Cruwy's Cross TA4 210 B7
Crypton Tech Bsns Pk TA6 209 B8
Cuck Hill BS25 70 E7
Cuckold's Row TA5 152 E8
Cuckoo Cnr TA1 213 B2
Cuckoo Hill Bruton BA10 160 D6
Frome BA11 119 E8
Cuckoo La Frome BA11 119 F8
High Littleton BS39 59 B3
Thorncombe TA20 199 C7
Wraxall BS48 9 A6
Cuffs Mead TA20 223 F1
Cufic La BS27 90 C8
Culliford Cl BA16 207 D7
Culliver's Grave BA22 197 C8
Culmhead Cl TA1 212 D1
Culmstock Prim Sch EX15 179 E1
Culvecliffe Ct TA24 125 C4
Culver Hill TA10 172 B7
Culver La
Carhampton TA24 131 B4
East Harptree BS40 74 F3
Culver St BS1 226 C2
Culver Street La TA5 134 A7
Culvercliffe Rd TA23 202 D7
Culverhay BS39 41 D6
Culverhay La TA4 210 B4
Culverhay Sch BA2 44 B2
Culverhayes TA20 223 C2
Culverhays La TA4 132 F1
Culverhill BA11 119 F3
Culverlake La EX13 199 A3
Culvers Cl Keynsham BS31 24 E6
Sherborne DT9 225 C4
Culvers Rd BS31 24 E6
Culvert Dro BS27 109 B6
Culverwell Cotts BA4 140 F3
Culverwell Rd BS13 22 A4
Cumberland Basin Rd BS8 11 F5
Cumberland Cl BS1 226 A1
Cumberland Ho BA1 228 A2
Cumberland Pl 6 BS8 11 F6
Cumberland Rd BS1 226 B1
Cumberland Row BA1 228 B2
Cumberland St BS2 227 B4
Cumhill Hill BA4 140 E3
Cumnock Cres BA7 214 C6
Cumnock Rd BA7 214 C6
Cumnock Terr BA7 214 C6
Cunningham Ave EX13 198 A2
Cunningham Rd TA8 104 C7
Curdleigh La TA3 181 D5
Curland Gr BS14 23 B5
Curlew Cl TA24 201 C4
Curlew Gdns BS22 31 F1
Currells La BS40 20 B1
Curriott Hill TA18 224 B4
Curriott Hill Rd TA18 224 B5
Curry Hole La BA22 197 C2
Curry La TA3 169 E6
Curry Mallet Prim Sch TA3 183 D8
Curry Rivel CE Prim Sch TA10 171 D4
Currymead La TA10 171 C2
Currypool La TA5 134 E1
Currywoods Way TA10 171 D4
Curtis Units BA11 119 E2
Curvalion House Gdns TA3 169 D4
Curvalion Rd TA3 169 D4
Cushuish La TA2,TA5 152 C2
Custom Cl BS14 23 A7
Cut Tongue La TA20 193 C7
Cutcombe CE Fst Sch TA24 129 E1
Cutcombe Cross TA24 129 E1
Cutcombe Hill TA24 129 F2
Cuthays La EX13 198 B1
Cuthbert St TA9 104 D3
Cutler Rd BS13 21 F6
Cutliff Cl TA1 212 E1
Cuts Rd TA3,TA7 170 E8
Cutt Mill La DT10 190 F3
Cutty Cotts BA22 175 D6
Cutty La BA22 175 D6
Cygnet Cres BS22 31 F1
Cynthia Rd BA2 44 D5
Cypress Ct Bristol BS9 5 D3
Somerton TA11 211 E4
Cypress Dr Puriton TA7 136 C4
Yeovil BA20 218 E2
Cypress Gdns BS8 11 E6
Cypress Terr BA3 78 D1
Cypress Way BA11 120 C7
Cyril St TA2 212 E6
Cyril St W TA2 212 E6

D

D'angers Lion TA4 210 D4
Dabinett Cl TA2 168 B5
Dafford St BA1 28 C2
Dafford's Bldgs BA1 28 C2
Dagg's La BS28 138 E8
Dagg's Lane Dro BA5, BS28 138 D7

Daghole BS27 90 C8
Daglands The BA2 78 E8
Dairs Orch TA20 198 C8
Dairy Cl BA5 203 B5
Dairy Ct 3 TA18 224 C5
Dairy Hill BA2 80 B5
Dairy House La TA3 182 E5
Dairycroft BS2 227 B4
Dairylands TA24 131 D4
Daisey Bank BA2 45 B4
Daisyfield BA22 188 A8
Dakota Dr BS14 23 A4
Dale La BA5 92 C3
Dale St BS2 227 C4
Daley Cl BS22 32 B3
Dalimores La BA11 143 B8
Dalleston BA3 114 C8
Dallimore Mead BA11 143 B8
Dalton Sq BS2 227 B4
Dalwood 12 BS22 32 A2
Dalwoods DT9 225 D3
Dame Court Cl BS22 31 F4
Dame Withycombe Villas
TA5 135 B5
Dampier Pl BA21 219 C5
Dampier St BA21 219 C5
Dampiet St TA6 208 F4
Damson Rd BS22 49 E7
Dancey Mead BS13 21 F6
Dancing Cross BA9 176 B5
Dancing Hill TA6 153 E4
Dancing La BA9 216 A4
DandO's La BS28 108 C4
Dandy's Mdw BS20 2 E4
Dane Cl BA15 64 E7
Dane Rise BA15 64 E7
Dane's Lea BS28 108 C4
Daneacre Rd BA3 79 A3
Danes Cl EX14 191 F2
Danesboro Rd TA6 208 C4
Danesborough View
TA4 202 D3
Danesborough View E
TA4 202 D3
Danesborough View W
TA4 202 D3
Danesfield CE Com Sch
TA4 202 D4
Dangerfield Ave BS13 21 F6
Daniel Cl BS21 6 F3
Daniel Mews BA2 45 B7
Daniel St BA2 45 B7
Daniels La BA5 111 A4
Danielsfield Rd BA20 218 F2
Dano View Gdns BS20 2 C5
Dapps Hill BS31 24 F5
Dapwell La BS14,BS31 24 A1
Darby Cl SP8 161 F1
Darby Way TA4 151 F1
Darby's Knap TA24 147 C5
Dare Cl TA2 213 A8
Dark La Backwell BS48 19 B5
Banwell BS29 51 C2
Berkley BA11 120 E8
Blagdon BS40 54 E3
Chew Magna BS40 38 F3
Freshford BA3 64 B5
Hockworthy EX16 178 B8
Holcombe BA3 97 C1
Kilmersdon BA11 98 A1
North Wootton BA4 140 C5
Sandford Orcas DT9 188 C7
Seavington TA19 184 E1
Stoke St Gregory TA3 170 F6
Stoke St Michael BA3 116 C2
Upton Noble BA4 142 F2
Wellington TA21 222 D5
Witham Friary BA11 143 D2
Darkey La BA10 215 F7
Darkfield Way TA7 136 E3
Darlington Mews BA2 45 B7
Darlington Pl BA2 45 B6
Darlington Rd BA2 45 B8
Darlington St BA2 45 B7
Darmead BS24 32 B1
Darshill Hospl BA4 204 F6
Dart Rd BS21 6 D1
Dartmouth Ave BA2 44 C5
Dartmouth Cl BS22 32 A2
Dartmouth Wlk BS31 24 D4
Darwin Cl TA2 212 B6
Dashwoods La TA4 132 E2
Daubeny Ct BS1 227 A1
Daunton Cl TA9 104 D4
David St BS2 227 C3
David's La TA19 184 F2
David's Rd BS14 23 C6
Davies Cl Bridgwater TA6 208 F2
Winsham TA20 194 E1
Davies Ct BA5 203 B4
Davin Cres BS20 4 C3
Davis La BS21 16 F8
Davis St BS11 4 B8
Davis Terr BA5 203 C4
Daw's La DT9 176 A3
Dawbins Dr TA7 136 E4
Dawes Cl BS21 6 D1
Dawes Ct 2 BS8 11 F6
Daws Cl TA6 208 E2
Daws La TA6 153 E3
Daws Mead TA1 212 A3
Day Cres BA2 43 F6
De Combe Ho TA18 224 D6
Deacon Rd TA6 209 C6
Deacon Way TA8 104 B6
Deacons Cl BS22 31 E2
Deacons Ct BS22 31 C1
Dead Maids Cross Rd
BA13 121 E5
Dead Woman's Cnr
BA12 161 F8
Deadlands La TA12,TA13 185 A6
Deadman's Hill DT9 176 A1
Deadmill La BA1 28 C3
Deal Cl TA6 209 D5
Dean Cl Frome BA11 120 C6
Weston-Super-Mare BS22 32 B3
Dean La Dunster TA24 201 D3
Milverton TA4 167 A6
Oakhill BA3 115 A3
Dean St BS2 227 B4
Dean's Cross TA24 124 E3
Dean's La Allerford TA24 124 E3
Brompton Ralph TA4 150 F4
Deane Cl TA4 150 D8
Deane Dr TA1 212 B2
Deane Gate Ave TA1 213 E5
Deane Pl BA5 203 D4
Deane Way TA20 198 D8
Deanery Rd BS1 226 C2
Deanery Wlk BA3 64 C6
Deanesly Way BA9 216 D3
Deanhill La BA1 27 A2
Deans Cross TA4 151 A4
Deans Mead BS11 5 A8
Deans The BS20 2 B4
Deansley Way BA9 216 E3
Debecca's La BS20 4 B4
Decoy La TA11 157 A2
Deep La BA12 121 E1
Deepleigh La TA4 210 C7
Deer Mead BS21 6 B1
Deer View TA24 201 C4
Deerleap Easton BA5 111 B6
Shipham BS25 70 F8
Deerswood Gdns BA16 207 A6
Delapre Rd BS23 48 D3
Delhorn La BS24 86 C7
Delius Gr BS4 22 D7
Dell The
Bristol, Westbury on Trym
BS9 5 F5
Minehead TA24 200 E6
Nailsea BS48 8 D2
Weston-Super-Mare BS22 31 E4
Deller's Wharf TA1 212 F5
Dellers Ct TA1 212 F5
Dellshore Cl TA20 223 D4
Delmore Rd BA11 119 E3
Delta Cl BA11 119 F5
Delta Rise TA4 151 E1
Demelza Ct BA22 174 D3
Dempier Mews BA22 218 B6
Dene Cl BS31 24 F3
Dene Cross TA4 167 F7
Dene Gdns TA24 201 B4
Dene Rd
Cotford St Luke TA4 167 F6
Whitchurch BS14 23 C4
Dening Cl TA20 223 C6
Denleigh Cl BS14 23 A4
Denman's La TA19 184 D5
Denman's La TA5 135 B2
Denmark Ave BS1 226 C2
Denmark Rd BA2 44 D6
Denmark St BS1 226 C2
Denmark Terr TA2 212 F7
Dennett Cl BA4 205 E4
Denning Cl TA1 212 B1
Denning Ct BS22 32 B4
Dennington La
Churchinford EX14 192 C6
Dulverton TA22 163 B4
Dennor Pk BS14 23 B7
Denny Cl BS20 2 A5
Denny La BS40 39 B1
Denny View BS20 2 A5
Dennyview Rd BS8 10 F8
Denston Dr BS20 2 E4
Denston Wlk BS13 22 A7
Dentwood Gr BS9 5 B8
Denvale Trad Pk BS4 22 E7
Denzil Cl BA22 197 A8
Derham Cl BS49 34 B8
Derham Ct BS49 34 B8
Derham Pk BS49 34 B8
Derham Rd BS13 22 A5
Derricke Rd BS14 23 F6
Dertfords BA12 144 D8
Derwent Gdns BA21 219 D6
Derwent Gr
Keynsham BS31 25 A5
Taunton TA1 213 E4
Derwent Rd BS23 49 A5
Derwent Way BA21 218 C6
Devenish La BA9 216 F4
Deveron Gr BS31 25 A4
Devonshire Bldgs BA2 44 F4
Devonshire Ct BS23 48 E4
Devonshire Dr BS20 1 F5
Devonshire Pl BA2 44 F4
Devonshire Rd
Bathampton BA2 28 E1
Weston-Super-Mare BS23 48 E4
Devonshire St TA6 209 B5
Devonshire Villas BA2 44 F3
Dew Water La TA11 211 D5
Dewar Cl TA8 104 C7
Dial Hill Rd BS21 6 D4
Dial La BS40 20 D1
Dial's Gate La BA6,TA11 158 D4
Diamond Batch BS24 32 B1
Dibbens Row BA9 161 A2
Dibbles La BA22 197 A8
Dickenson Rd BS23 48 E6
Dickenson's Gr BS49 34 E3
Digby Rd DT9 225 D3
Dighton Ct 3 BS2 227 A4
Dighton St BS2 227 A4
Digland La TA24 129 F5
Dilkes La TA11 174 C7
Dillons Rd TA3 169 D4
Dimmer La BA7 159 B2
Dinder Cl BS48 18 E8
Dinghurst Rd BS25 52 E4
Dingle Cl BS9 5 C6
Dingle Ct BS13 21 F7
Dingle Rd BS9 5 D7
Dingle The BS9 5 D7
Dingle View BS9 5 C7
Dinglewood Cl BS9 5 D7
Dinhay DT10 190 F6
Dipford Rd TA3 168 D1
Dipland Gr BS40 54 F2
Disraeli Pl TA1 212 D5
Ditch Furlong Rd TA7 137 A2
Ditcheat Prim Sch BA4 159 C7
Ditton St TA19 221 C3
Dixon Gdns BA1 27 F1
Dobree Pk TA21 222 A4
Dock Gate La BS8 226 A1
Doctor's Hill BA5 111 B1
Dod La BA6 206 E4
Dodd Ave BA5 203 F5
Dodge Cross DT9 225 F5
Dog Down Cross EX16 178 A8
Doleberrow BS25 52 F3
Dolemead La BS27 90 E2
Dolemoor La
Congresbury BS49 34 A4
Congresbury BS49 34 C3
Dolling Cl TA20 223 D6
Dolling's Rd TA3 181 B4
Dominion Rd BA2 44 A6
Dominy Cl TA20 223 D3
Dommett's La BA11 119 D4
Domus Dr BA4 205 E4
Donald Rd BS13 21 F7
Doniford Beach Halt
TA23 202 E6
Doniford Dr TA4 202 D3
Doniford Rd
Watchet TA23 202 E6
Williton TA4 202 D4
Donne La BA22 186 C2
Donnes Terr BA7 214 B5
Donnington Wlk BS31 24 D4
Donstan Rd TA9 104 E5
Donyatt Hill TA19 183 D1
Donyatt Hill Est TA19 183 D1
Doone Way TA24 201 B4
Dorchester Cl 6 BS48 8 D1
Dorchester Rd
Barwick BA22 197 F7
East Coker BA22 197 F5
Taunton TA2 213 A8
Yeovil BA22 219 A1
Dorchester St BA1 228 C1
Dorset Cl Bath BA2 44 D6
Frome BA11 119 E5
Dorset Ho BA2 44 D3
Dorset Rd TA6 209 C3
Dorset St BA2 44 D6
Doster's La TA2 169 C6
Double Gates Dro TA11 158 A3
Douglas Ct BS23 48 F5
Douglas Dr BA4 205 B5
Douglas Rd BS23 48 F5
Douglas Yates Ct BA3 116 F7
Doulting BA4 141 E6
Doulting Ct BA11 120 D7
Doulting Hill BA4 205 F4
Doulton Way BS14 23 B5
Dove Cots Cl BA16 207 C7
Dove La BS2 227 C4
Dove St BS2 227 A4
Dove St S BS2 227 A4
Dover Ho BA1 228 C4
Dover Pl 6 Bath BA1 28 A1
Bristol BS8 226 B3
Dover Rd TA2 213 A8
Dovers La BA1 29 C2
Dovers Pk BA1 29 C2
Dovery Manor Mus*
TA24 124 A3
Doveswell Gr BS13 22 A4
Dovetail Ct 1 TA1 212 E3
Dovetail Dr BS23 49 A7
Dovetons Cl TA4 202 E3
Dovetons Dr TA4 202 E3
Dowding Rd BA1 28 B1
Dowell Cl TA2 212 C6
Dowland 18 BS22 32 A2
Dowling La BA6 158 A5
Dowling Rd BS13 22 D3
Dowlish La TA19 194 F5
Down Ave BA2 45 A1
Down Cl BS20 1 F4
Down La Bathampton BA2 28 F1
Buckland Dinham BA11 99 C3
Shepton Montague BA9 160 B2
Sherborne DT9 188 A5
Trent DT9 187 F5
West Pennard BA4,BA6 140 C1
Down Rd BS20 1 F4
Down View BA3 97 F8
Down's Orch BA6 138 C4
Downash La EX13 198 E3
Downclose La TA18 196 C3
Downend Cres TA6 136 B4
Downend Rd TA6 136 B4
Downend Terr TA6 136 B4
Downey Field La TA18 196 D6
Downfield Bristol BS9 5 C7
Keynsham BS31 24 D5
Downhall Dr TA6 208 D6
Downhead La BA22 174 C5
Downland Cl Bristol BS4 22 D6
5 Nailsea BS48 8 D1
Downlands La TA3 181 A2
Downleaze
Bristol, Stoke Bishop BS9 5 F3
Portishead BS20 2 A5
Yeovil BA20 218 D2
Downleaze Rd BS9 5 F3
Downs Cl BS22 31 F1
Downs Cote Ave BS9 5 F6
Downs Cote Dr BS9 5 F6
Downs Rd BS41 21 D2
Downs Scn The BS48 9 C8
Downs The BS20 2 B4
Downside Portishead BS20 2 C5
Street BA16 207 D6
Downside Abbey* BA3 96 F2
Downside Cl
Bathampton BA2 28 F1
Chilcompton BA3 96 D3
Downside Rd
Backwell BS48 36 E8
Weston-Super-Mare BS23 48 F4
Downside Sch BA3 96 F2
Downslade La TA10 172 D5
Downsway BS39 77 D6
Downton Rd BS13 22 D8
Dowry Pl 3 BS8 11 F5
Dowry Rd BS8 226 A2
Dowry Sq BS8 226 A2
Dowsland Way TA1 213 C1
Dozen's Cnr TA17 195 A7
Dr White's Cl BS1 227 B1
Dragon Cross TA24 131 D3
Dragonfly Chase BA22 173 E2
Dragons Hill Cl BS31 24 F5
Dragons Hill Ct BS31 24 F5
Dragons Hill Gdns BS31 24 F5
Drake Ave BA2 44 F2
Drake Cl Saltford BS31 25 D2
Staplegrove TA2 212 B7
Weston-Super-Mare BS22 31 F4
Drake Rd BA5 203 F6
Drake's Cl TA3 169 C4
Drakes Cl TA6 208 F5
Drakes Cres TA20 198 D8
Drakes Mdw
East Coker BA22 197 C7
Yarcombe EX14 192 D3
Drakes Pk TA21 222 D7
Drakes Pk N TA21 222 D7
Drakes Way BS20 2 B5
Drang The Coxley BA5 139 E6
Porlock TA24 124 A3
Dransfield Way BA2 44 C4
Drapers Way TA24 129 D2
Dray Rd BA22 186 C2
Draycot Pl BS1 227 A1
Draycott & Rodney Stoke CE
First Sch BS27 90 F3
Draycott Ave TA2 213 A6
Draycott Moor Dro BS27 90 D1
Draycott Rd Cheddar BS27 90 D5
Shepton Mallet BA4 205 B6
Draydon Rd BS4 22 D8
Drayton BS24 49 A2
Drayton Cl BS14 23 B8
Drayton La TA10 171 D3
Drayton Rd BS9 5 C8
Drew's La DT10 190 B5
Drials La BA3 94 F6
Drift Rd TA24 201 D4
Drift The TA20 194 B3
Drill Hall La BA4 205 C5
Drimpton Cross DT8 199 F7
Dring The BA3 78 E2
Drive The
Bristol, Hengrove BS14 23 C6
Burnham-On-Sea TA8 85 A2
Churchill BS25 52 E4
Shipham BS25 70 E8
Stanton Drew BS39 39 F1
Taunton TA1 212 D1
Weston-Super-Mare BS23 48 F8
Woolavington TA7 136 E4
Dropping La BA10 160 D5
Drove Ct BS48 8 E3
Drove La
East Pennard BA4 158 E8
Shepton Beauchamp TA19 184 E4
Drove Rd
Stourton Caundle DT10 189 F2
Weston-Super-Mare BS23 48 F5
Drove Road Hospl BS23 48 F5
Drove The
Bridgwater TA6 209 A6
Portbury BS20 3 D6
Drove Way
Churchinford TA3 191 F8
Sandford BS24,BS25 51 E7
Droveway TA13 220 B5
Droveway Cl TA13 220 C5
Droveway La BA21 187 C7
Druid Cl BS9 5 E5
Druid Hill BS9 5 E5
Druid Rd BS9 5 D4
Druid Stoke Ave BS9 5 D5
Druid Woods BS9 5 C5
Druids Wlk TA20 223 C5
Druley Hill BA10 161 D8
Drum Ave BA6 206 C5
Drumhead Way The
BS25 70 E8
Dryleaze BS31 24 E7
Drysdale Cl BS22 31 D1
Duchy Cl BA3 78 E5
Duchy Rd Radstock BA3 78 E5
Shepton Mallet BA4 205 A5
Duck La Chard TA20 223 C3
Horsington BA8 176 E2
Ilchester BA22 173 F1
Kenn BS21 17 A6
Langford BS40 53 A8
Stalbridge DT10 190 B5
Westbury Sub Mendip BA5 110 E6
Duck Pool Dro BA6 206 B7
Duck Pool La BA11 102 B6
Duck St BS25 52 C5
Duckpool La TA18 196 B8
Ducks Hill TA10 172 B5
Ducks' Field Crossing
TA18 224 C1
Dudley Cl BS31 24 E4
Dudmoor TA12 185 B7
Dudwell La BA3 95 A5
Dugdale St TA24 200 F6
Duke Ave 7 TA5 135 B2
Duke Ho TA19 221 B3
Duke St Bath BA2 228 C2
Frome BA11 119 E5
Taunton TA1 213 A4
Duke's Cl BA9 216 E3
Duke's La
Horningsham BA12 144 A1
Kilmington BA12 161 F8
Dukes Field BA4 205 C5
Dukes Mead TA6 209 A2
Dull Cross TA4 151 D3
Dulverton Com Sch
TA22 163 D6
Dulverton La TA4 165 D7
Dumfries Pl BS23 48 E5
Dummis La BA5 111 A1
Dumper's La BA3 94 F7
Dumpers La BS40 39 B2
Dunbar Cl TA9 104 C4
Duncan Gdns BA1 27 A3
Duncart La BA5 204 C7
Duncliffe Cl DT10 190 B4
Duncombe Cl TA6 209 D5
Dundry CE Prim Sch
BS41 21 D2
Dundry La Dundry BS41 21 C3
Winford BS40 38 A7
Dunedin Way BS22 32 C4
Dunford Terr BA6 158 A5
Dungeon BS28 108 D7
Dungeon La BA5 204 C6
Dunkerry Rd BS26 88 C4
Dunkerton Cl BA6 206 F3
Dunkerton Hill BA2 61 E2
Dunkerton Rise TA2 168 B5
Dunkery Cl BS48 8 E1
Dunkery Rd
Bridgwater TA6 208 D4
Weston-Super-Mare BS23 30 F1
Dunkery Vineyard*
TA24 200 A1
Dunkleys Way TA1 213 C2
Dunn's Hill TA21 179 A6
Dunningham La BS28 107 E7
Dunns Cl BS28 108 C4
Dunsford Pl BA2 45 B6
Dunsgreen La EX15 191 A8
Dunsham La TA18 195 C2
Dunsley Hill EX16,EX36 162 D5
Dunstan Rd
Burnham-On-Sea TA8 104 B7
Glastonbury BA6 206 F5
Dunstan Way BS27 90 B6
Dunster Castle* TA24 201 E1
Dunster Cl
Minehead TA24 201 B4
Taunton TA2 213 B7
Dunster Cres BS24 49 A2
Dunster Ct BS25 70 A8
Dunster Fst Sch TA24 201 D2
Dunster Gdns 5 BS48 8 E1
Dunster Ho BA2 45 A2
Dunster Rd Bristol BS4 22 F8
Keynsham BS31 24 E4
Dunster Sta* TA24 201 F4
Dunster Steep
Dunster TA24 201 E2
Porlock TA24 123 F4
Porlock TA24 124 A3
Dunster Visitor Ctr*
TA24 201 E2
Dunster Working Water
Mill* TA24 201 E1
Dunsters Rd BS49 17 F1
Dunwear Ho 3 TA6 209 C4
Dunwear La TA6 209 D3
Durban Way BS49 17 B1
Durbin Park Rd BS21 6 D5
Durcott Rd BA2 78 D8
Durham Gr BS31 24 D4
Durham Pl 9 TA2 213 A8
Durhams Cotts TA4 210 C5
Durkheim Dr BA5 203 C4
Durleigh Cl
Bridgwater TA6 208 D3
Bristol BS13 22 A7
Durleigh Hill TA5 208 A2
Durleigh Rd TA6 208 C3
Durley Hill BS31 24 C7
Durley La BS31 24 D7
Durley Pk BA2 44 E4
Durleymoor Cross EX16 178 F4

Durnhill BS40 ... 73 F7
Durrant Cl DT9 ... 225 D3
Dursdon Dro Priddy BA5 ... 111 C8
　Wells BA5 ... 112 B6
Dursley Rd BS11 ... 4 E5
Durston Dro BS28 ... 49 A2
Durston Cl BA16 ... 207 C5
Durston Ho BA16 ... 207 C5
Durston Way TA1 ... 212 E1
Durville Rd BS13 ... 22 B6
Durweston Wlk BS14 ... 23 C8
Dutch Rd TA9 ... 105 E5
Dutton Cl BS14 ... 23 D6
Dutton Rd BS14 ... 23 D6
Dutton Wlk BS14 ... 23 D6
Dwelly Cl TA20 ... 223 C3
Dye La BA3 ... 115 A3
Dyehouse Cnr TA22 ... 164 A6
Dyehouse Cross TA22 ... 163 F5
Dyehouse La
　Dulverton TA22 ... 164 A5
　Glastonbury BA6 ... 206 C5
Dyer's La TA2 ... 213 E7
Dyers Cl Bristol BS13 ... 22 D4
　Curry Rivel TA10 ... 171 D4
　West Buckland TA21 ... 180 F7
Dyers Gn TA6 ... 153 F3
Dyers Rd TA10 ... 171 D4
Dyers' Close La BA11 ... 119 E5
Dyke Hill Terr TA20 ... 198 D8
Dyke's Way BA9 ... 216 B3
Dymboro Ave BA3 ... 77 F1
Dymboro Cl BA3 ... 77 F1
Dymboro Gdns BA3 ... 77 F1
Dymboro The BA3 ... 77 F1
Dyrham Cl TA8 ... 104 C7
Dyson Cl DT9 ... 34 B8

E

Eagle Cl Ilchester BA22 ... 173 E2
　Weston-Super-Mare BS22 ... 49 D8
Eagle Gdns BA22 ... 173 E2
Eagle La 1 BA11 ... 119 F4
Eagle Pk BA1 ... 28 F5
Eagle Rd BA1 ... 28 F5
Eagles The BS49 ... 34 B8
Eames Orch TA19 ... 221 C2
Earl St BS1 ... 227 A4
Earle St BA20 ... 219 C5
Earlesfield BS48 ... 8 C1
Earls Cl BS23 ... 49 A7
Earls Cl DT9 ... 225 F5
East Anstey Prim Sch
　EX16 ... 162 E5
East Approach Rd TA7 ... 136 D4
East La TA4 ... 104 C4
East Brent CE Fst Sch
　TA9 ... 86 C4
East Bridgwater Com Sch
　TA6 ... 209 C5
East Cl BA2 ... 44 A5
East Clevedon Triangle
　BS21 ... 6 F3
East Coker Com Prim Sch
　BA22 ... 197 C2
East Coker Rd BA20 ... 218 F2
East Coker Sawmills
　BA22 ... 197 C7
East Compton Rd
　Pilton BA4 ... 204 E1
　Shepton Mallet BA4 ... 205 B1
East Coombe La TA4 ... 165 D8
East Ct BS3 ... 11 F3
East Dr TA9 ... 86 B2
East Dundry La BS41 ... 22 A1
East Dundry Rd BS13,
　BS14 ... 22 F2
East End BS26 ... 88 D7
East End La BA3 ... 94 E4
East Gate 10 TA1 ... 213 A4
East Harptree Prim Sch
　BS40 ... 74 F4
East Huntspill Prim Sch
　TA9 ... 136 E8
East La TA18 ... 196 B7
East Lambrook Manor Gdns*
　TA13 ... 220 C7
East Lambrook St TA13 ... 220 D7
East Lanes BA21 ... 187 D6
East Lea Rd BA1 ... 44 A8
East Mead BA3 ... 78 B2
East Mead La
　Street BA16 ... 207 F5
　Walton BA16 ... 156 E6
East Mere Cross EX16 ... 178 B2
East Mill Ct DT9 ... 225 E4
East Mill La DT9 ... 225 E4
East Par BS9 ... 5 C6
East Quay TA6 ... 209 A6
East Quay Mews TA6 ... 209 A6
East Rd TA6 ... 207 E6
East Ride TA9 ... 86 B1
East Ridge Dr BS13 ... 21 F5
East Somerset Rly*
　BA4 ... 205 B3
East Somerset Way
　BA5 ... 203 D3
East St Banwell BS29 ... 51 C3
　Bourton SP8 ... 161 F1
　Bristol BS2 ... 227 C4
　Cannington TA5 ... 135 C2
　Chard TA20 ... 223 D4

East St continued
　Crewkerne TA18 ... 224 C6
　Drayton TA10 ... 171 E3
　East Coker BA22 ... 197 B8
　Ilminster TA19 ... 221 C4
　Martock TA12 ... 185 E6
　Milborne Port DT9 ... 217 D2
　North Perrott TA18 ... 196 C4
　Norton Sub Hamdon TA14 ... 185 F1
　Shepton Montague BA9 ... 160 B2
　Taunton TA1 ... 212 F3
　Templecombe BA8 ... 176 F1
East Stoke
　Stoke sub Hamdon TA14 ... 185 F4
　Stoke Sub Hamdon TA14 ... 186 A4
East Street Dro TA12 ... 185 E6
East Street La BA6 ... 140 A1
East Tapps La EX16 ... 163 B2
East Town La TA4 ... 150 E3
East Water La BA5 ... 92 F2
East Way BA2 ... 44 A5
East Wood Pl BS20 ... 2 E4
East Woodlands Rd
　BA11 ... 144 A7
Eastbourne Ct 12 TA1 ... 213 A4
Eastbourne Gate TA1 ... 213 A4
Eastbourne Terr 11 TA1 ... 213 A4
Eastbourne Terr 11 TA1 ... 213 A4
Eastbrook Terr TA3 ... 168 D1
Eastbury Hill TA24 ... 131 B5
Eastbury Rd TA24 ... 131 B5
Eastcombe Gdns BS23 ... 30 F1
Eastcombe La BA4 ... 142 E2
Eastcombe Rd BS23 ... 30 F1
Eastcote Pk BS14 ... 23 B5
Eastcourt Rd BS39 ... 76 F8
Eastcroft BS40 ... 54 E2
Eastcroft BS40 ... 54 E2
Eastdown Rd BA3 ... 78 D5
Easter La EX35 ... 122 B4
Eastdown Hall
　Dinnington TA17 ... 195 B8
　Seavington TA19 ... 184 E1
Eastern Ave TA6 ... 209 D4
Eastern Ho BS23 ... 30 E1
Eastern La TA24 ... 67 D1
Eastfield Bruton BA10 ... 215 F7
　10 Martock TA12 ... 185 E6
　Shepton Mallet BA4 ... 205 B6
Eastfield Ave BA1 ... 27 B2
Eastfield Cl 10 TA12 ... 185 E6
Eastfield Gdns BS23 ... 30 F1
Eastfield La
　Barrington TA19 ... 184 D5
　East Chinnock BA22 ... 196 D8
　Hambridge TA3 ... 184 B8
　Lydford-on-Fosse TA11 ... 158 D3
　North Perrott TA18 ... 196 C4
　Norton Sub Hamdon TA14 ... 185 F1
Eastfield Pk BS23 ... 30 F1
Eastfield Rd Hutton BS24 ... 49 E2
　Wincanton BA9 ... 216 D4
Eastgate Gdns 9 TA1 ... 213 A4
Easthams Rd TA18 ... 224 D6
Eastlay La TA20 ... 199 A4
Eastlea BA11 ... 120 B8
Eastland La TA4 ... 159 D5
Eastland Rd BA21 ... 219 C5
Eastlea BS21 ... 6 B1
Eastleigh Cl
　Burnham-On-Sea TA8 ... 104 C8
　Frome BA11 ... 120 A7
Eastleigh Rd TA1 ... 213 B3
Eastlyn Rd BS13 ... 22 B8
Eastmead Cir BS9 ... 5 E4
Eastmead La
　Banwell BS29 ... 51 C3
　Bristol BS9 ... 5 E4
Eastmoor La TA4 ... 164 E8
Eastmoor Rd BS14 ... 23 A3
Easton Cl BA3 ... 76 E1
Easton Ho 9 BA1 ... 28 C1
Easton La Pylle BA4 ... 141 C1
　Sampford Peverell EX16 ... 178 D1
Easton Rd BS20 ... 4 C4
Easton Town La BA4 ... 158 F4
Easton Trow La BA4 ... 159 B5
Eastop La DT10 ... 190 A3
Eastover Bridgwater TA6 ... 209 A5
　Langport TA10 ... 172 A6
Eastover Cl TA10 ... 172 A6
Eastover Com Prim Sch
　TA6 ... 209 B5
Eastover Gr BA2 ... 44 C1
Eastside Terr BS39 ... 59 D1
Eastside La BA1 ... 28 B1
Eastville BS6 ... 219 C5
Eastway BS48 ... 8 E3
Eastway Cl BS48 ... 8 D2
Eastway Sq BS48 ... 8 E3
Eastwick Ave TA2 ... 212 F7
Eastwick Rd TA2 ... 213 B7
Eastwood BA2 ... 45 E6
Eastwood Cl
　Bridgwater TA6 ... 209 C4
　Frome BA11 ... 119 C4
　High Littleton BS39 ... 59 C1
Eastwoods BA1 ... 29 B3
Eaton Cl BS14 ... 23 D5
Eaton Cres Bristol BS8 ... 226 A3
　Taunton TA2 ... 213 A6
Ebben La TA20 ... 194 F1
Ebbor Gorge Nature
　Reserve* BA5 ... 111 D6

Ebber La BA5 ... 111 B5
Ebden Lo 10 BS22 ... 32 A2
Ebdon Rd TA14 ... 31 F4
Ebenezer La BS9 ... 5 E5
Eckweek Gdns BA2 ... 79 D8
Eckweek La BA2 ... 79 D8
Eckweek Rd BA2 ... 79 D8
Ecos Ct BA11 ... 119 D4
Edbrook La TA5 ... 134 F3
Edbrooke Rd TA24 ... 147 C5
Eden Park Cl BA1 ... 29 A4
Eden Park Dr BA1 ... 29 A4
Edford Hill BA3 ... 116 C6
Edgar Bldgs BA1 ... 228 B3
Edgarley Ct BS21 ... 6 C5
Edgarley Field La BA6 ... 157 E8
Edgarley Rd
　Glastonbury BA6 ... 139 D1
　West Pennard BA6 ... 139 F1
Edgcot Rd TA24 ... 128 C1
Edgebury TA7 ... 136 E4
Edgecombe Ave BS22 ... 31 D2
Edgefield Cl BS14 ... 22 F3
Edgefield Rd BS14 ... 22 F3
Edgehill Rd BS21 ... 6 C5
Edgemoor Rd TA24 ... 201 B4
Edgewood Cl BS14 ... 23 B8
Edgeworth Rd BA2 ... 44 C2
Edinburgh Pl 11 BS23 ... 48 E8
Edinburgh Rd
　Bridgwater TA6 ... 208 E2
　Keynsham BS31 ... 24 E4
Edington & Shapwick Sch
　Burtle TA7 ... 137 D6
　Shapwick TA7 ... 137 F1
Edington Rd BA7 ... 137 D4
Edington Right Dro TA7 ... 155 B7
Edingworth Rd BS24 ... 86 F7
Edithmead La TA9 ... 105 A6
Edmond's Hill TA11 ... 173 D4
Edmund Hill La BA6 ... 206 F6
Edmunds Way BS27 ... 90 C7
Edward Cl BA22 ... 218 B6
Edward Ct BS31 ... 24 F4
Edward Rd BS21 ... 6 E5
Edward Rd S BS21 ... 6 E5
Edward Rd W BS21 ... 6 E6
Edward St Bath BA1 ... 44 C7
　Bath BA2 ... 45 B7
　Bridgwater TA6 ... 209 B5
　Weston Short St BS30 ... 25 E8
Egerton Rd BA2 ... 44 E4
Egford Hill BA11 ... 119 C5
Egford La BA11 ... 119 C5
Egg Moor La EX13 ... 198 A7
Eggwood La TA13,TA16 ... 195 E8
Egremont Rd BA8 ... 89 F7
Eglinton Rd BA16 ... 207 B4
Egrove Way TA4 ... 202 E4
Eight Acre Dro TA7,TA9 ... 137 A5
Eight Acre La
　Wellington TA21 ... 222 E5
　Wootton Courtenay TA24 ... 129 F8
Eighteen Arce La BA21 ... 218 C6
Eighth Ave BS14 ... 23 C7
Eileen Cl BA16 ... 207 E5
Eirene Terr BS20 ... 4 D4
Elberton Rd BS9 ... 5 C7
Elborough Ave BS49 ... 34 B8
Elborough Gdns BS24 ... 50 C3
Elbridge Ho 3 BS2 ... 227 C3
Elder Cl Chard TA20 ... 223 C5
　Highbridge TA9 ... 104 D5
Elder Ho TA1 ... 65 E2
Elderberry Wlk BS22 ... 31 F1
Eldergrove Cl TA6 ... 209 D7
Elderwood Rd BS14 ... 23 B7
Eldon Pl BA1 ... 28 B2
Eldred Cl BS9 ... 5 D5
Eleanor Cl BA2 ... 44 A5
Eleanor Cotts BA2 ... 44 A6
Electric Ho TA14 ... 185 E4
Eleven Ct TA6 ... 208 E4
Elfrida Terr BA5 ... 203 A5
Elgar Cl Bristol BS4 ... 22 D6
　Clevedon BS21 ... 6 F1
Eliot Cl BS23 ... 49 A3
Eliots Dr BA21 ... 218 E7
Elizabeth Cl BS24 ... 49 D3
Elizabeth Ct
　Burnham-On-Sea TA8 ... 104 B6
　4 Martock TA12 ... 185 E6
Elizabeth Flats BA21 ... 219 C6
Elizabeth Gdns 10 BA8 ... 190 A6
Elizabeth Ho BS20 ... 4 C4
Elizabeth Way
　Bridgwater TA6 ... 209 C5
　Chard TA20 ... 223 C5
Elizabeth St TA21 ... 222 D5
Elldridge Cl BS9 ... 5 E7
Ellen Cl 8 TA6 ... 153 F4
Ellen Ho BA2 ... 44 A5
Ellenborough Cres BS23 ... 48 E6
Ellenborough Ct BS23 ... 48 E6
Ellenborough Ho BS8 ... 226 A2
Ellenborough Park Rd
　Weston-Super-Mare BS23 ... 48 E6
Ellenborough Pk N BS23 ... 48 E6
Ellenborough Pk S BS23 ... 48 E6
Ellersdown La TA22 ... 163 E4
Ellesmere Rd Bristol BS4 ... 23 D8
　Weston-Super-Mare BS23 ... 48 F2
Ellfield Cl BS13 ... 21 F6
Ellick Rd BS40 ... 54 D1
Ellicombe La TA24 ... 201 C4
Ellicombe Mdw TA24 ... 201 C4
Elliot Cl TA11 ... 119 F6
Elliots La BA11 ... 119 B8
Elliott's Hill BA22 ... 196 D7
Enmore BS24 ... 49 A2

Ellis Ave BS13 ... 22 A8
Ellis Gr TA2 ... 168 B5
Ellis Pk BS22 ... 32 C4
Ellis's La TA5 ... 152 C6
Elliscombe Pk BA9 ... 176 B6
Elliston Dr BA2 ... 44 B4
Ellm Ave TA8 ... 104 B6
Ellsbridge Cl BS31 ... 25 B5
Ellsbridge Ho Norton
　Radstock Coll BS31 ... 25 B5
Elm Cl Banwell BS29 ... 50 E4
　Broadway TA19 ... 183 C2
　Nailsea BS48 ... 8 C1
　Star BS25 ... 52 D1
　Wells BA5 ... 203 A4
　Yatton BS49 ... 34 B7
Elm Ct
　Bristol, Hengrove BS14 ... 23 A6
　Keynsham BS31 ... 24 C4
　Radstock BA3 ... 79 B2
Elm Farm BS48 ... 9 A2
Elm Gr Bath BA2 ... 44 C4
　Locking BS24 ... 49 F4
　Minehead TA24 ... 201 A5
　Swainswick BA1 ... 28 C2
　Taunton TA1 ... 212 E5
Elm Hayes BS13 ... 21 F6
Elm La Great Elm BA11 ... 119 A6
　Wincanton BA9 ... 216 B7
　Woolavington TA7 ... 136 F4
Elm Lea Cl TA7 ... 136 C4
Elm Leigh BA11 ... 120 C6
Elm Lodge Rd BS48 ... 9 B2
Elm Pk TA1 ... 212 E5
Elm Rd BS39 ... 77 E5
Elm St TA20 ... 223 C5
Elm Terr BA3 ... 97 C8
Elm Tree Ave BA3 ... 78 D1
Elm Tree Pk BS20 ... 3 C3
Elm Tree Rd Clevedon BS21 ... 6 D2
　Locking BS24 ... 50 A4
Elm View
　Midsomer Norton BA3 ... 78 B1
　Temple Cloud BS39 ... 58 E1
Elm Way BA4 ... 205 A6
Elm Wlk Portishead BS20 ... 2 C4
　Yatton BS49 ... 34 B7
Elmdale Rd BS8 ... 226 B3
Elmgrove Cl TA6 ... 209 D7
Elmham Way BS24 ... 32 B1
Elmhurst Ave BA21 ... 219 B7
Elmhurst Est BA1 ... 28 F6
Elmhurst Gdns BS41 ... 20 F8
Elmhurst Jun Sch BA16 ... 207 D6
Elmhurst La BA16 ... 207 D6
Elmhurst Rd BS24 ... 49 E2
Elmhurst Rd BA21 ... 219 B8
Elmlea Ave BS9 ... 5 F5
Elmlea Jun & Inf Schs BS9 ... 5 F5
Elmleigh BA21 ... 218 C7
Elmleigh Rd 10 TA12 ... 185 E6
Elms Cl TA1 ... 212 E5
Elms Est TA2 ... 213 F8
Elms La TA24 ... 147 A8
Elms Rd TA21 ... 222 F5
Elms The BS29 ... 51 A4
Elmside Cl BA16 ... 207 D5
Elmside Ho TA6 ... 208 F2
Elmside Rd TA6 ... 208 E2
Elmsleigh Rd BS23 ... 48 E4
Elmsley La BS22 ... 31 C5
Elmswood BS23 ... 48 H8
Elmtree Dr BS13 ... 21 F5
Elmvale Dr BS24 ... 49 F3
Elmwood Ave TA6 ... 208 F3
Elmwood Sch TA6 ... 208 F3
Elsbert Dr BS13 ... 21 E6
Elscombe La
　Timberscombe TA24 ... 130 A4
　Wootton Courtenay TA24 ... 129 F4
Elton Ho 2 BS2 ... 227 C3
Elton Rd Bristol BS8 ... 226 C3
　Clevedon BS21 ... 6 C4
　Weston-Super-Mare BS22 ... 32 A4
Elton St BS2 ... 227 C4
Elvard Cl BS13 ... 22 A4
Elvard Rd BS13 ... 22 A4
Elwell La BS40,BS41 ... 21 A1
Elworthy Cross TA4 ... 150 C5
Elworthy Dr TA21 ... 222 D4
Elworthy La TA4 ... 150 C5
Ely Gr BS9 ... 5 B7
Embankment The TA10 ... 172 A5
Embercourt Dr BS48 ... 19 A6
Emery Gate BS29 ... 51 B3
Emlet DT9 ... 187 E1
Emley La BS40 ... 54 B6
Emley Cl 8 BS22 ... 32 D4
Emmanuel Ct BS8 ... 226 A4
Emmett Wood BS14 ... 23 B3
Empire & Commonwealth
　Mus The* BS1 ... 227 C1
Empress Menen Gdns
　BA1 ... 44 A8
Enderleigh Gdns BS25 ... 52 F4
Enfield Dr BA4 ... 141 E2
Enfield Rd BA4 ... 141 E2
England La BA22 ... 174 F3
Englands Mead BA22 ... 174 F3
Englands Rd TA24 ... 124 A3
Englands Way TA20 ... 223 D6
Englishcombe La BA2 ... 44 C3
Englishcombe Rd BS13 ... 22 C3
Englishcombe Tithe Barn*
　BA2 ... 44 A2
Englishcombe Way BA2 ... 44 E3
Enmore BS24 ... 49 A2

Enmore CE Prim Sch
　TA5 ... 152 E8
Enmore Cl TA8 ... 104 C8
Enmore Rd
　Bridgwater TA5 ... 153 B6
　Taunton TA2 ... 212 F7
Ennerdale Cl TA1 ... 212 C1
Enterprise Ctr The BS24 ... 49 A3
Enterprise Mews BA20 ... 218 D3
Entry Hill BA2 ... 44 F2
Entry Hill Dr BA2 ... 44 F3
Entry Hill Gdns BA2 ... 44 F3
Entry Hill Pk BA2 ... 44 F2
Entry Rise BA2 ... 44 F1
Erin Wlk BS4 ... 22 D8
Erion La BA5 ... 110 F4
Ermine St BA21 ... 218 D7
Ermine Way BS11 ... 4 C7
Ernest Ashman Pl TA20 ... 223 D5
Ervine Terr BS2 ... 227 C4
Escott Cl TA6 ... 208 F6
Escott La TA4 ... 132 D1
Esgar Rise BS22 ... 31 E3
Eskdale Cl BS22 ... 49 D8
Esmond Gr BS21 ... 6 D4
Esmonde Dr BA22 ... 173 E2
Esplanade
　Burnham-On-Sea TA8 ... 104 A7
　Minehead TA24 ... 201 A7
Esplanade La TA23 ... 202 C7
Esplanade Rd BS20 ... 2 C2
Essex Cl TA20 ... 223 C4
Essex Ct TA1 ... 212 C2
Essex Dr TA1 ... 212 C2
Estuary Pk TA5 ... 135 B5
Estune Wlk BS41 ... 11 A2
Esworthy Cross EX16 ... 162 F1
Ethel St BA5 ... 203 C3
Ethpark Gr 1 TA2 ... 212 F6
Eton La BS29 ... 50 E7
Eton Rd TA8 ... 104 B6
Etonhurst BS23 ... 48 D6
Etsome Ct TA11 ... 211 C4
Etsome Hill TA11 ... 211 C7
Etsome Rd TA11 ... 211 C5
Etsome Terr TA11 ... 211 C4
Ettlingen Way BS21 ... 6 F2
Eugene Flats 7 BS2 ... 227 A4
Eugene St Bristol BS2 ... 227 A4
　Bristol BS2, BS5 ... 227 C4
Evelyn Rd BA1 ... 44 B8
Evelyn Terr 21 BA1 ... 28 A1
Evening Post Rdbt The
　BS2 ... 227 C3
Evenlode Gdns BS11 ... 4 F5
Evenlode Way BS31 ... 25 A3
Evercreech Rd BS14 ... 23 B4
Evercreech Way TA9 ... 104 F2
Everett Cl BA5 ... 112 E1
Evergreen Cl BS25 ... 51 F1
Everton Rd BA20 ... 219 A4
Evesham Ave BA21 ... 218 C6
Evesham Dr TA9 ... 209 A1
Ewart Rd BS22 ... 49 C8
Ewell Cl TA19 ... 183 C1
Exbourne 10 BS22 ... 32 A2
Exbury Cl TA8 ... 104 C7
Excelsior St BA2 ... 45 B5
Excelsior Terr BA3 ... 78 B1
Exchange Ave 11 BS1 ... 227 A2
Exbridge Ind Est TA22 ... 163 F3
Exeter Cl
　Burnham-On-Sea TA8 ... 104 C7
　Nether Stowey TA5 ... 134 B2
Exeter Rd Portishead BS20 ... 2 E4
　Rockwell Green TA21 ... 222 B5
　Weston-Super-Mare BS23 ... 48 E2
Exford Cl BS23 ... 48 F1
Exford Fst sch TA24 ... 128 D1
Exford Rd TA24 ... 147 C6
Exmoor Falconry & Animal
　Farm* TA24 ... 124 B4
Exmoor Gdns TA22 ... 163 D6
Exmoor Rd BA2 ... 44 F2
Exmoor Way TA24 ... 200 E6
Exmouth Rd BS4 ... 22 F8
Exton BS24 ... 49 A2
Exton Cl BS14 ... 23 B5
Exton La TA22 ... 147 E4
Eyer's La BS2 ... 227 C3

F

Faber Gr BS13 ... 22 C4
Factory Hill SP8 ... 161 F2
Factory La
　East Huntspill TA9 ... 136 B8
　Tatworth TA20 ... 198 D8
Failand Cres BS9 ... 5 C5
Failand La Easton-in-G BS20 ... 4 A1
　Portbury BS20 ... 3 F2
Failand Wlk BS9 ... 5 C6
Fair Cl BA2 ... 81 E4
Fair Cross TA23 ... 131 F2
Fair Furlong BS13 ... 22 B4
Fair Furlong Prim Sch
　BS13 ... 22 B4
Fair Hill BS25 ... 70 F8
Fair Pl TA11 ... 158 D3
Fair View BA10 ... 161 A7
Fairacre Cl BS24 ... 50 B4
Fairacres BS31 ... 24 D5
Fairclose TA20 ... 193 D6
Fairdean Rd TA9 ... 104 E4
Fairfax Cl TA6 ... 209 C6
Fairfax Rd TA6 ... 209 C6
Fairfax St BS1 ... 227 B3

Fairfield Coleford BA3 ....116 E8
Crewkerne TA18 ....224 B5
Ilminster TA19 ....221 A4
7 Martock TA12 ....185 E6
Rode BA11 ....82 F1
Sampford Peverell EX16 .178 D1
Sherborne DT9 ....225 D5
Somerton TA11 ....211 E4
Fairfield Ave BA1 ....28 A2
Marshfield SN14 ....9 B7
Fairfield CI Backwell BS48 .19 D7
Frome BA11 ....120 A7
Marshfield SN14 ....9 B7
Weston-Super-Mare BS22 .31 B1
Fairfield Dr TA4 ....202 E3
Fairfield Gdns BA6 ....206 D4
Fairfield Gn TA3 ....192 A7
Fairfield Mdws BA14 .....83 F3
Fairfield Mead BS48 .....19 D7
Fairfield Mortessori Sch
BA6 ....206 D4
Fairfield Park Rd BA1 ....28 A2
Fairfield Pneu Sch BS48 .19 C6
Fairfield Rd Bath BA1 ....28 B1
Taunton TA2 ....213 B7
Fairfield Terr Bath BA1 ...28 A1
Freshford TA18 ....166 F5
Peasedown St John BA2 ..79 C7
Fairfield View BA1 ....28 A2
Fairfield Way BS48 ......19 C6
Fairford CI TA9 ....104 E4
Fairford Rd Bristol BS11 ..4 D7
Highbridge TA9 ....104 E4
Fairhouse Rd BA22 ......197 F8
Fairlands Mid Sch BS27 ..90 C7
Fairlands Way BS27 ......90 C7
Fairmead Rd BA21 ....219 C8
Fairmead Sch BA21 ......219 C8
Fairmont Terr DT9 ....225 E4
Fairseat Workshops
BS40 ....56 E7
Fairview Mells BA11 ......118 B7
Weston-Super-Mare BS22 .31 F4
Fairview Ho BS9 ....5 F8
Fairview Terr
Taunton TA3 ....168 D1
Yeovilton BA22 ....187 A8
Fairwater CI TA2 ....212 D6
Fairway BS4 ....23 D8
Fairway CI Berrow TA8 ....84 F4
Weston-Super-Mare BS22 .31 B2
Fairway Rise TA20 ....223 E5
Fairway View BA21 ....221 B4
Fairways Saltford BS31 ...25 E2
Wells BA5 ....203 C4
Fairways The TA1 ....212 F1
Fairwood Rd BA13 ....102 F5
Fairy Hill BS39 ....41 D6
Falcon CI
Bristol, Westbury on Trym
BS9 ....5 F8
Portishead BS20 ....2 D4
Falcon Cres BS22 ....49 D8
Falcon Ct BA1 ....212 C4
Falcondale Rd BS9 ....5 F7
Falconer Rd BA1 ....27 A3
Falconsmead Wlk BA21 .219 D8
Falkland Ho TA18 ....224 C6
Falkland Sq TA18 ....224 C6
Fallands Rise TA24 ......200 D7
Fallowfield Blagdon BS40 .54 E2
Weston-Super-Mare BS22 ..31 F3
Falmouth CI BS48 ....9 A1
Falmouth Ho BS14 ......23 A7
Faraday Rd **2** BS8 ......11 F5
Farleigh Coll BA2 ....82 D6
Farleigh Hungerford Castle*
BA2 ....
Farleigh Rd Backwell BS48 .19 C6
Clevedon BS21 ....6 B1
Keynsham BS31 ....24 D4
Norton St Philip BA2 ....81 F5
Farleigh Rise BA15 ......29 E1
Farleigh Wlk BS13 ......64 F3
Farleigh Wlk BS13 ......22 A8
Farler's End BS48 ....18 F8
Farley CI BA11 ....120 C6
Farley Dell BA3 ....116 E8
Farm CI TA11 ....211 B3
Farm Ct TA13 ....220 D5
Farm Dr TA11 ....211 B3
Farm Hill TA7 ....156 B8
Farm La
Buckland St Mary TA20 ...182 A2
Coultings TA5 ....134 E4
Stogursey TA5 ....134 D4
Street BA16 ....207 C7
Wellow BA2 ....62 E1
Farm Orch DT9 ....188 C7
Farm Rd
Bradford Abbas DT9 .....187 E1
Doulting BA4 ....141 E5
Hutton BS24 ....49 E2
Street BA16 ....207 C6
Weston-Super-Mare BS22 .31 F4
Farm St BA22 ....186 C6
Farm View TA2 ....168 F6
Farmborough Prim Sch
BA2 ....59 F6
Farmer Rd BS13 ....21 F4
Farmhouse Ct **1** BS48 ..8 E2
Farmhouse Ct **1** BS48 ..8 E1
Farmhouse Dr BA11 .....119 F7
Farmwell CI BS13 ....22 B5
Farnaby CI BS4 ....22 C7
Farningham Rd BS20 ....54 D8
Farncombe La BA9 ....160 B1
Farndale Rd BS22 ......49 D8
Farr St BS11 ....4 B8

Farr's La BS1 ....227 A2
Farr's Orch **6** TA16 ....195 F7
Farrant CI
Baltonsborough BA6 .....158 A5
Bristol BS4 ....22 D6
Taunton TA1 ....212 A4
Farrant Rd BA11 ....119 D5
Farriers Gn TA2 ....213 F7
Farringdon Hill La TA5 ..134 D6
Farrington Fields BS39 ..77 C3
Farrington Gurney CE Prim
Sch BS39 ....77 A4
Farrington La BA4 ......141 F6
Farrington Rd BS39 .....77 C5
Farrington Way BS39 ....77 A3
Farrow CI TA20 ....223 D3
Farrs La BA2 ....45 B2
Farthing Combe BS26 ...70 D2
Farthing Down TA21 ....179 E7
Farthing La EX13 ....193 D1
Farthing Rd TA6 ....208 E1
Farthing Row BA11 .....82 E1
Farthing's Pitts TA21 ...222 C4
Farthings CI TA21 ......167 C2
Faulkland View BA2 .....79 F7
Faulkland La BA2,BA3 ...80 C4
Faulkland Rd BA2 ......44 D5
Faversham Dr BS24 ....49 A1
Fawcus PI TA20 ....223 C4
Fawn Rd BA3 ....206 C3
Fayre Way BA5 ....204 B7
Fearnville Est BA21 .....6 C2
Featherbed La
Chew Stoke BS40 ....38 A3
Clayhanger EX16 ....165 C1
Clutton BS39 ....58 C6
Feddon Village BS21 ....1 F5
Felber Rd BA22 ....227 C1
Felcey Way BS27 ......90 C7
Feltham Dr BA11 ....120 A3
Feltham La BA11 ....148 B8
Felton Gr BS13 ....22 A8
Felton La BS40 ....37 E7
Felton St BS40 ....37 C7
Felton CI TA5 ....135 B5
Fenton **13** BS22 ......32 A2
Fennel La BS26 ....70 B2
Fennel Way BA22 ......218 A5
Fenners BS22 ....32 B4
Fennington La TA2 .....168 B8
Fenshurst Gdns BS41 ...20 F8
Fenswood CI BS41 .....10 F1
Fenswood Mead BS41 ..10 E1
Fenswood Rd BS41 .....10 E1
Fental La BA3 ....116 C1
Fenton CI BS31 ....25 D3
Ferenberge CI BA2 .....60 A6
Fermoy BA11 ....120 B6
Fern CI BA3 ....78 B1
Fern Gr BS48 ....18 C8
Fern Lea BS24 ....67 B6
Fern Lodge BS23 ......48 D6
Ferndale Dr TA1 ....168 D1
Ferndale Gdns BA21 ...218 E6
Ferndale Rd Bath BA1 ..28 C3
Portishead BS20 ....2 C5
Ferndown CI Bristol BS11 .5 A7
Taunton TA1 ....212 D1
Ferne Animal Sanctuary*
TA20 ....193 A2
Ferne Gdns BS20 ....4 B4
Fernlea Rd BS22 ....49 C7
Fernleigh Ave TA6 .....209 A3
Fernside BS48 ....19 A7
Fernsteed Rd BS13 .....21 F6
Ferry CI BA22 ....41 B6
Ferry La Bath BA2 ......45 B6
Lympsham BS24 ....67 C3
Ferry St BS1 ....227 B2
Ferryman Rd BA6 ......206 E7
Ferryman's Ct BS2 .....227 B2
Festival Units TA6 .....209 B1
Feversham Ave TA6 ....208 E6
Feversham La BA6 .....206 D5
Feversham Way TA2 ...213 A8
Fiddle La BA22 ....174 F1
Field CI BA3 ....116 A3
Field Dr BA22 ....169 C7
Field End Axminster EX13 .198 A1
Minehead TA24 ....201 A5
Field Gate TA13 ....183 C8
Field La
Chewton Mendip BA3 ...94 FB
Kington Magna SP8 .....177 E1
Penselwood BA9 ....161 D2
Field Rd TA10 ....156 A1
Field Vw BA5 ....140 F5
Fielders The BS27 .....32 B4
Fieldgardens Rd BS39 ..58 F1
Fieldgate La TA3 ....183 B8
Fielding Ct BA21 ......219 C6
Fielding Ho BA2 ....44 A6
Fielding Path BA6 .....206 C6
Fielding Rd Street BA16 .207 B7
Yeovil BA21 ....219 C6
Fielding's Rd BA2 .....44 C6
Fields End BA11 ....143 B2
Fieldway BS25 ....52 B4
Fifehead Bsns Ctr (Manor
Farm Trad Est) BA8 ....190 F8
Fifehead Hill BA8 .....190 F8
Filby Rd TA9 ....136 A8
Filer CI TA47 ....79 D8
Fillymead DT10 ....190 F5
Filwood Broadway BS4 ..22 E8

Finch CI
Shepton Mallet BA4 .....204 F6
Weston-Super-Mare BS22 .49 E8
Finches Way TA8 ....85 B1
Finger Cnr DT10 ....190 F5
Finger La DT9 ....225 D3
Finmere Gdns BS22 ....32 A4
Fir La BS40 ....72 B5
Fir Leaze BS48 ....8 E1
Fir Tor Ave BA5 ....203 C5
Fir Tree Ave BS24 .....49 E4
Fir Tree CI TA6 ....209 D4
Fircliff Pk BS20 ....2 D7
Firgrove La BA2 ....61 B1
Firs Ct BS31 ....24 C4
Firs The Bath BA2 ......45 B1
Langport TA10 ....172 A5
Limpley Stoke BA3 .....64 A5
Wheddon Cross TA24 ...129 E1
First Ave Axminster EX13 .198 A1
Bath BA2 ....44 E4
Bristol, Hengrove BS14 ..23 A7
Portbury BS20 ....3 E5
Radstock BA3 ....97 C8
First Dro TA7 ....155 D3
First Sedgemoor Dro
TA10 ....155 E4
Firtree Ave BS39 ......77 F4
Firtree CI TA5 ....134 A2
Firway Cross EX16 ....164 C3
Firwood Rd BA11 ......119 E4
Fisher's Hill
Glastonbury BA6 ....206 D4
Holywell Lake TA21 ....179 D7
Fisher's La
Dinnington TA17 ....195 A7
Mark TA9 ....106 D5
Fishers Brook BA11 ....120 A5
Fishers CI DT9 ....187 F5
Fishers Mead TA22 ....163 D6
Fisherway La TA19 ....195 A5
Fishpond Bottom Rd
DT6 ....199 A1
Fishwell La BA6 ....157 D4
Fitzharding Rd BS20 ....4 E3
Fivash CI TA1 ....168 D2
Five Acres **3** BA22 ....197 E8
Five Arches CI BA3 .....78 D2
Five Ashes BA22 ....186 C2
Five Barrows Cross
TA24 ....145 B7
Five Bells BA23 ....202 B5
Five Cross Way
East Anstey TA22 ......162 F7
West Buckland TA21 ....180 F6
Five Cross Ways TA22 ..163 A7
Five Hos TA21 ....222 B8
Five Lords TA5 ....134 B2
Five Yards **3** TA4 .....167 F8
Fiveways CI BS27 .....90 A7
Fiveways Rdbt BA21 ...219 A6
Fiveways Specl Sch
BA21 ....219 D6
Flagstaff Rd BS26 .....68 D7
Flamingo Cres BS22 ...49 E8
Flat The BS39 ....58 D5
Flatwoods Cres BA2 ...45 F3
Flatwoods Rd BA2 .....45 F3
Flax Bourton Prim Sch
BS48 ....19 F8
Flax Bourton Rd BS8 ...10 B3
Flax La DT9 ....188 A2
Flax Way BA21 ....218 C6
Flaxfield Dr TA18 .....224 C5
Flaxpool Hill TA4 ......151 C6
Fleet Air Arm Mus*
BA22 ....174 B3
Fletcher CI TA2 ....213 B8
Fletcher's La BS26 ....87 D6
Fleur De Lys Dr BA14 ...83 F4
Flingers La BA9 ....216 D4
Flint Cross TA14 ......149 C1
Flints CI BA11 ....119 D4
Florence Brown Specl Sch
BS4 ....22 D8
Florence Gr BS22 .....49 B8
Florence Rd **2** TA2 ...212 F6
Florida Fields BA7 ....216 B6
Florida St BA7 ....214 C5
Florida Terr BA3 ......78 C2
Flowerdale Rd TA23 ...202 C6
Flowerdown Bridge
BS22 ....49 D7
Flowerdown Rd BS24 ..50 D4
Flowers Hill BS4 ......23 E8
Flowers Ho **1** BA20 ...219 B4
Flowerwell Rd BS13 ....22 B5
Flushing Mdw BA21 ...219 E5
Foghamshire La BA11 ..143 D6
Foldhill CI BA22 ....185 E6
Foldhill La Ash BA22 ..186 A6
Martock TA12 ....185 F6
Folke La DT9 ....189 B1
Folleigh CI BS41 ......11 B2
Folleigh Dr BS41 ......11 B2
Folleigh La BS41 ......11 B2
Folliot Rd BA6 ....206 E6
Folly CI Cannington TA5 .135 B2
Midsomer Norton BA3 ..96 E7
Folly Dr BA4 ....159 C7
Folly Dro TA19 ....183 A5
Folly Farm Nature Reserve*
BS39 ....58 B5
Folly Fields BA21 .....219 B7
Folly La
Buckland St Mary TA20 .182 A1
Kington Magna SP8 ....177 F2

Folly La continued
Nether Compton DT9 ...187 F4
North Wootton BA4 .....140 C4
Shipham BS25 ....70 E7
South Cadbury BA22 ...175 D4
Weston-Super-Mare BS23 .48 E1
Folly Rd TA12 ....185 B7
Folly The Cold Ashton SN14 .12 F6
Ditcheat BA4 ....159 C7
Paulton BS39 ....77 F6
Saltford BS31 ....25 F2
Fons George TA1 ......212 F2
Fons George CI TA1 ...212 E2
Fons George Rd TA1 ...212 F2
Font La BA22 ....197 B7
Font Villas BA22 ......197 B8
Fonthill Rd BA1 ....27 E2
Fontmell Ct BS14 .....23 D7
Football La BA9 ....216 B4
Footlands CI TA1 ......212 B1
Forbes Fraser Hospl BA1 .44 B8
Forche's La TA24 .....131 D3
Forches Cnr EX15 .....181 A4
Ford La
Chewton Mendip BA3 ...94 D8
Dulcote BA5 ....140 F3
Stawell TA7 ....137 A1
Yarley BA5 ....139 B8
Ford Rd Bampton EX16 .164 C1
Peasedown St John BA2 .79 D8
Wellow BA2 ....62 F1
Wiveliscombe TA4 .....210 C4
Ford St TA21 ....222 F4
Forde Abbey* TA20 ....198 F8
Forde Pk BA21 ....218 C7
Fordhay BA22 ....196 E7
Fordhay Terr BA22 ....196 E7
Fordmill Cross EX16 ...164 D1
Fore Leaze Dro TA2 ...184 E7
Fore St **9** Bampton EX16 .164 B1
Bridgwater TA6 ....208 F5
Castle Cary BA7 ......214 C5
Chard TA20 ....223 C4
Dulverton TA22 ....163 D4
Holcombe Rogus TA21 .178 F5
Milverton TA4 ....167 A4
North Petherton TA6 ...153 E3
NonRoady TA7 ....155 C2
Tatworth TA20 ....198 D6
Taunton TA1 ....212 F4
Thorncombe TA20 .....199 B6
Wellington TA21 ......222 D6
West Camel BA22 .....174 D3
Westonzoyland TA7 ....154 F5
Williton TA4 ....202 D3
Wincanton BA9 ....216 C4
Windham TA20 ....194 E1
Forefield PI BA2 ......228 C1
Forefield Rise BA2 ....45 B4
Forehills Rd BS20 .....2 C4
Forelands BS23 ....30 B6
Forest Dr BS23 ....31 A1
Forest Dro TA3 ....182 F5
Forest Hill BA20 ......219 A4
Forest La TA20 ....193 E8
Forest Mill La TA19 ...183 B1
Forest Rd Frome BA11 .120 B7
Horningsham BA11,BA12 .144 B4
Forest Wlk BA13 ......121 C4
Forester Ave BA2 .....45 B8
Forester Ct BA2 ......228 C4
Forester La BA2 ......45 B8
Forester Rd BA2 ......45 B8
Portishead BS20 ....2 D4
Forge Cnr
Somerton TA11 ....211 C3
Stogursey TA5 ....134 B6
Forge End BS20 ....3 E3
Forge La
East Chinnock BA22 ....196 E8
Zeals SP8,BA12 ....161 F2
Forgotten World Mus*
BS26 ....68 D4
Fortescue Rd BA3 .....78 F2
Fortfield Rd BS14 .....23 B5
Forth CI BA16 ....207 A4
Forton La Chard TA20 ..223 F1
Tatworth TA20 ....194 A1
Forton Rd TA20 ....223 D2
Forts Orch BA22 ......186 E6
Forum Bldgs BS1 ......227 B1
Forward's La TA3 .....181 C5
Fosgrove La TA3 ......181 E7
Fosse Barton BS48 ....8 D2
Fosse CI Nailsea BS48 ..8 C2
Yeovil BA21 ....218 D7
Fosse Gdns BA2 ......62 D8
Fosse Gn BA3 ....78 E4
Fosse La Batheaston BA1 .29 A4
Clandown BA3 ....78 E4
Nailsea BS48 ....8 D2
Radstock BA3 ....78 D3
Shepton Mallet BA4 ...205 D4
Wedmore BS28 ....107 C3
Fosse La Trad Est BA4 .205 D5
Fosse Rd BA3 ....78 D3
Fosse The BA22 ....175 C4
Fosse Way Nailsea BS48 .8 C2
Yeovil BA21 ....218 D7
Fosse Way Cotts BA3 ..78 D2
Fosse Way Ct TA2 ....173 E2
Fosse Way Est BA2 ....44 D1
Fosse Way Sch BA3 ...79 B2
Fossedale Ave BS14 ..23 C6
Fossefield Rd BA3 .....97 B6
Fosseway Clevedon BS21 .6 C2
Midsomer Norton BA3 ..97 A5
Radstock BA3 ....97 C8

Fai – Fri 243

Fosseway continued
Radstock, Clandown BA3 .78 E4
Fosseway Ct BS8 ......226 A2
Fosseway Gdns BA3 ...78 D1
Fosseway Inf Sch BA2 ..44 C1
Fosseway S BA3 ....226 A3
Fosseway The BS8 ....226 A3
Foster CI BA5 ....112 E1
Foster Rd BA11 ....120 A3
Foster's La BA22 ......175 A7
Fothergills TA19 ......225 E4
Foundry Cotts BA2 ....60 B4
Foundry Mews **2** TA8 .224 C5
Foundry Rd TA1 ......212 F4
Foundry Sq **1** TA18 ..224 C5
Fountain La BS20 .....70 B7
Four Acre Mead **1** TA4 .167 F8
Four Acres CI Bristol BS13 .21 F4
Nailsea BS48 ....18 E8
Four Acres Prim Sch
BS13 ....21 E4
Four Elms TA21 ....179 A6
Four Forks La TA5 .....152 F7
Four Lanes TA20 .....193 F6
Four Oaks Inf Sch BS48 ..8 E2
Four Pools TA11 ......213 B1
Fourth Ave
Bristol, Hengrove BS14 ..23 B7
Radstock BA3 ....97 D8
Fourways CI BA2 ......214 D6
Fourts Cross TA19 ....184 F2
Fowey CI BS48 ....9 A8
Fowey Rd BS22 ....32 A4
Fowler St TA2 ....212 E6
Fownes Rd TA24 ......201 B5
Fox & Hounds La BS31 .24 F5
Fox CI TA21 ....222 A6
Fox Hill BA2 ....45 A2
Fox Mdws TA18 ......164 A8
Fox Rd BA16 ....207 A5
Fox Way TA5 ....134 B2
Fox's Dro BA11 ....102 C1
Foxbury CI BA11 ......119 F6
Foxcombe Rd Bath BA1 .44 B7
Bristol BS14 ....23 B4
Foxcote BA20 ....218 C7
Foxcote Gdns BA11 ...120 C7
Foxdon Hill TA20 .....223 A7
Foxdown Ho TA21 ....222 C4
Foxdown Ho TA21 ....222 C4
Foxdown Terr TA21 ...222 D4
Foxglove CI BS22 .....32 A5
Foxglove Way
Chard TA20 ....223 F5
Houndstone BA22 ....218 A5
Foxhanger La TA22 ...148 A2
Foxhill Ho BA2 ....45 A1
Foxhole La BA3 ....169 C5
Foxholes La BA2,BA11 .100 D5
Foxwell La BS24 ......196 C7
Foye Ho BS8 ....11 A6
Frampton Rd TA6 .....208 F2
Francis CI TA3 ....169 D5
Francis Fox Rd BS23 ..48 E7
Francis Ho BS2 ....227 A4
Francis Reed CI TA7 ..154 F5
Francolin CI TA1 ......168 E1
Francombe Ho BS1 ...227 A1
Frank Webber Rd TA21 .222 A5
Frankcom Ho BA2 .....45 B7
Frankland CI BA1 ......27 B1
Frankley Bldgs BA1 ...28 B1
Frankley Terr **2** BA1 ..28 B1
Franklin CI TA2 ....212 B7
Franklin Ct BS1 ....227 B1
Franklin's Way BS49 ..17 F1
Fraser CI
Burnham-On-Sea TA8 ..104 C7
Weston-Super-Mare BS22 .31 F4
Frederick Ave TA2 ....79 C7
Frederick Ct BA5 .....203 C4
Frederick PI BS8 .....226 B3
Frederick PI BS8 .....226 B3
Frederick Rd TA6 .....209 C6
Frederick PI BA3 .....219 B4
Free Hill BA5 ....110 E6
Free St BA22 ....173 E1
Free Tank BS2 ....227 C2
Freedom Ave BA21 ...219 E6
Freedom PI BS8 ......11 F6
Freelands BS21 ....16 C8
Freeling Ho BS1 ......227 B1
Freemans La BS48 ....20 B2
Freemantle Ho BS2 ...227 A4
Freeview Rd BA2 ......44 A5
Freezinghill La BS30 ..12 B4
Fremantle Rd TA1 ....213 B1
French CI Nailsea BS48 ..8 F3
Peasedown St John BA2 .79 D7
French Weir Ave TA1 ..212 E5
French Weir CI TA1 ...212 E5
Frenchay Rd BS22 ....48 E4
Frenchfield Rd BA2 ...79 D7
Freshford CE Prim Sch
BA3 ....64 B5
Freshford La BA3 .....64 A5
Freshford Sta BA3 ....64 C5
Freshmoor **6** BS21 ...6 E3
Frethey Rd TA1,TA4 ..168 B3
Friar Ave BS22 ....31 F4
Friar Ave TA24 ....208 F4
Friars CI TA24 ....208 F4
Friars Lawn TA6 ......208 F4
Friars Ave BA21 ......218 D6

Friars Cl BA22 ....173 D1
Friars Way TA8 ....104 B6
Friary BS1 ....227 C1
Friary Cl Clevedon BS21 ....6 C5
 Westwood BA15 ....64 E4
 Witham Friary BA11 ....143 C3
Friary Rd BS20 ....2 B5
Friday St TA24 ....200 F7
Friendly Row BS20 ....4 C5
Friendship Gr BS48 ....7 E2
Friendship Rd BS48 ....8 F3
Friggle St
 Corsley Heath BA11 .....144 C8
 Frome BA11 ....120 D1
Frithfield La BA4 ....205 C6
Frobisher Ave BS20 ....2 B5
Frobisher Cl
 Burnham-On-Sea TA8 ....104 D8
 Portishead BS20 ....2 A5
 Weston-Super-Mare BS22 .31 E4
Frobisher Way TA2 ....212 B6
Frog La Bristol BS1 ....226 C2
 Combe St Nicholas TA20 .193 D6
 Creech St Michael TA3 ..169 F6
 Dinnington TA17 ....195 B8
 Enmore TA5 ....153 A6
 Felton BS40 ....37 C8
 Galhampton BA22 ....175 E8
 Hasebury Plucknett TA18 196 C6
 Holcombe Rogus TA21 ...178 F5
 Ilminster TA19 ....221 C4
 Kingsdon TA11 ....173 D5
 Langport TA10 ....171 F5
 North Curry TA3 ....170 D5
 Shepton Mallet BA4 ....205 E4
 Stoke St Michael BA3 ...116 A4
 Ubley BS40 ....55 D1
 Wanstrow BA4 ....142 F4
 West Camel BA22 ....174 D3
 Winford BS40 ....37 F5
Frog St Bampton EX16 ...164 B1
 East Quantoxhead TA5 ..133 B6
 Lopen TA13 ....185 A1
Froglands La BS27 ....90 C7
Froglands Way BS27 ......90 C7
Frogmore St BS1 ....226 C2
Frogwell Cross TA4 ......164 D6
Frome Com Coll BA11 ...120 A7
Frome Mus* BA11 ....119 F5
Frome Old Rd BA3 ....79 A2
Frome Rd Bath BA2 ....44 D1
 Beckington BA11 ....101 D3
 Bruton BA10 ....215 F7
 Maiden Bradley BA12 ...144 B3
 Norton St Philip BA2 ....81 F3
 Nunney BA11 ....143 B8
 Radstock BA3 ....79 B2
 Rode BA11 ....101 F7
 Southwick BA14 ....83 F3
 Wingfield BA14 ....83 C7
Frome St BS2 ....227 C4
Frome Sta BA11 ....120 A4
Frome View BA12 ....144 C2
Fromefield BA11 ....120 A6
Front St Axbridge BS26 ..88 D1
 Chedzoy TA7 ....154 D8
 Churchill BS25 ....52 E4
 Monksilver TA4 ....150 B8
Frost Hill BS49 ....34 D7
Frost La TA19 ....183 F4
Fry's La BS40 ....53 F3
Fry's Well BA3 ....96 D3
Frys La TA7 ....154 E8
Fryth Ho BS48 ....9 B3
Fryth Way BS48 ....8 C2
Fulford Cl TA24 ....200 F7
Fulford Rd BS13 ....22 C5
Fulford Specl Sch BS13 ..22 C4
Fulford Wlk BS13 ....22 B5
Fullands Ave TA1 ....168 F1
Fullands Ct TA1 ....168 F1
Fullands Rd TA1 ....213 B1
Fullens Cl BS22 ....49 D7
Fuller Cl BA4 ....205 D5
Fuller Rd BA1 ....28 C2
Fullers La BS25 ....70 A6
Fullers Way BA2 ....62 D8
Fullwell Cl BA3 ....80 D1
Fulmar Rd BS22 ....31 F1
Fulwell La BA3 ....80 D1
Fulwood Cl TA1 ....212 D1
Furge Gr BA8 ....190 A6
Furge La BA8 ....190 A6
Furland Rd
 Crewkerne TA18 ....224 C5
 Weston-Super-Mare BS22 .31 C2
Furland Way TA18 ....224 C5
Furlong Cl BA3 ....96 F7
Furlong Cotts EX16 ......179 A4
Furlong Gn TA3 ....168 D1
Furlong La
 Curry Rivel TA10 ....171 C3
 Milborne Port DT9 ......217 B3
Furlongs Ave TA6 ....208 E2
Furlongs The DT9 ....225 D5
Furnham Cl TA20 ....223 D6
Furnham La TA20 ....223 C6
Furnham Rd TA20 ....223 D5
Furnleaze BS39 ....58 E3
Furpits La TA10 ....172 B6
Furringdons Cross TA18 .195 F6
Furze Cl Bridgwater TA6 .208 D4
 Weston-Super-Mare BS22 ..31 B2
Furze Rd BS22 ....31 A3
Furze The BA20 ....218 C2

Furzeclose La BA4 ....142 C7
Furzehill TA20 ....223 D5
Furzehill La TA24 ....147 C6
Furzeland Rd TA24 ......124 A4
Fylton Croft BS14 ....23 B3

G

Gables Cl BS29 ....51 B3
Gables The TA21 ....222 C6
Gabriel Cl BA11 ....120 C6
Gadd's La BS27 ....90 B8
Gagley La BA5 ....139 C5
Gainesmarsh La TA10 ...172 C5
Gainsborough Dr
 Gainsborough Ct BA1 ...27 B1
Gainsborough Dr
 Sherborne DT9 ....225 B3
 Weston-Super-Mare BS22 .31 F3
Gainsborough Gdns BA1 .44 C8
Gainsborough Hill DT9 ..225 E2
Gainsborough Rd BS31 ..24 F5
Gainsborough Way
 BA21 ....219 E8
Gale's Dro BA14 ....30 E3
Galhampton Hill BA7,
 BA22 ....214 C2
Galingale Way BS20 ......2 F5
Galleries The BS1 ....227 B3
Galley Batch BA3 ....114 F4
Galley Batch La BA3 ....114 F4
Galloping Bottom La
 TA23 ....149 E5
Galmington Cl TA1 ......212 C3
Galmington Dr TA1 .....212 C2
Galmington La TA1 .....212 C2
Galmington Rd TA1 .....212 C2
Gambyn Cross TA4 .....164 F4
Gammins Cotts TA24 ...129 E2
Gander Cl BS13 ....22 B5
Gardeanne Cross TA4 ...150 D2
Gange's Hill TA3 ....170 F2
Ganges Cl TA3 ....170 F2
Gannet Rd BS22 ....31 F1
Gants Mill La BA10 ......215 D5
Gaol La BA4 ....205 D6
Garamond Ct BS1 ....227 B1
Garden City TA10 ....172 A6
Garden Cl Bristol BS9 ....5 C5
 Norton Fitzwarren TA2 ..168 B4
 Weston-Super-Mare BS22 .31 E2
Garden Ct BS8 ....226 A4
Garden Ground BA4 ....205 C4
Garden Hurst CI TA8 ...104 B8
Garden Plot Hill TA3 ...183 E7
Garden Terr TA21 ....222 B7
Garden Way TA24 ......200 E6
Garden Wlk TA6 ....208 E2
Gardeners Cl BS27 ....90 B8
Gardeners Wlk BS41 ....11 B1
Gardenhurst TA8 ....85 B1
Gardens Rd BS21 ....6 C4
Gardens The
 Dulverton TA22 ....163 D7
 East Pennard BA4 ......158 F8
 Sherborne DT9 ....225 C3
 1 Wellington TA21 ....222 D5
Gardners Orch BS28 ...108 C4
Gardner Ave BS13 ....21 F7
Gardner Rd BS20 ....2 D6
Gardners CI TA4 ....167 F1
Garfield Terr BA1 ....28 B2
Garland Ho 8 BS21 ....6 C2
Garlandhayes La EX15 .180 E2
Garner Ct 4 BS22 ....32 B4
Garonor Way BS20 ....3 F5
Garre Ho BA2 ....43 F5
Garrett Rd BA20 ....218 D3
Garrick Rd BA2 ....43 F5
Garsdale BA11 ....120 A4
Garsdale Rd BS22 ....49 D8
Garston Cotts BS40 ......54 E3
Garston La Blagdon BS40 .54 E3
 Frome BA11 ....120 A4
 Marston Magna BA22 ..174 F1
Garston Rd BA11 ....120 A4
Garston St BA4 ....205 C6
Garstone La TA16 ......195 F8
Garstons Bathford BA1 ..29 B2
 8 Clevedon BS21 ....6 B1
 Wrington BS40 ....35 E1
Garstons CI BS40 ....35 C2
Garstons Orch BS40 ....35 C1
Garstons The BS20 ....2 D4
Garth Rd BS13 ....22 A8
Gartons Mead BA4 .....141 E1
Gartons Mead Rd BA4 ..141 E1
Garvins Rd BA6 ....206 C4
Gas La TA7 ....155 B8
Gasferry Rd BS1 ....226 B1
Gashay La EX13 ....199 B3
Gason La BA22 ....174 A2
Gasper St BA12 ....161 E3
Gaston Ave BS31 ....24 F6
Gaston La BA16 ....207 C4
Gaston's La TA12 ......185 D5
Gastons The BS11 ....4 D8
Gaswell La TA7 ....155 E8
Gatchell Gn TA3 ....168 D1
Gatchell Mdw TA3 .....168 D1
Gatchell's La TA3 ....181 B5
Gatcombe La TA14 ......132 F2
Gatcombe Rd BS13 ......22 B5
Gate Cl EX13 ....198 E3
Gate La BA5 ....203 D2

Gatehouse Ave BS13 .....22 A5
Gatehouse Cl BS13 ....22 A5
Gatehouse Ct BS13 ......22 B5
Gatehouse Sh Ctr BS13 ..22 A5
Gatehouse Way BS13 ....22 A5
Gaulden Manor* TA4 ...150 F2
Gaunt's La BA1 ....226 C2
Gaunton Cl TA1 ....212 D2
Gaunts Cl BS20 ....1 F4
Gaunts Rd TA6 ....135 E6
Gay Cl TA21 ....222 D6
Gay Ct BA1 ....28 E3
Gay Elms Prim Sch BS13 .22 A4
Gay Elms Rd BS13 ....22 A4
Gay St Bath BA1 ....228 B3
 Mells BA11 ....118 B7
 Wellington TA21 ....222 D6
Gay's Hill BA1 ....228 C4
Gaylard's La TA20 ......194 D4
Gazelle Rd
 Weston-Super-Mare BS24 ..49 B3
 Yeovil BA20 ....218 D3
Gefle Cl BS1 ....226 B1
Geldof Dr BA3 ....78 A2
Gelosia Cl TA7 ....154 F6
General Higgins Ho
 TA9 ....104 E3
General Hospl BS23 .....48 E2
Gennes Gr BA9 ....216 C4
Gentle St Frome BA11 ..119 F4
 Horningsham BA12 ....144 E4
Geoffrey Cl BS13 ....21 E6
George & Crown Cotts
 TA17 ....195 C2
George Cl BS48 ....19 D7
George La
 Marshfield SN14 ....13 E8
 South Petherton TA13 ..220 C4
George Sh Ctr The
 TA18 ....224 C6
George St Bath BA1 ....228 B3
 Bath BA2 ....45 B6
 Bridgwater TA6 ....208 F5
 Burnham-On-Sea TA8 ..104 A7
 Charlton Adam TA11 ...173 F7
 Glastonbury BA6 ......206 D5
 Portishead BS20 ....2 C2
 Sherborne DT9 ....225 D4
 Taunton TA2 ....212 F6
 Wellington TA21 ......222 D6
 Weston-Super-Mare BS23 .48 E7
George Sweetman Cl
 BA9 ....216 D4
George Whitefield Ct 5
 BS1 ....227 B3
George William Ct TA6 .208 F4
George's Pl BA2 ....45 B6
George's Rd BA1 ....28 A1
Georges Bldgs BA1 ......28 C2
Georges Ground BA11 .119 E2
Georges Mews TA1 .....213 C2
Georgian Ct BA11 ......119 D3
Georgian Ho BA2 ....228 C2
Georgian House (Mus)
 BS1 ....226 C2
Georgian View BA2 ......44 C2
Gerard Rd BS23 ....48 F8
Gerbestone La TA21 ....180 E6
Gerrard Bldgs BA2 ......45 B7
Gerrard Cl BS4 ....22 D7
Geys Hill BA12 ....144 D8
Giant's Grave TA20 ....193 A7
Giant's Grave Rd TA20 .193 A7
Gibbet La BS14 ....23 D1
Gibbet Rd BA9 ....75 B3
Gibbon Rd TA18 ....196 B6
Gilbert Scott Ho BA5 ...113 A1
Gilbert Scott Mews BA5 .113 A2
Gilbert Scott Rd BA5 ...113 A1
Gilberts Cnr BA6 ......138 D6
Gilberyn Dr BS22 ....32 A3
Gilda Cl BS14 ....23 C5
Gilda Cres BS14 ....23 B5
Gilda Par BS14 ....23 C5
Gilda Sq W BS14 ....23 B5
Giles Cl BA10 ....171 D4
Gill Cres TA1 ....212 B1
Gill Mews BS22 ....32 B4
Gillards La TA1 ....212 B4
Gillards Cl TA21 ....222 B4
Gillards Mead TA3 ....192 A7
Gillebank Cl BS14 ....23 D5
Gillingham La TA9 .....104 E3
Gillingham Terr 3 BA1 ..28 B1
Gillmore Cl BS22 ....31 B1
Gillmore Rd BS22 ....31 B1
Gills La BS26 ....87 B5
Gillson Cl BS24 ....49 D2
Gimblet Rd BS22 ....32 B4
Gipsy Cross TA4 ....166 A2
Gipsy Dro TA9 ....136 C4
Gipsy La Burcott BA5 ..139 E8
 Frome BA11 ....119 C6
 Glastonbury BA6 ......139 D1
 Halse TA4 ....167 B6
 Samford Arundel TA21 .179 F5
 Staplegrove TA2 ....212 D7
 Street BA16 ....207 E4

Gipsy La continued
 Taunton TA1 ....212 C3
 Wells BA5 ....203 A4
Gladstone Ct BA2 ....45 C2
Gladstone Rd Bath BA2 ..45 C2
 Bristol, Hengrove BS14 ..23 B6
Gladstone St
 Midsomer Norton BA3 ..78 B3
 Taunton TA2 ....212 E6
Gladstone Terr
 Minehead TA24 ....201 A5
 Wellington TA21 ......222 D6
Gladstone Villas BA3 ...115 C5
Glanfield Cl TA4 ....167 E8
Glanfield Terr BA22 ....173 F1
Glanvill Ave TA20 ......223 C5
Glanvill Rd BA16 ....207 C3
Glanville Dr BS39 ....75 E6
Glanville Rd BS28 .....108 C4
Glass House Hill DT9 ...225 E3
Glass's Cross TA4 ......149 E1
Glass's Rocks La TA4 ..149 D1
Glasses Mead TA1 .....212 B2
Glaston Ho BA16 ....207 D7
Glaston Rd BA16 ....207 D7
Glastonbury Abbey*
 Glastonbury Ct BS48 ....9 B1
 Glastonbury Ct BA21 ..218 D6
Glastonbury Rd
 Meare BA6 ....138 E1
 Wells BA5 ....203 B2
Glastonbury Tor* BA6 .139 D1
Glastonbury Way BS22 ..32 A2
Glebe Ave BS20 ....2 E4
Glebe Cl BA11 ....11 C2
Glebe Cotts TA3 ....169 E2
Glebe Ct BA11 ....11 C2
Glebe Ho BA18 ....45 B5
 Weston-Super-Mare BS22 .31 F3
Glebe Inf Sch BS49 ......34 C4
Glebe Paddock BA5 ....139 E8
Glebe Rd Bath BA2 ....6 C2
 Clevedon BS21 ....6 C2
 Long Ashton BS41 ......11 C2
 Portishead BS20 ....2 E4
 Weston-Super-Mare BS23 .48 E4
Glebe The Fivehead TA3 .170 F1
 Freshford BA3 ....64 B4
 Hinton Charterhouse BA2 .63 D2
 Queen Camel BA22 ....174 F3
 Timbercombe TA24 ....130 B4
 Timsbury BA2 ....60 B3
 Wrington BS40 ....35 D2
Glebe Way BS27 ....90 C6
Glebe Wlk BS31 ....24 C4
Glebe Yd TA10 ....172 E4
Glebeland Cl TA7 ......156 B8
Glebelands
 7 Merriott TA16 ....195 F7
 Minehead TA24 ....200 E8
 Norton Sub Hamdon TA14 .185 F3
 Nunney BA11 ....143 B7
 Radstock BA3 ....78 D1
Glebelands Cl BS27 ......90 B6
Glen Ave BS8 ....10 F8
Glen Brook BS9 ....5 D4
Glen Cl TA2 ....168 B5
Glen Dr Bristol BS9 ......5 D5
 Taunton TA2 ....168 A5
Glen The Salford BS31 ...25 F1
 Weston-Super-Mare BS22 ..31 B2
Glenavon Pk BS9 ....5 C4
Glencairn Ct BA2 ....45 B6
Glencoe Bsns Pk BS23 ..49 A7
Glencoe Terr TA3 ......168 D1
Glencot La BA5 ....203 A7
Glencot Rd BA5 ....203 A6
Glendale 8 BS8 ....11 F6
Glendevon Rd BS14 .....23 A3
Gleneagles BS48 ....9 A1
Gleneagles Cl Nailsea BS48 .9 A1
 Weston-Super-Mare BS22 .31 B2
Glenmore Rd TA24 .....201 A7
Glenthorne Ave BA21 ..219 B7
Glenthorne Rd BA21 ...219 B7
Glentworth Rd BS8 ....226 B2
Glenview Ho BA2 ....79 D8
Glenville Rd BA21 ......219 D6
Glenwood Dro TA7 ....155 C2
Glenwood Gdns TA2 ...212 F8
Glenwood Mans BS23 ..30 D1
Glenwood Rise BS20 ....1 D1
Globe Orch TA18 ......196 C6
Gloucester Ho 11 BS2 ..227 C3
Gloucester Rd Bath BA1 .28 A2
 Taunton TA1 ....168 F1
Gloucester Rd Bath BA1 .28 C3
Gloucester St Bath BA1 ..28 C3
 Bridgwater TA6 ....208 F2
 Burnham-On-Sea TA8 ..104 C7
 Upper Swainswick BA1 ..28 A7
Gloucester Row 8 BS8 ..11 F7
Gloucester St Bath BA1 ..28 C3
 5 Bristol BS2 ....227 B4
 8 Bristol, Clifton BS8 ...11 F7
 Taunton TA1 ....213 A4
 Weston-Super-Mare BS23 .48 D7
Glovers Cl
 Milborne Port DT9 ....217 D2
 4 Stoke sub Hamdon
  TA14 ....185 F4
Glovers Field TA14 ....185 E4
Glovers Walk 4 TA6 ...208 F5
Glynsmead TA20 ....198 C8
Glynswood TA20 ......223 C4
Goathill La BA8 ....176 C3
Goathill Rd DT9 ....189 B4
Goddard Dr BS22 ....32 B4
Godhams La TA4 ....165 A7
Godminster Ct BA10 ..215 E6

Godminster La BA10 ...215 E3
Godney Dro BA5 ....139 B6
Godney Rd BA5,BA6 ....139 A4
Godwin Dr BS48 ....8 C3
Goes La BA7 ....158 F2
Gogs Orch BS28 ....108 C3
Gold Corner Dro TA9 ..136 A2
Gold Hill Batcombe BA4 .142 D2
 Shepton Mallet BA4 ...205 B7
Gold St DT10 ....190 B4
Goldcroft BA21 ....219 B6
Golden Hill
 Stourton Caundle DT10 .189 F1
 Wiveliscombe TA4 ....210 C5
Golden Valley La BS30 ..25 F8
Golden Valley Prim Sch
 BA3 ....58 F2
Goldenhaye La TA20 ...194 D3
Goldfinches La BA6 ....139 D3
Golding Cl BA5 ....203 C4
Golding's La DT9 ....217 C1
Golding Ave BS8 ....58 E2
Goldney Cl BS39 ....58 E1
Goldney Rd BS8 ....226 A2
Goldney Way BS39 ......58 F1
Goldsmiths La EX14 ...198 A4
Goldsmoor Gate EX16 .178 E3
Golf Club La BS31 ....25 C2
Golf Course Rd BA2 ....45 D6
Golf Links La BA3 ......114 E3
Golf Links Rd TA8 ....85 A2
Gooch Cl Bridgwater TA6 .209 B4
 Frome BA11 ....120 D6
Good Hill BA4 ....142 E2
Good's La TA5 ....152 C5
Goodeaves Cl BA3 .....117 A7
Goodeaves Cotts BA3 ..117 A7
Goodeve Pk BS9 ....5 D3
Goodeve Rd BS9 ....5 D3
Goodlands La TA1 .....212 F4
Goodmoor Ave BA5 ...203 B5
Goodymoor La BA5 ....203 B5
Gooid Cl BA2 ....43 A8
Goosander Cl TA24 ....201 C4
Goosard La BS39 ....77 E8
Goose La
 Chilton Polden TA7 ....137 B3
 Horton TA19 ....183 C2
Goose St BA11 ....101 E5
Gooseacre La BA22 ....197 B8
Gooseacre La
 East Coker BA22 ....197 B8
 Yeovil BA22 ....218 A1
Gooseham La BS28 ....108 F4
Gooselade BA16 ....207 C3
Gooseland Cl BS14 .....22 F3
Gooseland La BS22 .....32 C2
Goose La BS22 ....32 C2
Gordano Gdns BS20 ....4 B4
Gordano Rd BS20 ....3 D7
Gordano Sec Sch BS20 ..2 D2
Gordano Way BS20 ......3 F5
Gordon Bldgs BA3 ......79 A3
Gordon Rd Bath BA2 ...45 B6
Gordano Sec Sch BS20 ..2 D2
Gordon Terr BA3 ....209 A5
Gordon's Cl TA1 ....213 B1
Gore La
 Chapmanslade BA13 ...121 B4
 Pitney TA10 ....172 C7
Gore Rd TA8 ....85 A1
Gore Sq TA4 ....167 E8
Gorefield TA13 ....220 D2
Gorehedge 8 BA11 ....119 F4
Gores Pk BS39 ....59 B2
Gorlangton Cl BS14 ....23 A7
Gorlegg TA21 ....179 E5
Gorpit La TA5 ....134 F8
Gorse La Bristol BS8 ...226 B2
 Cold Ashton BS30,SN14 .12 C7
Gort Rd TA2 ....168 B6
Goslet Rd BS14 ....23 E5
Goss Barton BS48 ....8 D1
Goss Cl BS48 ....8 C1
Goss La BS48 ....8 D1
Goss View BS48 ....8 C1
Goswell Cl BA16 ....207 C5
Goswell Rd BA16 ......207 C5
Goswell Sq WI TA11 ..173 F7
Goswell Way TA11 .....173 F7
Gough PI BS27 ....90 C8
Gough's Cave* BS27 ...90 D8
Gould Cl BA11 ....120 B7
Gould's Ground 2 BA11 .119 E5
Gouldsbrook Terr TA18 .224 B6
Goulston Rd BS13 ....22 A5
Goulston Wlk BS13 ......22 A5
Gournay Ct BS39 ....77 A3
Govenors Ho BA2 ....44 D6
Govier's La TA23 ......202 C7
Grace Cl BS49 ....34 B8
Grace Dr BA3 ....79 A3
Grace Martin's La BA22 .174 F3
Grace Rd BS22 ....32 C3
Gradwell Cl BS22 ......32 B3
Grafton Cl TA2 ....213 A8
Graham Way TA4 ......167 E6
Grainger Ct BS11 ....4 E7
Graitney Cl BS49 ....35 A8
Granary Orch DT9 .....217 C2
Granary Way TA3 ....181 D8

Gra – Han 245

Granby Hill BS8 . . . . .11 F6
Granby Rd BA22 . . . . .174 A2
Grand Par BA2 . . . . .228 C2
Grand Pier* BS23 . . . . .48 D7
Grand Western Canal (Country Pk)* EX16 . . . .178 F2
Grange (Millfield Sch) The TA11 . . . . .211 F3
Grange Ave
Highbridge TA9 . . . . .104 E3
Street BA16 . . . . .207 B6
Grange Cl
Cannington TA5 . . . . .135 C2
Wellington TA21 . . . . .222 E5
Weston-Super-Mare BS23 . . .48 E1
Grange Cnr DT8 . . . . .199 E7
Grange Dr
Bridgwater TA6 . . . . .208 D4
Taunton TA2 . . . . .213 A6
Grange End BA3 . . . . .97 B7
Grange Gdns TA2 . . . . . . .213 A7
Grange Paddock TA9 . . . .106 E4
Grange Rd Bristol BS8 . . . .226 A3
Bristol, Bishopsworth BS13 . .22 A5
Frome BA11 . . . . .120 A7
Saltford BS31 . . . . .25 C3
Street BA16 . . . . .207 D7
Taunton TA2 . . . . .213 A6
West Huntspill TA9 . . . . . .136 A8
Weston-Super-Mare BS23 . . .48 E1
Grange The Bristol BS9 . . . . .5 D7
Chilton Polden TA7 . . . . . .137 B2
Flax Bourton BS48 . . . . .19 F7
Kingston St Mary TA2 . . . . .168 E8
Grange Way TA6 . . . . .135 F5
Grange Wlk TA2 . . . . .213 A6
Grangefields BA16 . . . . . .207 D5
Grant's Hill EX16,TA22 . . .163 F2
Grant's La
Wedmore BS28 . . . . .108 D4
Wiveliscombe TA4 . . . . . . .210 D6
Grants Cl BA9 . . . . .216 B4
Grants La BA9 . . . . .216 D4
Granville Chapel 5 BS8 . . .11 F5
Granville Rd BA1 . . . . .27 E4
Granville Way DT9 . . . . . .225 E6
Grasmere TA6 . . . . .208 C5
Grasmere Dr BS23 . . . . .48 F4
Grass Meers Dr BS14 . . . . .23 A4
Grass Rd TA8 . . . . .65 F4
Grass Royal BA21 . . . . . . .219 C6
Grass Royal Jun Sch BA21 . . . . .219 C6
Grassmere Rd BS49 . . . . . .34 B8
Gratton La EX35 . . . . .122 A4
Gravel Hill BS40 . . . . .56 B7
Gravel La TA3,TA19 . . . . .183 F6
Gravel Pits DT9 . . . . .225 D3
Gravel Wlk BA1 . . . . .228 B3
Gravelands La TA3 . . . . . .169 D3
Gravenchon Way BA16 . .207 A6
Graves Cl 6 TA6 . . . . .209 B4
Gray Hollow BS40 . . . . .74 F4
Gray's Hill EX15 . . . . .180 D1
Gray's La EX15 . . . . .180 D1
Grayling Ho BS9 . . . . .5 F7
Grays Ave TA7 . . . . .154 E6
Grays Hill BA2 . . . . .80 B5
Grays Rd TA1 . . . . .213 B4
Grays Terr TA1 . . . . .213 B4
Great Ann St BS2 . . . . . . .227 C3
Great Barton BA4 . . . . . . .205 D6
Great Bedford St BA1 . . .228 B4
Great Brockeridge BS9 . . . . .5 F6
Great Cl EX15 . . . . .179 E1
Great Cnr BA21 . . . . .218 C6
Great Field La TA14 . . . . .185 F4
Great Gdns BA4 . . . . .205 C6
Great George St
Bristol BS1 . . . . .226 C2
Bristol BS2 . . . . .227 C3
Great Hayles Rd BS14 . . . .23 A6
Great Hill BA9 . . . . .161 D2
Great House Ct BA6 . . . .138 D4
Great House St TA24 . . . .130 B5
Great La Knole TA10 . . . . . .173 A4
Shepton Beauchamp TA19 .184 E4
Great Mdw TA22 . . . . .163 D6
Great Mead TA1 . . . . .212 B3
Great Orch BA22 . . . . . . .173 E2
Great Ostry BA4 . . . . .205 B6
Great Pit La BA22,DT9 . . .188 B7
Great Pulteney St BA2 . . .228 C3
Great Ringaton La EX36 .162 B6
Great St TA14 . . . . .185 E2
Great Stanhope St BA1 . .228 A2
Great Western Rd
Chard TA20 . . . . .223 D5
Clevedon BS21 . . . . .6 D2
Martock TA12 . . . . .185 E7
Great Western Terr BA21 . . . . .219 D5
Great Withy Dro BA5 . . . .206 C8
Greatstone La BS40 . . . . . .37 F5
Greatwood Cl TA6 . . . . . .209 A2
Grebe Cl TA6 . . . . .209 B4
Grebe Ct TA6 . . . . .209 B4
Grebe Rd Bridgwater TA6 .209 B4
Taunton TA2 . . . . .213 B6
Green Cl Holford TA5 . . . . .133 D4
Paulton BS39 . . . . .77 E6
Sparkford BA22 . . . . .175 A4
Green Cotts BA2 . . . . .45 C2
Green Ditch La BA3 . . . . . .96 B6
Green Dragon Ct 4 TA6 . . . . .208 F4
Green Dro TA11 . . . . .158 A4
Green Farm Ind Est BA13 . . . . .121 C4
Green Gate EX16 . . . . . . .178 C2
Green Knap La TA20 . . . .193 C2
Green La Blagdon BS40 . . . .55 A7
Brompton Regis TA22 . . . . . .148 B1
Castle Cary BA7 . . . . .214 F4
Chard TA20 . . . . .193 F1
Chard Junction TA20 . . . . . .198 D7
Chardstock EX13 . . . . .198 B7
Charlton Horethorne DT9 . .175 F2
Charlton Horethorne DT9 . .176 A2
Corfe TA3 . . . . .181 E7
Corsley Heath BA12 . . . . . .144 E7
Cricket St Thomas TA20 . . . .194 F3
East Chinnock BA22 . . . . . .186 B1
East Chinnock BA22 . . . . . .196 E8
East Coker BA22 . . . . .197 B8
Failand BS8 . . . . .10 C4
Farrington Gurney BS39 . . . .76 F6
Felton BS40 . . . . .37 C3
Fivehead TA3 . . . . .170 E2
Freshford BA3 . . . . .64 B2
Frome BA11 . . . . .119 D4
Hinton Charterhouse BA2 . . .63 E1
Kington Magna SP8 . . . . . .177 E2
Leigh upon Mendip BA3, BA11 . . . . .117 B2
Marshfield SN14 . . . . .13 E8
Oakhill BA3 . . . . .114 E4
Pitcombe BA7 . . . . .215 A1
Priddy BS40 . . . . .73 B7
Queen Camel BA22 . . . . . . .174 F3
Sampford Arundel TA21 . . .179 F4
Shepton Beauchamp TA19 .184 E3
Sherborne DT9 . . . . .188 E1
Southwick BA14 . . . . .83 D2
Stoke St Michael BA3 . . . . .116 B5
Stratton-on-the-Fosse BA3 . .96 E1
Street BA16 . . . . .207 C4
Tatworth TA20 . . . . .193 D1
Winsley BA15 . . . . .64 F6
Green Lane Ave BA16 . . .207 C4
Green Lane End TA19 . . . .184 E3
Green Lane Gate BA9 . . . .176 A8
Green Mead BA21 . . . . . . .218 C5
Green Ore Est BA5 . . . . . . .94 B1
Green Park La BA11 . . . . .101 F6
Green Park Mews BA1 . . .228 A2
Green Park Rd BA1 . . . . . .228 B2
Green Parlor Rd BA3 . . . . .79 D1
Green Pastures Rd BS48 . . .9 B2
Green Pits La BA11 . . . . .143 B7
Green Pk BA1 . . . . .228 B2
Green Ride BA12 . . . . .161 F7
Green St Bath BA1 . . . . . . .228 C2
Hinton St George TA17 . . . .195 D7
Peasedown St John BA2 . . . .79 E5
Ston Easton BA3 . . . . .95 E8
Green The Backwell BS48 . . .19 A5
Bath BA2 . . . . .44 D1
Bridgwater TA6 . . . . .208 E2
Brushford TA22 . . . . .163 E4
Coleford BA3 . . . . .116 F6
8 East Coker BA22 . . . . . . .197 E8
Easton BA5 . . . . .111 A4
Hinton Charterhouse BA2 . . .63 F1
Ilchester BA22 . . . . .173 E2
Locking BS24 . . . . .50 A4
Pill BS20 . . . . .4 D4
Pitminster TA3 . . . . .181 E6
1 Sherborne DT9 . . . . .225 D4
Williton TA4 . . . . .202 D3
Winscombe BS25 . . . . .70 A7
Green Tree Rd BA3 . . . . . . .78 B3
Green's Dro BA6 . . . . .206 C7
Green's Hill TA4 . . . . .151 C5
Greenacre
Wembdon TA6 . . . . .208 D6
Weston-Super-Mare BS22 . . .31 B2
Greenacre Rd BS14 . . . . . .23 A3
Greenacres Bath BA1 . . . . . .27 B3
Bristol BS9 . . . . .5 E7
Midsomer Norton BA3 . . . . .77 E1
Greenacres Pk BA21 . . . . .187 A5
Greenbank Gdns BA1 . . . . .27 B1
Greenbrook Terr TA1 . . . .212 E4
Greendale TA19 . . . . .221 B3
Greenditch Ave BS13 . . . . .22 C5
Greenditch Cl BA3 . . . . . . .96 C3
Greendown Pl BA2 . . . . . . .45 A1
Greenfield Cres BS48 . . . . . .8 E3
Greenfield La TA7 . . . . . .136 D2
Greenfield Pk BS20 . . . . . . .2 C3
Greenfield Pl BS23 . . . . . . .48 C8
Greenfield Terr TA20 . . . .198 D8
Greenfields TA18 . . . . . . .224 C7
Greenfields Ave BS29 . . . .51 A3
Greenfylde CE First Sch TA19 . . . . .221 C3
Greengage Cl BS22 . . . . . . .49 E8
Greenham La TA18 . . . . . .199 E7
Greenham Yd TA18 . . . . . .199 E7
Greenham's Cross TA14 . . . . .185 F2
Greenhayes BS27 . . . . .90 B8
Greenhays Foot EX13 . . . .198 B6
Greenhill DT9 . . . . .225 D4
Greenhill Cl Nailsea BS48 . . .8 D2
Weston-Super-Mare BS22 . . .32 A3
Greenhill Cross EX36 . . . .162 B2
Greenhill La
Axbridge BS26 . . . . .88 E5
Sandford BS25 . . . . .52 B4
Greenhill Pl BA3 . . . . .78 A3
Greenhill Rd
Midsomer Norton BA3 . . . . .78 A3
Sandford BS25 . . . . .52 B4
Greenhill Rd continued
Yeovil BA21 . . . . .219 D7
Greenland La TA24 . . . . . .131 B1
Greenland Rd BS22 . . . . . . .31 D1
Greenlands TA1 . . . . .213 B2
Greenlands Rd BA2 . . . . . .79 C8
Greenmoor La BA21 . . . . .187 A5
Greenridge BS39 . . . . .58 F3
Greenridge Cl BS13 . . . . . .21 E4
Greenslade Gdns BS48 . . . . .8 D3
Greenslade Inf Sch BS48 . .8 D3
Greenvale Cl BA2 . . . . .60 B1
Greenvale Dr BA2 . . . . .60 B1
Greenvale Rd BS39 . . . . . . .77 D5
Greenway
Bishops Lydeard TA4 . . . . . .167 E8
Faulkland BA3 . . . . .80 C1
Minehead TA24 . . . . .200 D6
Monkton Heathfield TA2 . . .169 B6
North Curry TA3 . . . . .170 B3
Watchet TA23 . . . . .202 B7
Greenway Ave TA2 . . . . . .212 E6
Greenway Cl BA9 . . . . . . .216 D4
Greenway Cotts TA4 . . . .167 E8
Greenway Cres TA2 . . . . .212 E7
Greenway Ct BA2 . . . . .44 F4
Greenway La
Angersleigh TA3 . . . . .181 B5
Barrington TA13 . . . . .184 E5
Bath BA2 . . . . .45 A4
Cold Ashton SN14 . . . . .12 D5
Combe St Nicholas TA20 . . .193 E6
Stoke St Mary TA3 . . . . . . .169 D2
Wiveliscombe TA4 . . . . . . .210 A5
Greenway Pk 3 BS21 . . . . . .6 F3
Greenway Rd
Castle Cary BA7 . . . . .214 B6
Rockwell Green TA21 . . . . .222 A5
Taunton TA2 . . . . .212 E6
Greenway Terr TA2 . . . . .168 D8
Greenways BA3 . . . . .96 C2
Greenwell La BS40 . . . . . . .53 C7
Greenwood Cl TA9 . . . . . .136 B8
Greenwood Rd
Weston-Super-Mare BS22 . . .31 E2
Yeovil BA21 . . . . .218 D7
Gregory Mead BS49 . . . . . .17 A1
Gregorys Gr BA2 . . . . .62 D8
Gregorys Tyning BS39 . . . .77 F6
Greinton BS24 . . . . .49 A2
Grenville Ave BS24 . . . . . . .50 A4
Grenville Cl BA6 . . . . .157 E4
Grenville Ho TA6 . . . . . . .208 F2
Grenville Pl 7 BS1 . . . . . . .11 F5
Grenville Rd TA8 . . . . . . .104 C7
Grenville View TA4 . . . . . .167 E6
Grey's Cnr BA9 . . . . .161 A3
Greyfield Comm BS39 . . . . .59 C2
Greyfield Rd BS39 . . . . .59 C2
Greyfield View BS39 . . . . . .58 F1
Greyhound Cl BA9 . . . . . .216 C4
Greylands Rd BS13 . . . . . . .21 F7
Greys Rd TA16 . . . . .195 F7
Grib La BS40 . . . . .54 F2
Gribb View TA20 . . . . . . .199 B6
Griffin Cl Wells BA5 . . . . . .203 B6
Weston-Super-Mare BS22 . . .32 B2
Griffin Ct BA1 . . . . .228 B2
Griffin La TA3 . . . . .182 F7
Griffin Rd Clevedon BS21 . . . .6 E3
Hatch Beauchamp TA3 . . . .182 F7
Griggfield Wlk BS14 . . . . . .23 A7
Grimsey La SP8 . . . . .177 F8
Grinfield Ave BS13 . . . . . .22 C4
Grinfield Cl BS13 . . . . .22 C4
Grinfield Ct BS13 . . . . .22 C4
Groats 9 TA4 . . . . .167 F8
Grooms Orch TA21 . . . . . .222 C5
Grosvenor Bridge Rd BA1 .28 C1
Grosvenor Ct BA22 . . . . . .173 E2
Grosvenor High Sch BA1 . .28 B1
Grosvenor Pk BA1 . . . . .28 C1
Grosvenor Pl BA1 . . . . .28 C1
Grosvenor Rd
Bristol BS2 . . . . .227 C4
Stalbridge DT10 . . . . .190 B4
Grosvenor Terr BA1 . . . . . .28 C2
Grosvenor Villas 9 BA1 . . .28 B1
Grove Alley BA10 . . . . . . .215 E6
Grove Ave Bristol BS1 . . . . .227 A1
Bristol, Coombe Dingle BS9 . . .5 C7
Yeovil BA20 . . . . .218 F5
Grove Cl TA23 . . . . .202 C6
Grove Ct BS9 . . . . .5 E5
Grove Dr Taunton TA2 . . . .212 F8
Weston-Super-Mare BS22 . . .31 C1
Grove Hill TA7 . . . . .155 B1
Grove Ho TA8 . . . . .104 A8
Grove Jun Sch BS48 . . . . . .18 D8
Grove La Faulkland BA3 . . . .80 D2
Frome BA11 . . . . .119 E3
Knole TA10 . . . . .173 A4
South Cheriton BA8 . . . . . .176 E5
Stalbridge DT10 . . . . .190 B4
West Anstey EX36 . . . . . . .162 D6
Weston-Super-Mare BS23 . . .48 D8
Grove Lane Cl DT10 . . . . .190 B4
Grove Leaze BS11 . . . . .4 D6
Grove Mead BA11 . . . . . . .119 E2
Grove Orch BS40 . . . . .54 E2
Grove Park Ct BS23 . . . . . .30 D1
Grove Park Rd BS23 . . . . . .30 D1
Grove Pl TA24 . . . . .201 B4
Grove Rd Banwell BS29 . . . .50 E4
Blue Anchor TA24 . . . . .131 B6
Bristol, Coombe Dingle BS9 . . .5 D8
Burnham-On-Sea TA8 . . . . .104 A8
Grove Rd continued
West Huntspill TA9 . . . . . . .136 A8
Weston-Super-Mare BS22 . . .31 C1
Weston-Super-Mare BS23 . . .48 D8
Grove St BA2 . . . . .228 C3
Grove Terr 5 TA2 . . . . . . .212 F6
Grove The Bath BA1 . . . . . . .27 C1
Bristol BS1 . . . . .227 A1
Burnham-On-Sea TA8 . . . . . .85 B1
Frome BA11 . . . . .119 E2
Paulton BS39 . . . . .77 B7
Ruishton TA3 . . . . .169 C3
Winscombe BS25 . . . . .51 F1
Wraxall BS48 . . . . .9 C3
Grove Wood Rd BA3 . . . . . .78 F1
Groves La TA24 . . . . .131 B6
Groves The BS13 . . . . .22 D4
Grughay La TA3 . . . . .182 E5
Grunter's La BA3 . . . . . . .114 F7
Gryphon Sch DT9 . . . . . . .225 E6
Guard Ave BA22 . . . . .218 B6
Guard House La BA5 . . . .203 D4
Gug The BS39 . . . . .59 C2
Guild Ct BS1 . . . . .227 B2
Guildford Pl TA1 . . . . . . .212 F3
Guildhall La BS28 . . . . . .108 C4
Guinea La BA1 . . . . .228 C3
Guinea St BS1 . . . . .227 A1
Guineagore La DT9 . . . . .188 B4
Guinevere Cl BA21 . . . . . .218 D7
Gullen BA2 . . . . .80 A6
Gulliford Cl TA9 . . . . .104 D4
Gulliford's Bank BS21 . . . . .6 F2
Gullimores Gdns BS13 . . . .22 B4
Gullock Tyning BA3 . . . . . .78 B1
Gullon Wlk BS13 . . . . .21 F5
Gullons Cl BS13 . . . . .22 A6
Gulway Mead TA20 . . . . . .198 D8
Gumbrells Ct TA6 . . . . . . .209 A4
Gunners La BA22 . . . . . . .218 A5
Gunning's La BA4 . . . . . . .142 F2
Gunville La
Charlton Horethorne DT9 . .176 A2
East Coker BA22 . . . . .197 D8
Gunwyn Cl BA6 . . . . .206 E6
Gurney St TA5 . . . . .135 C2
Gurnville Cotts BA11 . . . .119 F2
Guthrie Rd BS8 . . . . .226 A4
Gwynne La TA1 . . . . .213 A3
Gyffarde Ct 3 TA1 . . . . . .213 A4
Gyffarde St TA1 . . . . .213 A4
Gypsy La Axbridge BS28 . . .89 D6
Keynsham BS31 . . . . .42 B8
Marshfield SN14 . . . . .13 F7

H

Haberfield Hill BS8 . . . . .4 E2
Haberfield Ho 1 BS8 . . . . .11 F6
Hack La Holford TA5 . . . . . .133 F2
Nether Stowey TA5 . . . . . . .134 A2
Hack Mead La TA9 . . . . . .105 E1
Hacketty Way TA24 . . . . .124 B3
Hackness Rd TA9 . . . . . . .136 E8
Haddon Cl TA22 . . . . .148 B2
Haddon La
Brompton Regis TA4 . . . . . .164 C7
North Petherton TA6 . . . . . .153 C2
Stalbridge DT10 . . . . .190 C5
Hadley Rd BA2 . . . . .45 B2
Hadrian Cl BS9 . . . . .5 C4
Hadspen Gdn* BA7 . . . . . .160 A2
Hadworthy La TA6 . . . . . .153 F4
Hagget Cl TA6 . . . . .208 F1
Hagleys Gn TA4 . . . . .151 B7
Haig Cl BS9 . . . . .5 B7
Haig Rd TA2 . . . . .168 B6
Haines Hill TA1 . . . . .212 E2
Haines La DT8 . . . . .199 D5
Haines Pk TA1 . . . . .212 E1
Hains La DT10 . . . . .190 F7
Halcombe TA20 . . . . .223 C2
Halcon Cnr TA1 . . . . .213 D4
Halcon Com Prim Sch TA1 . . . . .213 D4
Hale La BA9 . . . . .177 C6
Hale Way TA2 . . . . .213 D7
Hales Mdw BA21 . . . . .187 D6
Halesleigh Rd TA6 . . . . . .208 E5
Half Acre TA4 . . . . .202 D2
Half Acre Cl TA4 . . . . . . .202 D2
Half Acres DT9 . . . . .225 C3
Half Moon St DT9 . . . . . .225 D3
Half Yd BS40 . . . . .53 D8
Halfacre Cl BS14 . . . . .23 A3
Halfacre La BS14 . . . . .23 B4
Halfpenny Row BA11 . . . . .82 E1
Halfway BA22 . . . . .186 F6
Hall Hill EX35 . . . . .122 B5
Hall La BA1 . . . . .12 B3
Hall Sch The BS25 . . . . . . .70 B8
Hall Terr TA8 . . . . .104 A8
Hallam Ct BS21 . . . . .6 C4
Hallam Rd BS21 . . . . .6 C4
Hallards Cl BS11 . . . . .4 F8
Hallatrow Rd BS39 . . . . . .77 C6
Hallen Dr BS9 . . . . .5 C7
Hallet Gdns BA20 . . . . . . .219 A4
Hallets Orch BA22 . . . . . .186 B6
Hallett Rd BA7 . . . . .214 B7
Halletts Way
Axminster EX13 . . . . .198 A1
Portishead BS20 . . . . .2 D5
Halliwell Rd BS20 . . . . .1 D4
Halse Cnr TA4 . . . . .167 D5
Halse La TA24 . . . . .147 B5
Halse Manor TA4 . . . . . . .167 B6
Halston Dr BS2 . . . . .227 C4
Halsway TA6 . . . . .209 C5
Halsway Hill TA4 . . . . . . .132 F1
Halsway La
Bicknoller TA4 . . . . .133 A1
Crowcombe TA4 . . . . .151 A8
Halswell Cl TA6 . . . . .208 E4
Halswell Gdns BS13 . . . . . .22 B4
Halswell Rd BS21 . . . . .6 D1
Halt End BS14 . . . . .23 C3
Halter Path Dro TA7 . . . .137 C7
Halves La BA22 . . . . .197 C7
Halwyn Cl BS9 . . . . .5 D5
Ham Cl BS39 . . . . .58 F1
Ham Gn Hambridge TA10 . . .184 D8
Pill BS20 . . . . .4 D3
Ham Gr BS39 . . . . .77 E5
Ham Green Hospl BS20 . . . .4 E4
Ham Hill Coleford BA3 . . . .116 D6
Combe St Nicholas TA20 . . .193 D8
High Ham TA10 . . . . .156 A2
Langford Budville TA21 . . . .166 A1
Ham Hill Ctry Pk* TA14 . . . . .186 A3
Ham Hill Rd
Higher Odcombe BA22 . . . .186 C2
Stoke sub Hamdon TA14 . . .185 F4
Ham La Bishop Sutton BS39 .57 C5
Burnham-On-Sea TA8 . . . . .104 B6
Compton Dundon TA11 . . . .157 A3
Croscombe BA4,BA5 . . . . . .204 E7
Dundry BS41 . . . . .21 D3
Farrington Gurney BS39 . . . .76 F5
Kingston Seymour BS21 . . . .16 B2
Marnhull DT10 . . . . .190 F6
North End BS49 . . . . .17 A3
Paulton BS39 . . . . .77 E5
Pawlett TA6 . . . . .135 E6
Rodhuish TA23 . . . . .149 C8
Shepton Mallet BA4 . . . . . .141 A7
Shepton Mallet BA4 . . . . . .205 A7
Sherborne DT9 . . . . .188 A5
Trent DT9 . . . . .187 F5
Wraxall BS48 . . . . .9 B4
Yatton BS49 . . . . .17 A3
Ham La E BA4 . . . . .204 F7
Ham Link BS40 . . . . .53 F3
Ham Mdw DT10 . . . . .190 E6
Ham Rd Brean BS24,TA8 . . . .66 B3
Burnham-On-Sea TA9 . . . . . .85 E4
Creech St Michael TA3 . . . .169 D4
Wellington TA21 . . . . .180 D8
Ham St BA6 . . . . .158 B5
Ham Wood Cl BS24 . . . . . .49 B2
Ham's La TA11 . . . . .174 D7
Hamber Lea TA4 . . . . .167 F8
Hambledon Rd BS22 . . . . .32 C4
Hambridge Com Prim Sch TA10 . . . . .184 D8
Hamdon Cl 12 TA14 . . . . .185 F4
Hamdon View TA14 . . . . .185 E3
Hamilton Ct Taunton TA1 .213 C4
Wells BA5 . . . . .203 B4
Hamilton Rd Bath BA1 . . . . .27 E2
Taunton TA1 . . . . .213 C4
Weston-Super-Mare BS23 . . .30 C1
Hamilton Terr BA2 . . . . . . .79 F5
Hamlands La TA21 . . . . . .167 D1
Hamlet The Nailsea BS48 . . . .9 A3
Templecombe BA8 . . . . . . .176 E1
Hamley La
Buckland St Mary TA20 . . . .193 B8
Combe St Nicholas TA20 . . .182 F1
Hamlyn Cl TA1 . . . . .212 C1
Hamlyn Rd BA6 . . . . .206 E6
Hammer La BA2,BA3 . . . .100 C8
Hammer St BA10 . . . . . . .161 B8
Hammet St
2 North Petherton TA6 . . .153 E3
Taunton TA1 . . . . .212 F4
Hammets Wharf 1 TA1 . .212 F4
Hammond Gdns BS9 . . . . . .5 E7
Hamp Ave TA6 . . . . .208 F3
Hamp Brook Way TA6 . . .208 E2
Hamp Com Jun Sch TA6 . . . . .208 F3
Hamp Green Rise TA6 . . .209 A3
Hamp Ind Est TA6 . . . . . .209 A3
Hamp Inf Sch TA6 . . . . . . .208 F3
Hamp St TA6 . . . . .208 F3
Hampden Rd BS22 . . . . . . .31 E2
Hampton Cl
5 Barwick BA22 . . . . .197 F8
Bridgwater TA6 . . . . .209 D7
Hampton Cnr BS11 . . . . . . .4 E6
Hampton Ho 10 BA1 . . . . . .28 C1
Hampton La BS8 . . . . .226 B4
Hampton Rd BS6 . . . . . . .226 C4
Hampton Row BA2 . . . . . . .45 B8
Hampton View BA1 . . . . . .28 B1
Hamrod La TA7 . . . . .154 E5
Hams La BS26 . . . . .68 C3
Hams Rd BS31 . . . . .24 F7
Hamway La TA20 . . . . . . .193 C8
Hamwood TA1 . . . . .212 B4
Hamwood Cotts TA1 . . . . .212 B4
Hamwood La TA3 . . . . . . .181 B8
Hamwood Terr TA1 . . . . . .212 B4
Hanbury Ct BS8 . . . . .226 A4
Hanbury Rd BS8 . . . . .226 A4
Handel Rd BS31 . . . . .24 E5
Handlemaker Rd BA11 . . .119 E2
Handy Cross TA4 . . . . . . .151 A2
Hanford Ct BS14 . . . . .23 D7
Hang Hill BA2 . . . . .80 A6

Hanger's Way TA24 ....201 D2
Hangerland La TA4 ....150 E6
Hanging Hill La TA13 ....184 F4
Hanglands La BA8 ....176 C2
Hanham La BS39 ....77 F7
Hanham Way BS41 ......203 B2
Hankridge Way TA1 .....213 E5
Hann Cl BA5 ....203 B2
Hanna Cl BA2 ....44 B6
Hannah More Cl
  Cheddar BS27 ....90 B7
  Wrington BS40 ....35 E2
Hannah More Inf Sch
  BS48 ....18 D8
Hannah More Prim Sch
  BS1 ....227 B2
Hannah More Rd BS48 ...18 C8
Hannan La BA3 ....110 E6
Hannay Rd BS27 ....71 B1
Hanning Cl TA19 ......221 F6
Hanning Pk TA19 ......183 C1
Hanning Rd TA19 ......183 C1
Hanny's La BS40 ......39 C3
Hanover Cl BS22 ......32 A4
Hanover Ct Bath BA1 ...28 B2
  Bristol BS1 ....227 B3
  Castle Cary BA7 .....214 C5
  Radstock BA3 ....79 C2
Hanover Gdns BA11 ...119 D3
Hanover Pl Bath BA1 ...45 B8
  Bristol BS1 ....226 B1
Hanover St **2** Bath BA1 ..28 B1
  2 Bristol BS1 ......227 A2
Hanover Terr **2** BA1 ...28 B1
Hans Price Cl BS23 ....48 E8
Hans Price Ho **16** BS23 ..48 E8
Hansetown Rd
  Brompton Regis TA4 ..148 F1
  Upton TA4 ....164 F8
Hansford Cl BA2 ......44 E1
Hansford Mews BA2 ...44 E1
Hansford Sq BA2 ......44 E1
Hanson's Way **6** BS21 ..6 C2
Hantone Hill BA2 .....45 F8
Happerton La BS20 ....4 D2
Hapsburg Cl BS22 ....32 A4
Hapsford Hill BA11 ...119 C8
Harbour Cl BA21 .....218 C5
Harbour Ct TA5 ......135 B5
Harbour Rd
  Portishead BS20 ......2 E6
  Sherborne DT9 ....225 E5
  Watchet TA23 ....202 C7
Harbour Road Trad Est
  BS20 ....2 E6
Harbour Terr DT9 .....225 E5
Harbour View TA5 ....135 B5
Harbour Wall BS9 ....5 B4
Harbour Way Bristol BS1 ..226 C1
  Sherborne DT9 ....225 E5
Harbourne Cl TA8 ....104 C8
Harbutts BA2 ....28 F1
Harcourt Cl BS31 ....25 E2
Harcourt Gdns BA1 ...87 B2
Harcourt Mews BA11 ..120 A4
Harcourt St TA2 .....212 E6
Harden Rd BS14 .....23 E5
Harding Pl BS31 .....25 B5
Harding's Hill TA10,TA11 ..172 F5
Harding's House La
  DT9 ....225 A6
Harding's La BA4 ....176 D4
Hardings Cl **8** TA6 ..153 F3
Hardings Ct TA13 ....220 C5
Hardington Dr BS31 ..25 A2
Hardmead La BS27 ...90 E8
Hardwarden Terr BA22 ..175 A5
Hardwick Rd BS20 ...4 C5
Hardy Cres DT10 .....190 B4
Hardy Ct TA18 ......224 C5
Hardy Mead Dro TA9 ..136 B7
Hare La TA20 ....182 E2
Hare Path TA24 .....147 F8
Hare Path Cross TA24 ..129 D1
Hare Pk TA24 ....124 C4
Hareclive Prim Sch BS13 ..22 C4
Hareclive Rd BS13 ...22 C4
Harepark Terr TA24 ..201 A5
Harepits La BA6 .....157 E3
Harestone Cross BA13 ..198 B7
Harewell Wlk BA5 ...203 B3
Harfield Terr **10** BA20 ..219 B4
Harford Cl BS9 ......5 C7
Harford Sq BS40 ....39 B3
Hargrove La DT10 ...190 C2
Harington Pl **7** BA1 ..228 B2
Harley Ct **3** BS8 ...11 F7
Harley La BS21 ......7 C6
Harley Mews **2** BS8 ..11 F7
Harley Pl **4** BS8 ...11 F7
Harley St BA1 ......228 B4
Harmony Dr BS20 ...1 F4
Harnell Cl TA1 .....213 C3
Harnhill Cl BS13 ...22 B4
Harp Chase TA1 ....213 B1
Harp Rd Brent Knoll TA9 ..105 E6
  South Petherton TA13 ..220 C3
Harper Rd TA18 ....224 C5
Harper's La TA23 ...131 D1
Harpitts La SP8 ....177 F2
Harptree BS24 .....49 A2
Harptree Ct BS48 ..18 D8
Harptree Hill BS40 ..74 B5
Harrington Ave BS14 ..23 E6
Harrington Cl BS30 ..25 E8

Harrington Gr BS14 ..23 E6
Harrington Rd BS14 ..23 E6
Harrington Wlk BS14 ..23 E6
Harris Cl EX16 ......179 A4
Harris La Abbots Leigh B58 ..10 F8
  Curry Mallet TA3 ...183 C8
Harris Vale BA3 ....116 F7
Harrison's La TA19 ..184 E1
Hart's La
  Huish Champflower TA4 ..165 D7
  Paulton BS39 ....77 B7
  Sherborne DT9 ....188 A3
Hartcliffe Rd BS4 ...22 E8
Hartcliffe Sch BS13 ..22 E7
Hartcliffe Way BS3,BS4,
  BS13 ....22 C7
Hartcliffe Wlk BS4 ..22 F8
Harter's Hill La BA5 ..139 E6
Harters Cl BA5 .....139 E6
Hartfield Ave BS6 ...226 C4
Hartgill Cl BS13 ....22 B3
Hartland **4** BS22 ..32 A2
Hartley Cotts BA4 ...204 B1
Hartley Way TA1 ...213 D2
Hartmoor Hill SP8 ..177 E3
Hartnor Ct TA1 ....212 C1
Harts Cl TA19 ......221 A4
Harts Paddock BA3 ..77 F3
Hartsfield TA20 ....223 D2
Hartswell TA4 .....210 C3
Harvest La
  Charlton Horethorne DT9 ..176 A2
  Weston-Super-Mare BS24 ..50 B8
Harvest Way BS22 ..32 A5
Harvesters Dr BA16 ..207 B4
Harvey Cl BS22 ....32 A4
Harvey Way TA19 ..183 B4
Harvey's Rd TA13 ..220 C4
Harwood Cross TA24 ..130 A4
Harwood Gdns BS22 ..31 E4
Harwood La
  Timberscombe TA24 ..130 A4
  Wootton Courtenay TA24 ..129 F4
Haselbury Gr BS31 ..25 E2
Haselbury Plucknett CE Fst
  Sch TA18 ....196 C5
Haseley Ct TA1 ....212 C2
Haslands BS48 .....18 D8
Hassage Hill BA2 ..80 E7
Hassock's La BA10 ..160 E8
Hastings Cross TA19 ..183 B3
Hatch Ct* TA3 .....183 A8
Hatch Green La TA3 ..183 A7
Hatch Mews Bsns Pk
  TA3 ....183 A7
Hatcher Cl TA8 ....104 D5
Hatchers Ct TA2 ...212 F7
Hatchet Hill BA3,BA11 ..98 E4
Hatfield Bldgs BA2 ..45 B5
Hatfield Rd Bath BA2 ..44 F3
  Weston-Super-Mare BS23 ..48 F8
Hathermead Gdns BA21 ..219 D7
Haunts TA18 ......196 C8
Havage Cl TA9 ....104 E5
Havage Dro BA22 ..51 D8
Haven Cl TA24 ....201 F3
Haversham Cl BA21 ..31 D1
Haviland Gr BA1 ..27 B3
Haviland Ho **7** BA2 ..227 C3
Haviland Pk BA1 ..27 B2
Havory BA1 ....28 C1
Havyat Rd BS40 ...53 E8
Hawarden Terr BA1 ..28 B1
Hawcombe View TA24 ..124 A3
Hawk's Worth Cl BA11 ..120 C7
Hawkchurch Cross
  EX13 ....198 E2
Hawkchurch Prim Sch
  EX13 ....198 E3
Hawkchurch Rd EX13 ..198 E3
Hawke Rd BS22 ...31 E4
Hawker's La BA5 ..112 E1
Hawkers Cl **1** TA5 ..135 B2
Hawkfield Bsns Pk BS14 ..22 D5
Hawkfield Cl BS14 ..22 D5
Hawkfield Rd BS13 ..22 D5
Hawkfield Way BS14 ..22 D5
Hawkin's La TA4 ...165 E8
Hawkins Cl
  Burnham-On-Sea TA8 ..104 C7
  Street BA16 ....207 E6
Hawkins Dr BS22 ...227 C3
Hawkins Way BA21 ..218 C6
Hawkmoor Hill DT6,
  EX13 ....199 B2
Hawkridge Cross TA22 ..146 D1
Hawkridge Rd TA6 ..208 B4
Hawksmoor Cl BS14 ..23 A6
Hawksworth Dr BS22 ..32 C4
Hawksworth Rd TA24 ..201 B6
Hawkwell Cross EX16 ..162 F4
Hawley Way TA8 ...104 C7
Hawthorn Cl
  Bridgwater TA6 .....209 D4
  Frome BA11 ....120 B6
  Portishead BS20 ....1 F5
Hawthorn Coombe BS22 ..31 E3
Hawthorn Cres
  Shepton Mallet BA4 ..205 A6
  Yatton BS49 ....17 A2
Hawthorn Gdns BS22 ..31 D3
Hawthorn Gr BA2 ..45 A1
Hawthorn Hill
  Kingsbury Episcopi TA13 ..185 B6
  Weston-Super-Mare BS22 ..31 D2
Hawthorn Hts BS22 ..31 D3
Hawthorn Pk BS22 ..31 E3

Hawthorn Rd
  Frome BA11 ....120 A6
  Minehead TA24 .....200 D7
  Radstock BA3 ......79 B2
  Street BA16 ....207 E6
  Taunton TA1 ....213 C1
  Yeovil BA21 ....219 D7
Hawthorn Way BS48 ..9 A2
Hawthorne Cl TA18 ..224 D7
Hawthorne Rd TA21 ..222 F5
Hawthorns La BS31 ..24 E5
Hawthorns The
  Clevedon BS21 ......6 C3
  Stalbridge DT10 ....190 C4
Haxen La TA17 .....195 A8
Hay Cl BS20 ....4 A4
Hay Hill Bath BA1 ..228 B3
  Croscombe BA5 ....204 B8
Hay La BS40 ....37 D6
Hay St BA3 ....96 A8
Hayboro Way BS39 ..77 E4
Haybridge Villas BA5 ..203 A5
Haycombe BS14 ...22 F6
Haycombe Dr BA2 ..44 A4
Haycombe La BA2 ..44 A3
Haycombe Cl BA2 ..228 A1
Haydon Cl TA1 ....212 B4
Haydon Dro
  Horrington BA5 ....112 F6
  Horrington BA5 ....113 C6
Haydon Gate BA3 ..97 B8
Haydon Hill BA3 ...98 A8
Haydon Hollow DT9 ..189 B3
Haydon Ind Est BA3 ..97 F8
Haydon La TA1,TA3 ..213 E2
Haydon Rd TA1 ....213 A4
Hayes End TA13 ...220 C4
Hayes End Manor TA13 ..220 D4
Hayes La TA11 ....156 F2
Hayes Park Rd BA3 ..77 F2
Hayes Rd
  Compton Dundon TA11 ..156 F3
  Midsomer Norton BA3 ..77 F1
Hayes The BS27 ...90 C6
Hayesdown Fst Sch
  BA11 ....120 B5
Hayesfield Pk BA2 ..228 B1
Hayesfield Sch BA2 ..44 D6
Hayesfield School Tech Coll
  BA2 ....228 A1
Hayeswood Rd BA2 ..59 E3
Hayfield Rd TA24 ..201 B6
Haygarth Ct BA1 ..208 C2
Haygrove La TA6 ...208 C3
Haygrove Rd TA6 ..208 C4
Haygrove Sch TA6 ..208 C4
Hayleigh Ho BS13 ..22 C5
Hayman Rd TA24 ...200 F7
Haymans Cl TA3 ...169 C3
Haymarket The BS1 ..227 A3
Haymarket Wlk **9** BS1 ..227 A4
Haymoor Dro BA5 ..139 D7
Haymoor La Cowley BA5 ..139 C6
  Long Sutton TA10 ..172 D4
Hayne Cross EX16 ..164 B4
Hayne La TA5 .....153 B7
Haynes Motor Mus*
  BA22 ....175 A6
Haytor Pk BS9 ....5 D6
Hayward Cl TA6 ...209 C5
Hayward Dr BA6 ..158 A6
Haywood Cl BS24 ..49 A1
Haywood Gdns BS24 ..49 B1
Haywood Rd TA1 ..213 D2
Hazel Cl TA1 .....213 C1
Hazel Cote Rd BS14 ..23 B4
Hazel Ct BA11 ....120 A3
Hazel Gr Bath BA2 ..44 D4
  Midsomer Norton BA3 ..97 B8
Hazel Terr BA3 ...97 C8
Hazel View TA18 ..224 D7
Hazel Way BA2 ...62 D8
Hazelbury Rd Bristol BS14 ..23 C7
  Nailsea BS48 ......8 D1
Hazeldene Rd BS23 ..49 A8
Hazelgrove House (Sch)
  BA22 ....174 F5
Hazell Cl BS21 ....6 E1
Hazelwell La TA19 ..221 A4
Hazelwood Ct BS9 ..5 D3
Hazelwood Dr TA6 ..209 C5
Hazelwood Rd BS9 ..5 D3
Head Croft BS48 ..20 B8
Head Dro Catcott TA7 ..137 D3
  NonRoady TA7 .....155 C1
  NonRoady TA7 .....155 D1
Head Rd BA22 .....186 B6
Headley Cl BS13 ...22 B6
Headley La BS13 ...22 B7
Headley Park Ave BS13 ..22 B7
Headley Park Prim Sch
  BS13 ....22 B6
Headley Park Rd BS13 ..22 A7
Headley Rd BS13 ..22 B6
Headley Wlk BS13 ..22 B7
Headon Cross TA24 ..129 F8
Headstock Cross TA20 ..198 C6
Headstock Rd TA20 ..198 C6
Headwell TA3 .....183 C8
Headwell Cl TA3 ..183 C8
Headwell Hill TA3 ..183 C8
Heal Cl TA8 ....104 D5
Heal's Field EX13 ..195 B2
Healeys TA21 .....124 A4
Healys Mdw TA4 ..167 E6
Hearn La BA22 ....175 D8

Heart Meers BS14 ..23 B5
Heath Cl BA12 ....144 D8
Heath Dr BA11 ...119 F6
Heath Rd BS48 ...8 F3
Heath Ridge BS41 ..11 A2
Heathcombe Rd TA6 ..208 B4
Heathcote Rd BA22 ..174 A2
Heather Cl
  Bridgwater TA6 ....209 B3
  Minehead TA24 ....201 C4
  Taunton TA1 ......169 A1
Heather Dr BA2 ..62 D8
Heather Rd BA21 ..219 D7
Heather Way BA22 ..218 A5
Heatherdene BS14 ..22 F7
Heathfield TA4 ...151 E4
Heathfield Cl Bath BA1 ..27 A3
  Creech St Michael TA3 ..169 D6
  Keynsham BS31 ....24 C5
  5 North Petherton TA6 ..153 F4
Heathfield Com Sch
  TA2 ....213 F8
Heathfield Cres BS14 ..23 B4
Heathfield Dr TA2 ..213 F8
Heathfield Rd BS48 ..8 E3
Heathfield Way BS48 ..8 E2
Heathgate BS49 ...34 B8
Heathgates BS23 ..48 D4
Heathstock Hill TA4 ..210 D5
Heathway BA12 ...144 D8
Heathway La BA6 ..138 B4
Heavitree Way TA2 ..213 A6
Hebden Rd BA15 ..64 F3
Heber's La TA19 ..195 A5
Heckley La BA3 ...115 B5
Hector Rd TA7 ....137 D2
Hectors La TA3 ...170 D8
Hectors Stones TA7 ..136 E4
Heddon Oak TA4 ..151 A8
Hedge Cl BS24 ...50 B8
Hedge La BA4 ....141 B2
Hedgemead Ct BA1 ..228 C4
Hedges Cl **3** BS21 ..6 B1
Hedges The BS22 ..32 C3
Hedgestocks BA4 ..160 C8
Hedging La TA7 ..170 A8
Heggard Cl BS13 ..22 B5
Heights The TA19 ..221 B4
Hele La Langport TA10 ..172 C4
  South Petherton TA13 ..220 C4
Helena Rd BA20 ...218 D1
Helens Rd BS25 ...70 A8
Helland Hill TA3 ..170 C3
Helland La TA3 ...170 D4
Helliar's La
  Curry Mallet TA3 ..183 D8
  Fivehead TA3 .....170 D1
Hellier Wlk BS13 ..22 C3
Hellier's Cl TA20 ..223 B4
Hellier's La TA27 ..89 E6
Helliers Rd TA20 ..223 C4
Helling's Cross TA4 ..166 A4
Helmstedt Way TA20 ..223 D6
Helston Rd BS48 ..9 A1
Helting Ct **7** BA1 ..228 B2
Helvier's La TA4 ..167 A7
Helwell Gn TA23 ..202 D6
Helyar Cl BA6 ....206 D5
Hembridge La BA4 ..158 E7
Hembury La BA5 ..139 C7
Hemington Prim Sch
  BA3 ....99 B7
Hemming Way BS24 ..49 E3
Hemp Gdn TA24 ...200 F8
Hempitts Rd BA16 ..156 E7
Hemplow Cl BS14 ..23 D7
Hemstich Hill TA7 ..138 C1
Hen La BS40 ......54 A3
Henacre Rd BS11 ..4 F8
Henbury Rd Henbury Hill
  BS9 ....5 F8
Henbury Road Henbury Hill
  BS9 ....5 F8
Hencliffe Rd BS14 ..23 D7
Henderson Cl TA1 ..212 C2
Henderson Dr TA20 ..223 D2
Henderson Ho **16** BS2 ..227 B4
Henderson Pl BA5 ..203 D4
Hendford BA20 ...219 A4
Hendford Gr BA20 ..219 A3
Hendford Hill BA20 ..219 A3
Hendre Rd BS3 ...11 F1
Hengrove Ave BS14 ..23 B8
Hengrove La BS14 ..23 B8
Hengrove Rd BS14 ..23 B7
Hengrove Way BS14 ..22 E6
Henhayes La TA18 ..224 C6
Henley Cl BS13 ...198 B7
Henley Gr TA1 ....212 E2
Henley La Butleigh BA6 ..157 E4
  Wookey BA5 ....139 E8
Henley Lodge Bath BA1 ..44 B8
  Yatton BS49 ....34 C7
Henley Pk BS49 ..34 C7
Henley Rd
  High Ham TA10 ...156 B5
  Kingsdon TA11 ....173 E5
  Taunton TA1 ......212 D3
Henley Rise BA4 ..205 D4
Henley View
  Crewkerne TA18 ..224 C4
  Wellow BA2 ....62 D1
Henmore La BS26 ..88 E6
Hennessy Cl BS14 ..22 F3
Henning Way DT9 ..217 D3

Henrietta Ct BA2 ..228 C4
Henrietta Gdns BA2 ..228 C3
Henrietta Mews BA2 ..228 C3
Henrietta Pl BA2 ..228 C3
Henrietta Rd BA2 ..228 C3
Henrietta St Bath BA2 ..228 C3
  Bristol BS2 ....227 A4
Henry Butt Ho **11** BS23 ..48 E8
Henry Rogers Ho **2**
  TA5 ....135 B2
Henry St BA1 .....228 C2
Hensley Gdns BA2 ..44 E4
Hensley Rd BA2 ..44 E3
Hensman's Hill BS8 ..226 A2
Henson Pk TA20 ..223 E5
Henson Dr BS23 ..223 E5
Hensman's Hill BS8 ..226 A2
Henson Pk TA20 ..223 E5
Henson Dr BS23 ..179 A3
Henstridge Trad Est
  BA8 ....190 C7
Hepburn Rd BS2 ..227 B4
Herald Cl BS9 ....5 D5
Herbert Ho TA22 ..163 D6
Herbert Rd Bath BA2 ..44 D5
  Burnham-On-Sea TA8 ..104 A8
  Clevedon BS21 .....6 D4
Herbert St TA2 ...212 E6
Herblay Cl BA21 ..219 E6
Hereford Dr TA2 ..213 A8
Heritage Cl BA2 ..79 D8
Heritage Ct BA6 ..206 D4
Heritage Ctyd BA5 ..203 D4
Heritage The
  Peasedown St John BA2 ..60 E1
  Peasedown St John BA2 ..78 E8
Herluin Way BS22,BS23 ..49 B6
Hermes Cl BS31 ..25 D2
Hermes Pl BA22 ..173 E2
Hermitage Cl BS11 ..4 E7
Hermitage Hill TA10 ..172 D6
Hermitage Rd Bath BA1 ..27 E1
  Langport TA10 ....172 D6
Hermitage St TA18 ..224 C5
Hern Gr BS14 ....22 E5
Herne Rise TA19 ..221 B2
Heron Cl Minehead TA24 ..201 C4
  Weston-Super-Mare BS22 ..49 E8
Heron Ct BS21 ...7 A4
Heron Dr TA1 ....212 B4
Heron Gate TA1 ..213 E6
Heron Gate Office Pk
  TA1 ....213 E5
Heron Gdns BS20 ..2 E4
Heron Ho **9** TA6 ..209 C4
Heron Pk TA8 ....54 A8
Heron Way TA19 ..221 C2
Herons La TA4 ...167 A4
Heronsmead Wlk BA21 ..219 D8
Herridge Cl BS13 ..22 B4
Herridge Rd BS13 ..22 B4
Hersey Gdns BS13 ..21 E3
Hertford Rd BA21 ..219 E8
Hervey Cl BS28 ..108 C4
Hervey Rd Chard TA20 ..223 D3
  Wells BA5 ....112 E1
Hestercombe Cl TA6 ..208 B4
Hestercombe Rd
  Bristol BS13 ......22 B6
  Kingston St Mary TA2 ..168 F7
Hewett Cl TA3 ...168 D1
Hewish Ct BS23 ..48 E5
Hewish La
  Crewkerne TA18 ..224 A5
  Crewkerne, Hewish TA18 ..195 D3
Hexton Rd BA6 ..206 E5
Heyron Wlk BS13 ..22 B4
Heywood Rd BS20 ..4 C4
Heywood Terr BS20 ..4 C4
Hibbs Cl SN14 ...13 F8
Hick's La TA22 ..214 D1
Hide Mkt BS2 ....227 C3
Hidewood La EX15 ..180 F1
Higgin's Grave La TA13 ..220 B1
High Acre BS39 ..77 F4
High Bank Porlock TA24 ..124 A3
  Watchet TA23 ....202 C7
High Bannerdown BA1 ..29 B4
High Cross EX16 ..164 A1
High Down Jun & Inf Schs
  BS20 ....2 A4
High Gn BS41 ....111 A4
High Gr BS9 .....5 B7
High Ham CE Prim Sch
  TA10 ....5 B7
High La
  Barton St David TA11 ..158 A2
  Shapwick TA7 ....155 F8
High Lea BA21 ...219 B8
High Mdws BA3 ..77 F1
High Mead Gdns BS39 ..57 D3
High Path BA22 ..174 D3
High Rd BA22 ...175 D8
High St Aller TA10 ..171 L8
  Ashcott TA7 ......156 B8
  Axbridge BS26 ...70 B2
  Bampton EX16 ...164 B1
  Banwell BS29 ....51 A2
  Bath BA1 ....228 C2
  Bath, Twerton BA2 ..44 B6
  Bath, Weston BA1 ..27 B1
  Bathampton BA2 ..28 F1
  Batheaston BA1 ..28 F3
  Bathford BA1 ....29 D2
  Bishops Lydeard TA4 ..167 E8
  Blagdon BS40 ...54 E3
  Bourton SP8 .....161 F2
  Bridgwater TA6 ..208 F5
  Bristol BS1 ......227 A2

High St continued
Bristol, Shirehampton BS11 . . . . 4 E6
Bruton BA10 . . . . 215 E6
Buckland Dinham B11 . . . . 100 A3
Burnham-On-Sea TA8 . . . . 104 A6
Butleigh BA6 . . . . 157 E4
Cannington TA5 . . . . 135 B2
Carhampton TA24 . . . . 131 A5
Castle Cary BA7 . . . . 214 C5
Chapmanslade BA13 . . . . 121 C4
Chard TA20 . . . . 223 B4
Charlton Adam TA11 . . . . 173 F7
Chew Magna BS40 . . . . 39 A3
Chewton Mendip BA3 . . . . 94 F7
Claverham BS49 . . . . 17 F1
Coleford BA3 . . . . 116 F6
Curry Mallet TA3 . . . . 183 D3
Dulverton TA22 . . . . 163 D6
Dunster TA24 . . . . 201 E2
East Chinnock BA22 . . . . 196 E8
East Harptree BS40 . . . . 74 F5
Evercreech BA4 . . . . 141 E1
Faulkland BA3 . . . . 80 D1
Freshford BA3 . . . . 64 B5
Frome BA11 . . . . 119 E5
Glastonbury BA6 . . . . 206 E4
Hardington Mandeville
BA22 . . . . 197 A6
Henstridge BA8 . . . . 190 A6
High Littleton BS39 . . . . 59 D1
Hinton Charterhouse BA2 . . . . . 63 E1
Hinton St George TA17 . . . . . . 195 D7
Ilchester BA22 . . . . 173 E1
Ilminster TA19 . . . . 221 B4
Keinton Mandeville TA11 . . . . . 158 A1
Keynsham BS31 . . . . 24 E6
Kingweston BA6 . . . . 157 E1
Lynford-on-Fosse BA11 . . . . . . 158 C2
Maiden Bradley BA12 . . . . 144 C2
Marshfield SN14 . . . . 13 F8
Midsomer Norton BA3 . . . . 78 B1
Milborne Port DT9 . . . . 217 D2
Milton Clevedon BA4 . . . . 160 A8
Milverton TA4 . . . . 166 F5
Monksilver TA4 . . . . 150 B8
Nailsea BS48 . . . . 8 F3
North Cadbury BA22 . . . . 175 D6
North Petherton TA6 . . . . 153 E4
North Wootton BA4 . . . . 140 C4
Norton St Philip BA2 . . . . 81 E4
Nunney BA11 . . . . 143 B8
Oakhill BA3 . . . . 115 A3
NonRoady TA7 . . . . 155 C2
Paulton, Plummer's Hill
BS39 . . . . 77 E6
Pensford BS39 . . . . 40 E4
Porlock TA24 . . . . 124 A3
Portbury BS20 . . . . 3 E3
Portishead BS20 . . . . 2 D5
Queen Camel BA22 . . . . 174 F3
Rimpton BA22 . . . . 188 A8
Rode BA11 . . . . 101 E8
Saltford BS31 . . . . 25 F3
Shepton Mallet BA4 . . . . 205 B5
Sparkford BA22 . . . . 175 A5
Spaxton TA5 . . . . 152 E7
Stalbridge DT10 . . . . 190 B5
Stogumber TA4 . . . . 150 D8
Stogursey TA5 . . . . 134 C5
Stoke sub Hamdon TA14 . . . . . 185 F4
Ston Easton BA3 . . . . 95 E8
Stoney Stratton BA4 . . . . 141 F2
Stourton BA12 . . . . 161 F5
Street BA16 . . . . 207 C6
Taunton TA1 . . . . 212 F3
Templecombe BA8 . . . . 176 E1
Thorncombe TA20 . . . . 199 B6
Timsbury BA2 . . . . 60 B2
Wedmore BS28 . . . . 107 E4
Wellington TA21 . . . . 222 E6
Wellow BA2 . . . . 62 D1
Wells BA5 . . . . 203 D4
West Coker BA22 . . . . 197 A8
Weston-Super-Mare BS22 . . . . 31 E2
Weston-Super-Mare BS23 . . . . 48 D8
Williton TA4 . . . . 202 D2
Wincanton BA9 . . . . 216 C4
Winford BS40 . . . . 38 A7
Winsham TA20 . . . . 194 E1
Wiveliscombe TA4 . . . . 210 C4
Wookey BA5 . . . . 139 D8
Wookey Hole BA5 . . . . 203 A8
Woolley BA1 . . . . 27 F6
Wrington BS40 . . . . 35 D2
Yatton BS49 . . . . 34 C8
Yenston BA8 . . . . 189 F8
Yeovil BA20 . . . . 219 B4
High View BS20 . . . . 2 A4
High View Dr TA7 . . . . 156 B8
Highaton Head Cross
EX36 . . . . 162 C4
Highbridge TA4 . . . . 202 F4
Highbridge Rd TA8 . . . . 104 B5
Highbridge Sta TA9 . . . . 104 E3
Highbrooks Rd TA11 . . . . 173 B5
Highburn Cl TA8 . . . . 104 C4
Highbury Cotts ⑧ BA1 . . . . . 28 A1
Highbury Par BS23 . . . . 30 C1
Highbury Pl BA1 . . . . 28 A1
Highbury Rd Paulton BS39 . . 77 F4
Weston-Super-Mare BS23 . . . . 30 C1
Highbury St BA3 . . . . 117 A7
Highbury Terr ⑩ BA1 . . . . . . 28 A1
Highbury Villas
⑤ BA1 . . . . 28 A1
Bristol BS2 . . . . 226 C4

Highcroft
Weston-Super-Mare BS23 . . . . 30 F1
Woolavington TA7 . . . . 136 E4
Highdale Ave BS21 . . . . 6 E3
Highdale Cl BS14 . . . . 23 B4
Highdale Rd BS21 . . . . 6 E3
Higher Actis BA6 . . . . 206 E3
Higher Backway BA10 . . . . . 215 E6
Higher Beacon TA19 . . . . 221 B4
Higher Beadon TA16 . . . . . . 195 E7
Higher Brooks BA16 . . . . 207 C2
Higher Bullen BA22 . . . . 197 F8
Higher Burton BA22 . . . . 197 C8
Higher Cheap St ⑧
DT9 . . . . 225 D4
Higher Coombses TA20 . . . . 198 D8
Higher Cross EX15 . . . . 179 C1
Higher Easthams La
TA18 . . . . 224 F7
Higher Farm La
Podimore BA22 . . . . 174 A4
Sparkford BA22 . . . . 175 B3
Higher Farm Trad Est
BA20 . . . . 218 C5
Higher Gunville DT9 . . . . 217 D2
Higher Heathfield TA4 . . . . . 151 E4
Higher Kingsbury DT9 . . . . . 217 D3
Higher Kingsbury Cl
DT9 . . . . 217 C3
Higher Kingston BA21 . . . . . 219 B5
Higher Mead TA19 . . . . 221 B3
Higher Millhayes EX15 . . . . 180 B1
Higher North Town La
BA22 . . . . 175 D7
Higher Orch
Martock TA12 . . . . 185 D4
Minehead TA24 . . . . 200 C8
Higher Palmerston Rd
TA1 . . . . 212 D6
Higher Park La TA24 . . . . . . 129 E2
Higher Pk TA24 . . . . 200 D6
Higher Rd Chedzoy TA7 . . . . 154 D8
Horsington BA8 . . . . 176 D3
Shepton Beauchamp TA19 . . 184 E3
Woolavington TA7 . . . . 136 E4
Higher Ream BA21 . . . . 218 C6
Higher Rodhuish Rd
TA24 . . . . 131 B3
Higher St
Curry Mallet TA3 . . . . 183 C8
East Quantoxhead TA5 . . . . . 133 B5
Martock TA12 . . . . 185 D4
Merriott TA16 . . . . 195 F7
Norton Sub Hamdon TA14 . . 185 E2
West Chinnock TA18 . . . . . . 196 B8
Higher Tolbury BA10 . . . . . . 215 E6
Higher Town EX16 . . . . 178 C1
Higher West Hatch La
TA3 . . . . 182 D7
Higher Westbury DT9 . . . . . 187 E1
Higher Westholme Rd
North Wootton BA4 . . . . 140 D4
Pilton BA4 . . . . 204 A1
Highfield Coleford BA3 . . . . 116 E8
Ilminster TA19 . . . . 221 B4
Taunton TA1 . . . . 212 A2
Taunton TA1 . . . . 212 C3
West Chinnock TA18 . . . . . . 196 B8
Highfield Cl Bath BA2 . . . . . . 44 B5
Somerton TA11 . . . . 211 C4
Taunton TA1 . . . . 212 A2
Highfield Cres
Chilcompton BA3 . . . . 96 C4
Taunton TA1 . . . . 212 A2
Highfield Dr BS20 . . . . 1 E3
Highfield La
Compton Martin BS40 . . . . . 74 B6
East Harptree BS40 . . . . 75 A3
Highfield Rd
Keynsham BS31 . . . . 24 F2
Peasedown St John BA2 . . . . 79 C8
Street BA16 . . . . 207 B5
Weston-Super-Mare BS24 . . 49 A1
Yeovil BA21 . . . . 219 C6
Highfield Terr TA12 . . . . . . 185 D5
Highfield Trad Est BA21 . . . 219 C6
Highfield View BA3 . . . . 116 E8
Highfield Way TA11 . . . . 211 C4
Highfields
Barrington TA19 . . . . 184 C5
Midsomer Norton BA3 . . . . . 78 D2
Radstock BA3 . . . . 78 E4
Stanton Drew BS39 . . . . 39 F1
Highgrove TA1 . . . . 212 E1
Highgrove Cl TA6 . . . . 209 A2
Highland Cl BS22 . . . . 31 B2
Highland Ct BA21 . . . . 219 C6
Highland Rd BA2 . . . . 44 B5
Highland Terr BA2 . . . . 44 D6
Highlands BA21 . . . . 219 A6
Highlands La TA24 . . . . 50 A8
Highlands Rd
Long Ashton BS41 . . . . 11 A2
Portishead BS20 . . . . 2 B5
Highmead Gdns BS13 . . . . . . 21 E4
Highmore Rd DT9 . . . . 225 C5
Highridge Cres BS13 . . . . . . 21 F5
Highridge Gn BS13 . . . . 21 E6
Highridge Inf Sch BS13 . . . . 21 F6
Highridge Jun Sch BS13 . . . 21 F6
Highridge Pk BS13 . . . . 21 E5
Highridge Rd BS13,BS41 . . . 21 E4
Highridge Wlk BS13 . . . . 21 E7
Highwall La BS14,BS31 . . . . 23 F1
Highwoods Cl TA14 . . . . 185 F2
Higson Cl BA22 . . . . 186 D3
Hilary Rd TA1 . . . . 212 D3
Hildesheim Bridge BS23 . . . . 48 F7
Hildesheim Cl BS23 . . . . 48 F6

Hildesheim Ct BS23 . . . . 48 E7
Hilhouse BS9 . . . . 5 C6
Hill Ave BA2 . . . . 44 F1
Hill Brow DT9 . . . . 225 B2
Hill Cl BA9 . . . . 216 D4
Hill Crest Rd BA21 . . . . 219 C6
Hill Cross BA22 . . . . 196 F6
Hill Cl BS39 . . . . 77 E6
Hill Dr BS8 . . . . 10 C3
Hill Gay Cl BS20 . . . . 1 F4
Hill Ground BA11 . . . . 119 E5
Hill Head BA6 . . . . 206 D3
Hill Head Cl
Glastonbury BA6 . . . . 206 D3
Taunton TA1 . . . . 213 A3
Hill House Cl DT9 . . . . 225 E5
Hill La Bicknoller TA4 . . . . . 132 F2
Brent Knoll TA9 . . . . 86 B3
Carhampton TA24 . . . . 131 A4
Chipstable TA4 . . . . 165 C6
Clevedon BS21 . . . . 7 C4
Cucklvarys TA4 . . . . 133 A1
Draycott BS27 . . . . 90 C2
Portishead BS20 . . . . 1 F1
Rodney Stoke BS27 . . . . 91 B2
Rowberrow BS25 . . . . 53 A1
Shepton Mallet BA4 . . . . . . 205 B6
Watercrow TA4 . . . . 165 E5
West Quantoxhead TA4 . . . 132 F4
Hill Lea Gdns BS27 . . . . 90 B8
Hill Moor BS21 . . . . 6 E2
Hill Pk BS49 . . . . 34 E5
Hill Rd Allerford TA24 . . . . . 124 E4
Clevedon BS21 . . . . 6 D4
Dundry BS41 . . . . 21 D2
Minehead TA24 . . . . 125 B4
Sandford BS25 . . . . 52 A3
Weston-Super-Mare BS22 . . . 31 D2
Weston-Super-Mare BS23 . . 48 F8
Hill Rd E BS22 . . . . 31 E2
Hill Side Cl BA5 . . . . 203 C5
Hill St Bristol BS1 . . . . 226 C2
Stogumber TA4 . . . . 150 D8
Hill Terr TA1 . . . . 212 A4
Hill The Freshford BA3 . . . . . 64 C5
Langport TA10 . . . . 172 A5
Hill Top BS20 . . . . 2 A4
Hill View Brean TA8 . . . . 65 E2
Bristol BS8 . . . . 226 B2
Brompton Ralph TA4 . . . . . . 150 C3
Farrington Gurney BS39 . . . . 77 B3
Marksbury BA2 . . . . 42 B1
Priston BA2 . . . . 61 A5
Yeovil BA21 . . . . 219 C5
Yeovil, Mudford BA21 . . . . . 187 D6
Hill View Cl Ilton TA19 . . . . 183 F4
⑦ Stoke sub Hamdon
TA14 . . . . 185 F4
West Chinnock TA18 . . . . . . 196 B8
Hill View Ct BS22 . . . . 49 D8
Hill View Park Homes
BS25 . . . . 49 D8
Hill View Rd Bath BA1 . . . . . 28 B2
Bristol BS13 . . . . 22 B8
Carhampton TA24 . . . . 131 A5
Weston-Super-Mare BS22 . . 49 A7
Hill View Terr
Ilminster TA19 . . . . 221 B4
Lyng TA3 . . . . 170 D7
Hill View Trad Est TA4 . . . . 151 E4
Hill's La ⑩ TA12 . . . . 185 E6
Hillborne Gdns BA21 . . . . . 218 C5
Hillbrook Cl DT9 . . . . 225 D4
Hillcrest Crowcombe TA4 . . 151 B7
Peasedown St John BA2 . . . . 79 C7
Pensford BS39 . . . . 40 E3
Hillcrest Cl Nailsea BS48 . . . 8 E1
Yeovil BA21 . . . . 219 C7
Hillcrest Dr BA2 . . . . 44 C4
Hillcrest Rd Nailsea BS48 . . . 8 E1
Portishead BS20 . . . . 2 B5
Templecombe BA8 . . . . 176 E1
Hillcroft Cl BS22 . . . . 31 A2
Hilldale Rd BS48 . . . . 19 E5
Hiller's La BA5 . . . . 139 C8
Hillfield BS27 . . . . 90 B7
Hillgrove Ave BA20 . . . . . . 218 F2
Hillgrove Cl TA6 . . . . 208 B5
Hillgrove Rd BA5 . . . . 93 C1
Hillgrove St BS2 . . . . 227 A4
Hillgrove St N BS2 . . . . 227 A4
Hillgrove Terr BS23 . . . . 48 D1
Hillhead Cotts TA2 . . . . 212 C8
Hillhead Cross TA24 . . . . . . 128 D3
Hillhouse EX14 . . . . 192 D3
Hillier's La TA24 . . . . 52 D4
Hillingdon Ct BA21 . . . . 218 C6
Hillmead Langford BS40 . . . . 33 A5
Shepton Mallet BA4 . . . . . . 205 B6
Hillmer Rise BS29 . . . . 50 F3
Hillpath BS29 . . . . 51 B2
Hills Cl BS31 . . . . 25 A5
Hills Cotts TA4 . . . . 167 A4
Hills Orch ⑧ TA12 . . . . 185 E6
Hillsboro TA7 . . . . 136 E4
Hillsborough BS8 . . . . 226 A2
Hillsborough Gdns TA8 . . . . 85 B1
Hillsborough Ho BS23 . . . . . 48 F4
Hillsdon Rd BS9 . . . . 5 F8
Hillside Bristol BS6 . . . . 226 C4
Chard TA20 . . . . 223 B4
Horrington BA5 . . . . 113 A2
Portbury BS20 . . . . 3 E3
Puriton TA7 . . . . 136 C4
Sherborne DT9 . . . . 225 E3
West Pennard BA6 . . . . 140 B1

Hillside Ave Frome BA11 . . . 119 F2
Midsomer Norton BA3 . . . . . 96 F8
Hillside Cl
Curry Rivel TA10 . . . . 171 D4
Paulton BS39 . . . . 77 F6
Hillside Cres
Midsomer Norton BA3 . . . . . 96 E8
Purton TA7 . . . . 136 C4
Hillside Dr TA7 . . . . 136 C4
Hillside Fst Sch BS22 . . . . . . 31 E2
Hillside Gdns
Bishop Sutton BS39 . . . . 57 C3
Weston-Super-Mare BS22 . . 31 B1
Hillside Gr TA1 . . . . 212 C1
Hillside Ho BA11 . . . . 119 F3
Hillside Rd Backwell BS48 . . 19 A4
Bath BA2 . . . . 44 D4
Bleadon BS24 . . . . 67 B8
Clevedon BS21 . . . . 6 D3
Long Ashton BS41 . . . . 11 B2
Midsomer Norton BA3 . . . . . 96 F8
Portishead BS20 . . . . 1 D4
Hillside Terr BA21 . . . . 219 C5
Hillside View
TA20 . . . . 193 C5
Holleys Cl TA20 . . . . 198 D8
Hollies Cl Martock TA12 . . . 185 D5
Middlezoy TA7 . . . . 155 B3
Shepton Mallet BA4 . . . . . . 205 C6
Hollies La BA1 . . . . 29 A6
Hollies The
Crewkerne TA18 . . . . 224 C4
Midsomer Norton BA3 . . . . . 78 A1
Yeovil BA21 . . . . 219 C7
Hollis Ave BS20 . . . . 2 C3
Hollis Cl Halstock BA22 . . . . 197 D3
Long Ashton BS41 . . . . 21 A8
Hollis Cres BS20 . . . . 2 C3
Hollis Way
Halstock BA22 . . . . 197 D3
Southwick BA14 . . . . 83 F3
Hollister's Dr BS13 . . . . 22 D4
Hollow La
Baltonsborough BA6 . . . . . . 158 B8
Dinnington TA17 . . . . 195 B7
Lopen TA13 . . . . 185 A1
Montacute TA15 . . . . 186 B3
Wembdon TA5,TA6 . . . . . . 208 C7
Weston-Super-Mare BS22 . . 31 F3
Hollow Marsh La BA3,
BS39 . . . . 76 B4
Hollow Rd
Shepton Beauchamp TA19 . 184 D3
Shipham BS25 . . . . 70 F8
Hollow The Bath BA2 . . . . . . 44 B4
Corsley Heath BA12 . . . . . . 144 E8
Peasedown St John BA2 . . . . 61 D4
Westbury Sub Mendip
BA5 . . . . 110 D7
Holloway Bath BA2 . . . . 228 B1
Lopen TA13 . . . . 185 A1
Minehead TA24 . . . . 200 F7
Holloway Rd TA7 . . . . 155 B2
Holloway St TA24 . . . . 200 F7
Holloway The TA21 . . . . 179 E7
Hollowbrook La BS39,
BS40 . . . . 57 D6
Hollowell Hill
Norton Sub Hamdon TA14,
TA18 . . . . 185 E1
West Chinnock TA18 . . . . . . 196 B8
Hollowmead BS49 . . . . 34 E8
Hollowmead Cl BS49 . . . . . . 34 F8
Hollowys BS14 . . . . 23 E5
Hollyway Rd BS14 . . . . 23 E5
Holly Cl Bridgwater TA6 . . . 209 E5
Nailsea BS48 . . . . 9 A3
⑦ North Petherton TA6 . . . 153 F3
Taunton TA1 . . . . 212 C1
Weston-Super-Mare BS22 . . 32 A1
Holly Cr Bristol BS2 . . . . . . 226 C4
Frome BA11 . . . . 120 B7
Holly Dr BA2 . . . . 62 D8
Holly Gr TA18 . . . . 224 D7
Holly Hill BA4 . . . . 142 C1
Holly La Clevedon BS21 . . . . 6 F6
Drimpton DT8 . . . . 199 F8
Holly Ridge BS20 . . . . 2 A5
Holly Terr Chard TA20 . . . . 223 C4
Higher Odcombe BA22 . . . . 186 C2
Holly Tree Wlk BA20 . . . . . 218 E3
Holly Wlk Keynsham BS31 . . 24 D4
Radstock BA3 . . . . 78 E1
Hollybush Cl BA15 . . . . 64 E7
Hollybush La Bristol BS9 . . . 5 F5
Leigh upon Mendip BA3 . . . 117 A2
Hollyman Wlk ⑤ BS21 . . . . 6 F3
Hollymead La BS9 . . . . 5 E4
Holyridge BS14 . . . . 23 C6
Holm La TA8 . . . . 104 B5
Holm Oaks BA6 . . . . 157 E4
Holm Rd BS24 . . . . 49 E2
Holman Cl BA6 . . . . 206 E6
Holman's BA6 . . . . 157 E4
Holmbush Cl BA14 . . . . 83 F3
Holmbush Ct TA24 . . . . 128 E8
Holmcroft TA24 . . . . 201 A5
Holmlea Portishead BS20 . . . 2 F5
Holmoak Rd BS31 . . . . 49 A5
Holms Rd BS23 . . . . 49 A5
Holsom Rd BS14 . . . . 23 F6
Holt Ball Steep TA24 . . . . . 129 D7
Holt Hill DT9 . . . . 189 C1
Holt La Halstock BA22 . . . . . 197 F3
South Perrott DT8 . . . . 196 D1

Holdscroft La DT6 . . . . 199 B1
Holeground Villas BA5 . . . . 203 A8
Holemore Cross EX14 . . . . . 191 F5
Holes La BA11 . . . . 118 B6
Holford Cl BS48 . . . . 8 E1
Holford Ct BS14 . . . . 23 B5
Holford La TA4 . . . . 151 C5
Holford Rd
Bridgwater TA6 . . . . 208 B4
Taunton TA2 . . . . 212 E8
Hollam Cross TA22 . . . . 163 E7
Hollam Dr TA22 . . . . 163 D6
Hollam La TA22 . . . . 163 D7
Holland Cl BA16 . . . . 207 D7
Holland Rd Bath BA1 . . . . . . 28 B1
Clevedon BS21 . . . . 6 B1
Holland St BS23 . . . . 49 A8
Holland's La
BA22 . . . . 149 E1
Hush Champflower TA4 . . . 165 E8
Holland's Wash Dro
TA20 . . . . 193 C5
Holleys Cl TA20 . . . . 198 D8

Holt La continued
Stourton Caundle DT9,
DT10 ....**189** E1
West Pennard BA6 ....**140** D2
Holt Rd Kilmington BA11 ..**161** E8
  Witham Friary BA11 ....**143** D1
Holten's La BA22 ....**196** E6
Holton Cross BA9 ....**176** C6
Holton St BA9 ....**176** C5
Holtsdown La BA1 ....**28** F7
Holvert La TA20 ....**194** F1
Holway
  North Petherton TA6 ....**153** F4
  Tatworth TA20 ....**198** D8
Holway Ave TA1 ....**213** B3
Holway Deane TA1 ....**213** D2
Holway Gn TA1 ....**213** D2
Holway Hill TA1 ....**213** B2
Holway Park Com Prim Sch
  TA1 ....**213** C3
Holway Rd TA1 ....**213** B3
Holwell Cl BS39 ....**77** E4
Holwell Hill BA11 ....**143** B7
Holwell La BS27 ....**89** F8
Holworthy La TA22 ....**148** E2
Holy Moor La EX36 ....**162** C1
Holy Tree Cross TA14 ....**185** E3
Holy Trinity CE Prim Sch
  Taunton TA1 ....**213** A3
  Yeovil BA20 ....**218** E2
Holy Well Rd TA7 ....**137** C2
Holyoake St TA21 ....**222** C7
Holyrood Com Sch (Lower)
  TA20 ....**223** C4
Holyrood Com Sch (Upper)
  TA20 ....**223** C3
Holyrood St TA20 ....**223** C3
Home Cl
  West Camel BA22 ....**174** D3
  Westbury Sub Mendip BA5 .**110** E6
  Wrington BS40 ....**35** E3
Home Cotts TA1 ....**212** D5
Home Dr Wincanton BA9 ..**216** C3
  Yeovil BA21 ....**218** E5
Home Farm Cl BA2 ....**79** B7
Home Farm La BA22 ....**188** A8
Home Farm Rd BS8 ....**11** B8
Home Farm Way TA18 ......**183** E2
Home Field Cl TA11 ....**157** B4
Home Ground BS11 ....**4** D7
Home Mdw TA24 ....**200** D7
Home Mead BS4 ....**222** E7
Home Orch
  Chew Stoke BS40 ....**56** D8
  Hatch Beauchamp TA3 ....**183** A7
Home Way Cnr BA6 ....**138** B4
Homeavon Ho BS31 ....**24** F5
Homecanton BA9 ....**216** C4
Homecastle Ho ② TA6 ....**208** F5
Homechine Ho BA5 ....**203** D3
Homeclose La EX13,
  TA20 ....**198** A8
Homefield
  Congresbury BS49 ....**34** E3
  Locking BS24 ....**50** A5
  Timsbury BA2 ....**60** C2
  Wellington TA21 ....**222** E4
Homefield Cl
  Beckington BA11 ....**101** E4
  Creech St Michael TA3 ......**169** D4
  Locking BS24 ....**50** A5
  Saltford BS31 ....**25** E3
  Winscombe BS25 ....**51** F1
Homefield Ind Est BS24 ....**50** A5
Homefield Rd BS31 ....**25** F3
Homelane Ho TA8 ....**85** A1
Homelea Pk E BA1 ....**44** A7
Homelea Pk W BA1 ....**44** A7
Homestead The
  Clevedon BS21 ....**6** C3
  Keynsham BS31 ....**24** F2
Homestead Way BS25 ....**70** A8
Homeville Ho BA20 ....**219** A4
Hone Cross EX16 ....**164** F5
Honey Crock La TA7 ....**155** E8
Honey Garston Cl BS13 ....**22** B4
Honey Garston Rd BS13 ...**22** B4
Honey Mead La BA6,
  TA11 ....**158** B4
Honey Pot La BA11 ....**144** A4
Honey Row La TA4 ....**132** C2
Honeycombe Rise DT9 ....**225** B2
Honeygar La BA6 ....**138** B5
Honeyhall La BS49 ....**34** D2
Honeyhurst La BS27 ....**109** F8
Honeylands
  Curry Rivel TA10 ....**171** D4
  Portishead BS20 ....**2** C5
Honeymead Bristol BS14 ...**23** C6
  Croscombe BA5 ....**204** B7
Honeypot La TA11 ....**158** C1
Honeysuckle Pl BS24 ....**50** A8
Honeywell La BA3 ....**94** F4
Honiton ⑨ BS22 ....**32** A2
Honiton Rd Clevedon BS21 ..**6** E1
  Taunton TA3 ....**168** D1
Hood Cl BA6 ....**206** E3
Hook Hill BA2 ....**60** D2
Hook La
  Hinton Blewett BA3, BS39 ..**75** E4
  Holton BA9 ....**176** C5

Hookedmead La BS26 ....**88** A1
Hooks Batch BS40 ....**54** C4
Hookway Hill TA24 ....**123** A3
Hooper Ave BA5 ....**112** E1
Hooper Cl
  Burnham-On-Sea TA8 ....**104** D5
  Highbridge TA9 ....**104** D4
Hooper Rd Bristol BS14 .....**23** D5
  Bristol BS4 ....**207** B5
Hooper's Cl TA1 ....**212** B2
Hooper's La
  Bridgwater TA7 ....**154** E3
  East Coker BA22 ....**197** F7
Hoopers Barton ⑨
  BA11 ....**119** E4
Hoopers Cross EX16 ....**164** D3
Hopcott Cl TA24 ....**200** E6
Hopcott Rd TA24 ....**200** F5
Hopcott Terr TA24 ....**201** A5
Hope Cl BA5 ....**203** B4
Hope Corner Cl TA2 ....**212** E8
Hope Corner La TA2 ....**212** F8
Hope Cotts TA9 ....**104** D3
Hope Cross SP8 ....**177** D3
Hope Ct BS1 ....**226** B1
Hope Sq BS8 ....**11** F6
Hope Terr BS3 ....**78** B1
Hopechapel Hill ⑯ BS8 ....**11** F6
Hopewell Gdns BS11 ....**4** F7
Hopkins La BA22 ....**173** E6
Hopkins St BS23 ....**48** E8
Hopton Ct BA4 ....**141** E1
Horesham Gr BS13 ....**22** C5
Horfield Rd BS2 ....**227** A4
Horn La TA20 ....**194** B2
Horn St BA11 ....**143** B8
Horn's La BS26 ....**70** B2
Hornbeam Cl
  Bridgwater TA6 ....**209** D5
  Frome BA11 ....**120** C6
  Taunton TA1 ....**213** D2
Hornbeam Wlk BS31 ....**24** C3
Horne Cl BA3 ....**96** F1
Horner Nature Trails★
  TA24 ....**129** E6
Horner Rd BA2 ....**213** B7
Horningsham Prim Sch
  BA12 ....**144** D4
Horns La BA4 ....**160** B2
Hornsbury Hill TA20 ....**223** E8
Hornsbury Mill Mus★
  TA20 ....**223** E8
Hornsey La TA20 ....**182** B1
Hornswell DT9 ....**189** D4
Horrington Prim Sch
  BA5 ....**113** B3
Horse Cl BA11 ....**101** D5
Horse La DT9 ....**176** A2
Horse Mill Cross DT6 ......**199** D3
Horse Pond TA6 ....**208** F4
Horse Race La BS8 ....**10** C6
Horsecastle Cl BS49 ....**17** A1
Horsecastle Farm Rd
  BS49 ....**17** A1
Horsecastles DT9 ....**225** D3
Horsecastles La DT9 ....**225** C3
Horsecombe Brow BA2 ......**45** A1
Horsecombe Gr BA2 ....**45** A1
Horsecombe Vale BA2 ....**45** A1
Horsecroft La BA3 ....**117** D5
Horsefair The BS1 ....**227** B3
Horsham La TA5 ....**134** E8
Horsehill La BA4 ....**142** D2
Horseland La TA24 ....**131** A5
Horseleaze La BS25 ....**52** D1
Horsepark La TA24 ....**130** A4
Horsepool Rd BS13 ....**21** E3
Horseshoe Cotts TA12 ....**185** E7
Horseshoe Dr BA2 ....**62** A8
Horseshoe La TA20 ....**199** A6
Horseshoe Wlk BA2 ....**45** B5
Horsey La
  Bridgwater TA7 ....**136** C2
  Langport TA10 ....**172** B4
  Yeovil BA20 ....**219** A4
Horsey Rdbt BA20 ....**219** A3
Horsington CE Prim Sch
  BA8 ....**176** E2
Hortmead La TA19 ....**183** E3
Horton Cl BA21 ....**218** D6
Horton Ho BA22 ....**218** A5
Horton St Bristol BS2 ......**227** C3
  Frome BA11 ....**119** F5
Horton Way TA7 ....**136** E4
Horts Rd TA1 ....**212** C1
Horwood Rd BS48 ....**8** F1
Hosey Wlk BS13 ....**22** A5
Hoskins Cl TA10 ....**171** E4
Hospital La
  Sherborne DT9 ....**225** D4
  South Petherton TA13 ......**220** D5
Hospital Rdbt BA20 ....**219** A5
Host St BS1 ....**227** A3
Hot Bath St ⑥ BA1 ....**228** B2
Hotwell Rd BS8 ....**226** A2
Hotwells Prim Sch BS8 ....**11** F6
Hotwells Rd BS26 ....**70** B1
Houlton St BS2 ....**227** C4
Hound St DT9 ....**225** D4
Houndmill BA8 ....**176** E2
Houndsmoor La TA4 ....**167** A4
Houndstone Bsns Pk
Houndstone Cl BA21 ....**218** C5
Houndstone Cnr BA22 .....**218** A5
Houndstone Ct BA22 ....**218** A5

Houndstone Mobile Home Pk
  BA22 ....**218** A5
Houndstone Ret Pk
  BA22 ....**218** B5
Houndwood Cl BA16 ....**207** A6
Houndwood Dro BA16 .....**207** A6
House Gate Rd BA11 ....**143** F2
House's La TA20 ....**193** F1
Housman Rd BA16 ....**207** D5
Houston Way BA11 ....**119** D5
Hoveland Cres TA1 ....**212** D2
Hoveland Ct TA1 ....**212** E2
Hoveland Dr TA1 ....**212** D1
Hoveland La TA1 ....**212** C2
How Hill BA2 ....**44** A6
Howard Cl
  Burnham-On-Sea TA8 ....**104** C7
  Saltford BS31 ....**25** D3
Howard Rd
  Wellington TA21 ....**222** D7
  Yeovil BA21 ....**219** E6
Howards Row TA20 ....**223** C4
Howecroft Gdns BS9 ....**5** E4
Howell Hill BA22 ....**174** D4
Howell's La TA2 ....**153** D1
Hownel La TA21 ....**147** F2
Hoyles Rd TA21 ....**222** E4
Hozzard La BS28 ....**107** E2
Huckeymead La BA4 ....**158** F7
Hudson St TA8 ....**104** B6
Hudson Way TA2 ....**212** C6
Huett Cl TA8 ....**65** F3
Hugdole La TA7 ....**137** D2
Hugh Littleton CE Prim Sch
  BS39 ....**59** C1
Hugh Sexey CE Mid Sch
  BS28 ....**107** E3
Hughenden Rd BS23 ....**49** A8
Hughes Cl ③ TA6 ....**209** B4
Hughes Ct BA11 ....**101** E8
Hugo St TA1 ....**213** A4
Huish Ball Steep TA24 ....**129** E8
Huish Cl Highbridge TA9 ..**104** D4
  Taunton TA1 ....**213** D4
Huish Cleeve TA4 ....**165** E7
Huish Ct BA3 ....**79** B2
Huish Episcopi Prim Sch
  TA10 ....**172** A5
Huish Episcopi Sec Sch
  TA10 ....**172** A5
Huish Gdns BA20 ....**219** A5
Huish La Alweston DT9 .....**189** B2
  Bruton BA10 ....**215** E5
  Huish Prim Sch BA20 ....**219** A5
Huish Rd TA11 ....**173** C7
Hukeleyhead Cross
  EX16 ....**164** D3
Hulk Moor Dro
  Glastonbury BA6,BA16 .....**206** A2
  Street BA16 ....**207** B8
Hulkshay La TA6 ....**153** E3
Hull La DT9,BA8 ....**176** B3
Humber Gr TA1 ....**213** D3
Humberstam Wlk BS11 ......**4** E8
Humphreys Rd TA21 ....**222** E7
Humphry Davy Way ⑥
  BS8 ....**11** F5
Humpy La DT9 ....**189** A1
Hundredstone Cl BA21 ....**219** B8
Hundry La TA10 ....**184** C8
Hung Rd BS11 ....**4** A5
Hungerford Cl BS4 ....**23** E8
Hungerford Gdns BS4 ....**23** E8
Hungerford Rd Bath BA1 ..**44** C7
  Bristol BS4 ....**23** E8
Hungerford Terr BA2 ....**62** D1
Hunstrete Rd BA2 ....**58** F7
Hunt's La BS49 ....**34** E8
Huntash La TA4 ....**167** A4
Huntenhull La BA13 ....**121** D4
Hunter's Wlk EX15 ....**179** E1
Hunter's Way EX15 ....**179** E1
Huntham Cl TA3 ....**170** E6
Huntham Ct TA3 ....**170** E6
Huntham La TA3 ....**170** E6
Huntingham Rd BS13 ....**21** F4
Huntley Cl BS13 ....**22** A4
Huntley La BA22 ....**9** A1
Huntley La
  Chardstock EX13 ....**198** A8
  Tatworth EX13,TA20 ....**193** D1
Hunts La TA5 ....**133** D5
Hunts Mead DT9 ....**225** B2
Huntsmans Ridge BS27 ....**90** C7
Huntspill Rd TA9 ....**104** D2
Huntworth Bsns Pk TA6 ..**154** E5
Huntworth La
  Bridgwater TA7 ....**154** C5
  North Petherton TA6 ....**153** F4
Hurcott Cross TA19 ....**183** C6
Hurcott La TA19 ....**183** C6
Hurd's Bldgs BA11 ....**119** F4
Hurdle Way TA1 ....**213** A3
Hurley La TA4 ....**151** E8
Hurlstone Pk TA24 ....**124** A8
Hurmans Cl TA7 ....**156** B8
Hurn Dro BA5 ....**139** B6
Hurn La Berrow TA8 ....**84** F7
  Keynsham BS31 ....**25** A3
  Pitcombe BA7 ....**215** A1
  Shepton Montague BA7 ....**160** A2
Hurn Rd BS21 ....**6** C4
Hursley Hill Bristol BS14 ...**40** D8
  Whitchurch BS14 ....**23** D1
Hursley La BS14 ....**23** E1
Hurst TA12 ....**185** D5

Hurst Dro
  Compton Dundon TA11 ....**157** A3
  Hambridge TA10,TA12 .....**184** C8
Hurst Mews TA12 ....**185** D5
Hurst Pk TA12 ....**185** D5
Hurst Rd Bristol BS4 ....**22** F8
  Weston-Super-Mare BS23 ..**49** A6
Hurst Wlk BS4 ....**22** F8
Hurston Rd BS4 ....**22** D7
Hussey's DT10 ....**190** F5
Hutchin's La BA10 ....**160** F8
Hutchings's La TA4 ....**167** D4
Hutton CE Prim Sch
  BS24 ....**49** E2
Hutton Cl Bristol BS9 ....**5** E7
  Keynsham BS31 ....**25** A5
Hutton Hill BS24 ....**49** F2
Hutton Moor La BS22, ...
Hutton Moor Rd BS22 ......**49** C7
Huxham La BA4 ....**158** F7
Hyacinth Terr TA21 ....**222** C5
Hyatt Pl BA4 ....**204** F5
Hyatts Wood Rd BS48 ......**19** F1
Hyde Ct BA21 ....**218** C6
Hyde La
  Monkton Heathfield TA2 ...**213** F6
  Taunton TA2 ....**213** F6
Hyde Gate Colla TA12 .....**169** C5
Hyde Park Ave ⑧ TA6 .....**153** E3
Hyde Pk TA6 ....**153** E3
Hyde Rd Minehead TA24 ..**200** E6
  Montacute TA15 ....**186** B4
Hyde The Clevedon BS21 ..**16** C8
  Keynsham BS31 ....**25** A5
Hyde's La SN14 ....**13** A6
Hyland Gr BS9 ....**5** F8
Hylton Cl TA1 ....**212** F8
Hylton La BA4 ....**141** E1
Hynicombe La TA4 ....**165** D6
Hythe La BS27 ....**89** E5

I

Iberry La TA3 ....**183** E8
Idwal Cl BA2 ....**79** C8
Iford Cl BS31 ....**25** E3
Iford Hill BA15 ....**64** E2
Iford La BA15,BA15 ....**64** C3
Ilchester Com Prim Sch (Inf)
  BA22 ....**173** E2
Ilchester Com Prim Sch (Jun)
  BA22 ....**173** E2
Ilchester Cres BS13 ....**22** B8
Ilchester La TA10 ....**172** F1
Ilchester Mead BA22 ....**173** D1
Ilchester Mus★ BA22 ......**173** E2
Ilchester Rd Bristol BS13 ..**22** B8
  Charlton Mackrell TA11 ....**173** C8
  Chilthorne Domer BA21, ...
  BA22 ....**186** F6
  Yeovil BA21 ....**218** F8
Ile Ct TA19 ....**221** C4
Ilex Ave BS21 ....**6** E3
Ilex Cl Bristol BS13 ....**21** F6
  West Huntspill TA9 ....**136** A8
Ilex La BS25 ....**51** F1
Ilford Cl TA1 ....**212** C2
Illustrious Cres BA22 ......**173** E2
Ilminster Cl Clevedon BS21 ..6 E2
  Nailsea BS48 ....**9** A2
Ilminster La BA20 ....**218** F1
Ilminster Rd BA21 ....**219** C6
Ilton Bsns Pk TA19 ....**183** F5
Ilton Fst Sch TA19 ....**183** E4
Imber Court Cl BS14 ....**23** B8
Immenstadt Dr TA1 ....**212** A4
Imperial Rd BS14 ....**23** C8
Improvement Pl ⑧
  TA21 ....**222** D5
Incline The TA19 ....**221** B3
Inclosures The BS24 ....**49** A1
Ingleside BS13 ....**198** A1
Ingleton Dr BS22 ....**32** A4
Ingrams Mdw TA20 ....**202** E4
Inman Ho BA1 ....**228** C4
Inn Cotts BS11 ....**5** A7
Inner Circ TA1 ....**213** D5
Inner Elm Terr BA3 ....**78** C1
Inner Gullands TA1 ....**212** B4
Innicks Cl BS40 ....**55** D1
Innox Gdns BS13 ....**22** A5
Innox Gr BA2 ....**43** F2
Innox Hill BA11 ....**119** E5
Innox La BA1 ....**28** A5
Innox Rd BA2 ....**44** B5
Inns Court Ave BS4 ....**22** D7
Inns Court Dr BS4 ....**22** D7
Insmead La TA7 ....**137** B1
Instow ⑦ BS22 ....**32** A2
Instow Rd BS4 ....**23** D8
Instow Wlk BS4 ....**23** D8
International Coll Sherborne
  Sch DT9 ....**225** E4
International Helicopter
  Mus★ BS24 ....**49** E5
Inverness Rd BA2 ....**44** C6
Inwood Rd TA6 ....**209** D7
Irene Cl TA6 ....**209** D7
Ireson Cl BA9 ....**216** C3
Ireson La BA9 ....**216** D4
Irnham Rd TA24 ....**201** A7
Iron Dish La TA13 ....**184** E6
Iron Mill La BA11 ....**101** A1

Iron Post TA22 ....**163** B5
Ironmould La BS31 ....**24** A8
Irvine Cl TA2 ....**212** C6
Irving Cl BS21 ....**6** F3
Irving Ho BS1 ....**226** C3
Irving Rd TA1 ....**158** A1
Irwell Gn TA1 ....**213** D4
Isaacs Cl BA16 ....**207** B4
Island The BA3 ....**78** A1
Islemoor Dro TA3 ....**184** A8
Islemoor La TA13 ....**220** B6
Islemoor Rd TA3 ....**183** F8
Isleport Bsns Pk TA9 ....**104** F4
Isleport Rd TA9 ....**104** F3
Isles La East Coker BA22 ..**197** C6
  East Coker BA22 ....**197** D6
Ivel Ct BA21 ....**219** C5
Ivel Gdns BA22 ....**173** E1
Ivel Sq BA20 ....**219** A5
Ivelway TA18 ....**224** C5
Ivo Peters Rd BA2 ....**228** A2
Ivors Way TA6 ....**153** E4
Ivy Ave BA2 ....**44** C4
Ivy Bank Pk BA2 ....**44** F2
Ivy Cl BS48 ....**21** D2
Ivy Cross TA21 ....**179** D7
Ivy Gn TA20 ....**223** C3
Ivy Gn TA20 ....**223** C3
Ivy La Bristol BS16 ....**9** C4
Ivy Grove Cl TA6 ....**209** D7
Ivy Ho TA21 ....**222** C6
Ivy House Cotts BS29 ......**50** D7
Ivy La BS24 ....**50** A8
Ivy Pl BA2 ....**44** C4
Ivy Thorn La BA16 ....**207** A1
Ivy Wlk Banwell BS29 ....**50** E4
  Midsomer Norton BA3 ....**97** B8
  Yeovil BA20 ....**218** E3
Ivybridge ⑧ BS22 ....**32** A2
Ivyleaf Rd TA1 ....**211** C4
Ivythorn Cl BA16 ....**207** C4
Ivythorn Rd BA16 ....**207** C4
Ivywell Rd BS9 ....**5** E3
Iwood La BS40 ....**35** A2

J

Jack White's Gibbet
  BA9 ....**176** B8
Jack's Dro BS28 ....**137** F8
Jack's La Croscombe BA5 ..**204** C7
  Frome BA11 ....**119** D7
Jackson's La TA5 ....**134** A2
Jacob St Bristol BS2 ....**227** B3
  Bristol BS2 ....**227** C3
Jacob's Cl BS1 ....**226** C2
Jacob's Wells Rd BS8 ......**226** B2
Jacobs Cl BA6 ....**206** E5
Jacobs Mdw BS20 ....**2** F4
Jagaar Ct TA7 ....**137** D5
Jamaica St BS2 ....**227** B4
James Cl Holcombe BA3 ...**116** C8
  Shepton Mallet BA4 ....**205** C4
James La EX14 ....**192** F2
James Lane Cross EX13 ..**193** A1
James St BS5 ....**227** C4
James St W BA1 ....**228** B2
James's Hill BA10 ....**161** A8
Janson Cl TA6 ....**209** D6
Japonica Cl TA6 ....**209** C5
Jarman Way TA20 ....**223** D6
Jarmany Hill BA6 ....**157** F3
Jarmyns TA1 ....**212** A3
Jarvis Cl DT10 ....**190** B4
Jarvis La TA9 ....**86** A3
Jarvis Way DT10 ....**190** B4
Jasmine Cl
  Crewkerne TA18 ....**224** D7
  Highbridge TA9 ....**104** D4
  Weston-Super-Mare BS22 ..**32** A1
Jasmine La ③ BS23 ....**48** E8
Jasmine La BA49 ....**32** A1
Jasmine Way BS24 ....**32** A1
Jay Cl BA11 ....**120** B6
Jaycroft Rd TA8 ....**104** B6
Jeffreys' Way TA1 ....**212** A2
Jeffries Cl TA19 ....**183** C4
Jeffs Way EX13 ....**198** A1
Jellalabad Ct TA1 ....**212** E3
Jellicoe Ct BS22 ....**31** E4
Jena Ct BS31 ....**25** D3
Jesmond Rd Clevedon BS21 ..6 C3
  Weston-Super-Mare BS22 ..**32** C4
Jesse Hughes Ct BA1 ....**28** C2
Jessop Underpass BS3 .....**11** F4
Jessop Underpass BS3 .....**11** F4
Jews La Bath BA2 ....**45** B4
  Churchill BS25 ....**52** F4
  Wiveliscombe TA4 ....**210** B5
Jill's Cl BA4 ....**142** A6
Jim O'Neil Ho BS11 ....**4** F7
Jocelin Dr BS22 ....**31** F4
Jocelin Rd BA5 ....**206** F5
Jocelyn Dr BA5 ....**203** B3
John Beales Hill BA4 ....**140** F3
John Cabot Ct BS1 ....**226** B1
John Carr's Terr BS8 ....**226** B3
John Cozens Ho ⑥ BS2 ...**227** C3
John Grinter Way TA21 ...**222** D4
John Gunn Cl TA20 ....**223** C5
John Slessor Ct BA1 ....**228** B4
John St Bath BA1 ....**228** B3
  Bristol BS1 ....**227** A3
  Burnham-On-Sea TA8 ....**104** B6
  Highbridge TA9 ....**104** D3
John St S TA8 ....**104** B6

John Wesleys Chapel
BS1 ....227 B3
Johnson Cl East Brent TA9 .86 D5
Wells BA5 ....203 F5
Johnson Flats BA21 ......219 C7
Johnson's Ctyd DT9 ....225 D3
Johnstone St BA2 ....228 C2
Joles La BA11 ....120 F1
Jones Cl BS49 ....17 A1
Joselin Ct DT9 ....225 D5
Joy Hill BS8 ....11 F6
Juan's La SP8 ....177 E1
Jubilee Cl
  Bridgwater TA6 ....209 C4
  Castle Cary BA7 ....214 C6
Jubilee Dr BS8 ....10 B4
Jubilee Gdns
  Milverton TA4 ....167 A4
  South Petherton TA13 ..220 C4
Jubilee La BS40 ....53 A6
Jubilee Pl Bristol BS1 ...227 A1
  Clevedon BS21 ....6 D1
  Yeovil BA21 ....218 D5
Jubilee Rd Axbridge BS26 ..70 C2
  Radstock BA3 ....78 D1
  Street BA16 ....207 C4
  Weston-Super-Mare BS23 ..48 E7
Jubilee St Bristol BS2 ....227 C2
  Burnham-On-Sea TA8 ..104 B6
  Taunton TA2 ....212 E6
Jubilee Terr Frome BA11 ..119 E5
  Hemington BA3 ....99 C6
  Paulton BS39 ....77 E6
Judy's Orch TA7 ....154 F5
Julian Cl Bristol BS9 ....5 E3
  Shepton Mallet BA4 ....205 C4
Julian Ct BS9 ....5 E3
Julian Rd Bath BA1 ......228 B3
  Bristol BS9 ....5 E3
Julian's Acres TA8 ....84 F4
Julier Ho BA1 ....228 C4
Junction Ave BA2 ....228 A1
Junction Dro TA3 ....170 C2
Junction Rd BA2 ....228 A1
Juniper Cl
  Bridgwater TA6 ....209 E4
  Yeovil BA20 ....218 F3
Juniper Pl BS22 ....31 F4
Juniper Rd TA1 ....213 C2
Jurston La
  Wellington TA21 ....222 E6
  Wellington TA21 ....222 F5
Jury Cross TA22 ....163 E6
Jury Hill TA22 ....163 E6
Jury Rd TA22 ....163 E6
Justice Ave BS31 ....25 E3
Justice La BA11 ....119 F5

Kale St BA4 ....142 D2
Kale Street Cotts BA4 ...142 D2
Karen Cl BS48 ....19 A4
Karen Dr BS48 ....19 A5
Kaynton Mead BA1 ....44 A7
Keats Ho B BS23 ....48 F4
Keats Rd Radstock BA3 ...97 C8
  Taunton TA1 ....213 C3
Kebby's Farm Cl TA4 ....202 E3
Keble Ave BS13 ....21 F5
Keeds La BS41 ....10 F1
Keedwell Hill BS41 ....10 F1
Keel's Hill BA2 ....79 C8
Keen's Elm La BA16 ......207 E4
Keene's Way BS21 ....6 C2
Keens Cl BA16 ....207 D5
Keens La TA7 ....155 C2
Keep St BA22 ....174 D3
Keep The BS22 ....32 A3
Keinton Mandeville Prim Sch
  TA11 ....158 A1
Kellways BS48 ....19 A4
Kelso Pl BA1 ....44 D7
Kelso Villas BA1 ....44 D7
Kelson's La BS28 ....108 B3
Kelston Cl BS31 ....25 D4
Kelston Gdns BS22 ....32 B5
Kelston Rd Bath BA1 ......26 C1
  Keynsham BS31 ....24 D5
Kelston View BA2 ....44 A5
Kelting Gr BS21 ....6 E2
Keltings TA6 ....208 C6
Kelway Rd TA21 ....222 E7
Kember's Hill BA22,DT9 .175 C3
Kemble Cl BS48 ....9 A1
Kemble Gdns BS11 ....4 F5
Kemm Cl BS27 ....90 B6
Kemp's La BA11 ....120 F7
Kempe's Cl BS41 ....11 A2
Kemps La TA24 ....147 B7
Kemps Way TA22 ....163 D6
Ken Cl Chard TA20 ....223 D3
  Wells BA5 ....140 C8
Kencot Wlk BS13 ....22 B3
Kendal Rd TA8 ....208 E6
Kendall Cl TA3 ....169 C2
Kendrick Ct BA5 ....203 D4
Kenilworth Cl BS31 ....24 D4
Kenilworth Ct BA1 ....45 B8
Kenmare Rd BS4 ....22 E8
Kenmeade Cl BS25 ....70 E8
Kenmore Dr BA21 ....219 B6
Kenn Cl BS23 ....49 A5
Kenn Moor Dr BS21 ....6 E1
Kenn Moor Rd BS49 ......17 B1

Kenn Rd BS21 ....16 F6
Kenn St BS21 ....16 F7
Kennard Cl BA6 ....206 F3
Kennard Moor Dro
  Butleigh BA6 ....157 E2
  Glastonbury BA6 ....206 F1
Kennaway Rd BS21 ....6 E2
Kennedy Cl TA9 ....104 E4
Kennel Batch BA5 ....111 D4
Kennel La
  Compton Bishop BS26 ....68 E3
  East Pennard BA4 ....158 F8
  Langport TA10 ....172 A6
  West Bagborough TA4 ..151 D4
Kennel Lodge Rd BS3 ....11 E4
Kennet Gr TA1 ....213 D4
Kennet Ho B BA1 ....228 B2
Kennet Pk BA2 ....28 E1
Kennford TA4 ....220 C4
Kennford B BS22 ....31 F2
Kennington Rd BA1 ....44 B7
Kennion Cl TA20 ....223 D3
Kennion Rd BA5 ....203 C5
Kenmore Rd BS21 ....17 A6
Kensington Ct Bath BA1 ..28 B2
  Bristol BS8 ....226 A3
Kensington Fields BA14 ..83 F7
Kensington Gdns
  Bath BA1 ....28 B1
  Bridgwater TA6 ....209 D6
Kensington Gr TA24 .....200 E6
Kensington Pl Bath BA1 ..28 B1
  Bristol BS8 ....226 A3
Kensington Rd BS23 ....48 F5
Kent Ave TA6 ....209 A2
Kent La Shapwick TA7 ...137 F1
  Shepton Mallet BA4 ....205 A5
Kent Rd Congresbury BS49 ..34 D5
  Tatworth TA20 ....198 D8
Kent St BS27 ....71 B1
Kent Way BS22 ....32 B4
Kent's Bglws TA20 ....198 D8
Kent's Cotts TA20 ....198 D8
Kent's Orch TA20 ....198 D8
Kentisworth Rd DT10 ..190 F5
Kents Cl TA20 ....198 C8
Kents La TA20 ....198 D8
Kentshare La BS40 ....38 B6
Kenwyn Cl TA1 ....213 D3
Keppel Cl BS31 ....25 D2
Kerry Croft BA11 ....143 C3
Kersham La BA4 ....130 A1
Kestrel Cl TA6 ....209 C3
Kestrel Dr BS22 ....31 E1
Kew Rd BS23 ....30 E1
Kew Wlk BS4 ....23 C8
Keward Ave BA5 ....203 B3
Keward Cl BA5 ....203 B3
Keward Hill Trad Est
  BA5 ....203 B2
Kewside BS22 ....31 B4
Kewstoke Prim Sch BS22 .31 B3
Kewstoke Rd Bath BA2 ..45 A2
  Bristol BS9 ....5 E4
  Weston-Super-Mare BS22 .31 C3
Key Hill BA22 ....197 E8
Keyes Path BS22 ....31 F4
Keyford Cotts B BA11 ..119 F4
Keyford Ct BA11 ....119 F2
Keyford Field Cotts
  BA11 ....119 F2
Keyford Gdns BA11 ......119 F3
Keyford Pl BA11 ....119 F4
Keyford Rdbt BA22 ....197 E8
Keyford Terr BA11 ....119 F3
Keyhaven Bglws BS22 ....31 B4
Keynsham By-Pass BS31 ..24 E7
Keynsham Hosp BA1 ....44 C6
Keynsham Prim Sch
  BS31 ....24 D5
Keynsham Rd BS30,BS31 ..25 A8
Keynsham Sta BS31 ....24 F6
Keyton Hill BS28 ....107 E2
Keyward Wlk BA5 ....203 C3
Kicks Hill TA7 ....155 B3
Kicks Hill La TA7 ....155 B4
Kid Gate Dro TA9,BS28 .137 D8
Kidd's La BA4 ....205 D6
Kidder Bank BA5 ....203 F5
Kiddles BA21 ....219 C5
Kidsbury Rd TA6 ....208 E5
Kielder Dr BS22 ....31 F3
Kilbirnie Rd BS14 ....23 A3
Kilburn Dr TA6 ....209 D6
Kildare Cl BA21 ....45 B7
Kildare Gdns TA24 ....200 F6
Kildare Rd BS13 ....22 D8
Kilkenny Ave B TA2 .....212 F6
Kilkenny Ct TA2 ....212 F6
Kilkenny La Bath BA2 .....62 B8
  Wraxall BA4 ....159 A6
Kilkenny St BS2 ....227 C2
Killams Ave
  Staplehay TA3 ....181 F8
  Taunton TA1 ....168 F1
Killams Cl TA1 ....168 F1
Killams Cres TA1 ....168 F1
Killams Dr TA1 ....168 F1
Killams Gn TA1 ....168 F1
Killams La TA1 ....168 F1
Killarney Ave TA8 ....104 C6
Killick Way TA4 ....202 D3
Kilmersdon CE Prim Sch
  BA3 ....98 A6
Kilmersdon Hill BA3 ......98 A5
Kilmersdon Rd
  Bristol BS13 ....22 B4
Kilmersdon Rd continued
  Radstock BA3 ....97 E8
Kilmington CE Fst Sch
  BA12 ....161 F7
Kilminster Rd BS11 ....4 D7
Kilmorie Cl TA1 ....212 C2
Kiln Cl TA5 ....135 B5
Kiln Dr Evercreech BA4 ..141 E1
  Highbridge TA9 ....104 D3
Kiln Pk BS23 ....49 A6
Kilton Cross TA5 ....133 E5
Kilton St BA4 ....49 A2
Kilve Cl TA2 ....212 F7
Kilve Cres TA2 ....212 F7
Kilve Ct TA5 ....133 C5
Kilver St BA4 ....205 D6
Kilver Street Hill BA4 ...205 D7
Kimber Cl TA9 ....104 D3
Kimberley Rd BS21 ....6 C2
Kimberley Terr TA6 ......209 B7
Kinber Cl BA15 ....27 A3
Kinder Cl TA7 ....136 E4
Kinforde TA20 ....223 C5
King Alfred Dr B TA6 ...153 F4
King Alfred Dr TA20 .....223 C2
King Alfred Sch The
  TA9 ....104 C5
King Alfred Way BA15 ....64 D7
King Alfreds Way BS28 .108 B4
King Arthur Dr BA21 .....218 D7
King Arthurs Com Sch
  BA9 ....216 A4
King Athelstan Dr TA20 .223 D2
King Ceol Cl TA20 ....223 D2
King Cerdic Cl TA20 .....223 D2
King Cuthred Cl TA20 ..223 D2
King Cuthred Dr TA20 ..223 C2
King Edward Cl BS14 ....23 A6
King Edward Rd Bath BA2 ..44 D4
  Minehead TA24 ....201 A6
King Edward's Jun Sch
  BA2 ....45 C7
King Edward's Senior Sch
  BA2 ....45 C7
King George Ave TA6 ...208 F2
King George Cl TA6 ......209 A2
King George Rd TA24 ...201 A6
King George St B TA2 ..219 B4
King George V Pl B
  BS1 ....227 A2
King George's Rd
  Bath BA2 ....44 C6
  Bristol BS13 ....21 F5
King Ina Rd TA11 ....211 D4
King Ine Cl N TA20 ....223 D2
King Ine Cl S TA20 ....223 C2
King La BS39 ....58 F4
King Rd BS49 ....52 E6
King Sq Bridgwater TA6 ..208 F5
King Square Ave BS2 ...227 A4
King St Bridgwater TA6 ..209 A5
  Bristol BS1 ....227 A2
  Frome BA11 ....119 F5
  Glastonbury BA6 ....206 D3
  Highbridge TA9 ....104 D3
  Yeovil BA21 ....219 B6
King William Ave BS1 ...227 A2
King William Rd TA7 ....137 D2
King's Castle Rd BA5 ....112 F1
King's Cnr TA22 ....163 D6
King's Coll TA1 ....213 B2
King's Head La BS13 ......21 F7
King's Hill BA3 ....94 F7
King's La Binegar BA3 ....95 E1
King's Rd Clevedon BS21 ..6 D5
  Weston-Super-Mare
  BS23 ....48 E8
King's Mill Rd DT10 ......190 D3
King's Pl TA6 ....208 F5
King's Rd Bristol BS8 ...226 A3
  Clevedon BS21 ....6 D5
  Doulting BA4 ....141 E7
  Portishead BS20 ....1 F4
King's Sch BA10 ....215 E6
Kingdom Barn La BS40 ..37 C5
Kingdom La BA5 ....203 B2
Kingdon Mead TA3 ....169 D4
Kingdown Rd BS40 ....37 C5
Kingfisher Cl TA6 ....209 C3
Kingfisher Ct BA3 ....64 C6
Kingfisher Dr BA3 ....97 B8
Kingfisher Rd BS22 ....31 F1
Kinghill CE Prim Sch
  BS48 ....8 D3
Kinglake Villas TA6 ......209 A2
Kings Castle Bsns Cent
  TA9 ....209 A6
Kings Cl
  Shepton Mallet BA4 ....205 B5
  Taunton TA1 ....212 D3
Kings Cres TA9 ....225 D5
Kings Ct Bath BA1 ....228 B2
  Bristol BS1 ....227 A2
Kings Dr TA7 ....154 F5
Kings Gn TA24 ....200 F7
Kingsettle Hill BA10 .....161 B5
Kingsfield BA2 ....44 C3
Kingsford Gate Cross
  TA24 ....145 B7
Kingsford Hill TA24 .....145 C7
Kingshams BA22 ....173 E1
Kingshill BS48 ....8 C2
Kingshill Gdns BS48 ....8 C1
Kingshill La BS40 ....56 C4
Kingsholme Ct BS23 ......30 E1
Kingsland TA23 ....202 D7
Kingsland Grange BA21 .218 C6
Kingsland La TA24 ....148 D5
Kingsley Cl TA1 ....212 C1
Kingsley Ho BS2 ....227 C2
Kingsland Trad Est BS2 .227 C3
Kingsmead TA24 ....48 F3
Kingsmead Ct B BA1 ....228 B2
Kingsmead Ho B BA1 ...228 B2
Kingsmead N BA1 ....228 B2
Kingsmead Sq BA1 ......228 B2
Kingsmead St BA1 ....228 B2
Kingsmead W BA1 ....228 B2
Kingsmill BS9 ....5 D5
Kingsmoor Prim Sch
  TA7 ....136 E2
Kingston Bath BA1 ....28 C8
Kingston Ave
  Clevedon BS21 ....6 D1
  Saltford BS31 ....25 C3
Kingston Dr BS48 ....18 C8
Kingston La Felton BS40 .37 F8
  Maiden Bradley BA12 ...144 C1
Kingston Mead BS40 ......37 F7
Kingston Rd Bath BA1 ...228 C2
  Nailsea BS48 ....18 C8
  Taunton TA2 ....213 A5
Kingston St Mary CE Prim
  Sch TA2 ....168 D8
Kingston View BA21 .....218 C6
Long Sutton TA10 ....172 F4
Kingston Well La TA20 ..194 C2
Kingstone Cross TA19 ..221 E1
Kingstone Hill TA19 .....221 F2
Kingsway Bath BA2 ....44 C3
Kingsway Ctr BA21 ......219 B6
Kingswood Chase BA14 ..83 F6
Kingswood Day Prep Sch
  BA1 ....27 E1
Kingswood Rd TA18 .....224 C4
Kingswood Sch BA1 ....27 E2
Kingswood View BA14 ..83 F6
Kingwell BS39 ....59 D2
Kingweston Rd
  Butleigh BA6 ....157 E3
  Charlton Mackrell TA11 ..173 E8
Kinsale Rd BS14 ....23 C7
Kinvara Rd BS4 ....22 D8
Kinver Terr TA8 ....104 A7
Kipling Ave BA2 ....44 F4
Kipling Rd Radstock BA3 .78 C1
  Weston-Super-Mare BS23 .49 A3
Kippax Ave BA5 ....203 D4
Kirby Cl TA6 ....209 D4
Kirkchurch Cross EX35 .122 A6
Kirk Dr TA7 ....154 E6
Kirke Gr TA2 ....213 B8
Kirkham St SI TA1 ....213 E4
Kirlegate BA6 ....138 C4
Kirtlington Rd BS5 ....64 A8
Kit's La TA4 ....166 A6
Kitchener Rd TA2 ....168 A6
Kitchens La TA13 ....220 C6
Kite La BA4 ....159 C6
Kite's Nest La SP8 ....161 F1
Kites Croft BA5 ....111 D7
Kithill TA19 ....221 A4
Kitley Hill BA3 ....78 C1
Kitridge La TA24 ....146 B7
Kitrow La TA24 ....130 D5
Kitswall La TA24 ....130 D5
Kitt Hill DT9 ....225 C4
Kings Sq BS30 ....25 D8
Kings Weston Ave BS11 ..4 E8
Kings Weston La BS11 ....5 A8
Kings Weston Rd BS9 .....5 B8
Kings Wlk BS13 ....21 E7
Kingsacre BA7 ....214 B5
Kingsbury Episcopi Prim Sch
  TA12 ....185 A6
Kingscliffe Terr TA6 ......209 A2
Kingscombe BA3 ....114 E6
Kingscourt Cl BS14 ....23 A4
Kingsdon CE Prim Sch
  TA11 ....173 D5
Kingsdon Hill TA11 ....173 D5
Kingsdon Manor Sch
  TA11 ....173 D4
Kingsdown TA6 ....209 D6
Kingsdown Gr SN13 ......29 F3
Kingsdown Par BS6 ....227 A4
Kingsdown View B BA1 ..28 A1
Kingsdown Pk BS29 ....69 F8
Knapps La Chard TA20 ..194 C4
Langport TA10 ....172 B5
Knaptons Hill BA11 ......118 C6
Knight Shute La TA20 ....194 C5
Knight's Cross TA21 .....181 A5
Knight's Ct BA11 ....119 F4
Knight's La
  Axminster EX13 ....198 A4
  Higher Chillington TA19 ..194 E5
Knightcott BS29 ....51 D3
Knightcott Gdns BS29 ....50 F3
Knightcott Ind Est BS29 ..50 E3
Knightcott Pk BS29 ....51 A3
Knightcott Rd
  Abbots Leigh BS8 ....10 F8
  Banwell BS29 ....50 F3
Knightlands La TA10 ....172 F4
Knighton Dro TA10 ......184 D7
Knights Cl BS22 ....32 A5
Knights Rd TA21 ....180 D8
Knights Templar CE Meth
  Com Fst Sch TA23 ......202 D6
Knights Yd BA7 ....214 C5
Knightsbridge Pk BS13 ..22 E4
Knightsbridge Way TA6 .209 D6
Knightstone Cswy B
  BS23 ....48 C8
Knightstone Ho
  Burnham-On-Sea TA8 ..104 B6
  Clevedon BS21 ....6 D1
  Standige DT10 ....190 B4
  Taunton TA2 ....213 A6
  Weston-Super-Mare BS23 .30 D1
Knightstone Ho
  B Bristol BS2 ....227 A4
  Weston-Super-Mare BS23 .48 C8
Knightstone Hts BA11 ...119 F3
Knightstone Pk B BS23 ..48 E5
Knightstone Rd BA11 .....27 B1
  B Weston-Super-Mare
  BS23 ....31 F2
Knob Hill BA3 ....23 C5
Knobsbury Hill BA3 ....98 D6
Knobsbury La BA3 ....98 C8
Knole Cswy Knole TA10 ..173 A4
  Long Sutton TA10 ....172 F4
Knole Pit La TA10 ....173 A4
Knoll Ct BS9 ....5 D3
Knoll Green TA5 ....134 F2
Knoll Hill BS9 ....5 D3
Knoll La BA4 ....142 E3
Knoll Pk TA8 ....65 F2
Knoll The BS20 ....2 D7
Knoll View TA8 ....104 C8
Knotcroft La TA2 ....168 D1
Knotts Paddock DT9 .....225 E4
Knowle Cross DT8 ....199 F6
Knowle Dro
  Middlezoy TA7 ....155 A4
  Westonzoyland TA7 ....155 F4
Knowle End TA7 ....136 E3
Knowle La Chard TA20 ..194 B6
  Crewkerne DT8,TA18 ..224 E2
  Dunster TA24 ....201 B1
  Shepton Mallet BA4 ....205 E2
  Wookey BA5 ....110 E1
Knowle Moor Dro BA5 ..110 C2
Knowles Rd BS21 ....6 C2
Knowleyards Rd TA7 ....155 B4
Kuchina Rd BA22 ....174 A2
Kylross Ave BS14 ....23 B5
Kyrle Gdns BA1 ....28 C3
Kyte Rd BA4 ....205 C5
Kitton La DT9 ....188 A4
Kitts TA21 ....222 D4
Knacker's Hole La
  Churchinford TA3 ....192 A6
  Thorncombe DT6,TA20 ..199 C4
Knap Hill BA3 ....117 B2
Knap The BA8 ....176 E1
Knapp TA16 ....195 F7
Knapp Hill Cl BA5 ....113 A2
Knapp La
  Bishops Lydeard TA4 ...151 E1
  North Curry TA3 ....170 B4
Knapp Rd
  Creech St Michael TA3 ..169 F4
  North Curry TA3 ....170 A4
Knapps Cl BS25 ....69 F8
Knapps Dr BS25 ....69 F8

Knowle Dro
La Ciotat Ho BA16 ....209 A4
Labbott The BS31 ....24 E5
Laburnham Dro BS27 .....90 B5
Laburnham Way BS27 ....90 B6
Laburnum Ave TA1 ....213 A4
Laburnum Cl
  Bridgwater TA6 ....209 D4
  Frome BA11 ....120 B7
  Midsomer Norton BA3 ..96 F8
  Somerton TA11 ....211 D4
Laburnum Cres TA18 ....224 D7
Laburnum Gr
  B Taunton TA1 ....213 A4

Laburnum Ct continued
Weston-Super-Mare BS23 ....49 B7
Laburnum Dr TA11 ....211 D4
Laburnum Gr BA3 ....96 F8
Laburnum Lodges TA9 ....136 A8
Laburnum Rd
Wellington TA21 ....222 E5
Weston-Super-Mare BS23 ....49 B7
Laburnum Terr TA3 ....169 D4
Laburnum Way BA20 ....218 D2
Laburnum Wlk BS31 ....24 C3
Lacey Rd BS14 ....23 F6
Ladd Cl TA9 ....104 D3
Ladies Mile BS8 ....5 F1
Ladman Gr BS14 ....23 E6
Ladman Rd BS14 ....23 E5
Lady Harriet Acland's Dr
TA22 ....164 A8
Lady Lawn TA3 ....168 D8
Lady St TA22 ....163 D7
Lady Victoria's Dr TA22 ....163 E6
Ladycroft 4 BS21 ....6 B1
Ladye Bay BS21 ....6 D7
Ladye Wake BS22 ....31 F4
Ladymead BS20 ....2 F5
Ladymead Cl TA6 ....208 B4
Ladymead Com Sch
TA2 ....168 E6
Ladymead La BS40 ....52 F5
Ladymead Rd TA2 ....168 F6
Ladymeade Backwell BS48 ....19 A7
Ilminster TA19 ....221 B3
Ladywell BS40 ....35 D2
Laggan Gdns BA1 ....27 E1
Lagger Hill TA5 ....133 C5
Lahs Pl BA11 ....101 E4
Lake Mews BA22 ....219 B1
Lake Rd BS20 ....2 D7
Lake Wall TA7 ....154 E4
Lakefields BA22 ....197 B8
Lakemead Gdns BS13 ....21 F4
Lakemead Gr BS13 ....21 F6
Lakeside TA9 ....104 E4
Lakeside BS40 ....55 D5
Lakeside Pk BA11 ....117 E8
Lakeview Cres TA9 ....104 E3
Lamb La TA6 ....208 F4
Lamb St BS2 ....227 C3
Lambert Cl DT9 ....217 C2
Lambert Dr DT9 ....217 D2
Lambert La TA19 ....194 F5
Lambert Pl BS4 ....22 D6
Lambert's Hill BA4 ....204 F3
Lamberts Marsh BA14 ....83 E2
Lambourn Rd BS31 ....25 A4
Lambourne Cl TA8 ....224 D7
Lambourne Way BS20 ....2 F5
Lambpark Ct TA3 ....191 F6
Lambridge 6 BA1 ....28 C1
Lambridge Bldgs 5 BA1 ....28 C1
Lambridge Mews 5 BA1 ....28 C1
Lambridge Pl BA1 ....28 C1
Lambridge St BA1 ....28 C1
Lambrook Cl BA14 ....83 F6
Lambrook Ct TA1 ....213 B4
Lambrook Gate TA13 ....184 F5
Lambrook Rd
Shepton Beauchamp TA19 ....184 E4
Taunton TA1 ....213 B4
Lambrook St BA6 ....206 E4
Lambrook Way TA1 ....213 C4
Lambs Field DT9 ....225 E5
Lamont Ho 7 BA1 ....28 C1
Lampard's Bldgs BA1 ....28 B4
Lamparts Way TA19 ....183 C2
Lampley Rd BS21 ....16 D2
Lampreys La TA13 ....220 C3
Lampton Ave BS13 ....22 E3
Lampton Gr BS13 ....22 E3
Lampton Rd BS41 ....10 F1
Lancaster House Sch
BS23 ....48 F8
Lancer Ct TA21 ....222 D6
Lanch La SP8 ....177 F5
Lancock St TA21 ....222 A5
Lancombe La BA10 ....215 C3
Landacre La TA24 ....146 A7
Landemann Cir BS23 ....30 E1
Landemann Path 2
BS23 ....48 E8
Landford Budville CE Prim
Sch TA21 ....166 F1
Landlord's Hill TA21 ....179 E7
Landmead BA6 ....206 D6
Landmoor La TA10 ....172 D4
Landsdown Mews BA11 ....119 D5
Landsdown Pl BA11 ....119 D5
Landsdown View BA3 ....80 D1
Landseer BA8 ....176 E1
Landseer Cl BS22 ....31 F3
Landseer Rd BA2 ....44 B6
Landshire La
Charlton Horethorne DT9 ....176 A1
Chilton Polden TA7 ....137 A3
Henstridge BA8 ....190 C6
Higher Odcombe BA22 ....186 C1
Lane End BA12 ....144 D8
Lane Foot TA24 ....129 D7
Lane Head TA24 ....123 E4
Lanes End Hill BA11,
BA12 ....144 D8
Lanesborough Rise BS14 ....23 D7
Laneys Dro BS24 ....49 E5
Lang Rd TA18 ....224 C4

Lang's Cnr TA19 ....183 B1
Langaller Hill TA22 ....163 D4
Langdon Cl TA20 ....223 D6
Langdon Rd BA2 ....44 B4
Langdons DT9 ....225 E5
Langdons Way TA20 ....198 C8
Langford Gr BS14 ....23 E5
Langer's La TA19 ....194 E5
Langford Cl TA3 ....170 F1
Langford Ct TA1 ....213 A4
Langford Gate TA4 ....166 F2
Langford House Sch of Vet
Science BS40 ....53 B6
Langford La
Fivehead TA3 ....170 F2
Langford Rd BS40 ....53 E5
Norton Fitzwarren TA2 ....168 C6
Langford Rd Bristol BS13 ....21 F8
Weston-Super-Mare BS23 ....49 A6
Langford's La BS39 ....59 D1
Langfords La BS39 ....77 C8
Langham Dr TA1 ....212 C1
Langham Gdns TA1 ....212 C1
Langham La SP8 ....177 F5
Langham Pl BA11 ....82 F1
Langhill Ave BS4 ....22 D7
Langland La TA7 ....137 D2
Langland's La TA9 ....104 B1
Langlands TA14 ....185 F4
Langlands La TA13 ....169 F2
Langley Cres BS31 ....24 C5
Langley Cross TA4 ....210 B6
Langley's La BA3, BS39 ....77 C1
Langleys Cotts BA3 ....96 D7
Langmead Dro
Middlezoy TA7 ....155 A4
Westonzoyland TA7 ....154 F5
Langmead La TA7 ....155 A4
Langmead Pl TA18 ....224 C4
Langmead Rd TA18 ....224 C4
Langmead Sq TA18 ....224 C4
Langmoor La EX13 ....198 D2
Langport Gdns BS48 ....18 E8
Langport Rd
Long Sutton TA10 ....172 E5
Middlezoy TA7 ....155 B4
Somerton TA11 ....211 B4
Weston-Super-Mare BS23 ....48 E5
Langridge La BA1 ....27 D8
Langton Ho 9 BS2 ....227 C3
Langworthy Orch TA19 ....183 C1
Lansdown Cres Bath BA1 ....27 F1
Timsbury BA2 ....60 C2
Lansdown Ct BS23 ....48 F8
Lansdown Gdns BS22 ....32 B5
Lansdown Gr BA1 ....228 B4
Lansdown Grove Ct
BA1 ....228 B4
Lansdown Hts BA1 ....27 F1
Lansdown La Bath BA1 ....27 B4
Upton Cheyney BS30 ....26 D8
Lansdown Mans BA1 ....228 B4
Lansdown Pk BA1 ....27 E3
Lansdown Pl Bristol BS8 ....226 A3
High Littleton BS39 ....59 D1
Lansdown Pl E BA1 ....228 B4
Lansdown Pl W 2 BA1 ....27 F1
Lansdown Pl W Bath BA1 ....27 F1
Bristol BS8 ....226 A3
Saltford BS31 ....25 F3
Lansdown View Bath BA2 ....44 C5
Timsbury BA2 ....60 C2
Lansdowne Rd TA2 ....213 A6
Lapwing Cl BS24 ....50 A8
Lapwing Cl TA24 ....201 C5
Lapwing Gdns BS22 ....31 F1
Larch Ave TA20 ....223 B5
Larch Cl Bridgwater TA6 ....209 D6
Langford BS40 ....53 A5
Nailsea BS48 ....8 F3
Taunton TA1 ....213 D2
Larches The BS22 ....32 A3
Larchfield Cl BA11 ....120 B7
Larchgrove Cres BS22 ....31 F1
Larchgrove Wlk BS22 ....31 F1
Lark Cl BA3 ....97 B8
Lark Pl BA1 ....44 D7
Lark Rd BS22 ....31 F1
Larkhall Pl BA1 ....28 C2
Larkhall Terr BA1 ....28 C2
Larkhill Rd Locking BS24 ....50 B6
Yeovil BA21 ....218 F7
Larks Mdw DT10 ....190 C4
Larkspur Cl TA1 ....213 C1
Larkspur Cres BS21 ....218 D7
Larkspur Cl TA2 ....212 D7
Larviscombe Cl TA4 ....202 D4
Larviscombe Rd TA4 ....202 D4
Lasbury Gr BS13 ....22 D5
Lascot Hill BS28 ....108 C5
Latcham Dro BS27,BS28 ....109 E4
Latches La BS27 ....140 B8
Latham Ct BS13 ....22 A8
Late Broads BA15 ....64 D7
Lauder Cl DT9 ....217 D2
Launcherley Cross BA5 ....140 A6
Launcherley Rd BA4,BA5 ....140 B5
Launder Cl BS48 ....18 E8
Laura Pl BA2 ....228 C3
Laurel Ave TA9 ....86 A2
Laurel Cl
East Coker BA22 ....197 B8
Frome BA11 ....120 B7
Laurel Dr Nailsea BS48 ....8 F2
Paulton BS39 ....77 E5

Laurel Dr continued
Weston-Super-Mare BS23 ....48 E2
Laurel Gdns Chard TA20 ....223 B5
Yatton BS49 ....17 B1
Laurel La BA22 ....174 F3
Laurel St BA6 ....140 A1
Laurel Terr BS49 ....17 B1
Laurels The
Crewkerne TA18 ....224 D7
Wembdon TA6 ....208 C6
Weston-Super-Mare BS23 ....48 E2
Lavender Cl BS22 ....32 A5
Lavender Cl BS22 ....32 A5
Lavender Ct Frome BA11 ....120 B7
Street BA16 ....207 B4
Lavender Rd TA1 ....212 C3
Laver's La BS40 ....198 F5
Laverley Cotts BA6 ....140 C2
Laverock Ct TA1 ....212 E5
Lavers Ct TA12 ....186 A7
Lavers Oak TA12 ....185 E7
Lavington Cl BS21 ....6 B1
Law La Drayton TA10 ....171 F3
Lawford St BS2 ....227 C3
Lawfords Gate BS2 ....227 C3
Lawfords Gate Ho 17
BS2 ....227 C3
Lawn La
Galhampton BA22 ....175 D8
Shapwick TA7 ....137 F1
Lawn Mdw TA3 ....169 D4
Lawn Rd TA2 ....212 C8
Lawns The 1 TA21 ....222 D6
Lawnmoor La TA10 ....184 C6
Lawns The Bristol BS11 ....4 E7
Combe St Nicholas TA20 ....193 D6
Weston-Super-Mare BS22 ....32 B3
Yatton BS49 ....17 A1
Lawnside BS48 ....19 B5
Lawpool Ct BA5 ....203 D4
Lawrence Cl
Burnham-On-Sea TA8 ....104 D5
Highbridge TA9 ....104 D4
Lawrence Hayes BA9 ....216 D3
Lawrence Hill BA9 ....216 D3
Lawrence Hill Bsns Ctr
BA9 ....216 A3
Lawrence Mews BS22 ....31 E2
Lawrence Rd
Coleford BA3 ....116 F7
Weston-Super-Mare BS22 ....31 E2
Wrington BS40 ....35 C2
Lawson Cl
5 Martock TA12 ....185 E6
Saltford BS31 ....25 C2
Lawyer's Hill TA5 ....152 C7
Lax Cl BA5 ....203 B4
Laxton Cl TA1 ....213 D5
Laxton Rd TA1 ....213 E5
Laxton Way BA2 ....79 D7
Laycock Hill DT9 ....217 D7
Layfield La TA3 ....170 C3
Layne Terr TA18 ....196 B8
Lays Bsns Ctr BS31 ....24 C4
Lays Dr BS31 ....24 C5
Lays La BS40 ....54 D4
Lays The BA11 ....101 E5
Lea Cl BA21 ....219 B8
Lea Croft BS13 ....22 A4
Lea Grove Rd BS21 ....6 C4
Leach Cl BS21 ....6 F6
Leach Rd TA20 ....223 D7
Leach's Field TA2 ....168 D8
Leaches Cl BA22 ....186 B6
Leacroft La TA13 ....210 A4
Leafy Way BS24 ....50 B4
Leaholme Gdns BS14 ....23 A3
Leaze House Mews
BA11 ....119 F5
Leaze La Blagdon BS40 ....72 E8
West Chinnock TA18 ....196 B8
Leaze Rd BA11 ....119 D5
Leaze The Radstock BA3 ....78 D1
Rode BA3 ....82 C1
Leazemoor La TA10 ....172 B8
Leazeway Dro TA7 ....155 C3
Lecher La DT8,TA18 ....196 B1
Leda Ave BS14 ....23 A7
Lee Pk TA21 ....180 F7
Leedham Rd BS24 ....50 C5
Leeford La EX35 ....122 B5
Leeming Way BS11 ....4 C8
Leeside BS20 ....2 C4
Leet Ct DT9 ....225 B2
Leeward Cl TA6 ....209 C4
Leewood Rd TA2 ....30 F1
Leg La BS40 ....54 E8
Leg Of Mutton Rd BA6 ....206 D3
Leg Sq BA4 ....205 C6
Leg Square Ct BA4 ....205 C6
Leggar The TA6 ....209 A6
Leggar The TA6 ....209 A6
Legion Rd BA21 ....218 F6
Leigh Cl BA1 ....28 A2
Leigh Court Bsns Ctr BS8 ....5 A2
Leigh Furlong Rd BA16 ....207 B4
Leigh La Cold Ashton BA1 ....13 E8
Crowcombe TA4 ....151 A2
Halstock BA22 ....197 C3
Winford TA22 ....147 C2
Winsham TA20 ....199 A8

Leigh on Mendip Fst Sch
BA3 ....117 A3
Leigh Rd Bristol BS8 ....226 B4
Leigh upon Mendip BA11 ....117 C2
Street BA16 ....207 C5
Leigh View Rd BS20 ....2 E7
Leigh Woods Forest Walks *
BS8 ....5 C1
Leighton Cl BA4 ....141 E1
Leighton Cres BS24 ....67 A8
Leighton La BA4 ....141 E1
Leighton Lane Ind Est
BA4 ....141 E2
Leinster Ave BS4 ....22 D8
Lemon La BS2 ....227 C4
Lenover Gdns BS13 ....22 B4
Lenthay Cl DT9 ....225 C2
Lenthay Ct DT9 ....225 C3
Lenthay Rd DT9 ....225 B3
Leonard Houlden Ct 7
TA2 ....213 A8
Leonard La BS1 ....227 A3
Leonard's Barton BA11 ....119 E6
Leopold Bldgs BA1 ....228 C4
Lerburne The BS28 ....108 C4
Les Rosiers Gdns BA9 ....216 C4
Leslie Ave TA2 ....212 E6
Leslie Rise BA15 ....64 F3
Lester Dr BS22 ....32 A3
Lester La DT9 ....176 A2
Letham Ct TA19 ....221 B4
Lethbridge Pk TA4 ....151 D1
Lethbridge Rd BA5 ....203 C3
Level La DT9 ....176 A2
Level View TA10 ....172 C5
Leversedge Rd BA11 ....120 A7
Lewins Mead BS1 ....227 A3
Lewis Cres BA11 ....119 F6
Lewis St Bristol BS13 ....22 A8
Taunton TA2 ....212 E7
Lewis's Dro TA5 ....138 E7
Lewisham Gr BS23 ....49 A8
Lewmond Ave BA5 ....203 C5
Leycroft Cl TA1 ....213 B4
Leycroft Gr TA1 ....213 B4
Leycroft Rd TA1 ....213 B4
Leyland Wlk BS13 ....21 F4
Leys Hill BA11 ....120 A6
Leys La BA11 ....119 F7
Leystone Cl BA11 ....120 A6
Leyton Dr TA6 ....209 D6
Lias Rd BA16 ....207 B4
Liberty Gdns BS1 ....226 C1
Liberty La BS40 ....54 E2
Liberty Pl TA6 ....209 B4
Liberty The BA5 ....203 E5
Liddon Hill TA18 ....195 C5
Liddymore La
Watchet TA23 ....202 D5
Williton TA4 ....202 E4
Liddymore Rd TA23 ....202 D6
Lightgate La TA13 ....220 D5
Lightgate Rd TA13 ....220 D5
Lilac Cl TA1 ....213 C2
Lilac Ct BS31 ....24 C4
Lilac Terr BA3 ....78 C2
Lilac Way BS22 ....32 A5
Lilian Terr BS39 ....77 E5
Lillebonne Cl TA21 ....222 F6
Lillesdon Terr TA3 ....170 A2
Lillington Cl BA3 ....79 B2
Lillington Rd BA3 ....79 B2
Lillington Way TA20 ....223 C5
Lilly Batch BA11 ....119 F7
Lillycombe La TA3 EX15 ....191 B8
Lillypool Cheese & Cider
**Farm ***BS25 ....70 F6
Lily La BA8 ....176 E4
Limber Gate BA22 ....218 A6
Limbers La BA5 ....139 B8
Limbury B TA12 ....185 E6
Limbury Cotts 3 TA12 ....185 E6
Lime Cl Frome BA11 ....120 B7
Locking BS24 ....50 B4
Minehead TA24 ....201 B5
Street BA16 ....207 C5
Weston-Super-Mare BS22 ....32 A1
Lime Cres TA1 ....213 C2
Lime Gr Bath BA2 ....45 B6
Lime Grove Gdns BA2 ....45 B6
Lime Grove Sch BA2 ....45 B6
Lime Kiln La
Castle Cary BA7 ....214 E4
Clevedon BS21 ....6 D1
Henstridge BA8 ....190 A6
Wookey Hole BA5 ....203 A8
Lime St
Nether Stowey TA5 ....134 B2
Stogursey TA5 ....134 C5
Lime Terr BA3 ....78 D1
Lime Tree Cl TA6 ....209 D5
Lime Tree Gr BS20 ....4 D3
Limebreach Wood BS48 ....8 D3
Limeburn Hill BS40 ....38 E5
Limekiln La Bath BA2 ....45 F8
Chard TA20 ....223 D1
Cricket St Thomas TA20 ....194 E2

Limekiln La continued
Leigh upon Mendip BA11 ....117 C3
Oakhill BA3 ....114 E5
Stoke St Michael BA3 ....115 F4
Tatworth TA20 ....193 F1
Limekilns Ct BS31 ....24 F5
Limepits La TA10 ....172 D5
Limerick Cl DT9 ....217 D2
Limerick La BA11 ....101 F2
Limes Cl TA4 ....202 E3
Limestone Hill TA5 ....135 C1
Limington Rd BA22 ....173 E1
Limpetshell La TA4 ....202 E3
Limpley Stoke Rd BA15 ....64 D6
Linch La BA4 ....142 D2
Lincoln Hill TA19 ....184 E4
Lincoln Cl BS31 ....24 C4
Lincombe Rd BA3 ....97 D8
Lincott View BA2 ....79 C8
Linden Ave BS23 ....49 B8
Linden Cl Bridgwater TA6 ....209 C4
Bristol, Stockwood BS14 ....23 E6
Frome BA11 ....119 D5
Radstock BA3 ....97 E8
Linden Ct BS21 ....6 D4
Linden Gdns BA1 ....44 D8
Linden Gr TA1 ....212 E5
Linden Hill TA21 ....222 A6
Linden Rd Clevedon BS21 ....6 D4
Yeovil BA20 ....218 F5
Lindens The BS27 ....31 E4
Lindisfarne Cl BA15 ....64 E6
Lindsey Cl BS20 ....1 F4
Lindsey Cres 1 TA6 ....153 F3
Linemere Cl BS48 ....19 D6
Lines Way BS14 ....23 C3
Liney Rd TA7 ....154 F6
Lingfield Ave BA21 ....219 D7
Linham Rd TA6 ....208 F6
Linhay Cl EX15 ....179 E1
Link La Burrington BS40 ....53 F3
Monkton Farleigh BA15 ....46 F8
Link Rd Nailsea BS48 ....8 F2
Portishead BS20 ....2 E7
Link The BS27 ....90 B8
Linkhay TA20 ....198 D8
Linkhay Cl TA20 ....198 D8
Linkmead BA3 ....96 F2
Links Cl BS23 ....48 D4
Links Gdns TA8 ....84 F3
Links Rd BS23 ....48 C2
Linkside TA8 ....6 E6
Linley Cl Bath BA2 ....44 A5
Bridgwater TA6 ....209 D7
Linleys The BA1 ....44 C7
Linne Ho BA2 ....44 A5
Linnet Cl Taunton TA1 ....212 B4
Weston-Super-Mare BS22 ....31 E1
Linnet Way Frome BA11 ....120 B6
Midsomer Norton BA3 ....97 B8
Linsvale Cl BA11 ....120 C5
Linsvale Dr BA11 ....120 C5
Linton La BA14 ....159 C7
Lion Cl BS48 ....8 D2
Lion Ho 20 BA4 ....205 B6
Lion Mews TA11 ....211 E4
Lipe Hill La TA3,TA4 ....168 B1
Lipe La TA3 ....169 C3
Lipgate Pl BS20 ....2 D3
Lippetts Way TA7 ....137 D1
Lippiat La Cheddar BS27 ....90 C7
Shipham BS25 ....70 F8
Lippiatt La BS27 ....90 B3
Lippiatt The BS27 ....90 C8
Lisieux Ct TA1 ....213 D2
Lisieux Way TA1 ....213 C3
Lisle Rd BS22 ....32 B4
Lister Gr BA15 ....64 F3
Lister's Hill TA19 ....221 C2
Listercombe Cl TA19 ....221 C2
Litfield Pl BS8 ....11 F7
Litfield Rd BS8 ....11 F8
Litt Hill BA3 ....75 F2
Little Ann St BS2, BS5 ....227 C4
Little Birch Croft BS14 ....23 A3
Little Bishop St BS2 ....227 B4
Little Brooks La BA4 ....205 C4
Little Burrow Dro TA7 ....155 A1
Little Caroline Pl 4 BS8 ....11 F5
Little Cl TA2 ....212 C8
Little Elm Rd TA7 ....155 C4
Little England TA7 ....155 D3
Little Entry BA5 ....203 F5
Little Headley Cl BS13 ....22 B7
Little Keyford La BA11 ....119 E2
Little King St BS1 ....227 A2
Little Lester TA19 ....221 A4
Little Marston Rd BA22 ....174 F1
Little Mead
1 Bishops Lydeard TA4 ....167 F8
Ilchester BA22 ....173 E1
Little Mead Cl BS24 ....49 E3
Little Meadow End BS48 ....18 E8
Little Moor Rd TA7 ....155 B3
Little Orch Cheddar BS27 ....90 C8
Street BA16 ....207 D7

Little Orch *continued*
Weston-Super-Mare BS23 ...48 D1
Little Paul St BS2 ......226 C4
Little Pen TA8 ....84 F5
Little Sammons BA22 .....186 E5
Little Silver Ct TA23 ....202 C7
Little Silver La TA21 ....222 D2
Little St TA14 ....185 E2
Little Stanhope St BA1 ...228 A2
Little Stoke Rd BS9 ....5 E4
Little Trumps BA22 ....186 B7
Little Withey Mead BS9 ...5 F5
Little Wiveliscombe La
TA4 ....165 D6
Littlebrook BS39 ....77 E6
Littlefield DT9 ....225 B3
Littlefield Cl BA16 ......156 E7
Littlefield La TA10 ......172 E4
Littlefields La TA19 .....184 F3
Littlefields Rise BS29 ...51 B3
Littleham Cotts TA3 ......181 E6
Littlemore Dro TA7 ....154 C3
Littleton Hill TA11 ......211 E6
Littleton La Wellow BA2 ..80 C7
Winford BS40 ....38 D5
Littlewood Cl BS24 ....23 B3
Littlewood La BS49 ....18 C2
Littlewoods BA11 ....143 C4
Litton BS24 ....49 A2
Liver Moor Dro TA11 .....156 E2
Livingstone Rd BA2 ......44 D5
Livingstone Terr BA2 ....228 A1
Livingstone Way TA2 .....212 B6
Llewellyn Way BS22 ......32 B3
Llewellyns Almshouses
BA5 ....203 D4
Lloyd Cl TA1 ....212 B1
Load Pool TA7 ....154 E5
Lobelia Cl TA9 ....104 D5
Lock Gdns BS13 ....21 E7
Lock's Hill BA11 ....119 F3
Lock's La BA9 ....216 C4
Lockemor Rd BS13 ....22 F4
Locketts Barton TA3 .....170 D7
Lockey Rd BA4 ....205 B4
Locking Farm Ind Est
BS24 ....50 A5
Locking Head Dro BS24 ...49 F5
Locking Moor Rd
Locking BS24 ....50 B5
Weston-Super-Mare BS22 ..49 D8
Locking Prim Sch BS24 ...50 B4
Locking Rd BS22,BS23 ....49 B7
Lockingwell Rd BS31 .....24 D5
Locks Way TA7 ....136 F3
Locksbrook Ct Bath BA1 ..44 B6
Weston-Super-Mare BS22 ..32 B5
Locksbrook Trad Est BA1 ..44 B6
Lockswell TA7 ....156 A5
Lockyer Dro TA7 ....156 A5
Lodes La TA2 ....168 E8
Lodge Cl Taunton TA1 ....212 A2
Wellington TA21 ....222 D6
Yatton BS49 ....34 B8
Lodge Ct BS9 ....5 E4
Lodge Dr
Long Ashton BS41 ....11 B2
Weston-Super-Mare BS23 ..31 A1
Lodge Gdns BA2 ....44 D1
Lodge Hill
Bratton Seymour BA9 .....176 A7
Chapmanslade BA11,BA13 ...120 F5
Somerton TA11 ....211 F4
Westbury Sub Mendip
BA5 ....110 D5
Lodge Hill Ind Pk BA5 ...110 D6
Lodge La Kenmarton EX13 .198 B2
Wraxall BS48 ....9 B2
Lodge Pl BS1 ....226 C3
Lodge Rd
Horningsham BA12 ....144 D4
Kingsdon TA11 ....173 D3
Lodge Rocks TA24 ....131 D3
Lodge St BS1 ....226 C3
Lodway BS20 ....4 C4
Lodway Cl BS20 ....4 C5
Lodway Gdns BS20 ....4 C4
Lodwells Orch TA3 ......170 B4
Lombardy Cl BS22 ....49 E8
London Cross TA4 ....151 E4
London Dro BA6,BS28 ....138 D7
London Rd BA1 ....29 A3
Milborne Port DT9 ....217 E1
London Rd E BA1 ....29 A3
London Rd W BA1 ....28 C2
London Sq ⊞ TA22 ......185 E6
London St BA1 ....228 C3
Long Acre BA5 ....205 C4
Long Acre Ho BA1 ....228 C4
Long Acres Cl BS9 ......5 D7
Long Ashton Rd BS41 ....11 B2
Long Ave BS21 ....6 B2
Long Barnaby BA3 ....78 A2
Long Cl ⑪ Ilminster TA19 .221 C2
Yeovil BA21 ....218 C5
Long Cross Doulting BA4 .141 F8
Felton BS40 ....37 D7
Nether Stowey TA5 ....134 A3
Long Cross Bottom
Doulting BA3 ....142 A8
Stoke St Michael BA3 ....115 A1
Long Dro
Broadway TA19,TA20 ......183 A2
Buckland St Mary TA20 ...182 F2

Long Dro *continued*
Glastonbury BA5 ....139 E4
Westbury Sub Mendip
BS27 ....110 A4
Long Eaton Dr BS14 .....23 B7
Long Furlong La
East Coker BA22 ....197 C8
Long Sutton TA10 ....172 E5
Long Ground BA11 ....119 F3
Long Hay Cl BA2 ....44 B5
Long Hill Ashton-under-Hill BS28 .89 D2
Shepton Mallet BA4 ......141 C8
Long La Backwell BS48 ...19 C2
Bourton SP8 ....161 D1
Cucklington BA9 ....177 D5
Dinder BA5 ....140 D7
Felton BS40 ....37 B5
Marshwood DT6 ....199 B1
Walton BA16 ....156 D7
Wanstrow BA4 ....142 F5
West Chinnock TA18 .....196 B7
Wootton Courtenay TA24 ..129 E8
Wrington BS40 ....36 B2
Long Lakes TA4 ....202 E4
Long Lane Cross TA24 ...129 E8
Long Load Rd TA12 ......185 E8
Long Mead BA21 ....218 C5
Long Moor Dro TA7,TA9 ..137 A7
Long Orchard Hill TA19 ..221 E3
Long Ride Dro BA6 ......157 F3
Long Row BS1 ....227 B2
Long Run BA22 ....186 C2
Long St Croscombe BA5 ..204 B7
Galhampton BA22 ....175 E8
High Ham TA10 ....156 A1
Sherborne DT9 ....225 E4
Williton TA4 ....202 E3
Long Sutton CE Prim Sch
TA10 ....172 E4
Long Thorn La BS40 .....55 E7
Long Valley Rd BA2 .....43 F5
Long-Thorn BS48 ....116 F6
Longacre BS21 ....16 B8
Longacre Dro TA7 ....212 E7
Longacre La TA19 ....194 F6
Longacre Rd BS14 ......23 A3
Longbottom BS25 ....71 A6
Longbridge ⑩ BA4 ......205 B6
Longcombe Dr BA12 .....144 F6
Longcroft Rd BA21 ......219 C6
Longcross Dr BS22 ......32 B4
Longfellow Ave BA2 .....44 F4
Longfield BA11 ....118 A7
Longfield Cl TA4 ....202 E2
Longforward Hill
Dinnington TA17 ....195 A8
Seavington St Mary TA19 ..184 D3
Longforward La
Dinnington TA17 ....195 B8
Seavington St Mary TA19 ..184 D1
Longlands La
East Coker BA22 ....197 C8
Westbury Sub Mendip BA5 .110 E2
Longleat Cl BA11 ....119 F3
Longleat Ho★ BA12 .....144 D6
Longleat La BA11 ....119 E4
Longleat Ho★ BA12 .....144 D6
Longman's Lea BA4 ......159 C7
Longmarsh La TA10 ......172 E6
Longmead Cl
Norton St Philip BA2 ....81 F4
Taunton TA1 ....212 D2
Wellington TA21 ....222 B8
Longmead Cotts TA21 ....222 B8
Longmead Croft BS13 ....21 F4
Longmead Way TA1 ....212 D2
Longmeadow Rd BS31 .....24 D4
Longreach Gr BS14 ......23 D6
Longridge Way BS24 .....50 A8
Longrun La TA1 ....212 D2
Longs Field TA3 ....170 C4
Longstone Ave TA6 ......209 C5
Longstone Cl TA5 ....134 B2
Longstrings La TA18 ....224 C8
Longthorne Pl BA2 ......44 F2
Longton Grove Rd ⑤
BS23 ....48 E8
Longton Ind Est BS23 ...48 F6
Longvernal BA3 ....77 F1
Longvernal Prim Sch
BA3 ....77 F1
Longway Ave BS13,BS14 ..22 F4
Longwood Ho BS8 ....10 C4
Longwood La
Burlescombe TA21 ....179 C4
Long Ashton BS41 ....11 A1
Lonsdale Ave BS23 ......48 F4
Lonsdale Rd TA6 ....135 C2
Look's La BA6 ....157 C6
Lopen Head TA13 ....220 A1
Lopen La TA13 ....220 A1
Lopen Rd TA13,TA17 ....195 D8
Lords Meadow La ⑥
EX16 ....164 B1
Lordsleaze La TA20 .....223 D3
Loretto Rd BS11 ....198 A1
Lorne Pl BA5 ....203 E5
Lorne Rd BA2 ....44 D6
Lotment Hill TA11 .....173 D5
Lottisham La BA6 ......158 D6
Lottisham Rd BA6 ......158 C6

Lotts' Ave BS48 ....19 B5
Lotus St BS23 ....227 C2
Louisa Gate TA22 ....163 F7
Louisa St BS2 ....227 C2
Loundshay La TA4 ......167 A4
Love La
Burnham-On-Sea TA8 .....104 C7
Ilminster TA19 ....221 C3
Marnhull DT10 ....190 F6
Shepton Beauchamp TA19 ..186 E4
Wincanton BA9 ....216 F5
Love's La BA2 ....59 F6
Lovelands DT2 ....197 A1
Lovelinch Gdns BS41 ...10 F1
Lovells Mead DT10 .....190 F6
Lovells Mill BS39 .....57 D4
Loveridge La TA20 .....198 D8
Lovers La BA3,BS39 ....78 A5
Lovers Wlk BS25 ....203 D5
Lovers' Wlk
⑷ Cannington TA5 ......135 B2
Weston-Super-Mare BS23 ..48 D8
Loves Hill BA2 ....60 A1
Lovington CE Prim Sch
BA7 ....214 C5
Low Ham Rd TA10 ......172 B8
Low's Hill La DT9 .....188 B3
Lowbourne BA2 ....60 A1
Lower Acreman St DT9 ..225 D3
Lower Actis BA6 ....206 E3
Lower Ansford BA7 .....214 B7
Lower Backway BA10 ....215 E6
Lower Bath Rd BS23 ....48 E6
Lower Bath Rd TA6 .....209 B6
Lower Beadon TA16 ....195 F7
Lower Borough Walls
BA1 ....228 C2
Lower Boyston La DT9 ..188 F5
Lower Bristol Rd
Bath BA2 ....44 B6
Clutton BS39 ....58 F4
Lower Camden Pl BA1 ...228 C4
Lower Castle St BS1 ...227 B3
Lower Chapel Ct BA5 ...113 A1
Lower Cheriton La BA8 ..176 D4
Lower Church Rd BS23 ..227 A3
Lower Church Rd BS23 ..48 D8
Lower Claverham BS49 ..17 F3
Lower Clifton Hill BS8 ..226 B2
Lower College St BS1 ...226 C2
Lower Coombses TA20 ...198 D8
Lower Cross EX15 ......179 C1
Lower Down Rd BS20 ....2 B5
Lower East Coker Rd
BA20 ....218 F1
Lower East Hayes BA1 ..45 B8
Lower Fairmead Rd
BA21 ....219 D8
Lower Fallow Cl BS14 ..22 F3
Lower Farm La BA2 .....59 E7
Lower Foxmoor Rd
TA21 ....222 B5
Lower Gay St BS2 ......227 A4
Lower Guinea St BS1 ...227 A1
Lower Gully Dro BS28 ..89 F3
Lower Gunville DT9 ....217 D2
Lower Hedgemead Rd
BA1 ....228 C4
Lower High St BS11 ....4 D7
Lower Holway Cl TA1 ...213 D3
Lower Hyde Rd TA15 ....186 B4
Lower Innox BA11 ......119 E6
Lower Keyford BA11 ....119 F3
Lower Kingsbury DT9 ...217 D3
Lower Kingsdown Rd
SN13 ....29 F3
Lower Knowles Rd BS21 ..6 C2
Lower La
Shepton Mallet BA4 .....205 C6
Wanstrow BA4 ....142 F5
Lower Lamb St BS1 .....226 C2
Lower Linden Rd BS21 ...6 D3
Lower Lodfin EX16 .....164 B2
Lower Marshfield Rd
TA24 ....201 B6
Lower Maudlin St BS1 ...227 A3
Lower Meadow Rd
TA24 ....201 B6
Lower Middle St TA1 ...212 F4
Lower New Rd BS27 .....90 A7
Lower North St BS27 ...90 B8
Lower North Town La
BA22 ....175 D7
Lower Northend BA1 ....28 F5
Lower Oakley BA5 ......204 B7
Lower Odcombe BA22 ...196 D8
Lower Parade Ground Rd
BS24 ....50 C5
Lower Park La TA24 ....129 E1
Lower Park Row BS1 ....227 A3
Lower Pk TA24 ....200 E7
Lower Queen's BS21 ....6 D3
Lower Rd
Hinton Blewett BS39 ....75 E6
Horsington BA8 ....176 D3
Kingsdon TA11 ....173 D5
Stalbridge DT10 ....190 C4
Lower Rocke's Cotts
BA6 ....157 D4

Lower Silk Mill BA4 ....204 F6
Lower Somerton TA11 ...211 F3
Lower St
Buckland Dinham BA11 ...100 A2
Carhampton TA24 ....131 B4
Chewton Mendip BA3 ....94 F7
Curry Mallet TA3 ......183 C8
Merriott TA16 ....195 F7
Pilton BA4 ....139 E7
Rode BA11 ....101 E8
Upton Noble BA4 ....142 F2
West Chinnock TA18 ....196 B8
Lower Stoke BA2,BA3 ...64 A8
Lower Strode BS40 .....56 A7
Lower Strode Rd BS21 ..16 A7
Lower Touches TA20 ....223 E5
Lower Town EX16 ....178 D1
Lower Turners Barn La
BA20 ....218 F2
Lower Vellow TA4 ......132 D2
Lower Westholme Rd
BA4 ....140 D3
Lower Whitelands BA3 ..79 B3
Lowtrow Cross TA4 .....165 A8
Loxhams TA10 ....156 B2
Loxleigh Ave TA6 ......209 B4
Loxleigh Gdns TA6 .....209 B4
Loxley Batch TA7 ......156 A8
Loxley Gdns BA2 ....44 C4
Loxley Terr TA6 ....209 F7
Loxton Dro BS26 ....88 A6
Loxton Rd BS23 ....48 F2
Loxton Sq BS14 ....23 A6
Lubborn La BA6 ....158 B5
Lucas Cnr TA20 ....193 D6
Luckes La TA4 ....132 E3
Luckington Cross BA11 ..98 B2
Lucklands Rd BA1 ......27 C1
Luckley Ave BS13 ......22 C5
Luckwell Cross TA24 ...128 C6
Ludbourne Rd DT9 ......225 E4
Ludlow Cl
Bridgwater TA6 ....209 A2
Frome BA11 ....120 C6
Keynsham BS31 ....24 D5
Ludney Cross TA19 .....194 F7
Ludney La
Ilminster TA19 ....194 F7
Kingstone TA19 ....194 F7
Ludwells Orch BS39 ....77 E6
Lufton Heights Com Pk
BA22 ....218 A4
Lufton Trad Est BA22 ..218 A7
Lufton Way BA22 ....218 A6
Lugshorn La TA11 ......211 C8
Luke St EX16 ....164 B1
Lullington La BA11 ....101 B3
Lulsgate Rd BS13 ......22 A8
Lulworth Rd BS31 ......24 D4
Lundy Dr TA8 ....104 B5
Lunty Mead BS48 ......18 F8
Lupin Way BA22 ....218 B5
Lusty Gdns BA10 ......215 E5
Luttrell Cl TA2 ....213 B8
Luttrell Gdns TA24 ....200 F6
Luvers La BS40 ....54 C2
Lux Furlong BS9 ......5 B7
Luxborough Rd TA6 .....208 B4
Luxhay Cl TA2 ....213 B8
Luxton's La BA3,BA4 ...116 F5
Lyatt La BA5 ....140 E8
Lyatts Hill BA22 ......197 B6
Lychgate Pk BS24 .....50 A4
Lyddon Cl TA21 ....222 D4
Lyddon Rd BS22 ....32 B4
Lyddons Mead TA20 ....223 D4
Lyde Ct BA21 ....219 E6
Lyde La BA21 ....219 F6
Lyde Rd BA21 ....219 E6
Lydeard Cross TA5 ....152 E3
Lydeard Down Hill TA4 ..151 A8
Lydeard St Lawrence Com
Prim Sch TA4 ....151 A3
Lydford La TA11 ......165 D5
Lydon's Hill TA22 ....148 A1
Lye Cross BS40 ....36 C1
Lye Hole La BS40 .....36 D4
Lye La BA4 ....159 C6
Lye Mead BS40 ....38 A6
Lyefield Rd BS22 .....31 E4
Lyes The BS49 ....34 D3
Lyewater TA18 ....224 B5
Lyme Gdns BA1 ....44 B7
Lyme Rd Axminster EX13 .198 A1
Bath BA1 ....44 B7
Crewkerne TA18 ....224 B4
Lymore Ave BA2 ......44 C5
Lymore Gdns BA2 .....44 C5
Lymore Terr BA2 .....44 C4
Lympsham CE Fst Sch
BS24 ....67 B1
Lympsham Gn BA2 .....62 D8

Lympsham Rd BS24 ......67 B1
Lynbrook BS41 ....10 F1
Lynbrook La BA2 ......44 F3
Lynch Cl BS22 ....31 F3
Lynch Cres BS25 ......69 F7
Lynch Hill BA3 ....96 A3
Lynch La Cheddar BS27 ..90 C8
Hardington Mandeville
BA22 ....197 A6
Westbury Sub Mendip
BA5 ....110 D8
Lynch The BS25 ......69 F7
Lynchcombe La BA5 ...110 F6
Lynchmead BS25 ......70 A7
Lyncombe Hill BA2 ...228 C1
Lyncombe Vale BA2 ...45 B4
Lyncombe Vale Rd BA2 ..45 A4
Lyndale Ave
Bridgwater TA6 ....208 E5
Bristol BS9 ....5 D5
Lynde Cl BS13 ....22 B4
Lyndhurst Cres TA6 ..208 C5
Lyndhurst Gr TA11 ...185 D7
Lyndhurst Rd Bath BA2 ..44 C6
Bristol BS9 ....5 F7
Keynsham BS31 ....24 F3
Midsomer Norton BA3 ...97 B8
Weston-Super-Mare BS23 ..48 E4
Lyndhurst Terr BA1 ...228 C4
Lynfield Pk BA1 .....27 C1
Lynfield Rd BA11 ....119 D5
Lynford La TA11 .....158 C1
Lyngford Cres TA2 ...213 A7
Lyngford La TA8 ....168 F6
Lyngford Park Prim Sch
TA2 ....213 B8
Lyngford Pl TA2 .....213 A7
Lyngford Rd TA2 ....213 A7
Lyngford Sq TA2 ....213 A7
Lynmouth Cl BS22 ...32 A2
Lynor Cl TA1 ....213 D3
Lynton Cl BS20 .....2 E4
Lynton Rd
Burnham-On-Sea TA8 ..104 B6
Midsomer Norton BA3 ..97 B8
Lynwood Cl Frome BA11 .119 D4
Midsomer Norton BA3 ..97 A8
Lynx Cres BS24 .....49 B2
Lynx Trad Est BA20 ..218 D3
Lynx West Trad Est
BA20 ....218 C3
Lyons Court Rd BS14 ..23 D7
Lyons Ct BS23 ......48 F7
Lype La TA22 ....147 E4
Lypstone Cl BS24 ...50 A8
Lypyatt La BA6 .....206 F4
Lysander Rd BA20 ...218 E3
Lysander Rd Rdbt BA20 .218 E3
Lytchett La BA22 ...173 E1
Lyte's Cary★ TA11 ..173 E5
Lytes Cary Rd BS31 ..25 A3
Lytton Gdns BA2 ....44 B4
Lytton Gr BS31 .....25 A5
Lyveden Gdns BS13 ..22 B5
Lyvedon Way BS41 ...11 B1

M

Macaulay Bldgs BA2 ...45 C4
Macey's Rd BS13 .....22 D3
Machine Cross TA22 ..163 F6
Macies The BA1 ......27 B3
Mackley La BA2 .....81 E3
Mackley Way BS22 ...6 A2
Macquarie Farm Cl BS49 .17 A1
Macrae Rd BS20 .....4 E4
Madam La
Weston-Super-Mare BS22 ..31 F2
Weston-Super-Mare BS22 ..32 A4
Madam's Paddock BS40 ..39 B3
Madden Cl TA8 ......104 C7
Maddocks Pk BA9 ....216 C3
Maddocks Slade TA8 ..104 A8
Madeira Ct BS23 ....48 C8
Madeira Rd Clevedon BS21 .6 C3
Weston-Super-Mare BS23 ..30 C1
Madgeon La TA20 ....192 C8
Madwoman's La BS28 ..108 B2
Maes Down Ho ⑧ BA4 ..205 B6
Maesbury Rd BS31 ...25 A2
Maesdown Cl BA4 ...141 E2
Maesdown Cotts BA4 ..141 E2
Maesdown Hill BA4 ..141 E3
Maesdown Rd
Doulting BA4 ....141 E4
Evercreech BA4 ......141 E2
Maesknoll La BS14,BS39 ..40 B8
Magdalen Ave BA2 ...228 B1
Magdalen La BA2 ....83 B7
Magdalen Rd BA2 ....228 B1
Magdalene Cl BA6 ...206 D4
Magdalene Cl ⑩ TA1 ..212 F4
Magdalene La ⑦ TA1 ..212 F4
Magdalene Rd BA3 ...78 D1
Magdalene St
Glastonbury BA6 .....206 D4
Taunton TA1 ....212 F4
Magellan Cl BS22 ...31 F4
Maggs Hill BA2 .....62 A6
Maggs La
Castle Cary BA7 .....214 C7
Whitchurch BS14 ....23 C4

Maglands Rd TA23 . . . . .202 D6
Magna Cl BA21 . . . . .219 D8
Magnolia Ave BS22 . . . . .32 A1
Magnolia Cl Frome BA11 120 C7
  Weston-Super-Mare BS22 . .49 E7
Magnolia Rd BA3 . . . . . . .78 E1
Magnolia Tree Rd TA6 . .209 E5
Magpie Cl
  Burnham-On-Sea TA8 . . . . .85 B1
  Weston-Super-Mare BS22 . .49 E8
Maiden Beech Mid Sch
  TA18 . . . . .224 B4
Maiden Croft La BA6 . . .139 D2
Maiden Way BS11 . . . . . . .4 C8
Maidenbrook La TA2 . .169 A6
Maidenhead Cross
  EX16 . . . . .179 C2
Maidenhead Rd BS13 . . .22 D3
Maidstone Gr BS24 . . . . . .49 A1
Main Rd Brockley BS49 . . . .18 D2
  Burrowbridge TA7 . . . . . .154 F1
  Cannington TA5 . . . . .135 C1
  Coxley BA5 . . . . .139 E6
  Flax Bourton BS48 . . . . . . .19 F7
  Hutton BS24 . . . . .49 E2
  Kilve TA5 . . . . .133 C5
  Lyng TA3,TA7 . . . . .170 C7
  Middlezoy TA7 . . . . .155 B3
  NonReady TA7 . . . . .155 B2
  Shapwick TA7 . . . . .155 F8
  West Huntspill TA9 . . . . . .136 B8
  Westhay BA6 . . . . .138 B5
  Westonzoyland TA7 . . . . . .154 F5
Main St Babcary TA11 . . .174 C7
  Barton St David TA11 . . . .158 A3
  Chilthorne Domer BA22 . .186 E6
  Farrington Gurney BS39 . . .77 A4
  Martock TA12 . . . . .185 F7
  Walton BA16 . . . . .156 D7
Maincombe Cl TA18 . . . .224 C4
Mal's Mead La TA20 . . . .194 E2
Malago Wlk BS13 . . . . . . .21 E4
Malherbie Ct TA20 . . . . .194 B6
Mall The Bath BA1 . . . . . .228 C2
  Bristol, Clifton BS8 . . . . . . .11 F7
Mallard Pl TA9 . . . . .104 C4
Mallard Rd TA24 . . . . . .201 C5
Mallard Way TA6 . . . . . .209 B4
Mallory Ct TA2 . . . . .212 C6
Mallow Cl BS21 . . . . .6 E2
Malmesbury Ct BA21 . .218 C6
Malmesbury Way BA21 .218 C6
Malta Way BA22 . . . . . . .174 A2
Malthouse Ct BA9 . . . . .216 C4
Malthouse Ct
  Frome BA11 . . . . .119 E3
  Taunton TA1 . . . . .212 A4
Malthouse La DT9 . . . . .187 E5
Maltings Ind Est The BA1 .44 B6
Maltings The
  Chard TA20 . . . . .223 C3
  Frome BA11 . . . . .119 F4
  Sherborne DT9 . . . . .225 D5
  Weston-Super-Mare BS22 . .31 F2
Maltlands BS22 . . . . .49 D8
Malvern Bldgs BA1 . . . . .28 A2
Malvern Cl TA6 . . . . .209 D6
Malvern Ct BA21 . . . . . .218 D6
Malvern Rd BS23 . . . . . . .48 E5
Malvern Terr **3** Bath BA1 .28 A1
  Taunton TA2 . . . . .212 F6
Malvern Villas **3** BA1 . . .28 A1
Mamsey La TA4 . . . . .202 C3
Mancroft Ave BS11 . . . . . .4 F7
Mandarin La TA6 . . . . . .209 B4
Mandy Mews BA3 . . . . . .77 F1
Mangle Cave Hill TA18 .195 C5
Manilla Cres BS23 . . . . . .30 C1
Manilla Pl BS23 . . . . .30 C1
Manilla Rd BS23 . . . . . . .30 C1
Manmoor La BS21 . . . . . . .7 A1
Manning Cl BA5 . . . . . . .203 F5
Manning Rd TA4 . . . . . . .167 E6
Manning's La BA3 . . . . . .94 F3
Manor Barton TA14 . . . .185 E2
Manor Bldgs TA18 . . . . .196 C4
Manor Cl Berrow TA8 . . . .84 F6
  Bradford Abbas DT9 . . . . .187 E1
  Chard TA20 . . . . .223 C2
  Charlton Horethorne DT9 .176 E2
  Cossington TA7 . . . . .136 F3
  Ditcheat BA4 . . . . .159 C7
  East Brent TA9 . . . . .86 D5
  Easton-in-G BS20 . . . . .4 A4
  Farrington Gurney BS39 . . .77 A3
  Glastonbury BA6 . . . . . . .206 D5
  Kingsdon TA11 . . . . .173 D5
  Portishead BS20 . . . . .2 A5
  South Perrott DT8 . . . . . .196 C1
  Sparkford BA22 . . . . .175 A4
  Taunton TA1 . . . . .212 E3
  Templecombe BA8 . . . . . .189 E8
  Wellow BA2 . . . . .62 D1
Manor Cl The BS8 . . . . . . .11 A8
Manor Copse Rd BA3 . . . .79 C2
Manor Court Prim Sch
  TA20 . . . . .223 C3
Manor Ct Backwell BS48 . .19 A4
  Burnham-On-Sea TA8 . . . .104 B7
  Easton BA5 . . . . .111 A4
  Horsington BA8 . . . . .176 D2
  Locking BS24 . . . . .50 B4
  Sherborne DT9 . . . . .225 D5
  Stawell TA7 . . . . .137 A1
  Weston-Super-Mare BS23 . .49 A8

Manor Dr Bathford BA1 . . .29 C2
Berrow TA8 . . . . .84 F6
Chedzoy TA7 . . . . .154 D8
East Coker BA22 . . . . .197 B8
10 Merriott TA16 . . . . . . .195 F7
Staplegrove TA2 . . . . .212 C7
Taunton TA1 . . . . .212 E3
Manor Farm Chard TA20 .223 C3
  East Coker BA22 . . . . .197 B8
Manor Farm Barns TA7 .169 E8
Manor Farm Cl
  Tatworth TA20 . . . . .198 C8
  Weston-Super-Mare BS24 . .49 B2
Manor Farm Cres BS24 . .49 B2
Manor Furlong BA11 . . .119 C2
Manor Gdns
  Farmborough BA2 . . . . . . .59 F6
  Farrington Gurney BS39 . . .77 A3
  Ilchester BA22 . . . . .173 E1
  Locking BS24 . . . . .50 A4
  Weston-Super-Mare BS24 . .31 B4
Manor Gn EX14 . . . . . . .191 F2
Manor Grange BS24 . . . . .67 B7
Manor House Gdns TA1 . .212 C7
Manor House Sacred Heart
  Sch BS40 . . . . .39 A3
Manor La Abbots Leigh BS8 .10 F8
  Wedmore BS28 . . . . .108 D5
  Weston-Super-Mare BS24 . .31 B4
Manor Mews TA1 . . . . . .212 DB
Manor Orch TA1 . . . . . . .212 D2
Manor Pk Bath BA1 . . . . . .44 BB
  Keinton Mandeville TA11 . .158 B1
  Norton Fitzwarren TA2 . . .168 B4
  Pawlett TA6 . . . . .135 F6
  Radstock BA3 . . . . .79 C2
Manor Pl TA11 . . . . .158 B1
Manor Rd
  Abbots Leigh BS8 . . . . . . .10 F7
  Bath BA1 . . . . .27 C1
  Bridgwater TA6 . . . . .209 C6
  Bristol, Bishopsworth BS13 .22 A6
  Burnham-On-Sea TA8 . . . .104 B7
  Chedzoy TA7 . . . . .154 DB
  Edington TA7 . . . . .137 D2
  Frome BA11 . . . . .119 E2
  Isle Abbotts TA3 . . . . .183 F7
  Kingsdon TA11 . . . . .173 D5
  Milborne Port DT9 . . . . . .217 C3
  Minehead TA24 . . . . .201 B4
  Pawlett TA6 . . . . .135 F6
  Radstock BA3 . . . . .79 C2
  Saltford BS31 . . . . .25 C2
  Staplegrove TA2 . . . . .212 C8
  Taunton TA1 . . . . .212 D3
  Weston-Super-Mare BS23 . .48 A8
  Yeovil BA20 . . . . .219 A4
Manor Ride TA6 . . . . .86 B2
Manor St BA22 . . . . .197 A8
Manor Terr TA1 . . . . .79 C2
Manor Valley BS23 . . . . . .31 A1
Manor View
  Crewkerne TA18 . . . . .224 C4
  Golsoncott SA23 . . . . .131 D1
Manor Villas BA1 . . . . . . .27 C1
Manor Way Berrow TA8 . . .84 F6
  Failand BS8 . . . . .10 C4
  Frome BA11 . . . . .119 E2
Manse La TA7 . . . . .136 C4
Mansel Cl BS31 . . . . .25 C3
Mansfield Ave BS23 . . . . .49 A8
Mansfield Rd TA1 . . . . . .213 A3
Mansford La DT6 . . . . . . .199 D1
Manship Gn BA4 . . . . . . .205 B4
Mansion Cl BS14 . . . . .23 C7
Mantle St TA21 . . . . .222 C5
Mantle VC Rd BA22 . . . . .174 A2
Manvers St BA1 . . . . .228 C1
Manworthy Cross TA4 . .166 C4
Maperton Rd DT9 . . . . . .176 A2
Maple Cl
  Bristol, Stockwood BS14 . . .23 D5
  North Petherton TA6 . . . . .153 F3
  Taunton TA1 . . . . .136 C4
  Street BA16 . . . . .207 C5
  Weston-Super-Mare BS23 . .49 A8
  Wincanton BA9 . . . . .216 C2
Maple Ct **1** Bridgwater TA6 .209 D6
  Bristol BS9 . . . . .5 FB
Maple Dr
  Burnham-On-Sea TA8 . . . .104 B5
  Crewkerne TA18 . . . . .224 D7
  Radstock BA3 . . . . .78 E1
  Yeovil BA20 . . . . .218 F3
Maple Gdns BA2 . . . . .44 E4
Maple Gr BA2 . . . . .44 E4
Maple Leaf Ct BS8 . . . . .226 A3
Maple Rd
  Curry Rivel TA10 . . . . . . .171 D4
  Langport TA10 . . . . .172 A6
Maple Rise BA3 . . . . .79 B2
Maple Tree Ct TA7 . . . . .136 F3
Maple Wlk BS31 . . . . .24 D4
Maples The Nailsea BS48 . . .8 C1
  Shepton Mallet BA4 . . . . .205 C6
Maplestone Rd BS14 . . . .23 A3
Mapstone Cl BA6 . . . . . .206 E3
Marchant Cl BA22 . . . . .175 D8
Marchant's Hill BA3 . . . . .95 F2
Marchant-Holliday Sch
  BA8 . . . . .176 C5
Marchants Pass BA1 . . . .228 C1
Marchfields Way BS23 . . .49 A5
Marconi Cl BS23 . . . . .49 B7
Marconi Rd BS20 . . . . .1 F5
Marden Gr TA1 . . . . .213 D3

Marden Rd BS31 . . . . .25 A4
Mardi's La TA11 . . . . . . .158 C2
Mardyke Ferry Rd BS1 .226 B1
Mare La TA13 . . . . .220 C5
Mares La BA5 . . . . .110 E7
Margaret Cres TA8 . . . . .104 A5
Margaret Rd BS13 . . . . . .21 F4
Margaret's Bldgs BA1 . . .228 B3
Margaret's Hill BA1 . . . .228 C4
Marguerite Rd BS13 . . . . .21 F7
Marholm Rd BA22 . . . . .209 B4
Marindin Dr BS22 . . . . . .32 B4
Marine Ct BA21 . . . . .219 D5
Marine Dr TA8 . . . . .104 B5
Marine Hill BS21 . . . . .6 C5
Marine Par Clevedon BS21 . .6 C4
  Pill BS20 . . . . .4 C5
  Weston-Super-Mare BS23 . .30 B1
  Weston-Super-Mare BS23 . .48 D6
Mariner's Cl BS22 . . . . . .31 D1
Mariner's Ct TA9 . . . . . . .106 A4
Mariners Cl Backwell BS48 .19 A4
  Bridgwater TA6 . . . . .209 A5
  Wraxall TA6 . . . . .209 A5
Mariners Dr
  Backwell BS48 . . . . .19 A6
  Bristol BS9 . . . . .5 D4
Mariners Way TA23 . . . .202 D6
Mariners' Path BS9 . . . . . .5 E3
Mark CE Fst Sch TA9 . . .106 A4
Mark Coll TA9 . . . . .106 A4
Mark Cswy TA9 . . . . .106 B4
Mark La BS1 . . . . .226 C2
Mark Rd Burtle TA7 . . . . .137 D6
  Highbridge TA9 . . . . .105 A2
Market Cl
  4 Bampton EX16 . . . . .164 B1
  Brushford TA22 . . . . .163 E4
Market Ct
  Crewkerne TA18 . . . . .224 C6
  8 Shepton Mallet BA4 . .205 B6
Market House La TA24 . .200 F7
Market Ind Est BS49 . . . .17 B1
Market Pl
  Burlescombe EX16 . . . . . . .179 B3
  Castle Cary BA7 . . . . .214 C5
  Frome BA11 . . . . .119 F5
  Glastonbury BA6 . . . . . . .206 D4
  Ilchester BA22 . . . . .173 E1
  2 Shepton Mallet BA4 . .205 B6
  Somerton TA11 . . . . .211 E4
  Wells BA5 . . . . .203 E4
  Wiveliscombe TA4 . . . . . .210 C4
Market Pl The BA11 . . . .143 B8
Market Sq
  Crewkerne TA18 . . . . .224 C6
  South Petherton TA13 . . . .220 C4
Market St
  Bridgwater TA6 . . . . .208 F5
  Crewkerne TA18 . . . . .224 C6
  Highbridge TA9 . . . . .104 E3
  Watchet TA23 . . . . .202 C7
  Wells BA5 . . . . .203 D4
  Yeovil BA20 . . . . .219 B5
Market Terr TA4 . . . . . . .104 E3
Markham Cl BS11 . . . . . . .4 C7
Marklands BS9 . . . . .5 E3
Marksbury Rd BS4 . . . . . .22 F4
Marksbury CE Prim Sch
  BA2 . . . . .42 B1
Marksview Bsns Ctr
  BA21 . . . . .219 F7
Marl Cl BA21 . . . . .218 E7
Marl La DT9 . . . . .187 E3
Marl Pits La BA11 . . . . . .143 C7
Marlborough Ave TA6 . .209 A2
Marlborough Bldgs
  Bath BA1 . . . . .228 A3
  Langport TA10 . . . . .171 F5
Marlborough Cl TA6 . . . .209 A2
Marlborough Ct TA8 . . . . .85 B1
Marlborough Dr BS22 . . .32 B2
Marlborough Flats **8**
  BS2 . . . . .227 A4
Marlborough Hill BS2 . .227 A4
Marlborough Hill Pl
  BS2 . . . . .227 A4
Marlborough La BA1 . . .228 A3
Marlborough Rd BA21 . .219 E6
Marlborough St
  Bath BA1 . . . . .228 A4
  Bristol BS2 . . . . .227 A4
Marlepit Gr BS13 . . . . . . .21 F6
Marley Cl TA24 . . . . .201 A5
Marley's Row TA24 . . . . .201 A5
Marlfield Wlk BS13 . . . . .21 E7
Marlowe Ho **3** BS23 . . . .48 F4
Marne Cl BS14 . . . . .23 D5
Marnhull Cl DT10 . . . . . .190 F6
Marron Cl BS26 . . . . .70 C2
Marsden Rd BA2 . . . . . . .44 B3
Marsh Cross TA24 . . . . . .200 D1
Marsh Hill TA22 . . . . . . .163 C8
Marsh La
  Barrington TA19 . . . . . . .184 E5
  Barton St David TA11 . . . .158 A3
  Bridgwater TA6 . . . . .209 B1
  Huntspill TA9 . . . . .136 C6
  Cossington TA7 . . . . .154 C6
  Easton-in-G BS20 . . . . .4 A4
  Farrington Gurney BS39 . . .77 A3

Marsh La continued
  Henstridge BA8 . . . . .190 B7
  Holcombe BA3 . . . . .116 C5
  Penselwood BA9 . . . . . . .161 D2
  Pitney TA10 . . . . .172 D7
  Portbury BS20 . . . . .3 C6
  South Cheriton BA8 . . . . .176 E4
  Temple Cloud BS39 . . . . . .59 A1
  Tintinhull BA22 . . . . .186 A5
  Yeovil BA21 . . . . .218 F8
  Yeovil Marsh BA21 . . . . . .187 A5
Marsh Lane Trad Est BS20 .3 F7
Marsh Pottinson Ho **16**
  BA20 . . . . .219 B4
Marsh Rd Bristol BS3 . . . . .11 F3
  Rode BA11 . . . . .82 F1
  Standerwick BA11 . . . . . .102 D1
  Yatton BS49 . . . . .34 B8
Marsh St Avonmouth BS11 . .4 C8
  4 Bristol BS1 . . . . .227 A2
  Dunster TA24 . . . . .201 E3
Marshall Wlk BS4 . . . . . . .22 D7
Marshalsea Est DT6 . . . .199 C3
Marshbridge Cross
  TA22 . . . . .163 C7
Marshclose Hill TA22 . . .146 E7
Marshfield Rd TA24 . . . .201 B5
Marshfield Way BA1 . . . . .28 A1
Marshway TA7 . . . . .170 D1
Marshwood CE Prim Sch
  DT6 . . . . .199 C2
Marshwood Cross DT6 .199 E1
Marson Rd BS21 . . . . .6 D3
Marston Cl Frome BA11 .119 D2
  Taunton TA1 . . . . .212 E1
Marston La BA11 . . . . . . .119 D2
Marston Mead BA11 . . . .119 D2
Marston Rd Frome BA11 .119 D1
  Nunney BA11 . . . . .143 D8
  Sherborne DT9 . . . . .225 B5
Marston Trad Est BA11 .119 E2
Mart Rd TA24 . . . . .201 B7
Mart The BS23 . . . . .48 E7
Martcombe Rd BS20 . . . . .4 C2
Martin St BA6 . . . . .158 A5
Martin's Cl TA8 . . . . .85 A3
Martindale Ct BS22 . . . . .49 D8
Martindale Rd BS22 . . . . .49 D8
Martins TA3 . . . . .169 C4
Martins Bldgs **4** TA21 . .222 D5
Martins TA3 . . . .
Evercreech BA4 . . . . .141 E1
  Wellington TA21 . . . . .222 D5
  Wells BA5 . . . . .203 B3
Martins Gr BS22 . . . . .31 E2
Martins La BA4 . . . . .141 E1
Martins Paddock BA4 . .142 A6
Martland Cl TA7 . . . . . . .136 E3
Martlet Rd TA24 . . . . . . .200 F7
Martock BS24 . . . . .48 F2
Martock CE Prim Sch
  TA12 . . . . .185 F7
Martock La TA12 . . . . . . .185 F7
Martock Rd
  Keynsham BS31 . . . . .25 A3
  Long Sutton TA10 . . . . . . .172 E4
Martyn Cl TA5 . . . . .135 C2
Marwin Cl TA12 . . . . . . .185 E7
Marwood Cl TA8 . . . . . . .104 C8
Marwood Rd BS4 . . . . . . .22 E8
Mary Brown Davis La **7**
  BA5 . . . . .139 D8
Mary Elton Prim Sch BS21 . .6 C2
Mary Hart Cl BA16 . . . . .207 B7
Mary La **10** EX16 . . . . . . .164 B1
Mary Rd BA5 . . . . .203 C5
Mary St Taunton TA1 . . . . .213 B5
  Yeovil BA21 . . . . .219 B5
Marybush La **7** BS2 . . . .227 B3
Masefield Ho BS23 . . . . . .49 A4
Mason La TA15 . . . . .186 B4
Mason Way BA4 . . . . . . .205 A4
Mason's Way BS27 . . . . . .90 C7
Masons Way BA11 . . . . .119 D1
Materman Rd BS14 . . . . .23 E5
Matfurlong Cl TA12 . . . .185 E7
Matt's La TA14 . . . . .185 F4
Matthews Cl BS14 . . . . . .23 F6
Matthews Rd
  Taunton TA1 . . . . .212 B1
  Yeovil BA21 . . . . .219 B5
Mattock's Tree Hill TA3 .169 E1
Mattys Cross BS14 . . . . .194 D3
Maudlin Cross TA20 . . . .199 C8
Maudlin La TA20 . . . . . . .199 C8
Maudslay Field BA22 . . .197 F8
Maunsel Rd
  Bridgwater TA7 . . . . .154 A1
  North Newton TA7 . . . . . .153 F1
Max Mill La BS25 . . . . . . .69 C8
Maxwell St BA22 . . . . . . .185 E7
Maxwell St TA2 . . . . .212 E6
May Pole Knap TA11 . . . .211 C4
May Tree Cl BS48 . . . . . . .8 D1
May Tree Rd BA3 . . . . . . .78 E1
May Tree Wlk BS31 . . . . .24 C3
May's La BA5 . . . . .33 C3
Maybrick Rd BA2 . . . . . . .44 D5
Mayfair Ave BS48 . . . . . . .8 E1
Mayfield Ave BS22 . . . . . .31 E1
Mayfield Cl TA6 . . . . . . .208 B4
Mayfield Dr TA6 . . . . . . .208 B4
Mayfield Rd Bath BA2 . . . .44 E6
  Yeovil BA21 . . . . .219 B5
Mayfields BS31 . . . . .24 C5
Mayflower Gdns BS48 . . .9 A2
Maynard Cl Bristol BS13 . .22 C5

Maynard Cl continued
  4 Clevedon BS21 . . . . . . .6 F3
Maynard Rd BS13 . . . . . .22 C5
Maypole Cl BS39 . . . . . . .58 E3
Maysfield Cl BS20 . . . . . . .2 D3
Maysgreen La BS24 . . . . .33 B3
Maysmead La BS40 . . . . .53 C6
Maytree Ave BS13 . . . . . .22 B7
Maytree Cl Bristol BS13 . .22 B7
  Frome BA11 . . . . .120 B7
Mc Creery Rd DT9 . . . . .225 D6
McAdam Way BS1 . . . . . .11 F5
McCrae Rd BS24 . . . . .50 B5
McCreath Cl **3** TA6 . . . .153 F3
McKinley Terr TA23 . . . .131 C4
Mead Ave BA22 . . . . .218 B6
Mead Cl Bath BA2 . . . . . . .44 E3
  Bristol BS11 . . . . .4 E6
  Cheddar BS27 . . . . .90 B6
  East Huntspill TA9 . . . . . .136 E8
  Stoke St Michael BA3 . . . .116 D2
Mead Ho BA2 . . . . .44 A5
Mead La Blagdon BS40 . . .54 E3
  Lydford-on-Fosse TA11 . . .158 C3
Saltford BS31 . . . . .25 E4
Sandford BS25 . . . . .51 E4
Stocklinch TA19 . . . . .184 C4
Wanstrow BA4 . . . . .142 F4
West Pennard BA6 . . . . . .140 C2
Mead Lands BA2 . . . . .43 B7
Mead Rd BS20 . . . . .2 C2
Mead St BS3 . . . . .227 C1
Mead Terr BS40 . . . . .54 E2
Mead The Clutton BS39 . . .58 E3
  Dundry BS41 . . . . .21 D2
  East Brent TA9 . . . . .86 E5
  Farmborough BA2 . . . . . . .60 A6
  Holcombe BA3 . . . . .116 C8
  Ilminster TA19 . . . . .221 B3
  Paulton BS39 . . . . .77 D5
  Rode BA11 . . . . .101 E8
  R Shepton Mallet BA4 . .205 B6
  Shipham BS25 . . . . .70 E8
  Stoke St Michael BA3 . . . .116 B2
  Stratton-on-the-Fosse BA3 . .96 F2
  Street BA16 . . . . .207 D7
  Timsbury BA2 . . . . .60 C3
  Winsley BA15 . . . . .64 F7
Mead Vale BS22 . . . . .49 E8
Mead Vale Prim Sch
  BS22 . . . . .31 E1
Mead Way TA2 . . . . .169 B6
Meade Cl TA6 . . . . .153 F3
Meade La TA19 . . . . .184 E1
Meadow Cl Backwell BS48 . .19 A6
  Chilton Trinity TA5 . . . . . .135 F2
  Farrington Gurney BS39 . . .77 A3
  Henstridge BA8 . . . . .190 A7
  Highbridge TA9 . . . . .104 D4
  Kingston St Mary TA2 . . . .168 E8
  Langport TA10 . . . . .172 A6
  Nailsea BS48 . . . . .8 E3
Nether Stowey TA5 . . . . . .134 A2
  Portishead BS20 . . . . .2 C1
  Stalbridge DT10 . . . . .190 B4
  Street BA16 . . . . .207 B4
  Wincanton BA9 . . . . .216 C4
Meadow Cotts TA24 . . . .131 B4
Meadow Croft BS24 . . . . .49 B2
Meadow Dr Bath BA2 . . . .62 D8
  Locking BS24 . . . . .50 B4
  Portishead BS20 . . . . .1 F1
Meadow Gdns Bath BA1 . .27 A1
  Stogursey TA5 . . . . .134 C6
Meadow Gr BS11 . . . . . . .4 D7
Meadow La
  Bathampton BA2 . . . . .28 E2
  Walton BA16 . . . . .156 E7
Meadow Pk Bathford BA1 . .29 B3
  Wembdon TA6 . . . . .208 C5
Meadow Rd Clevedon BS21 . .6 E3
  Paulton BS39 . . . . .77 F4
  Yeovil BA21 . . . . .219 E7
Meadow Rise BA4 . . . . . .205 B7
Meadow St Axbridge BS26 .70 C2
  Bristol BS2 . . . . .227 C4
  Weston-Super-Mare BS23 . .48 E7
Meadow Terr TA1 . . . . . .201 A5
Meadow View
  2 Bampton EX16 . . . . .164 B1
  4 Barwick BA22 . . . . . .197 F8
  East Coker BA22 . . . . .197 C8
  Glastonbury BA6 . . . . . . .206 E3
  Radstock BA3 . . . . .79 A1
  Timberscombe TA24 . . . . .130 A5
Meadow View Cl BA1 . . . .44 A8
Meadow Villas BS23 . . . . .48 E8
Meadowbank BS22 . . . . . .31 F3
Meadowcroft Dr TA8 . . . .85 B2
Meadowlands BS22 . . . . .32 C2
Meadows End BS25 . . . . .52 D4
Meadows Prim Sch The
  BS30 . . . . .25 D8
Meadows The
  Drayton TA10 . . . . .171 E3
  Porlock TA24 . . . . .124 A3
Meadowside
  Carhampton TA24 . . . . . .131 A5
  Rockwell Green TA21 . . . .222 B5
Meadowside Cl TA1 . . . .212 B4
Meadowside Dr BS14 . . . .23 A3
Meads Droveway TA3 . . .169 D5
Meads The DT9 . . . . .217 D2
Meadway Bristol BS9 . . . . .5 C5
  Farmborough BA2 . . . . . . .60 A6

Meadway continued
Temple Cloud BS39 . . . . .58 E1
Woolavington TA7 . . . . .136 E4
Meadway Ave BS48 . . . . .8 D2
Mearcombe La BS24 . . . . .67 F6
Meardon Rd BS14 . . . . .23 E6
Meare BS24 . . . . .48 F2
Meare Prim Sch BA6 . . . . .138 D4
Meare Rd Bath BA2 . . . . .45 A2
Glastonbury BA6 . . . . .206 B6
Mearway BA6 . . . . .138 C5
Mearn's Cross BA3 . . . . .94 B6
Mede Cl BS1 . . . . .227 B1
Medical Ave BS2, BS8 . .226 C3
Medway Cl
Keynsham BS31 . . . . .25 A3
Taunton TA1 . . . . .213 D4
Medway Dr BS31 . . . . .25 A3
Meetinghouse La BS49 . . . . .18 A1
Melbourne House Mews
BA5 . . . . .203 D4
Melbourne Pl TA6 . . . . .209 B6
Melbourne Terr 2 BS21 . . . . .6 D2
Melcombe Ct BA2 . . . . .44 D4
Melcombe La TA6 . . . . .153 E3
Melcombe Rd BA2 . . . . .44 D4
Mellanby Cl BA16 . . . . .207 D5
Mellent Ave BS13 . . . . .22 C3
Mells CE Fst Sch BA11 . . . . .118 A6
Mells Cl BS31 . . . . .25 A2
Mells La BA3 . . . . .79 B1
Melrose Ave Bristol BS8 . . . .226 B4
Wells BA5 . . . . .203 C4
Melrose Cl BS23 . . . . .203 C4
Melrose Gr BA2 . . . . .44 B3
Melrose Pl BS8 . . . . .226 B4
Melrose Rd BA21 . . . . .219 B6
Melrose Terr 28 A2
Melsbury La BA5 . . . . .139 E6
Memorial Ave TA18 . . . . . .224 C5
Memorial Rd
Houndstone BA22 . . . . .218 B6
Wrington BS40 . . . . .35 E2
Mendip Ave
Shepton Mallet BA4 . . . . .205 E4
Weston-Super-Mare BS22 . . .31 F2
Mendip Centre (Coll) The
BS40 . . . . .54 D2
Mendip Cl Axbridge BS26 . . .70 D2
Frome BA11 . . . . .120 A4
Keynsham BS31 . . . . .24 D5
3 Nailsea BS48 . . . . .8 E1
Paulton BS39 . . . . .77 E4
Yatton BS49 . . . . .34 B7
Mendip Dr BA11 . . . . .120 A7
Mendip Edge BS24 . . . . .66 F8
Mendip Fields BA3 . . . . .96 C2
Mendip Gdns Bath BA2 . . . . .62 D8
Frome BA11 . . . . .120 A7
Yatton BS49 . . . . .34 B7
Mendip Green Fst Sch
BS22 . . . . .31 E1
Mendip Ho TA1 . . . . .212 F3
Mendip Lea Cl BS27 . . . . .90 F2
Mendip Lodge BS25 . . . . .70 A8
Mendip Rd
Bridgwater TA6 . . . . .209 C4
Locking BS24 . . . . .50 D4
Portishead BS20 . . . . .2 B5
Rockbridge BS26 . . . . .87 A6
Stoke St Michael BA3 . . . . . .116 A2
Weston-Super-Mare BS23 . . .49 A7
Yatton BS49 . . . . .34 B7
Mendip Rise BA3 . . . . .3 A4
Mendip Vale BA3 . . . . .116 E7
Mendip Vale Sta* BA4 . . . . .205 F3
Mendip Vale Trad Est
BS27 . . . . .90 A7
Mendip View
Coleford BA3 . . . . .116 F7
Street BA16 . . . . .207 B7
Mendip Villas
Cheddar BS27 . . . . .71 A1
Compton Martin BS40 . . . . . .73 F7
Emborough BA3 . . . . .95 E3
Mendip Way
Burnham-On-Sea TA8 . . . . . .104 B7
Radstock BA3 . . . . .78 F3
Menlea BS40 . . . . .54 D3
Mercer Ct BS14 . . . . .23 B8
Merchant St BS1 . . . . .227 B3
Merchants Barton Ind Est
BA11 . . . . .119 F4
Merchants Ct BS8 . . . . .226 A1
Merchants Quay BS1 . . . . . .227 A1
Merchants Rd
Bristol BS8 . . . . .226 A3
Bristol, Hotwells BS8 . . . . . . .226 A1
Merchants Row* BS1 . . . . . .227 A1
Merchants' Barton 3
BA11 . . . . .119 F4
Meredith Cl BA22 . . . . .197 C3
Meredith Ct BS1 . . . . .226 A1
Meriden BA1 . . . . .44 D8
Meridian Pl BS8 . . . . .226 B3
Meridian Vale BS8 . . . . .226 B3
Meriet Ave BS13 . . . . .22 B4
Merle Cl TA6 . . . . .209 B4
Merlin Cl Bristol BS9 . . . . .5 F8
Weston-Super-Mare BS22 . . .49 E8
Merlin Dr BA5 . . . . .203 B5
Merlin Pk BA TA2 . . . . .213 B6
Merlin Pk BS20 . . . . .2 A4
Merrick Ct BS1 . . . . .227 A1
Merrick Rd BA4 . . . . .206 E7
Merridge Cl TA6 . . . . .208 A4
Merridge Hill TA5 . . . . .152 D6
Merrifields TA4 . . . . .167 E6

Merriman Gdns BA16 . . . . . .207 C5
Merriman Rd BA16 . . . . .207 C5
Merrimans Rd BS11 . . . . .4 D8
Merriott Fst Sch TA16 . . . . .195 F7
Merriott Rd
Hinton St George TA17 . . . . .195 D4
Merriott TA16 . . . . .195 F6
Merry La TA9 . . . . .136 F8
Merry-field BA3 . . . . .116 E8
Merryfield La
Doulting BA4 . . . . .141 F5
Ilton TA19 . . . . .183 E4
Merryfield Rd BS24 . . . . .50 B6
Merryfields TA9 . . . . .106 D5
Merthyr Guest Cl BA8 . . . . .176 E1
Merton Dr BS24 . . . . .50 A8
Mervyn Ball Cl TA20 . . . . . . .223 C5
Methwyn Cl BS22 . . . . .49 C7
Mews The Bath BA1 . . . . .44 A8
4 Bridgwater TA6 . . . . .209 B4
East Coker BA22 . . . . .197 C7
Minehead TA24 . . . . .201 A7
Wiveliscombe TA4 . . . . .210 C4
Meyrick Dr BS27 . . . . .71 B1
Michaels Mead BA1 . . . . .27 B2
Middle Ave BS1 . . . . .227 A2
Middle Brooks BA16 . . . . . . .207 C3
Middle Dro
Baltonsborough BA6 . . . . . . .158 B4
Compton Dundon TA11 . . . . .156 F3
Glastonbury BA6 . . . . .206 B5
Hambridge TA10,TA12 . . . . . .184 F8
Lydford-on-Fosse TA11 . . . . .158 C3
Rodney Stoke BS27 . . . . .109 C6
Street BA6 . . . . .157 C7
Middle Field La DT9 . . . . . . .188 B7
Middle Gate TA10 . . . . .172 D8
Middle Green Rd TA21 . . . . .222 E3
Middle Leaze BA16 . . . . .28 B1
Kingston Seymour BS21 . . . . .15 F4
Middle Leaze Dro TA12 . . . .185 F7
Middle Leigh BA16 . . . . .207 C5
Middle Moor Dro TA5 . . . . . .134 D7
Middle Moor La BS27 . . . . . . .89 E7
Middle Path TA18 . . . . .224 B5
Middle Rd TA7 . . . . .137 A3
Middle Ridge La DT9 . . . . . . .175 D1
Middle St Ashcott TA7 . . . . .156 B7
Burnham-On-Sea TA9 . . . . . . .85 E5
Crewkerne TA18 . . . . .224 F3
East Harptree BS40 . . . . .74 F4
East Lambrook TA13 . . . . . . .220 C8
Galhampton BA22 . . . . .175 D8
Kingsdon TA11 . . . . .173 D5
Martock TA12 . . . . .185 D4
Minehead TA24 . . . . .200 F8
Montacute TA15 . . . . .186 B3
North Perrott TA18 . . . . .196 C4
Puriton TA7 . . . . .136 C4
Shepton BA22 . . . . .184 E8
Shepton Beauchamp TA19 . .184 E3
Taunton TA1 . . . . .212 F4
Yeovil BA20 . . . . .219 B4
Middle Stoke BA3 . . . . .64 A6
Middle Touches TA20 . . . . . .223 E5
Middle Way TA11 . . . . .157 B4
Middle Yeo Gn BS48 . . . . .8 D3
Middle's La BA4 . . . . .140 C4
Middlecombe Cross
TA24 . . . . .200 C6
Middlefield La TA10 . . . . . . .184 D6
Middlefield Rd TA10 . . . . . . .172 C7
Middleford Ho BS13 . . . . .22 C4
Middlegate Rd TA10 . . . . . . .172 C7
Middlemead BA3 . . . . .96 F3
Middlepiece La BA2,BS31 . . .42 F7
Middleroom Dro TA3 . . . . . . .182 E4
Middlestream Cl TA6 . . . . . .208 D2
Middleton La
Clatworthy TA4 . . . . .149 C2
Shepton Mallet BA4 . . . . . . .205 B4
Middleton Rd BS11 . . . . .4 F8
Middleway TA1 . . . . .212 E2
Middleway Ct TA1 . . . . .212 E2
Middleway Rd BA4 . . . . .158 E8
Midelney La
TA7 . . . . .155 B3
Midelney Rd TA10 . . . . .171 E2
Midford BS24 . . . . .48 F2
Midford Hill BA2,BA3 . . . . . . .63 C5
Midford La BA2,BA3 . . . . .63 E7
Midford Rd
Southstoke BA2 . . . . .63 B7
Taunton TA1 . . . . .213 B4
Midhaven Rise BS22 . . . . .31 E4
Midland Bridge Rd BA1,
BA2 . . . . .228 A2
Midland Rd Bath BA1 . . . . . . .44 D7
Bristol BS2 . . . . .227 C3
Midland St BS2 . . . . .227 C2
Midleaze DT9 . . . . .225 A3
Midney La BA22 . . . . .174 D8
Midsomer Ent Pk BA3 . . . . . .78 C2
Midsomer Norton Prim Sch
BA3 . . . . .78 B1
Midsomer Norton Railway
Ctr* BA3 . . . . .97 A8
Midsummer Bldgs BA1 . . . .28 B2
Milborne Port Bsns Ctr
DT9 . . . . .217 D2
Milborne Port Prim Sch
DT9 . . . . .217 D2
Milbourne Cl BA15 . . . . .64 D7
Milburn Rd BS23 . . . . .48 F7
Milbury Gdns BS22 . . . . .31 C2
Mildmay Dr BA22 . . . . .174 F3
Mildmay's Rd TA10 . . . . .155 F1
Mildred Rd BA16 . . . . .156 E7

Mile Wlk BS14 . . . . .23 A6
Miles St BA2 . . . . .228 C1
Miles's Bldgs BA1 . . . . .228 B3
Milestone Cl TA6 . . . . .153 F4
Milestone Ct BS22 . . . . .32 D2
Milford Inf Sch BA21 . . . . . .219 B7
Milford Jun Sch BA21 . . . . . .219 B7
Milford Pl 2 TA1 . . . . .213 A4
Milford Rd BA21 . . . . .219 C7
Milk St Bath BA1 . . . . .228 B2
Frome BA11 . . . . .119 E5
Milking La BS27 . . . . .90 E2
Mill Ave BS1 . . . . .227 A2
Mill Batch Farm Ind Est
TA9 . . . . .86 F4
Mill Cl Cannington TA5 . . . . .135 B2
East Coker BA22 . . . . .197 C8
Frome BA11 . . . . .119 F6
Nether Stowey TA5 . . . . .134 B2
Portbury BS20 . . . . .3 D2
Mill Cotts TA3 . . . . .169 D4
Mill Cross Halstock BA22 . . .197 C3
Kingston St Mary TA2 . . . . . .168 E7
Mill Ct TA23 . . . . .202 B7
Mill Farm Hill TA5 . . . . .134 F1
Mill Gdns BA22 . . . . .201 D1
Mill Hill BA2 . . . . .62 E1
Mill La Alhampton BA4 . . . . .159 C5
Axbridge BS26 . . . . .88 D4
Axminster EX13 . . . . .198 F3
Batcombe BA4 . . . . .142 C1
Bath BA2 . . . . .44 B6
Bathampton BA2 . . . . .28 F2
Beckington BA11 . . . . .101 D5
Bishops Lydeard TA4 . . . . . . .167 F8
Bitton BS30 . . . . .25 E8
Bourton SP8 . . . . .161 F1
Bradford Abbas DT9 . . . . . . .187 E1
Bruton BA10 . . . . .215 E6
Cannington TA5 . . . . .135 B2
Chard TA20 . . . . .223 C3
Chard, Wambrook TA20 . . . .193 C2
Charlton Mackrell TA11 . . . .173 E7
Chew Stoke BS40 . . . . .56 E1
Clatworthy TA4 . . . . .149 E2
Compton Martin BS40 . . . . . .74 A7
Congresbury BS49 . . . . .34 D4
Corfe TA3 . . . . .181 F6
Corsley Heath BA12,BA11 . .144 C8
Creech St Michael TA3 . . . . .169 D4
Crewkerne TA18 . . . . .224 D5
Crewkerne, Misterton
TA18 . . . . .196 B3
Dinnington TA17 . . . . .195 B8
Dunster TA24 . . . . .201 D1
East Coker BA22 . . . . .197 B8
East Coker BA22 . . . . .197 C7
Exford TA24 . . . . .128 C2
Higher Chillington TA19 . . . .194 E5
Ilchester BA22 . . . . .173 F1
Ilminster TA19 . . . . .221 B7
Ilminster, Dowlish Wake
TA19 . . . . .194 E2
Ilminster, Kingstone TA19 . .221 F1
Logen TA13 . . . . .185 A1
Lynford-on-Fosse TA11 . . . . .158 C2
Maiden Bradley BA12 . . . . . .144 B3
Marnhull DT10 . . . . .190 F6
Monkton Combe BA2 . . . . . . .45 F1
Monkton Combe BA2 . . . . . . .63 E8
Nether Stowey TA5 . . . . .134 A2
North Wootton BA4 . . . . . . .140 D5
NonRoady TA7 . . . . .155 C2
Pitcombe BA10 . . . . .215 C3
Porlock TA24 . . . . .124 A3
Portbury BS20 . . . . .3 E3
Priston BA2 . . . . .61 A7
Redhill BS40 . . . . .55 A8
Shepton Mallet BA4 . . . . . . .205 A6
Shepton Mallet BA4 . . . . . . .204 E4
Somerton BA4 . . . . .211 D2
South Petherton TA13 . . . . .220 E6
Stoke St Michael BA3 . . . . . .116 B3
Taunton TA1 . . . . .212 B3
Thurloxton TA2 . . . . .153 D1
Timsbury BA2 . . . . .60 B1
Trent DT9 . . . . .187 F5
Watchet TA23 . . . . .202 C7
Wellington TA21 . . . . .222 B8
Wells BA5 . . . . .203 A1
West Monkton TA2 . . . . .169 D8
Wiveliscombe TA4 . . . . .210 C4
Wrington BS40 . . . . .53 F8
Yeovil BA20 . . . . .219 B3
Mill La Trad Est BA20 . . . . . .219 C4
Mill Lane Cl TA3 . . . . .168 D1
Mill Leat BA6 . . . . .157 F5
Mill Leg BS49 . . . . .34 A6
Mill Rd
Barton St David TA11 . . . . . .158 A3
Radstock BA3 . . . . .79 B2
Mill Rise Bourton SP8 . . . . . .161 F1
Staplegrove TA2 . . . . .212 B7
Mill Road Ind Est BA3 . . . . . .79 B3
Mill St Cannington TA24 . . . .131 A4
North Petherton TA6 . . . . . .153 F3
Rimpton BA22 . . . . .188 A8
Watchet TA23 . . . . .202 C7
Wells BA5 . . . . .203 D4
Wincanton BA9 . . . . .216 C4
Mill Stream Cl BS26 . . . . .70 C1
Mill Stream Gdns TA21 . . . . .222 B7
Mill Wlk TA7 . . . . .136 E3
Millands La TA5 . . . . .133 C6
Millands The TA11 . . . . .211 E4
Mitchell Gdns TA20 . . . . . . .223 B3

Millard's Hill
Batcombe BA4 . . . . .142 D2
Midsomer Norton BA3 . . . . . .78 C3
Millards Ct BA3 . . . . .78 B3
Millards Hill BA3 . . . . .78 B3
Millbatch BA6 . . . . .138 C4
Millbourne Rd BS27 . . . . .90 C7
Millbridge Gdns TA24 . . . . .200 F7
Millbridge Rd TA24 . . . . .200 F7
Millbrook BA20 . . . . .219 A4
Millbrook Cross EX13 . . . . . .198 A1
Millbrook Ct BA2 . . . . .228 C1
Millbrook Dale EX13 . . . . . . .198 A1
Millbrook Gdns BA7 . . . . . . .214 B5
Millbrook Pl BA2 . . . . .228 C1
Millcross BS21 . . . . .16 C8
Millennium Cl BA3 . . . . .116 A3
Millennium Sq BS1 . . . . .226 C2
Miller Cl BS23 . . . . .48 F8
Miller Ho BS8 . . . . .226 A2
Miller Wlk BA2 . . . . .28 F1
Miller's Hill DT9 . . . . .217 A5
Millers Cl BS20 . . . . .4 C4
Millers Orch BA22 . . . . .203 E5
Millers Orch TA3 . . . . .170 F1
Millers Rise BS22 . . . . .32 A4
Millers Way TA4 . . . . .167 F8
Milletts Cl 2 TA24 . . . . .131 A5
Millfield Chard TA20 . . . . . . .223 D3
Ilchester BA22 . . . . .173 E2
Midsomer Norton BA3 . . . . . .96 F8
Millfield Cl TA20 . . . . .223 D3
Millfield Pre Prep Sch
BA6 . . . . .206 D4
Millfield Prep Sch Edgerley
Hall BA6 . . . . .139 D1
Millfield Sch
Glastonbury BA6 . . . . .206 E5
Street BA16 . . . . .207 E5
Millfield Sch (Chindit Ho)
BA6 . . . . .206 E5
Millford La BA4 . . . . .159 C6
Millgreen Cl TA9 . . . . .136 B8
Millground Rd BS13 . . . . .21 F5
Millham La TA22 . . . . .163 D6
Miller Rd BS49 . . . . .35 B8
Milliman Cl BS13 . . . . .22 C5
Milliner Ct BA4 . . . . .205 B5
Millmead Ho BS13 . . . . .22 C4
Millmead Rd BA2 . . . . .44 C5
Millmoot La TA7 . . . . .136 F3
Millstream Cl TA24 . . . . .200 F6
Millward Terr BS39 . . . . .77 E6
Millway Cl TA3 . . . . .168 D1
Millway BS27 . . . . .110 B8
Millwey Ave EX13 . . . . .198 A2
Millwood Cl TA6 . . . . .208 E2
Milne Cl TA6 . . . . .208 F2
Milsom Pl TA4 . . . . .167 F6
Milsom St BA1 . . . . .228 B3
Milton Ave Bath BA2 . . . . .44 F4
Weston-Super-Mare BS23 . . .49 A8
Milton Brow BS22 . . . . .31 B2
Milton CI Nailsea BS48 . . . . . . .8 E3
Taunton TA1 . . . . .213 C3
Milton Ct BA4 . . . . .205 B7
Milton Gn BS22 . . . . .31 C1
Milton Hill
Monkton Heathfield TA2 . . .213 E7
Weston-Super-Mare BS22 . . .31 B2
Milton Ho BS23 . . . . .187 D6
Milton Jun & Inf Schs
BS22 . . . . .31 C1
Milton La Martock TA12 . . . .185 E8
Wells BA5 . . . . .203 D5
Milton Lane BA5 . . . . .203 B8
Milton Lease TA10 . . . . .172 E2
Milton Lodge Gdn*
BA5 . . . . .203 D7
Milton Park Rd BS22 . . . . .31 C1
Milton Pk BS22 . . . . .31 C1
Milton Rd Bath BA2 . . . . .78 C1
Taunton TA1 . . . . .213 C3
Weston-Super-Mare BS23,
BS23 . . . . .49 B8
Milton Rise BS22 . . . . .31 C1
Milton Terr BA2 . . . . .78 C1
Milverton Com Prim Sch
TA4 . . . . .166 F4
Milverton Rd TA21 . . . . .222 B8
Milward Rd BS31 . . . . .24 E6
Minchinton's Cl TA14 . . . . . .185 F2
Minehead First Sch
TA24 . . . . .200 F6
Minehead Hospl TA24 . . . . .200 F7
Minehead La TA22 . . . . .164 A7
Minehead Mid Sch
TA24 . . . . .201 A6
Minehead Rd
Bishops Lydeard TA4 . . . . . . .167 E8
Bridgwater TA6 . . . . .209 B4
Minehead Sta* BS24 . . . . . .201 B7
Miners Cl BS41 . . . . .10 F2
Minerva Gdns BA2 . . . . .44 C4
Minnows The TA20 . . . . .223 C3
Minsmere Rd BS31 . . . . .25 A4
Minster Ct BA7 . . . . .214 B5
Minster Cl TA1 . . . . .212 C1
Minster Way BA2 . . . . .45 C8
Mint The BA11 . . . . .119 E5
Minton Cl BS14 . . . . .23 B5
Mintons Ct BA20 . . . . .223 B3
Mintons Orch TA20 . . . . .223 B3
Misburg Cl BA4 . . . . .205 A5
Misterton CE Fst Sch
TA18 . . . . .224 F3
Mitchell Gdns TA20 . . . . . . .223 B3

Mitchell La BS1 . . . . .227 B2
Mitchell St TA21 . . . . .222 C7
Mitchell Terr BA5 . . . . .112 L1
Mitchell's Row BA22 . . . . . . .175 D6
Mitchelmore Rd BA21 . . . . . .219 B5
Mitford-Slade Ct BS49 . . . . .34 C7
Mizzymead Cl 1 BS48 . . . . . . .8 D1
Mizzymead Rd BS48 . . . . .8 E1
Mizzymead Rise BS48 . . . . . . .8 E1
Moffats Dr BA5 . . . . .113 A2
Molesworth Cl BS13 . . . . .22 A4
Molesworth Dr BS13 . . . . .22 A4
Molly Cl BS39 . . . . .76 E8
Monarch Ctr TA2 . . . . .213 C6
Monday's Court La
TA10 . . . . .172 E5
Money Pit La EX13 . . . . .193 A1
Monger Cotts BS39 . . . . .77 F4
Monger La
Midsomer Norton BA3 . . . . . .78 A3
Paulton BS39 . . . . .78 A4
Monington Rd BA6 . . . . .206 E6
Monk Cross TA24 . . . . .128 D1
Monkley La BA11 . . . . .83 C1
Monks Cl
Rooksbridge BS26 . . . . .87 B5
Taunton TA1 . . . . .213 B5
Monks Dale BA21 . . . . .218 D6
Monks Dr TA7 . . . . .137 F1
Monks Ford BA5 . . . . .139 D8
Monks Hill BS22 . . . . .31 B3
Monks Way TA8 . . . . .104 B6
Monks' Path TA23,TA24 . . . .131 E4
Monksdale Rd BA2 . . . . .44 D4
Monksford La BA5 . . . . .139 C8
Monkstone Dr TA8 . . . . .84 F5
Monksway TA23 . . . . .131 E4
Monkton Ave BS24 . . . . .49 A2
Monkton Combe Jun Sch
BA2 . . . . .45 C1
Monkton Combe Jun Sch
(Pre-Prep) BA2 . . . . .45 C1
Monkton Combe Senior Sch
BA2 . . . . .45 D2
Monkton Farleigh Prim Sch
BA15 . . . . .46 E7
Monkton La TA5 . . . . .134 D5
Monmouth Cl
Chard TA20 . . . . .223 E4
Glastonbury BA6 . . . . .206 D5
Portishead BS20 . . . . .1 F4
Westonzoyland TA7 . . . . .154 F5
Monmouth Ct Bath BA1 . . . .228 A2
Chard TA20 . . . . .223 E4
Monmouth Dr BA11 . . . . .120 B6
Monmouth Farm Cl TA6 . . . .135 F5
Monmouth Paddock BA2 . . . .81 E5
Monmouth Pl BA1 . . . . .228 B2
Monmouth Rd
Keynsham BS31 . . . . .24 D5
Pill BS20 . . . . .4 C5
Shepton Mallet BA4 . . . . . . .205 A4
Taunton TA1 . . . . .213 B5
Westonzoyland TA7 . . . . .154 F6
Yeovil BA20 . . . . .219 D7
Monmouth St Bath BA1 . . . .228 B2
Bridgwater TA6 . . . . .209 A5
Montacute Ho* TA15 . . . . . .186 B4
Montacute Rd
Montacute TA14,TA15 . . . . .186 B4
Tintinhull BA22 . . . . .186 B6
Montague Ct 4 BS2 . . . . . . .227 A4
Montague Flats 6 BS2 . . . . .227 A4
Montague Gdns BA7 . . . . . . .214 B5
Montague Hill BS2 . . . . .227 A4
Montague Hill S 5 BS2 . . . .227 A4
Montague Pl BS6 . . . . .227 A4
Montague Rd
Peasedown St John BA2 . . . . .79 E5
Saltford BS31 . . . . .25 D2
Montague St BS1 . . . . .227 A4
Montague Way TA20 . . . . . . .223 C3
Montacliffe CE Jun Sch
TA11 . . . . .211 E3
Montpelier BS23 . . . . .48 F8
Montgomery Ct BA11 . . . . . .120 A4
Montgomery La BA11 . . . . . .120 A4
Montrose Rd BA21 . . . . .219 E7
Montrose Villas BS27 . . . . . . .90 C7
Montsurs Cl BA3 . . . . .96 E3
Monument Cl TA21 . . . . .222 E4
Monument Rd TA21 . . . . .222 E4
Moorlham La
Ilminster TA19 . . . . .221 D1
Ilminster, Moolham TA19 . . .194 D7
Moon La TA7 . . . . .153 E1
Moon St BS2 . . . . .227 B4
Moon's Dro TA7 . . . . .155 A1
Moondown La TA13 . . . . .220 B2
Moonhayes Cross EX14 . . . . .191 F4
Moonraker Cl 7 TA6 . . . . . .209 B4
Moons Hill BA3 . . . . .116 A4
Moonshill Cl BA3 . . . . .116 A3
Moonshill Ct BA3 . . . . .116 A3
Moonshill Rd BA3 . . . . .116 A3
Moor Cl
Compton Dundon TA11 . . . . .156 F2
Langport TA10 . . . . .172 A6
Wincanton BA9 . . . . .216 D3
Moor Croft Rd BS24 . . . . .49 B3
Moor Dro TA7 . . . . .155 F6
Moor End Spout BS48 . . . . . . .8 D2
Moor Gn BS20 . . . . .70 C1
Moor Gr BS11 . . . . .5 A8

Moor House La TA5 .....133 E4
Moor La Alhampton BA4 ..159 C5
Backwell BS48 ...18 F6
Batcombe BA4 ...142 D1
Brushford TA22 ...163 F4
Churchinford TA3 ...192 A7
Clapton In Gordano BS20 ...2 E1
Clevedon BS21 ...6 E2
Clevedon BS21 ...7 A2
Cucklington SP8 ...177 E5
Draycott BS27 ...90 F1
East Coker BA22 ...197 D7
Hardington Mandeville BA22 ...197 A7
Higher Chillington TA20 ...194 F5
Hutton BS24 ...49 D3
North Curry TA3 ...170 B4
South Petherton TA13 ...220 B3
Tickenham BS21 ...7 F4
Westbury Sub Mendip BA5 .110 C5
Weston-Super-Mare BS24 ...49 F7
Wincanton BA9 ...216 C2
Moor Lane Cl TA3 ...170 B4
Moor Park Rd TA10 ...171 F5
Moor Pk Clevedon BS21 ...6 E2
Langport TA10 ...171 F5
Moor Rd Banwell BS29 ...51 B5
Bridgwater TA7 ...154 F8
Middlezoy TA7 ...155 B4
Minehead TA24 ...200 E8
Moorlinch TA7 ...155 D7
Sutton Mallet TA7 ...155 B8
Yatton BS49 ...17 B2
Moor Sherd BS28 ...110 C1
Moor Villas TA13 ...220 B3
Moorclose Dro TA7 ...137 C3
Moorclose La BA4 ...158 E6
Moore's La TA5,TA6 ...208 C7
Moorend Gdns BS11 ...4 F7
Moores Yd BA14 ...83 C6
Moorfield Gdn TA24 ...146 C6
Moorfield Rd BS48 ...19 A6
Moorfields Cl BA2 ...44 D3
Moorfields Ct BS48 ...8 D2
Moorfields Ho BS48 ...8 D2
Moorfields Rd Bath BA2 ...44 D4
Nailsea BS48 ...8 D2
Moorgrove Ho BS9 ...5 C7
Moorham Rd BS25 ...52 A1
Moorhouse La TA4 ...165 A8
Moorings The BS20 ...4 C4
Moorland Cl TA1 ...213 C5
Moorland Cotts BS26 ...69 F2
Moorland Pl TA1 ...213 C5
Moorland Rd Bath BA2 ...44 D5
Bridgwater TA6 ...209 D4
Street BA16 ...207 B7
Taunton TA1 ...213 C5
Weston-Super-Mare BS23 ...48 E4
Moorland St BS26 ...70 C1
Moorland Way TA6 ...209 D5
Moorlands TA4 ...167 F8
Moorlands Cl
16 Martock TA12 ...185 E6
Nailsea BS48 ...8 D2
Moorlands Dr BA3 ...64 B6
Moorlands Inf Sch BA2 ...44 D4
Moorlands Jun Sch BA2 ...44 D3
Moorlands Pk 18 TA12 ...185 E6
Moorlands Pk Sh Ctr 19 TA12 ...185 E6
Moorlands Rd TA16 ...195 E6
Moorledge La BS39,BS40 ...57 F7
Moorledge Rd BS40 ...39 B1
Moorlinch Right Dro TA7 ...155 D6
Moorside BS49 ...17 B1
Moorside Ct BS21 ...6 E2
Moorside Villas BS21 ...6 E2
Moortown La TA10 ...171 B2
Moorview Cl BA6 ...138 C4
Moorway La DT9 ...188 C6
Moots La TA6 ...209 D4
Morangis Way TA20 ...223 B6
Morden Wlk BS14 ...23 D7
Moreton Cl BS14 ...23 A4
Moreton La BS40 ...56 E2
Morford St BA1 ...228 B4
Morgan Cl Saltford BS31 ...25 D2
Weston-Super-Mare BS24 ...50 B8
Morgan Way BA2 ...79 E7
Morgan's La
East Harptree BS40 ...74 F2
8 Frome BA11 ...119 E5
Morgans Bldgs BS20 ...8 F8
Morgans Hill Cl BS48 ...18 D8
Morgans Rise TA1 ...212 A3
Morland Rd TA9 ...104 D4
Morlands Ind Pk TA9 ...104 D4
Morley Terr Bath BA2 ...44 D6
Radstock BA3 ...79 A3
Mornington Pk TA21 ...222 E5
Morpeth Rd BS4 ...22 D8
Morrell's Cross EX16 ...164 B4
Morrell's La EX16 ...178 B6
Morris Cl TA19 ...184 C5
Morris La BA1 ...29 B3
Mortimer Cl Bath BA1 ...27 B2
Woolavington TA7 ...136 E4
Mortimer Rd BS8 ...226 A3
Morton's La TA10 ...156 C1
Moseley Gr BS23 ...48 E2
Moss Cl TA6 ...209 C6
Moss La TA3 ...169 C3
Mosterton Down La DT8 ...196 A1
Moulton Cl BA4 ...205 A4
Mounsdon Cl BA6 ...157 E4
Mount Beacon Row 1 BA1 ...28 A1
Mount Gr BA2 ...44 B3
Mount Hey TA11 ...211 E3
Mount Hindrance Cl TA20 ...223 D6
Mount Hindrance La TA20 ...223 D6
Mount Ho TA1 ...212 F3
Mount La
Charlton Horethorne DT9 ..176 A1
Golsoncott TA23,TA24 ...131 C1
Mount Nebo TA1 ...212 E2
Mount Pleasant Bath BA2 .45 D1
Castle Cary BA7 ...214 C5
Crewkerne TA18 ...224 D6
Frome BA11 ...119 F2
Kilmington BA12 ...161 F6
Pill BS20 ...4 D4
Pilton BA4 ...140 F3
Radstock BA3 ...79 B2
Yeovil BA21 ...219 C5
Mount Pleasant Ave BA5 ...203 B5
Mount Rd Bath BA1 ...228 B4
Nether Stowey TA5 ...134 A2
Mount St
Bishops Lydeard TA4 ...167 E8
Bridgwater TA6 ...208 F5
Taunton TA1 ...212 F3
Mount Terr TA1 ...213 A3
Mount The Frome BA11 ...119 F2
Taunton TA1 ...212 F3
Yatton BS49 ...34 C8
Mount View Bath BA1 ...28 A1
Bath BA2 ...44 B3
Woolavington TA7 ...136 E4
Mount View Terr TA6 ...135 F6
Mountain Ash BA1 ...27 D1
Mountain Wood BA1 ...29 C2
Mountain's La BA2 ...59 E6
Mountbatten Cl
Burnham-On-Sea TA8 ...85 A1
Weston-Super-Mare BS22 ...31 E4
Mountbatten Ho TA6 ...209 C5
Mounter's Hill EX13, TA20 ...193 B2
Mounters Cl DT10 ...190 F5
Mountery Cl BA5 ...203 D5
Mountery Rd BA5 ...203 D5
Mountfields Ave TA1 ...213 B1
Mountfields Pk TA1 ...213 B1
Mountfields Rd TA1 ...213 B1
Mountsfield BA11 ...120 A2
Mountway TA1 ...213 A3
Mountway Cl TA1 ...212 C4
Mountway La TA1 ...212 C4
Mountway Rd TA1 ...212 C4
Movey La BA22 ...173 F1
Mow Barton Bristol BS13 ..21 F6
8 Martock TA12 ...185 E6
Mow Barton Rd TA11 ...173 D5
Mowbray Rd BS14 ...23 C7
Mowcroft Rd BS13 ...22 D4
Mowes La DT10 ...190 F4
Mowground La TA7 ...137 A3
Mowleaze 11 BA22 ...197 F8
Mowries Ct TA11 ...211 D4
Moxham Dr BS13 ...22 C4
Muchelney Abbey* TA10 ...172 A3
Muchelney Hill BA6 ...158 B5
Muchelney Ho TA19 ...221 B3
Muchelney Way BA21 ...218 C7
Muckleditch La TA19 ...184 D3
Mud La BS49 ...17 D2
Muddicombe Cross TA24 ...128 B2
Muddicombe La TA24 ...128 B2
Muddy La BS22 ...32 A8
Muddyford La TA4 ...151 A3
Mudford Hill BA21 ...187 C5
Mudford Rd BA21 ...219 B8
Mudgley Cross Roads BS28 ...108 F1
Mudgley Hill BS28 ...108 E1
Mudgley Rd
Rooksbridge BS26 ...87 A4
Wedmore BS28 ...108 E3
Mulberry Ave BS20 ...2 E5
Mulberry Cl
Backwell BS48 ...19 A6
Portishead BS20 ...2 F5
Taunton TA1 ...213 C2
Weston-Super-Mare BS22 ..32 A1
Mulberry Ct BA11 ...120 B7
Mulberry Farm BA6 ...140 B1
Mulberry Gdns
4 Crewkerne TA18 ...224 C5
Sherborne DT9 ...225 C5
Mulberry La Bleadon BS24 .67 C6
Stoke Sub Hamdon TA14 ...186 A4
Mulberry Rd BS49 ...34 E3
Mulberry Tree Cl TA6 ...209 D5
Mulberry Wlk BS9 ...5 C8
Mullins Cl BA5 ...203 B3
Mullins Way BA7 ...214 B6
Mundays Mead BA9 ...216 D3
Munden's La DT9 ...189 A1
Murford Ave BS13 ...22 B4
Murford Wlk BS13 ...22 B4
Murhill BA3 ...64 C6
Muriel Terr BA5 ...203 D3
Murray-Smith Dr BA22 ..218 A6
Murtry Hill La BA11 ...100 C2
Mus of Bath at Work* BA1 ...228 B4
Mus Of Costume* BA1 ..228 B3
Mus of East Asian Art* BA1 ...228 B3
Musbury Cl DT10 ...190 F6
Musbury La DT10 ...190 F6
Museum Of South Somerset* BA20 ...219 B4
Musgraves TA22 ...163 E6
Musgrove Rd TA1 ...212 C3
Musmoor La BA22 ...174 F7
Mutton La BS28 ...108 D4
Mutton St DT6 ...199 D1
Mux's La TA4 ...151 B3
Myrtle Cl TA6 ...209 D5
Myrtle Dr Bristol BS11 ...4 E5
Burnham-On-Sea TA8 ...104 A7
Myrtle Gdns BS49 ...34 C8
Myrtle Hill BS20 ...4 C5
Myrtle La TA21 ...179 E7
Myrtle Rd Bristol BS2 ...226 C4
22 Martock TA12 ...185 E6
Myrtle Tree Cres BS22 ...31 A6
Myrtleberry Mead BS22 ..32 A5
Myrtles The BS24 ...49 D2

N

Nag's La TA18 ...195 B1
Nailsea & Backwell Sta BS48 ...18 F7
Nailsea Cl BS13 ...22 A7
Nailsea Com Sch BS48 ...8 E1
Nailsea Moor La BS48 ...17 F7
Nailsea Pk BS48 ...8 F2
Nailsea Wall BS21 ...17 C8
Nailsea Wall La BS48 ...17 E7
Naish Hill BS20 ...2 F1
Naish Ho BA2 ...44 A6
Naish La BS48 ...20 D3
Naish Rd TA8 ...85 A3
Naish's Cross BA3 ...96 D3
Naish's St BA11 ...119 E5
Naishes Ave BA2 ...79 D7
Naisholt Rd BA4 ...204 F6
Nanga-gat Rd BA22 ...174 A2
Nanny Hurn's La BS39 ...58 A1
Napier Ct Bristol BS1 ...226 B1
Sherborne DT9 ...225 B2
Napier Miles Rd BS11 ...5 A8
Napier Rd BA1 ...27 A3
Narfords La TA20 ...193 C1
Narrow Plain BS2 ...227 B2
Narrow Quay BS1 ...227 A2
Nash Barton BA22 ...197 C8
Nash Cl BS31 ...25 A5
Nash Gn TA2 ...212 B7
Nash La
Dinnington TA17,TA19 ...195 A6
East Coker BA22 ...197 C8
Marshwood DT6 ...199 B2
Yeovil BA20 ...218 D1
Nates La BS40 ...35 F1
Nathan Cl BA20 ...218 D2
Naunton Way BS22 ...31 B2
Neale's Way BA4 ...141 E2
Neat La BA4 ...204 D1
Neathem Rd BA21 ...219 C7
Nedge Cnr BA3 ...94 D4
Nedge La BA3 ...94 C4
Needhams Patch TA4 ...167 E6
Nelson Bldgs BA1 ...228 C4
Nelson Ct Bridgwater TA6 .208 F5
Weston-Super-Mare BS22 ...31 E4
Nelson Ho BA1 ...228 A3
Nelson Pl BA1 ...228 C4
Nelson Pl W BA1 ...228 A2
Nelson St BS1 ...227 A3
Nelson Terr BA1 ...228 C4
Nelson Villas BA1 ...228 A2
Nempnett St BS40 ...55 D5
Neroche View TA3 ...183 A7
Nerrols Dr TA2 ...213 C7
Neston Wlk BS4 ...22 F8
Nether Stowey CE Prim Sch TA5 ...134 A2
Netherclay TA1 ...212 A4
Netherclay La TA3 ...182 B7
Nethercoombe La DT9 ...225 C5
Nethercott La TA4 ...151 C3
Nethercott Way TA4 ...151 A3
Netherhay La DT8 ...199 F8
Nethermoor Rd TA7 ...155 B3
Netherstoke La BA22 ...197 C3
Netherton Cross BA22 ...197 E6
Netherton La
East Coker BA22 ...197 F6
Marston Magna BA22 ...175 A1
Netherton Rd BA21 ...219 D7
Netherton Wood La BS48 .18 A6
Netherways BS21 ...6 B1
Netley BA21 ...218 D6
Nettle Combe View BA5 ...113 A2
Nettlebridge Hill BA3 ...115 D5
Nettlecombe Hill
Castle Cary BA7 ...214 F6
Pitcombe BA7 ...215 A2
Nettlecombe Ho BA5 ...113 A1
Nettlecombe Park Rd
Monksilver TA4 ...132 A1
Sticklepath TA4 ...149 F7
Neva Rd BS23 ...48 E6
Neville Cl 1 TA11 ...173 F7
Neville Pk BA6 ...158 A5
Nevys La TA4 ...150 E8
New Bglws TA20 ...223 C3
New Bldgs
Bampton EX16 ...164 C1
Bridgwater TA7 ...209 D1
Frome BA11 ...119 F3
Ilminster TA19 ...221 B1
Oake TA4 ...167 C4
New Bond St BA1 ...228 C2
New Bond Street Pl BA1 ...228 C2
New Bristol Rd BS22 ...31 E1
New Buildings La BA11 ..119 F3
New Church Rd BS23 ...48 D2
New Cl Bourton SP8 ...161 F1
Haselbury Plucknett TA18 ..196 B5
Horrington BA5 ...113 A4
Street BA16 ...207 B4
New Cotts
Milton Clevedon BA4 ...160 A8
West Chinnock TA18 ...196 B8
New Cross TA11 ...211 C3
New Cross Hill
Barrington TA12,TA13 ...184 F6
Kingsbury Episcopi TA12 ...185 A6
New Cut BA5 ...203 D7
New Cut Bow BS21 ...16 A6
New Fosseway Rd BS14 .23 B6
New Fosseway Sch BS14 .23 B6
New Friary Cotts BA11 ..143 C3
New Hill TA11 ...211 E4
New King St BA1 ...228 B2
New Kingsley Rd BS2 ...227 C2
New La Bampton EX16 ...163 F2
Charlton Horethorne DT9 ..176 A1
Creech St Michael TA3 ...169 D5
Cricket St Thomas TA20 ...194 E4
Haselbury Plucknett TA18 ..196 C6
Tatworth TA20 ...198 C8
Witham Friary BA11 ...143 C4
New Orchard St BA1 ...228 C2
New Park Ho BS21 ...6 D5
New Pit Cotts BA2 ...60 F1
New Rd Axbridge BS26 ...88 C2
Banwell BS29 ...50 E4
Barwick BA22 ...197 F8
Bathford BA1 ...29 D2
Bawdrip TA7 ...136 D2
Brendon EX35 ...122 D4
Bridgwater TA6 ...209 A5
Burrowbridge TA3,TA7 ...170 E8
Burrowbridge TA7 ...154 F1
Cannington TA5 ...135 C1
Carhampton TA24 ...131 A5
Chard Junction TA20 ...198 F8
Churchill BS25 ...52 F4
Clevedon BS21 ...6 D2
Combe St Nicholas TA20 ...193 D6
Crewkerne TA18 ...195 B4
Draycott BS27 ...91 C3
East Huntspill TA9 ...136 D8
Freshford BA3 ...64 B5
Hambridge TA12 ...184 E7
Haselbury Plucknett TA18 ..196 E6
High Littleton BS39 ...59 C3
Higher Odcombe BA22 ...186 D3
Hinton St George TA17 ...195 C7
Houndstone BA22 ...218 A5
Ilminster TA19 ...221 B4
Kilmersdon BA3 ...98 E4
Kilmington BA12 ...161 E7
Lyng TA3 ...170 B6
North Wootton BA4 ...140 A4
Norton Sub Hamdon TA14 ...185 E3
Norton Sub Hamdon TA14 ...185 F1
NonRoady TA7 ...155 C2
Pensford BS39 ...40 D3
Pill BS20 ...4 C4
Porlock TA24 ...123 E3
Redhill BS40 ...37 A4
Seavington TA19 ...184 E1
Sherborne DT9 ...225 E3
Shipham BS25 ...52 E1
South Cadbury BA22 ...175 E4
Stalbridge DT10 ...190 B4
Staple Fitzpaine TA3 ...182 D5
Taunton TA3 ...168 D1
Upottery EX14 ...191 E1
Wanstrow BA4 ...142 D5
Waterrow TA21 ...165 F4
Wedmore BS28 ...108 D8
West Bagborough TA4 ...151 E4
Wiveliscombe TA4 ...166 A6
New Rock Ind Est BA3 ...96 D2
New Sq BA5 ...113 A2
New St Bath BA1 ...228 B2
Bristol BS2 ...227 C3
Long Sutton TA10 ...172 E4
Marnhull DT10 ...190 F5
Mells BA11 ...118 B7
North Perrott TA18 ...196 C4
Somerton TA11 ...211 E4
Wells BA5 ...203 D5
New Street Flats 4 BS2 ...227 C3
New Thomas St BS2 ...227 C2
New Way TA10 ...172 B7
Newark St BA1 ...228 C1
Newbarn Park Rd TA1 ...212 B1
Newberry's Patch TA3 ...192 A7
Newbery Cl EX13 ...198 A1
Newbery La TA18 ...224 F3
Newbolt Cl BS23 ...49 B4
Newbourne Rd BS22 ...49 C8
Newbridge Ct BA1 ...44 B7
Newbridge Dro TA9 ...105 A1
Newbridge Gdns BA1 ...44 A8
Newbridge Hill BA1 ...44 B7
Newbridge Ho BS9 ...5 C4
Newbridge Jun Sch BA1 ..44 B7
Newbridge La TA9 ...104 F1
Newbridge Rd BA1,BA2 ...44 B7
Newbridge St John's Inf Sch BA1 ...44 B7
Newbury BA12 ...144 E4
Newbury Cotts BA3 ...117 A3
Newbury Terr BA21 ...218 F7
Newchester Cross TA16 .195 E7
Newclose La BS40 ...56 D1
Newcombe Dr BS9 ...5 C4
Newcombe Rd BS9 ...5 F7
Newcot Cross EX15 ...191 A5
Newditch La BS40 ...20 C1
Newell DT9 ...225 C4
Newell House Sch DT9 ..225 C4
Newfields BS40 ...72 C8
Newfoundland Rd BS2 ..227 C4
Newfoundland St BS2 ...227 C4
Newfoundland Way BS2 ...227 C4
Newgate BS1 ...227 B3
Newgate Cross TA22 ...163 D7
Newgate La TA4 ...210 C5
Newhaven Pl BS20 ...1 E4
Newhaven Rd BS20 ...1 D4
Newhouse La TA4 ...165 E6
Newington Cl BA11 ...119 E3
Newington Terr BA11 ...119 E4
Newland DT9 ...225 E4
Newland Cross TA24 ...128 B1
Newland Dr BS13 ...22 A4
Newland Flats DT9 ...225 E4
Newland Gdn DT9 ...225 E4
Newland Rd Bristol BS13 ..22 A3
Weston-Super-Mare BS23 ...48 F6
Newland Wlk BS13 ...22 A3
Newlands Cl BS20 ...2 C5
Newlands Cres TA3 ...169 C3
Newlands Gn BS21 ...6 E1
Newlands Gr TA3 ...169 C3
Newlands Hill BS20 ...2 C4
Newlands Rd
Keynsham BS31 ...24 D4
Ruishton TA3 ...169 C3
Newlyn Ave BS9 ...5 D5
Newlyn Cres TA7 ...136 B4
Newman Cl BA6 ...206 E6
Newmans La
East Huntspill TA9 ...105 C1
Timsbury BA2 ...60 B2
Newmarket Ave 5 BS1 ..227 A3
Newnham Cl BS14 ...23 D7
Newport Cl Clevedon BS21 ..6 C2
Portishead BS20 ...1 F4
Newport Hill TA3 ...170 B2
Newport Rd BS20 ...4 C5
Newsome Ave BS20 ...4 C4
Newton Cl
Burnham-On-Sea TA8 ...85 A2
West Harptree BS40 ...74 E6
Newton Gn BS48 ...18 C8
Newton La Bicknoller TA4 .132 E1
Corfe TA3 ...181 F6
Newton Rd Barwick BA22 .197 F8
Bath BA2 ...43 F6
North Petherton TA6 ...153 F3
Taunton TA1 ...213 E4
Weston-Super-Mare BS23 ...48 E6
Yeovil BA20 ...219 D3
Newton Sq 8 EX16 ...164 B1
Newton's Rd
Weston-Super-Mare BS22 ...31 E3
Weston-Super-Mare BS22 ...31 E4
Newtown La BA6 ...140 A1
Newtown Pk TA10 ...172 A6
Newtown Rd
Highbridge TA9 ...104 D3
Langport TA10 ...172 A6
Nibley Rd BS11 ...4 E5
Nichol Pl TA4 ...167 F6
Nichol's Rd BS20 ...1 F5
Nicholas Cl TA22 ...163 E4
Nicholls Cl TA6 ...208 D4
Nick Reed's La EX15 ...180 D1
Nidon La TA7 ...137 D3
Nigel Pk BS11 ...4 E7
Nightingale Acre TA3 ...183 A7
Nightingale Ave BA11 ...120 B6
Nightingale Cl
1 Bridgwater TA6 ...209 C4
Burnham-On-Sea TA8 ...85 B1
Wells BA5 ...203 B3
Weston-Super-Mare BS22 ...31 E1
Nightingale Ct 15 TA1 ...213 A4
Nightingale Gdns BS48 ...8 D2
Nightingale Gr BA4 ...205 D5
Nightingale La BA22 ...174 F6
Nightingale Rise BS20 ...1 F3
Nightingale Way BA3 ...97 B8
Nightingales TA4 ...167 E6
Nile St BA1 ...228 A2
Nine Acre Dro TA7 ...138 B2
Nine Acre La TA3 ...170 B3
Nine Barrows La BA5 ...92 E4
Nippors Way BS25 ...69 F8
Nithsdale Rd BS23 ...48 F2
Nixon Trad Units BS24 ...49 A3
No 1 Royal Cres Mus* BA1 ...228 B3
No Place La TA5 ...152 E5
Noake Rd DT9 ...225 B3
Noble St TA1 ...213 B4
Noel Coward Cl TA8 ...104 C6
Nomis Pk BS49 ...34 E2
Norbins Rd BA6 ...206 D5
Nordens Mdw TA4 ...210 D4

Nore Gdns BS20 2 C6
Nore Park Dr BS20 1 F5
Nore Rd BS20 2 A6
Norfolk Ave BS2 227 B4
Norfolk Bldgs BA1 228 A2
Norfolk Cl TA6 209 C3
Norfolk Cres BA1 228 A2
Norfolk Gr BS31 24 C4
Norfolk Rd Portishead BS20 2 E4
Weston-Super-Mare BS23 48 F5
Norland Rd BS8 11 F8
Norman La TA7 156 B7
Norman Rd BS31 25 E3
Normandy Ave TA23 202 E6
Normandy Dr TA1 213 C3
Normandy Mews BA16 207 B6
Normans The BA2 28 F1
Normans Way BS20 3 E7
Norrington Way TA20 223 D2
North Ave TA9 104 C4
North Bank BA5 203 A8
North Cadbury CE Prim Sch BA22 175 D6
North Chew Terr BS40 39 B3
North Chine Dro BA5 138 D8
North Cl BS27 90 F3
North Cres DT9 217 D3
North Croft TA4 202 D3
North Curry CE Sch TA3 170 B3
North Down Cl BS25 70 F8
North Down La BS25 70 F8
North Dro BS48 8 A2
North End
Charlton Horethorne DT9 176 A2
Creech St Michael TA3 169 D5
Yatton BS49 17 A2
North End Rd BS49 16 F3
North Gr Pill BS20 4 C4
Wells BA5 203 E5
North Green St 11 BS8 11 F6
North Hill Mews BA11 120 A5
North Hill Rd TA24 200 F8
North Hill Woodland Trail* TA24 125 B4
North Hills Cl BS24 49 B2
North La Bath BA2 45 D5
Berrow TA8 65 F1
East Coker BA22 197 A7
Nailsea BS48 8 B1
NonRoady TA7 155 C2
Shoulsbarrow Common EX31,TA24 126 B4
Stogursey TA5 134 C7
Weston-Super-Mare BS23 48 E7
Yeovil BA20 219 B5
North Leaze BS41 11 B2
North Leaze La BA22 175 C7
North Mdws BA2 79 E8
North Mills La TA13 220 C5
North Par Bath BA2 228 C2
Frome BA11 119 F5
North Parade Bldgs BA1 228 C2
North Parade Pas BA1 228 C2
North Parade Rd BA2 45 B6
North Perrott Rd TA18 196 C5
North Petherton Com Jun Sch TA6 153 F3
North Petherton Inf Sch TA6 153 F3
North Rd Banwell BS29 51 A3
Bath BA2 45 B2
Bathampton BA2 45 C6
Charlton Horethorne DT9 176 A2
Leigh Woods BS8 11 D7
Lympsham BS24 67 D2
Midsomer Norton BA3 78 A1
Minehead TA24 201 A7
Sherborne DT9 225 E5
Timsbury BA2 60 C2
Wells BA5 203 E5
Williton TA4 202 D4
Wookey BA5 139 D8
North Side Rd BS48 36 F8
North St Axminster EX13 198 A2
Babcary TA11 174 C7
Bradford Abbas DT9 187 E1
Bridgwater TA6 208 E4
Bristol BS1 227 B4
Castle Cary BA7 214 C5
Crewkerne TA18 224 C7
Drayton TA10 171 E3
Haselbury Plucknett TA18 196 C6
Ilminster TA19 221 C4
Langport TA10 172 A5
Martock TA12 185 E6
Milborne Port DT9 217 D2
Milverton TA4 167 A4
Nailsea BS48 8 B1
North Petherton TA6 153 E4
Norton St Philip BA2 81 E4
Norton Sub Hamdon TA14 185 E1
Shepton Beauchamp TA19 184 E4
Somerton TA11 211 E4
South Petherton TA13 220 C5
Stoke sub Hamdon TA14 185 F4
Taunton TA1 212 F4
Wellington TA21 222 D6
Weston-Super-Mare BS23 48 E8
Williton TA4 202 D3
Wincanton BA9 216 C4
Wiveliscombe TA4 210 B4
North Stoke La BS30 26 B8
North Terr BA21 219 C6
North Town TA11 173 D5
North Town Com Prim Sch TA1 212 E4
North Town Mews TA1 212 E5
North View BA3 79 B2
North View Cl BA2 44 B5
North View Dr BS29 51 A2
North Villas TA4 167 F6
North Way Bath BA2 44 A5
Midsomer Norton BA3 78 A1
North Wootton Vineyard* BA4 140 C5
Northampton Bldgs BA1 228 B4
Northampton Ho BS48 9 D3
Northampton St BA1 228 B4
Northay Cross EX13 199 B3
Northay La
Axminster EX13 199 A3
Combe St Nicholas TA20 193 B6
Northbrook Dr TA7 137 F1
Northbrook Rd
Cannington TA5 135 C2
Shapwick TA7 138 A1
Yeovil BA21 219 D7
Northcombe La TA22 163 E7
Northcote Cres BA11 120 A7
Northcote Rd BS8 5 F1
Northdown Rd BA3 78 E5
Northern Path BS21 6 F3
Northern Way BS21 6 F3
Northfield
Bridgwater TA6 208 E4
Radstock BA3 79 A3
Somerton TA11 211 C4
Timsbury BA2 60 C3
Winsley BA15 64 F7
Northfield Ave TA1 212 E4
Northfield Cl TA5 134 C6
Northfield Gdns TA1 212 E5
Northfield Ho BA1 27 F1
Northfield La
Dinnington TA17 195 B8
South Petherton TA13 220 C2
Northfield Rd
Minehead TA24 201 A8
Portishead BS20 1 E3
Taunton TA1 212 E5
Northfield Way TA11 211 C5
Northfields Bath BA1 27 F1
Taunton TA1 212 B3
Northfields Cl BA1 27 F1
Northgate
Bridgwater TA6 208 F5
Wiveliscombe TA4 210 C5
Northgate St BA1 228 C2
Northleach Wlk BS11 4 F5
Northleaze CE Prim Sch BS41 11 B2
Northleaze Ho BA16 207 C6
Northleigh Ave BS22 31 C1
Northleigh Rd TA1 213 B3
Northload Bridge BA6 206 C5
Northload Bridge Rdbt BA6 206 D5
Northload Dro BS28 109 E2
Northload La BS28 109 D1
Northload St BA6 206 D5
Northload Terr BA6 206 D5
Northmead Ave BA3 77 F2
Northmead Cl BA3 77 F2
Northmead Dro TA3 170 A1
Northmead Rd BA3 77 F2
Northmoor La TA3 170 C7
Northmoor Rd
Dulverton TA22 163 D7
NonRoady TA10 155 D1
Northover Dr TA20 223 B5
Northside
Castle Cary BA7 214 C6
Rockwell Green TA21 222 B5
Northtown Rd BA4 140 C4
Northumberland Bldgs 1 BA1 228 B2
Northumberland Pl BA1 228 C2
Northwick Gdns BS39 57 D4
Northwick Rd
Chew Magna BS39,BS41 39 D7
Mark TA9 106 B5
Northwood Cl TA2 168 B4
Northwood Dro BA6 158 A6
Norton Cl
Chew Magna BS40 39 B3
Shepton Mallet BA4 205 A5
Norton Down La BA3 96 F5
Norton Dro TA12 185 B8
Norton Fitzwarren CE Com Prim Sch TA2 168 B5
Norton Hill Sch BA3 97 B8
Norton Ho 7 BS1 227 B1
Norton La
Chew Magna BS39,BS40 39 D5
Wellow BA2 81 B7
Weston-Super-Mare BS22 31 C4
Whitchurch BS14 23 C2
Norton Radstock Coll BA3 78 F2
Norton Rd TA14 185 E3
Norton St Philip CE Prim Sch BA2 81 E4
Norton sub Hamdon CE Prim Sch TA14 185 F3
Nortons Wood La BS21 7 A5
Norville Cl BS27 90 B8
Norville La BS27 90 B8
Norwich Cl TA1 212 C1
Norwich Ct TA1 212 D2
Norwood Ave BA2 45 E5
Norwood Farm* BA2 81 F7
Norwood Gr BS20 1 F5
Notgrove Cl BS22 31 B2
Notlake Dro BS27 89 E4
Notting Hill Way BS26 88 D6
Nova Scotia Pl BS1 226 A1
Nover's Lane Inf Sch BS4 22 C7
Nover's Lane Jun Sch BS4 22 C7
Novers Cres BS4 22 C8
Novers Hill BS4 22 C8
Novers La BS4 22 D7
Novers Park Dr BS4 22 C8
Novers Park Rd BS4 22 D8
Novers Rd BS4 22 C8
Nowers La TA21 222 C3
Nowhere La BS48 9 A1
Number 15 BA21 219 F7
Nunney Cl
Burnham-On-Sea TA8 85 C1
Keynsham BS31 25 A2
Nunney Fst Sch BA11 143 B8
Nunney Rd BA11 119 D4
Nurcott La TA24 147 C7
Nursery Cl TA5 135 B5
Nursery Gdns TA20 223 E4
Nursery Rd BA20 219 A3
Nursery Rise BA3 96 E4
Nursery Terr TA6 208 E5
Nut Tree Cl TA9 136 E8
Nut Tree La TA18 224 D7
Nutgrove La BS40 39 A4
Nutshole La TA20 194 B2
Nutts La BA11 101 F8
Nutwell Rd BS22 31 E2
Nutwell Sq BS22 31 E2
Nydon The TA7 137 D3
Nye Cl BS27 90 C7
Nye Dro BS24 51 E8
Nye Rd BS25 51 F5
Nyland Dro BS27 90 B1
Nyland La BA8 190 C8
Nynehead Hollow TA21 167 C1
Nynehead Prim Sch TA21 167 B1
Nynehead Rd
Nynehead TA21 167 C1
Wellington TA21 222 F8
Nythe Rd TA7 156 A5

O

Oak Ave BA2 44 C3
Oak Cl TA24 200 D7
Oak Ct BS14 23 A5
Oak Dr BS20 2 B4
Oak End Way TA20 223 C5
Oak Gr BS20 4 C5
Oak Ho Brean TA8 65 E2
Bristol BS13 22 D4
Oak La East Anstey TA22 162 E6
Rodhuish TA24 131 A3
Oak Rd
Nether Stowey TA5 134 B2
Winscombe BS25 70 A8
Oak St BA2 228 B1
Oak Terr BA3 78 D1
Oak Tree Ho 13 TA14 185 F4
Oak Tree Pl TA8 85 A3
Oak Tree Way TA5 135 B2
Oak Tree Wlk BS31 24 D3
Oak Vale La BA8 190 A6
Oak Way BA22 218 A7
Oak's Dro BA5 138 E8
Oakdale Gdns BS22 31 F2
Oakdale Rd BS14 23 A8
Oake Acres TA4 167 D4
Oake Cl TA4 167 D4
Oake Gn TA4 167 D4
Oake Prim Sch TA4 167 D4
Oaken Ground TA21 222 B5
Oakfield Cl Bath BA1 44 D8
Frome BA11 119 D5
Oakfield Gr BS8 226 B4
Oakfield Mid Sch BA11 119 D4
Oakfield Pk TA21 222 E4
Oakfield Pl BS8 226 B4
Oakfield Rd
Bridgwater TA6 208 C4
Bristol BS8 226 B4
Frome BA11 119 D4
Keynsham BS31 24 F2
Street BA16 207 B4
Oakford Ave BS23 48 F8
Oakgrove Way TA6 209 D6
Oakhill BS24 49 A2
Oakhill CE Prim Sch BA3 115 B3
Oakhill Cl BS48 9 B1
Oakhill Ct BA3 116 E3
Oakhill Rd BA2 44 F2
Oakhurst Rd BS9 5 F5
Oakland Ct TA12 185 E7
Oakland Dr Hutton BS24 49 E3
Martock TA12 185 E7
Oakland Rd TA12 185 E7
Oaklands Cheddar BS27 90 A8
Clevedon BS21 6 C4
Paulton BS39 77 E4
Temple Cloud BS39 58 E1
Oaklands Ave TA20 223 F4
Oaklands Rd BA21 219 D7
Oakleigh BA20 218 D2
Oakleigh Cl BS48 19 B5
Oakley Bath BA2 45 E5
7 Clevedon BS21 6 B1
Oakley Cl TA7 154 F5
Oakley La BA22 186 F6
Oakridge Cl BS25 70 B7
Oakridge La BS25 70 C6
Oakridge Pk BA21 219 A6
Oaks The Nailsea BS48 9 A2
Taunton TA1 213 C1
Wembdon TA6 208 C6
Winford BS40 37 F7
Oaksey Gr BS48 9 A1
Oaktree Cl EX14 191 F2
Oaktree Ct BS11 4 E7
Oaktree Gdns BS13 21 E5
Oare Post TA24 123 B3
Oatfield BS48 19 F1
Oathill Cotts BA4 140 F3
Oathill La Clapton TA18 195 C1
Winsham TA18 199 E8
Oatlands Ave BS14 23 A6
Oatley La TA5 134 F2
Oborne Rd DT9 225 F5
Obridge Cl TA2 213 A6
Obridge Cres TA2 213 A6
Obridge La TA2 213 A6
Obridge Rd TA2 213 A6
Obridge Viaduct TA2 213 B6
Ocean Way BA22 174 B3
Octagon The 5 TA1 212 F4
Odcombe Hollow BA22 196 E8
Odins Rd BA2 44 D1
Olands Rd TA21 222 D6
Old App BA7 159 A3
Old Banwell Rd BS24 50 B4
Old Barn La Felton BS40 37 A5
Hatch Beauchamp TA3 182 F6
Old Barn Way BA20 218 E3
Old Barrow Hill BS11 4 D7
Old Bond St 4 BA1 228 B2
Old Bowden Way DT9 217 D4
Old Bread St BS2 227 C2
Old Brewery Ind Est The TA4 210 C4
Old Brewery Rd TA4 210 C4
Old Brewhouse The BA1 27 B2
Old Bridge Cl BA6 206 D5
Old Bristol Rd
East Brent TA9 86 E4
Oakhill BA3,BA4 114 E1
Priddy BA5,BS40 93 A6
Shepton Mallet BA4 141 C8
Wells BA5 112 B5
Weston-Super-Mare BS22 32 A2
Old Bull La BA4 141 F7
Old Burnham Rd TA9 104 D4
Old Chapel BA1 228 C4
Old Chapel Rd TA7 155 B3
Old Chelsea La BS8 10 C4
Old Church Rd
Axbridge BS26 70 C1
Clevedon BS21 6 C3
Nailsea BS48 18 D8
Weston-Super-Mare BS23 48 D2
Old Cleeve Fst Sch TA23 131 E4
Old Co-op Cotts BA3 117 A7
Old Coach Rd BS26 69 E2
Old Combe Hill TA3 181 F5
Old Ditch BA5 110 E7
Old Ditch La TA7 155 E7
Old Down La BA4 142 A6
Old England Way BA2 79 E8
Old Farm DT9 225 C4
Old Farm Cl TA24 200 E6
Old Farm Ct
Queen Camel BA22 174 F3
Wedmore BS28 107 E4
Old Farm Pl TA17 195 C7
Old Farm Rd
Minehead TA24 200 E6
Nether Stowey TA5 134 B2
Old Ferry Rd BA2 44 C6
Old Forge Way BA2 79 E8
Old Fosse Rd BA2 44 C1
Old Frome Rd Bath BA2 62 E8
Doulting BA4 141 E8
Horrington BA5 113 D3
Oakhill BA3,BA4 115 B1
Old Gore La BA3 95 E3
Old Green The 2 DT9 225 D4
Old Hill Wincanton BA9 216 C5
Winford BS40 37 D6
Wrington BS40 35 F3
Old Hitchen 5 TA16 195 F7
Old King St BA1 228 B3
Old King Street Ct 3 BS1 227 B3
Old La Farmborough BA2 60 A6
Nailsea BS21 8 C4
Porlock TA24 124 B3
Old Main Rd TA6 135 F5
Old Maltings The BA3 115 A3
Old Manor Est BA3 116 C8
Old Market 6 TA12 185 E6
Old Market Ct BA6 206 D5
Old Market Mews DT10 190 B4
Old Market Rd BA4 205 B6
Old Market St BS2 227 C3
Old Midford Rd BA2 63 B7
Old Mill Rd Portishead BS20 2 D5
Woolavington TA7 136 E4
Old Mill Way Wells BA5 203 B2
Weston-Super-Mare BS24 50 A8
Old Millard's Hill BA3 78 B3
Old Mills Ind Est BS39 77 E2
Old Mills La BS39 77 D3
Old Mixon Rd BS24 49 C2
Old Newbridge Hill BA1 44 A8
Old Orch Bath BA1 228 C3
Chard TA20 223 F1
Old Orch The TA13 220 D4
Old Orchard Cl TA19 183 F4
Old Orchard St BA1 228 C2
Old Orchards TA20 223 E4
Old Park Hill BS2 226 C3
Old Park Rd Bristol BS11 4 D7
Clevedon BS21 6 E4
Old Pawlett Rd TA9 136 A7
Old Pit Rd BA3 97 C8
Old Pit Terr BA3 78 E4
Old Pk BS2 226 C3
Old Police Station The BA9 216 C4
Old Post Office La BS23 48 D8
Old Pound Ct SP8 161 E1
Old Print Works 6 BA11 119 E5
Old Priory Rd BS20 4 B4
Old Quarry BA2 44 D2
Old Quarry Rd BS11 4 E7
Old Quarry Rise BS11 4 E7
Old Rd
Higher Odcombe BA22 186 C2
North Petherton TA6 153 F4
Radstock BA3 79 C1
South Cadbury BA22 175 E4
Old Rd The BA8 189 D6
Old Rectory The TA9 86 C4
Old Saw Mills The BA3 117 A3
Old Sawmill The BA12 161 F6
Old School Cl
Alweston DT9 189 A1
Ashcott TA7 156 B8
Yeovil BA21 218 C5
Old School Ho BA21 219 C5
Old School Ho The BA1 228 B4
Old School La
Bleadon BS24 67 C6
Catcott TA7 137 D2
Lynford-on-Fosse TA11 158 C2
Old School Pl BA5 203 E5
Old School The BA11 119 E4
Old Schoolhouse The BA11 118 A3
Old Sneed Ave BS9 5 D4
Old Sneed Cotts BS9 5 E4
Old Sneed Pk BS9 5 D4
Old Sneed Rd BS9 5 D4
Old St Clevedon BS21 6 E3
Croscombe BA5 204 B7
Old Station Cl
Cheddar BS27 90 A7
Wrington BS40 35 D1
Old Station Ct TA20 223 D5
Old Station Gdns BA8 190 A7
Old Station La BA10 215 C4
Old Station Rd BA20 219 C4
Old Tarnwell BS39 40 B2
Old Taunton Rd TA6 209 A4
Old Threshing Mill The BA4 141 B2
Old Tiverton Rd EX16 164 C1
Old Tk BA2 63 F7
Old Town TA20 223 C3
Old Vicarage Cl TA7 137 B2
Old Vicarage Ct BS14 23 C4
Old Vicarage Gdns TA13 220 C4
Old Vicarage Gn BS31 24 E6
Old Vicarage La TA4 167 E8
Old Walcot Sch BA1 228 B3
Old Wall BS24 66 D5
Old Water Gdns The BS40 54 E2
Old Way Chipstable TA4 165 D6
Stogumber TA4 150 D8
Old Wells Rd Bath BA2 44 F3
Croscombe BA5 204 D6
Doulting BA4 142 A8
Glastonbury BA6 206 F6
Leigh upon Mendip BA3, BA4,BA11 117 B2
Shepton Mallet BA4 205 A5
Old Weston Rd
Congresbury BS49 34 B5
Flax Bourton BS48 20 B8
Oldacre Rd BS14 23 A3
Oldbarn La
Bampton EX16 163 E1
Compton Martin BS40 56 D1
Oldberry La TA22 163 D6
Oldbridge Rd BS14 23 C3
Oldbroach La TA3 213 F2
Oldfield BS21 6 E1
Oldfield Girls Sch BA1 26 F1
Oldfield La BA2 44 E4
Oldfield Park Halt BA2 44 D6
Oldfield Park Inf Sch BA2 44 D6
Oldfield Park Jun Sch BA2 44 C4
Oldfield Pl BS8 11 F5
Oldfield Rd Bath BA2 228 A1
Bristol BS8 226 A1
Oldford Hill BA11 101 B1
Oldmead La BS26 87 C5
Oldmead Wlk BS13 21 E7
Oldmixon Cres BS24 49 A3
Oldmixon Prim Sch BS24 49 A2
Oldmixon Rd BS24 49 B1
Oldrey La TA24 147 C8
Oldshute La TA22 163 C7
Oldville Ave BS21 6 D2
Oldway La TA3 183 A8
Oldway Pk TA21 222 F4
Oldway Pl TA9 104 D4

Oldway Rd
East Anstey TA22 ....162 F5
Wellington TA21 ....212 E4
Oliver Brooks Rd BA3 ...96 E7
Oliver's La TA19 ....183 B2
Olivier Cl TA8 ....104 C6
One Elm TA10 ....172 B7
Onega Ctr BA1 ....228 A3
Onega Terr BA1 ....228 A3
Oolite Gr BA2 ....44 D1
Oolite Rd BA2 ....44 D1
Orange Gr BA1 ....228 C2
Orange St BS2 ....227 C4
Orchard Ave Bristol BS1 .226 C2
 Midsomer Norton BA3 ....77 F1
 Portishead BS21 ....7 F4
Orchard Cl Banwell BS29 .51 B3
 Bishop Sutton BS39 .....57 C3
 Bradford On Tone TA4 ..167 F1
 Bristol, Westbury on Trym
  BS9 ....5 E5
 Carhampton TA24 ....131 B5
 Castle Cary BA7 ....214 B7
 Cheddar BS27 ....90 B8
 Coleford BA3 ....117 A7
 Congresbury BS49 ......34 D4
 Cossington TA7 ....137 A3
 Coxley BA5 ....139 E6
 Drimpton DT8 ....199 F8
 East Brent TA9 ....86 E4
 East Huntspill TA9 ....136 E8
 Felton BS40 ....37 C8
 Flax Bourton BS48 ....20 A8
 Frome BA11 ....119 D4
 Highbridge TA9 ....104 E4
 Higher Odcombe BA22 ..186 C2
 Keynsham BS31 ....24 D6
 Long Sutton TA10 .....172 E4
 ◤ North Petherton TA6 .153 E3
 Portishead BS20 ......2 D5
 Rockwell Green TA21 ..222 A5
 South Petherton TA13 .220 C5
 Sparkford BA22 ....175 A5
 Taunton TA3 ....168 D1
 Wedmore BS28 ....108 C4
 West Coker BA22 ......197 A8
 Weston-Super-Mare, Kewstoke
  BS22 ....31 B3
 Weston-Super-Mare, Worle
  BS22 ....31 F2
 Westwood BA15 ......64 F3
 Wincanton BA9 ......216 D3
 Wrington BS40 ....35 E2
 Yeovil Marsh BA21 ...187 A5
Orchard Cl The BS24 ...49 F4
Orchard Cotts
 Croscombe BA5 ......204 B7
 Timsbury BA2 ....60 F1
Orchard Cres BS11 ...4 D7
Orchard Ct
 Cannington TA5 ......135 B2
 Claverham BS49 .....17 F1
 Minehead TA24 ......201 B4
 Street BA16 ....207 C6
 Wellington TA21 ....222 E6
Orchard Dr Sandford BS25 .52 A4
 Southwick BA14 ....83 E3
 Taunton TA1 ....212 A3
Orchard End BS40 ...74 F4
Orchard Gdns
 Paulton BS39 ....77 E6
 West Buckland TA21 .180 F7
Orchard Ho BA2 ....212 F8
Orchard Ho BA21 ...219 A6
Orchard La
 Allerford TA24 ......124 B4
 Bristol BS1 ....226 C2
 Chewton Mendip BA3 .94 F6
 Crewkerne TA18 ....224 C6
 Evercreech BA4 .....141 E1
 Kingsbury Episcopi TA12 .185 B8
 Thorncombe TA20 ...199 B6
 Weston-Super-Mare BA20 .208 D5
Orchard Lea Coxley BA5 .139 E7
 Pill BS20 ....4 D4
 Wells BA5 ....203 C5
Orchard Mdw TA23 ..202 F6
Orchard Mead TA19 .183 C1
Orchard Paddock BA5 .203 A7
**Orchard Pk Mobile Home
 Site** BA20 ....174 D3
Orchard Pl Aller TA10 .171 D8
 Queen Camel BA22 ..174 F3
 Weston-Super-Mare BS23 .48 E7
Orchard Rd Axbridge BS26 .70 C1
 Backwell BS48 ......19 A6
 Carhampton TA24 ...131 B5
 Clevedon BS21 .....6 D2
 Hutton BS24 ....49 E2
 Long Ashton BS41 ..10 F1
 Milborne Port DT9 ..217 C2
 Minehead TA24 ....200 F8
 Nailsea BS48 ......8 D1
 Paulton BS39 ......77 E6
 Somerton TA11 ....211 B4
 Street BA16 ....207 C6
Orchard Rise
 Crewkerne TA18 ...224 C5
 Firehead TA3 ......170 F2
 Porlock TA24 ......124 A3
 Ruishton TA3 ......169 C4
Orchard St Bristol BS1 .226 C3
 Frome BA11 ....119 E5
 Weston-Super-Mare BS23 .48 E8
 Yeovil BA20 ......219 A4

Orchard Terr Bath BA2 ...44 B6
 Glastonbury BA6 ...206 D5
Orchard The
 Banwell BS29 ......51 A3
 Bath BA2 ....45 B1
 Freshford BA3 .....64 C5
 Holywell Lake TA21 .179 E7
 Locking BS24 .....50 A5
 Meare BA6 ....138 D4
 Pensford BS39 ....40 E4
 Pill BS20 ....4 C4
 Stanton Drew BS39 .40 A2
 Weston-Super-Mare BA2 .50 A8
Orchard Vale
 Ilminster TA19 ....221 B3
 Langport TA10 ....172 A5
 Midsomer Norton BA3 .77 F1
Orchard View
 Baltonsborough BA6 .158 B6
 Haselbury Plucknett TA18 .196 C6
Orchard Way
 Charlton Horethorne DT9 .176 A2
 Cheddar BS27 .....90 B8
 Crewkerne TA18 ...224 F3
 Keinton Mandeville TA11 .158 A1
 Peasedown St John BA2 .79 D7
 Shapwick TA7 .....137 F1
 Taunton TA1 ......212 B8
 Timberscombe TA24 .130 B5
 Williton TA4 ......202 E4
 Woolavington TA7 .136 E3
Orchard Wlk
 Churchill BS25 ....52 E4
 Milborne Port DT9 .217 C2
Orchardleigh BA22 .196 E8
Orchardleigh View
 BA11 ....119 D6
Orchards The
 Bristol, Shirehampton BS11 .4 E6
 Stockinch TA19 ...184 C4
Orchid Cl TA1 ....169 A1
Orchids The TA8 ..85 A2
Oriel Dr BA6 .....206 D4
Oriel Gdns BA1 ...28 C2
Oriel Gr BA2 .....44 B4
Oriel Rd BA1 .....207 C5
Orme Dr BS21 ....6 D5
Ormerod Rd BA4 .197 B7
Orneage Cl BA11 .101 E8
Orwell Dr BS31 ..25 A4
Osborne Ave BS23 .48 F7
Osborne Gr BA1 ..212 E3
Osborne Pl TA16 .195 F7
Osborne Rd Bath BA1 .47 B8
 Bridgwater TA6 ...208 F6
 Bristol BS3 ....226 C1
 Weston-Super-Mare BS23 .48 F7
 Yeovil BA20 .....219 A5
Osborne Villas BS2 .226 C4
Osborne Wallis Ho BS8 .226 A1
Osborne Way TA1 .212 E3
Osborne Wlk TA1 .104 C6
Oslings La BA1 ..29 B2
Osmond Dr BA5 .203 B3
Osprey Ct BS14 .22 D5
Osprey Gdns BS22 .31 F1
Ostrey Mead BS27 .90 B7
Othery Village Prim Sch
 TA7 ....155 C2
Ottawa Rd BS27 .83 B5
Otter Rd ◤ BS21 .6 E1
Otter Vale Cl EX14 .191 F1
Otterford Cl BS14 .23 B5
Otterham La TA3 .183 F8
Otterhampton Prim Sch
 TA5 ....135 B5
Ottery La DT9 ...225 C3
**Our Lady of Mount Carmel
 RC Prim Sch** BA2 .216 C3
**Our Lady of the Rosary Cath
 Prim Sch** BS11 ..5 A8
Outer Circ TA1 ..213 D5
Outer Gullands TA1 .212 D2
Oval The BA2 ...44 C4
Over Innox BA11 .119 F6
Overbrook Bsns Ctr
 BS28 ....107 D4
Overcombe BA8 .189 E8
Overdale
 Peasedown St John BA2 .60 F3
 Radstock BA3 ...78 E5
Overhill BS20 ...4 D4
Overland La TA3 .169 C4
Overlands
 North Curry TA3 ..170 C4
 Ruishton TA3 ....169 C4
Overleigh Street BA16 .207 C3
 Street BA16 .....207 C4
Overton BA9 ....216 D4
Owen Dr BS8 ...10 B4
Owen St TA21 ..222 C6
Owl St
 South Petherton TA13 .220 B8
 Stocklinch TA19 .184 C3
Owlaborough La EX36 .162 B2
Owsley Cotts TA19 .180 E4
Oxen La TA3 ...170 B3
Oxen Rd TA18 ..224 C6
Oxendale BA16 .207 B5
Oxenpill BA6 ...138 C6
Oxford Pl
 ◤ Bristol, Clifton BS8 .11 F6
 ◤ Taunton TA2 ....212 E6
 Weston-Super-Mare BS23 .48 D7
Oxford Rd BA21 .219 E7
Oxford Row BA1 .228 B3
Oxford Sq BS20 .50 B6
Oxford St Bristol BS2 .226 C4

Oxford St continued
 Burnham-On-Sea TA8 .104 B6
 Evercreech BA4 ...141 E1
 Weston-Super-Mare BS23 .48 D7
Oxford Terr ◤ TA6 .209 B4
Oxhayes DT8 ...199 F8
Oxhouse La Failand BS8 .10 B6
 Winford BS40 ....37 D6
Oxleaze
 ◤ Bishops Lydeard TA4 .167 F8
 Bristol BS13 .....22 C4
Oxleaze La BS41 .22 B3
Oxley Cotts DT9 .225 C4
Ozenhay BS39 ...75 E6

P

Pack Horse La BA2 .62 F7
Packers' Way TA18 .196 B3
Packsaddle Way BA11 .119 F7
Paddles La BA11 .119 D1
Paddock Cl TA3 .169 D5
Paddock Dr TA9 .104 D4
Paddock Gdn BS14 .22 F7
Paddock Park Homes
 BS22 ....32 B2
Paddock The
 Banwell BS29 ...51 A3
 Clevedon BS21 ..6 D2
 Corston BA2 .....43 B7
 Dulverton TA22 .164 C5
 Galhampton BA22 .175 D8
 Portishead BS20 .2 D4
 Taunton, Dowsland TA1 .168 F1
 Taunton, Trull TA3 .168 D1
Paddock Wlk DT9 .217 C2
Paddock Woods BA2 .45 D8
Paddocks Cvan Pk The
 BS26 ....87 A7
Paddocks The BA2 .45 B1
 Ilchester BA22 ...173 E1
 Sandford BS25 ..52 C4
 Wellington TA21 .222 E5
 North Petherton TA6 .153 F4
 Seavington TA19 .184 C1
 Thorncombe TA20 .199 A7
 Wellington TA21 .222 C1
 Wellington, Chelston TA21 .180 F7
 Yenston BA8 ....189 F8
Park Lane TA24 .131 A5
Park Pl Bath BA1 .228 A4
 Bristol BS2 .....226 C4
 Bristol BS8 .....226 B3
 Castle Cary BA7 .214 C5
 Weston-Super-Mare BS23 .48 D8
Park Prep Sch for Boys
 BA1 ....44 B8
Park Rd Bath BA1 .44 B7
 Bridgwater TA6 .208 D4
 Bristol BS3 .....226 B1
 Bristol, Shirehampton BS11 .4 F6
 Bruton BA10 ...215 E5
 Chard TA20 ....212 C3
 Clevedon BS21 .6 D4
 Congresbury BS49 .34 E3
 Frome BA11 ...119 E4
 Henstridge BA8 .190 A6
 Keynsham BS31 .24 F6
 Paulton BS39 ..77 D5
 Shepton Mallet BA4 .205 B5
 Stalbridge DT10 .190 B4
 Street BA16 ...207 D5
 Yeovil BA20 ...219 B5
Park Row BS1 ..228 B3
Park St BA20 ...226 C4
 Bristol BS1 ....228 A4
 Castle Cary BA7 .214 C5
 Dunster TA24 ..201 D1
 Exford TA24 ...128 C1
 Minehead TA24 .200 F7
 Taunton TA1 ...212 E3
 Yeovil BA20 ...219 B4
Park Street Ave BS1 .226 C3
Park Street Mews BA1 .228 A4
Park Terr Chard TA20 .223 B4
 Glastonbury BA6 .206 D4
 Taunton TA1 ...193 F1
Park The Castle Cary BA7 .214 B4
 Keynsham BS31 .24 E6
 Portishead BS20 .2 D5
 Yatton BS49 ...17 B1
 Yeovil BA20 ...219 A5
Park View
 Axminster EX13 .198 A3
 Chard TA20 ....223 B4
 Crewkerne TA18 .224 C4
 Crewkerne, Misterton
  TA18 ....195 D6
 Montacute TA15 .186 B3
 Stogursey TA5 .134 C5
Park Villas BS23 .48 D8
Park Wall BA10 .215 F5
Park Wall Dro TA7 .209 D8
Park Water La DT8 .199 F5
Park Way Bruton BA10 .215 E5
 Midsomer Norton BA3 .97 A8
 Ruishton TA3 ..169 D5
Park Wood Cl BS14 .22 F4
Parker Cl TA21 .222 E6
Parkes Rd BS24 .50 C5
Parkfield Cl TA6 .153 F4
Parkfield Cres TA1 .212 D2
Parkfield Dr TA1 .212 D3
Parkfield Gdns BS39 .57 D3
Parkfield Prim Sch TA1 .212 D3

Parkfield Rd
 Axbridge BS26 ...70 D1
 Taunton TA1 .....212 D3
Parkfields Residential Home
 BA6 ....157 E4
Parkgate La BA11 .101 E7
Parkhouse La BS31 .24 C2
Parkhouse Rd TA24 .200 E7
Parkhurst Rd BS23 .49 A7
Parkland Wlk TA18 .224 C4
Parklands BS39 ..59 D2
Parklands Ave BS22 .32 A4
Parklands Rd Bristol BS3 .11 E4
 Wellington TA21 .222 D7
Parklands Rise TA24 .200 D7
Parklands Way TA11 .211 B4
Parkmead TA2 ..213 E8
Parks Cotts TA2 .168 D8
Parks La
 Brompton Ralph TA4 .150 C3
 Minehead TA24 .200 F7
Parks The
 Bridgwater TA6 .208 D4
 Minehead TA24 .200 E7
Parks View TA24 .124 A4
Parkside Inf Sch BA1 .228 B3
Parkstone Ave TA6 .209 A2
Parksway Ct TA24 .200 E7
Parkway BA11 ..209 C5
Parkway La BA2 .60 D3
Parlour Ho TA1 .213 B5
Parmin Cl TA1 ..213 C3
Parmin Way TA1 .213 C3
Parnell Rd BS21 .6 D3
 Combe St Nicholas TA20 .193 C6
 Downhead BA4 .117 A1
 Faulkland BA3 ..80 B1
 Goathurst TA5 ..153 C4
 Henstridge BA8 .190 A8
 High Ham TA10 .156 D1
 Ilminster TA19 .183 E1
 Kingsdon TA11 .173 E5
 Kingston St Mary TA2 .168 C8
 Langport TA10 .171 E4
 Montacute BA22, TA15 .186 B3
 North Petherton TA6 .153 F4
 Thorncombe TA20 .199 A7
 Wellington TA21 .222 C1
 Wellington, Chelston TA21 .180 F7
 Yenston BA8 ...189 F8
Parrett Mead
 South Perrott DT8 .196 C1
 Taunton TA1 ...213 D3
Parrett Way TA6 .209 B3
Parrett Works Cotts
 TA12 ....220 F8
Parricks La TA20 .198 D3
Parrocks La TA20 .198 C8
Parry Cl BA2 ...44 B4
Parry's Cl BS9 ..5 F5
Parry's La BS9 ..5 F5
Parson's Batch BA4 .140 E3
Parson's Dro BS28 .138 C7
Parson's La TA11 .173 D5
Parson's St TA14 .124 A3
Parsonage Cl
 Langport TA10 .172 A5
 Somerton TA11 .211 E3
 Winford BS40 ..37 F6
Parsonage Cotts TA2 .168 D8
Parsonage Cres BA7 .214 B6
Parsonage Ct
 Puriton TA7 ....136 F4
 Taunton TA1 ...212 A4
Parsonage Hill TA21 .211 E3
Parsonage La
 Axhall TA19 ...183 C4
 Axbridge BS26 .70 E2
 Bath BA1 ......228 B2
 Chilcompton BA3 .96 C4
 Kingston St Mary TA2 .168 D8
 Milverton TA4 .167 A4
 Pensford BS39 .40 D6
 Staple Fitzpaine TA3 .182 C4
 Wincanton BA9 .161 B1
 Winford BS40 ..37 F6
Parsonage Pl TA10 .171 D4
Parsonage Rd Berrow TA8 .84 F5
 Long Ashton BS41 .11 C2
 West Camel BA22 .174 D3
Parsons Cl Bicknoller TA4 .132 F2
 Long Sutton TA10 .172 F4
Parsons Gate BA7 .214 B7
Parsons Grn Clevedon BS21 .16 C8
 Weston-Super-Mare BS22 .32 C3
Parsons Mead BS48 .19 F7
Parsons Paddock BS14 .23 A7
Parsons Pen BS27 .90 B7
Parsons Rd TA9 .104 C4
Parsons Way Wells BA5 .203 B4
 Winscombe BS25 .69 E6
Parsons' La TA5 .152 A7
Partis Coll BA1 .44 A8
Partis Way BA1 .44 A8
Partition St BS1 .226 C2
Partman's Hill BA3 .116 B3
Partridge Cl BS22 .31 F1
Partway La
 Chard Junction TA20 .198 F6
 East Chinnock BA22 .196 F7
Passage Leaze BS11 .4 D6
Passage St BS2 .227 B2
Pastures The BA15 .64 E3
Patch Croft BS21 .16 C8
Pathe Rd TA7 ..155 B1
Pathfinder Terr ◤ TA6 .209 B4
Patrick's Way TA3 .181 D8
Patten Cl TA1 ..212 B3
Patson Hill La DT9 .188 B5
Patterson Ho ◤ BS1 .227 B1
Pattinson Cl BA21 .219 D6
Pattons TA3 ...169 C1
Patwell La BA10 .215 E6
Paul St BA10 ..215 E6
Paul St BS2 .....226 C4
 Frome BA11 ...119 F4
 Shepton Mallet BA4 .205 B6
Paul's Cnr TA11 .212 F3
Paul's Cswy BS49 .34 C4
Paull's La TA19 .183 B2
Paulet Rd TA6 .209 B4

Paulls Cl TA10 172 A6
Paulman Gdns BS41 20 F8
Paulmont Rise BS39 58 E1
Pauls Rd TA11 211 C3
Paulto' Hill BA3, BS39 78 B6
Paulton Inf Sch BS39 77 E5
Paulton Jun Sch BS39 77 E5
Paulton La BA2,BA3 78 D7
Paulton Meml Hospl BS39 77 F4
Paulton Rd
Farrington Gurney BS39 77 B4
Midsomer Norton BA3 77 F1
Paulton BS39 77 B7
Paulwood Rd BS39 58 E1
Pavement The TA3 170 B4
Pavey Cl BS13 22 C4
Pavey Rd BS13 22 C4
Pavyotts La BA22 197 E8
Pawelski Cl BA4 142 B7
Pawlett BS24 49 A2
Pawlett Mead Dro TA6 136 A5
Pawlett Prim Sch TA6 135 F5
Pawlett Rd Bristol BS13 22 C3
Puriton TA6 136 B4
West Huntspill TA6,TA9 136 A7
Pawlett Wlk BS13 22 C3
Pawletts Almshouses TA5 134 C5
Paybridge Rd BS13 21 F4
Payne Rd BS24 49 D2
Payne's La TA12 185 E8
Paynes La TA7 155 C2
Payton Rd
Holywell Lake TA21 179 F7
Rockwell Green TA21 222 A5
Peace Cl TA6 209 D6
Peacehay La TA21 179 E4
Peach Tree Cl TA6 209 E5
Peacocks Cl TA21 180 F7
Peacocks Hill TA11 158 A2
Peadon La TA5 134 C4
Peak La
Compton Dundon TA11 157 A2
Shepton Beauchamp TA19 184 D3
Pear Ash La BA9 161 E2
Pear Tree Cl TA6 209 D4
Pear Tree Gdns BS24 67 C6
Pear Tree Ind Est BS40 53 C4
Pearce Dr TA9 104 D4
Pearmain Rd BA16 207 B4
Pearse Cl BS22 32 B5
Pearson Ho BA21 219 A6
Peart Cl BS13 21 E5
Peart Dr BS13 21 E4
Peartree Field BS20 2 F5
Peartwater Hill TA5 152 D8
Peartwater Rd TA5 152 D7
Peasedown St John Prim Sch BA2 79 C7
Peat Moors Visitor Ctr* BA6 138 A4
Pebbles Orch TA19 184 E4
Pecking Mill Rd BA4 141 E1
Pedder Rd BS21 6 D1
Peddles Cl TA10 171 D8
Peddles La TA11 173 E8
Pedlars Gr
Chapmanslade BA13 121 C4
Frome BA11 119 E7
Pedwell Hill TA7 156 A7
Pedwell La TA7 156 A7
Peel St BS5 227 C4
Peerage Ct TA24 201 A6
Peggy's La TA18 196 C5
Peile Dr TA2 212 E7
Pelham Ct TA6 209 D7
Pelican Cl BS22 49 F8
Pelting Dro BA5 92 C1
Pembroke Ave BS11 4 E6
Pembroke Cl
Burnham-On-Sea TA8 85 B1
Taunton TA1 212 C1
Yeovil BA21 219 E7
Pembroke Ct BS21 6 C4
Pembroke Gr BS8 226 A3
Pembroke Mans BS8 226 A4
Pembroke Pl BS8 226 A1
Pembroke Rd
Bridgwater TA6 209 C3
Bristol BS8 226 A4
Bristol, Shirehampton BS11 4 E6
Portishead BS20 1 E4
Weston-Super-Mare BS23 48 F4
Pembroke St BS2 227 B4
Pembroke Vale BS8 226 A4
Pemswell Rd TA24 200 F8
Pen Cross BA22 197 B6
Pen Elm Cotts TA2 168 B5
Pen Elm Hill TA2 168 B6
Pen Hill BA9 161 C4
Pen Mill Hill SP8,BA12 161 F2
Pen Mill Inf Sch BA21 219 D6
Pen Mill Sta BA21 219 E5
Pen Mill Trad Est BA21 219 F6
Penarth Dr BS24 49 A1
Penarth Rd TA6 208 D4
Pendlesham Gdns BS23 31 A1
Pendomer Rd BA22 197 B5
Pendragon Pk BA6 206 D5
Penel Orlieu TA6 208 F4
Penfield BA21 219 C5
Penlea Ave TA6 208 E2
Penlea Cl TA6 208 E2
Penlea Ct BS11 4 D7
Penmoor Pl TA8 84 F5
Penmoor Rd TA8 84 F5
Penmore Rd BA22,DT9 188 B7
Penn Cl Cheddar BS27 90 C7
Wells BA5 112 E2
Penn Gdns BA1 44 A8
Penn Hill BA20 219 B4
Penn Hill Pk BA20 219 B4
Penn Hill Rd BA1 27 A1
Penn La BA22 197 A6
Penn Lea Ct BA1 44 B8
Penn Lea Rd BA1 44 B8
Penn Rd BS27 90 C7
Penn St BS1 227 B3
Penn View BA9 216 D4
Penn Way BS26 70 C1
Pennard BS24 49 A2
Pennard Ct BS14 23 B5
Pennard Gn BA2 44 A6
Pennard La BA6 140 A2
Penneys Piece BA11 120 C6
Pennine Gdns BS23 31 A1
Pennlea BS13 22 C7
Penns The BS21 6 E2
Penny Batch La BA5 139 E8
Penny Cl TA21 222 D7
Penny Lea TA23 202 C6
Penny's Meade TA19 183 F4
Pennycress BS22 49 D7
Pennyquick BA2 43 D6
Pennyquick View BA2 43 F6
Pennywell Est 3 BS21 6 D2
Pennywell Rd BS2 227 C4
Penpole Ave BS11 4 E6
Penpole Cl BS11 4 D7
Penpole La BS11 4 E7
Penpole Pk BS11 4 E7
Penpole Pl BS11 4 E6
Penrice Cl BS22 31 C2
Penrose BS14 22 F7
Penrose Sch TA6 208 E4
Pensford Ct BS14 23 D5
Pensford Hill BS39 40 D5
Pensford La BS39 40 A3
Pensford Old Rd BS39 40 E3
Pensford Prim Sch BS39 40 D4
Pensford Way BA11 120 D7
Pentagon The BS9 5 B5
Pentire Ave BS13 22 A6
Pentridge La DT10 190 E3
Penzoy Ave TA6 209 B4
Pepperall Rd TA9 104 D4
Peppershells La BS39 41 C6
Pepys Cl BS31 25 D2
Pera Pl BA1 228 C4
Pera Rd BA1 228 C4
Perch Hill BA5 110 E6
Percival Rd BS8 11 F8
Percy Pl 18 BA1 28 B1
Percy Rd BA21 219 D6
Peregrine Cl BS22 31 F1
Perfect View BA1 28 A1
Periton Cross TA24 200 D6
Periton Ct TA24 200 D6
Periton La TA24 200 D7
Periton Rd TA24 200 D6
Periton Rise TA24 200 D6
Periton Way TA24 200 D6
Perkins Ct BA5 203 B4
Perley La TA23 148 D8
Perrett Way BS20 4 E4
Perretts Ct BS1 226 C1
Perridge Hill BA4 140 D4
Perrin Cl BS39 76 E8
Perrings The BS48 18 E8
Perrot Hill Sch TA18 196 B4
Perrow La BS28 89 C2
Perry Court Inf Sch BS14 23 A6
Perry Court Jun Sch BS14 23 A6
Perry Hill TA11 174 D8
Perry Hill Rd TA11 211 D2
Perry La TA9 106 F5
Perry Lake La BA5 139 B7
Perry New Rd TA22 163 F4
Perry Pl BA21 219 C5
Perry Rd Bristol BS1 227 A3
Wedmore TA9 107 A6
Perry St TA20 198 D8
Perry's Cider Mills* TA19 194 E7
Perry's Cl BS27 90 A7
Perrycroft Ave BS13 22 A6
Perrycroft Rd BS13 22 A6
Perrymead Bath BA2 45 B3
Weston-Super-Mare BS22 32 B5
Perrymead Ct BA2 45 B4
Pesley Cl BS13 22 A4
Pesters La TA11 211 E3
Pestlefield La TA3 170 C1
Peter St
Shepton Mallet BA4 205 B6
Taunton TA2 212 F6
Yeovil BA20 219 B4
Peter's Gore DT6 199 B1
Petercole Dr BS13 22 A6
Peterside BS39 76 E8
Peterson Sq BS13 22 C3
Petherton Gdns BS14 23 B7
Petherton Rd Bristol BS14 23 B7
North Newton TA7 153 F2
Petherton Road Inf Sch BS14 23 B7
Pethick Ho BS4 22 F8
Peto Garden at Iford Manor The* BA15 64 E3
Petrel Cl TA6 209 D7
Petter's Way BA20 219 B4
Petticoat La BA4 205 B6
Pettitts Cl DT9 187 E1
Petton Cross EX16 165 A3
Petvin Cl BA16 207 D4
Pevensey Wlk BS4 22 D7
Phelps Cl TA20 223 D6
Philadelphia Ct 6 BS1 227 B3
Philippa Cl BS14 23 A7
Philips Ho 2 BS2 227 B4
Phillip Ho TA6 208 F2
Phillip's Dro TA3 170 D7
Phillips Cl TA6 208 D4
Phillips Rd BS23 49 A6
Phillis Hill BS39 77 F4
Phippen St 1 BS1 227 B1
Phoenix Ct Frome BA11 119 D4
Taunton TA1 212 F3
Phoenix Ho Bath BA1 228 B4
Frome BA11 119 D4
Phoenix Rd TA6 209 B3
Phoenix Terr TA8 104 B6
Piccadily Ho 13 BA4 205 B6
Pickeridge Cl TA2 213 B7
Picket La DT8 196 C1
Pickett La BA21 219 A7
Pickney La TA2 168 B7
Pickpurse La TA4 150 E8
Pickwick Rd BA1 28 A2
Piece TA19 184 E4
Piece La TA19 184 E4
Piece Rd DT9 217 C3
Piece The 2 TA16 195 F7
Pier Rd BS20 2 E7
Pier St TA8 104 A6
Pierrepont Pl BA1 228 C2
Pierrepont St BA1 228 C2
Piers Rd BA4 142 A6
Pig Hill BA22 197 A7
Pig La TA7 154 D8
Pig Market La TA1 212 F3
Pigeon House Dr BS13 22 D4
Pigeon La BS40 36 E1
Pightley La TA5 152 F6
Pightley Rd TA5 152 E7
Pigott Ave BS13 22 A4
Pigs Hill La TA5 134 D1
Pike Cl BA6 206 C5
Pike Hill BA4 205 A7
Pike La BA4 205 B6
Pikes Cres TA1 212 E1
Pilcorn St BS28 108 C4
Pile La Curry Mallet TA3 183 C8
Stourton Caundle DT10 189 F3
Piley La TA21 179 D8
Pilgrim's Way TA6 135 F5
Pilgrims Way
Chew Stoke BS40 56 D8
Lovington BA7 158 E2
Shirehampton BS11 4 C7
Weston-Super-Mare BS22 31 E3
Pill Bridge La BA22 173 D1
Pill Head La TA18 196 C4
Pill Mdw SP8 177 E2
Pill Rd Abbots Leigh BS8 4 F1
Pill BS20 4 E2
Rooksbridge BS26,TA9 87 C2
Pill St BS20 4 D4
Pill Way BS21 6 B2
Pillar La BA11 99 D4
Pillmead La BS28 108 D5
Pillmoor Dro BA5 139 F6
Pillmoor La BA5 139 F6
Pillmore La
Highbridge TA9 105 A4
Watchfield TA9 105 C4
Pilots Helm TA6 153 E4
Pilsdon La DT6 199 F3
Pilton Hill BA4 140 C4
Pilton Manor Vineyard* BA4 140 E3
Pimm's La BS22 31 B2
Pimms La BS22 31 B3
Pimpernel Cl BA16 207 B7
Pince's Knap TA20 198 F5
Pinchay La BS40 38 A4
Pincushion Cnr BA22 197 E6
Pine Ave TA20 223 C5
Pine Cl Street BA16 207 B3
Taunton TA1 213 D2
Weston-Super-Mare BS22 31 D2
Pine Ct Chew Magna BS40 39 B3
Frome BA11 120 B7
Keynsham BS31 24 C4
Radstock BA3 79 A2
Pine Hill BS22 31 D2
Pine Lea BS24 67 B6
Pine Ridge Cl BS9 5 C4
Pine Tree Ave BA20 218 F3
Pine Tree Cl TA6 209 D4
Pine Wlk BA3 78 E1
Pinecroft Bristol BS14 22 F7
Portishead BS20 1 F6
Pines Cl Chilcompton BA3 96 D3
Wincanton BA9 216 C3
Pines Residential Site The BA11 120 D8
Pines Way Bath BA2 228 A2
Radstock BA3 79 A2
Pines Way Ind Est BA2 228 A2
Pinetree Rd BS24 50 D4
Pinewood TA11 211 D4
Pinewood Ave BA3 77 F1
Pinewood Dr TA11 211 D4
Pinewood Gr BA3 77 F1
Pinewood Rd BA3 77 F1
Pinewood Way TA8 65 F3
Pinford La DT9 188 F3
Pinhay Rd BS13 22 B6
Pink Knoll Hollow DT9 188 C8
Pinkham Hill TA20 194 B6
Pinkhams Twist BS14 23 A5
Pinksmoor La TA21 179 E7
Pinkwood La BA10 160 E7
Pinmore BA11 119 E2
Pinney Cl TA1 212 B1
Pinnockscroft TA8 84 F5
Pintail Rd TA24 201 C5
Pinter Cl TA8 104 C6
Pioneer Ave BA2 44 F1
Pipe La BS1 226 C2
Pipehouse La BA2 63 F4
Piper's Alley TA19 221 B4
Pipers Cl BS26 88 E6
Pipers Pl EX14 191 F2
Pippard Cl BA16 207 E5
Pippin Cl BA2 79 D7
Pippins The TA6 208 D6
Pipplepen La DT8,TA18 196 B2
Pit Hill TA17 195 B7
Pit Hill La TA7 155 C7
Pit La Sticklepath TA23 149 D7
Sutton Mallet TA7 155 C7
Ubley BS40 55 F5
Pit Rd Dinnington TA17 195 C7
Midsomer Norton BA3 78 B1
Pitch & Pay La BS9 5 E3
Pitch & Pay Pk BS9 5 E3
Pitchcombe Gdns BS9 5 D7
Pitcher's Hill TA2 168 F7
Pitching The BA3 96 D5
Pitcombe Hill BA10 215 B2
Pitcombe La TA4 165 B5
Pitcombe Rock BA10 215 C3
Pitcot La BA3 115 F7
Pitfield Cnr BA22 188 A7
Pitfour Terr BA2 60 B2
Pithay Cl BS1 227 A3
Pithay The Bristol BS1 227 A3
Paulton BS39 77 E6
Pitman Ct BA1 28 C2
Pitman Ho BA2 44 D4
Pitman Rd BS23 48 E6
Pitminster Prim Sch TA3 181 C5
Pitney Hill TA10 172 C6
Pitsham La TA4 164 E6
Pitt Ct TA10 171 B3
Pitt La
Huish Champflower TA4 165 E8
Porlock TA24 123 C3
Waterrow TA4 165 F5
Pitt's La BS40 39 B1
Pitten St BA3 116 E3
Pitts Cl TA1 212 C1
Pitts La TA3 183 F7
Pitway TA13 220 D5
Pitway Cl BS39 76 F4
Pitway Hill TA13 220 D6
Pitway La BS39 76 E4
Pix La TA4 167 B4
Pixash Bsns Ctr BS31 25 B5
Pixash La BS31 25 C5
Pixton Way TA22 163 E6
Pizey Ave
Burnham-On-Sea TA8 85 A1
Clevedon BS21 6 B2
Pizey Ave Ind Est BS21 6 C2
Pizey Cl BS21 6 B2
Place Dro TA7 154 F4
Placket La BA20 218 D1
Plain Pond TA4 210 C5
Plain The BA2 81 E4
Plais St TA2 212 F6
Plantagenet Chase BA20 218 D2
Plantagenet Pk BA20 218 E3
Platterwell La BA4 141 B3
Players La TA8 85 A1
Playfield Cl 2 BA8 190 A6
Playford Gdns BS11 4 E8
Playses Gn TA10 184 D8
Pleasant Pl BA1 29 D2
Pleshey Cl BS22 31 D2
Plimsoll Ho 3 BS1 227 B1
Plot La DT9 187 F5
Plott La BA8 190 B7
Plough Cl BA16 207 A4
Ploughed Paddock BS48 8 D1
Plover Cl
Milborne Port DT9 217 C2
Minehead TA24 201 C5
Weston-Super-Mare BS22 31 F1
Plover Ct BA21 218 D6
Plover Rd DT9 217 C2
Plovers Rise BA3 79 A3
Plowage La BA22 174 D3
Plox BA10 215 E6
Plud St BS28 108 B3
Plum La TA6 209 C2
Plum Orch DT9 187 F4
Plum Tree Cl TA6 209 E5
Plumber's Barton 5 BA11 119 F4
Plumers Cl 4 BS21 6 E1
Plumley Cres BS24 50 A4
Plumley Ct BS23 48 D4
Plummer's La BA5 92 D5
Plumptre Ave BA5 203 F5
Plumptre Cl BS39 77 E5
Plumptre Rd BS39 77 E5
Plumtree Cl BS25 52 A1
Plumtree Rd BS22 49 E8
Plunder St BS49 35 B7
Plunging Dr BA6 206 F1
Plymor Rd TA9 136 A8
Poachers End TA24 201 C4
Pococks Yd TA10 171 F5
Podger's La TA19 183 F4
Podgers Dr BA1 27 B2
Podium The BA1 228 C2
Polden Bsns Ctr The TA6 136 B2
Polden Cl BS48 8 E1
Polden Rd Portishead BS20 2 B5
Weston-Super-Mare BS23 48 F8
Polden St TA6 209 B5
Polden View BA6 206 E3
Polden Wlk TA7 136 E3
Pole Rue La TA20 193 C6
Polestar Way BS24 50 A8
Polham La TA11 211 D3
Polkes Field TA3 170 F6
Pollard Rd TA6 209 D6
Pollard Way BS22 49 F8
Pollard's La TA21 180 F7
Pollards Ct TA24 124 A3
Pollards Way TA1 212 E4
Polygon Rd BS8 226 A2
Polygon The 15 BS8 11 F6
Pomeroy La BA14 83 B6
Pomfrett Gdns BS14 23 E5
Pond Cl 5 BA8 190 A6
Pond La TA21 179 D3
Pond Orch TA4 150 B8
Pond Wlk DT10 190 B4
Pondhead Cross TA4 202 E3
Pondpool La TA3 170 C3
Ponsford Rd Bristol BS14 23 B8
Minehead TA24 201 A6
Pookfield Cl BA11 143 B7
Pool Cl TA7 136 C4
Pool Hill TA21 165 E1
Pool La BS40 38 A2
Poolbridge Rd BS28 107 C4
Poole Hill TA22 163 B5
Poole Ho BA2 43 F5
Poole St BS11 4 B8
Pooles Cl TA5 134 A2
Pooles La TA20 194 E1
Pooles Wharf BS8 226 A1
Pooles Wharf Ct BS8 226 A1
Poolmead Rd BA2 43 F5
Poop Hill TA18 196 C8
Poop Hill La TA18 196 C8
Poor Hill BA2 59 F6
Poorhouse La DT6 199 E1
Pop La EX13,TA20 198 B8
Pope Cl TA1 168 D1
Pope's La
Milborne Port DT9 217 D2
Rockwell Green TA21 222 B4
Pope's Wlk BA2 45 B3
Popery La TA24 129 E1
Popham Cl
Bridgwater TA6 209 D5
East Brent TA9 86 D5
Popham Flats TA21 222 D6
Poplar Ave BS9 5 D6
Poplar Cl Bath BA2 44 D4
Frome BA11 120 B7
Poplar Dr BA21 218 C7
Poplar Est TA9 104 D3
Poplar Farm BA5 111 A4
Poplar La TA9 105 E3
Poplar Pl 16 BS23 48 E8
Poplar Rd Bath BA2 62 D8
Bridgwater TA6 209 D7
Bristol, Highridge BS13 21 F7
Burnham-On-Sea TA8 104 A8
Street BA16 207 C3
Taunton TA1 213 D2
Poplar Tree La BA14 83 C2
Poplar Wlk BS24 49 E5
Poplars Cl BA21 187 A5
Poplars The
Easton-in-G BS20 4 B4
Porlock TA24 124 A3
Weston-Super-Mare BS22 32 A1
Pople's La BA11 117 F8
Pople's Well TA18 224 B6
Poples Bow TA9 104 E5
Poppy Cl
Houndstone BA22 218 B5
Weston-Super-Mare BS22 32 A5
Porch EX13 198 A3
Porchestall Dro BA6 206 B4
Porlock Cl
3 Clevedon BS21 6 E1
Weston-Super-Mare BS23 48 F2
Porlock Dr TA1 212 E1
Porlock Gdns BS48 8 E1
Porlock Hill TA24 123 F3
Porlock Rd Bath BA2 45 A1
Minehead TA24 200 C7
Port La TA22 164 A5
Port View BS20 4 C5
Port Way BA2 100 D7
Portal Rd BS24 50 D4
Portbury Comm BS20 2 F4
Portbury Gr BS11 4 D6
Portbury Hundred The BS20 3 C4
Portbury La BS20 9 E7
Portbury Way BS20 3 E5
Portbury Wlk BS11 4 D6
Portcullis Rd TA10 172 A6
Porter's Hatch BA6 138 D4
Portfield La TA10 171 F5
Portishead Bsns Pk BS20 2 E5
Portishead Lo BS20 2 D6
Portishead Prim Sch BS20 2 C5
Portishead Rd BS22 32 B4
Portishead Way BS3 11 E3

Portland Cl
Cannington TA5 .... 135 B2
Nailsea BS48 .... 8 D1
Portland Ct BS31 .... 226 B1
Portland Dr BS20 .... 2 C4
Portland Grange [6] TA1 212 E3
Portland Ho TA8 .... 85 A1
Portland Pl Bath BA1 .... 228 B4
Brent Knoll TA9 .... 86 B1
Bridgwater TA6 .... 208 D5
Frome BA11 .... 119 D5
Portland Rd Bath BA1 .... 228 B4
Frome BA11 .... 119 D5
Langport TA10 .... 172 B5
Street BA16 .... 207 A6
Portland Sq BS2 .... 227 B4
Portland St
Bristol, Clifton BS8 ...... 11 F7
Taunton TA1 .... 212 E4
Portland Terr Bath BA1 .. 228 B4
Watchet TA23 .... 202 C7
Portman Cres [9] TA6 .. 153 F3
Portman Ct BA22 .... 196 E8
Portman Dr TA6 .... 153 E3
Portman Ho TA6 .... 153 E3
Portman St TA2 .... 212 F6
Portmans TA3 .... 170 B3
Portmeade Dro BS26 .. 70 C1
Portmeirion Cl BS14 .... 23 B5
Portnell's La BA12 ...... 161 F2
Portobello Bldgs TA20 223 B4
Portreeve Dr BA21 ...... 219 B6
Portview Rd BS11 .... 4 B8
Portwall Dro TA7 .... 209 F5
Portwall La BA1 .... 227 B1
Portwall La E [10] BS1 .. 227 B1
Portway
Bristol, Shirehampton BS11 .. 4 C6
Bristol, Sneyd Park BS8 .. 5 C3
Frome BA11 .... 120 A4
Street BA16 .... 207 D4
Wells BA5 .... 203 C4
Portway Ave BS5 .... 203 D4
Portway Hill
Batcombe BA4 .... 142 C1
Bruton BA4 .... 159 F6
Portway La Binegar BA3 .. 95 E1
Holford TA5 .... 133 E4
Portway Rdbt BS11 ...... 4 C8
Portway Villas BA11 .... 120 A4
Post Cl TA21 .... 222 E4
Post La Brendon EX35 .. 122 C4
Upton TA4 .... 164 E7
Post Office La
Blagdon BS40 .... 54 D3
Flax Bourton BS48 ...... 19 F7
Minehead TA24 .... 200 F7
Tatworth TA20 .... 198 C8
Post Office Rd BS24 .... 50 C5
Post Office Yd DT8 ...... 199 F7
Poston Way BA15 .... 64 E7
Pot La BA11 .... 120 E8
Potter's Cross TA4 ...... 165 C2
Potters Ho [1] BA4 ...... 205 B6
Potterton Cl TA6 .... 208 F1
Pottery Cl BS23 .... 49 A6
Pottery Rd TA19 .... 183 C1
Pottery View TA19 ...... 183 C1
Pottle St BA12 .... 144 D3
Potts Cl BA1 .... 28 F3
Poulett Cotts TA17 .... 195 D7
Pound Cl
Glastonbury BA6 .... 206 D5
Stalbridge DT10 .... 190 B4
Yeovil BA21 .... 218 C5
Pound Fold BA5 .... 204 C2
Pound Hill TA11 .... 179 A5
Pound La
Bishops Lydeard TA4 .... 151 F1
Bratton Seymour BA9 .. 175 F8
Buckland St Mary TA20 .. 193 A8
Downhead BA4 .... 117 A1
Easton BA5 .... 111 A4
Lydford-on-Fosse TA11 .. 158 C3
Martock TA12 .... 185 D6
Nailsea BS48 .... 8 D3
Oakhill BA3 .... 115 B5
Upottery EX14 .... 191 F1
Yarcombe EX14 .... 192 E2
Yeovil BA22 .... 218 A2
Pound Mead BS40 ...... 37 C8
Pound Orch TA4 .... 151 C7
Pound Pool TA11 .... 211 C4
Pound Rd
Axminster EX13 .... 198 F2
Broadway TA19 .... 183 C2
Frome BA11 .... 135 F5
Pound Terr [3] TA21 .. 222 D5
Pound The BS40 .... 36 D3
Pound Way TA10 .... 172 B3
Poundfield Rd TA24 .... 200 E6
Poundisford Cl TA1 .... 212 D1
Poundsclose TA22 ...... 163 E4
Pounsell La TA10 .... 172 B5
Pow's Hill BA3 .... 78 D5
Pow's Orch BA3 .... 78 A1
Powell Cl TA3 .... 169 C4
Powell Ct BA5 .... 203 B4
Powis Cl BS22 .... 31 C2
Powlett Cl BA2 .... 45 B7
Powlett Rd BA2 .... 45 B8
Powy's Gn DT9 .... 225 C4
Powy's La DT9 .... 225 C4
Poyntz Rd BS4 .... 22 F8

Prankerds Rd DT9 ...... 217 C2
Preachers Vale BA3 .... 116 F7
Preanes Gn BS22 .... 32 A2
Precinct The BS20 ...... 2 D5
Prescot Cl BS22 .... 31 B2
Prescott Rd EX15 ...... 179 D1
Prestleigh La BA4 ...... 141 E4
Prestleigh Rd BA4 ...... 141 E2
Preston CE Prim Sch
BA21 .... 218 C7
Preston Cross TA4 ...... 150 E6
Preston La TA4 .... 150 E6
Preston Rd
Houndstone BA22 ...... 218 B5
Yeovil BA20 .... 218 E5
Preston Rd Rdbt BA21 .. 218 C5
Prestor EX13 .... 198 A1
Pretwood Cl TA19 ...... 221 C3
Prewett St [1] BS1 .... 227 B1
Prey La TA3 .... 182 D7
Preywater Rd BA5 ...... 139 D8
Prices Bldgs TA6 .... 209 A4
Priddles La TA20 .... 193 C8
Priddy Cl Bath BA2 ...... 44 B5
Frome BA11 .... 120 C7
Priddy Ct BS14 .... 23 B5
Priddy Dr BS14 .... 23 B5
Priddy Prim Sch BA5 .. 92 D3
Priddy Rd BA5 .... 112 E8
Priddy Veal La BA5 .... 111 A5
Priest Row BA5 .... 203 D4
Priest St TA4 .... 202 C2
Priest's Ho* TA10 ...... 172 A3
Priestlands DT9 .... 225 D5
Priestlands La DT9 .... 225 D5
Priestley Way TA8 ...... 104 D6
Priests Way BS22 ...... 31 D2
Prigg La TA13 .... 220 C4
Primmerfield La BA3 .. 94 C8
Primrose Hill Bath BA1 .. 27 D1
Charlton Mackrell TA11 .. 173 F7
East Coker BA22 .... 197 B7
Nunney BA11 .... 143 B8
Primrose Hill Pk TA11 .. 173 F7
Primrose La
Midsomer Norton BA3 .. 78 A6
Yeovil BA21 .... 187 D5
Prince St BS1 .... 227 A1
Prince Street Rdbt BS1 227 A2
Prince's Bldgs [7] BS8 .. 11 F6
Prince's Cl [11] TA14 .. 185 F4
Prince's Rd Clevedon BS21 .. 6 D3
Shepton Mallet BA4 .... 205 C6
Street BA16 .... 207 B5
Prince's St Bristol BS2 .. 227 C4
Radstock BA3 .... 78 E5
Princes Bldgs BA1 ...... 228 B3
Princes St Bath BA1 .... 203 D4
Princes St Bath BA1 .... 228 B2
Taunton TA1 .... 213 B4
Yeovil BA20 .... 219 B5
Princes' La BS8 .... 11 F6
Princess Anne Rd BA11 .. 120 A7
Princes Cl
Keynsham BS31 .... 24 E4
North Petherton TA6 .. 153 F4
Princess Rd TA1 .... 212 D2
Princess Row BS2 ...... 227 A4
Princess St TA8 .... 104 B7
Princess Victoria St BS8 .. 11 F6
Prior Park Bldgs BA2 .. 45 B5
Prior Park Coll BA2 .... 45 C2
Prior Park Cotts BA22 .. 228 C1
Prior Park Gdns BA2 .... 45 B5
Prior Park Landscape Gdn*
.... 45 C3
Priors Hill BA2 .... 60 A2
Priorswood Ind Est TA2 213 B6
Priorswood Pl [8] TA2 .. 213 A8
Priorswood Prim Sch
TA2 .... 212 F6
Priorswood Rd TA2 .... 213 A6
Priory TA1 .... 222 E6
Priory Ave TA1 .... 213 A4
Priory Bridge Rd TA1 .. 213 A4
Priory Cl Bath BA2 ...... 45 B2
Cannington TA5 .... 135 C2
Castle Cary BA7 .... 214 B5
Chilton Polden TA7 .... 137 B2
Ilchester BA22 .... 173 E1
Midsomer Norton BA3 .. 78 A1
Yeovil BA20 .... 218 D1
Priory Corn Sch BS22 .. 32 B3
Priory Ct Bridgwater TA6 .. 208 F4
[8] Stoke sub Hamdon
TA14 .... 185 F4
[4] Taunton TA1 .... 213 A4
Wellington TA21 .... 222 E7
Priory Farm Trad Est
.... 3 D3
Priory Gdns
Bristol, Shirehampton BS11 .. 4 D7
Burnham-On-Sea BA8 .. 104 B6
Easton-in-G BS20 ...... 4 B4
Wellington TA21 .... 222 E6
Priory Glade BA21 ...... 218 C6
Priory Gn TA24 .... 201 E2
Priory Hill TA5 .... 134 C5
Priory Hospl BA5 ...... 203 C3
Priory Mead BA10 ...... 215 F8
Priory Mews BA23 ...... 49 B7
Priory Path BA7 .... 214 C5
Priory Pl BA5 .... 203 D4
Priory Rd Bristol BS8 .. 226 C4
Bristol, Shirehampton BS11 .. 4 D6
Chilton Polden TA7 .... 137 B2

Priory Rd continued
Easton-in-G BS20 .... 4 B4
Ilchester BA22 .... 173 E1
Keynsham BS31 .... 24 E7
Portbury BS20 .... 3 D3
Wells BA5 .... 203 D3
Weston-Super-Mare BS23 .. 49 A7
Priory Spec Sch The
TA2 .... 213 B7
Priory View BA7 .... 214 B6
Quaker's La TA4 .... 216 C3
Priory Way TA1 .... 213 B5
Priory Way Ind Est TA1 .. 213 B5
Priory Wlk BS20 .... 3 D3
Priorygate Ct BA7 ...... 214 B6
Priorygate Ct BS22 .... 32 B5
Priston La BA2,BA3 .... 61 A5
Priston Hill* BA2 .... 61 B8
Priston Rd BA2 .... 61 D6
Pritchard St BS2 .... 227 B4
Private Rd TA2 .... 212 D7
Proctor Ho BS1 .... 226 C1
Prophet's La TA14 ...... 185 E3
Prospect
East Brent TA9 .... 86 E5
Shepton Mallet BA4 .... 205 A6
Prospect Gdns BA1 .... 28 F5
Prospect Pl
Bath, Bathwick BA1 .... 28 A1
Bath, Weston BA1 ...... 27 C2
Bathford BA1 .... 29 B2
[9] Weston-Super-Mare
BS23 .... 48 E8
Prospect Rd BA2 ...... 45 C4
Prospect Row TA18 .... 224 F3
Prospect Terr TA1 ...... 212 F5
Prospect Villas BA4 .... 159 C7
Proud Cross BS40 ...... 74 E4
Providence La BS41 .... 10 F2
Providence Pl
Bristol BS2 .... 227 C2
Bruton BA10 .... 215 E6
Providence View BS41 .. 11 A1
Provident Pl TA6 ...... 208 E5
Prowle's Cross BA22 .. 197 F5
Prowse La TA9 .... 106 C7
Prowse's La BS26 ...... 70 B2
Prowses Mdw TA2 .... 168 B4
Publow La BS39 .... 40 E5
Pud Brook DT9 .... 217 D1
Pudding Pie Cl BS40 .. 53 A6
Pudding Pie La BS40 .. 53 A6
Puddle La TA20 .... 223 B8
Puffin Cl Minehead TA24 .. 201 C5
Weston-Super-Mare BS22 .. 49 F8
Pullen Ct BA4 .... 205 B4
Pulmans La TA18 ...... 224 C5
Pulpitsway Dro TA10 .. 185 A8
Pulteney Ave BA2 ...... 45 B6
Pulteney Gdns BA2 .... 45 B6
Pulteney Gr BA2 .... 45 B6
Pulteney Mews BA2 .... 45 B7
Pulteney Rd BA2 .... 45 B6
Pulteney Terr BA2 ...... 45 B6
Pump La Bathford BA1 .. 29 B2
Bristol BS1 .... 227 B1
Combe St Nicholas TA20 .. 193 D6
Pump Sq BS20 .... 4 D5
Punnel Cl BS27 .... 90 B7
Puppy Cross Ways BA3 .. 94 F5
Puppy La BA3 .... 94 F5
Purcell Wlk BS4 .... 22 D7
Purdue Cl BS22 .... 32 B3
Purewell TA7 .... 136 C4
Puriton CE Prim Sch
TA7 .... 136 C3
Puriton Hill TA7 .... 136 C4
Puriton Prim Sch TA7 .. 136 C4
Puriton Rd Pawlett TA6 .. 136 A5
West Huntspill TA9 ...... 136 B7
Purlewent Dr BA1 ...... 27 C1
Purley Dr TA6 .... 209 D6
Purn La BS24 .... 67 A8
Purn Rd BS24 .... 66 F8
Purnell Way BS24 ...... 67 B7
Pursey Ave BA16 ...... 207 E5
Purving Row BS24 .... 67 C1
Purving Row La BS24 .. 67 C1
Putham La TA24 .... 129 F1
Putsham Hill TA5 .... 133 D5
Putsham Mead TA5 .... 133 D5
Putt's La DT9 .... 188 D8
Puttingthorpe Dr BS22 .. 49 C7
Putts La DT9 .... 175 D1
Puxley Cl BS14 .... 23 D6
Puxton La BS24 .... 33 D3
Puxton Moor La BS24 .. 33 E2
Puxton Rd BS24 .... 33 C2
Pyde La TA10 .... 184 D6
Pye Cnr Churchill BS25 .. 52 D4
Somerton TA11 .... 211 D4
Pye La TA20 .... 198 E8
Pyle La BA22 .... 174 A2
Pyle Well La TA11 ...... 174 E8
Pyleigh La TA4 .... 151 A1
Pyles Thorne TA21 .... 222 F4
Pyles Thorne Cl TA21 .. 222 F5
Pyles Thorne Rd TA21 .. 222 F5
Pylewell La BS25 ...... 52 D1
Pylle Hill BA4 .... 141 A1
Pyle La BA4 .... 141 A1
Pyle Rd BA4 .... 141 A2
Pyncombe La TA4 ...... 210 B3
Pyne Point BS21 .... 6 C3
Pynne Cl BS14 .... 23 F5
Pynne Rd BS14 .... 23 F5
Pyracantha Wlk BS14 .. 23 A6
Pyrland Ave TA2 .... 212 F8

Pyrland Pl TA2 .... 213 A8
Pyrland Wlk TA6 .... 208 B4

Q

Quab La Axbridge BS26 .. 88 F3
Wedmore BS28 .... 108 B5
Quab La Cl BS28 .... 108 B4
Quaish La BA4 .... 140 C4
Quaker's La TA4 .... 216 C3
Quakers' Friars BS1 .... 227 B3
Quakinghouse La TA4 .. 166 E5
Quantick Gdns TA24 .. 201 B5
Quantock Ave TA6 .... 208 D4
Quantock Cl
Burnham-On-Sea TA8 .. 104 B7
North Petherton TA6 .. 153 E4
Quantock Ct
Burnham-On-Sea TA8 .. 104 A5
Ilminster TA19 .... 221 C4
Street BA16 .... 207 B5
Williton TA4 .... 202 D2
Quantock Gr TA4 ...... 202 E2
Quantock Hills (YH)*
TA5 .... 133 C4
Quantock Ho TA6 ...... 153 E4
Quantock Mdw TA6 .. 208 C5
Quantock Rd
Bridgwater TA5,TA6 .... 208 B5
Cannington TA5 .... 135 C1
Portishead BS20 .... 2 B4
Taunton TA2 .... 212 E8
Wellington TA21 .... 222 D7
Weston-super-Mare BS23 .. 48 E4
Quantock Rise
Kingston St Mary TA2 .. 168 E8
Pawlett TA6 .... 135 F5
Quantock Terr TA6 .... 209 A6
Quantock View
Bishops Lydeard TA4 .. 167 F8
Highbridge TA9 .... 104 D3
Quantock Way
Bridgwater TA6 .... 208 C5
Kingston St Mary TA2 .. 168 D8
Quantocks BA2 .... 62 D8
Quaperlake St BA10 .. 215 F7
Quarme La TA24 ...... 147 E7
Quarr BA4 .... 205 A6
Quarr Cross SP8 ...... 177 E4
Quarr Dr BS19 .... 225 D6
Quarr La DT9 .... 225 D6
Quarry Batch
Street BA16 .... 207 A5
Walton BA16 .... 156 E7
Quarry Cl Bath BA2 .... 44 F1
Limpley Stoke BA3 .... 64 D6
Minehead TA24 .... 201 B5
Quarry Hay BS40 ...... 56 D8
Quarry Hill
Charlton Horethorne BA22 .. 175 F4
Charlton Horethorne BA22 .. 176 A4
Quarry La
Blagdon Hill TA3 ...... 181 D4
Bradford Abbas DT9 .. 187 E1
Butleigh BA6 .... 157 D3
Combe St Nicholas TA20 .. 193 D6
Kingston St Mary TA2 .. 168 F7
Quarry Rd Bath BA2 .... 45 D6
Kingdon TA11 .... 173 D5
Sandford BS25 .... 52 A2
Washford BA23 .... 32 A8
Washford TA23 .... 131 F4
Quarry Rock Gdns Cvn Pk
BA2 .... 45 D4
Quarry Vale Cotts BA2 .. 45 B1
Quarry Way BS48 ...... 8 D2
Quarrylands La BS26 .. 88 B4
Quarrymans Cl BA2 .... 45 B1
Quartley Hill EX16 .... 164 E4
Quay La TA24 .... 201 A8
Quay St Bristol BS1 .... 227 A3
Minehead TA24 .... 201 A8
Quay W TA24 .... 125 D4
Quayside TA6 .... 208 F5
Queen Anne Ct TA24 .. 200 F7
Queen Charlotte St BS1 .. 227 A2
Queen Charlton La BA23 .. 23 E2
Queen Elizabeth Ct
Bridgwater TA6 .... 209 A5
Street BA16 .... 207 C6
Queen Elizabeth's Hospital
Sch BS8 .... 226 B3
Queen Quay BS1 ...... 227 A2
Queen Sq Bath BA1 .. 228 B2
Bristol BS1 .... 227 A2
Salford BS31 .... 25 F3
Queen Square Ave [7]
BS1 .... 227 A2
Queen Sq Pl BA1 ...... 228 B3
Queen St Bath BA1 .... 228 B2
Bratton Seymour BA9 .. 175 F8
Bridgwater TA6 .... 208 F5
Bristol BS2 .... 227 C3
Keinton Mandeville TA11 .. 158 C1
North Petherton TA6 .. 153 F4
Taunton TA1 .... 213 B4
Tintinhull BA22 .... 186 B7
Wells BA5 .... 203 D4
Queen's Ave Bristol BS8 .. 226 B3
Portishead BS20 .... 2 C5
Queen's Ct BS8 .... 226 B3
Queen's Down TA13 .. 169 C4
Queen's Dr BA2 .... 45 A2

Queen's Par BA1 ...... 228 B3
Queen's Parade Pl BA1 .. 228 B3
Queen's Rd
Bridgwater TA6 .... 208 F2
Bristol BS8 .... 226 B3
Bristol, Bishopsworth BS13,
BS41 .... 21 F4
Clevedon BS21 .... 6 D3
Evercreech BA4 .... 141 E2
Radstock BA3 .... 79 B2
Shepton Mallet BA4 .. 205 A5
Weston-Super-Mare BS23 .. 30 D1
Queen's Terr TA9 ...... 225 D6
Queen's Way BS23 .... 31 F4
Queens Coll TA1 ...... 212 D1
Queens Coll Jun Sch
TA1 .... 212 D1
Queens Cres TA4 ...... 185 F5
Queens Dr TA1 .... 168 D1
Queens Gate BS9 ...... 5 D5
Queens Gr BA9 .... 161 E2
Queens Par BS1 ...... 226 C2
Queens Rd Banwell BS29 .. 51 A3
Bradford Abbas DT9 .. 187 E1
Frome BA11 .... 119 D4
Keynsham BS31 .... 24 D4
Minehead TA24 .... 201 A6
Nailsea BS48 .... 8 D1
Portishead BS20 .... 1 E4
Somerton TA11 .... 211 D4
Street BA16 .... 207 B5
Wellington TA21 ...... 222 E4
Queens Row BS27 .... 90 C8
Queens Sq TA9 .... 104 C4
Queens Terr TA1 ...... 213 A3
Queens Way BS20 ...... 1 E4
Queenscote BS20 ...... 2 E4
Queensway Taunton TA1 .. 212 B1
Taunton TA2 .... 212 D8
Queensway PI BA20 .. 219 A4
Queensway Rd TA6 .. 208 C5
Queenswood Rd TA1 .. 213 C3
Queenwood Ave BA1 .. 28 A1
Quicksilver Rdbt BA20 .. 218 F2
Quickthorn Cl BS14 .. 23 A6
Quiet St BA1 .... 228 B2
Quilter Gr BS4 .... 22 D7
Quirke St TA24 .... 200 F7

R

Raby Mews BA2 .... 45 B7
Raby Pl BA2 .... 45 B7
Rackclose Gdns TA20 .. 223 B4
Rackclose Ho TA20 .... 223 A4
Rackclose Pk TA20 .... 223 B4
Rackfield TA21 .... 222 A5
Rackfield Pl BA2 .... 44 B6
Rackhay BS1 .... 227 A2
Rackley La
Buckland St Mary TA20 .. 182 B1
Compton Bishop BS26 .. 69 B2
Rackstile TA20 .... 223 A7
Rackvernal Ct BA3 ...... 78 B1
Rackvernal Rd BA3 .... 78 B1
Raddon Cl BA4 .... 205 B6
Radford Hill
Peasedown St John BA2,
BA3 .... 78 C7
Timsbury BA2 .... 60 C3
Radigan La TA3,TA19 .. 183 C5
Radlet Cl TA2 .... 213 B7
Radnidge La EX16 .... 162 D4
Radsbury La EX35 .... 126 B8
Radstock Inf Sch BA3 .. 79 A3
Radstock Rd BA3 ...... 79 D5
Rag La Babcary BA22 .. 174 B6
Yarcombe EX14 .... 192 D2
Ragged Dro BA6 ...... 158 A7
Raglan Cl
Bridgwater TA6 .... 209 D7
Chilcompton BA3 ...... 96 C4
Raglan Ct [3] TA2 .... 212 F6
Raglan La BS40 .... 37 E7
Raglan Pl BS23 .... 30 C1
Raglan Terr Bath BA1 .. 28 A2
Yeovil BA21 .... 218 F7
Raglan Wlk BS31 ...... 24 D4
Raglan's Cross TA4 .. 202 F2
Ragland La BA22 ...... 28 A2
Ragland St BA1 .... 28 A2
Railford Mill BA11 .... 118 B3
Railway Cotts BA3 .... 143 C3
Railway La BA2 .... 62 D1
Railway Pl BA1 .... 228 C1
Railway St Bath BA1 .. 228 C1
Taunton TA2 .... 212 F6
Railway View Pl BA3 .. 78 B2
Rainbow La TA3 .... 191 C7
Rainbow Wood Farm
BS1 .... 227 A2
Rainham CI BS23 ...... 48 F2
Rains Batch BS40 ...... 72 E6
Rainey La [3] TA2 .... 193 C7
Raleigh Cl
Bridgwater TA6 .... 209 C5
Salford BS20 .... 25 D2
Raleigh Ct
Sherborne DT9 .... 225 E4
[3] Weston-Super-Mare
BS23 .... 48 E5
Raleigh Ho TA6 .... 153 E4
Raleigh Rd DT10 ...... 190 B4
Raleigh Rise BS20 ...... 2 B6
Ralph Allen Dr BA2 .... 45 B3
Ralph Allen Sch BA2 .. 45 E2

Ramon Ave TA23 .... 202 D7
Ramsay Cl BS22 .... 31 E4
Ramsay Way TA8 .... 104 C8
Ramscombe La BA1 ...... 28 F6
Ramsey La TA21 .... 179 F8
Ramshorn Cl TA1 ...... 212 C2
Ramshorn Gn TA1 ...... 212 D2
Ramshorn Pl TA1 ...... 212 D3
Ranchways BS20 .... 1 F4
Randall Rd BS8 .... 226 B2
Randolph Ave BS13 ..... 22 B5
Randolph Cl BS13 ...... 22 B5
Randolph Rd BA11 ...... 119 F4
Ranger Rd BA6 .... 206 C3
Rank Rd TA23 .... 202 E6
Rank The Coxley BA5 ... 139 F6
  Vobster BA3 .... 117 D6
Rankers La BS39 ...... 41 C5
Ranscombe Ave BS22 ... 31 D2
Ransford BS21 .... 6 B1
Raphael Ct BS1 ...... 227 B1
Raps Cl TA1 .... 213 E5
Raps Gn TA1 .... 213 E5
Rashwood La BA11 ..... 118 B6
Ratleigh La DT9 ...... 188 A3
Rattigan Cl TA8 ...... 104 C6
Rattle Row TA24 ...... 131 B4
Raven Cl BS22 .... 31 E1
Raven Ct BS9 .... 5 F8
Ravenhead Dr BS14 .... 23 B8
Ravensmead TA20 ..... 223 C5
Ravenswood Special Sch
  BS48 .... 8 D3
Ravensworth Terr TA8 .. 104 B7
Rawlings La BS26 ..... 88 E2
Rawlins Ave BS22 ..... 32 A5
Rayens Cl BS41 ...... 10 F1
Rayens Cross Rd BS41 .. 10 F1
Rayleigh Rd BS9 ...... 5 E7
Raymond St TA2 ...... 212 E6
Raymoor Rise BS41 .... 10 F1
Raysmoor BS25 .... 48 F8
Read Mead BA6 .... 206 E3
Reakes Cl BA5 .... 203 C4
Rebels Way BA6 ...... 206 D5
Reckleford BA20,BA21 .. 219 B5
Reckleford Inf Sch
  BA21 .... 219 C5
Rector's Cl TA8 ...... 65 F3
Rector's Way BS23 .... 48 F6
Rectory Cl
  Farmborough BA2 ..... 60 A6
  North Petherton TA6 ... 153 E3
  Staplegrove TA2 ..... 212 C8
  Wraxall BS48 .... 9 A2
Rectory Ct TA20 ...... 193 D6
Rectory Dr
  Burnham-On-Sea TA8 .. 104 B8
  Staplegrove TA2 ..... 212 C7
  Yatton BS49 .... 34 C7
Rectory Farm Cl BA22 .. 174 F3
Rectory Gdns TA20 .... 193 D6
Rectory Hill
  Axbridge BS26 ...... 88 D2
  Pitney TA10 .... 172 C7
  South Cadbury BA22 .. 175 C3
Rectory La Bleadon BS24 67 C6
  Compton Martin BS40 .. 74 B6
  Hardington Mandeville
  BA22 .... 197 A6
  Horsington BA8 ...... 176 E2
  Norton Sub Hamdon TA14 185 F2
  Sparkford BA22 ..... 175 A3
  Timsbury BA2 .... 60 B2
  Wincanton BA9 ...... 216 E6
Rectory Lawn TA8 ..... 104 B8
Rectory Pl TA8 ...... 104 C8
Rectory Rd
  Ashbrittle TA21 ..... 178 F8
  Burnham-On-Sea TA8 .. 104 B8
  Easton-in-G BS20 ..... 4 B3
  Norton Fitzwarren TA2 .. 168 B5
  Shepton Mallet BA4 ... 205 B6
  Staplegrove TA2 ..... 212 C8
Rectory Way
  Lympsham BS24 ...... 66 F2
  Yatton BS49 .... 34 C7
Recurium Lodge BS26 .. 70 B2
Red Barn La TA20 ..... 193 D4
Red Cotts BA12 ...... 144 E8
Red Cross Post TA11 ... 173 D4
Red Hill
  Peasedown St John BA2 . 60 E1
  Redhill BS40 .... 36 D2
Red Hill La TA7 ...... 155 E7
Red House Cl TA9 ..... 5 E6
Red House Rd TA9 ..... 86 D5
Red La Churchinford TA3 191 F7
  Hemyock EX15 ...... 180 E3
  Seaborough DT8 ..... 195 E1
  Staplehay TA3 ...... 181 E8
Red Poor TA24 ...... 124 B3
  Isle Abbotts TA3 ..... 183 E7
Red Post Cl BA2 ..... 79 B7
Red Rd Berrow TA8 .... 85 A7
  Brean TA8 .... 66 A2
Red Way The BA2 ..... 144 F6
Red Wing Rd DT9 ..... 217 C2
Redacre BS40 .... 36 D3
Redcliff Backs BS1 .... 227 B2
Redcliff Hill BS1 .... 227 B1
Redcliff Mead La BS1 .. 227 B1
Redcliff Par E BS1 .... 227 B1
Redcliffe Cl BS20 ..... 1 E3
Redcliffe Par W BS1 ... 227 A1
Redcliffe St BS27 ..... 90 C7

Redcliffe Way BS1 ..... 227 B1
Redcroft BS40 .... 36 D3
Redcross Mews 16 BS2 . 227 C3
Redcross St BS2 ...... 227 C3
Redding Pit La BS40 ... 37 E4
Reddings The BS40 .... 74 B7
Redfield Gr BA3 ...... 97 A8
Redfield Rd BA3 ...... 97 A8
Redford Cres BS13 .... 21 F3
Redford Wlk BS13 ..... 21 F3
Redgate Pk TA18 ..... 224 C8
Redgate St TA6 ...... 209 B4
Redgates Rd TA24 .... 200 E7
Redhill La BA3 ...... 95 A2
Redhole La DT9 ...... 225 D8
Redlake Dr TA1 ...... 213 D3
Redland La TA3 ...... 183 C8
Redland Pk BA2 ...... 43 F6
Redland Rd BS20 ..... 3 F6
Redland Terr BA11 .... 119 F3
Redlands La TA7 ..... 137 C2
Redlands Terr BA3 .... 96 F8
Redlynch Cross BA10 .. 160 E4
Redlynch La BS31 ..... 24 D2
Redmans Hill BS28 .... 107 E4
Redmans Way BA1 ..... 53 B7
Redstart Prim Sch The
  TA20 .... 223 C5
Redstart Rd TA20 ..... 223 C6
Redwing Dr BS22 ..... 31 F1
Redwood Cl Nailsea BS48 9 A2
  Radstock BA3 ...... 97 E8
Redwood Ho BS13 ..... 22 D3
Redwood La BS48 ..... 20 C7
Redwood Rd BA21 .... 219 E8
Reed Cl Bridgwater TA6 . 208 F2
  Chard TA20 .... 223 D6
  Watchet TA23 ...... 202 D6
Reedley Rd BS9 ...... 5 F5
Reeds Dr TA7 .... 136 F4
Rees Way BS26 ...... 87 F7
Reeves Cl BS27 ...... 90 F2
Regal Way 2 BA4 .... 205 B6
Regency Cl TA8 ...... 85 A2
Regency Ct BS23 ..... 203 C4
Regent Ct BA20 ...... 173 E2
Regent St
  Bradford On Tone TA4 .. 167 F1
  Bristol BS8 .... 226 A2
  Burnham-On-Sea TA8 .. 104 A7
  Weston-Super-Mare BS23 48 E7
Regent Way TA6 ...... 209 A2
Regents The
  Keynsham BS31 ...... 24 F6
  Yeovil BA21 .... 218 C6
Regil La BS40 .... 38 A6
Regil Rd BS40 ...... 37 F3
Regine The BA1 ...... 228 B3
Reid Ct BA5 .... 203 B4
Remaland Ct BA7 ..... 214 B5
Remdcomb Cl BS22 ... 31 B2
Rennison Ct BS23 .... 48 E4
Reservoir La BA5 ..... 203 C6
Retford Ho BA2 ...... 45 E4
Rete Gr BA15 ...... 64 F3
Retreat The Frome BA11 120 B4
  Radstock BA3 .... 79 E3
  Taunton TA2 .... 168 F6
Reubens Ct BS22 ..... 31 F3
Rex Rd BA22 .... 186 C2
Rex's La Barwick BA22 . 197 F8
  Yeovil BA22 ...... 219 C1
Rexton La TA4 ...... 150 F5
Reynald's Way
  Butleigh BA6 ...... 157 C4
  Street BA16 ...... 207 D1
Reynolds Cl BS31 .... 25 A5
Rhode Cl BS31 ...... 25 A3
Rhode La TA6 ...... 208 E2
Rhodes Cl TA2 ...... 212 C7
Rhodyate BS40 ...... 54 E3
Rhodyate Hill BS49 ... 34 F6
Rhodyate La BS49 .... 35 A7
Rhodyate The BS29 ... 51 C1
Rhydderch Way TA18 .. 224 C5
Rhyll Gate Cross TA22 . 162 E7
Rhyne Terr BS23 ..... 48 D2
Rhyne View BS48 ..... 8 B1
Rich's Farmhouse Cider
  Farm * TA9 .... 105 D3
Richard Beadon Cl TA4 . 210 B4
Richard Huish Coll TA1 . 213 A2
Richards Cl
  Wellington TA21 ..... 222 C8
  Weston-Super-Mare BS22 32 B4
Richards Cres TA2 .... 169 A6
Richmond Cl Bath BA1 . 27 F1
  Bridgwater TA6 ...... 208 F7
  Keynsham BS31 ...... 24 E4
  Minehead TA24 ...... 200 E6
  Portishead BS20 ..... 2 C3
  Samford Peverell EX16 178 D1
  Sherborne DT9 ...... 225 C3
Richmond Ct BA22 .... 173 E2
Richmond Hill Bath BA1 27 F1
  Bristol BS8 .... 226 B3
Richmond Hill Ave BS8 . 226 B3
Richmond Ho
  Crewkerne TA18 ..... 224 C6
  6 Shepton Mallet BA4 . 205 B6
  Yeovil BA20 .... 219 A4
Richmond La Bath BA1 . 27 F1
  Bristol BS8 .... 226 B3

Richmond La continued
  Bristol BS8 .... 226 B3
Richmond Mews BS8 ... 226 A3
Richmond Park Rd BS8 . 226 A3
Richmond Pl TA1 ..... 212 C4
Richmond Pl BA1 ..... 27 F1
Richmond Rd Bath BA1 . 27 F1
  2 Frome BA11 ..... 119 E3
  Sherborne DT9 ...... 225 C3
  Taunton TA1 .... 212 D5
  Yeovil BA20 .... 219 A4
Richmond St BS23 .... 48 D7
Richmond Terr BS8 ... 226 A3
Richmond Way BA21 .. 218 C6
Ricketts La BS22 ..... 32 A2
Rickford La BS40 ..... 54 A3
Rickford Rd BS48 ..... 8 F1
Rickford Rise BS40 ... 54 A3
Rickhay Rise TA18 .... 196 B8
Rickhayes BA9 ...... 216 B4
Rickney Cl TA11 ..... 211 B3
Ricksey La TA11 ..... 211 B3
Ricksmead Dro TA7 ... 155 B2
Rickyard Rd BS40 .... 35 E2
Ridge Cl BS20 ...... 2 A4
Ridge Gn BS40 ...... 74 E6
Ridge Green Cl BA2 ... 62 D8
Ridge Highway TA4 ... 166 A3
Ridge Hill TA4 ...... 210 D5
Ridge La
  Charlton Horethorne DT9 175 D1
  East Chinnock BA22 ... 196 F8
  East Coker BA22 ..... 197 A7
  Pitcombe BA7,BA10 ... 215 A2
  Shepton Mallet BA4 ... 205 B3
  West Harptree BS40 ... 74 D5
Ridge Rd
  Croscombe BA4,BA5 ... 204 D5
  West Anstey TA22 .... 162 D7
Ridge The Bristol BS11 . 4 E7
  Porlock TA24 ...... 124 A3
  Poyntington DT9 ..... 188 F7
  Yatton BS49 .... 34 B8
Ridgemead BA20 ..... 218 D2
Ridgemeade BS14 .... 23 B4
Ridgeview BS41 ..... 11 B2
Ridgeway Ashcott TA7 . 156 B8
  Nailsea BS48 ...... 8 C1
  Sherborne DT9 ...... 225 B3
Ridgeway Ave BS23 ... 48 E6
Ridgeway Cl BS40 .... 74 E6
Ridgeway Gdns
  Bristol BS14 ...... 23 C5
  Glastonbury BA6 .... 206 F5
Ridgeway La Bristol BS14 23 B5
  Moorlinch TA7 ...... 155 F7
  North Cadbury BA22 .. 175 D6
  Nunney BA11 ...... 143 C8
  Shillingford EX16 .... 164 D2
  Stolford TA5 ...... 134 B8
Ridgeway Rd BS41 .... 11 A2
Ridgeway The BS22 ... 32 C2
Ridgewood BS9 ...... 5 D3
Ridgewood Cross EX15 . 191 B8
Ridgewood La EX15 ... 191 A8
Ridgway TA18 ...... 196 B8
Ridings The BS13 .... 21 E4
Ridley Cnr TA10 ..... 171 C5
Ridlington Rd BS10 ... 4 C1
Riec-Sur-Belon TA19 .. 221 A4
Rigg La DT9 .... 187 F5
Rigga Cotts DT9 ..... 187 D3
Riggles Cross EX14 ... 191 D3
Rimpton Hill BA22 ... 188 A7
Rimpton Rd BA22 .... 174 F1
Ring St DT10 ...... 190 B4
Ringdown La EX15 ... 180 F2
Ringolds Way BA16 ... 207 B4
Ringspit La BS14,BS39 . 40 E8
Ringstone TA9 ...... 136 B8
Ringswell Gdns BA1 .. 28 B1
Ringwell BA2 ...... 81 E4
Ringwell La BA2 ..... 81 E4
Ringwood Gr BS23 ... 31 A1
Ringwood Rd Bath BA2 . 44 C5
Ripley Close TA22 .... 163 E3
Ripple The BS21 ..... 8 D4
Rippleside BS20 ..... 2 C5
Rippleside Rd BS21 ... 6 E5
Risdale Rd BS3 ..... 11 F1
Risdon Rd BS20 ..... 2 C2
Risedale Cl TA6 ..... 208 C5
Risedale Rd BS25 .... 70 A8
Risemoor Rd TA6 .... 208 E2
Ritchie Rd BA22 .... 218 A5
Rivendell BS22 ..... 32 A4
River Dro TA7 ...... 155 E4
River La TA7 .... 209 E1
River Rd
  East Huntspill TA7 ... 137 B8
  Mark TA9 .... 106 D1
River St BS2 .... 227 C3
River Street Pl BA1 ... 228 B3
River View
  Bridgwater TA6 ..... 208 F6
  Brushford TA22 ..... 163 F3
  Combwich TA5 ...... 135 B5
Riverbed Ho TA9 .... 21 F5
Riverleaze Bristol BS9 . 5 C5
  Portishead BS20 ..... 1 F6
Rivers Rd BA21 ..... 219 D8

Rivers Reach BA11 .... 120 A5
Rivers St BA1 ...... 228 B3
Rivers Street Mews
  BA1 .... 228 B3
Riverside
  Banwell BS24,BS29 ... 51 B5
  Burrowbridge TA7 .... 154 F1
  Combwich TA5 ...... 135 C5
  Dinder BA5 .... 140 D7
  Horton TA19 ...... 183 C2
  Meare BA5 .... 138 F5
  Taunton TA1 .... 212 E4
  Wellington TA21 ..... 222 B7
Riverside Cl Bristol BS11 4 F5
  Clevedon BS21 ...... 6 E1
  Midsomer Norton BA3 .. 96 F7
Riverside Cotts BA3 ... 79 A2
Riverside Ct BA2 ..... 228 B1
Riverside Gdns Bath BA1 228 B2
  Dunster TA24 ...... 201 D3
  Midsomer Norton BA3 .. 96 F7
Riverside Pl 2 TA1 ... 212 F4
Riverside Rd Bath BA2 . 228 B2
  Midsomer Norton BA3 .. 96 F7
Riverside Terr BA11 ... 119 F5
Riverside Wlk BA3 .... 96 F7
Riverton Rd TA7 ..... 136 B4
Riverway BS48 ...... 8 F3
Roachill Cross EX36 ... 162 C1
Road Hill Colerne SN13 . 29 E8
  Langford Budville TA4 .. 166 B3
Roath Rd BS20 ...... 2 D5
Rob-Lynne Ct BS25 ... 69 F8
Robbins Cl SN14 ..... 13 F8
Robert Ct BS8 ...... 11 D7
Robert Rd TA6 ...... 209 C7
Roberts Dr TA6 ..... 209 A2
Roberts Rd TA2 ..... 168 A6
Robin Cl
  Bristol, Stockwood BS14 23 D6
  Midsomer Norton BA3 .. 97 B8
  Taunton TA1 .... 212 B4
  Weston-Super-Mare BS22 49 E8
Robin Dr BS24 ...... 49 E2
Robin La BS21 ...... 6 D5
Robina Wlk BS14 .... 23 A7
Robins Ct Chard TA20 .. 223 C5
  Frome BA11 .... 119 D5
Robins Dr
  Bridgwater TA6 ..... 209 A6
  Burtle TA7 .... 137 D6
Robins La Burtle TA7 .. 137 C6
  Frome BA11 .... 119 D5
  Shepton Beauchamp TA19 184 E4
Robinson Cl BS48 .... 19 A5
Robinson Hts DT10 ... 190 B4
Robinson Way BS48 ... 19 A5
Rochester Cl BS24 .... 49 A1
Rochester Rd TA2 .... 213 A8
Rochfort Ct BA1 ..... 45 B8
Rock Ave BS48 ...... 8 C2
Rock Cotts BS20 ..... 4 E4
Rock Hall La BA2 .... 45 B1
Rock La Bath BA2 .... 45 B1
  West Bagborough TA4 . 151 E5
Rock Rd Chilcompton BA3 96 D3
  Keynsham BS31 ..... 24 F5
  Midsomer Norton BA3 .. 78 B2
  Yatton BS49 .... 34 C7
Rock Terr BA3 ...... 116 F6
Rock Villas BS20 .... 2 B1
Rock's Dro BA16 .... 138 F3
Rockeries The BS25 ... 69 F8
Rocketts Cl TA3 ..... 169 C4
Rocketts Cotts TA3 ... 169 C4
Rockfield Cotts TA21 .. 179 F7
Rockfield Dr BA21 ... 218 D7
Rockhaven Gdns BS11 . 5 A8
Rockingham Gr BS23 .. 31 A1
Rockleaze Bristol BS9 .. 5 E2
  Evercreech BA4 ..... 141 E2
Rockleaze Ave BS9 ... 5 E3
Rockleaze Ct BS9 .... 5 E3
Rockleaze Mans BS23 . 30 C1
Rockleaze Rd BS9 .... 5 E3
Rockley La EX32 ..... 126 A1
Rockliffe Ave BA2 .... 45 B8
Rockliffe Rd BA2 .... 45 B8
Rocks La BS40 ...... 20 E1
Rocks The BS40 ..... 54 C4
Rocks St BA5 .... 204 C7
Rockwell Green Prim Sch
  TA21 .... 222 B5
Rocky Hill TA11 ..... 173 D5
Rockyfields BA4 .... 141 E2
Rod La TA19 ...... 183 F4
Rodber Cl BA9 ...... 216 B4
Rodber Gdns BA9 .... 216 B4
Rodden Rd BA11 .... 120 A5
Roddenbury Cl BA11 .. 144 D8
Rodden Bird Gdns* BA22 187 D1
Rode Hill Rode BA11 .. 82 E1
  Southwick BA11 ..... 83 A1
Rodfords Mead BS14 .. 23 A7
Rodhuish Hill La TA24 . 131 A3
Rodmead La BA6 ..... 110 E4
Rodmead Wlk BS13 ... 22 A4
Rodmoor Rd BS20 .... 2 D5
Rodmore Cres BA4 ... 142 A6
Rodmore Rd BA4 ..... 141 E1
Rodney Cl BS31 ..... 24 F5
Rodney Cres TA6 .... 208 F6
Rodney Ho BA2 ..... 44 A6

Ram – Ros 259

Rodney Pl BS8 ...... 226 A3
Rodney Rd Backwell BS48 19 A6
  Saltford BS31 ...... 25 E2
Rodney Stoke National
  Nature Reserve* BS27 . 91 B2
Rodway TA5 .... 135 B3
Rodwell La TA13 ..... 184 E5
Roe Ave BA22 ...... 218 A5
Roe Cl TA6 .... 209 D4
Roe La BA22 ...... 188 B8
Roebuck Cl BS22 .... 32 B4
Roebuck Gate La TA4 . 151 B6
Roemead La BA3 ..... 114 C5
Roemead Rd BA3 .... 114 C5
Rogers Cl
  Buckland Dinham BA11 . 100 A3
  Clutton BS39 ...... 58 C3
Rokeby Terr 11 TA6 .. 153 F3
Roland Cl TA1 ..... 212 C2
Roman Baths & Pump
  Room* BA1 .... 228 C2
Roman La BA11 ..... 219 D6
Roman Farm Rd BS4 .. 22 E7
Roman Ho BA1 ...... 228 C4
Roman La TA6 ...... 208 C3
Roman Rd Bath BA1 .. 228 C3
Roman Villas BA4 .... 205 E4
Roman Way Bristol BS9 . 5 C4
  Coleford BA3 ...... 116 F7
  Paulton BS39 ...... 77 C6
  Watchet TA23 ...... 202 C7
Roman Way The BA6 .. 206 C3
Romney Mead TA1 ... 213 D4
Romsey Rd BA21 .... 219 E8
Ron Jones Ho 8 BS1 .. 227 B4
Rook La BA11 ...... 119 F4
Rook's Meade La TA9 . 184 E1
Rookery Cl Puriton TA7 . 136 C4
  Rooksbridge BS26 ... 87 A6
  Weston-Super-Mare BS22 31 E3
Rookery La
  Croscombe BA5 ..... 204 B7
  Drimpton DT8 ...... 199 F6
Rookery Terr TA21 ... 222 C5
Rookery The BA5 .... 140 D7
Rookery Way BS14 ... 22 D7
Rooks La BA11 ..... 120 E7
Rooksbridge Rd BS26 . 87 B6
Room Hill Rd TA24 ... 146 D2
Rope Wlk Backwell BS48 19 A5
  Bridgwater TA6 ..... 209 A5
  Evercreech BA4 ..... 141 E1
  4 Martock TA12 .... 185 E6
  Stogursey TA5 ...... 134 C5
Rope Wlk The TA23 ... 202 C7
Roper's La BS40 ..... 35 E3
Ropewalk The TA20 .. 223 B5
Roping Rd BA21 .... 219 B6
Rosary Dr TA6 ...... 208 B4
Rose & Crown Cotts
  BA3 .... 116 F6
Rose Cotts BS22 .... 32 C2
Rose Ct
  Keinton Mandeville TA11 158 A1
  Shepton Mallet BA4 .. 205 B6
Rose Dale Wlk BA11 .. 119 F6
Rose Gdns BS22 ..... 32 B4
Rose Hill Bath BA1 ... 28 C3
  Spaxton TA5 ...... 152 F2
Rose La TA18 ...... 224 B6
Rose Meare Gdns BS13 . 21 E7
Rose Terr BA21 ..... 218 D7
Rosebank La BA22 ... 186 C2
Rosebery Cl BS22 .... 32 A3
Rosebery Cotts BA3 .. 117 A7
Rosebery Pl BA2 .... 44 C6
Rosebery Rd Bath BA2 . 44 C6
Rosebery Terr TA11 .. 212 D5
Rosebery Ave
  Bridgwater TA6 ..... 209 B5
Roselyn Cres DT9 ... 189 A1
Rosemary La
  Dulverton TA22 ..... 163 D6
  Freshford BA3 ...... 64 B4
Rosemary St DT9 .... 217 C2
Rosemarylane Cross
  EX15 .... 180 D1
Rosemont Terr BS8 ... 226 A2
Rosemount La BA2 ... 45 B4
Rosemount Rd BS48 .. 20 B8
Roseneath Ave TA8 .. 84 F4
Rosetree Paddock TA5 . 134 B5
Rosette Cotts TA12 .. 185 E7
Rosevean Cl TA6 .... 209 D7
Rosevear Rd BA22 ... 44 A4
Rosewell Ct BA1 .... 228 B2
Rosewood Ave TA8 .. 104 C8
Rosewood Cl TA8 ... 104 C6
Roslyn Ave BS22 .... 31 C1
Rosshayne La EX14 .. 192 C2
Rossholme Sch TA9 .. 86 D4

Rossiter Rd BA2 ....228 C1
Rossiter's Hill BA11 ....119 F3
Rossiter's Rd BA11 ....119 E3
Rosslyn Rd BA1 ....44 B7
Rotcombe La BS39 ....59 D2
Rotcombe Vale BS39 ....59 D2
Rotton Row TA4 ....210 C4
Roughmoor TA4 ....202 E4
Roughmoor Cl TA1 ....212 D5
Roughmoor Cres TA1 ....212 D5
Roughmoor La BA5 ....110 C7
Round Oak Gr BS27 ....90 A8
Round Oak Rd BS27 ....90 A8
Round Pool La TA4 ....151 B7
Round Well Cl BA4 ....204 F6
Roundhill Gr BA2 ....44 B3
Roundhill Pk BA2 ....44 A4
Roundmoor Cl BS31 ....25 D3
Roundmoor Gdns BS14 ....23 D7
Roundoak Gdns TA21 .....167 C2
Roundwell St TA13 ....220 C4
Row La
  Keinton Mandeville TA11 ...158 A1
  Laverton BA2 ....100 D8
Row Of Ashes La BS40 .....36 F4
Row The
  Hambridge TA10 ....184 D8
  Langport TA10 ....172 B3
Rowacres Bath BA2 ....44 B3
  Bristol BS14 ....22 F6
Rowan Cl Nailsea BS48 ......9 A2
  Puriton TA7 ....216 A3
  Wincanton BA9 ....216 D2
Rowan Ct Frome BA11 .....120 B7
  Radstock BA3 ....78 E1
Rowan Dr TA1 ....213 D1
Rowan Ho BS13 ....22 D4
Rowan Pl BS24 ....32 B1
Rowan Way Langford BS40 ..53 A5
  Yeovil BA20 ....218 F3
Rowan Wlk BS31 ....24 C4
Rowans Cl TA6 ....209 C6
Rowans The BS20 ....2 C4
Rowbarrow Hill
  Rimpton DT9 ....188 A7
  Trent DT9 ....187 F6
Rowbarton Cl TA2 ....212 F7
Rowberrow BS14 ....22 F7
Rowberrow La BS25 ....70 F8
Rowberrow Way BS48 ....8 E1
Rowcliffe Cotts TA21 .....178 F8
Rowden Mill La DT10 .....189 F1
Rowdens Rd BA5 ....203 D3
Rowditch La TA5 ....133 D5
Rowe Cl TA21 ....222 A4
Rowe's Hill BA12 ....144 E4
Rowlands Cl BA1 ....29 B2
Rowlands Rise TA7 ....136 C4
Rowley Rd BA6 ....206 E5
Rowls La BA9 ....177 E6
Rowmarsh La TA10 ....172 D5
Rownham Cl BS3 ....11 E4
Rownham Ct BS8 ....226 A1
Rownham Hill BS8 ....11 E6
Rownham Mead BS8 ....226 A1
Rows La EX16 ....164 A1
Rows The BS22 ....31 E2
Royal Ave BA1 ....228 B3
Royal Cl BA21 ....219 C6
Royal Cres* Bath BA1 .....228 A3
  Weston-Super-Mare BS23 ..48 D8
Royal Ct BS23 ....48 D4
Royal Fort Rd BS2, BS8 ..226 C3
Royal High Sch The
  BA1 ....228 B4
Royal Ho B BA4 ....205 B6
Royal Hospl for Sick Children
  BS2 ....226 C3
Royal National Hospl for
  Rheumatic Diseases
  BA1 ....228 B2
Royal Par BA1 ....48 D8
Royal Photographic Society*
  BA1 ....228 B2
Royal Pk BS8 ....226 A3
Royal Portbury Dock Rd
  BS20 ....3 E5
Royal Prom BS8 ....226 B3
Royal Sands BS23 ....48 D4
Royal Sch The BA1 ....22 F2
Royal Terr BS20 ....2 E7
Royal United Hospl BA1 ...44 B8
Royal West of England Acad
  BS8 ....226 B3
Royal York Cres BS8 ....11 F6
Royal York Ho BS8 ....226 A2
Royal York Mews BS8 .....226 A2
Royal York Villas BS8 .....226 A2
Royces La TA19 ....184 C5
Royston Way BS27 ....90 B7
Royston Lodge BS23 ....48 D6
Royston Rd TA13 ....192 A7
Rubbery La TA11 ....158 D1
Rubens Cl BS31 ....25 A5
Ruborough Rd TA6 ....209 C4
Ruddock Cl BA22 ....197 B8
Ruddock Way BA22 ....197 B8
Ruddymead BS21 ....6 D2
Rudge Hill BA11 ....102 D5
Rudge La
  Beckington BA11 ....102 B6
  Standerwick BA11 ....102 D3
Rudge Rd BA11 ....102 B2
Rudgeway Rd BS39 ....77 E4
Rudgewood Cl BS13 ....22 D4

Rudgleigh Ave BS20 ....4 C4
Rudgleigh Rd BS20 ....4 C4
Rudhall Gn BS22 ....32 B3
Rudmore Pk BA1 ....44 A7
Rue La Alveston DT9 .....189 C2
  Hambridge TA3 ....184 B7
Ruett La BS39 ....77 B4
Rugg's Dro Chedzoy TA7 ..154 D7
  West Huntspill TA9 ......136 B1
Rugg's Hill TA4 ....136 E2
Rughill BS28 ....108 D8
Rugosa Dr TA8 ....84 F4
Ruishton CE Sch TA3 ......169 C3
Ruishton La TA3 ....169 C4
Ruishton Lane Cotts
  TA3 ....169 C3
Runnymede Rd BA21 .....219 D8
Rupert St Bristol BS1 .....227 A3
  Taunton TA2 ....212 E6
Rush Ash La BA3 ....116 E8
Rush Hill Bath BA2 ....44 C2
  Farrington Gurney BS39 ...76 F3
Rush Hill La BS28 ....107 F3
Rusham BS13 ....21 F4
Rushgrove Gdns BS39 .....57 C4
Rushmoor BS21 ....6 A1
Rushmoor Gr BS48 ....19 A5
Rushmoor La BS48 ....19 A5
Rushway BS40 ....53 F4
Ruskin Cl TA1 ....213 C4
Ruskin Rd BA3 ....78 C1
Ruskway La TA10 ....184 C6
Russ La BS21 ....16 E4
Russ St BS2 ....227 C2
Russell Cl BS40 ....38 A6
Russell Pl
  Bridgwater TA6 ....208 F6
  Milborne Port DT9 ....217 C3
Russell Pope Ave TA20 ...223 D2
Russell Rd Clevedon BS21 ..6 C3
  Locking BS24 ....50 C6
Russell St BA1 ....228 B3
Russell's TA4 ....210 C4
Russell's Barton BA11 ...143 B8
Russet Way
  Peasedown St John BA2 ...79 D7
  Yeovil BA20 ....218 D2
Russett Cl BS48 ....19 B6
Russett Gr BS48 ....18 C8
Russett Rd Street BA16 ..207 C4
St Bartholomew's CE Fst
  Sch TA18 ....224 D5
Rusty Wall BA20 ....218 F3
Rusty Wall Mobile Home Pk
  BA6 ....206 D4
Rutherford Bd BS4 ....22 E8
Rutland Cl BS22 ....49 C8
Rutters La TA19 ....221 B4
Ryburn Cl TA1 ....213 D3
Rydal Ave BS24 ....50 A4
Rydal Rd BS23 ....48 F4
Rydon Cres TA5 ....135 C2
Rydon La Lopen TA13 ....185 A1
  South Petherton TA13 ...220 A5
  Taunton TA2 ....212 F8
Rye TA7 ....136 C4
Rye Cl BS13 ....21 E6
Rye Gdns BA20 ....218 D2
Rye La TA7 ....155 C2
Rye Water La DT2 ....197 A1
Ryecroft Rise BS41 ....11 B1
Ryefields Cl BA22 ....197 B8
Ryepool TA4 ....167 F8
Ryesland Way TA3 ....169 D4
Rylands BA11 ....101 E4
Rylands La BA14 ....202 D2
Rylestone Gr BS9 ....5 F5
Rysdale Rd BS9 ....5 F6

S

Sabrina Way BS9 ....5 C4
Sackmore Gn DT10 ....190 F6
Sackmore La DT10 ....190 F5
Sadborow La BA8 ....199 B4
Sadborow Pound TA20 ..199 B5
Sadbury Cl BS22 ....32 B4
Sadler St BA5 ....203 D4
Sadlier Cl BS11 ....5 A8
Saffron Cl TA1 ....168 F1
Saffron Ct Bath BA1 .....228 C4
  Sherborne DT9 ....225 E4
Saffron Ho ■ BS22 ....32 B4
Saffrons The ■ BS22 ......32 B4
Sage Cl BS20 ....1 E4
Sage's La BA3 ....94 D6
Sainsbury Cl TA24 ....200 D7
Sainsbury Rd TA24 ....200 D7
SS Gt Britain* BS1 ....226 B1
SS Peter & Paul RC Cath*
  BS8 ....226 A4
St Agnes Cl BS48 ....9 A1
St Albans Pl TA2 ....212 F8
St Aldhelm's Cl BA11 ....119 D4
St Aldhelm's Rd DT9 ....225 D6
St Aldhelms CE Prim Sch
  BA4 ....141 E6
St Andrew's CE Jun Sch
  BA5 ....203 D4
St Andrew's CE Jun Sch
  Bath BA1 ....228 B4
  Taunton TA2 ....212 F6

St Andrew's Cl
  Curry Rivel TA10 ....171 D4
  High Ham TA10 ....156 A2
St Andrew's Ct BA5 ......203 F5
St Andrew's Dr BS21 ....6 A4
St Andrew's Jun Sch
  ....104 B7
St Andrew's Par ■ BS23 ..48 F4
St Andrew's Rd
  Burnham-On-Sea TA8 ...104 B7
  Stogursey TA5 ....134 C5
  ⑥ Taunton TA2 ....212 F6
St Andrew's Sch EX13 ...198 A7
St Andrew's Terr BA1 ....228 B3
St Andrews CE Nailsea BS48 ..9 A1
  Weston-Super-Mare BS22 ..31 F3
St Andrews Ct TA6 ......200 F7
St Andrews Dr EX13 ......198 A2
St Andrews La TA24 .....200 F7
St Andrews Pk BA5 ......203 D3
St Andrews Rd
  Backwell BS48 ....19 B5
  Cheddar BS27 ....90 C7
  Yeovil BA20 ....218 F5
St Andrews View TA2 ....212 F6
St Ann's Cl TA2 ....212 E7
St Ann's Dr BA4 ....85 A1
St Ann's Pl BA1 ....228 B2
St Ann's Way BA2 ....45 C6
St Anne's Ave BS31 ......24 D6
St Anne's CE Prim Sch
  BS24 ....33 B5
St Anne's Cl BA6 ....158 A5
St Anne's Ct BS31 ....24 D6
St Anne's Gdns BA21 ...218 E6
St Anthony's Cl BA3 ......78 A2
St Antonys Sq DT9 ......225 D3
St Aubyn's Ave BS23 .....48 D2
St Audries Cl TA5 ....134 C6
St Augustine of Canterbury
  RC Sch TA2 ....213 A7
St Augustine St TA1 ......213 A4
St Augustine's Par BS1 ..227 A2
St Augustine's Pl ■
  BS1 ....227 A2
St Austell Cl BS48 ....19 A8
St Austell Rd BS22 ....49 B8
St Barnabas CE Prim Sch
  BS20 ....2 C6
St Barnabas Cl BA3 ....78 B3
St Bartholomew's CE Fst
  Sch TA18 ....224 D5
St Benedict's Cl BA6 ....206 D4
St Benedict's Jun Sch
  BA6 ....206 D4
St Bernard Rd BS11 ....4 E6
St Bernadette RC Prim Sch
  BS14 ....23 B6
St Bernard's RC Sch
  BS11 ....4 E6
St Bernard's Rd BS11 .....4 E6
St Brandon's Sch BS21 ....6 B3
St Brides Cl BA6 ....206 D5
St Bridget's Cl TA6 ....65 F5
St Cadoc Ho BS31 ....24 F5
St Catherine's CE Prim Sch
  BA11 ....119 E5
St Catherine's Mead BS20 ..4 D3
St Catherine's Way DT9 ..225 B3
St Catherines Hill BA10 ..215 E6
St Chad's Ave BA3 ....78 A1
St Chad's Gn BA3 ....97 A8
St Charles Cl BA2 ....78 A2
St Christopher's Ct BA6 ..205 C5
St Christopher's Sch
  TA8 ....85 A2
St Christopher's Way
  TA8 ....85 A2
St Christophers Cl BA2 ...45 C8
St Cleer's Orch TA11 ....211 C3
St Cleers Way TA11 ......211 C3
St Cleers La TA11 ....211 C3
St Clements Cl Bath BA1 ..27 C1
  Bridgwater BS21 ....6 C4
  Keynsham BS31 ....24 E4
  ☑ Weston-Super-Mare
    BS22 ....32 A2
St Cuthbert Ave BA5 .....203 B5
St Cuthbert St BA5 ......203 D4
St Cuthbert Way BA5 ....203 D4
St Cuthbert's CE Inf Sch
  BA5 ....203 C3
St Cuthbert's Villas
  BA5 ....203 C3
St David's Cl BA6 ....206 E4
St David's Ct
  Taunton TA2 ....213 A8
  Weston-Super-Mare BS22 ..31 B2
St David's Cres BA21 ....219 B7
St David's Ct BS20 ....203 A2
St David's Ct EX13 ......198 A2
St Davids Ct TA6 ....209 D3
St Davids Pl BA10 ....215 E7
St Decuman's Rd TA23 ...202 C7
St Decumans Sch TA23 ..202 C7
St Dunstan's Com Sch
  TA24 ....124 A3
St Dunstan's Pk BA6 .....158 A5
St Dunstans CE BA6 .....206 D5

St Edmund's Rd BA6 .....206 D5
St Edmund's Terr BA3 ...117 C7
St Edmunds Rd BA6 ......206 E5
St Edward's Rd BS6 .....226 C4
St Edward's Rd BS8 ......226 B2
St Edyth's Rd BS9 ....5 C6
St Elizabeth's Way TA13 ..220 C4
St Frances Prim Sch BS48 ..8 F1
St Francis Rd BS31 ....24 D6
St George CE Prim Sch
  BS1 ....226 B2
St George's Ave
  Taunton TA2 ....212 F8
  Yeovil BA21 ....219 B7
St George's Cl TA24 .....201 D2
St George's Cross
  BA11 ....101 E1
St George's Hill Bath BA2 ..45 D8
  Easton-in-G BS20 ....4 A3
St George's Ho BS8 ......226 B2
St George's Pl TA1 ....213 A4
St George's Prim Sch
  TA6 ....208 C6
St George's RC Prim Sch
  TA1 ....213 A3
St George's Rd
  Keynsham BS31 ....24 D6
  Portbury BS20 ....3 E2
St George's St TA24 .....201 D2
St Georges Ave TA13 ....198 A2
St Georges CE Sch SP8 ..161 E1
St Georges Ct BA6 ......206 D5
St Georges Mews TA1 ...212 F3
St Georges Rd BS1 ......226 C2
St Georges Sq TA1 ....212 F3
St Georges Way TA1 .....212 G2
St Gilda's Cl TA10 ....172 A5
St Gilda's Way BA6 ......206 D4
St Gildas TA20 ....223 D4
St Gildas RC Prim Sch
  BA21 ....219 B5
St Gildes Ct TA10 ....172 A5
St Gregory's CE Prim Sch
  DT10 ....190 F5
St Gregory's RC Sch
  BA2 ....62 D8
St Hilary Cl BS9 ....5 D5
St Ives Cl BS48 ....9 A1
St Ives Rd BS23 ....49 A5
St James Cl TA1 ....212 F4
St James Ct
  Bridgwater TA6 ....209 D3
  ☑ Taunton TA1 ....212 F4
St James Mews TA13 ...220 C4
St James St Taunton TA1 ..212 F4
  Weston-Super-Mare BS23 ..48 D7
St James Terr BA22 .....197 B8
St James' Barton BS1 ...227 B4
St James' Sq BA6 ....157 D4
St James' St BA21 ....218 D5
St James's Par BA1 ......228 B2
St James's Pk Bath BA1 ..228 B4
  Yeovil BA20 ....218 C5
St James's Sq BA1 ......228 B4
St James's St BA11 ......228 B4
  South Petherton TA13 ...220 C4
St John & St Francis CE Prim
  Sch TA6 ....208 C4
St John St
  Bridgwater TA6 ....209 B4
  Wells BA5 ....203 D4
St John the Evangelist CE
  Prim Sch BS21 ....6 C1
St John's Ave BS21 ....6 D3
St John's Bridge ☑ BS1 ..227 A3
St John's CE Fst Sch
  BA11 ....119 F4
St John's CE Jun Sch
  TA9 ....104 D6
St John's CE Prim Sch
  TA21 ....222 E6
St John's CE Sch BA1 .....78 A1
St John's Cl
  Peasedown St John BA2 ...79 B7
  Weston-Super-Mare BS23 ..30 D1
St John's Cres
  Midsomer Norton BA3 ....78 A2
  Trowbridge BA14 ....102 C8
St John's Pl BA1 ....228 B2
St John's Rd
  Backwell BS48 ....19 B5
  Bath BA2 ....228 C3
  Burnham-On-Sea TA8 ...104 B7
  Clevedon BS21 ....6 D3
  Frome BA11 ....120 B5
  Yeovil BA21 ....219 B7
St John's Sq BA6 ....206 D5
St John's Terr BA11 ......119 F4
St Johns CE Inf Sch
  BA5 ....206 D5
St Johns Cl TA19 ....183 C2
St Johns Ct Axbridge BS26 ..70 B2
  Keynsham BS31 ....24 E6
  Wells BA5 ....203 D3
St Johns Rd BS20 ....2 E4
St Johns Ret Pk TA1 .....213 B5
St Johns Wlk BA6 ....206 D5
St Joseph & St Teresa's RC
  Sch BA5 ....203 D4

St Joseph's RC Prim Sch
  Bridgwater TA6 ....208 D4
  Burnham-On-Sea TA8 ...104 B6
St Joseph's RC Prim Sch
  BS20 ....2 C6
St Joseph's Rd BS23 ......30 E1
St Jude's Terr BS22 ......31 C1
St Julian's CE Prim Sch
  BA2 ....62 E1
St Julian's Rd BA2 ....79 F5
St Julians Cl BS39 ....77 E4
St Julians Ct BS39 ....77 E4
St Katherine's CE Prim Sch
  BA10 ....197 C3
St Katherine's Sch BS20 ..4 E3
St Kenya Ct BS31 ....24 F5
St Keyna Rd BS31 ....24 E5
St Kilda's Rd BA2 ....44 D5
St Ladoc Rd BS31 ....24 D6
St Laud Cl BS9 ....5 D5
St Lawrence's CE Prim Sch
  BA5 ....110 E6
St Louis RC Prim Sch
  BA11 ....119 E5
St Luke's Cl TA8 ....104 B7
St Luke's Rd Bath BA2 ...44 F3
  Midsomer Norton BA3 ....77 F2
St Lukes Mews TA4 ......167 E6
St Lukes Rd BA11 ....101 E5
St Margaret's Cl BS48 ....19 A5
St Margaret's La BS48 ...19 A5
St Margaret's Prim Sch
  BA22 ....186 C6
St Margaret's Rd BA22 ..186 B6
St Margaret's Terr BS23 ..48 D8
St Margarets Cl BS48 .....19 A5
St Margarets Ct TA1 .....213 A4
St Margarets La TA20 ...198 C8
St Mark's CE Sch BA1 ....28 B2
St Mark's CE/Methodist
  Ecumenical Prim Sch
  BS22 ....31 E4
St Mark's Rd Bath BA2 ..228 C1
  Midsomer Norton BA3 ...78 A2
  Weston-Super-Mare BS22 ..32 A3
St Marks CE Chedzoy TA7 ..154 E8
  Keynsham BS31 ....24 E6
St Marks Ct TA6 ....209 D3
St Marks Gdns BA21 ....228 C1
St Martin's Cl TA5 ....170 F1
St Martin's Ct BA2 ....44 E1
St Martin's Garden Prim Sch
  BA2 ....44 E1
St Martin's La SN14 ......13 F8
St Martin's Pk SN14 .....13 F8
St Martin's Sch TA18 ....224 B6
St Martins BS21 ....6 C4
St Martins CE Jun Sch
  BS22 ....31 D2
St Martins Hospl BA2 ....44 E1
St Martins Rd BS20 .....218 D2
St Martins Way BA20 .....48 A3
St Mary Redcliffe & Temple
  CE Sch BS1 ....227 B1
St Mary St
  Bridgwater TA6 ....208 F4
  Nether Stowey TA5 ......134 B2
St Mary's Bldgs BA2 ....228 B1
St Mary's CE Prim Sch
  Bradford Abbas DT9 .....187 E1
  Bridgwater TA6 ....208 C4
St Mary's CE Fst Sch
  BA3 ....79 C1
St Mary's Ct BA20 ....60 C3
St Mary's Cl
  Axminster EX13 ....198 A1
  Bath BA2 ....45 B6
  Cossington TA7 ....136 F3
  Timsbury BA2 ....60 B2
St Mary's Cres
  Chard TA20 ....223 C3
  ☑ North Petherton TA6 ..153 F4
  Yeovil BA21 ....219 C8
St Mary's Ct BA20 ....60 C3
St Mary's Ct St ■ TA6 ...208 F4
St Mary's Gdns BS40 ....35 A5
St Mary's Gr BS48 ....18 C8
St Mary's Hospl BS8 .....226 B3
St Mary's Park Rd BS20 ..2 C4
St Mary's Pk
  Langport TA10 ....172 A5
  Nailsea BS48 ....18 C8
  ☑ North Petherton TA6 ..153 F4
St Mary's RC Prim Sch
  Axminster EX13 ....198 A1
  Bath BA1 ....228 B1
  Burnham-On-Sea TA8 ...104 B7
  Frome BA11 ....120 B5
  Hutton BS24 ....49 D2
  Leigh Woods BS8 ....11 C6
  Meare BA6 ....138 D4
  Oxenpill BA6 ....138 C4
  Portishead BS20 ....2 D4
  Sherborne DT9 ....225 B3
  Westonzoyland TA7 .....155 B3
St Mary's Sch TA20 ......199 B6
St Mary's Se BS26 ....70 C2
St Mary's Wlk BS11 ....4 E6
St Mary's St Hutton BS24 ..49 D2
  Seavington TA19 ....184 D1
  Wedmore BS28 ....108 C4
St Marys Ct TA6 ....153 E4

St Marys Pl BA4 ....142 F4
St Marys Rise BA3 ....79 C2
St Mathew's Pl BA2 ....45 B5
St Mathias Ho BS2 ......227 C3
St Matthew's Cl BS23 ....30 D1
St Matthew's Field TA6 .208 E4
St Matthew's Rd BS6 ....227 A4
St Matthews Gn TA6 ....208 E4
St Matthias Pk BS2 ......227 C3
St Medard Rd BS28 ....108 C4
St Michael Cl TA3 ......169 D4
St Michael Rd TA3 ......169 D4
St Michael's Ave
  Clevedon BS21 ....6 D1
  Weston-Super-Mare BS22 .32 A3
  Yeovil BA21 ....219 C7
St Michael's CE First Sch
  TA24 ....200 F7
St Michael's CE Jun Sch
  BA2 ....44 A6
St Michael's Cl
  Buckland Dinham BA11 ..100 A3
  Glastonbury BA6 ......206 E3
  Nether Stowey TA5 ....134 A2
St Michael's Cres TA2 ..213 A8
St Michael's Ct BA2 ......63 E8
St Michael's Gdns BA13 220 D5
St Michael's Hill
  Bristol BS2 ....226 C4
  Milverton TA4 ....167 A4
St Michael's Hospl BS2 226 C4
St Michael's Pk BS2 ....226 C4
St Michael's Pl BA1 ....228 B2
St Michael's Rd Bath BA1 44 D7
  Burnham-On-Sea TA8 ...104 B7
  Minehead TA24 ....200 F8
  Yeovil BA21 ....219 D6
St Michael's View
  TA15 ....186 B4
St Michaels Cl
  Nether Compton DT9 ....187 F3
  Stoke St Michael BA3 ....116 B3
St Michaels Ct TA7 ....136 E2
St Michaels Rd BA2 ....44 A5
St Nicholas CE Prim Sch
  Combe St Nicholas TA20 .193 D6
  Henstridge BA8 ....190 F7
St Nicholas Chantry Prim Sch
  BS21 ....6 E3
St Nicholas Cl
  ▲ Henstridge BA8 .....190 A6
  Winsley BA15 ....64 D7
St Nicholas Ct BA2 ....28 F1
St Nicholas Pk BA20 ..219 B4
St Nicholas Rd
  Weston-Super-Mare BS23 .48 D2
  Whitchurch BS14 ....23 C4
St Nicholas St BS1 ....227 A2
St Nicholas Way BS48 ..18 B3
St Nicholas' Rd BA1 ....78 F2
St Nicholas's Church Mus
  BS1 ....227 A2
St Oswald's Ct BS13 ....22 A8
St Patrick's Ct BA2 ....45 B6
St Patrick's Rd
  Taunton TA2 ....213 A8
  Yeovil BA21 ....218 D7
St Patricks Cl ▲ TA2 .213 A8
St Patricks Ct BS31 ....24 E5
St Paul St BS2 ....227 A4
St Paul's Cl DT9 ......225 E6
St Paul's Flats DT9 ....225 E6
St Paul's Gn DT9 ......225 E6
St Paul's Rd Bristol BS8 .226 B3
  Burnham-On-Sea TA8 ...104 B7
  Weston-Super-Mare BS23 .48 E5
St Paul's Terr BA1 ....111 A4
St Pauls CE Jun Sch
  BA4 ....205 B5
St Pauls Ct TA13 ......220 D4
St Pauls Ct TA6 ....209 D3
St Pauls Pl Bath BA1 ..228 B2
  Midsomer Norton BA3 ....78 A2
St Peter's Cl BS23 ....30 D1
St Peter's Cl
  Horton TA19 ....183 C1
  Taunton TA2 ....213 B7
St Peter's Ho BS8 ....226 B2
St Peter's Rise
  Bristol BS13 ....22 B7
  South Petherton TA13 ..220 D4
St Peter's Terr BA2 ....44 D6
St Peters CE Fst Sch
  TA4 ....202 D4
St Peters Cl
  BS20 ....2 D4
St Peters Cl Ilton TA19 .183 F4
  Staple Fitzpaine TA3 ..182 F5
  Williton TA4 ....202 D2
St Peters Ct TA6 ......209 D3
St Peters Rd
  Portishead BS20 ....2 D4
  Shepton Mallet BA4 ....205 A6
St Peters Terr ▲ BA4 ..205 B6
St Philip's CE Prim Sch
  BA2 ....44 C4
St Pias X RC Prim Sch
  BS13 ....22 A5
St Quintin Pk TA20 ....223 B4
St Rayn Hill TA17 ......195 B4
St Saviour's Ave TA6 ..209 A4
St Saviour's Inf Sch BA1 ..28 B2
St Saviour's Jun Sch
  BA1 ....28 B2
St Saviour's Rd BA1 ....28 C2

St Saviour's Terr ⑩ BA1 ..28 B1
St Saviour Way ④ BA1 .28 C1
St Stephen's Ave ③
  BS1 ....227 A2
St Stephen's CE Prim Sch
  BA1 ....227 F1
St Stephen's Ct BA1 ....227 F1
St Stephen's Ct BA1 ....228 B4
St Stephen's Pl BA1 ....228 B4
St Stephen's Rd BA1 ..228 B4
St Stephen's St BS1 ....227 A2
St Swithin's Pl BA1 ....228 C4
St Swithin's Rd DT9 ..225 E4
St Swithin's Yd BA2 ..228 C3
St Swithins Ct BS19 ..225 E4
St Thomas Cross BA1 ..219 C5
St Thomas Ct TA6 ......209 D3
St Thomas Rd BA3 ......78 B2
St Thomas St Bristol BS1 227 B2
  Dunster TA24 ....201 E2
  Wells BA5 ....203 E5
St Thomas St E BA1 ....227 B2
St Thomas St W BA1 ..227 B2
St Thomas' Ct BA5 ....203 E5
St Vigour & St John Prim Sch
  BA3 ....96 E3
St Vincent's Rd BS8 ..226 A2
St Whytes Rd BS4 ......22 D8
St Winifreds Dr BA2 ....63 D8
Salcombe Gdns BS22 ....32 A2
Sales Ho ⑤ BA4 ......205 B6
Salisbury Rd Bath BA1 ..28 C2
  Burnham-On-Sea TA8 ..104 C7
  Paulton BS39 ....77 F4
  Weston-Super-Mare BS22 .31 C1
Salisbury St TA2 ......212 E6
Salisbury Terr
  Castle Cary BA7 ......214 B5
  ④ Frome BA11 ....119 E3
  Gurney Slade BA3 ......114 E8
  Weston-Super-Mare BS23 .48 D7
Sally Hill BS20 ....2 D7
Sally In The Wood BA1,
  BA15 ....46 D6
Sally Lovell's La BA8 ..189 F8
Sally Lunn's Kitchen Mus*
  BA1 ....228 C2
Sallysmead Cl BS13 ....22 B4
Salmon Par TA6 ......209 A4
Saltford CE Prim Sch
  BS31 ....25 E2
Saltford Ct BS31 ......25 E2
Salthouse Ct BS21 ....6 B2
Salthouse La BA20 ....219 A4
Salthouse Rd BS21 ....6 B2
Saltings Cl BS21 ......6 B2
Saltlands TA6 ....208 F7
Saltlands Ave TA6 ....208 F7
Saltlands Ho TA6 ......208 F7
Saltry La TA24 ....146 A3
Saltwell Ave BS14 ....23 C5
Salway Gdns EX13 ....198 A1
Sambourne La BS20 ....4 C4
Sampford Arundel Com Prim
  Sch TA21 ....179 E5
Sampford Peverell CE Prim
  Sch EX16 ....178 C1
Sampford Rocks TA4 ..202 F1
Sampsons Rd BS13 ....22 D4
Samuels Ct TA2 ......212 C6
Samways Cl BA22 ......218 B5
Sanctuary Gdns BS9 ....5 D3
Sanctuary La TA22 ....148 A2
Sand Farm La BS22 ....31 A6
Sand Rd Wedmore BS28 .108 C3
  Weston-Super-Mare BS22 .31 B5
Sand St TA4 ....166 F4
Sandbrook La BA22 ....175 D7
Sandburrows Rd BS13 ..21 F6
Sandburrows Wlk BS13 .21 F6
Sandcroft BS14 ......22 E6
Sandcroft Ave BS23 ....48 D2
Sandene Ct TA2 ......212 C8
Sandford Cl ② BS21 ..6 B1
Sandford Hill TA5,TA6 .208 A6
Sandford Orcas Rd DT9 225 B7
Sandford Pk BA14 ......83 F7
Sandford Prim Sch BS25 .52 B4
Sandford Rd Bristol BS8 226 A1
  Weston-Super-Mare BS23 .49 A7
  Winscombe BS25 ....70 E5
Sandhill La TA14 ......131 C4
Sandhills Dr TA8 ......84 F4
Sandhurst Rd BA20 ....218 F1
Sanding's La
  Chapel Leigh TA4 ......167 A8
  Fitzhead TA4 ....166 F8
  Lydeard St Lawrence TA4 .151 A1
Sandlewood Cl BA21 ..219 E8
Sandmead Rd BS25 ....52 A4
Sandown Cl
  Bridgwater TA6 ....209 A2
  Yeovil BA20 ....219 A5
Sandpiper Cl
  Bridgwater TA6 ....209 A4
Sandpiper Dr BS22 ....31 F1
Sandpiper Rd TA6 ....209 A4
Sandpits Rd BA16 ....207 C5
Sandringham Ct TA6 ..209 C7
Sandringham Ct BS23 ..48 F5
Sandringham Rd
  Weston-Super-Mare BS23 .48 F5
  Yeovil BA21 ....219 E6
Sandrocks La TA24 ....131 B3
Sandscross La BA11 ..100 A3
Sandy Cl TA9 ....104 D4
Sandy Hole TA16 ......195 F7

Sandy La
  Beckington BA11 ....101 E4
  Cannington TA5 ....135 A3
  Easton-in-G BS20 ....4 A1
  Easton-In-Gordano BS8 ..10 A8
  Failand BS8 ....10 C7
  Stanton Drew BS39,BS40 ..39 E3
  Vriveliscombe TA4 .....210 C7
Sandy View BA11 ......101 E4
Sandy's Hill La BA11 ..119 E1
Sandy's La EX14 ......191 F2
Sandyleaze BS9 ....5 E7
Sandys Moor TA4 ......210 D4
Sansom's Cross DT6 ..199 F1
Sansome's Hill DT9 ..217 D2
Sarabeth Dr BA2 ......61 A4
Saracen St BA1 ......228 C3
Saunder's Piece La
  TA8 ....224 A7
Saunters Cl BA9 ......216 B4
Saunton Wlk BS4 ......22 E8
Savernake Rd BS22 ....31 F3
Savery or Cottage Row
  TA1 ....213 B3
Saville Cres BS22 ....49 C8
Saville Gate Cl BS9 ....5 F4
Saville Mews BS6 ......227 A4
Saville Pl BS8 ....226 A2
Saville Rd Bristol BS9 ..5 F3
  Weston-Super-Mare BS22 .49 C8
Saville Row BA1 ......228 B3
Saw Cl BA1 ....228 B2
Sawmill Cotts BA11 ..143 B8
Sawmill Gdns BA3 ....96 D3
Sawpit La BA6 ....140 C2
Sawpits Cl TA4 ....150 D8
Sawyers Cl
  Chilcompton BA3 ......96 D3
  Wincanton BA9 ....9 A2
Sawyers Ct BS21 ......6 E3
Sawyers Leigh TA2 ....168 D8
Sawyers Mill EX16 ....164 E2
Saxby Cl Clevedon BS21 ..6 B1
  Weston-Super-Mare BS22 .32 B4
Saxon Cl Ilton TA7 ....167 D4
  Watchet TA23 ....202 B7
Saxon Gn TA6 ....209 C4
Saxon Pl BS27 ....90 B7
Saxon Rd Bridgwater TA6 209 C4
  Weston-Super-Mare BS22 .49 C8
Saxon Ridge TA23 ....202 B7
Saxon St BS40 ....53 D6
Saxon Way Cheddar BS27 .90 B6
  Peasedown St John BA2 ..79 E8
Wedmore BS28 ....108 C4
Wincanton BA9 ....216 B3
  Winsley BA15 ....64 F7
Saxondale Ave TA8 ....85 A3
Saxonvale BA11 ......119 F4
Says La BS40 ....54 A3
Scadden's La BS27 ....91 B1
Scafell Cl Taunton TA1 212 C1
Scamel Ho ① BA4 ..205 B6
Scaurs The BS22 ......31 F2
School Cl Bampton EX16 .164 B1
  Banwell BS29 ....51 B3
  Bristol, Whitchurch BS14 .22 F4
  Tintinhull BA22 ....186 C6
  Watchet TA23 ....202 C7
School Cotts
  ⑯ East Coker BA22 ..197 E8
  Taunton TA6 ....168 F6
School Fields
  Cannington TA5 ....135 C2
  North Petherton TA6 ..153 F3
School Hill Ashcott TA7 .156 B8
  Crewkerne TA18 ....224 F3
  Cucklington BA9 ......177 D6
  South Perrott DT8 ....196 F2
  Westbury Sub Mendip BA5 .110 E6
  Wookey Hole BA5 ......203 A8
School La
  Barrow Gurney BS48 ....20 D5
  Batheaston BA1 ....28 F4
  Brushford TA22 ....163 E6
  Chew Stoke BS40 ......56 D8
  Combwich TA5 ....135 B5
  Compton Dundon TA11 ..157 A3
  Doulting BA4 ....141 E6
  East Brent TA9 ....86 E5
  Farrington Gurney BS39 ..77 A4
  Horrington BA5 ....113 A1
  Lopen TA13 ....185 A1
  North Petherton TA6 ..153 F4
  Rowberrow BS25 ......53 A1
  Seavington TA19 ....184 E2
  Shapwick TA7 ....137 F1
  Sherborne DT9 ....225 D3
  Tatworth TA20 ....198 C8
  Templecombe BA8 .....176 E1
  Wedmore BS28 ....108 D4
  Woolavington TA7 .....136 E4
School of Christ the King RC
  Prim Sch BS4 ....22 D7
School Rd
  Kingsdon TA11 ....173 D5
  Monkton Heathfield TA2 213 F8
  Parbrook BA6 ....158 C7
  Westonzoyland TA7 ....154 E5
  Wrington BS40 ....35 E2
School St
  Curry Rivel TA10 ....171 D4
  Drayton TA10 ....171 E3
School View BS48 ......9 B1
Scimitar Rd BA22 .....218 B6

Scobell Rise BS39 ......59 C2
Score La BS40 ....54 E2
Score The BS40 ......54 E2
Scornfield La BS40 ....56 D7
Scot Cl TA6 ....135 F5
Scot Elm Dr BS24 ......32 D1
Scot La BS40 ....38 D1
Scotch Horn Cl BS48 ....8 F2
Scotch Horn Way BS48 ..8 F2
Scotland La
  Axbridge BS26 ....107 D8
  Rudge BA11 ....102 C4
Scots Pine Ave BS48 ....8 F2
Scott Cl TA1 ....212 C6
Scott Rd Frome BA11 ..119 F5
  Highbridge TA9 ....104 D3
  Weston-Super-Mare BS23 ..49 A4
Scott's Hill
  Huish Champflower TA4 .165 E8
  Seavington TA19 ....184 D1
Scott's La
  Baltonsborough BA6 ..158 A8
  Wellington TA21 ....222 E6
Scotts Cl BS13 ....116 C8
Scotts La TA7 ....137 D1
Scotts Way TA18 ......196 B8
Scouse Cross EX13 ....198 E2
Scouse La EX13 ....198 D2
Scrapton La TA20 ......193 D5
Scrubbitts La TA7 ....137 B2
Scumbrum La BS39 ....59 C2
Sea Hay Rd BA20 ......218 D3
Sea La Carhampton TA24 ..131 A4
  Dunster TA24 ....201 F4
  Kilve TA5 ....133 C6
  Watchet TA23 ....132 D5
Sea Mills Inf Sch BS9 ....5 C7
Sea Mills Jun Sch BS9 ...5 C5
Sea Mills La BS9 ......5 C5
Sea Mills Sta BS9 ......5 B4
Sea View Rd TA8 ......104 A8
Seaborough View TA18 224 C4
Seabrook Rd BS22 ....31 D1
Seagrove Cl BS27 .....90 F7
Sealey Cres BA5 ......112 E1
Sealeys Cl TA9 ......136 A8
Searle Cres BS23 ......49 A6
Searle Ct BS23 ......6 E2
Seat La BA4 ....142 C2
Seaton Ct BA20 ......219 A4
Seaton Rd BA20 ......218 F4
Seavale Mews BS21 ....6 C4
Seavale Rd BS21 ......6 C4
Seaview Rd
  Portishead, Redcliffe Bay
  BS20 ....1 F4
  Portishead, West Hill BS20 ..1 F6
Seawalls BS9 ....5 D2
Seawalls Rd BS9 ......5 D2
Seaward Dr TA6 ......208 F6
Seaward Way TA24 ....201 C6
Second Ave
  Axminster EX13 ....198 A2
  Bath BA2 ....44 D5
  Bristol BS14 ....23 B7
  Radstock BA3 ....97 C7
Second Dro TA7 ......155 D3
Sector Hill BS13 ......198 B1
Sector La EX13 ....198 A1
Sedge Cl TA6 ....208 D2
Sedge Dro TA7 ....137 C3
Sedgemoor Dr Yeovil BA21 ..219 C7
Sedgemoor Coll TA3 ..170 A2
Sedgemoor Dro
  Sutton Mallet TA7 ....155 A6
  Wrantage TA3 ....170 E2
Sedgemoor Hill Dr TA7 155 B7
Sedgemoor Manor Com Jun
  Sch TA6 ....209 D3
Sedgemoor Manor Inf Sch
  TA6 ....209 D5
Sedgemoor Rd Bath BA2 ..44 F2
  Bridgwater TA6 ....209 C3
  Weston-Super-Mare BS23 ..30 F1
  Woolavington TA7 .....136 E3
Sedgemoor Way
  Glastonbury BA6 ......206 D5
  Woolavington TA7 .....136 E3
Sedgemount Ind Pk
  TA6 ....136 A2
Sedgwick Ho BS11 ......4 F7
Seeley Cres BS23 ......207 B3
Sefton Sq BS24 ......50 B8
Selbourne Cl BA1 ......44 A8
Selbourne Pl TA24 ....200 F6
Selbourne Rd BS23 ....48 E4
Selden Rd BS14 ......23 E5
Selley Wlk BS13 ......22 A5
Selway Ct BA2 ....45 B2
Selwood TA20 ....223 C5
Selwood Cl BA11 ......120 A7
Selwood Cres BA11 ....120 A7
Selwood Rd Frome BA11 .119 E5
  Glastonbury BA6 ......206 F6
Selwood St BA11 ......118 B7
Selworthy Cl
  Bridgwater TA6 ....208 F1
  Keynsham BS31 ....24 D5
Selworthy Gdns ④ BS48 ..8 E1
Selworthy Ho BA2 ......44 F2
Selworthy Rd
  Taunton TA2 ....213 B8
  Weston-Super-Mare BS23 ..49 A4

Selworthy Specl Sch
  TA2 ....213 A8
Selworthy Terr BA2 ....44 F2
Semington Cl TA1 .....213 D4
Septimus Blgss BS14 ..22 D5
Serbert Cl BS20 ....2 E5
Serbert Rd BS20 ......2 E5
Serbert Way BS20 ......2 E5
Sercombe Pk BS21 ......6 E1
Serel Dr BA5 ....203 B3
Serlo Ct BS22 ....32 A4
Seven Acres La BA1 ....28 F5
Seven Acres The BA21 ..49 F7
Seven Dials BA1 ......228 B2
Seven Thorns EX35 ....122 D5
Sevenacres TA11 ......211 C3
Seventh Ave BS14 ......23 A7
Severalls Park Ave
  TA18 ....224 C5
Severn Ave BS23 ......48 E5
Severn Cl TA6 ....209 D7
Severn Dr TA1 ....213 C3
Severn Gr TA8 ....104 B5
Severn Rd Bristol BS11 ...4 D6
  Portishead BS20 ....2 C5
  Weston-Super-Mare BS23 .48 E5
Severn Terr TA23 ......202 C7
Severn Way BS31 ......25 A5
Severnleigh Gdns BS9 ...5 F3
Severnmeade BS20 ....1 F5
Sevier Rd BS26 ....68 C3
Seville Ct BS20 ....2 E7
Seville Rd BS20 ......2 E7
Seward Terr BA3 ......79 C2
Seward Way BS25 ......70 A8
Sexey's Hospl BA10 ..215 E6
Sexey's Mid Sch BA10 .215 D5
Sexey's Rd BS28 ......107 E4
Seymour Cl Clevedon BS21 ..6 E3
  Wells BA5 ....203 C5
  Weston-Super-Mare BS22 .31 F4
Seymour Rd Bath BA1 ..228 C4
  Bridgwater TA6 ....209 D5
  Street BA16 ....207 D4
Seymour St BS2 ......227 C4
Shackel Cross EX15 ..191 B8
Shadow Wlk BS24 ......50 C3
Shadwell Ct BA9 ......216 C4
Shadwell La BA9 ......216 C4
Shaft Rd BA2 ....45 E1
Shaftesbury Ave BA1 ..44 C7
Shaftesbury Cl BS48 ..18 D8
Shaftesbury La BA9 ..177 B6
Shaftesbury Rd Bath BA2 ..44 D5
  Weston-Super-Mare BS23 .49 B8
Shaftesbury Terr BA3 ..79 A3
Shaftgate Ave BA4 ....205 A6
Shakespeare Ave
  Bath BA2 ....44 F4
  Taunton TA1 ....213 C3
Shakespeare Rd BA3 ..78 C1
Shaking Dro TA9 ....137 B6
Shalford La
  Wincanton BA9 ....161 A2
  Wincanton BA9 ....216 D8
Shallows The BS31 ....25 F3
Sham Castle La BA2 ....45 C7
Shambles The TA3 ....170 B4
Shapcott La BS36 .....162 C2
Shapcott Wood Hill
  EX36 ....162 A2
Shaplands BS9 ....5 F4
Shapway Cross TA19 ..184 F3
Shapway Cross TA19 ..184 F3
Shapway La BA4 ......141 F2
Shapway Rd BA4 ......141 F2
Shapwick Heath National
  Nature Reserve* BA6 ..138 A3
Shapwick Hill TA7 ....155 F8
Shapwick Rd BA6 ......138 A4
Shapwick Right Dro
  TA7 ....155 C5
Sharland Cl BS9 ......5 E3
Sharland Gr BS13 ......22 C4
Sharlands TA19 ......184 C5
Sharpenton La TA7 ....155 D6
Sharpham Dro BA16 ..138 C1
Sharpham La
  Glastonbury BA16 ....138 D1
  Stoke St Gregory TA3 ..170 E5
Sharpham Rd BS27 ....90 B8
Shatt La SN5 ....152 F3
Shatterwell Cotts BA9 .216 C4
Shatwell La
  Bratton Seymour BA9 ..175 F8
  Galhampton BA7 ......214 F1
Shaulders The TA2 ....213 C7
Shave Cross DT6 ......199 F1
Shave Hill SP8 ....177 D4
Shave La
  Crewkerne TA18 ....224 A3
  Donyatt TA19 ....183 D1
  Horton TA19 ....183 D1
  North Brewham BA10 ..161 A6
Shaw Path TA8 ....104 C6
Shawford La BA11 ....103 F7
Shaws Way BA2 ......43 F5
Sheafhayne Cross EX14 192 F4
Shearing Cross TA20 ..199 A5
Shearn La TA6 ....208 E3
Shearwater Cl TA6 ....209 D3
Shedrick Hill TA20 ....199 B8
Sheep Fair La SN14 ..113 F8

Sheep Way TA19 ....**184** E3
Sheephouse Caravan Pk
BS20 .... 3 E7
Sheeplands La DT9 ....**225** B5
Sheeplands The DT9 ...**225** B5
Sheeps Croft BS13 ......**22** A5
Sheepstealing La TA4 ..**150** E5
Sheepway BS20 .... 3 B5
Sheepway La BS20 .... 3 C5
Sheldon Cl BS21 .... 6 F2
Sheldon Ct TA1 ....**212** E4
Sheldon Dr BA5 ....**203** C3
Sheldon's La TA22 ....**163** A7
Shelduck Cl TA24 ......**201** C5
Shell's La Chard TA20 ..**193** A3
   Shepton Beauchamp TA19 **184** E4
Shelley Ave BS21 .... 6 D2
Shelley Cl BA21 ....**218** D6
Shelley Dr TA8 ....**85** B2
Shelley Gr TA1 ....**213** B3
Shelley Rd Bath BA2 ....**44** F4
   Radstock BA3 ....**78** C1
   Weston-Super-Mare BS23 ..**49** A4
Shellthorn Gr TA6 ......**208** F2
Shelthorne TA5 ....**152** F3
Shelway La TA19 ....**184** C4
Shepherd's Cnr TA23 ..**157** A4
Shepherd's Dro TA7 ...**155** A3
Shepherd's Hay TA1 ...**212** C2
Shepherd's Mill SP8 ...**177** E4
Shepherd's La
   Chard TA20 ....**223** B4
   Frome BA11 ....**144** B7
   Hemyock EX15 ....**180** F1
Shepherds Cl TA6 ......**208** D6
Shepherds Cross BA8 ..**176** C5
Sheppard's Barton
   BA11 ....**119** E5
Sheppard's Cnr TA5 ...**153** B5
Sheppards Gdns BA1 ....**27** B1
Sheppards Wlk BA3 .....**96** D3
Sheppy's Cider Farm Ctr
   TA4 ....**167** F5
Sheppy's Mill BS49 .....**34** D5
Shepton BS24 ....**49** A2
Shepton Beauchamp CE Fst
   Sch **184** E4
Shepton Mallet Inf Sch
   BA4 ....**205** C6
   Shepton Mallet Mus*
   BA4 ....**205** B5
Shepton Old Rd
   Croscombe BA5 ....**204** A6
   Dinder BA5 ....**140** D7
Shepton Rd BA4,BA5 ...**204** D7
   Sherborne Abbey*
   DT9 ....**225** D3
Sherborne Abbey CE Prim
   Sch DT9 ....**225** B2
   Sherborne Castle* DT9 ..**225** F3
Sherborne Hill DT9 ....**225** E1
   Sherborne Mus* DT9 .....**225** D4
   Sherborne Old Castle*
   DT9 ....**225** D4
Sherborne Prep Sch
   DT9 ....**225** D3
Sherborne Prim Sch
   DT9 ....**225** E5
Sherborne Rd
   Henstridge BA8 ....**189** E6
   Milborne Port DT9 ....**217** C2
   Yeovil BA21 ....**219** D5
Sherborne Sch for Girls
   DT9 ....**225** C4
Sherford Rd TA1 ....**212** E1
Sherford Terr TA1 .....**212** E1
Sheridan Ct TA6 ....**209** D3
Sheridan Gdns BA14 ....**83** F6
Sheridan Rd Bath BA2 ...**43** F5
   Burnham-On-Sea TA8 ......**104** C6
Sherlands 4 TA16 ......**195** F7
Sherlands Gdns 3 TA16 **195** F7
Sherrin Way BS13 ....**21** E3
Sherston Cl BS48 ....**9** A1
Shervage Ct TA6 ....**209** C5
Sherwood Cl BS31 ....**24** E5
Sherwood Cres BS22 ....**31** F3
Sherwood Rd BS31 ......**24** E5
Shetland Way BS48 ....**9** A1
Shickle Gr BA2 ....**44** D1
Shiller's La BA7 ....**188** C7
Shillingford Fst Sch
   EX16 ....**164** F3
Shiners Elms BS49 ......**34** B8
Ship La Bristol BS1 ....**227** B1
   Combwich TA5 ....**135** B5
Shipham CE Fst Sch
   BS25 ....**70** E8
Shipham Cl Bristol BS14 **23** B5
   Nailsea BS48 ....**18** F8
Shipham La BS25 ....**52** B1
Shipham Rd BS27 ....**71** A3
Shiplate Rd BS24 ....**67** E6
Shipney La DT10 ....**190** C5
Shircombe La TA22 .....**147** F2
Shire Gdns BS11 ....**4** D8
Shirehampton Inf Sch
   BS11 ....**4** D6
Shirehampton Rd BS9 ....**5** C6
Shirehampton Sta BS11 ..**4** D5
Shiremoor Hill TA16 ...**195** F7
Shires Yd BA1 ....**228** B3
Shockerwick La BA1 .....**29** D4

Shoe La TA7 ....**209** E7
Shoot Hill TA17 ....**195** C8
Shop La Pilton BA4 .....**140** E3
   Wingfield BA14 ....**83** C6
Shophouse Rd BA2 ......**44** B5
Shopland Ho 9 BS21 .....6 C2
Shoreditch BS40 ....**56** C7
Shoreditch Rd
   Stoke St Mary TA3 ....**169** A1
   Taunton TA1 ....**213** B1
Shoredown La DT9,BA8 ..**217** E6
Short Dro Mudgley BS28 **138** C7
   Westbury Sub Mendip BA5,
   BS27 ....**110** B4
Short La Axbridge BS26 ..**88** C2
   Draycott BS27 ....**90** E3
   Litton BA3 ....**75** F2
   Long Ashton BS41 ....**11** A2
Short Way BS8 ....**10** B4
Shortland La BS28 ......**108** C3
Shortmarsh La BA22 ...**196** F4
Shortwood Rd BS13 .....**22** E3
Shortwood Wlk BS13 ....**22** E3
Shoscombe CE Prim Sch
   BA2 ....**79** C5
Shoscombe Gdns BA11 **120** C7
Shovel La TA6 ....**153** E3
Showell Pk TA2 ....**212** B7
Showering Cl BS14 ......**23** D5
Showering Rd BS14 .....**23** D5
Showground Rd TA6 ....**209** B1
Shrewsbury Bow BS24 ...**50** A8
Shrubbery Ave BS23 ....**30** D1
Shrubbery Cl TA8 ....**84** E8
Shrubbery Rd BS23 .....**30** D1
Shrubbery Terr BS23 ....**30** C1
Shrubbery Wlk BS23 ....**30** D1
Shrubbery Wlk W BS23 ..**30** D1
Shudrick La TA19 ......**221** C3
Shurtland La TA4 ......**150** C3
Shute La Lamyatt TA5 ..**134** C6
   Shute La Bruton BA10 ....**215** D6
   Huish Champflower TA4 ...**165** C8
   Long Sutton TA10 ....**172** E4
Shute Lake La TA18 ....**224** D5
Shute Row TA21 ....**222** E5
Shute's La SP8 ....**177** E4
Shuteleigh TA21 ....**222** E5
Shutemead TA1 ....**212** A4
Shuter Rd BS13 ....**21** E5
Shutewater La TA1 .....**212** A4
Shutewater Hill TA1 ...**212** A4
Shuttern 2 TA1 ....**212** E3
Shuttern Bridge 3 TA1 **212** E3
Shutwell La BA4 ....**140** E3
Shyners Terr TA6 ......**195** F7
Sidcot BS25 ....**70** A7
Sidcot La BS25 ....**70** A7
Sidcot Sch BS25 ....**70** B7
Side Wood La EX36 ....**162** A1
Sideland Cl BS14 ....**23** E6
Sidelings The BS40 .....**73** D8
Sidings The DT10 ......**190** C4
Sidmouth Cl TA8 ....**104** C8
Sidney Hill Cottage Homes
   BS25 ....**52** E4
Silbury Rd BS3 ....**11** E2
Silbury Rise BS31 ....**25** A2
Silcox Rd BS13 ....**22** C4
Silk Cl BA4 ....**205** B7
Silk House Barton DT10 **190** B4
Silk Mills La TA2 ....**212** A4
Silk Mills Rd TA1 ......**212** A4
Silklands Gr BS9 ....5 C6
Silton Rd SP8 ....**161** F1
Silver Ct BS48 ....8 C2
Silver Mead BS49 ....**34** D2
Silver Moor La BS29 ....**50** F7
Silver Rd BA16 ....**207** C5
Silver Springs TA19 ...**184** E3
Silver St
   1 Bampton EX16 ....**164** B1
   Barrington TA19 ....**184** D5
   Barton St David TA11 ....**158** A3
   Barwick BA22 ....**197** F8
   Bridgwater TA6 ....**208** E4
   Bristol BS1 ....**227** A3
   Bruton BA10 ....**215** E6
   Chard TA20 ....**223** C3
   Cheddar BS27 ....**90** B8
   Chew Magna BS40 ....**39** B3
   Congresbury BS49 ....**34** D2
   Crewkerne TA18 ....**196** B3
   Curry Mallet TA3 ....**183** C8
   Ditcheat BA4 ....**159** C7
   East Lambrook TA13 ......**220** C8
   Fivehead TA3 ....**170** F8
   Glastonbury BA6 ....**206** D4
   Holcombe BA3 ....**97** C1
   Ilminster TA19 ....**221** B4
   Kilmersdon BA3 ....**98** B5
   Kingsbury Episcopi TA12 ..**185** B8
   Kingsdon TA11 ....**173** D5
   Langport TA10 ....**172** A3
   Midsomer Norton BA3 .....**97** A7
   Milverton TA4 ....**167** A4
   Portishead BS20 ....**1** F1
   Shepton Beauchamp TA19 ..**184** E3
   South Petherton TA13 ....**220** D4
   Taunton TA1 ....**213** A3
   Wells BA5 ....**203** E3
   West Buckland TA21 ......**180** F7
   West Huntspill TA9 ......**136** A8
   Wincanton BA9 ....**216** C4
   Wiveliscombe TA4 ....**210** C4
   Wrington BS40 ....**35** E2

Silver St continued
   Yeovil BA20 ....**219** B5
Silverberry Rd BS22 ....**32** A1
Silvercombe 1 BS23 ....**48** E5
Silverdale Cl
   Brushford TA22 ....**163** E4
   Wembdon TA6 ....**208** C5
Silverdown Hill TA4 ...**150** C7
Silverlake Cotts DT9 ..**188** B2
Silverlow Rd BS48 ....**8** D2
Silvermead TA4 ....**201** B5
Silverstone Way BS49 ..**34** D3
Simbriss Rd BA3 ....**114** F5
Simmons Cl BA16 ......**207** D5
Simon's Cl BS39 ....**77** F3
Simons Cl BS22 ....**32** A2
Simons Mews TA20 ....**223** E4
Simons Rd DT9 ....**225** D5
Sinclair Ho BS8 ....**226** A2
Singapore Rd BS23 .....**48** E5
Singer's Knoll BA11 ...**119** F4
Singleton St BA1 ......**203** C5
Sion Hill Bath BA1 ......**27** E1
   Bristol BS8 ....**11** F7
Sion Hill Pl BA1 ....**27** E1
Sion La BS8 ....**11** F7
Sion Pl Bath BA2 ....**45** B6
   Bristol BS8 ....**11** F7
Sion Rd BA1 ....**27** E1
   Sir Bevil Grenville's Mon*
   BA1 ....**12** A1
Sisters The BA4 ....**205** A6
Six Acres Cl TA1 ....**213** C5
Six Streams BA1 ....**27** B2
Six Ways BS21 ....6 C4
Sixpence BS39 ....**59** D2
Sixteen Acre La TA20 ..**193** D8
Sixth Ave BS14 ....**23** A7
Sixty Acres Cl BS8 ......**10** B4
Skilgate La TA4 ....**185** E1
Skimmerton La TA5,TA6 **208** A5
Skinner's Hill BA2 ....**78** F7
Skinner's La TA14 ......**185** F2
Skinners La BS25 ....**52** F4
Skitmoor Dro BS28 ....**109** C2
Skylark Cl TA6 ....**209** B4
Sladacre La BS40 ....**54** E2
Slade Cl TA4 ....**150** E8
Slade La
   Barrow Gurney BS48 ......**20** C4
   Golsoncott TA23 ....**131** A1
   Hawkridge TA22 ....**146** D1
   Lympsham BS24 ....**67** B1
   Rimpton BA22 ....**188** A7
   Rooksbridge BS26 ....**87** E4
   West Anstey EX36 ....**162** B6
Slade Rd BS20 ....2 D5
Slade Way TA4 ....**202** E4
Slade's Cross TA20 ....**193** D7
Sladebrook Ave BA2 ....**44** C3
Sladebrook Ct BA2 .....**44** C2
Sladebrook Rd BA2 .....**44** B4
Slades Hill BA8 ....**176** E1
Slades Orch TA19 ......**183** C1
Slait Hill BA4 ....**142** C7
   Midsomer Chase BA16 ....**156** C7
Slapes Cl TA2 ....**168** F6
Slate La BS14,BS31 ......**41** B7
Sleep La BS14 ....**23** D3
Sleight Cl BA21 ....**218** C6
Sleight La BA5 ....**140** E8
Slippery Batch TA11 ...**211** A6
Sloe Cl BS22 ....**49** D8
Slopers La BA9 ....**176** D5
Slough Hill TA3 ....**182** D6
Slough La
   Cold Ashton SN14 ....**12** F5
   Crowcombe TA4 ....**151** A8
   North Wootton BA4 ......**140** B3
   Stoke St Gregory TA3 ....**170** F6
   Upottery EX14 ....**191** F5
Slow Court La BA22 ....**174** D3
Sloway La TA6,TA9 ....**136** A8
Slowland La BA5 ......**110** D8
Slugg Hill BA16 ....**207** C3
Small Down End BS25 ...**51** F2
Small Down La BA4 ....**142** C6
Small La EX16 ....**179** B2
Small Mead Dro BA6 ..**157** F4
Small Moor La BA16 ...**156** E7
Small St BS1 ....**227** A3
Small Way La BA22 ....**214** C1
Smallbrook La BS39 ....**41** A6
Smallcombe Cl BA3 ....**78** F3
Smallcombe Rd BA3 ....**78** E4
Smallcombe View BA3 ..**78** F4
Smallmoor Chase BA16 **156** E7
Smallmoor Dro TA7 ....**155** A3
Smallridge Rd EX13 ...**198** A4
Smalls Mead 2 TA11 ...**173** F7
Smallway BS49 ....**34** D5
Smallways La TA7 ......**137** B3
Smeathy La EX15 ......**180** F3
Smeaton Rd BS1 ....**11** F5
Sminhays Cnr TA23 ....**149** B5
Smith Way TA9 ....**104** D3
   Smith's Forge Ind Est
   TA7 ....**137** D2
Smith's Hill TA18 .....**196** C8
Smith's La BA4 ....**159** C6
Smith's Terr BA21 .....**219** C6
Smithfield Rd BA16 ....**207** B4
Smithick's La BA11 ....**143** E6
Smithmead BS13 ....**22** B5
Smiths Cl BS27 ....**91** A1
Smithy TA1 ....**212** B3
Smithyard La TA4,TA23 **202** A3

Smokeham La TA4 .....**151** D5
Smoky Hole La TA18,
   BA22 ....**185** F1
Smurl La TA9 ....**104** C1
Smythe Croft BS14 .....**23** A3
Smythes Cross EX15 ...**191** C7
Snag La BA9 ....**216** E3
Snagg La BA4 ....**159** D5
Snake La BS28 ....**108** C6
Snakelake Hill BA10 ...**160** C7
Snap Hill TA11 ....**173** D8
Snathe Lea 4 TA4 .....**167** F8
Snedden Gr TA1 ....**213** B5
Snipefield La BS28 .....**108** A6
Snow Hill BA1 ....**28** A1
Snow Hill Ho BA1 ......**228** C4
Snowberry Cl BS22 .....**32** A1
Snowdon Cottage La
   TA20 ....**223** B4
Snowdon Hts TA20 ....**223** B4
Snowdon Vale BS23 .....**31** A1
Society Rd BA4 ....**205** A6
Sock Hill BA21 ....**187** C6
Sock La BA21 ....**187** C6
Sock's La BA10 ....**160** B6
Solomon's Hollow TA3 .**169** F2
Solon Ct BS13 ....**21** F5
Solsbury Ct BA1 ....**28** F3
Solsbury La BA1 ....**28** F4
Solsbury View 17 BA1 ..**28** A1
Solsbury Way BA1 ......**28** A2
Somer Ave BA3 ....**77** F2
Somer Ct BA3 ....**78** B1
Somer Ho BA3 ....**78** A1
Somer Lea BA3 ....**96** D5
Somer Rd BA3 ....**77** F2
Somer's Hill BA11 .....**117** D3
Somerdale Ave Bath BA2 **44** D2
   Bristol BS4 ....**22** F8
   Weston-Super-Mare BS22 ..**49** C8
Somerdale Cl BS24 .....**49** F4
Somerdale Rd BS31 .....**24** F7
Somerdale Rd N BS30,
   BS31 ....**24** F8
Somerdale View BA3 ...**44** C2
Somerleaze Cl BA5 ....**203** B3
Somerleaze Cl BA5 .....**51** E2
Somer Ho BA3 ....**78** A1
Somerset Ave
   Taunton TA1 ....**212** B2
   Weston-Super-Mare BS22,
   BS24 ....**49** E8
   Somerset Brick & Tile Mus*
   TA6 ....**209** A2
Somerset Bridge Prim Sch
   TA6 ....**209** A2
Somerset Cl BA4 ....**205** C5
Somerset Coll of Art & Tech
   (Annexe) TA1 ....**212** E4
Somerset Coll of Art & Tech
   (Bishops Hull Annexe)
   TA1 ....**212** A3
Somerset County Mus*
   TA1 ....**212** F4
Somerset Cty Cricket Gd
   TA1 ....**212** F4
Somerset Folly BA2 ....**60** B2
Somerset Gdns TA6 ...**209** C3
Somerset Ho Bath BA2 .**44** D3
   2 Bristol BS2 ....**227** C3
Somerset La BA1 ....**27** E2
Somerset Mews BS23 ...**48** F6
Somerset Nuffield Hospl
   TA2 ....**212** D8
Somerset Pl Bath BA1 ...**27** E2
   Taunton TA1 ....**213** B4
   Yeovil BA20 ....**219** A3
Somerset Rd
   Bridgwater TA6 ....**209** C3
   Clevedon BS21 ....6 E3
   Frome BA11 ....**119** E4
   Portishead BS20 ....2 D2
   Somerset Rural Life Mus*
   BA6 ....**206** E4
Somerset Sq Bristol BS1 **227** B1
   8 Nailsea BS48 ....8 F2
Somerset St Bath BA1 ..**228** C1
   Bristol BS1 ....**227** B1
   Bristol BS2 ....**227** C3
Somerset Way BS39 .....**77** E6
   Somerset Wildlife Trust*
   TA5 ....**152** E3
Somerton BS24 ....**49** A2
Somerton Cl TA6 ......**209** D4
Somerton Door Dro
   Compton Dundon TA11 ...**156** E1
   Somerton TA11 ....**211** A7
Somerton Dro TA11 ...**156** E1
Somerton Gdns BA11 ..**120** C6
Somerton Hill
   Langport TA10 ....**172** E7
   Somerton TA11 ....**211** A3
   Somerton Inf Sch TA11 ..**211** C4
Somerton Rd
   Clevedon BS21 ....6 E1
   Langport TA10 ....**172** E4
   Street BA16 ....**207** B7
Somertonfield Rd TA11 **172** E7
Somervale Rd BA3 ....**78** B3
Somervale Sch BA3 .....**78** A1
Somerville Cl
   Saltford BS31 ....**25** E3
   Shepton Mallet BA4 .....**205** D4
Somerville Cotts BA5 ..**204** B8
Somerville Rd
   Sandford BS25 ....**52** A4

Somerville Rd continued
   Wells BA5 ....**203** C5
Somerville Way TA6 ...**209** D3
   Sommertaun Cross
   EX36 ....**162** A4
Sopers Field TA20 .....**223** D2
Sophia Gdns BS22 ......**32** B4
South Ave Bath BA2 ....**44** D5
   Highbridge TA9 ....**104** C4
   Portishead BS20 ....2 D6
   Sherborne DT9 ....**225** B2
South Bank
   Castle Cary BA7 ....**214** B3
   Wookey Hole BA5 ....**203** A8
South Brent Cl TA9 .....**85** F3
South Bristol Trad Pk
   BS3 ....**11** F3
South Cary La BA7 ....**214** A5
South Cl Draycott BS27 ..**90** E2
   Lympsham BS24 ....**86** B8
   Walton BA16 ....**156** D7
South Combe BS24 ......**67** B6
South Common La
   EX13 ....**198** A5
South Croft BS25 ....**54** D2
South Dene BS9 ....5 E6
South Dro TA10 ....**171** B4
South Espl TA8 ....**104** A5
South Fields BA6 ......**206** E3
South Green St 8 BS8 .**11** F6
South Harp TA13 ......**220** E1
South Hele Cross EX16 **165** C1
South Hills BS25 ....**51** F2
South La
   Nether Stowey TA5 ......**134** B2
   Shoulsbarrow Common
   EX31 ....**126** A3
South Lawn BS24 ....**49** F4
South Lawn Cl BS24 ....**49** F4
South Lea Rd BA1 ....**44** A8
South Mdw BA5 ....**113** A1
South Mdws BS40 ....**35** E2
South Molton Rd EX16 **164** B1
South Moors La TA7 ...**137** B2
South Parr Bath BA2 ...**228** C2
   Chew Magna BS40 ....**39** B3
   Frome BA11 ....**119** E4
   Weston-Super-Mare BA2 ..**48** D8
South Parade Cotts BA2 .**45** C1
South Petherton Hospl
   TA13 ....**220** D5
South Petherton Inf Sch
   TA13 ....**220** C4
   South Petherton Jun Sch
   TA13 ....**220** D3
South Pk Taunton TA4 ..**200** D6
South Rd Brean TA8 .....**65** F3
   Lympsham BS24 ....**67** B1
   Midsomer Norton BA3 .....**78** B1
   Portishead BS20 ....2 D2
   Taunton TA1 ....**213** A2
   Timsbury BA2 ....**60** B2
   Watchet TA23 ....**202** C6
   Weston-Super-Mare BS23 ..**30** C1
South Road Villas BA9 .**216** C4
South Rock Ind Est BA3 .**96** D1
South Side BS49 ....**34** E5
South St
   Burnham-On-Sea TA8 ....**104** A6
   Castle Cary BA7 ....**214** B4
   Crewkerne TA18 ....**224** D5
   Hinton St George TA17 ..**195** D7
   Holcombe Rogus TA21 ...**178** F5
   Kington Magna SP8 ......**177** E1
   Milborne Port DT9 ....**217** D2
   Montacute TA15 ....**186** B3
   Sherborne DT9 ....**225** E3
   South Petherton TA13 ....**220** D4
   Stratton-on-the-Fosse BA3 ..**96** F2
   Taunton TA1 ....**213** A2
   Wellington TA21 ....**222** E5
   Wells BA5 ....**203** D4
   West Camel BA22 ....**174** D3
   Wincanton BA9 ....**216** C3
   Wiveliscombe TA4 ....**210** C4
   Yeovil BA20 ....**219** B4
South Terr
   Burnham-On-Sea TA8 ....**104** B6
   Weston-Super-Mare BS23 ..**48** D8
   Yeovil BA20 ....**219** B4
South Veiw BA5 ....**113** A1
South View Bath BA2 ....**45** E1
   Bawdrip TA7 ....**136** E2
   Bradford Abbas DT9 .....**187** E1
   Broadway TA19 ....**183** C2
   1 East Coker BA22 ....**197** E8
   Lynford-on-Fosse TA11 ..**158** C1
   Paulton BS39 ....**77** F5
   Portishead BS20 ....2 D2
   Queen Camel BA22 ......**174** F3
   Radstock BA3 ....**78** E5
   Taunton TA3 ....**168** D1
   Timsbury BA2 ....**60** B2
   Westleigh EX16 ....**179** A3
South View Pl BA3 ......**78** B2
South View Rd Bath BA2 **44** B6
   Milborne Port DT9 ....**217** C3
South View Terr
   Taunton TA1 ....**168** D1
   Yatton BS49 ....**17** B1
South Villas TA4 ......**150** C1
   South Wansdike Sp Ctr
   BA3 ....**78** B1
South Well TA3 ....**168** D1
   South Western Bsns Pk
   DT9 ....**225** D3

South Western Terr
  BA20 ....219 C4
Southampton Row **5**
  TA2 ....213 A8
Southay Cross TA20 ....193 A4
Southay La TA20 ....192 F4
Southbourne Gdns BA1 ...28 B1
Southbourne Ho BA1 .....208 E4
Southbourne Mans BA2 ..228 C2
Southbrook TA5 ....135 C2
Southbrook Cl TA5 ....135 C2
Southbrook Cotts BA9 ...216 F4
Southcombe House (Queens
  Coll) TA1 ....168 D1
Southcombe Way BA22 ..186 B6
Southcot Pl BA2 ....228 C1
Southcroft Dr BA13 ....121 D4
Southdown
  Charlton Horethorne DT9 .176 A1
  Weston-Super-Mare BS22 ..31 F4
Southdown Ave BA2 ....44 B3
Southdown Cross EX16 ..179 B2
Southdown Inf Sch BA2 ...44 B3
Southdown Jun Sch BA2 .44 B3
Southdown Rd Bath BA2 ..44 B4
  Bristol BS9 ....5 F8
Southend Gdns TA9 ....104 E5
Southend Rd BS23 ....48 E4
Southern Lea Rd TA8 .....104 C8
Southern Ring Path **4**
  BS21 ....6 B1
Southern Way BS21 ....6 C1
Southernhay BS8 ....226 B2
Southernhay Ave BS8 ....226 B2
Southernhay Cres BS8 ...226 B2
Southey Rd BS21 ....6 D2
Southfield Cheddar BS27 ..90 B8
  Norton St Philip BA2 ......81 F4
  Radstock BA3 ....79 A2
  Southwick BA14 ....83 F2
  Wiveliscombe TA4 ....210 C3
Southfield Cl Nailsea BS48 ..8 E3
  Taunton TA1 ....168 F4
  Weston-Super-Mare BS23 ..48 D2
  Woolavington TA7 ....136 E3
Southfield Hill BA3 ....99 A6
Southfield Rd Nailsea BS48 ..8 F3
  Shepton Mallet BA4 ....205 A5
Southfield Rd Trad Est
  BS48 ....8 F3
Southfields Frome BA11 ..120 A2
  Ilminster TA19 ....183 E2
Southgate Bath BA1 ....228 C2
  Wiveliscombe TA4 ....210 C3
Southgate Ave TA6 ....209 A3
Southgate Dr BA9 ....216 C3
Southgate Rd BA9 ....216 C3
Southlands Bath BA1 ......27 B1
  Carhampton TA24 ....131 B5
Southlands Dr BA2 ....60 B2
Southlands Way BS49 ....34 E5
Southleaze BS25 ....70 A6
Southleaze Orch BA16 ...207 D6
Southleaze Rd BA16 ......207 B6
Southleigh BS25 ....69 F8
Southleigh Rd
  Bristol BS8 ....226 B4
  Taunton TA1 ....213 B3
Southmead
  West Camel BA22 ....174 D3
  Winscombe BS25 ....70 A8
Southmead Cres TA18 ...224 C5
Southmead La BA8 ....190 A6
Southmead Rd BA22 ......49 B7
Southmead Terr TA18 ....224 C5
Southover BA5 ....203 D3
Southover Rd BS39 ....59 D1
Southridge Hts BS24 ......67 A8
Southside BS23 ....48 E8
Southside Cl BS9 ....5 B8
Southside Cres BS22 ......31 A4
Southview La BA2 ....62 F8
Southstoke Rd BA2 ....44 F1
Southtown La TA6 ....158 B8
Southview Cl Hutton BS24 ..49 F2
  Westonzoyland TA7 ....154 F5
Southview Rd TA7 ....154 F5
Southville BA21 ....219 C5
Southville Rd BS23 ....48 E6
Southville Terr BA2 ....45 B4
Southway Cl BA21 ....218 F6
Southway Cres BA21 .....218 F6
Southway Cl BS21 ....6 D2
Southway Dr BA21 ....218 F6
Southwell Cl TA3 ....168 D1
Southwell Cres TA9 ......104 E3
Southwell La TA9 ....104 E3
Southwell St BS2 ....226 C4
Southwick Ctry Pk*
  BA14 ....83 F3
Southwick Rd TA9 ....106 C1
Southwood Ave BS9 ....5 C8
Southwood Dr BS9 ....5 B8
Southwood Dr E BS9 ....5 C8
Southwood Gr TA1 ....212 C2
Southwood Way TA3 .....168 D1
Southwoods BA20 ....219 A3
Sovereign Rd BA16 ....208 D7
Sovereign Sh Ctr BS23 ..48 D7
Sowden Hill TA5 ....134 D4
Spanish Hill TA4 ....150 C4
Spargrove La BA4 ....142 B1
Sparkford Hill La BA22 ..175 A7
Sparkford BA22 ....175 A6
Sparkhayes La TA24 .....124 A3

Sparks Way TA9 ....104 D3
Sparrow Hill Way BS26 ...88 E6
Sparrow La TA24 ....146 C7
Sparrow Rd BA21 ....219 B6
Spartley Dr BS13 ....21 F6
Spartley Wlk BS13 ....21 F6
Spaxton CE Prim Sch
  TA5 ....152 E7
Spaxton Cl TA8 ....104 C8
Spaxton Rd TA5 ....153 C7
Spear Mead DT8 ....199 F7
Spearcey Cl TA3 ....181 D8
Spearcey La TA3 ....181 D8
Spearhay La TA20 ....198 F5
Spears La
  Waterrow TA21 ....165 F4
  Weston-Super-Mare TA24 .166 A4
Specket La DT8 ....199 E5
Speckington La BA22 ...174 B2
Specklemead BS39 ....77 D5
Speedwell Est **2** BS21 ...6 C2
Speke Cl Ilminster TA19 ..221 B4
  Merriott TA16 ....195 F7
  Staplegrove TA2 ....221 B6
Speke Ct TA19 ....221 B4
Spencer Ave TA2 ....212 E6
Spencer Dr TA20 ....204 D3
Spencer Dr
  Midsomer Norton BA3 .....78 A2
  Weston-Super-Mare BS22 ..32 B3
Spencer Ho **8** BS23 ....48 E7
Spencers Belle Vue
  BA1 ....228 B4
Sperry Cross TA4 ....149 B1
Spicer Way TA20 ....223 D2
Spillers Cl TA6 ....208 E2
Spindleberry Gr BS48 .....9 A2
Spinners End BS22 ....32 B4
Spinners Ho **8** BA4 ...205 B6
Spinney Croft BS13 ....21 F5
Spinney Rd TA19 ....221 A4
Spinney The Ashcott TA7 .156 A8
  Portishead BS20 ....2 C4
  Taunton TA1 ....212 D2
  Weston-Super-Mare BS24 ..48 F1
  Yeovil BA20 ....218 F2
Spinneyfield TA4 ....167 F7
Spire Cross TA24 ....147 A4
Splatt La TA5 ....152 E8
Splott BS26 ....88 F6
Spoonbill Rd TA6 ....209 B4
Spratts Bridge BS40 ....39 A3
Spring Cres BA2 ....228 C3
Spring Field Cres DT9 ...225 C3
Spring Gardens Rd BA2 ..228 C2
Spring Gdns
  Minehead TA24 ....201 B5
  Weston-Super-Mare TA24 .210 C5
Spring Ground Rd BS39 ...77 F5
Spring Hill BS22 ....31 D2
Spring Hill Dr BS22 ....31 E1
Spring La Bath BA1 ....28 B2
  Dundry BS41 ....22 A1
  Sandford Orcas DT9 ......188 C7
Spring Rd BA11 ....119 F6
Spring Rise
  Portishead BS20 ....2 C3
  Puriton TA7 ....136 C4
  Wells BA5 ....203 C3
Spring Terr Frome BA11 .119 D2
  Weston-Super-Mare BS22 ..31 D2
Spring Valley BS22 ....31 D2
Spring Wood Gdns BS24 .49 E3
Springbok Cl BA10 ....227 A3
Springer's Hill BA3 ....116 E6
Springfield
  East Chinnock BA22 ......196 E8
  Ilminster TA19 ....221 B2
  Norton St Philip BA2 .....81 F4
  Peasedown St John BA2 ..79 C7
Springfield Ave
  Bridgwater TA6 ....208 C3
  Bristol, Shirehampton BS11 ..4 D6
  Weston-Super-Mare BS22 ..31 D1
Springfield Bldgs
  Midsomer Norton BA3 .....77 D2
  Radstock BA3 ....79 A3
Springfield Cl
  Axbridge BS26 ....69 F2
  Bath BA2 ....44 A6
  Cheddar BS27 ....90 A8
Springfield Cotts BS30 ..26 A8
Springfield Cres BA3 .....79 A3
Springfield Ct BA4 ....205 A5
Springfield Dr BS28 ......108 D4
Springfield Flats TA20 ..223 C4
Springfield Gdns BS29 ...51 A3
Springfield Ho
  Bristol BS6 ....226 C4
  Portishead BS20 ....2 C3
Springfield Hts BA3 ......78 E4
Springfield Lawn BS11 ...4 D6
Springfield Pl
  Bath BA1 ....78 E4
  Yeovil BA21 ....218 E7
Springfield Rd
  Cheddar BS27 ....90 A8
  Highbridge TA9 ....104 E4
  Milborne Port DT9 ....217 D3
  Portishead BS20 ....2 B5
  Wellington TA21 ....222 C7
  Wincanton BA9 ....216 B4
  Yeovil BA21 ....218 E7

Springfield Terr
  Street BA16 ....207 B5
  Tatworth TA20 ....198 D8
Springfields DT10 ....190 C4
Springhill Cl BS39 ....77 C6
Springley Rd TA6 ....209 D6
Springmead TA20 ....223 B3
Springway Ind Est TA7 ..155 A5
Springwell Cotts **3**
  BA11 ....119 E5
Spruce Way Bath BA2 .....62 E8
  Weston-Super-Mare BS22 ..49 E8
Spurwells TA19 ....183 F4
Square The Axbridge BS26 ..70 C2
  Bath BA2 ....228 B1
Stathe Cl TA7 ....215 F7
Stathe Rd TA7 ....171 A8
Station App Frome BA11 .120 A4
  Ilminster TA19 ....183 E1
  Pensford BS39 ....40 D5
  Weston-Super-Mare BS23 ..48 E7
Station Cl Backwell BS48 ..18 F7
  Congresbury BS49 ....34 C4
Station Cotts TA24 ....201 A7
Station Lodge BS23 ....48 E7
Station Mead BA3 ....96 D3
Station Path BA11 ....211 D3
Station Rd Ashcott TA7 ..156 B8
  Axbridge BS26 ....70 C2
  Backwell BS48 ....19 A6
  Bampton EX16 ....164 B1
  Bath BA1 ....44 C7
  Binegar BA3 ....114 D7
  Bishops Lydeard TA4 ....167 E8
  Blagdon BS40 ....54 E3
  Bristol, Shirehampton BS11 ..4 E5
  Bristol, Shirehampton BS11 ..4 C6
  Bruton BA10 ....215 F6
  Burlescombe EX16 ....179 B3
  Burnham-On-Sea TA9 ....85 F3
  Burtle TA7 ....137 D6
  Castle Cary BA7 ....214 B5
  Chard Junction TA20 ....198 D8
  Cheddar BS27 ....90 B7
  Clevedon BS21 ....6 D3
  Clutton BS39 ....58 E3
  Congresbury BS49 ....34 C4
  Cossington TA7 ....136 F3
  Crewkerne TA18 ....224 E4
  Draycott BS27 ....90 E2
  Dunster TA24 ....201 E4
  Flax Bourton BS48 ....20 A8
  Freshford BA3 ....64 C5
  Hatch Beauchamp TA3 ...183 A7
  Henstridge BA8 ....190 A7
  Ilminster TA19 ....183 D2
  Keynsham BS31 ....24 E6
  Meare TA7 ....138 C1
  Midsomer Norton BA3 .....78 B2
  Milborne Port DT9 ....217 D4
  Milverton TA4 ....167 A5
  Nailsea BS48 ....8 D1
  Norton Fitzwarren TA2 ..168 B4
  Pill BS20 ....4 C4
  Portbury BS20 ....3 D3
  Portishead BS20 ....2 D6
  Puriton TA6 ....136 B3
  Sandford BS25 ....51 F4
  Shapwick TA7 ....137 F2
  Shepton Mallet BA4 ......205 B5
  Sherborne DT9 ....225 E3
  Stalbridge DT10 ....190 B4
  Taunton TA1 ....212 F5
  Templecombe BA8 ....176 E1
  Wanstrow BA4 ....142 F4
  Washford TA23 ....131 A2
  Wellington TA21 ....222 C7
  Wellow BA2 ....62 D1
  Westbury Sub Mendip BA5 .110 E5
  Weston-Super-Mare, St Georges
   BS22 ....31 F2
  Weston-Super-Mare, Worle
   BS22 ....32 A3
  Williton TA4 ....202 E3
  Wincanton BA9 ....216 C3
  Wiveliscombe TA4 ....210 C6
  Wrington BS40 ....35 D2
  Yatton BS49 ....17 B1
Station Rd Ind Est BA10 .215 F6
Station Road Bsns Pk
  TA9 ....104 E4
Station Way BA4 ....141 E1
Station Wlk TA4 ....167 A5
Staundle La TA3 ....183 B8
Staunton Fields BS14 ...23 C4
Staunton La
  Minehead TA24 ....201 A4
  Whitchurch BS14 ....23 C3
Staunton Rd TA24 ....201 A5
Staunton Rise TA24 ......201 A4
Staunton Way BS14 ......23 D4
Staverdale Gr BS14 ....23 B6
Stawell Rd TA7 ....154 E5
Stawley Prim Sch TA21 .179 B8
Steam Mills BA3 ....96 F5
Steam Packet Terr **1**
  TA6 ....209 A4
Steamalong TA3 ....183 E7
Steart Ave TA8 ....104 B6
Steart Cl TA8 ....104 B6
Steart Ct TA8 ....104 A7
Steart Dr TA8 ....104 B6
Steart Gdns TA8 ....104 B6
Steart Hill BA22 ....174 D5
Steart La Babcary TA11 ..174 B5

Stapleton Cl TA12 ....185 E7
Stapleton Cross TA12 ...185 E7
Stapleton Rd TA12 ....185 E7
Stapley Cross TA3 ....181 B1
Stapling La TA24 ....130 F3
Star La BS20 ....4 D4
Starcross Rd BS22 ....32 A2
Starling Cl BS22 ....49 E8
Starling Way BA4 ....205 C4
Starrs Cl BS26 ....70 B2
Stars La BA20 ....219 C4
Statham Cl Cheddar BS27 ..90 B7
  Taunton TA1 ....212 C2
Stathe Cl TA7 ....171 A7
Stathe Rd TA7 ....171 A8
Station App Frome BA11 .120 A4
Stearts Cotts TA3 ....169 C3
Steeds Terr BA3 ....115 D6
Steel La TA7 ....137 D2
Steel Mills BS31 ....24 F4
Steel Well La BA8 ....190 A6
Steep La BA9 ....161 D2
Steep La BA22 ....164 C8
Steep The TA24 ....147 C5
Steeple View BA13 ....116 A3
Steevens Ho (almshouses) **15**
  BS2 ....227 C3
Stembridge Rd TA10 .....156 B1
Stembridge Tower Mill*
  TA10 ....156 B1
Stembridge Way TA2 ...168 B4
Stephen St TA1 ....213 A4
Stephen Way **4** TA1 ..213 A4
Stephen's Hill TA10 ......172 E4
Stephenson Dr BA11 ....120 B6
Stephenson Rd TA24 ...201 B6
Steppes Cres **16** TA12 ..185 E6
Steppes Mdw TA12 .....185 E6
Steps La BA22 ....100 E7
Stert Dro TA5 ....135 B7
Steven's Cl BA4 ....205 A5
Stevens La Frome BA11 ..119 F3
  Lympsham BS24 ....67 C3
Steway La BA1 ....29 B6
Stibbear La TA19 ....194 A8
Stiby Rd BA21 ....218 E7
Stickland BS21 ....6 C1
Stickle Hill TA4 ....151 B2
Stickle Path EX16 ....165 C1
Stickleball La BA4,BA6 ..140 D1
Sticklinch Rd BA6 ....140 C2
Stilemead La BS40 ....55 D1
Stiles Ct BA5 ....203 B4
Stileway BA6 ....138 E4
Stiling Cl TA9 ....104 E4
Stillingfleet Rd BS13 .....22 C5
Stillington Cl BA5 ....203 B3
Stillman Cl BS13 ....21 E4
Stirling Way Frome BA11 ..120 B6
  Keynsham BS31 ....24 C2
Stirtingale Ave BA2 ......44 C3
Stirtingale Rd BA2 ....44 C3
Stitching La BS28 ....138 C8
Stitchings La BA2 ....63 D7
Stitchings Shord La
  BS39 ....57 C4
Stoate Cl TA23 ....202 C5
Stoberry Ave BS49 ....203 E5
Stoberry Cres BA5 ....203 E5
Stoberry Park Sch BA5 .203 E5
Stock Hill BA3 ....115 B8
Stock Hill CP BA3 ....117 B7
Stock La
  Buckhorn Weston SP8 ...177 F5
  Langford BS40 ....33 C4
Stock Moor Dro TA6 ....209 A1
Stock Way N BS48 ....8 F2
Stock Way S BS48 ....8 E2
Stock's La
  Hatch Beauchamp TA3,
   TA19 ....183 B6
  Leigh upon Mendip BA3 ..116 E3
  North Wootton BA4 ....140 C4
Stockbridge La BA6 ......140 B2
Stockditch Rd TA12 .....185 B7
Stockers Cl TA4 ....210 B7
Stockham Cross TA4 ....151 D3
Stockham Hill TA22 .....163 E8
Stockhill Cl BA3 ....96 C3
Stockhill Rd BA3 ....96 C3
Stockland Hill EX14 .....192 A1
Stockland Manor TA5 ..134 F6
Stockman La TA20 ....198 C2
Stockmead BS40 ....53 B5
Stockmoor Cl TA6 ....208 A2
Stockstyle La EX13 ......198 A8
Stockton Cl BS14 ....22 F3
Stockwitch Cross BA22 .174 B3
Stockwood Green Prim Sch
  BS14 ....23 D4
Stockwood Hill BS31 ....24 C7
Stockwood Rd BS4,BS14 ..24 A7
Stodden's La TA8 ....104 E8
Stodden's Rd TA8 ....85 C1
Stodden's Wlk TA8 ......104 E8
Stodeleigh Cl BS22 ....32 B3
Stoford La
  Broadway TA19 ....183 C2
  West Buckland TA21 ......181 A7
  Yeovil BA21 ....218 A3
Stogursey CP Prim Sch
  TA5 ....134 A5
Stogursey La TA5 ....134 A3
Stoke Bishop CE Prim Sch
  BS9 ....5 D5
Stoke Cotts BS9 ....5 E3
Stoke Gr BS9 ....5 E6
Stoke Hamlet BS9 ....5 E6
Stoke Hill Bristol BS9 ......5 E3
  Chew Stoke BS40 ....56 C2
  Stoke St Mary TA3 ....169 D1
  Stoke St Michael BA3 ...116 A2
  Wincanton BA9 ....160 C3
Stoke La
  Bratton Seymour BA9 ....175 C4
  Bristol, Westbury on Trym
   BS9 ....5 E5
  Stoke St Mary TA3 ....169 A1
  Wincanton BA9 ....216 F5

Stoke Mead BA2 . . . . .63 F7
Stoke Moor Dro BS27 . . .109 D6
Stoke Paddock Rd BS9 . . . .5 D6
Stoke Park Rd BS9 . . . . .5 E4
Stoke Park Rd S BS9 . . . . . .5 E3
Stoke Rd Bristol BS9 . . . . .5 F8
  Martock TA12 . . . . .185 E5
  North Curry TA3 . . . . .170 C4
  Portishead BS20 . . . . .2 D5
  Ruishton TA3 . . . . .169 C2
  Stoke St Mary TA3 . . . . . . .169 B1
  Street BA16 . . . . .207 E6
  Taunton TA1 . . . . .213 B1
  Westbury Sub Mendip
  BA5 .110 D6
Stoke St BS27 . . . . .110 B8
Stoke St Gregory Prim Sch
  TA3 . . . . .170 E6
Stoke St Michael Prim Sch
  BA3 . . . . .116 A3
Stoke sub Hamdon Castle
  Prim Sch TA14 . . . . .185 F4
Stoke sub Hamdon Priory*
  TA14 . . . . .185 F4
Stokeleigh Wlk BS9 . . . . . .5 C5
Stokes Croft BS1 . . . . .227 B4
Stokes La DT10 . . . . .189 F2
Stolford Hill TA2 . . . . .148 A4
Stonage La TA18 . . . . .196 C5
Stone Allerton Dro BS26 . .88 B2
Stone Cl TA1 . . . . .168 D1
Stone Cross TA24 . . . . . . .128 E1
Stone Down La BA6 . . . . .139 D1
Stone Hill Ct TA24 . . . . . .200 F7
Stone Hill La TA4 . . . . . . .166 D3
Stone La
  East Pennard BA4 . . . . . . .158 E6
  Winsford TA24 . . . . .147 E6
  Yeovil BA21 . . . . .187 B5
Stone Mead La TA10 . . . .173 A4
Stone Rd TA8 . . . . .104 D5
Stoneable Rd BA3 . . . . .79 A3
Stoneage La BA2 . . . . .61 B1
Stonebarrow La EX13 . . .198 F2
Stonebridge BS21 . . . . .6 D1
Stonebridge Dr BA11 . . . .120 B7
Stonebridge Rd BS23 . . . .48 F4
Stonedene DT9 . . . . .225 D6
Stonegallows TA1 . . . . . . .212 A3
Stonehenge La BS48 . . . . . .8 E4
Stonehill
  South Cadbury BA22 . . . . .175 C3
  Stoke Sub Hamdon TA14 . .186 A4
  Street BA16 . . . . .207 B5
Stonehouse Cl BA2 . . . . . .45 B2
Stonehouse La BA2 . . . . . .45 B2
Stoneleigh
  Chew Magna BS40 . . . . . . .39 B3
  Wellington TA21 . . . . .222 B8
Stoneleigh Cl
  Burnham-On-Sea TA8 . . . .104 C8
  Staplegrove TA2 . . . . .212 C8
Stoneleigh Ct Bath BA1 . .27 E3
  Taunton TA1 . . . . .212 C1
Stoneleigh Rise BA11 . . .120 A6
Stoneridge La TA4 . . . . . .165 D5
Stones Cross BA22 . . . . . . .78 B2
Stones Paddock BA3 . . . .116 C7
Stonewall Terr BA11 . . . .119 F2
Stonewell Dr BS49 . . . . . . .34 D3
Stonewell Gr BS49 . . . . . . .34 D3
Stonewell La BS49 . . . . . . .34 D3
Stonewell Park Rd BS49 . .34 D3
Stoney Furlong TA3 . . . .213 B8
Stoney La
  Bishops Lydeard TA4 . . . .167 E8
  Curry Rivel TA10 . . . . .171 C3
  East Coker BA22 . . . . .197 D6
  Stockinch TA19 . . . . .184 C4
Stoney Lane Cross
  EX16 . . . . .178 B3
Stoney Steep BS48 . . . . . . .9 A5
Stoneyard La BA3 . . . . .79 D7
Stoneyfield Cl BS20 . . . . . .4 B5
Stoneyfields BS20 . . . . . . .2 D4
Stoneyhurst Dr TA10 . . . .171 C3
Stony La Axminster EX13 .198 A1
  Hawkridge TA22 . . . . .146 E3
  Whitley BA11 . . . . .118 D2
Stony Littleton Long
  Barrow* BA2 . . . . .80 C7
Stony St BA11 . . . . .119 F5
Stonyhead Hill TA3 . . . . .169 F1
Stoodham TA13 . . . . .220 C5
Stoodly La
  North Wootton BA4 . . . . . .140 D4
  Pilton BA4 . . . . .204 A2
Stooper's Hill TA20 . . . . .193 C4
Stopgate Cross EX14 . . . .192 C4
Stoppard Rd TA8 . . . . . . .104 C6
Stopper's La BA5 . . . . . . .139 F6
Stormont Cl BS23 . . . . . . .48 F3
Stormore BA13 . . . . .121 F8
Storridge La
  Axminster EX13 . . . . .198 B6
  Brompton Regis TA22 . . . .148 A1
Storridge View TA22 . . . .148 A2
Stour Hill SP8 . . . . .177 E1
Stour Hill Pk SP8 . . . . . . .177 F1
Stourhead* BA12 . . . . . . .161 F5
Stourton Cl BA21 . . . . . . .119 E3
Stourton Gdns 🔳 BA11 .119 E3
Stourton La BA21 . . . . . . .161 F4
Stourton View BA11 . . . .119 E3

Stourton Way BA21 . . . . .218 D6
Stout Cross EX14 . . . . . . .192 C5
Stout's Way La
  Kingsbridge TA23 . . . . . . .148 F8
  Rodhuish TA24 . . . . .131 A1
Stowborough Cotts BA2 . .79 C7
Stowell Hill DT9 . . . . .176 C1
Stowell La TA20 . . . . .198 D8
Stowey Bottom BS39 . . . .57 E5
Stowey La
  Curry Mallet TA3 . . . . .183 E8
  Fivehead TA3 . . . . .170 E1
Stowey Pk BS49 . . . . .34 D3
Stowey Rd Pitney TA10 . .172 D7
  Taunton TA2 . . . . .212 E8
  Yatton BS49 . . . . .34 C8
Stradling Ave BS23 . . . . . .48 F5
Stradling Cl TA7 . . . . .137 B2
Stradling's Hill TA5 . . . . .135 B3
Straight Dro
  Burrowbridge TA7 . . . . . . .155 B1
  Chilton Trinity TA5 . . . . . .135 F2
  West Huntspill TA9 . . . . . .136 B7
  Woolavington TA9 . . . . . . .137 A6
Straight La BA11 . . . . .101 D7
Straight St BS2 . . . . .227 C2
Strap La Ston Easton BA3 . .95 F7
  Upton Noble BA4,BA10 . . .143 A1
Stratford Cl BS14 . . . . .22 F3
Stratford Ct BS9 . . . . .5 F8
Stratford La BS40 . . . . .56 E1
Stratford Rd BA21 . . . . . .218 D5
Stratheden BS8 . . . . .226 A4
Stratton Cl TA6 . . . . .209 D3
Stratton Rd
  Holcombe BA3 . . . . .116 B8
  Saltford BS31 . . . . .25 E3
Stratton St BS2 . . . . .227 B3
Strawberry Bank TA19 . .221 C4
Strawberry Cl BS48 . . . . . . .8 D1
Strawberry Field BS26 . . .70 D2
Strawberry Gdns BS48 . . .18 D8
Strawberry Hill
  Clevedon BS21 . . . . .6 F4
  Street BA16 . . . . .207 B7
Strawberry La BS13,BS41 . .21 E3
Strawberry Way N BA5 . .203 C4
Strawberry Way S BA5 . .203 D3
Streaked La TA3 . . . . .170 C6
Streamcombe La TA22 . .163 B5
Streamcross BS49 . . . . . . .17 D1
Streamleaze BS40 . . . . . . .39 B3
Streamside
  Chew Magna BS40 . . . . . . .39 B3
  🔳 Clevedon BS21 . . . . .6 F3
  Taunton TA1 . . . . .213 C2
Stredlings Yd BS2 . . . . . .226 C4
Street Ash La TA20 . . . . .193 C8
Street Dro Street BA16 . .207 B1
  Walton BA16 . . . . .207 E7
Street End BA40 . . . . .54 D2
Street End La BS40 . . . . . .54 D2
Street Ho TA19 . . . . .221 B3
Street La
  Higher Odcombe BA22 . . .186 C2
  North Brewham BA10 . . . .161 A7
Street Rd
  Glastonbury BA6 . . . . .206 D3
  Street BA6 . . . . .207 D8
Street Shoe Mus*
  BA16 . . . . .207 C6
Street The
  Bishop Sutton BS39 . . . . . .57 D4
  Bishop Sutton, Stowey BS39 .57 F4
  Chew Stoke BS40 . . . . .56 D3
  Chilcompton BA3 . . . . .96 D5
  Compton Martin BS40 . . . .74 B7
  Draycott BS27 . . . . .90 F2
  Farmborough BA2 . . . . .59 F6
  Kilmington BA12 . . . . .161 F6
  Radstock BA3 . . . . .78 F2
  Ubley BS40 . . . . .55 D1
  Wanstrow BA4 . . . . .142 F4
  West Monkton TA2 . . . . . .169 C7
  Winford BS40 . . . . .37 E5
Stretcholt La TA6 . . . . . . .135 F6
Stretford La TA19 . . . . . . .194 F7
Stringfellow Cres TA20 . .223 D5
Stringfellow Mews
  TA20 . . . . .223 C3
Stringland's La TA24 . . . .131 B2
Strode Coll BA16 . . . . . . .207 D6
Strode Ho 🔳 BA4 . . . . . . .205 B6
Strode Rd Clevedon BS21 . . .6 C2
  Street BA16 . . . . .207 D6
Strode Way Clevedon BS21 . .6 B1
  Shepton Mallet BA4 . . . . . .205 A5
Stroud Rd BS11 . . . . .4 E6
Strowland La BS24 . . . . . . .86 F6
Strowlands BS24,TA9 . . . .86 E6
Struthers Cl BA16 . . . . . . .207 D7
Strutter's Hill BA10 . . . . .215 D2
Stuart Pl BA2 . . . . .44 D6
Stuart Rd BS23 . . . . .49 A5
Stuarts Cl BA5 . . . . .203 B3
Stubb's La BA11 . . . . .101 D4
Studley La BA4 . . . . .142 B7
Studley Mdws BA4 . . . . . .142 F4
Stump Cross
  Pitcombe BA7 . . . . .215 A1
  Shepton Mallet BA4 . . . . . .204 D5
Sturford La BA12 . . . . . . .144 E1
Sturmey Way BS20 . . . . . . .4 E3
Sturminster Cl BS14 . . . . .23 D6
Sturminster Rd BS14 . . . .23 D7
Stutts End TA4 . . . . .167 E6
Style Flats TA4 . . . . .210 C5

Style Rd TA4 . . . . .210 C5
Styles Ave BS11 . . . . .120 D4
Styles Cl BA11 . . . . .120 B4
Styles Hill BA11 . . . . .120 B4
Styles Mdw BA11 . . . . . . .120 C5
Styles Pk BA11 . . . . .120 B4
Sub Rd BA6 . . . . .157 D4
Suffolk Cl TA6 . . . . .209 C5
Suffolk Cres TA1 . . . . . . .212 C1
Suffolk Ct TA1 . . . . .212 C1
Sugg's La TA19 . . . . .183 C2
Sulis Manor Rd BA2 . . . . .62 D8
Sullivan Cl BS4 . . . . .22 D6
Sully Cl TA6 . . . . .209 D6
Sumerleaze Cres TA2 . . .213 C8
Sumerlin Dr BS21 . . . . .6 F3
Summer Hill Frome BA11 .119 F3
  Hinton St George TA17 . . .195 D7
Summer House Terr
  BA20 . . . . .219 B4
Summer La Banwell BS29 . .50 E5
  Chard TA20 . . . . .194 C4
  Hinton St George TA13,
  TA17 . . . . .195 C8
  Monkton Combe BA2 . . . . .63 D8
  Weston-Super-Mare BS22, . . .
  BA2 . . . . .32 B1
  Walton BA16 . . . . .106 D6
Summer Shard TA13 . . . .220 C4
Summerfield BS22 . . . . . . .32 A3
Summerfield Cl TA7 . . . . .154 F5
Summerfield Ct TA1 . . . . .212 E4
Summerfield Rd BA1 . . . . .28 A1
Summerfield Sch BA1 . . . .27 D1
Summerfield Terr BA1 . . . .28 A1
Summerfields Rd BA22 . .223 C3
Summerhedge Cres
  TA7 . . . . .155 A3
Summerhedge Rd TA7 . . .155 C1
Summerhill BA1 . . . . .28 E1
Summerhouse BS21 . . . . . .8 D4
Summerhouse View
  BA22 . . . . .219 C6
Summerland Ave TA4 . . .201 A7
Summerland Pl TA24 . . . .200 F7
Summerland Rd TA24 . . .200 F7
Summerlands
  Backwell BS48 . . . . .19 B5
  Yeovil BA21 . . . . .218 E6
Summerlands Hospl
  BA21 . . . . .218 F6
Summerlands Park Ave
  TA19 . . . . .221 B4
Summerlands Park Cl
  TA19 . . . . .221 B4
Summerlands Park Dr
  TA19 . . . . .221 B4
Summerlays Ct BA2 . . . . . .45 B6
Summerlea BA2 . . . . .61 A5
Summerleaze BS31 . . . . . .24 E7
Summerleaze Cres TA2 . .213 C7
Summers Hill La BA4 . . . .204 C2
Summerville Terr TA8 . . .104 B6
Summerway Dro TA7 . . . .209 E4
Summerway Rd BA16 . . .207 B4
Sun Batch BS27 . . . . .91 A3
Sun St TA11 . . . . .119 E5
Sunderland Pl BS8 . . . . . .226 B3
Sunderland St BA2 . . . . .228 C3
Sunderland St TA1 . . . . . .213 C1
Sunfield Rd BS24 . . . . .49 E3
Sunningdale BS8 . . . . . . .226 B4
Sunningdale Cl BS48 . . . . .9 A1
Sunningdale Rd
  Weston-Super-Mare BS22 . .31 F3
  Yeovil BA21 . . . . .219 C6
Sunny Bank TA4 . . . . .150 B8
Sunny Bank Way BS24 . . .32 B1
Sunny Cl TA9 . . . . .136 B8
Sunny Hill Bristol BS9 . . . .5 C7
  Pitcombe BA10 . . . . .215 C4
Sunny La BA10 . . . . .215 C4
Sunnybank BA2 . . . . .45 B4
Sunnybank Rd TA6 . . . . . .209 B5
Sunnybow Cl 🔳 TA6 . . . .153 F4
Sunnyhill Dr BS11 . . . . .4 E6
Sunnyhill Ho W BS11 . . . .4 E6
Sunnyhill Ho W BS11 . . . .4 E6
Sunnymead
  Bridgwater TA6 . . . . .208 E2
  Keynsham BS31 . . . . .24 F3
  Midsomer Norton BA3 . . . .77 F2
  Oakhill BA3 . . . . .114 F3
  Stratton-on-the-Fosse BA3 .96 F3
Sunnymede Rd BA6 . . . . .138 C4
Sunnyside
  Barrington TA19 . . . . .184 C5
  Bristol BS9 . . . . .5 C8
  Burlescombe EX16 . . . . . .179 C2
  Clevedon BS21 . . . . .59 B4
  Farrington Gurney BS39 . . .77 B3
  Frome BA11 . . . . .119 F3
Sunnyside Cotts TA24 . . .129 A8
Sunnyside Cres 🔳 BS21 . .6 D3
Sunnyside Gdns TA24 . . .129 A8
Sunnyside Rd BS23 . . . . . .48 E5
Sunnyside Rd N BS23 . . . .48 E6
Sunnyside Terr DT9 . . . . .225 E4

Sunnyside View BA2 . . . .79 C7
Sunnyvale Clevedon BS21 . .6 B1
  Peasedown St John BA2 . .78 E8
Sunridge Cl BA3 . . . . .96 F8
Sunridge Pk BA3 . . . . .96 F8
Sunset Cl BA11 . . . . .79 C7
Suprema Ave TA7 . . . . . .137 C2
Suprema Est TA7 . . . . . . .137 C2
Surrey St BS2 . . . . .227 B4
Susanna's Cross BA3 . . . .116 B2
Susanna's La BA3 . . . . . . .116 C2
Sussex Ave TA6 . . . . .209 B3
Sussex Cl TA6 . . . . .209 B3
Sussex Lodge TA1 . . . . . .212 F5
Sussex Rd BA21 . . . . .228 C1
Sutherland Ave TA8 . . . .104 B6
Sutherland Cl TA1 . . . . . .212 C1
Sutherland Ct TA1 . . . . . .212 C1
Sutherland Dr BS24 . . . . .49 D2
Sutton Cl Frome BA11 . . .120 B7
  Weston-Super-Mare BS22 . .49 E8
Sutton Cross TA10 . . . . . .172 F4
Sutton Grange BA21 . . . .218 C6
Sutton Hill
  East Coker BA22 . . . . .197 D6
  Long Sutton TA10 . . . . . . .172 E3
Sutton Hill Rd BS39 . . . . .57 B2
Sutton La Redhill BS40 . . .36 F1
  Walton BA16 . . . . .106 D6
Sutton Pk BS39 . . . . .57 D4
Sutton Rd TA11 . . . . .211 C2
Sutton St BA2 . . . . .45 B7
Swain St TA23 . . . . .202 C7
Swains La BA22 . . . . .222 D4
Swains La TA11 . . . . .222 D4
Swainswick BS14 . . . . .22 F6
Swainswick Gdns BA1 . . . .28 C2
Swainswick La BA1 . . . . . .28 C4
Swainswick Prim Sch
  BA1 .28 B3
Swallow Cl BA3 . . . . .97 B8
Swallow Ct BS14 . . . . .23 A5
Swallow Dr BA11 . . . . . . .120 B6
Swallow Gdns BS22 . . . . . .49 E8
Swallow Hill TA10 . . . . . .172 A6
Swallow St BA1 . . . . .228 C2
Swallowcliffe Ct BA20 . . .219 A5
Swallowcliffe Gdns
  BA20 . . . . .219 A5
Swallows The BS22 . . . . . .49 D7
Swan Cl BS22 . . . . .49 E8
Swan Down TA10 . . . . . . .194 E4
Swan Hill TA18 . . . . .196 C5
Swan Ho 🔳 BA4 . . . . .205 B6
Swan Prec TA19 . . . . .221 C3
Swan Yd DT9 . . . . .225 D4
Swancombe Blagdon BS40 . .54 E2
  Clapton In Gordano BS20 . .8 E8
Swane Rd BS14 . . . . .23 F6
Swanmead Com Sch
  TA19 . . . . .221 C3
Swans La BS27 . . . . .90 F2
Swanshard La BA5 . . . . . .139 D6
Swedish Hos TA13 . . . . . .220 D1
Sweetgrass Rd BS24 . . . . .32 B1
Sweethay Cl TA3 . . . . . . .181 D8
Sweethay Cross TA3 . . . .181 C8
Sweethay La TA3 . . . . . . .181 C8
Sweetleaze BA3 . . . . .116 A2
Swell Cl TA9 . . . . .136 A8
Swell La TA3 . . . . .171 A2
Swift Cl BS22 . . . . .31 F1
Swift Lodge BA20 . . . . . . .219 A4
Swifts TA21 . . . . .166 F1
Swindridge BA3 . . . . .213 E7
Swiss Dr BS3 . . . . .11 F2
Swiss Rd Bristol BS3 . . . . .11 F1
  Weston-Super-Mare BS23 . .48 F7
Sycamore Cl
  Bridgwater TA6 . . . . .209 D5
  Burnham-On-Sea TA8 . . . .104 A5
  Nailsea BS48 . . . . .8 E2
  Shipham BS25 . . . . .70 E8
  Taunton TA1 . . . . .213 C2
  Weston-Super-Mare BS23 . .49 A8
  Westonzoyland TA7 . . . . .154 E5
Sycamore Ct TA20 . . . . . .222 E7
Sycamore Dr
  Crewkerne TA18 . . . . .224 D7
  Frome BA11 . . . . .120 B7
  Langport TA10 . . . . .172 A6
  Yeovil BA20 . . . . .218 F2
Sycamore Rd
  Minehead TA24 . . . . .200 D7
  Radstock BA3 . . . . .79 B2
Sycamore Sq TA20 . . . . . .223 D5
Sydenham La BA4 . . . . . .141 D4
Sydenham Bldgs BA2 . . .228 A2
Sydenham Cl
  Bridgwater TA6 . . . . .209 D6
  Porlock TA24 . . . . .124 B4
Sydenham Terr BA2 . . . . .45 C2
Sydling Rd BA21 . . . . .219 C6
Sydnalls La BS21 . . . . .43 C4
Sydney Bldgs BA2 . . . . . .45 B6
Sydney Ho Bath BA2 . . . . .45 B7
  Pill BS20 . . . . .4 C5
Sydney Mews BA2 . . . . . . .45 B7
Sydney Pl BA2 . . . . .45 B7
Sydney Rd BA2 . . . . .45 B7
Sydney Row BS1 . . . . . . .226 B1
Sydney Wharf BA2 . . . . . .45 B7
Sylvan Rd TA21 . . . . .222 E6
Sylvan Way Bristol BS9 . . . .5 B7

Sylvan Way continued
  Monkton Heathfield TA2 . .213 E8
Symes Ave BS13 . . . . .22 C4
Symes Ct TA18 . . . . .196 C4
Symes Pk BA1 . . . . .27 A2
Symons Way
  Bridgwater TA6 . . . . .209 A6
  Cheddar BS27 . . . . .90 C7
Syndercombe La TA4,
  TA23 . . . . .149 D2

T

Tabernacle La 🔳 BA20 . .219 B4
Tacchi Morris Arts Ctr
  TA2 . . . . .213 F8
Tadhill La BA3 . . . . .116 D2
Tadwick La BA1 . . . . .28 B4
Tail Mill TA16 . . . . .195 F7
Tailor's Ct 🔳 BS1 . . . . . .227 A3
Talbot Cl TA9 . . . . .104 D3
Tallis Gr BS4 . . . . .22 D6
Tallowood BA4 . . . . .205 D5
Tamar Ave TA1 . . . . .213 B1
Tamar Dr BS31 . . . . .25 A4
Tamar Rd BS22 . . . . .32 A2
Tamblyn Cl BA3 . . . . .79 A3
Tamsin Ct BA15 . . . . .64 F5
Tamworth Rd BS31 . . . . . .24 E4
Tan La SP8 . . . . .161 F1
Tan Yard La TA13 . . . . . . .184 F5
Tancred St TA1 . . . . .213 A4
Tangier TA1 . . . . .212 E4
Tankard's Cl BS8 . . . . . . .226 C3
Tankey's Cl BA11 . . . . . . .120 A7
Tanner's Hill TA4 . . . . . . .165 E7
Tanners La SN14 . . . . .13 F8
Tanners Wlk Bath BA2 . . .43 F5
  Marshfield SN14 . . . . .13 F8
Tannery Cl BA16 . . . . .207 C5
Tannery Ct TA18 . . . . .224 C7
Tanorth Cl BS14 . . . . .23 A3
Tanorth Rd BS14 . . . . .22 F3
Tansee Hill TA20 . . . . .199 B6
Tansey BA4 . . . . .142 A6
Tanyard Broadway TA19 . .183 C2
  Nether Stowey TA5 . . . . . .134 B2
Tanyard La
  Langport TA10 . . . . .172 A5
  North Wootton BA4 . . . . . .140 C4
  North Wootton, Lower Westholme
  BA4 . . . . .140 D3
Tanyard The BA16 . . . . . .207 C5
Tanyards BA10 . . . . .215 D3
Tape La BA3 . . . . .114 F7
Taphouse La DT6 . . . . . . .199 E1
Tapmoor Rd TA7 . . . . . . .155 C8
Tappers La 🔳 TA6 . . . . . .153 E3
Tapps La TA7 . . . . .136 A4
Tapstone Rd TA20 . . . . . .223 D4
Taranto Hill BA22 . . . . . .173 E2
Taranto Way BA22 . . . . . .174 A2
Taras Cl TA12 . . . . .185 D4
Target La TA12 . . . . .185 D4
Tarnock Ave BS14 . . . . . . .23 A7
Tarnwell BS39 . . . . .40 A2
Tarr Steps* TA22 . . . . . . .146 E3
Tarr Water Cotts TA23 . .148 E8
Tarrant La BA20 . . . . .218 F1
Tarratt La
  East Coker BA22 . . . . .197 E8
  Yeovil BA20,BA22 . . . . . . .219 A1
Tarratt Rd BA20 . . . . .218 F1
Tatham Ct TA1 . . . . .212 E4
Tatworth Prim Sch
  TA20 . . . . .198 C8
Tatworth Rd TA20 . . . . . .223 C2
Tatworth St TA20 . . . . . . .198 C8
Tauntfield Cl TA1 . . . . . . .213 A3
Taunton & Somerset Hospl
  Musgrove Pk TA1 . . . . . . .212 C3
  Taunton TA1 Ashcott TA7 . .156 B7
  Bishops Lydeard TA4 . . . .167 F7
  Bridgwater TA6 . . . . .153 F4
  Bridgwater TA6 . . . . .209 A3
  North Petherton TA6 . . . . .153 E2
  Wellington TA21 . . . . .222 F2
  Weston-Super-Mare BS22 . .32 D5
  Wiveliscombe TA4 . . . . . .210 D4
Taunton Sch TA2 . . . . . . .212 D6
Taunton Sta TA1 . . . . .213 B4
Taunton Trad Est TA2 . . .212 A7
Taunusstein Way 🔳
  BA20 . . . . .219 B4
Taveners Wlk BS48 . . . . . . .9 B2
Taverner Cl BS4 . . . . .22 D7
Tavistock Rd BS22 . . . . . . .32 A2
Tawny Way BS22 . . . . .49 E8
Taylor Cl TA12 . . . . .168 B5
Taylor Ct Bridgwater TA6 .209 A5
  Taylor Gdns BS13 . . . . . . .21 F4
Taylor Ho TA19 . . . . .221 B3
Taylor's Meade TA20 . . . .198 D8
Taylor's Orch TA14 . . . . . .185 E1
Tayman Ridge BS30 . . . . .25 D8
Teagle Cl BA5 . . . . .203 F5
Teak Cl TA6 . . . . .209 C4
Teal Cl Bridgwater TA6 . .209 A4
  Weston-Super-Mare BS22 . .31 F1
Teal Rd TA24 . . . . .201 C5
Tealham Moor Dro
  BS28 . . . . .137 E8
Teals Acre 🔳 TA15 . . . . .185 B2
Teapot Lane (Worms Lane)
  BA6 . . . . .158 B6
Teasel Wlk BS22 . . . . .49 D7
Technical St TA8 . . . . . . .104 B6

Teck Hill TA6 153 E2
Teckhill La TA6 153 E2
Teddington Cl BA2 44 C4
Teesdale Cl BS22 49 D8
Teign Ct BA16 156 D7
Teignmouth Rd BS21 6 E3
Telephone Ave BS1 227 A2
Telford Ho BA2 44 D3
Tellis Cross BA22 197 D8
Tellis La BA3 114 D8
Tellisford La BA2 81 F4
Temblett Gn TA6 208 C5
Templars Barton BA8 176 E1
Templars Pl BA8 176 E1
Templars Way BS25 70 E7
Temple Back BS1 227 B2
Temple Back E BS1 227 C2
Temple Circus Giratory
BS1 227 C1
Temple Ct BS31 24 E5
Temple Field TA23 202 C6
Temple Gate BS1 227 B1
Temple Inf Sch BS31 24 F5
Temple Inn La BS39 58 E1
Temple Jun Sch BS31 24 F6
Temple La BA8 176 F1
Temple Rose St BS1 227 B2
Temple St Bristol BS1 227 B2
Keynsham BS31 24 F5
Temple Way BS2 227 B2
Temple Way Underpass
BS2 227 C3
Templecombe La SP8 177 C3
Templecombe Sta BA8 176 E1
Templeland Rd BS13 21 F5
Tenby Rd BS31 24 D4
Tengore La TA10 172 C6
Tennis Corner Dro
BA11 102 D2
Tennis Court Ave BS39 77 D5
Tennis Court Rd BS39 77 D5
Tennyson Ave BS21 6 B2
Tennyson Cl BS31 24 F6
Tennyson Rd Bath BA1 44 D7
Weston-Super-Mare BS23 49 A3
Tenterk Cl BS24 67 B6
Tents Hill BA11 118 B6
Tenyard Cotts TA24 131 A5
Terhill La TA4 151 F3
Termare Cl BA22 218 B6
Terrace The
Minehead TA24 201 A5
Shipham BS25 70 E7
Terrace View DT9 225 E5
Terrace Wlk BA1 228 C2
Terrell St BS2 227 A4
Terry Hill BA3 98 D8
Terry Ho BS1 226 C3
Tetbury Gdns BS48 9 A1
Tetton Cl TA6 208 B4
Teviot Rd BS31 25 A4
Tewkesbury BA21 218 D6
Tewther Rd BS13 22 D3
Teyfant Com Sch BS13 22 E4
Teyfant Rd BS13 22 E4
Teyfant Wlk BS13 22 E4
Thackeray Ave BS21 6 E4
Thackeray Ho BS23 49 A5
Thackeray Rd BS21 6 E4
Thames Dr TA1 213 D4
Thatch The TA11 211 C4
Thatcham Cl BA21 218 F7
Thatcham Ct BA21 218 F7
Thatcham Pk BA21 218 F7
Thatcher Cl BS20 2 D4
Theaks Mews TA1 213 A3
Theatre Royal BS1 227 A2
There-and-Back-Again La
BS1 226 C3
Theynes Croft BS41 11 B1
Thicket Mead BA3 78 A2
Thickthorn Cross TA19 183 C3
Thimble La DT9 217 D2
Third Ave Bath BA2 44 D5
Bristol, Hengrove BS14 23 B7
Radstock BA3 97 D7
Thirlmere Rd BS23 49 A4
Thistle Pk TA6 209 B1
Thistledoo Vine TA7 136 F2
Thomas Cl BS29 51 A3
Thomas La BS1 227 B2
Thomas St Bath BA1 228 C4
Bristol BS2 227 B4
Taunton TA2 212 F6
Thomas Way BA6 206 B4
Thompson Cl TA6 209 D6
Thompson Rd BS14 23 E6
Thomson Dr TA18 224 D5
Thong La TA10 184 D6
Thorn Cl BS22 32 B2
Thorn Cross Way TA21 178 D8
Thorn La TA3 169 D2
Thornash Cl TA2 213 F8
Thornbank Ct DT9 225 E4
Thornbank Pl BA2 228 A1
Thornbury Dr BS23 48 D2
Thornbury Rd BS23 48 C2
Thornbush Cross TA4 150 F3
Thorncombe Cres TA6 209 C5
Thorncombe Thorn
TA20 199 B5
Thorndale BS8 226 A4
Thorndale Cl BS22 49 D8
Thorndale Mews BS8 226 A4
Thorndun Park Dr TA20 223 D6
Thorne Cross BA22 218 B7
Thorne Gdns BA21 218 C7
Thorne La
Wheddon Cross TA24 147 C8
Winsford TA24 147 C8
Yeovil BA21 218 C8
Thorne Pk TA8 104 B5
Thorney Rd TA12 185 B8
Thorneymoor La TA10 172 A3
Thornhill Dro TA12 173 A1
Thornhill Rd DT10 190 B4
Thornton Rd BA21 218 D7
Thornwell La BA9 216 D3
Thornwell Way BA9 216 C3
Thorny La BA21 187 E8
Thornymarsh La BA7 175 B8
Three Ashes DT8 199 D7
Three Ashes La TA11 157 B4
Three Corner Mead
BA21 218 C5
Three Gates Cross
TA22 163 C6
Three Hill View BA6 206 E5
Three Horse Shoes Hill
TA5 152 C4
Three Oaks Cross TA19 183 C4
Three Queens' La BS1 227 B2
Three Wells Rd BS13 21 F4
Thrift Cl DT10 190 C4
Throgmorton Rd BS4 22 F8
Throop Rd BA8 176 F1
Thrubwell La BS40 37 B4
Thrupe La BA5 114 A2
Thrush Cl BS22 49 E8
Thumb La BA4 158 E7
Thurlbear CE Prim Sch
TA3 182 C8
Thurlestone BS14 23 A6
Thurlocks BA22 186 B6
Thynne Cl BS27 90 B6
Tibbott Rd BS14 23 D5
Tibbott Wlk BS14 23 D5
Tichborne Rd BS23 30 E1
Tickenham Hill BS48 8 E4
Tickenham Prim Sch BS21 7 F4
Tickenham Rd BS21 7 A4
Tide Gr BS11 5 A8
Tiffany Ct BS1 227 B1
Tile Hill BA10 161 A7
Tile House Rd
East Huntspill TA7 137 B8
Mark TA9 106 C1
Tiledown BS39 58 E1
Tiledown Cl BS39 58 F1
Tilery EX14 192 D3
Tilham St BA6 158 B6
Tilley Cl Farmborough BA2 60 A5
Keynsham BS31 25 A2
Tilley La BA2 60 A5
Tilleys Dro BA5 138 F7
Tilsey La TA4 150 C5
Timbers The BA3 97 B7
Timberscombe Way
TA6 208 B4
Timberscombe Wlk BS14 23 C5
Timberyard TA7 137 F1
Timewell Hill EX16 164 C4
Timsbury Rd
Farmborough BA2 60 B5
High Littleton BS39 59 D1
Tin Bridge Rdbt BA6 139 D3
Tinker's La
Compton Martin BS40 74 B7
Cucklington BA9 177 D7
Halse TA4 167 C6
Kilmersdon BA11 98 B1
Tinneys La DT9 225 E4
Tintagel Cl BS31 24 D4
Tintagel Rd BA21 218 D7
Tintern BA21 218 C6
Tintinhull Rd Yeovil BA21 186 F5
Yeovil BA21 218 E8
Tipcote Hill 17 BA4 205 B6
Tipnoller Hill TA4 210 F7
Tippacott La EX35 122 A4
Tiptoft 3 TA14 185 F4
Tirley Way BS22 31 B2
Titan Barrow BA1 29 C2
Tithe Barn Cross EX15 179 D2
Tithe Mdw TA4 167 A7
Tithill La TA4 167 F7
Titlands La BA5 203 A7
Tiverton Gdns BS22 32 A2
Tiverton Rd
1 Bampton EX16 164 C1
2 Clevedon BS21 6 E1
Tivington Cross TA24 129 F8
Tivoli Ho BS23 48 E8
Tivoli La BS23 48 E8
Toghill La BS30 12 A8
Tolbury La BA10 215 D6
Tolbury Mill BA10 215 E6
Toll Bridge Rd BA1 28 E3
Toll House Rd 1 TA5 135 B2
Toll Rd Porlock TA24 124 A3
Weston-Super-Mare BS23 66 F8
Tolland BS24 49 A2
Tolley's La TA20 194 C3
Tom Tit's La TA11 211 C3
Toms Cl TA20 223 B3
Tone Dr TA6 209 B3
Tone Gn TA4 167 E2
Tone Hill TA21 222 B8
Tone Rd BS21 6 D1
Tonedale Bsns Pk TA21 222 B7
Toneway TA2 213 C6
Toose The BA21 218 C6
Top Hill BA4 142 F2
Top La Mells BA11 118 B6
Stourton BA12 161 E4
Top Rd
Charlton Adam TA11 173 F7
Cheddar BS27 90 E5
Shipham BS25 70 F7
Westbury Sub Mendip BA5 110 E6
Top St Kingsdon TA11 173 D5
Pilton BA4 140 F3
Top Wood BA3 116 B7
Tor Cl BS22 32 A2
Tor St BA5 203 E4
Tor View Cheddar BS27 90 C7
Woolavington TA7 136 E4
Tor View Ave BA6 206 D3
Tor Wood View BA5 203 E5
Torbay Cl BA7 214 B5
Torbay Rd BA7 214 A5
Torbay Road Ind Est
BA7 214 A5
Torbay Villas BA7 214 A5
Torhill La BA5 203 F4
Torhole Bottom BA3 94 A4
Tormynton Rd BS22 31 E3
Torre Rocks TA23 131 E2
Torre The BA21 218 C6
Torridge Mead TA1 213 D4
Torridge Rd BS31 25 A4
Torrington Ave BS4 22 F8
Torrington Cres BS22 32 A3
Totnes Cl BS22 32 A2
Totney Dro BS28 137 E8
Totshill Dr BS13 22 E4
Totshill Gr BS13 22 E4
Tottenham Pl BS8 226 B3
Totterdown La
Pilton BA4 204 B1
Weston-Super-Mare BS24 49 A1
Totterdown Rd BS23 48 F4
Touch La TA10 156 C1
Touches La TA20 223 E5
Touches Mdw TA20 223 E5
Touching End La SN14 13 F8
Touchstone Cl TA20 223 B4
Touchstone La TA20 223 B4
Tout Hill BA9 216 C3
Tout La BA22TA11 174 A6
Tovey Cl BS22 31 E4
Tower Cl Cheddar BS27 90 B6
Stoke St Michael BA3 116 A3
Tower Hill Bristol BS2 227 B3
Bruton BA10 215 D6
Holcombe Rogus TA21 178 D5
Horsington BA8 176 E2
Locking BS24 50 D4
Stogursey TA5 134 B5
Stoke St Michael BA3 116 A3
Williton TA4 202 E2
Tower Hill Rd TA18 224 B5
Tower House La BS48 9 A4
Tower La Bristol BS1 227 A3
Taunton TA1 212 E4
Tower Rd
Kilmington BA12 161 D6
Portishead BS20 2 A4
Stawell TA7 137 B1
Yeovil BA21 219 C8
Tower St Bristol BS1 227 B2
Taunton TA1 212 E4
Tower View Frome BA11 119 F2
South Cheriton BA8 176 D3
Wanstrow BA4 142 E4
Tower Wlk BS23 30 D1
Towerhead Rd BS29 51 D3
Towerleaze BS9 5 D3
Town Barton BA2 81 F4
Town Cl North Curry TA3 170 B4
Stogursey TA5 134 B6
Town End BA2 81 F4
Town Hill EX36 162 C6
Town La BA4 205 C6
Town St BA4 205 B6
Town Tree La TA10,
TA12 185 D8
Townend Villas TA14 185 F2
Townhall Bldgs BA5 203 E4
Townrise 15 BA20 219 B4
Townsend
East Harptree BS40 75 A5
Ilminster TA19 221 D3
Marston Magna BA22 174 F1
Middlezoy TA7 155 C3
Montacute TA15 186 B3
Shepton Mallet BA4 205 B5
Westonzoyland TA7 154 F5
Williton TA4 202 E3
Townsend Cl Bristol BS14 23 F5
Bruton BA10 215 F7
Townsend Gn 10 BA8 190 A6
Townsend La
Chilton Polden TA7 137 B2
Emborough BA3 95 B2
Theale BS28 109 A2
Townsend Orch
Merriott TA16 195 F8
Street BA16 207 B5
Townsend Pk BA10 215 F7
Townsend Rd Bristol BS14 23 F5
Minehead TA24 201 A6
Townsend Rise BA10 215 F7
Townshend Rd BS22 32 B5
Trackfordmoor Cross
TA22 163 B3
Tracy Cl BS14 22 F7
Trafalgar Rd BA1 27 B1
Traits La BA22 174 E4
Trajan's Way BA4 205 E5
Transform Ind Est TA6 209 A6
Transom Ho BS1 227 B2
Travers Cl BS4 22 D6
Trawden Cl BS23 31 A1
Treasure Ct TA8 85 A1
Treasurer's Ho* TA12 185 E6
Treborough Cl TA2 213 B8
Treefield Rd BS21 6 D2
Tregarth Rd BS3 11 F1
Tregelles Cl TA9 104 C4
Tregonwell Rd TA24 201 A7
Trelawn Cl BS22 32 D2
Trellech Ct BA21 218 C6
Tremes Cl SN14 13 F8
Tremlett Mews 3 BS22 32 B4
Trenchard Rd
Locking BS24 50 D4
Saltford BS31 25 D3
Trenchard St BS1 226 C3
Trendle La Bicknoller TA4 132 F2
Wincanton BA9 160 E3
Trendle Rd TA1 212 B1
Trendle St DT9 225 D3
Trendlewood Way BS48 9 A1
Trenleigh Dr BS22 32 A2
Trent Cl BA21 219 E8
Trent Ct TA1 213 D4
Trent Gr BS31 25 A4
Trent Mdw TA1 213 E4
Trent Path La DT9 225 A5
Trent Youngs Sch DT9 187 F5
Tresco Spinney BA21 218 C6
Trevanna Rd BS3 11 F1
Trevelyan Rd BS23 48 F7
Trevett Rd TA1 212 C2
Trevithick Cl BA11 120 C6
Trevor Rd TA6 209 C6
Trevor Smith Pl TA1 213 A3
Trewartha Cl BS23 48 F8
Trewartha Pk BS23 48 F8
Trewint Gdns BS4 22 F8
Triangle Ct BA2 44 D5
Triangle Ctr The BS21 6 D3
Triangle E BA2 44 D5
Triangle N BA2 44 D5
Triangle S BS8 226 B3
Triangle The
Clevedon BS21 6 D3
North Curry TA3 170 A4
Somerton TA11 211 D4
Wrington BS40 35 D2
Triangle W Bath BA2 44 D5
Bristol BS8 226 B3
Tribunal & Lake Village
Mus* BA6 206 D4
Trickey Warren La TA3 181 C1
Trim Bridge 3 BA1 228 B2
Trim St BA1 228 B2
Trin Mills BS1 227 A1
Trinder Rd BS20 4 B4
Trindlewell La TA18 196 C4
Trinity Bsns Ctr TA1 213 A3
Trinity CE Fst Sch BA11 119 C4
Trinity Cl Bath BA1 228 B2
Burnham-On-Sea TA8 85 A1
Wedmore BS28 107 D4
Wellington TA21 222 C5
Trinity Coll BS9 5 E4
Trinity Ct Bridgwater TA6 208 F6
Nailsea BS48 8 C1
18 Yeovil BA20 219 B4
Trinity Mews 15 BS2 227 C3
Trinity Pl Bristol BS8 226 A2
Weston-Super-Mare BS23 30 C1
Trinity Rd Bath BA2 45 B2
Nailsea BS48 8 D1
Taunton TA1 213 B3
Weston-Super-Mare BS23 30 C1
Trinity Rise TA8 85 A1
Trinity Row Frome BA11 119 E5
Wellington TA21 222 C5
Trinity St Bath BA1 228 B2
Frome BA11 119 E5
Taunton TA1 213 B3
Trinity Wlk Bristol BS2 227 C3
Frome BA11 119 E5
Tripps Cnr BS49 34 D7
Tripps Dro BA5 139 A6
Triscombe Ave TA6 208 D4
Triscombe Rd TA2 212 E8
Tristram Dr TA3 169 D4
Tropical Bird Gdn* TA8 47 F2
Tropicana Leisure Pool*
BS23 48 D6
Trossachs Dr BA2 45 D8
Trotts La TA19 183 B2
Trottsway Cross TA24 129 C2
Trow La BA12 144 C2
Trowbridge Cl TA9 104 D4
Trowell La TA4 165 E4
Truckwell La TA4 150 D4
Trull CE Prim Sch TA3 168 D1
Trull Green Dr TA3 168 D1
Trull Rd TA1 212 E2
Trumps Cross EX16 178 E3
Truro Cl TA8 104 C7
Truro Rd BS48 9 A1
Trym Bank BS9 5 D7
Trym Cross Rd BS9 5 C5
Trym Side BS9 5 C5
Trymleaze BS9 5 C5
Trymwood Par BS9 5 D6
Tucker St Bristol BS2 227 C3
Wells BA5 203 C4
Tucker's Cross DT9 188 A4
Tucker's La
Baltonsborough BA6 157 F6
Compton Martin BS40 73 E8
Tucker's Moor Cross
EX16 162 F3
Tuckers La BA7 214 B7
Tuckerton La TA7 153 F1
Tuckingmill La BS39 41 E5
Tuckmarsh La BA11 143 E7
Tuckmill BS21 6 B1
Tuddington Gdns BA5 203 B4
Tudor Ct Chard TA20 223 C6
Yeovil BA20 219 A4
Tudor Rd Portishead BS20 2 E4
Weston-Super-Mare BS22 32 A4
Tudor Way TA6 209 A1
Tudway Cl BA5 203 C4
Tufton Ave BS11 5 A8
Tugela Rd BS13 21 F7
Tuggy's La BA2 63 E1
Tulip Tree Rd TA6 209 E5
Tulse Hill BA12 161 F2
Tunbridge Cl BS40 39 B2
Tunbridge Rd BS40 39 B2
Tuncombe La TA18 195 D4
Tunley Hill BA2 60 E2
Tunley Rd BA2,BA3 61 D5
Tunnel The TA24 128 B2
Tunscombe La BA4 142 D8
Tunstall Cl BS9 5 E4
Turkey Ct 5 TA1 212 E3
Turn Hill TA10 155 F2
Turnbury Ave BS48 9 A1
Turnbury Cl BS22 31 F3
Turner Cl Bridgwater TA6 209 A4
Keynsham BS31 25 A5
Turner Ct Wells BA5 203 D3
Weston-Super-Mare BS22 31 F3
Turner Rd TA2 212 E7
Turner Way BS21 6 B1
Turner's Barn La BA20 218 F2
Turner's Court La BA3 114 D8
Turner's La DT6 199 B2
Turner's Terr BA3 80 A1
Turnhill Rd TA10 156 A2
Turnpike Milverton TA4 167 A4
Sampford Peverell EX16 178 C1
Turnpike Cl TA18 196 B3
Turnpike Cnr BA3 95 B8
Turnpike Cross TA14 185 E2
Turnpike Gn TA18 196 B3
Turnpike La BA4 142 B6
Turnpike Rd
Axbridge BS26 69 E1
Shipham BS25 70 E8
Turstin Rd BA6 206 F6
Turtlegate Ave BS13 21 E4
Turtlegate Wlk BS13 21 E4
Tut Hill DT9 189 C1
Tutton Way BS21 6 D1
Tuttors Hill BS27 71 C1
Tuxwell La TA5 152 C8
Tweed Rd BS21 6 C1
Tweed Rd Ind Est 2 BS21 6 C1
Tweentown BS27 90 B8
Twelve Acre Post TA22 163 A4
Twerton Farm Cl BA2 44 B6
Twerton Inf Sch BA2 44 A5
Twinell La TA5 152 D7
Twines Cl BA22 175 A5
Twinhoe La BA2 62 E2
Twistgates La EX14 192 A4
Twitchens La BS27 90 F2
Two Acres Cvn Pk BS21 1 B1
Two Acres Rd BS14 23 A7
Two Ash Hill TA20 193 F1
Two Ash La TA20 194 A1
Two Elms BA21 187 E8
Two Tower La BA22 219 B2
Two Trees BS40 72 E8
Twyford Pl TA21 222 D5
Tydeman Rd BS20 2 F5
Tyler Gn 2 BS22 32 B4
Tyler Way TA9 104 D3
Tyler's La TA4 167 A7
Tylers End TA9 104 F3
Tyndall Ave BS8 226 C4
Tyndall Ho 5 BS2 227 C3
Tyndall's Park Rd BS8 226 C4
Tyndalls Park Mews
BS2 226 C4
Tyne Pk TA1 213 D3
Tyning Cl BS14 23 A7
Tyning Cotts BA3 116 C7
Tyning End BA2 45 B5
Tyning Hengrove Jun Sch
BS14 23 A7
Tyning Hill Hemington BA3 99 C8
Radstock BA3 79 B3
Tyning La BA1 28 B1
Tyning Pl BA2 45 C2
Tyning Rd Bath BA2 45 C2
Bathampton BA2 28 F2
Peasedown St John BA2 79 D7
Saltford BS31 25 E2
Winsley BA15 64 E7
Tyning The Bath BA2 45 B5
Freshford BA3 64 B4
Tynings BS39 58 D3
Tynings La BA5 203 C8
Tynings Mews BS23 48 E4
Tynings Rd BA16 207 B4
Tynings The Clevedon BS21 6 A1
Portishead BS20 1 F1
Tynings Way Clutton BS39 58 E3
Westwood BA15 64 F3
Tynning Terr 15 BA1 28 A1
Tynte Ave BS13 22 E3
Tynte Rd TA6 209 D6
Tyntesfield Rd BS13 22 A8
Tyrone Wlk BS4 22 E8

Tythe St BA6 ....206 E3
Tytherington La BA11 ...143 E8
Tything Way BA9 ......216 D3
Tythings Ct TA24 ......200 F7

U

Ubley CE Prim Sch BS40 ..55 D1
Ubley Dro BS40 ....73 B7
Uillcombe La EX14 ....191 F4
Ullswater Cl BS23 .....49 A4
Ullswater Dr BA1 ......28 A2
Uncombe Cl BS48 .....19 D7
Under Knoll BA2 ......79 E8
Under La BS40 ....36 D1
Under Way TA20 ......193 D6
Underbanks BS20 ......4 D4
Underdown BA21 ......219 F5
Underdown Ho BS1 ....227 A1
Underdown Hollow
  Bradford Abbas DT9 ....187 E2
  Yeovil BA21 ....219 F4
Underdown La DT9 ....225 F6
Underhill
  Gurney Slade BA3 ....114 E7
  Hambridge TA10 ......184 D8
  Pensehwood BA9 ....161 D1
Underhill Ave BA3 ......77 F2
Underhill Cl BA16 .....207 B5
Underhill Dr BS23 .....49 A3
Underhill La
  Midsomer Norton BA3 ...77 F2
  Staple Fitzpaine TA3 ...182 B4
Underhill Rd BA16 .....207 B5
Underleaf Way BA2 ....79 D7
Undertown BS40 ......74 A7
Underwood Ave BS22 ..31 B1
Underwood Bsns Pk
  BA5 ....203 B6
Underwood End BS25 ..52 A4
Underwood La TA10 ...172 C8
Underwood Rd
  Glastonbury BA6 ....206 D6
  Kingsdon TA11 ......173 D5
  Portishead BS20 ......2 C3
Union Dro TA10 ......172 B6
Union La TA4 ....202 E4
Union Pas BA1 ....228 C2
Union Pl BS23 ....48 D7
Union St Bath BA1 ....228 C2
  Bridgwater TA6 ......209 B6
  Bristol BS1 ....227 B3
  Cheddar BS27 ....90 B7
  Dulverton TA22 ......163 D6
  Nailsea BS48 ....8 C1
  Wells BA5 ....203 D4
  Weston-Super-Mare BS23 ..48 D7
  Yeovil BA20 ....219 B4
Unity Ct BS31 ....25 A5
Unity Rd BS31 ....25 A6
Unity St Bristol BS1 ...226 C2
  Bristol BS2 ....227 C3
Univ of Bath BA2 ......45 E5
Univ of Bristol BS8 ...226 C3
Univ of Bristol Dept of
  Economics BS8 ......226 C3
Univ of Bristol Dept of Ed
  BS8 ....226 C3
Univ of Bristol Sch of
  Vetinary Science BS2 .226 C4
Univ of the West of England
  BS3 ....11 E4
University Cl BS9 ....5 N4
University Rd BS8 .....226 C3
University Wlk BS8 ....226 C3
Upcot Cres TA1 ....212 B2
Upcott La Bicknoller TA4 .132 F1
  Winsford TA24 ......147 D7
Upcott Rd TA1,TA4 ...168 B3
Uphill Ct BS23 ....48 D2
Uphill Dr BA1 ....28 C2
Uphill Prim Sch BS23 ..48 D2
Uphill Rd N BS23 .....48 D4
Uphill Rd S BS23 .....48 D2
Uphill Way BS23 ....48 D1
Uphills BA10 ....215 E7
Upjohn Cres BS13 .....22 D3
Uplands BA4 ....176 B8
Uplands Cl BA2 ....63 F7
Uplands Dr BS31 ......25 F2
Uplands Rd BS31 .....25 F2
Uplands Terr BA22 ....197 B8
Uplowman CE Prim Sch
  EX16 ....178 B2
Uplowman Rd EX16 ...178 A4
Upottery Prim Sch EX14 .191 F2
Upper Berkeley Pl BS8 .226 B3
Upper Bloomfield Rd
  BA2 ....44 D1
Upper Borough Walls
  BA1 ....228 C2
Upper Breach BA5 ....113 A2
Upper Bristol Rd
  Bath BA1 ....44 D7
  Clutton BS39 ....58 E4
  Weston-Super-Mare BS22 ..31 B1
Upper Byron Pl BS8 ...226 B3
Upper Camden Pl BA1 .228 C4
Upper Church La
  Bristol BS2 ....226 C3
  Hutton BS24 ....49 D2
Upper Church Rd BS23 ..30 D1

Upper Church St BA1 ..228 B3
Upper Crannel Dro BA6 .139 C4
Upper East Hayes BA1 ..28 B1
Upper Farm Cl BA2 .....81 F4
Upper Furlong BA2 .....60 B3
Upper Green La BA5 ...204 B7
Upper Hedgemead Rd
  BA1 ....228 B4
Upper High St
  Castle Cary BA7 ....214 C5
  Taunton TA1 ....212 F3
Upper Holway Rd TA1 .213 C2
Upper Kewstoke Rd
  BS23 ....30 B1
Upper Lambridge St BA1 .28 C2
Upper Lansdown Mews
  BA1 ....228 A4
Upper Maudlin St BS2 ..227 A3
Upper Merrifield BA3 ..116 E8
Upper Mount Pleasant
  BA3 ....64 A4
Upper Myrtle Hill BS20 ..4 C4
Upper New Rd BS27 ....90 A8
Upper North St BS27 ...90 B8
Upper Oldfield Pk BA2 ..228 A1
Upper Pitching BA3 .....66 A5
Upper Rd BS39 ....75 E6
Upper Stanton BS39 ....40 A2
Upper Strode BS40 .....55 F7
Upper Town La BS40 ...37 C8
Upper Wells St BS1 ...226 C2
Upper Whatcombe
  BA11 ....119 E6
Upper Wood St TA1 ...212 E4
Upper York St BS2 ....227 B4
Upton BS24 ....49 A2
Upton La Dundry BS41 ..39 A8
  Seavington TA19 ....184 E2
Upton Noble Prim Sch
  BA4 ....142 F2
Urchinwood La BS49 ...34 F4

V

Vagg Hill BA22 ....186 E5
Vagg La BA22 ....186 F5
Vagg Pk BA22 ....186 F6
Valda Rd BS22 ....31 C2
Vale Cl TA18 ....224 C4
Vale Cres BS22 ....32 C2
Vale Ct BS8 ....226 A4
Vale End BS48 ....8 D1
Vale La BS3 ....22 C8
Vale Mill Way BS24 ...49 F8
Vale Rd Stalbridge DT10 .190 B4
  Yeovil BA21 ....219 E6
Vale St BA8 ....190 A6
Vale View Aller TA10 ..171 E8
  Henstridge BA8 ......190 A7
  Radstock BA3 ....79 A2
  Wincanton BA9 ......216 F5
Vale View Cotts TA4 ..151 E4
Vale View Gdns BA9 ..216 C2
Vale View Terr BA1 ....28 F3
Valentine Cl BS14 .....23 B5
Valentines TA22 ......163 E6
Valerian Cl BS11 ....4 F6
Valetta Cl BS23 ....48 F3
Valetta Pl TA6 ....208 F5
Valley Cl [6] Nailsea BS48 ..8 C2
  Wells BA5 ....203 C4
Valley Gdns BS22 .....219 A6
Valley Line Ind Pk BS27 .90 A7
Valley Rd
  Bristol, Bedminster Down
  BS13 ....22 A8
  Clevedon BS21 ....6 F5
  Crewkerne TA18 .....224 C4
  Leigh Woods BS8 ....11 C7
  Portishead BS20 ......2 A2
  Taunton TA1 ....213 C5
Valley View
  Axminster EX13 .....198 A1
  Bampton EX16 ......164 B3
  Clutton BS39 ....58 E3
  Frome BA11 ....119 D6
  Millmoor EX15 ......179 E1
Valley View Cl BA1 .....28 B3
Valley View Rd Bath BA1 .28 C3
  Paulton BS39 ....77 E6
Valley Way Rd BS48 ....8 C2
Valley Wlk BA5 ....79 B2
Vallis Cl [7] BA11 .....119 E5
Vallis Fst Sch BA11 ...119 E5
Vallis Mills Trad Est
  BA11 ....119 D5
Vallis Rd BA11 ....119 D5
Vallis Way BA11 ......119 E5
Van Diemen's La BA1 ..27 F2
Vandyck Ave BS31 .....24 F6
Vane St BA2 ....45 B7
Vanguard Cl BA22 ....218 A5
Varsity Way BS24 .....50 B6
Vaughan Ct BA5 ......203 B4
Veal La Horrington BA5 .113 B2
  Walton BA16 ....156 E6
Veale Cl TA18 ....224 C5
Veales DT10 ....189 F2
Vedal Dro TA10 ......172 D4
Vee La BS40 ....37 D8
Vellore La BA2 ....45 C8
Venford Hill
  East Anstey TA22 ...162 E8

Venford Hill continued
  Hawkridge TA22 .....146 D1
Venn Cl TA4 ....167 E6
Venn Cross TA4 ......165 D3
Venn Hill DT6,TA20 ...199 C6
Vennland Way TA24 ..201 A6
Venns Cl BS27 ....90 B7
Venns Gate BS27 ......71 A1
Venture 20 BA20 .....218 C3
Venture 7 BA20 ......218 C3
Venture Eleven The
  TA2 ....213 B6
Venture Way TA2 .....213 B6
Venus La BS39 ....58 E3
Venus St BS49 ....34 D2
Verbena Way BS22 ....32 A1
Verdun Terr TA23 ....131 E4
Vereland Rd BS24 .....49 E3
Verlands BS49 ....34 E5
Vernal La BA11 ......119 D4
Vernalls Rd DT9 ......225 D5
Vernham Gr BA2 .....44 C1
Vernon Cl BS31 ....25 D3
Vernon La BS26 ....69 B3
Vernon Pk BA2 ....44 C6
Vernon Terr BA2 .....44 C6
Vernslade BA1 ....27 A2
Verriers TA4 ....153 E4
Verrington La BA9 ...216 B5
Verrington Park Rd
  BA9 ....216 B4
Vesey's Hole Hill SP8 ..177 E4
Vestry Cl BA16 ....207 C5
Vestry Rd BA16 ......207 C5
Vian End BS22 ....31 F4
Vicar's Cl BA5 ....203 E5
Vicar's La TA1 ....184 F7
Vicarage Cl Chard TA20 .223 C3
  Coxley BA5 ....139 E6
  Creech St Michael TA3 .169 C4
  Stogursey TA5 ....134 C6
  Weston-Super-Mare BS22 .32 A3
  Westonzoyland TA7 ..154 F5
Vicarage Ct
  Burnham-On-Sea TA8 ..104 A7
  Timberscombe TA24 .130 B5
Vicarage Gdns BA2 ....79 B7
Vicarage Hill
  Combe St Nicholas TA20 .193 D6
  Winney La BA11 ....143 F8
Vicarage La
  Barrow Gurney BS48 ..20 C6
  Compton Bishop BS26 ..69 B3
  Compton Dando BS39 ..41 D6
  Creech St Michael TA3 .169 D4
  Drayscott BS27 ......90 F7
  Mark TA9 ....106 E5
  Norton St Philip BA2 ..81 E4
  Pawlett TA6 ....135 F5
  Shapwick TA7 ....137 F1
  Stogursey TA5 ....139 D8
Vicarage Lawns TA3 ..169 D4
Vicarage Rd
  Bristol, Bishopsworth BS13 ..22 A6
  Carhampton TA24 ...131 B5
  Leigh Woods BS8 ....11 C6
  Minehead TA24 ......200 F8
  Stogursey TA5 ....134 C6
  Wookey BA5 ....139 E8
  Woolavington TA7 ...136 E4
Vicarage St
  Burnham-On-Sea TA8 ..104 A7
  Frome BA11 ....119 F4
  Tintinhull BA22 ......186 C6
  [6] Yeovil BA20 .....219 B4
Vicarage Wlk BA20 ...219 B5
Vicars La TA4 ....208 D5
Vickery Cl
  Bridgwater TA6 ......208 D3
  Curry Rivel TA10 ....171 D4
Victoria Ave TA20 ....223 D4
Victoria Bldgs Bath BA2 ..44 D6
  Taunton TA1 ....213 C5
Victoria Bridge Rd BA1,
  BA2 ....228 A2
Victoria Bsns Pk TA20 .223 D4
Victoria Cl Bath BA2 ....44 C5
  Portishead BS20 ......2 D5
  Yeovil BA21 ....219 D6
Victoria Cotts BA2 ....62 F7
Victoria Ct
  Castle Cary BA7 .....214 B5
  Frome BA11 ....120 A4
  Ilminster TA19 ......221 C4
  Portishead BS20 ......2 D6
Victoria Gate TA1 ....213 B4
Victoria Gr
  Batheaston BA1 ....28 F3
  Castle Cary BA7 .....214 B6
  [9] Henstridge BA8 ..190 A6
Victoria Gr BA4 ......205 D5
Victoria Ho Bath BA1 ..44 D8
  Keynsham BS31 ......24 F4
Victoria Hospl BA11 ..119 F4
Victoria Jubilee Homes
  BS40 ....53 C6
Victoria La BA14 .....111 F8
Victoria Lodge BS22 ...31 E2
Victoria Mews BA7 ...214 B5
Victoria Park BS31 ....24 F4
  BA1 ....44 D7
Victoria Parkway TA1 .213 B4
Victoria Pk
  Castle Cary BA7 .....214 B5
  Weston-Super-Mare BS23 ..30 C1
Victoria Pl [2] Bath BA1 ..28 C1
  Bath BA2 ....45 C1

Victoria Pl continued
  Chardstock EX13 ....198 A7
  Highbridge TA9 .....104 D3
  Paulton BS39 ....77 D5
  Weston-Super-Mare BS23 ..48 D8
Victoria Quadrant BS23 ..48 E8
Victoria Rd Avonmouth BS11 ..4 B7
  Bath BA2 ....44 D6
  Bridgwater TA6 .....208 E5
  Castle Cary BA7 .....214 A5
  Clevedon BS21 ....6 C3
  Frome BA11 ....120 A4
  Minehead TA24 ......201 A5
  Saltford BS31 ....25 D3
  Yeovil BA21 ....219 D6
Victoria Sh Mews TA18 .224 C6
Victoria Sq Bristol BS8 .226 A3
  Evercreech BA4 .....141 E1
  Portishead BS20 ......2 D5
  Weston-Super-Mare BS23 ..48 D7
Victoria St Bristol BS1 ..227 B2
  Burnham-On-Sea TA8 ..104 A7
  Taunton TA1 ....213 B4
  Wellington TA21 ....222 D6
Victoria Terr Bath BA2 ..44 D6
  [3] Bristol, Clifton BS8 ..11 F6
  [4] Henstridge BA8 ..190 A6
  Paulton BS39 ....77 E6
Victoria Way TA5 ....152 E7
Victory Rd TA2 ......213 A7
Vigor Rd BS13 ....22 B5
Viking Cl TA21 ......200 D7
Vilberie Cl TA2 ......212 A7
Villa Rosa BS23 ....30 C1
Village Rd TA3 ......182 F6
Villes La TA24 ......163 A5
Villice La BS40 ....74 A7
Vincent Cl TA6 ......104 C7
Vincent Pl BA20 .....219 B5
Vincent St [5] BA20 ..219 B5
Vine Cotts TA21 .....169 C1
Vine Gdns Frome BA11 .119 F6
  Weston-Super-Mare BS22 .32 A2
Vine Gr BA8 ....176 E1
Vine St BA8 ....176 E1
Vinery The BS25 ......70 A7
Viney La EX14 ....191 F1
Viney St TA1 ....213 B3
Viney's Yd BA10 .....215 F6
Vining's Hill BA4 ....142 D1
Vinney La BA11 ......143 F8
Violet La DT9 ....176 A2
Virginia Cl [1] BA11 ..190 A6
Virginia Orch TA3 ...169 C3
Vivary Ct TA1 ....212 E3
Vivary Gate TA1 ....212 F3
Vivary Mrs TA1 .....212 E3
Vivary Rd TA1 ......212 E3
Vivien Ave BA3 ......78 A2
Vixen Cl BA22 ......174 A3
Vobster Cross BA3 ...117 D7
Vobster Hill BA3 ....117 D7
Vole Rd Brent Knoll TA9 ..86 D1
  Mark TA9 ....106 B7
Volis Cross TA5 .....152 F1
Volis Hill TA2 ....168 F8
Vowell Cl BS13 ....22 B4
Voxmoor Cl BS48 ......9 A2
Vulcan Ho BA2 ......228 C3
Vulcan Rd TA24 .....201 B6
Vynes Cl BS48 ....9 A1
Vynes Ind Est BS48 ....9 A1
Vynes Way BS48 ....9 A1
Vyvyan Rd BS8 ......226 A3
Vyvyan Terr BS8 ....226 A3

W

Wadbrook Cross EX13 .198 C4
Wade Cl TA7 ....154 E6
Wade St BS2 ....227 C3
Wadham Cl TA20 ....193 D5
Wadham Com Sch
  TA18 ....224 D7
Wadham Cross
  Knowstone EX36 ....162 A2
  West Anstey EX36 ..162 A4
Wadham Hill EX36 ...162 A2
Wadham St BS23 .....48 D8
Wadham's Almshouses
  TA19 ....183 E4
Wagg Dro TA10 .....172 B5
Waggs Plot EX13 ....198 B4
Wagon & Horses Hill
  BA4 ....141 E8
Wagtail Gdns BS22 ....49 E8
Wains Cl [4] BS21 .....6 C2
Wainwright Cl [5] BS22 .32 B4
Wainwright Ct BA1 ..205 B4
Wainwright Dr BA11 .120 C7
Wake Cl BS29 ....75 D8
Wakedean Gdns BS49 ..17 A1
Walcombe La BS49 ...203 E6
Walcot Bldgs BA1 ...228 C4
Walcot Gdns BA1 ....228 C4
Walcot Gate BA1 ....228 C4
Walcot Ho BA1 ......228 C4
Walcot Inf Sch BA1 ..228 C4
Walcot Par BA1 .....228 C4
Walcot St BA1 ....228 C3
Walcot Terr BA1 ....228 C4
Waldegrave Rd BA1 ..27 E1
Waldegrave Terr BA11 ..79 A3
Walden Rd BS31 .....25 A5

Waldock Barton TA13 ..220 D4
Waldron's Cross TA21 ..165 E1
Wales La BA22 ....174 E3
Walford Ave BS22 .....32 C4
Walford Cross Roads
  TA1 ....169 D7
Walk La TA13 ....184 F1
Walker Rd BA11 .....120 A3
Walker St BS2 ....226 C4
Walkers Gate TA1 ...222 D5
Wall Ditch La TA16 ..196 A8
Wall Gn BS26 ....70 C1
Wall The TA9 ....106 D5
Wallace La BS40 ......74 E3
Wallace Rd BA1 ......28 B1
Wallace Wells Rd TA8 .104 D5
Wallbridge BA11 .....120 B4
Wallbridge Ave BA11 .120 A4
Wallbridge Gdns BA11 .120 A4
Wallbridge Rd BA11 ..120 A4
Wallbridge Ind Est
  BA11 ....120 B4
Wallenge Cl BS39 .....77 F6
Wallenge Dr BS39 ....77 F6
Walley La BS40 ....57 B7
Wallingford Rd BS4 ...22 D7
Walliscote Grove Rd
  BS23 ....48 E7
Walliscote Prim Sch
  BS23 ....48 E7
Walliscote Rd BS23 ...48 D6
Walliscote Rd S BS23 .48 D4
Walls La BS28 ....108 B8
Walls The TA7 ....137 C2
Wallycourt Rd BS40 ...56 E8
Walmsley Terr [4] BA1 .28 C2
Walnut Bldgs BA3 .....79 A3
Walnut Cl Axbridge BS26 ..70 B1
  Cheddar BS27 ....90 B7
  Easton-in-G BS20 ......4 A3
  Keynsham BS31 ......24 C4
  Nailsea BS48 ....18 E8
  Puriton TA7 ....136 C4
  Rode BA11 ....101 E8
  Taunton TA1 ....212 B4
  Weston-Super-Mare BS24 ..49 B2
Walnut Dr Bath BA1 ...44 E4
  Bridgwater TA6 .....209 D3
  Somerton TA11 .....211 D4
Walnut La TA7 ....136 F3
Walnut Tree Cl BS25 ..35 F1
Walnut Tree Cnr TA23 .131 F4
Walnut Tree Dr TA24 .131 A5
Walnut Wlk Bristol BS13 ..21 F5
  Frome BA11 ....120 B7
  Keynsham BS31 ......24 C4
Walnuts The TA7 ....137 B2
Walridge Cross TA4 ..166 A4
Walrond Ct TA19 ....221 B3
Walrond's Pk TA3 ...184 B7
Walrow TA9 ....104 E3
Walrow Ind Est TA9 .104 F2
Walrow Terr TA9 ....104 E3
Walscombe Cl [1] TA14 .185 F4
Walsh Ave BS14 ......23 A7
Walsham Cl BS24 .....49 B2
Waltham End BS24 ...50 A8
Walton BS24 ....49 A2
Walton Bay House Park
  Homes BS21 ....1 B1
Walton CE Prim Sch
  BA16 ....156 E7
Walton Cl
  Bridgwater TA6 ......209 D5
  Keynsham BS31 ......24 D4
Walton Dro Clevedon BS21 ..7 C6
  Walton BA16 ....156 D5
Walton Rd Bristol BS11 ..4 D6
  Clevedon BS21 ....7 B6
Walwyn Cl BA2 ....44 A6
Wambrook Cl TA1 ...212 E1
Wandsdyke Prim Sch
  BS14 ....22 F4
Wansbeck Rd TA1 ...213 D3
Wansbeck Rd BS31 ...25 A4
Wansbrough Rd BS22 ..32 B4
Wansdyke Bsns Ctr BA2 ..44 D4
Wansdyke Ct BS14 ...23 B5
Wansdyke Rd BA2 .....44 D1
Wansdyke Sch BA2 ...62 E8
Wansdyke Workshops
  BS31 ....25 A6
Wapping Rd BS1 ....227 A1
War Meml Hospl TA8 .104 B7
Ward La TA7 ....154 E8
Warden Rd TA24 ....200 F6
Wardlewreth Way TA21 .222 C7
Wardour Rd BS4 ......22 D8
Wareham Cl BS48 ......8 D1
Wareham Cross EX13 .198 E1
Wareham Rd EX13 ...198 E2
Wares La TA6 ....208 D6
Waring Ho BS1 ......227 A1
Warleigh Cl BA11 ....119 D4
Warleigh Dr BA1 ......29 A3
Warleigh La BA1 ......46 C5
Warleigh Manor Sch
  BA1 ....46 C6
Warman Cl BS14 ......23 F6
Warman Rd BS14 ....23 F6
Warmington Rd BS14 ..23 C8
Warminster Rd
  Bath BA2,BA3 ....46 B5
  Beckington BA11 ....101 E4
  Frome BA11 ....120 B4
Warne Pk BS23 ....49 A6

Warne Rd BS23 .... 49 A6
Warner Cl BS49 .... 35 A7
Warren Cl
  Bridgwater TA6 .... 208 F6
  Bruton BA10 .... 215 E6
  Charlton Horethorne DT9 .. 176 A2
  Hutton BS24 .... 49 D2
Warren Gdns BS14 .... 23 F5
Warren La BS41 .... 20 E8
Warren Rd Brean TA8 .... 65 F6
  Minehead TA24 .... 201 B7
Warren St TA21 .... 222 A4
Warren The BA16 .... 207 A5
Warren's Cl BS27 .... 71 B1
Warrens Hill BS27 .... 71 B1
Warrens Hill Rd BS27 .... 71 D4
Warrens Way BA5 .... 113 A1
Warres Rd TA2 .... 213 C8
Warrilow Cl BS22 .... 32 B5
Warrior Ave BA22 .... 218 B6
Warry Cl BS48 .... 9 B2
Warth La BS22 .... 32 A8
Warwick Ave TA6 .... 209 C3
Warwick Cl BS22 .... 49 C8
Warwick Gdns
  Burnham-On-Sea TA8 .... 85 B1
  Clutton BS39 .... 58 D3
  Taunton TA1 .... 213 C2
Warwick Rd Bath BA1 .... 44 B7
  Keynsham BS31 .... 24 D4
  Taunton TA2 .... 213 A8
Wash La TA15 .... 186 B4
Washcross La TA19 .... 184 E3
Washford Cross TA23 .... 131 F3
Washford Hill TA23 .... 202 A5
Washford Sta TA23 .... 131 E4
Washing Pound La
  Bristol BS14 .... 23 B4
  Nailsea BS48 .... 8 F8
Washington Gdns TA6 .... 208 E5
Washington Terr TA20 .... 223 B5
Washpool La BA2 .... 43 F2
Wassail Cl 5 TA24 .... 131 A5
Wassail View TA2 .... 168 B4
Watchet Boat Mus*
  TA23 .... 202 C7
Watchet Sta TA23 .... 202 C7
Watchhouse Rd BS20 .... 4 F4
Watchill Ave BS13 .... 21 F6
Watchill Cl BS13 .... 21 F6
Watchill Cl BS13 .... 22 F6
Water Hill TA4 .... 150 F7
Water La Bristol BS1 .... 227 B2
  Butleigh BA6 .... 157 E4
  Charlton Horethorne DT9 .. 176 A2
  Crowcombe TA4 .... 151 A7
  Frome BA11 .... 119 E3
  Horningsham BA12 .... 144 D4
  Keenthorne TA5 .... 134 C1
  Lopen TA13 .... 185 A1
  Nether Stowey TA5 .... 134 A1
  Paulton BA3, BS39 .... 78 A8
  Pill BS20 .... 4 C4
  Somerton TA11 .... 211 C3
  Stogumber TA4 .... 150 F7
Water St Burrington TA4 .. 184 D5
  Curry Rivel TA10 .... 171 C4
  East Harptree BS40 .... 74 F4
  East Lambrook TA13 .... 220 C8
  Hambridge TA10 .... 171 D1
  Lopen TA13 .... 185 A1
  Martock TA12 .... 185 E6
  Seavington TA19 .... 184 E1
Waterbridge Rd BS13 .... 21 F4
Watercombe Hts BA20 .. 218 D2
Watercombe La
  Yeovil BA20 .... 218 C2
  Yeovil BA20 .... 218 D5
Watercombe Pk BA20 .. 218 D2
Watercress Cl BS48 .... 9 B2
Waterfield Cl TA1 .... 212 B3
Waterfield Dr TA1 .... 212 B3
Waterford Beck BA14 .. 83 F6
Waterford Cl TA6 .... 209 A2
Waterford Pk BA3 .... 78 E1
Waterhouse La BA2 .... 63 F8
Waterlake DT10 .... 190 B4
Waterlake La TA10 .... 198 C8
Waterlands La TA18 .... 224 C8
Waterleaze TA2 .... 213 D7
Waterlip BA4 .... 141 F7
Waterloo Frome BA11 .. 119 F5
  Puriton TA7 .... 136 C4
Waterloo Bldgs BA2 .... 44 B6
Waterloo Cl TA7 .... 136 C4
Waterloo Cotts TA1 .... 212 B4
Waterloo Ho BS20 .... 4 D5
Waterloo La DT10 .... 190 A2
Waterloo Pl 8 BS2 .... 227 C3
Waterloo Rd Bristol BS2 .. 227 C3
  Radstock BA3 .... 79 A2
  Shepton Mallet BA4 .... 205 B7
  Wellington TA21 .... 222 C5
Waterloo St Bristol BS2 .. 227 C3
  9 Bristol, Clifton BS8 .... 11 F7
  Weston-Super-Mare BS23 .. 48 E8
Watermead TA20 .... 198 D8
Watermead Cl 3 BA1 .. 228 B2
Waters La BS27 .... 90 C8
Waterside Cres BA3 .... 78 D1
Waterside La BA3 .... 98 A6
Waterside Ms BS20 .... 2 C4
Waterside Rd
  Radstock BA3 .... 78 D1
  Wincanton BA9 .... 216 C4
Waterside Way BA3 .... 97 D8
Watersmeet TA1 .... 212 E4

Watery Combe BA3 .... 94 E7
Watery La
  Axminster EX13 .... 198 A3
  Bath BA2 .... 44 A6
  Broadway TA19 .... 194 B8
  Charlton Horethorne DT9 .. 176 C1
  Clatworthy TA4 .... 149 C2
  Coultings TA5 .... 134 E3
  Crewkerne TA18 .... 195 D3
  Doynton BS30 .... 12 A8
  Halstock BA22 .... 197 D3
  Langford Budville TA4,
  TA21 .... 166 C2
  Minehead TA24 .... 200 F7
  Nailsea BS48 .... 8 B3
  North Petherton TA6 .... 153 E4
  Sherborne DT9 .... 225 D1
  Spaxton TA5 .... 152 F4
  Stogursey TA5 .... 134 C5
  Stratton On The Fosse BA3 .. 97 A3
  Williton TA4 .... 202 E4
  Winford BS40 .... 38 B4
  Wiveliscombe TA4 .... 210 C6
Watling St BA21 .... 218 D7
Watling Way BS11 .... 4 D7
Watsons La TA4 .... 209 A5
Watts La TA4 .... 151 E1
Watts's Quarry La TA10,
  TA11 .... 173 A5
Watts's Rd TA7 .... 137 B6
Waveney Rd BS31 .... 25 A3
Waverley TA11 .... 211 C4
Waverley Cl Frome BA11 .. 120 C6
  Somerton TA11 .... 211 C4
Waverley St BS49 .... 34 D3
Waverley Rd
  Backwell BS48 .... 19 A7
  Bridgwater TA6 .... 208 F6
  Bristol, Shirehampton BS11 .. 4 E6
  Weston-Super-Mare BS23 .. 48 F4
Waverney Cl TA1 .... 213 D3
Way Terr TA23 .... 131 E3
Wayacre Dro TA24 .... 66 E6
Wayclose La BA9 .... 177 D5
Waycroft Prim Sch TA4 .. 23 E5
Waydown Cross TA24 .... 130 A4
Waydown La TA24 .... 130 A4
Wayfield Gdns TA4 .... 28 F4
Wayford Cl BS31 .... 25 A3
Wayford Hill TA18 .... 195 C1
Waylands Rd TA1 .... 212 B5
Waysdown La TA4 .... 149 D1
Wayside Staplehay TA3 .. 181 D8
  Weston-Super-Mare BS22 .. 31 D2
Wayside Cl BA11 .... 120 C6
Wayside Dr BS21 .... 6 E5
Weacombe Rd
  Bridgwater TA6 .... 209 C5
  Taunton TA2 .... 212 F7
Weal Terr BA1 .... 27 B2
Weal The BA1 .... 27 B2
Weare CE Fst Sch BS26 .. 88 D7
Weare Ct BS1 .... 226 A1
Weares La TA1 .... 137 D2
Weatherley Dr BS20 .... 1 F3
Weatherly Ave BA2 .... 44 B2
Weavers Cl
  Crewkerne TA18 .... 224 D5
  Shepton Mallet BA4 .... 205 D4
Weavers Ct BA11 .... 119 E3
Weavers The BA11 .... 101 E4
Webb's Cl BA5 .... 203 D3
Webb's Hill BA11 .... 119 B5
Webber Rd BA4 .... 205 D4
Webber's Post TA24 .... 129 C6
Webbers TA4 .... 167 F7
Webbers CE Prim Sch
  TA21 .... 178 F5
Webbers Cl TA21 .... 222 E4
Webbers Way TA7 .... 136 B4
Webbington Rd BS26 .... 69 C3
Webbs Mead
  Beckington BA11 .... 101 E4
  Chew Stoke BS40 .... 56 D8
Wedgwood Cl BS14 .... 23 B5
Wedgwood Rd BA2 .... 44 A5
Wedlakes TA23 .... 202 C6
Wedmore Cl
  Burnham-On-Sea TA8 .... 104 C8
  Frome BA11 .... 120 C7
  Weston-Super-Mare BS23 .. 48 F2
Wedmore Pk BA2 .... 44 A3
Wedmore Rd
  Cheddar BS27 .... 90 A7
  Clevedon BS21 .... 6 B1
  Nailsea BS48 .... 18 A8
  Saltford BS31 .... 25 D4
Week La TA22 .... 147 D4
Weekes Mdw TA21 .... 179 E6
Weekesley La BA2 .... 60 D1
Weetwood Rd BS49 .... 34 D5
Weind The BS22 .... 31 D2
Weir Head Cotts TA22 .. 163 D7
Weir La Abbots Leigh BS8 .. 10 F7
  Marshfield SN14 .... 13 F8
  Pilton BA4 .... 140 E3
  Yeovilton BA22 .... 174 B5
Weir Rd BS49 .... 34 E3
Weirfield Gn TA1 .... 212 D5
Weirfield Rd TA24 .... 201 A8
Welbeck Rd BA21 .... 219 C6
Well Cl Long Ashton BS41 .. 11 B1
  Weston-Super-Mare BS22 .. 49 B2
  Winscombe BS25 .... 70 A8
Well House Cl BS9 .... 5 E3
Well La Banwell BS29 .... 50 E3

Well La continued
  Purse Caundle DT9 .... 189 D4
  Timbercombe TA24 .... 130 A5
  Yatton BS49 .... 34 C8
Well Pk BS49 .... 34 E4
Well The TA21 .... 222 B5
Welland Cl TA1 .... 213 D4
Welland Rd
  Keynsham BS31 .... 24 F4
  Yeovil BA21 .... 219 D2
Wellard Cl 1 BS22 .... 32 B4
Wellesley Cl TA1 .... 212 C1
Wellesley Gn BA10 .... 215 E6
Wellesley Park Prim Sch
  TA21 .... 222 E4
Wellesley Pk TA21 .... 222 D4
Wellesley St TA2 .... 212 F6
Wellesley Way TA3 .... 192 A7
Wellfield Hill DT6,EX13 .. 199 B2
Wellhouse La BA6 .... 206 F4
Welling Cl TA20 .... 198 C8
Wellings Cl TA20 .... 198 C8
Wellington Bldgs 27 B2
Wellington Cottage Hospl
  TA21 .... 222 D5
Wellington Ct BS21 .... 6 C5
Wellington Flats BA20 .. 219 A4
Wellington Hill TA21 .... 222 F2
Wellington Jun Sch
  TA21 .... 222 E5
Wellington Mews BS11 .. 4 D5
Wellington Mus TA21 .... 222 D6
Wellington New Rd TA1 .. 212 B3
Wellington Pl
  Cheddar BS27 .... 90 B7
  Weston-Super-Mare BS23 .. 48 D7
Wellington Rd
  Bridgwater TA6 .... 209 B5
  Bristol BS2 .... 227 C4
  Taunton TA1 .... 212 D4
  Taunton TA21 .... 222 E5
Wellington Terr
  10 Bristol BS8 .... 11 F6
  Clevedon BS21 .... 6 D5
  Wiveliscombe TA4 .... 210 C5
Wellow Brook Mdw BA3 .. 78 B2
Wellow Dr BA11 .... 120 C7
Wellow La
  Hinton Charterhouse BA2 .. 63 D1
  Norton St Philip BA2 .... 81 D5
  Peasedown St John BA2 .. 79 C6
  Peasedown St John BA2 .. 79 E6
Wellow Mead BA2 .... 79 B7
Wellow Rd BA2 .... 80 B8
Wellow Tyning BA2 .... 79 D7
Wells & District Hospl
  BA5 .... 203 F5
Wells Cathedral* BA5 .. 203 E4
Wells Cathedral Sch
  BA5 .... 203 E5
Wells Cl Bristol BS14 .... 23 C5
  Burnham-On-Sea TA8 .... 104 C7
  Nailsea BS48 .... 9 B1
  Taunton TA1 .... 213 A8
Wells Mus* BA5 .... 203 E4
Wells Rd Bath BA2 .... 228 B1
  Bristol BS14 .... 23 C7
  Chilcompton BA3 .... 96 F4
  Clevedon BS21 .... 6 D1
  Dundry BS40,BS41 .... 38 F7
  Glastonbury BA5,BA6 .... 139 D4
  Glastonbury BA6 .... 206 E6
  Norton St Philip BA2,BA3 .. 81 C3
  Paulton BS39 .... 77 B7
  Priddy BA5 .... 92 E2
  Radstock BA3 .... 78 E2
  Stoke St Michael BA3 .... 94 F1
  Shepton Mallet BA4 .... 204 E6
  Theale BS28 .... 109 B1
  Westbury Sub Mendip BA5 .. 110 C6
  Wookey Hole BA5 .... 203 A7
  Yarley BA5 .... 139 C8
Wells Road Trad Est
  BA5 .... 206 E2
Wells Sq BA3 .... 78 D1
Wells Sq BA3 .... 78 D1
Wells Way BS28 .... 107 F3
Wellsea Gr BS23 .... 49 B7
Wellshead La TA24 .... 128 A3
Wellsprings Prim Sch
  TA2 .... 212 F8
Wellsprings Rd TA2 .... 212 F7
Wellsway BA2 .... 44 F3
Wellsway Bath BA2 .... 44 F3
Wellsway Pk BA2 .... 44 E2
Wellsway Rd BA4 .... 205 B6
Wellsway Sec Sch BS31 .. 25 A5
Welsford Ave BA5 .... 203 C5
Welsford Cl BA5 .... 203 B5
Welsh Back BS1 .... 227 B2
Welsh Ct BA5 .... 203 B4
Welshmill La BA11 .... 119 F5
Welshmill Rd BA11 .... 119 F5
Welton TA7 .... 78 B3
Welton Inf Sch BA3 .... 78 B2
Welton Prim Sch BA3 .... 78 B2
Welton Rd BA3 .... 78 C2
Welton Vale BA3 .... 78 B2
Welwyn Gdns BS15 .... 22 C3
Wembdon Ct TA6 .... 208 E4
Wembdon Hill TA6 .... 208 D4
Wembdon Rise TA6 .... 208 D5
Wembdon St TA6 .... 208 F5
Wemberham Cres BS49 .. 17 A1
Wemberham La BS49 .... 33 E8
Wendick Dro TA10 .... 171 E3
Wentwood Dr BS24 .... 49 A1
Wentworth Cl BS22 .... 32 A3
Wentworth Rd BA21 .... 219 C6
Werren Cl TA7 .... 202 B7
Wesley Ave BA3 .... 78 C1

Wesley Cl Brean TA8 .... 65 F3
  Frome BA11 .... 119 F4
  Southwick BA14 .... 83 E2
  Taunton TA1 .... 212 C1
  Wanstrow BA4 .... 142 F4
Wesley Dr BS22 .... 32 A3
Wesley La BA14 .... 83 E2
Wesley Mews BS27 .... 90 B7
Wesley Rd BA3 .... 78 D1
Wesley Slope 7 BA11 .. 119 F4
Wesley Villas BA3 .... 116 F6
Wessex Bldgs TA11 .... 211 B5
Wessex Bsns Ctr BS27 .. 90 A6
Wessex Cl
  Bridgwater TA6 .... 209 C4
  Chard TA20 .... 223 C2
  Street BA16 .... 207 D6
Wessex Ct DT9 .... 225 D3
Wessex Dr DT9 .... 187 E1
Wessex Fields BA11 .... 119 D2
Wessex Ho 10 BS2 .... 227 C3
Wessex Pk TA11 .... 211 B5
Wessex Rd
  Stalbridge DT10 .... 190 C4
  Taunton TA1 .... 168 E1
  Weston-Super-Mare BS23 .. 49 B2
  Yeovil BA21 .... 218 D8
Wessex Rise TA11 .... 211 E3
Wessex Way BA9 .... 216 B3
West Anstey School Cross
  EX36 .... 162 C5
West Approach Rd TA7 .. 136 D4
West Ave Bath BA2 .... 44 C5
  Highbridge TA9 .... 104 C4
West Bank BA5 .... 203 A8
West Bourton Rd SP8 .. 177 E8
West Bow Ho TA6 .... 208 E4
West Bower La TA5 .... 153 C7
West Brook BA21 .... 218 D6
West Buckland Com Prim
  Sch TA21 .... 180 F7
West Buckland Rd
  TA21 .... 180 D7
West Camel Farm BA22 .. 174 E3
West Camel Rd BA22 .. 174 E3
West Charlton TA11 .... 173 C7
West Chinnock CE Prim Sch
  TA18 .... 196 B8
West Cl Bath BA2 .... 44 A5
  Dunster TA24 .... 201 D2
West Coker CE Prim Sch
  BA22 .... 197 A8
West Coker Rd BA20 .. 218 E2
West Compton La BA4 .. 204 E3
West Coombe Bristol BS9 .. 5 C6
  Yeovil BA21 .... 218 D6
West Coombe La TA4 .. 165 D8
West Cornmoor Dro
  TA9 .... 136 D7
West Cotts TA24 .... 127 A2
West Cres TA19 .... 221 B2
West Croft Blagdon BS40 .. 54 E2
  Clevedon BS21 .... 6 E5
West Ct Horrington BA5 .. 112 F1
  Weston-Super-Mare BS23 .. 48 D8
  Yeovil BA20 .... 219 A5
West Dene BS9 .... 5 C5
West Dro TA7 .... 137 D4
West Dundry La BS41 .. 21 E2
West End Bristol BS2 .... 227 A4
  Bristol BS1 .... 226 C1
  Somerton TA11 .... 211 C4
  Street BA16 .... 207 B5
  Wedmore BS28 .... 108 C3
West End Cl
  Somerton TA11 .... 211 C4
  South Petherton TA13 .... 220 B4
West End Ct
  Taunton TA1 .... 136 D1
  South Petherton TA13 .... 220 B4
West End La BS48 .... 18 A8
West End Trad Est BS48 .. 8 B1
West End View
  Barrington TA19 .... 184 C5
  South Petherton TA13 .... 220 B4
West End Way TA13 .... 220 B4
West Field CI TA1 .... 212 A2
West Field Lawn TA8 .. 104 B8
West Ford Dr TA21 .... 222 A5
West Garston BS29 .... 51 A3
West Gdns BS20 .... 2 D5
West Harptree Rd BS40 .. 74 F5
West Hatch La TA3 .... 182 F8
West Hay BS40 .... 35 C3
West Hendford BA20 .. 219 A4
West Hill
  Milborne Port DT9 .... 217 D2
  Nailsea BS48 .... 9 A5
  Portishead BS20 .... 2 B5
  Wincanton BA9 .... 216 B4
West Hill Gdns
  Radstock BA3 .... 78 D1
  Radstock BA3 .... 78 E1
West Hill La
  Winsham TA20 .... 199 B8
  Wraxall BS48 .... 10 B4
West Howetown La
  TA24 .... 147 D5
West Huntspill Com Prim Sch
  TA9 .... 104 C1
West La Alhampton BA4 .. 159 C5
  Alweston DT9 .... 189 A2
  Barrington TA13 .... 184 F5
  Croscombe BA5 .... 140 F8
  Felton BS40 .... 37 C8
  Lynford-on-Fosse TA11 .... 158 D2
  Sherborne DT9 .... 188 F1
West Leaze Rd BA4 .... 27 A1
West Leaze BA16 .... 207 C6
West Leigh Inf Sch BS48 .. 19 A6
West Links BS23 .... 48 D2

West Links Cl BS22 .... 31 B3
West Lynne BS27 .... 90 B8
West Mall BS8 .... 11 F7
West Mill La
  Marnhull DT10 .... 190 D6
  Sherborne DT9 .... 225 D2
West Monkton CE Prim Sch
  TA2 .... 213 F8
West Par BS9 .... 5 C7
West Park Cl TA24 .... 200 E7
West Pennard CE Prim Sch
  BA6 .... 140 B1
West Pk Bristol BS8 .... 226 B4
  Butleigh BA6 .... 157 E4
  Castle Cary BA7 .... 214 B6
  Minehead TA24 .... 200 E7
West Quay BA20 .... 218 F5
West Quay Taunton TA6 .. 208 F5
West Rd
  East Brent BS24,TA9 .... 86 B7
  Lympsham BS24 .... 67 B1
  Midsomer Norton BA3 .... 78 A3
  Wiveliscombe TA4 .... 210 B4
  Yatton BS49 .... 34 B7
West Rocke Ave BS9 .... 5 D6
West Rolstone Rd BS24 .. 33 A1
West Sedgemoor Rd
  TA3 .... 170 D3
West Shepton BA4 .... 205 A5
West Somerset Com Coll The
  TA24 .... 201 B5
West Somerset Rly*
  Crowcombe TA4 .... 151 C4
  * Dunster TA24 .... 201 D5
West Somerset Rural Life
  Mus* TA24 .... 124 C4
West St Ashcott TA7 .... 156 B8
  Axbridge BS26 .... 70 B2
  Bampton EX16 .... 164 B1
  Banwell BS29 .... 51 B3
  Bishops Lydeard TA4 .... 167 E8
  Bratton Seymour BA9 .... 175 F7
  Bridgwater TA6 .... 208 E4
  Bristol BS2 .... 227 C3
  Carhampton TA24 .... 131 B4
  Crewkerne TA18 .... 224 B6
  Ilton St George TA17 .... 195 C7
  Ilchester BA22 .... 173 E1
  Ilminster TA19 .... 221 B4
  Kington Magna SP8 .... 177 E1
  Martock TA12 .... 185 E8
  Minehead TA24 .... 200 E7
  Seavington TA19 .... 184 D1
  Somerton TA11 .... 211 D4
  South Petherton TA13 .... 220 B4
  Stoke sub Hamdon TA14 .. 185 E3
  Templecombe BA8 .... 189 D8
  Watchet TA23 .... 202 B7
  Wells BA5 .... 203 C3
  Weston-Super-Mare BS23 .. 48 D8
  Wiveliscombe TA4 .... 210 C4
  Yeovil BA20 .... 219 C4
West Town Gr BS4 .... 23 D8
West Town La BA4 .... 157 F5
West Town Pk BS4 .... 23 D8
West Town Rd
  Backwell BS48 .... 19 A5
  Bristol BS11 .... 4 C7
West Tyning BA2 .... 42 B1
West View
  Creech St Michael TA3 .... 169 D5
  Long Sutton TA10 .... 172 E4
  Queen Camel BA22 .... 174 F4
  South Cadbury BA22 .... 175 D4
  West Monkton TA2 .... 169 D8
West View Cl TA7 .... 155 B4
West View Rd
  Batheaston BA1 .... 29 A3
  Keynsham BS31 .... 24 E5
West Villas TA4 .... 167 F6
West Way BS21 .... 6 C3
West Ways BA22 .... 196 E8
West Well La BS28 .... 109 C1
West Wick BS24 .... 32 C1
West Wick Rdbt BS24 .. 50 B8
Westacre BA16 .... 207 A4
Westacre Cl BS27 .... 90 B8
Westacre Rd BS27 .... 90 B8
Westaway Cl BS49 .... 34 C7
Westaway Pk BS49 .... 34 D7
Westbourne Ave
  Clevedon BS21 .... 6 B2
  Keynsham BS31 .... 24 E5
Westbourne Cres BS21 .. 6 B2
Westbourne Gr BA20 .. 218 E5
Westbourne Pl BS8 .... 226 B3
Westbridge Pk DT9 .... 225 B2
Westbrook Pk BA1 .... 27 A2
Westbrook Rd Bristol BS4 .. 23 D8
  Evercreech BA4 .... 141 E1
  Weston-Super-Mare BS22 .. 31 D1
Westbrook Vale BA4 .... 141 E1
Westbury
  Bradford Abbas DT9 .... 187 E1
  Sherborne DT9 .... 225 D3
Westbury Cres BS23 .... 48 F2
Westbury Gdns BA22 .. 186 C2
Westbury Pl BS23 .... 48 E2
Westbury Terr DT9 .... 225 D3
Westbury View BA2 .... 79 E7
Westcliff Coll F Ed BS23 .. 30 B1
Westcombe BA8 .... 176 E1

Westcombe Hill BA4 ....142 C2
Westcombe Rd
　Evercreech BA4 ....141 F2
　Westcombe BA4 ....142 A2
Westcombe Trad Est
　TA19 ....183 E1
Westcombes EX13 .....198 B7
Westcott Cl BA11 ......100 C6
Westcott La TA4 ....148 F2
Westend BA22 ....174 E1
Westend La BA11 ......143 C6
Westerkirk Gate TA2 ...212 C7
Westerleigh Rd BA22 ..45 B1
　Clevedon BS21 ....6 B2
Western Approaches
　BA22 ....174 A2
Western Ave BA21 .....218 B6
Western Cl Clevedon BS21 ..6 D3
　Shepton Mallet BA4 .....205 B6
Western Dr BS14 ....22 E6
Western Gate TA10 ....172 C7
Western La
　East Harptree BS40 .....74 C3
　Minehead TA24 ....200 F7
Western Retreat BA5 ...203 B5
Western St DT9 ....187 E4
Western Way
　Bridgwater TA6 ....208 F7
　Winsham TA20 ....194 E1
Westex Ho BS23 ....49 B5
Westfield Bruton BA10 ..215 D5
　Clevedon BS21 ....16 D8
　Curry Rivel TA10 ....171 C3
　Shepton Mallet BA4 .....205 A6
　Sherborne DT9 ....225 B2
Westfield Ave BA21 ....218 E6
Westfield Cl
　Backwell BS48 ....19 A6
　Bath BA2 ....44 E3
　Bridgwater TA6 ....208 E4
　Burnham-On-Sea TA8 ..104 B8
　Keynsham BS31 ....24 C5
　Weston-Super-Mare BS22 ..31 F3
Westfield Com Sch
　BA21 ....218 E6
Westfield Cres
　Banwell BS29 ....51 A3
　Yeovil BA21 ....218 F6
Westfield Ct TA8 ....104 B8
Westfield Dr
　Backwell BS48 ....19 A6
　Burnham-On-Sea TA8 ..104 B8
Westfield Est BA12 .....161 F2
Westfield Pk TA4 ....44 A7
Westfield Pl Bristol BS8 ..11 F7
　Yeovil BA21 ....218 E6
Westfield Prim Sch BA3 ..97 C8
Westfield Rd
　Backwell BS48 ....19 A6
　Banwell BS29 ....51 A3
　Burnham-On-Sea TA8 ..104 B8
　Frome BA11 ....119 D3
　Wells BA5 ....203 C4
　Weston-Super-Mare BS23 ..48 D2
Westfield Terr BA11 ....78 D1
Westfields TA19 ....184 C5
Westford Cl BA21 ......222 A5
Westgate Bldgs BA1 ...228 B2
Westgate St Bath BA1 ...228 B2
　4 Taunton TA1 ....212 E3
Westhall Rd BA1 ....44 D7
Westhaven Sch BS23 ...48 D2
Westhay Broad Dro TA7 ..137 E6
Westhay Cross EX13 ....198 F3
Westhay Moor Dro BA5,
　BA6 ....138 D6
Westhay Rd BA6 ....138 C4
Westhill La TA9 ....105 C2
Westholm Rd TA11 .....211 B4
Westlake Cl TA7 ....155 C2
Westland Rd BA20 .....218 F4
Westleigh Gdns BA4 ...205 A6
Westleigh Pk BS14 .....22 A8
Westleigh Rd TA1 ......213 B3
Westmans Est TA8 .....104 C7
Westmarch Way BS22 ..32 A4
Westmead Gdns BA1 ...27 A2
Westmere Cres TA8 ....104 C8
Westminster BA21 .....218 C7
Westminster Bldgs
　DT10 ....190 B4
Westminster Cotts
　DT10 ....190 B4
Westminster St BA20 ..219 A4
Westmoor Dro TA10,
　TA12 ....184 E7
Westmoor La TA10 .....184 F4
Westmoreland Dr BA2 ..228 A2
Westmoreland Rd BA2 ..228 A1
Westmoreland St BA2 ..228 A1
Westmoreland Station Rd
　BA2 ....228 A1

Weston All Saints CE Prim
　Sch BA1 ....27 A2
Weston Bsns Pk BS24 ..49 E5
Weston Cl Bristol BS9 ...5 C7
　East Chinnock BA22 ....196 E8
Weston Dro BS20 ....7 F8
Weston Euro Pk BS24 ...49 B4
Weston Express Bsns Pk
　BS22 ....49 C2
Weston Farm La BA1 ...27 C2
Weston Hill SP8 ....177 D3
Weston Ind Est BS24 ...49 B2
Weston La Bath BA1 ....44 C8
　East Coker BA22 ....197 E5
　Halstock DT2 ....196 F1
Weston Lock Ret BA2 ...44 C6
Weston Lodge BS23 ....48 D8
Weston Miiature Rly
　BS23 ....49 B6
Weston Milton Sta BS22 ..49 C7
Weston Park Ct BA1 ...27 A2
Weston Park Prim Sch
　BS11 ....4 F8
Weston Pk BA1 ....27 C1
Weston Pk E BA1 ....27 C1
Weston Pk W BA1 ......27 C1
Weston Rd Bath BA1 ...44 D8
　Brean TA8 ....66 A5
　Congresbury BS49 ......34 B5
　East Brent BS24,TA9 ...86 D6
　Failand BS8 ....10 C3
　Long Ashton BS41 .....20 D8
Weston Ret Pk BS22 ....49 A6
Weston Sixth Form Coll
　BS23 ....48 F2
Weston St
　Buckhorn Weston SP8 ..177 D3
　East Chinnock BA22 ....196 E8
Weston Town BA4 .....141 E1
Weston Way BS24 ......49 F2
Weston Wood Rd BS20 ..2 C3
Weston-Super-Mare Sea Life
　Ctr* BS23 ....48 D6
Weston-Super-Mare Sta
　BS23 ....48 E7
Weston-Super-Mare Tech
　Coll & Sch of Art BS23 ..48 D8
Westonia BS22 ....31 E2
Westonian Ct BS9 ......5 C4
Westonzoyland Prim Sch
　TA7 ....154 F5
Westonzoyland Rd TA6,
　TA7 ....209 E4
Westover BA11 ....119 D4
Westover Gdns BS9 ....5 F8
Westover Gn Sch BS24 ..49 B2
Westover Green Prim Sch
　TA6 ....208 E4
Westover La
　Crewkerne TA18 ....224 B7
　Martock TA12 ....185 E8
Westover Rd BS9 ......5 F8
Westover Trad Est TA1 ..171 F5
Westover View TA18 ...224 C7
Westover's Cnr BS28 ..108 B4
Westowe Hill TA4 ......151 A3
Westridge DT9 ....188 C6
Westridge Way TA4 ....167 E7
Westview BS30 ....77 C5
Westview Orch BA3 ....64 B5
Westville BA21 ....219 C5
Westward BS41 ....12 A8
Westward Cl BS40 ......35 D2
Westward Dr BS20 ......4 C4
Westward Gdns BS41 ..11 B2
Westward Rd BS13 .....21 F7
Westway Nailsea BS48 ..8 E2
　Street BA16 ....207 B6
Westway Ctr BA11 ......119 F5
Westway La BA4 ....205 B4
Westwood Ave BS39 ...59 C2
Westwood Cl **2** BS22 ..31 F2
Westwood Cotts BA8 ...76 E1
Westwood Dr BA11 ....119 C4
Westwood Dro TA11 ...158 C3
Westwood Rd
　Bridgwater TA6 ....209 D7
　Bristol BS4 ....23 D8
Westwood with Iford Prim
　Sch BA15 ....64 F3
Westwoods BA1 ....29 B3
Wet La BS27 ....90 F2
Wetherell Pl BS8 ......226 B3
Wetlands La BS20 ......2 C2
Wetmoor La
　Langport TA10 ....172 C2
　　Westbury Sub Mendip
　BA5 ....110 E1
Wexford Rd BS4 ....22 D8
Weycroft Ave EX13 ....198 A2
Weymont Cl TA7 ....155 B3
Weymouth Cl TA6 .....45 B8
Weymouth Rd
　Evercreech BA4 ....141 E1
　Frome BA11 ....119 D3
Weymouth St BA1 .....45 B8
Whaddon Hill BA10 ...160 C7
Wharf Cotts TA21 .....222 B8
Wharf La Ilminster TA19 ..221 B3
　Portbury BS20 ....3 E5
Wharfside BS24 ....66 E3
Wharnecliffe Cl BS14 ..23 B5
Wharnecliffe Gdns BS14 ..23 B5
Whatcombe Rd BA11 ..119 E6
Whatcombe Terr BA11 ..119 E6
Whatley TA10 ....171 F5
Whatley Cross TA20 ..194 C1

Whatley La
　Buckland St Mary TA20 ..192 D7
　Langport TA10 ....172 A5
　Tatworth TA20 ....194 C1
　Winsham TA20 ....199 A8
Whatley Vineyard & Herb
　Gdn* BA11 ....118 D4
Wheatfield Dr BS22 ....32 A5
Wheatfield La BA3 .....95 A6
Wheathill Cl
　Keynsham BS31 ....24 D5
　Milborne Port DT9 ....217 D2
Wheathill La DT9 ......217 E3
Wheathill Way DT9 ....217 D2
Wheatleigh Cl TA1 ....212 D2
Wheatley Cres TA1 ....213 B5
Wheatstones **10** TA4 ..167 F8
Wheel House La TA20 ..199 B7
Wheeler Gr BA5 ....203 B4
Wheelers Ct BA3 ......78 C2
Wheelers Dr BA3 ......78 C2
Wheelers Rd BA3 ......78 C2
Whellers Mdw TA12 ...185 E7
Whetham Mill Cross
　DT8 ....199 F5
Whetham Mill La DT8 ..199 F6
Whetstones Almshouses
　TA19 ....183 F4
Whippington Ct **1** BS1 ..227 B3
Whirligig La TA1 ....212 F4
Whirligig Pl **7** TA1 .....212 F4
Whistley La BS40 ......74 F6
Whitbourne Moor BA12 ..144 E8
Whitbourne Springs
　BA12 ....144 F7
Whitchey Dro TA9 .....137 A5
Whitchurch District Ctr
　BS14 ....22 A5
Whitchurch La
　Bristol, Bishopsworth BS13 ..22 B5
　Bristol, Hartcliffe BS13 ..22 C5
　Bristol, Whitchurch BS14 ..22 E5
　Dundry BS41 ....22 C1
　Yenston BA8 ....189 F8
Whitchurch Prim Sch
　BS14 ....22 A6
Whitchurch Rd BS13 ...22 A6
Whitcombe Farm La
　DT9 ....175 D2
Whitcombe La TA12 ...185 F8
Whitcross **10** BA22 ....197 F8
White Ash La TA20 ....193 A5
White Cats Cotts BA8 ..176 F3
White Cross
　Brent Knoll TA9 ....105 C8
　Exford TA24 ....43 B8
White Cross Gate BS39 ..76 F6
White Hart La TA21 ....222 D6
White Hill Dro TA10 ...193 C5
White Horse Dr BA11 ..120 C6
White Horse La BS28 ..138 D8
White Horse Rd BA15 ..64 E7
White House La
　East Huntspill TA9 .....136 E7
　Loxton BS26 ....68 A3
White House Rd
　Claverham BS49 ....34 F8
　Pawlett TA5,TA6 ......135 D5
White Lodge Pk BS20 ..2 D6
White Mead BA21 .....218 D6
White Ox Mead La BA2 ..61 A3
White St Bristol BS5 ...227 C4
　Creech St Michael TA3 ..169 E4
　Horningsham BA12 ....144 E4
　North Curry TA3 ......170 C4
White's Dro BA5 ......138 F7
White's La TA4 ....133 A1
Whitebeam Cl TA6 ....209 D5
Whitebrook La BA2 ....79 A8
Whitebrook Terr BA11 ..178 F5
Whitechapel La BA11 ..143 E5
Whitechurch La BA8 ..190 A7
Whitecroft TA4 ....202 E4
Whitecross Ave BS14 ..23 C6
Whitecross La
　Banwell BS29 ....51 A4
　Minehead TA24 ....200 E7
Whitecross Rd
　East Harptree BS40 .....74 F4
　Weston-Super-Mare BS23 ..48 E6
Whitecross Way TA24 ..200 E7
Whitedown Cross EX15 ..191 B4
Whitefield Cl BA1 ......29 B4
Whitefield Cross EX36 ..162 D3
Whitefield La TA19 ....184 D4
Whitefield Rocks TA4 ..150 B1
Whitegate Cl
　Bleadon BS24 ....67 B6
　Minehead TA24 ....200 E7
Whitegate Rd TA24 ...201 A6
Whitehall Taunton TA1 ..212 F5
　Watchet TA23 ....202 B7
Whitehall Cl TA13 .....220 C4
Whitehall Ct TA18 ....224 C7
Whitehole Hill BA3 ....116 E4
Whitehouse Com Sch
　BS13 ....22 C5
Whitehouse La Litton BA3 ..75 D3
　Wraxall BS48 ....9 B4
Whiteladies Rd BS26 ..226 B4
Whitelands Hill BA3 ...79 B3
Whiteleaze La
　Thurloxton TA2 ....153 C1
　West Monkton TA2 ....169 D8
Whitemill La BA11 ....119 C3
Whitemoor Hill TA20 ..194 C4

Whitemoor La TA4 ....150 F3
Whiteoak Way BS48 ...18 D8
Whitepost Gate DT9 ...188 D6
Whites Cl TA6 ....208 E2
Whitesfield Cl BS48 ....8 D1
Whitesfield Rd BS48 ....8 D1
Whitesome's Dro BS27 ..109 C6
Whitestaunton Cross
　TA20 ....193 B5
Whitestone Rd BA11 ..120 B6
Whitewall Cnr TA3 ....181 D2
Whiteway BA2 ....193 E6
Whiteway Ave BA2 ....44 A3
Whiteway Rd BA2 .....44 A3
Whitewell Pl BA11 ....119 E3
Whitewell Rd BA11 ....119 E3
Whitewells Rd BA1 ....28 A2
Whitewick La TA5 .....134 F8
Whitfield Rd TA6 ......209 D6
Whitford Hill Corfe TA3 ..182 A4
　Pitminster TA3 ....181 F5
Whitford La TA3 ....182 A4
Whitys The BA16 ......207 C7
Whiting La **1** TA6 .....153 E3
Whiting Rd Bristol BS13 ..22 A4
　Glastonbury BA6 ......206 F5
Whiting Way BA5 .....203 D4
Whitland Ave BS13 ....22 B5
Whitland Rd BS13 .....22 B5
Whitley Rd TA7,BA16 ..156 C8
Whitling St BS40 ......53 B7
Whitmead Gdns BS13 ..22 C4
Whitmore La TA2 .....212 D8
Whitmore Rd TA2 .....212 E8
Whitnage La EX16 .....178 C2
Whitnell Cnr BA5 .....113 F6
Whitnell La Binegar BA3 ..114 B8
　Keenthorne TA5 ....134 D2
Whitney Hill TA19 .....193 F8
Whitson Ho **1** BS2 ....227 C3
Whitson St BS1 ....227 A4
Whitstone Cl BA4 .....205 C6
Whitstone Com Sch
　BA4 ....205 C5
Whitstone Ct BA4 ....205 D5
Whitstone Hill BA4 ...204 C1
Whitstone La BA4 .....205 E1
Whitstone Rd BA4 ....205 C6
Whitstone Rise BA4 ...205 D5
Whitswood Steep TA24 ..130 D4
Whittakers Ho **6** BA4 ..205 B6
Whitting Rd BS23 .....48 E4
Whittington Dr BS22 ..31 D2
Whittock Rd BS14 .....23 D6
Whittock Sq BS14 .....23 D7
Whittox La BA11 ......119 E5
Whitwell Rd BS14 .....23 B8
Whitworth Rd
　Frome BA11 ....119 F2
　Minehead TA24 ....200 D7
Wick Hill
　Charlton Horethorne DT9 ..176 A1
　Milborne Port DT9 ....217 B6
Wick Hollow BA6 .....206 F5
Wick House Cl BS31 ...25 D3
Wick La
　Burnham-On-Sea TA9 ..85 E6
　Camerton BA2,BA3 ....61 A4
　Glastonbury BA6 ......139 E2
　Lympsham BS24 ......66 E1
　Pensford BS39 ....40 D3
　Upton Cheyney BS30 ..26 A8
Wick Moor Dro TA5 ...134 C7
Wick Rd
　Bishop Sutton BS39 ...57 C3
　Lympsham BS24 ......66 D2
　Milborne Port DT9 ....217 C4
Wicketsbeer Rd BA22 ..197 C6
Wickfield BS21 ....6 C1
Wickham Ct BS21 .....6 C3
Wickham Rise BA11 ...119 F6
Wickham Way
　East Brent TA9 ....86 D4
　Shepton Mallet BA4 ...205 A6
Wickham's Cross or
　Beggar's Grave BA6 ..157 C3
Wickhill Rd TA10 .....171 D5
Wicklow Rd BS4 ......22 E8
Widcombe BS14 ....23 A6
Widcombe CE Jun Sch
　BA2 ....45 B5
Widcombe Cres BA2 ..45 B5
Widcombe Hill BA2 ...45 C5
Widcombe Inf Sch BA2 ..45 B5
Widcombe Par BA2 ...228 C1
Widcombe Rise BA2 ..45 B5
Widcombe Terr BA2 ...45 B5
Wideatts Rd BS27 .....90 A7
Widmore Rd BS13 .....22 A4
Wigeon Cl TA24 ....201 C5
Wigmore Gdns BS22 ..31 D2
Wilbye Gr BS4 ....22 D7
Wild Oak Ho TA3 .....168 D1
Wild Oak La TA3 ......168 D1
Wildcountry La BS48 ..20 E6
Wilde Cl TA8 ....104 C6
Wilder Ct BS2 ....227 B4
Wilder St BS2 ....227 B4
Wilders Ho TA24 .....128 C2
Wilderness The DT10 ..190 B4
Wildmoor La TA21 ....181 A6
Wilfred Rd TA1 ....213 A4
Wilfrid Rd BA16 ......207 D6
Wilkins Cl TA20 ......223 E4
Wilkins Rd TA6 ....209 D5
Wilkinthroop Hill BA8 ..176 C2
Will La TA4 ....151 A3
Willcocks Cl **6** BA21 ..222 D5
Willcox Cl BA6 ....206 E5

Willet Cl TA9 ....104 D3
Willet's La BA3 ....94 D6
Willett Hill Cross TA4 ..150 D5
Willey Rd TA3 ....170 E6
William Daw Cl BS29 ..50 F3
William Herschel Mus*
　BA1 ....228 B2
William Reynolds Ho
　BA6 ....207 D7
William St Bath BA2 ..228 C3
　Taunton TA2 ....212 F6
Williamstowe BA2 ....45 C1
Willie Gill Ct TA1 .....212 E4
Willinton Rd BS4 .....22 F8
Willis Hay DT9 ....225 D3
Willis's La TA18 ......196 C4
Williton & District Hospl
　TA4 ....202 D3
Williton Cres BS23 ....48 F3
Williton Sta TA4 ......202 F4
Willmott Cl BS14 .....22 F4
Willmotts Cl TA7 .....137 B2
Willoughby Cl BS13 ..22 B7
Willoughby Pl TA20 ..223 D3
Willoughby Rd TA6 ..208 C4
Willoway La BA4 ......62 E8
　Clevedon BS21 ....6 E3
　East Huntspill TA9 ....136 E7
　Langport TA10 ....172 A6
　Long Ashton BS41 .....10 F1
　Portishead BS20 ......2 F4
　Radstock BA3 ....78 E2
　Taunton TA1 ....213 D1
　Weston-Super-Mare BS22 ..32 D2
　Weston-Super-Mare BS23 ..48 E2
　Westonzoyland TA7 ...154 F5
　Williton TA4 ....202 E3
Willow Ct TA6 ....209 D5
Willow Dr Bleadon BS24 ..67 C6
　Hutton BS24 ....49 E2
　Shepton Mallet BA4 ...205 A6
　Weston-Super-Mare BS24 ..49 E5
Willow Gdns BS22 ....32 D2
Willow Gn TA7 ....154 D8
Willow Gr TA23 ......131 E4
Willow Ho BS13 ......22 C4
Willow La* EX15 .....180 F2
Willow Rd Bleadon BS24 ..207 B3
　Yeovil BA21 ....218 F6
Willow The BA3 ......96 F2
Willow Tree Cl BA22 ..174 A4
Willow Vale BA11 ....119 F5
Willow Wlk
　Bridgwater TA6 ....209 C4
　Keynsham BS31 ....24 D4
Willowbank TA24 .....130 B4
Willowdown BS22 ....31 E4
Willowfalls The BA1 ..28 E3
Willows The
　Brent Knoll TA9 ....86 A2
　Nailsea BS48 ....8 F3
Wills Ind Est TA6 .....209 A4
Wills Rd TA6 ....209 D3
Willway St BS2 ....227 C3
Wilmots Way BS20 ....4 D4
Wilmott Ho BS20 ....4 C4
Wilsham Cross EX35 ..122 A5
Wilshay Cl BS24 .....122 A5
Wilson Pl BS2 ....227 C4
Wilson St BS2 ....227 C4
Wilsons Cl TA5 ......134 B2

Wilton Cl
　Burnham-On-Sea TA8 ..104 C8
　Street BA16 ....207 D5
　Taunton TA1 ....212 E3
Wilton Gdns BS23 ....48 D7
Wilton Gr TA1 ....212 E3
Wilton Orch Street BA16 ..207 D5
　Taunton TA1 ....212 E2
Wilton Rd BA21 ......219 E8
Wilton St BA1 ....212 E3
Wiltons BS40 ....35 D2
Wiltown La TA11 .....171 D3
Wiltown La EX15 .....180 F3
Wiltshire Cl TA1 ......212 C2
Wiltshire Ct TA1 .....212 C2
Wiltshire Way BA1 ...28 A2
Wiltshires Barton **4**
　BA11 ....119 E5
Wilway La TA22 ......163 C6
Wimbledone Rd BS25 ..51 F2
Wimborne Cl TA1 ....213 D3
Wimborne Rd BA21 ..196 F6
Winash Cl BS14 ......23 C7
Wincanton Bsns Pk BA9 ..216 B3
Wincanton Cl BS48 ...9 A1
Wincanton Prim Sch
　BA9 ....216 C3
Wincanton Town Mus*
　BA9 ....216 C4
Winchcombe Cl BS48 ..9 A1
Winchester Cotts TA19 ..184 E1
Winchester Gdns BA21 ..219 C7
Winchester Ho **11** TA1 ..213 A4
Winchester Rd Bath BA2 ..44 C5
　Burnham-On-Sea TA8 ..104 C8
Winchester St TA1 ....213 A4
Wind Down Cl TA6 ...208 C4
Windcliff Cres BS11 ...4 E7
Windermere Ave BS23 ..48 F4
Windermere Cl BA20 ..218 F2
Windmill TA3 ....170 F5
Windmill Cl TA24 ....136 C3
Windmill Hill La
　Ashill TA19 ....183 B3

Windmill Hill La continued
Westbury Sub Mendip
BA5 .....110 D4
Windmill Hill Rd BA6 .....206 E5
Windmill La
Langport TA10 .....172 C5
Montacute TA15 .....186 C4
West Pennard BA6 .....140 C1
Windmill Rd TA10 .....126 A4
Windmill Rise TA18 .....224 C7
Windrush Cl BA2 .....43 F4
Windrush Gn BS31 .....25 A4
Windrush Rd BS31 .....25 A4
Windsor Ave BS31 .....24 E5
Windsor Bridge Rd BA1,
BA2 .....44 D7
Windsor Cl
Burnham-On-Sea TA8 .....85 B1
Clevedon BS21 .....6 D2
Minehead TA24 .....200 E6
Taunton TA1 .....212 C11
Windsor Cres BA11 .....120 A5
Windsor Dr Nailsea BS48 .....8 E2
Bridgwater TA6 .....209 D7
Windsor Hill La BA4 .....141 B8
Windsor Ho TA6 .....209 C5
Windsor La TA14 .....186 A4
Windsor Pl Bath BA1 .....44 C7
Bristol, Clifton BS8 .....11 F6
Windsor Rd
Bridgwater TA6 .....209 D7
Weston-Super-Mare BS22 .....31 C2
Windsor Terr
Bristol, Clifton BS8 .....11 F6
7 Henstridge BA8 .....190 A6
Paulton BS39 .....77 E5
Windsor Villas BA1 .....44 C7
Windway Hill TA4 .....164 D6
Windwhistle Circ BS23 .....48 F4
Windwhistle La
Sticklepath TA4 .....149 F6
Weston-Super-Mare BS23 .....48 E3
Windwhistle Prim Sch
BS23 .....
Windwhistle Rd BS23 .....48 D3
Windy Ridge TA17 .....195 D7
Windyridge La TA11 .....211 B1
Wine St Bath BA1 .....228 C2
Bristol BS1 .....227 A3
Frome BA11 .....119 E4
Yeovil BA20 .....219 B4
Winford CE Prim Sch
BS40 .....37 F7
Winford Cl BS20 .....2 E4
Winford Gr BS13 .....22 A8
Winford La BS41 .....21 C1
Winford Rd BS40 .....38 F3
Winford Rural Workshops
BA22 .....197 A2
Winford Terr BA11 .....21 C5
Wingard Cl BS23 .....48 D2
Wingard Ct 6 BS23 .....48 E5
Wingate Ave BA21 .....219 C7
Wingfield CE Prim Sch
BA14 .....83 C6
Wingfield Rd DT9 .....225 C3
Winifred Cliff Ct 1
EX16 .....164 B1
Winifred's La BA1 .....27 E1
Winkworth Way TA1,
TA2 .....213 A5
Winnibrook La TA4 .....131 A5
Winnowing End BS25 .....52 A3
Winpenny La TA2 .....168 E8
Winsbeer La
Rockwell Green TA21 .....222 A6
Runnington TA21 .....179 F8
Winsbury View BA2 .....42 B1
Winscombe Cl BS31 .....24 D6
Winscombe Ct BA11 .....120 B5
Winscombe Dro
Shipham BS25 .....70 D6
Winscombe BS25 .....70 A5
Winscombe Hill BS25 .....69 F5
Winscombe Rd BS23 .....49 A7
Winscombe Woodborough
Prim Sch BS25 .....70 A8
Winsham CE Prim Sch
TA20 .....194 E1
Winslade Cl TA2 .....213 B7
Winsley CE Prim Sch
BA15 .....64 E7
Winsley Hill BA3 .....64 B6
Winsley Rd BA15 .....64 E7
Winsors La TA24 .....131 A5
Winstitchen Cross TA24 .....127 C2
Winstitchen La TA24 .....127 C2
Winston Cl TA2 .....212 E6
Winston Dr BA21 .....218 F8
Winstone Ct BA22 .....226 C3
Wint Hill BS29 .....51 B2
Winter La DT9 .....188 C8
Winter's La TA4 .....150 C3
Winterfield TA18 .....196 B5
Winterfield Pk BS39 .....77 E4
Winterfield Rd BS39 .....77 E5
Winterhay La TA19 .....221 A5
Winters Cross TA4 .....165 C8
Winters Hill La BA4 .....204 C3
Winters Orch TA3 .....169 C1
Winterstoke Commercial Ctr
BS23 .....49 A6
Winterstoke Rd
Bristol BS3 .....11 F3

Winterstoke Rd continued
Weston-Super-Mare BS23,
BS24 .....49 B4
Winterstoke Underpass
BS3 .....11 F4
Winterwell La BA4 .....141 F4
Winyards View TA18 .....224 D4
Wireworks Est The TA6 .....136 A2
Wirral Park Rd BA6 .....206 C6
Wirral Park Rdbt BA6 .....206 C3
Wisteria Ave BS24 .....49 D2
Wisteria Cl BA22 .....218 B5
Wiston Cross EX36 .....162 D2
Witch Hazel Rd BS13 .....22 E3
Witches Wlk TA6 .....208 E2
Witcombe Dro TA12 .....172 F1
Witham Cl TA1 .....213 D3
Witham Rd BS31 .....25 A3
Withey Cl W BS9 .....5 F5
Witheys The TA6 .....23 C4
Withial Hill BA4 .....158 D8
Withiel Dr TA5 .....135 B2
Withiel Hill TA24 .....148 F6
Withies La BA3 .....97 A8
Withies Pk BA3 .....96 F8
Withmoor Dro TA10 .....172 E4
Withy Cl BS48 .....8 F3
Withy Cl E BS9 .....5 F6
Withy Cotts BA3 .....115 C5
Withy Gr TA7 .....136 C7
Withy Grove Cl TA6 .....209 D7
Withy Mead 3 TA11 .....173 F7
Withy La
Barton St David TA11 .....158 A3
Clatworthy TA4 .....149 B2
Hemyock EX15 .....180 B1
Oakhill BA3 .....115 C5
Withy Rd TA9 .....136 C7
Withy Wood La BA4 .....142 C5
Withybed La BA9 .....177 E6
Withycombe Cross
TA24 .....131 C4
Withycombe La TA5 .....135 A5
Withycombe Hill Gate
TA24 .....130 F4
Withycombe La TA4 .....131 B5
Withyditch La BA2 .....61 C4
Withypool Gdns BS14 .....23 B5
Withys The BS20 .....4 D4
Withywine La TA22 .....164 C5
Withywood Com Sch
BS13 .....22 A5
Withywood Gdns BS13 .....21 F4
Withywood Rd BS13 .....21 F4
Witney La Chard TA20 .....223 D8
Tatworth TA20 .....193 F1
Wittey's La TA20 .....199 B6
Wiveliscombe Prim Sch
TA4 .....210 B5
Wivenhoe Ct BA11 .....120 C6
Woburn Rd BA21 .....219 E7
Wolfester Terr BA22 .....174 F4
Wollens Cl BA6 .....206 C4
Wolmer Cl TA6 .....208 E2
Wolsey Cl BA5 .....203 B3
Wolvers Hill Rd BS29 .....50 E6
Wolvershill Ind Units
BS29 .....50 C6
Wolvershill Pk BS29 .....51 A3
Wonhouse Dro BS28 .....138 B6
Wood Cl BA5 .....203 B4
Wood Close La TA7 .....195 A8
Wood Dro TA10 .....171 E8
Wood End TA4 .....167 D6
Wood End Wlk BS9 .....34 E6
Wood Hill BS49 .....34 E6
Wood Hill Pk BS20 .....2 D7
Wood Kilns The BS49 .....17 A1
Wood La Axbridge BS26 .....70 D2
Blue Anchor TA24 .....121 A5
Butleigh BA6 .....157 C4
Carhampton TA24 .....131 B4
Chapmanslade BA13 .....121 D4
Clapton In Gordano BS20 .....8 E8
Crowcombe TA4 .....151 C7
Drimpton DT8 .....199 F7
High Ham TA10 .....155 E1
Marnhull DT10 .....190 F2
Moorlinch TA7 .....155 E8
Rodney Stoke BS27 .....91 B1
South Cheriton BA8 .....176 F4
Stalbridge DT10 .....190 B4
Stawell TA7 .....137 A1
Stogumber TA4 .....150 D7
Weston-Super-Mare BS24 .....30 F1
Wood Rd Ash Hill TA19 .....183 B4
High Ham TA10 .....172 A8
Wood Rock EX36 .....162 C5
Wood St Bath BA1 .....228 B2
Bath BA2 .....228 B1
Milverton TA4 .....166 F4
Taunton TA1 .....212 E4
Wood Way EX35 .....122 D4
Wood's Cross EX36 .....162 C5
Woodadvent La TA23 .....131 E1
Woodbarton 4 TA4 .....166 F4
Woodbirds Hill La TA10 .....172 C8
Woodborough Cres BS25 .....70 A7
Woodborough Ct BS25 .....70 A8
Woodborough Dr BS25 .....70 A8
Woodborough La BA3 .....79 A4
Woodborough Rd
Radstock BA3 .....79 A3
Winscombe BS25 .....69 F8
Woodburn Cross EX16 .....162 F2
Woodburn Hill EX16 .....162 F2

Woodburn Water Cross
EX16 .....162 F1
Woodbury Ave BA5 .....203 F5
Woodbury Cl BA5 .....203 F5
Woodbury Rd TA6 .....208 D4
Woodcliff Ave BS22 .....31 C1
Woodcliff Rd BS22 .....31 C1
Woodcock St BA7 .....214 C5
Woodcock Way EX13 .....198 B7
Woodcombe Brake
TA24 .....200 D7
Woodcombe La TA24 .....200 C8
Woodcote BA20 .....218 D2
Woodcroft BS39 .....57 C2
Woodcroft Mdws TA20 .....192 E7
Wooddene BS25 .....70 A8
Woodfield Cl TA8 .....104 C5
Woodford Cl BS48 .....9 A1
Woodford Cotts TA4 .....132 A1
Woodford Ct 3 BS23 .....48 E5
Woodford La Coxley BA5 .....139 F6
Wells BA5 .....203 B1
Woodhayes Rd BA8 .....190 A6
Woodhayes Ho 1 BA8 .....190 A6
Woodhayes Rd BA11 .....120 C6
Woodhenge BA22 .....218 B5
Woodhill Ave BS20 .....2 D6
Woodhill Ct BS20 .....2 D6
Woodhill Rd BS20 .....2 D6
Woodhill Terr TA3 .....170 F6
Woodhill Views BS48 .....8 F2
Woodhouse Cross SP8 .....177 F6
Woodhouse La
Axminster EX13 .....198 D1
Chard TA20 .....194 B6
Marston Magna BA22 .....175 B1
Montacute TA15 .....186 C3
Woodhouse Rd
Axminster EX13 .....198 D1
Bath BA2 .....44 A6
Woodhurst Rd BS23 .....49 A7
Woodington Rd BS21 .....6 C1
Woodland Ave TA7 .....154 F5
Woodland Cl
4 Carhampton TA24 .....131 A5
Failand BS8 .....10 B4
Woodland Ct BS9 .....5 C3
Woodland Glade BS21 .....6 E5
Woodland Gr Bath BA1 .....27 A2
Bristol BS9 .....5 D6
Yeovil BA20 .....219 B4
Woodland Pl BA2 .....45 D5
Woodland Rd
Bristol BS8 .....226 C4
Frome BA11 .....119 F4
Nailsea BS48 .....8 E3
Woodland Way BS8 .....10 B4
Woodlands Axbridge BS26 .....70 D2
Wellington TA21 .....222 F3
Weston-Super-Mare BS23 .....30 D1
Woodlands Bsns Pk
EX16 .....179 C3
Woodlands Dr TA3 .....169 C3
Woodlands La
Holcombe BA3 .....116 B7
Isle Abbotts TA3 .....183 E6
Woodlands Mead DT10 .....190 F6
Woodlands Pk BA1 .....28 C2
Woodlands Rd
Baltonsborough BA6 .....158 A8
Clevedon BS21 .....6 C4
Portishead BS20 .....2 D8
Woodlands The BA7 .....60 D3
Woodleaze BS9 .....5 B6
Woodleigh Gdns BS14 .....23 C6
Woodmansh Cl BS14 .....23 A4
Woodmead Gdns BS13 .....22 C4
Woodmill BS49 .....17 A1
Woodpecker Ave BA3 .....97 B8
Woodpecker Dr BS22 .....49 E8
Woodram La TA3 .....181 E5
Woodridge Mead TA4 .....167 F8
Woodrush Cl TA1 .....213 C1
Woods Batch BA16 .....207 B6
Woods Hill BA3 .....64 A6
Woodside Bristol BS9 .....5 D3
Midsomer Norton BA3 .....77 E1
Woodside Ave BS24 .....49 B2
Woodside Cl TA4 .....202 E2
Woodside Ct BS23 .....49 A8
Woodside Gdns BS20 .....1 E5
Woodside Rd BS4 .....6 E5
Woodspring Ave BS22 .....31 B3
Woodspring Cres BS22 .....31 A3
Woodspring Mus *
BS23 .....48 E8
Woodspring Priory *
BS22 .....14 C1
Woodstock Rd
Taunton TA1 .....212 E5
Weston-Super-Mare BS22 .....49 B8
Yeovil BA21 .....219 C7
Woodview
Chilcompton BA3 .....96 E5
2 Clevedon BS21 .....6 F3
Paulton BS39 .....77 C5
Woodview Cl BS11 .....4 E7
Woodview Dr BS49 .....35 B8
Woodview Rd BS27 .....90 C7

Woodview Terr
Nailsea BS48 .....8 F2
Weston-Super-Mare BS23 .....49 A6
Woodwell Rd BS11 .....4 E5
Wookey Cl BS48 .....18 F8
Wookey Hole Cave *
BA5 .....111 E5
Wookey Hole Papermill
(Mus)* BA5 .....203 A8
Wookey Hole Rd BA5 .....203 B5
Wookey Prim Sch BA5 .....139 D8
Woolavington Rd TA7 .....136 E3
Woolavington Rd TA7 .....136 D4
Woolavington Right Dro
TA7 .....154 D6
Woolavington Village Prim
Sch TA7 .....136 E4
Woolcott La SP8 .....161 E1
Wooler Rd BS23 .....48 E8
Wooley La TA19,TA20 .....194 C6
Woolhayes La TA20 .....223 A8
Woollard La
Bristol BS14,BS39 .....41 A7
Whitchurch BS14 .....23 E1
Woollen La BA22 .....174 F1
Woolley La BA1 .....28 A4
Woolley Rd BS14 .....23 E5
Woolpit La TA24 .....146 B7
Woolston Rd BA22 .....175 E6
Woolstone La TA5 .....134 F7
Woolvers Way BS24 .....50 B6
Wooton Hall BA6 .....157 C5
Wootton Cross EX13 .....198 F1
Wootton Gr DT9 .....225 E5
Wootton Rd BS4 .....157 C6
Worberry La BA3 .....95 B7
Worcester Bldgs BA1 .....28 B2
Worcester Cl BA2 .....79 D7
Worcester Cres BS8 .....226 A4
Worcester Gdns BS48 .....18 C8
Worcester Pk BA1 .....28 B2
Worcester Pl BA1 .....28 B2
Worcester Rd BS8 .....226 A4
Worcester Terr BA1 .....28 B2
Worcester Villas BA1 .....28 A2
Wordsworth Ave TA6 .....208 E6
Wordsworth Cl TA8 .....85 B2
Wordsworth Dr TA1 .....213 B3
Wordsworth Rd
Clevedon BS21 .....6 C2
Weston-Super-Mare BS23 .....49 A3
World's End La BS31 .....25 C5
Worle Ct BS22 .....31 F3
Worle Inf Sch BS22 .....31 E2
Worle Moor Rd BS24 .....49 F8
Worle Parkway Sta BS22 .....32 B1
Worle Parkway Sta BS22 .....32 B2
Worle Sch BS22 .....31 E1
Worlebury CE Inf Sch
BS22 .....31 B2
Worlebury Cl BS22 .....31 B3
Worlebury Hill Rd BS22,
BS23 .....31 B3
Worlebury Park Rd BS22 .....31 A2
Wormcliff La SN13 .....29 F3
Wornmester Batch BA4 .....140 D5
Worston La TA8 .....104 C5
Worston Mdws TA9 .....104 E4
Worston Rd TA9 .....104 E5
Worth La TA22,TA24 .....146 C4
Worthings The BS24 .....67 B3
Worthington Cl BS28 .....108 D5
Worthy Cres BS24 .....67 B1
Worthy La
Creech St Michael TA3 .....169 D5
Bath BA4 .....140 F3
West Pennard BA4,BA6 .....140 D1
5 Weston-Super-Mare
BS23 .....48 E8
Worthy Pl 4 BS23 .....48 E8
Worthy Toll Rd TA24 .....123 B4
Wouldham Rd TA23 .....202 D6
Wragcombe La TA21 .....180 A4
Wrangcombe Rd TA21 .....180 A4
Wrangle Farm Gn BS21 .....6 E2
Wrangle The BS24 .....49 F7
Wrangway Rd EX15 .....180 A3
Wraxall CE Prim Sch BS48 .....9 B4
Wraxall Cross Rds BA4 .....159 A7
Wraxall Gr BS13 .....22 A8
Wraxall Hill Ditcheat BA4 .....159 A8
Wraxall BS48 .....9 C5
Wraxall Rd BA4 .....159 B7
Wraxhill Cl BA16 .....207 D5
Wrawhill Rd Street BA16 .....207 C5
Yeovil BA20 .....218 E1
Wreath La TA20 .....194 A6
Wren Cl Frome BA11 .....120 B6
Taunton TA1 .....212 C4
Weston-Super-Mare BS22 .....49 D8
Wrenmoor Cl TA6 .....209 C3
Wrington CE Prim Sch
BS40 .....35 E2
Wrington Cres BS13 .....22 A7
Wrington Hill BS40 .....35 F5
Wrington La BS49 .....34 E5
Wrington Mead BS49 .....34 F5
Wrington Rd BS49 .....34 F4
Wristland Rd TA23 .....202 D7
Writh Rd DT9 .....189 B1
Writhlington Ct BA3 .....79 C2
Writhlington Sch BA3 .....79 C2
Wrough Dro BS21 .....22 D4
Wroughton Gdns BS14 .....23 D6
Wry La TA4 .....149 F2
Wyatt Ave BS13 .....21 F5
Wyatt Cl BS13 .....21 F5
Wyatt's Cl BS48 .....8 D2

Wyatt's Ct BA11 .....195 C7
Wyatts Field TA3 .....168 D1
Wyatts Way TA19 .....183 C4
Wych Ct EX13 .....198 E3
Wych Elm Rd BA11 .....120 C6
Wychford Dr BS22 .....225 B3
Wydon La BA22 .....124 F3
Wye Ave TA6 .....209 D3
Wyedale Ave BS9 .....5 C7
Wyke La BS13 .....215 A5
Wyke Rd Bruton BA10 .....215 B7
Castle Cary BA7,BA10 .....214 E7
Wylds Rd TA6 .....209 A7
Wyllie Ct BS22 .....32 A5
Wymbush Cres BS13 .....22 C5
Wymbush Gdns BS13 .....22 C5
Wyndam Ct BS2 .....227 B4
Wyndeats La TA5 .....134 B5
Wyndham Cres BS20 .....4 A4
Wyndham Rd
Bridgwater TA6 .....209 C6
Taunton TA2 .....212 E7
Watchet TA23 .....202 C6
Wyndham St BA20 .....219 D5
Wyndham View BA21 .....219 D5
Wyndham Way BS20 .....2 E5
Wyndham's La TA24 .....210 C4
Wynford Rd BA11 .....120 B5
Wynnes Cl BA6 .....157 C5
Wynnes Rise DT9 .....225 C3
Wynsome St SA14 .....83 F3
Wynter Cl BS22 .....32 A3
Wyrral Cl BA6 .....206 D3
Wytch Gn EX13 .....198 E3
Wythburn Rd BA11 .....120 C5
Wyvern Cl Bruton BA10 .....215 F7
Weston-Super-Mare BS23 .....48 F7
Yeovil BA20 .....218 C11
Wyvern Com Sch BS23 .....48 F5
Wyvern Ct TA18 .....224 C6
Wyvern Rd TA1 .....168 E1
Wyville Rd BA11 .....120 C6

Y

Yadley Cl BS25 .....70 A7
Yadley La BS25 .....70 A6
Yadley Way BS25 .....70 A7
Yallands Hill TA2 .....213 F8
Yanel La BS25 .....52 B5
Yanhey Hill EX16 .....162 F4
Yanleigh Cl BS13 .....21 D6
Yarbury Way BS24 .....32 B1
Yard La Marshwood DT6 .....199 F3
Wiveliscombe TA4 .....210 C4
Yarde Farm Est TA4 .....213 C6
Yarde Pl TA1 .....212 F4
Yardleigh Cross EX13 .....198 D4
Yardwall Rd TA9 .....106 A3
Yarley Field La BA5 .....139 B7
Yarley Hill BA5 .....139 B7
Yarlington Ct TA2 .....168 B4
Yarn Barton BA20 .....219 C4
Yarnbarton BA8 .....176 E1
Yarrow Ct BS22 .....32 A5
Yarrow Rd TA9 .....106 D3
Yatton Jun & Inf Schs
BS49 .....34 C8
Yatton Sta BS49 .....17 A1
Yeabsleys Way BA7 .....214 C6
Yealscombe La TA24 .....128 B2
Yeamen's Ho BS1 .....227 B1
Yeap's Dro BA5 .....139 A7
Yearmoor La TA5 .....134 F8
Yearnor Mill La TA24 .....123 B5
Yeaman Hospl DT9 .....225 D4
Yellingmill La BA4 .....141 C8
Yellow Way Rd
Maiden Bradley BA11,
BA12 .....144 A3
Witham Friary BA11 .....143 F3
Yellow Wood Cross
TA4 .....132 D2
Yenston Hill BA8 .....189 F8
Yeo Bank La BS21 .....15 F1
Yeo Cl Clevedon BS21 .....6 E2
Congresbury BS49 .....34 D4
Yeo La Bridgwater TA6 .....209 B2
Long Ashton BS41 .....10 F1
Yeo Mill Cross EX36 .....162 C5
Yeo Moor BS21 .....6 E2
Yeo Moor Dro BS27,
BS28 .....109 D3
Yeo Moor Jun & Inf Sch
BS21 .....6 E2
Yeo Rd TA6 .....209 B2
Yeo Valley 2 BA22 .....197 F8
Yeo Valley Way BS48 .....9 B2
Yeo Way BS21 .....6 B2
Yeolands Dr BS21 .....6 B1
Yeomanry Way BA4 .....205 D5
Yeomans Cl BS9 .....5 D5
Yeomans Lodge BA11 .....119 C4
Yeomans Orch BS40 .....35 E3
Yeomanside Cl BS14 .....23 D5
Yeovil Bsns Ctr BA21 .....219 F7
Yeovil Coll BA21 .....219 A6
Yeovil District Hospl
BA21 .....219 B5

Yeovil Junction Sta
  BA22 . . . .**219** E1
Yeovil Marsh Pk BA21 . .**187** A5
Yeovil Rd
  Crewkerne TA18 . . . .**224** E7
  Halstock BA22 . . . .**197** D3
  Montacute TA15 . . . .**186** B3
  Sherborne DT9 . . . .**225** C4
  Tintinhull BA22 . . . .**186** C6
  Yeovil BA22 . . . .**218** F1
Yeovil Small Bsns Ctr
  BA22 . . . .**218** B6

Yeovil Trinity Foyer 7
  BA20 . . . .**219** B4
Yeoward Rd BS21 . . . .**6** E1
Yet Mead La
  BS27 . . . .**110** B7
Yew Tree Cl
  Bishop Sutton BS39 . . . .**57** D4
  Langford BS40 . . . .**53** E6
  Nailsea BS48 . . . .**8** C1
  Yeovil BA20 . . . .**218** E2
Yew Tree Ct BS14 . . . .**23** B5
Yew Tree Gdns
  Easton-in-G BS20 . . . .**4** C4
  Nailsea BS48 . . . .**8** C1
  Sandford BS25 . . . .**52** A4

Yew Tree La
  Compton Martin BS40 . . . . . .**74** A7
  Kingston Seymour BS21 . . . .**16** B1
  Taunton TA2 . . . .**213** E6
Yew Tree Pk BS49 . . . .**34** D3
Yewcroft Cl BS14 . . . .**23** A4
Yewtree Batch BS40 . . . . . .**37** A1
Yomede Pk BA1 . . . .**44** A7
Yonder Dro TA10 . . . .**184** E8
Yonder Mead TA4 . . . .**167** F7
York Bldgs TA6 . . . .**208** F5
York Cl Axminster EX13 . . .**198** A1
  Weston-Super-Mare BS22 . .**32** A4
York Ct BS2 . . . .**227** B4
York Gdns BS8 . . . .**11** F6

York Lodge BA20 . . . .**219** A5
York Pl Bristol BS1 . . . .**226** C2
  Bristol BS8 . . . .**226** B3
  Yeovil BA20 . . . .**219** A5
York Rd Bridgwater TA6 . . .**208** F2
  Bristol BS2 . . . .**227** C1
  Taunton TA1 . . . .**213** C5
York St Bath BA1 . . . .**228** C2
  Bristol BS2 . . . .**227** B4
  5 Frome BA11 . . . .**119** E5
  Weston-Super-Mare BS23 . .**48** D7
York's La BA3 . . . .**94** B6
Youngwood La BS48 . . . . .**18** D7

Zeals Rise BA12 . . . .**161** F2
Zembard La TA20 . . . .**223** C4
Zeta Cl TA7 . . . .**209** E8
Zig Zag BS21 . . . .**6** D4
Zion Hill
  Midsomer Norton BA3 . . . . .**96** B7
  Oakhill BA3 . . . .**115** A3
  10 Shepton Mallet BA4 . . .**205** B6